Fundamentals of Organizational Behaviour

FIFTH CANADIAN EDITION

D1122209

Fundamentals of Organizational Behaviour

FIFTH CANADIAN EDITION

Nancy Langton

University of British Columbia

Stephen P. Robbins

San Diego State University

Timothy A. Judge

University of Notre Dame

With contributions by

Katherine Breward, Ph.D.

University of Winnipeg

PEARSON

Toronto

Vice-President, Editorial Director: Gary Bennett
Acquisitions Editor: Carolin Sweig
Marketing Manager: Jessica Saso
Developmental Editor: Mary Wat
Project Manager: Andrea Falkenberg
Production Editor: Claudia Forgas
Copy Editor: Claudia Forgas
Proofreader: Kelli Howey
Compositor: Cenveo® Publisher Services
Photo and Permissions Researcher: Joanne Tang
Art Director: Julia Hall
Cover and Interior Designer: Anthony Leung
Cover Image: Credit: Harper Collins Publishers/The Art Archive at Art Resource, NY

Credits and acknowledgments of material borrowed from other sources and reproduced, with permission, in this textbook appear on the appropriate page within the text and on p. 431.

6   17

Library and Archives Canada Cataloguing in Publication

Langton, Nancy
    Fundamentals of organizational behaviour / Nancy Langton,
Stephen P. Robbins, Timothy A. Judge.—5th Canadian ed.

Includes index.
ISBN 978-0-13-420493-2

    1. Organizational behavior--Textbooks.   I. Robbins, Stephen P., 1943-
II. Judge, Tim   III. Title.

HD58.7.L34 2013   658.3   C2012-908075-6

ISBN : 978-0-13-420493-2

BRIEF CONTENTS

CONTENTS

PART 4 Sharing the Organizational Vision — 264

CHAPTER 8 Leadership — 264

CHAPTER 9   Decision Making, Creativity, and Ethics   300

CHAPTER 10   Organizational Culture and Change   336

PREFACE

Welcome to the fifth Canadian edition of *Fundamentals of Organizational Behaviour*. From its first edition, this text has enjoyed widespread acclaim across the country for its rich Canadian content and its emphasis on the material's relevance beyond a "9-to-5" job.

Fundamentals of Organizational Behaviour continues to be a vibrant and relevant text because it is truly a Canadian product with an abundance of examples and research from the Canadian workplace. It has retained the features of the previous edition that instructors say that they like, and there is also a great deal that is new.

Pedagogical Approach in Writing the Textbook

- *Relevance.* This textbook was the first to emphasize that OB is for anyone who has to interact with others to accomplish a task—in others words, OB *is* for everyone, from the bottom-rung employee to the CEO, and even for activities outside the workplace. We continue to emphasize this theme throughout this edition. For instance, each chapter includes a summary of the implications of chapter concepts for the workplace, while **OB for You** provides applications for individuals in their daily lives. In addition, the feature **OB in the Street**, clearly demonstrates how OB applies outside of the workplace.

- *Writing style.* Clarity and readability are the hallmarks of this text. Our reviewers find the text "interesting," "student-friendly," and "very clear." Students say that they really enjoy the text's informal style and personal examples.

- *Examples, examples, examples.* From our teaching experience, we know that while students may have trouble remembering a concept, they will remember an example. This textbook is packed full of recent real-world examples drawn from a variety of organizations: business and nonprofit, large and small, and local and international. We also use examples taken from the world at large, to illustrate the broader applicability of OB material.

- *Comprehensive literature coverage.* This textbook is regularly singled out for its comprehensive and up-to-date coverage of OB from both academic journals as well as business periodicals.

- *Skill-building emphasis.* At the end of each chapter is the **OB at Work** section, which is full of exercises to help students make the connections between theories and real-world applications. Exercises at the end of each chapter reinforce critical thinking, behavioural analysis, and team building.

Highlights of the Fifth Edition

Conceived as a "break out" revision, this edition has been designed to evolve with today's students. As such, the authors made a concerted effort to update every dimension of the book—from the interior design, through the new chapter-opening vignettes, to updated theory coverage, to the new **The Big Idea** margin features, and the continued emphasis on providing the latest research findings. In this edition, we have

- Updated the chapter vignettes to reflect companies and individuals relevant to today's students.

- Added **The Big Idea** and **Lessons Learned** margin features. **The Big Idea** margin note in each chapter opener provides a big picture view of the upcoming chapter topic. At the end of each chapter, a **Lessons Learned** margin note provides a brief recap of key chapter takeaways.

- Overhauled the boxed features as well as the examples and research referenced in the text extensively to ensure that that the fifth edition reflects the ever-changing world of OB in Canada.

Chapter-by-Chapter Highlights: What's New

Each and every aspect of the book was thoroughly updated for the fifth edition. Each chapter offers new examples, new cutting-edge research, improved discussions of current issues, and a wide variety of application material. The key *changes* are listed below.

Chapter 1: What Is Organizational Behaviour?

- Kicked off the chapter with a new *Opening Vignette* that introduces Yellow House Events (Toronto, Ontario) and some of the OB-related challenges faced by its founder

- Expanded the discussion of the importance of interpersonal skills

- Incorporated a new *OB in the Workplace* box: Habañero's Employees Help Set Policies

- Addressed the importance of customer service

- Expanded discussion of the importance of fostering innovation and change in organizations

- Established a new *Ethical Dilemma Exercise* about misrepresentation and withholding information in business ("Lying in Business")

- Offered a new suggested book list on leadership in *Point/Counterpoint*

- Revised *Case Incident* "How a UPS Manager Cut Turnover"

- Revised the following glossary definitions: job satisfaction, ethical dilemmas, and ethical choices

Chapter 2: Perception, Personality, and Emotions

- Revised the *Opening Vignette*, which describes perceptions of Walmart Canada and ties into the chapter subject (how our perceptions, personalities, and emotions affect our behaviour)

- Updated the *Focus on Diversity* box to discuss what types of questions employers can ask about a person's mental health history (see "Law Society's Questions About Mental Health Challenged")

- Expanded the description of the Big Five Personality Model

- Discussed a 2011 study on narcissism and how it affects organizational behaviour

- Added a new *OB in the Street* box on how perceived emotions can affect relationships (see "How Perception Causes Fights in Relationships")

- Presented a new *Case Incident* that examines negative emotions in the workplace (see "The Upside of Anger?")

- Revised the following glossary definition: affect

Chapter 3: Values, Attitudes, and Their Effects in the Workplace

- Set the stage for the chapter by including a new *Opening Vignette* about casino operator SaskGaming (Saskatchewan). The vignette explores the relationship between organizational values and attitudes and the impact of those aspects on workplace diversity
- Added a new *OB in the Street* box on whether lapses in ethics outside of work should affect a person's day job (see "Stanley Cup Rioting Leads to Employee Firing")
- Incorporated a new *OB in the Workplace* box on diversity and values in the nonprofit sector (see "The Nonprofit Sector Looks to Diversify Its Workforce")
- Updated the section on generational differences
- Offered a new *Case Incident* that examines job satisfaction as a state of mind (see "Thinking Your Way to a Better Job")
- Added/updated glossary definitions: value system, collectivism, core self-evaluation, job involvement, affective commitment, normative commitment, and continuance commitment

OB on the Edge: Stress at Work

- Provided new research findings on the effects of stress on job performance
- Featured statistics describing stress levels by province and gender (see "Stressed Quite a Lot, 2010")
- Incorporated new research on the physiological symptoms of stress
- Expanded the section on "role stress" and physical and mental wellness programs
- Updated the box offering tips for how to reduce stress in the workplace (see "Toward Less Stressful Work")

Chapter 4: Motivating Self and Others

- Included a new *Opening Vignette* that discusses the success of figure skater Patrick Chan and explores what motivates him to continue skating and participating in competitions
- Incorporated a new figure exploring Maslow's Hierarchy of Needs as applied to the workplace (see Exhibit 4-1: "Maslow's Hierarchy of Needs Applied to the Workplace")
- Revised and expanded the section on McClelland's theory of needs
- Created a new section on the importance of providing performance feedback, including tips on how to do so effectively (see "OB in Action: Giving More Effective Feedback")
- Introduced a new *OB in the Workplace* box that examines the benefits of results-only work environments (see "Results-Only Work Environments")
- Revised the *Research Findings* section on inequitable pay
- Presented new research findings on extrinsic vs. intrinsic rewards
- Updated the *Point/Counterpoint* feature on the subject of failure (see "Praise Motivates!/Praise Is Highly Overrated")
- Added/revised glossary definitions: motivation, hierarchy of needs, lower-order needs, self-actualization, higher-order needs, and goal-setting theory

Chapter 5: Working in Teams

- Introduced Cirque du Soleil (Montreal, Quebec) and its recipe for successful teamwork in the new *Opening Vignette*

- Updated discussion of "Roles" and "Diversity"

- Included new facts and findings in the *Point/Counterpoint* feature (see "Sports Teams Are Good Models for Workplace Teams/Sports Teams Are Not the Model for All Teams")

- Explored how Toyota integrates teamwork as one of its core values in the new *Case Incident* (see "Toyota's Team Culture")

- Added the following new glossary definition: mental models

Chapter 6: Communication, Conflict, and Negotiation

- Opened the chapter with a new story that explores the communication plan developed by the Toronto Leaside Girls Hockey Association to win more ice time for practice

- Presented a new *OB in the Workplace* box that describes how the selection of an inappropriate communication channel can have disastrous effects (see "Some Emails Should Be Left Unsent")

- Expanded the section on barriers to effective communication to discuss language, silence, and nonverbal communication

- Described the time-consuming nature of email and offered strategies for keeping the volume of email under control

- Explored how new technologies like social networking, blogs, and Twitter affect the workplace

- Included a new *OB in the Workplace* box that describes how one RCMP officer was disciplined for his Facebook posts (see "An RCMP Officer's Facebook Posts Land Him in Trouble")

- Added the following glossary definitions: formal channels, informal channels, and blog

Chapter 7: Power and Politics

- Introduced a new *Opening Vignette* that explores a Tim Hortons franchise that brought a class-action lawsuit against the company, arguing abuse of power by senior management

- Updated opening definition of power

- Revised the section on workplace harassment to include new research findings about sexual harassment

- Established a new *Case Incident* that discusses the changing attitudes toward dress codes and the impact of dress on image management (see "Dressing for Success")

OB on the Edge: The Toxic Workplace

- Introduced a new *Opening Vignette* that tells the story of one person's poor workplace behaviour (in this case, that of a BC Lions football player) and how the situation was handled by the manager (the team coach)

- Added a new section on workplace bullying

- Presented two new *Fact Boxes*: one lists the possible negative effects associated with the experience of rudeness in the workplace, and the other presents statistics revealing the frequency of some inappropriate management behaviours

- Featured a new box that lists the behaviours commonly associated with poor managers (see "Do You Have a Bad Boss?")

- Included a box with tips for how to deal with a toxic manager (see "How to Deal with a Toxic Boss")

- Included a box that lists the typical characteristics of a toxic organization (see "What Does a Toxic Organization Look Like?")

Chapter 8: Leadership

- Introduced a new *Opening Vignette* that discusses Lieutenant Colonel Maryse Carmichael, who was recently appointed the first female Commanding Officer (CO) of Canada's Snowbirds, and explores the factors that affect one's ability to lead and inspire others

- Updated the discussion of Situational Leadership®

- Integrated new research findings on path-goal theory

- Added a new *Research Findings* box: "Transformational leadership" addresses the strengths and weaknesses of this leadership approach

- Expanded the discussion of the effectiveness of formal and informal mentoring

- Expanded the discussion of transformational and charismatic leadership

- Questioned whether the ends justify a leader's ethically ambiguous means in a new *Ethical Dilemma Exercise* (see "Do the Ends Justify the Means?")

- Added a new *Case Incident* "Moving from Colleague to Supervisor"

- Added/revised glossary definitions: charismatic leadership theory, trait theories of leadership, identification-based trust, and vision

Chapter 9: Decision Making, Creativity, and Ethics

- Introduced a new *Opening Vignette* exploring the value-based business decisions of the founders of Kicking Horse Coffee, a fair trade coffee company

- Revised the explanations of "bounded rationality" and "satisficing" as applied to decision making

- Included a new *OB in the Street* box that explores whether intuition can help you win at chess (see "Intuition Comes to the Chess Board")

- Addressed the topic of risk aversion and its implications on decision making

- Added a new *OB in the Street* box to exemplify the implications of groupthink among market analysts (see "Groupthink among Analysts")

- Described in an *OB in the Workplace* box the Canadian army's written code of ethics, which underscores the need for ethical behaviour in warfare (see "Ethics and the Army")

- Presented a new *Point/Counterpoint* section that weighs action against inaction (see "When in Doubt, Do!/Wait! Not so Fast")

- Added a new glossary definition: risk aversion

Chapter 10: Organizational Culture and Change

- Updated the *Opening Vignette*, which discusses the strong organizational culture created by the co-founders of the successful Boston Pizza franchise

- Listed the seven primary characteristics that capture the essence of an organization's culture

- Included a new "Culture Creates Climate" section that discusses how an organization's culture creates a climate (shared perceptions of environment) that affects an individual's job satisfaction, involvement, commitment, and motivation

- Added a new *OB in the Workplace* box to address what can happen when employees do not buy into their organization's culture (see "Making Culture Work")

- Included a new *OB in the Workplace* box: "The NRC Changes Its Research Focus to 'Market Drivers'"

- Added a new *OB in Action* box: "How to Speed Up the Pace of Change"

- Explored the concept of the "5S" principles and how they are incorporated into organizational culture in the new *Case Incident* (see "Is a 5S Culture for You?")

- Revised the following glossary definition: organizational climate

Pedagogical Features

This textbook offers the most complete assortment of pedagogy available for any OB book on the market.

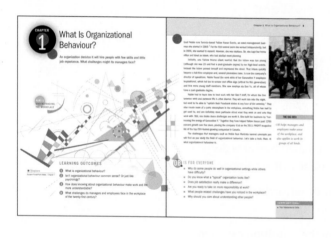

- The text is developed in a "story-line" format that emphasizes how the topics fit together. Each chapter opens with a list of learning outcomes related to a main example that threads through the chapter. The opening vignette is carried throughout the chapter to help students apply a real-life example to the concepts they are learning. The learning outcome questions appear in the margin of the text, to indicate where they are addressed. The opening questions are repeated and answered at the end of each chapter to summarize the chapter content.

- **OB Is for Everyone** in the chapter-opener highlights the integrated questions that students will encounter throughout each chapter (in the form of margin notes). Right from the start, these questions encourage students to think about how OB applies to everyday lives.

- NEW! **Personal Inventory Assessment (PIA)** is a collection of online exercises designed to promote self-reflection and engagement in students, enhancing their ability to connect with the concepts taught in the text. PIA marginal icons appear throughout the text.

- NEW! **The Big Idea/Lessons Learned** features appear at the beginning and end of each chapter. These new resources are designed to work hand-in-hand. At the beginning of the chapter, a "Big Idea" item appears in the margin that is meant to give students a big picture view of the topic at hand. Then, at the end of the chapter a "Lessons Learned" item appears in the margin to recap the key takeaways from the chapter.

- Exclusive to the Canadian edition, **OB in the Street**, **OB in the Workplace**, **Focus on Ethics**, **Focus on Diversity**, and **Focus on Research** boxes help students see the links between theoretical material and applications.

- **OB in Action** features provide tips for using the concepts of OB in everyday life, such as Giving More Effective Feedback, How to Speed Up the Pace of Change, and Increasing Group Cohesiveness.

- **Summary and Implications** provides responses to the outcomes-based questions at the beginning of each chapter, while the **Snapshot Summary** provides a study tool that helps students to see the overall connections among concepts presented within each chapter.

- Each chapter concludes with **OB at Work**, a set of resources designed to help students apply the lessons of the chapter. Included in **OB at Work** are the following features:

  - **For Review** and **For Critical Thinking** provide thought-provoking questions to review the chapter and consider ways to apply the material presented.

  - **OB for You** outlines how OB can be used by individuals in their daily lives.

  - **Point/Counterpoint** promotes debate on contentious OB issues. This feature presents more focused arguments.

  - **Learning About Yourself, Breakout Group, Working with Others**, and **Ethical Dilemma** exercises are valuable application exercises for the classroom. The many new exercises included here are ones that we have found particularly stimulating in our own classrooms. Our students say they like these exercises *and* they learn from them. Additional exercises can be found on MyManagementLab at **www.pearsoned.ca/mymanagementlab**.

  - **Case Incidents** deal with real-world scenarios and require students to exercise their decision-making skills. Each case enables an instructor to quickly generate class discussion on a key theme within the chapter.

  - **From Concepts to Skills** provides a wide range of applications for students. The section begins with a practical set of tips on topics such as reading emotions, setting goals, and solving problems creatively, which demonstrate real-world applications of OB theories. These tips are followed by the features *Practising Skills* and *Reinforcing Skills*. *Practising Skills* presents an additional case or group activity to apply the chapter's learning outcomes. *Reinforcing Skills* asks students to talk about the material they have learned with others, or to apply it to their own personal experiences.

- **OB on the Edge** (which appears at the close of parts one and three) takes a close look at two of the hottest topics in the field: work-related stress, and the behavioural pathologies that can make an organization "toxic." Since this is a stand-alone feature, these topics can be introduced at the instructor's discretion.

Supplements

We have created an outstanding supplements package for *Fundamentals of Organizational Behaviour*, fifth Canadian edition. We have provided access to MyManagementLab, which provides students with an assortment of tools to help enrich and expedite learning. MyManagementLab is an online study tool for students and an online homework and assessment tool for faculty. MyManagementLab lets students assess their understanding through auto-graded tests and assignments, develop a personalized study plan to address areas of weakness, and practise a variety of learning tools to master management principles. New and updated MyManagementLab resources include the following:

- *New Personal Inventory Assessment (PIA).* Students learn better when they can connect what they are learning to their personal experience. PIA is a collection of online exercises designed to promote self-reflection and engagement in students, enhancing their ability to connect with concepts taught in principles of management, organizational behaviour, and human resource management classes. Assessments can be assigned by instructors, who can then track students' completions. Student results include a written explanation along with a graphic display that shows how their results compare to the class as a whole. Instructors will also have access to this graphic representation of results to promote classroom discussion.

- *New Personalized Study Plan.* As students work through MyManagementLab's new Study Plan, they can clearly see which topics they have mastered—and, more importantly, which they need to work on. Each question has been carefully written to match the concepts, language, and focus of the text, so students can get an accurate sense of how well they've understood the chapter content.

- *New Learning Catalytics.* Learning Catalytics is a "bring your own device" student engagement, assessment, and classroom intelligence system. It allows instructors to engage students in class with a variety of question types designed to gauge student understanding.

- *Assignable Mini-Cases and Video Cases.* Instructors have access to a variety of case-based assessment material that can be assigned to students, with multiple-choice quizzes or written-response format in MyManagementLab's new Writing Space.

- *eText.* Students can study without leaving the online environment. They can access the eText online, including videos and simulations. The interactive eText allows students to highlight sections, bookmark pages, or take notes electronically just as they might do with a traditional text. Instructors can also add their own notes to the text and then share them with their students.

- *Glossary Flashcards.* This study aid is useful for students' review of key concepts.

- *Simulations.* Simulations help students analyze and make decisions in common business situations; the simulations assess student choices and include reinforcement quizzes, outlines, and glossaries.

The following materials are available for instructors:

- *Instructor's Resource Manual with Video Guide.* The Instructor's Manual includes learning objectives, chapter outlines and synopses, video cases, annotated lecture outlines, teaching guides for in-text exercises, a summary and analysis of

Point/Counterpoint features, and answers to questions found under **OB at Work**'s *For Review* and *For Critical Thinking* sections, and **Case Incidents**. There are additional cases, exercises, and teaching materials as well.

- *MyTest* from Pearson Canada is a powerful assessment generation program that helps instructors easily create and print quizzes, tests, exams, as well as homework or practice handouts. Questions and tests can all be authored online, allowing instructors ultimate flexibility and the ability to efficiently manage assessments at any time, from anywhere. MyTest for the fifth Canadian edition of *Fundamentals of Organizational Behaviour* includes 1000 questions in MyTest format, including multiple choice, true/false, and essay questions. These questions are also available in Microsoft Word format and can be downloaded from a password-protected section of Pearson Canada's online catalogue (**www.pearsoned.ca/highered**).

- *Pearson Canada Video Library.* Pearson Canada has developed an exciting video package consisting of segments from CBC programs and from Prentice Hall's Video Library for Management and Organizational Behaviour. These segments show students issues of organizational behaviour as they affect real individuals and companies. Teaching notes are provided in the Instructor's Resource Manual with Video Guide. The videos are available in DVD (0-13-315372-X) format.

- *Image Gallery.* This package provides instructors with images to enhance their teaching. Most of these instructor supplements are available for download from a password-protected section of Pearson Canada's online catalogue (**www.pearsoncanada.ca/highered**). Navigate to your textbook's catalogue page to view a list of those supplements that are available. See your local sales representative for details and access.

- *Learning Solutions Managers.* Pearson's Learning Solutions Managers work with faculty and campus course designers to ensure that Pearson technology products, assessment tools, and online course materials are tailored to meet your specific needs. This highly qualified team is dedicated to helping schools take full advantage of a wide range of educational resources, by assisting in the integration of a variety of instructional materials and media formats. Your local Pearson Education sales representative can provide you with more details on this service program.

- *CourseSmart for Instructors.* CourseSmart goes beyond traditional expectations—providing instant, online access to the textbooks and course materials you need at a lower cost for students. And even as students save money, you can save time and hassle with a digital eText that allows you to search for the most relevant content at the very moment you need it. Whether it's evaluating textbooks or creating lecture notes to help students with difficult concepts, CourseSmart can make life a little easier. See how when you visit **www.coursesmart.com/instructors**.

Acknowledgments

A number of people worked hard to give this fifth Canadian edition of *Fundamentals of Organizational Behaviour* a fresh look. I received incredible support for this project from a variety of people at Pearson Canada. Nick Durie, Senior Acquisitions Editor, Mary Wat, Developmental Editor, and Andrea Falkenberg, Project Manager, worked hard to keep this project on track. Anthony Leung, Senior Designer, was responsible for the beautiful interior and cover design. Steve O'Hearn, President of Higher Education, and

Gary Bennett, Vice President, Editorial Director of Higher Education, were extremely supportive on the management side of Pearson Canada. This kind of support makes it much easier for an author to get work done and meet dreams and goals.

There are a variety of other people at Pearson who also had a hand in making sure that the manuscript would be transformed into this book and then delivered to you. To all of them I extend my thanks for jobs well done. The Pearson sales team is an exceptional group, and I know they will do everything possible to make this book successful. I continue to appreciate and value their support and interaction. Claudia Forgas was the Production Editor and Copyeditor for the project and continues to amaze for how well she makes sure everything is in place and written clearly. Claudia provided a wealth of support, great ideas, and goodwill throughout the production process. Turning the manuscript into the textbook you hold in your hands could not have happened without her inspired leadership. I am grateful for the opportunity to work with her again. Kelli Howey, as the proofreader, was extremely diligent about checking for consistency throughout the text. Both performed a number of helpful fact-checking activities. Their keen eyes helped to make these pages as clean as they are. I also want to acknowledge my divisional secretary, Nancy Tang, who helps keep me on track in a variety of ways. I could not ask for a better, more dedicated, or more cheerful assistant. She really helps keep things together.

Nancy Langton received her Ph.D. from Stanford University. Since completing her graduate studies, Dr. Langton has taught at the University of Oklahoma and the University of British Columbia. Currently a member of the Organizational Behaviour and Human Resources division in the Sauder School of Business, UBC, she teaches at the undergraduate, MBA, and Ph.D. level and conducts executive programs on attracting and retaining employees, time management, family business issues, as well as women and management issues. Dr. Langton has received several major three-year research grants from the Social Sciences and Humanities Research Council of Canada, and her research interests have focused on human resource issues in the workplace, including pay equity, gender equity, and leadership and communication styles. She is currently conducting longitudinal research with entrepreneurs in the Greater Vancouver Region, trying to understand the relationship between their human resource practices and the success of their businesses, and she is also looking at how social media can affect social movements. Her articles on these and other topics have appeared in such journals as *Administrative Science Quarterly, American Sociological Review, Sociological Quarterly, Journal of Management Education,* and *Gender, Work and Organizations.* She has won Best Paper commendations from both the Academy of Management and the Administrative Sciences Association of Canada.

Dr. Langton routinely wins high marks from her students for teaching. She has been nominated many times for the Commerce Undergraduate Society Awards, and has won several honourable mention plaques. She has also won the Sauder School of Business's most prestigious award for teaching innovation, The Talking Stick. The award was given for Dr. Langton's redesign of the undergraduate organizational behaviour course as well as the many activities that were a spin-off of these efforts. She was also part of the UBC MBA Core design team that won the Alan Blizzard award, a national award that recognizes innovation in teaching.

In Dr. Langton's "other life," she engages in the artistry of quiltmaking, and one day hopes to win first prize at *Visions,* the juried show for quilts as works of art. When she is not designing quilts, she is either reading novels recommended by her book club colleagues, or studying cookbooks for new ideas. All of her friends would say that she makes from scratch the best pizza in all of Vancouver, and one has even offered to supply venture capital to open a pizza parlour.

Stephen P. Robbins

Education

Ph.D., University of Arizona

Professional Experience

Academic Positions: Professor, San Diego State University, Southern Illinois University at Edwardsville, University of Baltimore, Concordia University in Montreal, and University of Nebraska at Omaha.

Research: Research interests have focused on conflict, power, and politics in organizations, behavioural decision making, and the development of effective interpersonal skills.

Books Published: World's best-selling author of textbooks in both management and organizational behaviour. His books have sold more than 5 million copies, have been translated into 20 languages, and editions have been adapted for Canada, Australia, South Africa, and India, such as these:

- *Essentials of Organizational Behavior,* 10th ed. (Prentice Hall, 2010)
- *Management,* 10th ed. with Mary Coulter (Prentice Hall, 2009)
- *Human Resource Management,* 10th ed., with David DeCenzo (Wiley, 2010)
- Prentice Hall's Self-Assessment Library 3.4 (Prentice Hall, 2010)
- *Fundamentals of Management,* 7th ed., with David DeCenzo and Mary Coulter (Prentice Hall, 2011)
- *Supervision Today!* 6th ed., with David DeCenzo (Prentice Hall, 2010)
- *Training in Interpersonal Skills,* 5th ed., with Phillip Hunsaker (Prentice Hall, 2009)
- *Managing Today!* 2nd ed. (Prentice Hall, 2000)
- *Organization Theory,* 3rd ed. (Prentice Hall, 1990)
- *The Truth About Managing People,* 2nd ed. (Financial Times/Prentice Hall, 2008)
- *Decide and Conquer: Make Winning Decisions and Take Control of Your Life* (Financial Times/Prentice Hall, 2004).

Other Interests

In his "other life," Dr. Robbins actively participates in masters' track competition. Since turning 50 in 1993, he has won 18 national championships and 12 world titles. He is the current world record holder at 100 metres (12.37 seconds) and 200 metres (25.20 seconds) for men 65 and over.

Timothy A. Judge

Education

Ph.D., University of Illinois at Urbana-Champaign

Professional Experience

Academic Positions: Visiting Franklin D. Schurz Professor of Management, Mendoza College of Business, University of Notre Dame; Matherly-McKethan Eminent Scholar in Management, Warrington College of Business Administration, University of Florida; Stanley M. Howe Professor in Leadership, Henry B. Tippie College of Business, University of Iowa; Associate Professor (with tenure), Department of Human Resource Studies, School of Industrial and Labor Relations, Cornell University; Lecturer, Charles University, Czech Republic, and Comenius University, Slovakia; Instructor, Industrial/Organizational Psychology, Department of Psychology, University of Illinois at Urbana-Champaign.

Research: Dr. Judge's primary research interests are in (1) personality, moods, and emotions, (2) job attitudes, (3) leadership and influence behaviours, and (4) careers (person-organization fit, career success). Dr. Judge has published more than 120 articles in these and other major topics in journals such as *Journal of Organizational Behavior*, *Personnel Psychology*, *Academy of Management Journal*, *Journal of Applied Psychology*, *European Journal of Personality*, and *European Journal of Work and Organizational Psychology*.

Fellowship: Dr. Judge is a fellow of the American Psychological Association, the Academy of Management, the Society for Industrial and Organizational Psychology, and the American Psychological Society.

Awards: In 1995, Dr. Judge received the Ernest J. McCormick Award for Distinguished Early Career Contributions from the Society for Industrial and Organizational Psychology. In 2001, he received the Larry L. Cummings Award for mid-career contributions from the Organizational Behavior Division of the Academy of Management. In 2007, he received the Professional Practice Award from the Institute of Industrial and Labor Relations, University of Illinois.

Books Published: H. G. Heneman III and T. A. Judge, *Staffing Organizations*, 6th ed. (Madison, WI: Mendota House/Irwin, 2009).

Other Interests

Although he cannot keep up (literally!) with Dr. Robbins' accomplishments on the track, Dr. Judge enjoys golf, cooking and baking, literature (he's a particular fan of Thomas Hardy, and is a member of the Thomas Hardy Society), and keeping up with his three children, who range in age from 20 to 6.

CHAPTER 1

What Is Organizational Behaviour?

An organization decides it will hire people with few skills and little job experience. What challenges might its managers face?

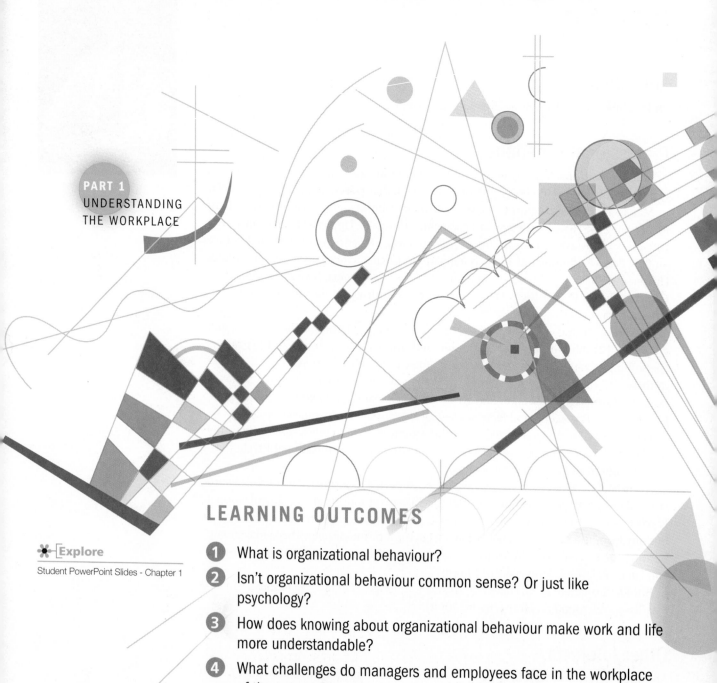

Explore

Student PowerPoint Slides - Chapter 1

LEARNING OUTCOMES

1. What is organizational behaviour?
2. Isn't organizational behaviour common sense? Or just like psychology?
3. How does knowing about organizational behaviour make work and life more understandable?
4. What challenges do managers and employees face in the workplace of the twenty-first century?

Grail Noble runs Toronto-based Yellow House Events, an event-management business she started in 2003.[1] For the first several years she worked independently, but in 2006, she wanted to expand. However, she was cautious. So, she kept her home office and hired an intern, who had studied event planning.

Initially, one Yellow House client worried that the intern was too young (although she was 23 and had a post-graduate degree) to run high-level events. Instead the intern proved herself and impressed the client. That intern quickly became a full-time employee and, several promotions later, is now the company's director of operations. Noble found the work ethic of her Generation Y employee inspirational, which led her to secure cool office digs (critical for this generation) and hire more young staff members. She now employs six Gen Ys, all of whom have a post-graduate degree.

Noble had to learn how to best work with her Gen-Y staff, for whom the line between work and personal life is often blurred. They will work late into the night, but want to be able to "update their Facebook status at any hour of the workday." They also create more of a party atmosphere in the workplace, something Noble has had to get used to, and are definitely more particular about *what* they work on and *who* they work with. Still, she thinks these challenges are worth it. She built her business by "harnessing the energy of Generation Y." Together they have helped Yellow House post 1200 percent growth over five years, placing the company 41st on the 2011 *PROFIT* magazine list of the top-200-fastest-growing companies in Canada.

The challenges that managers such as Noble face illustrate several concepts you will find as you study the field of organizational behaviour. Let's take a look, then, at what organizational behaviour is.

THE BIG IDEA

OB helps managers and employees make sense of the workplace, and also applies to work in groups of all kinds.

OB IS FOR EVERYONE

- Why do some people do well in organizational settings while others have difficulty?
- Do you know what a "typical" organization looks like?
- Does job satisfaction really make a difference?
- Are you ready to take on more responsibility at work?
- What people-related challenges have you noticed in the workplace?
- Why should you care about understanding other people?

LEARNING ABOUT YOURSELF

- Your Interpersonal Skills

Defining Organizational Behaviour

1 What is organizational behaviour?

Organizational behaviour (often abbreviated as OB) is a field of study that looks at the impact that individuals, groups, and structure have on behaviour within organizations for the purpose of applying such knowledge toward improving an organization's effectiveness. Because the organizations studied are often business organizations, OB is frequently applied to topics such as jobs, absenteeism, turnover, productivity, motivation, working in groups, and job satisfaction. Although debate exists about their relative importance, OB also examines the core topics of motivation, leader behaviour and power, interpersonal communication, group structure and processes, learning, attitude development and perception, change processes, conflict, work design, and work stress.[2]

Why do some people do well in organizational settings while others have difficulty?

OB Is for Everyone

It may seem natural to think that the study of OB is for leaders and managers of organizations. However, OB is for everyone. For instance, many organizations also have informal leadership opportunities. In organizations in which employees are asked to share in a greater number of decision-making processes rather than simply follow orders, the roles of managers and employees are becoming blurred.[3] For instance, employees in some retail stores are asked to make decisions about when to accept returned items on their own, without involving the manager.

OB is not just for managers and employees. Entrepreneurs and self-employed individuals may not act as managers, but they certainly interact with other individuals and organizations as part of their work. In fact, much of OB is relevant beyond the workplace.

OB applies equally well to all situations in which you interact with others. In fact, OB is relevant anywhere that people come together and share experiences, work on goals, or meet to solve problems. The study of OB can shed light on the interactions among family members, the voluntary group that comes together to do something about reviving the downtown area, students working as a team on a class project, the parents who sit on the board of their child's daycare centre, or even the members of a lunchtime pickup basketball team. Throughout this text, a feature called *OB in the Street* will help you understand these broader connections.

The Importance of Interpersonal Skills

Until the late 1980s, business school curricula emphasized the technical aspects of management, focusing on economics, accounting, finance, and quantitative techniques. Course work in human behaviour and people skills received minimal attention. Over the past three decades, however, business faculty have come to realize the role that understanding human behaviour plays in determining organizational effectiveness, and required courses on people skills have been added to many curricula. Employers are looking for people skills as well. In a recent survey of Canadian chief financial officers, 34 percent said a job candidate's people skills were more important than industry experience and software proficiency. Five years earlier, only 1 percent cared about interpersonal skills.[4]

Organizations that invest in the development of employees' interpersonal skills are more likely to attract and keep high-performing employees. Regardless of labour market conditions, outstanding employees are always in short supply.[5] Companies known as good places to work—such as Toronto-based Royal Bank of Canada, Fredericton-based NB Power, Lunenburg, Nova Scotia-based High Liner Foods, Winnipeg-based

organizational behaviour A field of study that investigates the impact of individuals, groups, and structure on behaviour within organizations; its purpose is to apply such knowledge toward improving an organization's effectiveness.

Ceridian Canada, Regina-based SaskTel, Calgary-based Agrium, and Vancouver-based Ledcor[6]—have been found to generate superior financial performance.[7] A recent survey of hundreds of workplaces, and over 200 000 respondents, showed that the social relationships among co-workers and supervisors were strongly related to overall job satisfaction. Positive social relationships also were associated with lower stress at work and lower intentions to quit.[8] So, having managers with good interpersonal skills is likely to make the workplace more pleasant, which in turn makes it easier to hire and keep qualified people. Creating a pleasant workplace appears to make good economic sense, particularly because wages and benefits are not the main reasons people like their jobs or stay with an employer.[9]

Succeeding in the workplace takes good people skills. This text has been written to help managers and employees develop those people skills. To learn more about the kinds of skills needed in the workplace, see the *Working with Others Exercise* on page 26. To find out about the strengths and weaknesses in your people skills, see the *Learning About Yourself Exercise* on page 25.

What Do We Mean by Organization?

An **organization** is a consciously coordinated social unit, made up of a group of people who work together on common goals on a relatively continuous basis. Manufacturing and service firms are organizations, and so are schools, hospitals, churches, military units, retail stores, police departments, volunteer organizations, start-ups, and local, provincial, and federal government agencies. Thus, when we say "organization" throughout this text, we are referring not only to large manufacturing firms but also to small mom-and-pop stores, as well as to the variety of other forms of organization that exist. Businesses that employ no more than 100 people made up 98 percent of the employers in Canada in 2011.[10] These businesses employed 48 percent of the workforce.[11] Less than .05 percent of employers have more than 500 employees, and they employ 36.3 percent of the workforce. Most of these large organizations are in the public sector.[12]

Do you know what a "typical" organization looks like?

The examples in this text present various organizations so that you gain a better understanding of the many types that exist. Though you might not have considered this before, the college or university you attend is every bit as much a "real" organization as is lululemon athletica or Air Canada or the Vancouver Canucks. A small, for-profit organization that hires people with limited skills to renovate and build in the inner city of Winnipeg is as much a real organization as is London, Ontario-based EllisDon, one of North America's largest construction companies. Therefore, the theories we cover should be considered in light of the variety of organizations you may encounter. We try to point out instances where the theory may be less applicable (or especially applicable) to a particular type of organization. For the most part, however, you should expect that the discussions in this text apply across the broad spectrum of organizations. Throughout, we highlight applications to a variety of organizations in our feature *OB in the Workplace*.

 2 Isn't organizational behaviour common sense? Or just like psychology?

OB: Making Sense of Behaviour in Organizations

As Grail Noble encouraged her employees to act more like owners of Yellow House Events, it meant that she had to listen to feedback that she did not necessarily like.[13] In one case, the employees complained about one of her largest clients. They found it demotivating to manage the client's events because of the way the client interacted with them. Noble listened to her employees, reviewed the email exchanges employees and the client had written, and reflected on her own experiences with the client. She decided

organization A consciously coordinated social unit, made up of a group of people who work together on common goals on a relatively continuous basis.

to fire the client after Yellow House finished the work they had already committed to doing. "That was a very tough decision," she acknowledges. "But my people are my brand and product. At that point, the money wasn't worth their unhappiness." What can Noble learn from organizational behaviour to do an even better job of managing her employees?

So far, we have considered why OB applies to a variety of settings. In this next section, we consider the other fields of study that have contributed to OB and discuss the fact that OB is a scientific discipline, with careful research that is conducted to test and evaluate theories.

The Building Blocks of OB

OB is an applied behavioural science that is built upon contributions from a number of behavioural disciplines. The main areas are psychology, sociology, social psychology, anthropology, and political science.[14] As we will learn, psychology's contributions have been mainly at the individual or micro level of analysis. The other four disciplines have contributed to our understanding of macro concepts, such as group processes and organization. Exhibit 1-1 presents an overview of the major contributions to the study of OB.

Explore

Exhibit 1-1: Toward an OB Discipline

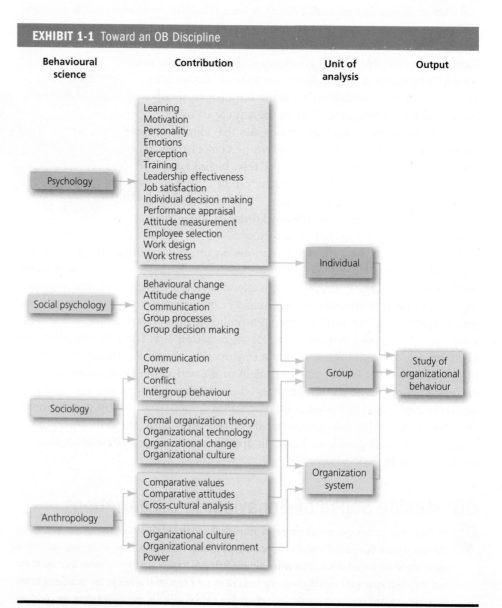

EXHIBIT 1-1 Toward an OB Discipline

The Rigour of OB

Whether you want to respond to the challenges of the Canadian workplace, which we discuss later in this chapter, manage well, guarantee satisfying and rewarding employment for yourself, or know how to work better in groups and teams, it pays to understand organizational behaviour. OB provides a systematic approach to the study of behaviour in organizations, as well as groups and teams. Underlying this systematic approach is the belief that behaviour is not random. Thus, research studies are conducted and are the basis for all of the claims made in this text. OB is even being adopted by other disciplines, as *OB in the Street* shows.

in the STREET
Is OB Just for the Workplace?

Can finance learn anything from OB? It may surprise you to learn that, increasingly, other business disciplines are employing OB concepts.[15] Marketing has the closest overlap with OB. Trying to predict consumer behaviour is not that different from trying to predict employee behaviour. Both require an understanding of the dynamics and underlying causes of human behaviour, and there is a lot of correspondence between the disciplines.

What is perhaps more surprising is the degree to which the so-called hard disciplines are making use of soft OB concepts. Behavioural finance, behavioural accounting, and behavioural economics (also called *economic psychology*) all have grown in importance and interest in the past several years.

On reflection, the use of OB by these disciplines should not be so surprising. Your common sense will tell you that humans are not perfectly rational creatures, and in many cases, our actions do not conform to a rational model of behaviour. Although some elements of irrationality are incorporated into economic thought, finance, accounting, and economics researchers find it increasingly useful to draw from OB concepts.

For example, investors have a tendency to place more weight on private information (information that only they, or a limited group of people, know) than on public information, even when there is reason to believe that the public information is more accurate. To understand this phenomenon, finance researchers use OB concepts. In addition, behavioural accounting research might study how feedback influences auditors' behaviour, or the functional and dysfunctional implications of earnings warnings on investor behaviour.

The point is that while you take separate courses in various business disciplines, the lines between them are becoming increasingly blurred as researchers draw from common disciplines to explain behaviour. We think that this is a good thing because it more accurately matches the way managers actually work, think, and behave. ●

OB Looks at Consistencies

Certainly there are differences among individuals. Placed in similar situations, people do not all act exactly alike. However, there are certain fundamental consistencies underlying the behaviour of most individuals that can be identified and then modified to reflect individual differences.

These fundamental consistencies are very important because they allow predictability. For instance, when you get into your car, you make some definite and usually highly accurate predictions about how other people will behave.

What may be less obvious is that there are rules (written and unwritten) in almost every setting. Thus, it can be argued that it's possible to predict behaviour (undoubtedly, not always with 100 percent accuracy) in supermarkets, classrooms, doctors' offices, elevators, and in most structured situations. For instance, do you turn around and face the doors when you get into an elevator? Almost everyone does. Is there a sign inside the elevator that tells you to do this? Probably not! Just as we make predictions about drivers, where there are definite rules of the road, so we can make predictions about the behaviour of people in elevators, where there are few written rules. This example supports a major foundation of this text: Behaviour is generally predictable, and the *systematic study* of behaviour is a means to making reasonably accurate predictions.

OB Looks Beyond Common Sense

Each of us watches the actions of others and attempts to interpret what we see. Unfortunately, a casual or commonsensical approach to reading others can often lead to erroneous predictions. However, you can improve your predictive ability by supplementing intuition opinions with a more systematic approach.

Underlying the systematic approach used in this text is the belief that behaviour is not random. Behaviour is generally predictable in that even seemingly random behaviour is guided by an underlying probability of whether that behaviour will occur. When we use the phrase **systematic study**, we mean looking at relationships, attempting to attribute causes and effects, and basing our conclusions on scientific evidence—that is, on data gathered under controlled conditions and measured and interpreted in a reasonably rigorous manner. Exhibit 1-2 illustrates the common methods researchers use to study topics in OB.

Evidence-based management (EBM) complements systematic study by basing managerial decisions on the best available scientific evidence. We would want doctors to

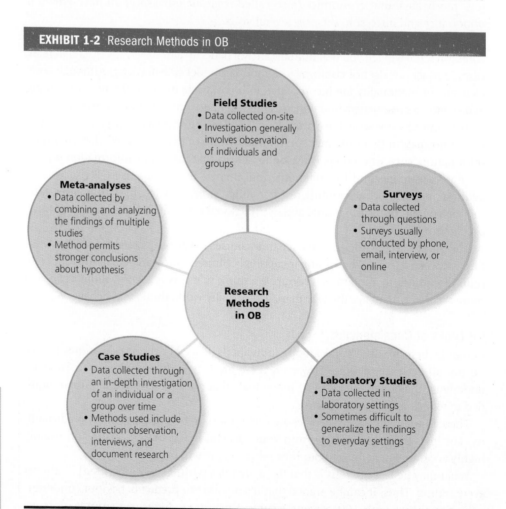

EXHIBIT 1-2 Research Methods in OB

Field Studies
- Data collected on-site
- Investigation generally involves observation of individuals and groups

Meta-analyses
- Data collected by combining and analyzing the findings of multiple studies
- Method permits stronger conclusions about hypothesis

Surveys
- Data collected through questions
- Surveys usually conducted by phone, email, interview, or online

Research Methods in OB

Case Studies
- Data collected through an in-depth investigation of an individual or a group over time
- Methods used include direction observation, interviews, and document research

Laboratory Studies
- Data collected in laboratory settings
- Sometimes difficult to generalize the findings to everyday settings

systematic study Looking at relationships, attempting to attribute causes and effects, and drawing conclusions based on scientific evidence.

evidence-based management (EBM) Basing managerial decisions on the best available scientific evidence.

make decisions about patient care based on the latest available evidence, and EBM argues that managers should do the same, becoming more scientific in how they think about management problems. For example, a manager might consider a managerial question, search for the best available evidence based on research conducted that applies to that question, and apply the research results to the question or case at hand. You might think it's difficult to argue against this (what manager would say that decisions should not be based on evidence?), but the vast majority of management decisions are still made "on the fly," with little or no systematic study of available evidence.[16]

Systematic study and EBM add to **intuition**, or those "gut feelings" about "what makes others (and ourselves) tick." If we make all decisions with intuition or gut instinct, we are likely working with incomplete information, comparable to making a decision with only half the data. Relying on intuition is made worse because we tend to overestimate the accuracy of what we think we know. In a recent survey, 86 percent of managers thought their organization was treating their employees well, but only 55 percent of employees thought they were well treated.[17]

Some of the conclusions we make in this text, based on reasonably substantive research findings, will support what you always knew was true. But you will also be exposed to research evidence that runs counter to what you may have thought was common sense. One of the objectives of this text is to encourage you to enhance your intuitive views of behaviour with a systematic analysis, in the belief that such analysis will improve your accuracy in explaining and predicting behaviour.

If understanding behaviour were simply common sense, we would not observe many of the problems that occur in the workplace, because managers and employees would know how to behave. Unfortunately, as you will see from examples throughout the text, many individuals and managers exhibit less than desirable behaviour in the workplace. With a stronger grounding in OB, you might be able to avoid some of these mistakes. This chapter's *Point/Counterpoint* on page 24 looks at how systematic OB is.

OB Has Few Absolutes

There are few, if any, simple and universal principles that explain OB. In contrast, the physical sciences—chemistry, astronomy, and physics, for example—have laws that are consistent and apply in a wide range of situations. Such laws allow scientists to generalize about the pull of gravity or to confidently send astronauts into space to repair satellites. However, as one noted behavioural researcher concluded, "God gave all the easy problems to the physicists." Human beings are complex. Because we are not alike, our ability to make simple, accurate, and sweeping generalizations is limited. Two people often act differently in the same situation, and the same person's behaviour changes in different situations.

OB Takes a Contingency Approach

Just because people can behave differently at different times does not mean, of course, that we cannot offer reasonably accurate explanations of human behaviour or make valid predictions. It does mean, however, that OB must consider behaviour within the context in which it occurs—known as a **contingency approach**. In other words, OB's answers "depend upon the situation." For example, OB scholars would avoid stating that everyone likes complex and challenging work (the general concept). Why? Because not everyone wants a challenging job. A job that is appealing to one person may not be to another, so the appeal of the job is contingent on the person who holds it. OB theories mirror the subject matter with which they deal. People are complex and complicated, and so too must be the theories developed to explain their actions.

Consistent with the contingency approach, the *Point/Counterpoint* feature included in each chapter presents debates on some of the more controversial issues in OB. These debates highlight the fact that within OB there is disagreement on many issues.

intuition A gut feeling not necessarily supported by research.

contingency approach An approach taken by OB that considers behaviour within the context in which it occurs.

The *Point/Counterpoint* format gives you the opportunity to explore different points of view on an issue, discover how diverse perspectives complement and oppose each other, and gain insight into some of the current debates in the OB field.

How Will Knowing OB Make a Difference?

When we talk about the impact of OB in each chapter, we consider the impact on both the workplace and the individual (see our features *OB in the Workplace* and *OB in the Street*). So let's begin our discussion of OB's impact by looking broadly at how knowing about OB makes a difference in the workplace, before we look at how OB affects us individually.

3 How does knowing about organizational behaviour make work and life more understandable?

In the Workplace

From a management point of view, understanding OB can help you manage well. The evidence indicates that managing people well makes for better corporations overall.

Each year, Aon Hewitt publishes a list of the "50 Best Employers in Canada." According to the 2011 survey's results, each of the top companies emphasizes the importance of employee engagement. "One area that our research has shown is critical to high engagement is manager effectiveness—how people are coached and motivated by their direct supervisor."[18] Managing well also makes a difference to the bottom line. Despite the recent economic challenges, companies that were ranked in the Best Employers list exceeded the industry average annual total shareholder return by more than 14 percent.[19]

While surveys show that managing well adds to the bottom line, it also shows that managing well provides managers with day-to-day returns. Companies ranked as "best employers" tend to have low turnover, and employees want to stay there—even when they are offered higher-paying jobs by other companies. Employees with the 50 best employers who participated in the survey did not mention money. Instead, they noted that the company recognizes their performance in little ways that make a difference.

The simple message is this: Managing people well pays off. Doing so may also lead to greater **organizational commitment**. We use this term to describe the degree to which an employee identifies with the organization and wishes to maintain membership in the organization.[20] This type of commitment is often called **affective commitment**, which describes the strength of an individual's emotional attachment to, identification with, and involvement in the organization. Employees who are highly committed go beyond expected behaviours to provide extra service, extra insight, or whatever else is needed to get the job done. There is some concern that extreme organizational commitment can have negative effects, in that employees with strong organizational commitment may behave unethically to protect the organization. However, this concern should not be a reason to avoid encouraging commitment. One benefit of having committed employees is that they are less resistant to change when organizations need to carry out changes.

Finally, managing well may improve organizational citizenship behaviour, a topic we discuss later in this chapter.

organizational commitment The degree to which an employee identifies with the organization and wishes to remain with the organization.

affective commitment The strength of an individual's emotional attachment to, identification with, and involvement in the organization.

For You as an Individual

You may be wondering exactly how OB applies to you if you are still in school and not yet working. Or you may want to know how OB applies to you if you are planning to run your own business or work for a small nonprofit organization, rather than a large organization. Or you may be asking yourself how OB applies to you if you are not planning on being a manager. We look at each of these scenarios below to help you see that OB is relevant in a variety of situations.

"What if I Am 'Just' a Student?"

You may think that OB is only useful once you reach the workplace. However, many of the concepts that apply to organizations also apply to teamwork, something many students have to do. As a team member, it's important to know how personality differences affect the ability of people to work together. You may need to motivate members of your team. Or you may want to know how to create a more effective team or solve conflict in a team. Individually or as part of a team, you also have decisions to make and need to know how to communicate with others. All of these topics are covered by OB.

"What if I Am Not Going to Work in a Large Organization?"

You may think that when we say "organization" we are referring to large financial firms in office towers, to the exclusion of the variety of other forms of organization that exist. You may be thinking that you want to work in a small business, or in your family's business, so OB has no relevance for you. But this would be short-sighted. Throughout your life you will work with a variety of organizations, and OB will help you better understand how those organizations work.

"What if I Do Not Want to Be a Manager?"

Many of us carry around a simplistic view of work organizations, with the participants divided into set categories: owners, leaders and/or managers, and employees. These distinct roles are found most often in large, publicly held organizations. Distinct organizational roles become more blurred when we discuss smaller, privately owned firms.

When we talk about leadership in organizations, we typically mean the person or persons responsible for setting the overall vision of the organization, although leadership can come from informal sources as well. While managers and leaders have seen their roles expand as a result of factors such as globalization and e-commerce, employees are also being asked to take on more responsibility and be more accountable. Thus, leadership skills are sought out in all levels of the organization.

You may be thinking that you are not planning to work in an organization at all because you would prefer to be self-employed. While self-employed individuals often do not act as managers, they certainly interact with other individuals and organizations as part of their work. Thus, the study of OB is just as important for the sole proprietor or entrepreneur as for those who work in large organizations. It gives all of us more insight into how to work with others, and how to prepare to become employees in the twenty-first-century workplace.

Today's Challenges in the Canadian Workplace

Shortly after Grail Noble of Yellow House Events hired her first Gen-Y full-time employee, she realized that she needed to know more about the work habits of this younger generation.[21] She worked carefully with her early hires to learn about their work preferences. What she found was that Gen Ys like to be empowered, and they want to work in entrepreneurial cultures. She opened her financial records to the employees, so that they could really understand the business. "I think business owners who try to shield employees from both good and bad news are making a mistake," she says.

That openness helped Noble when times got tough. During late 2008 and all of 2009, companies stopped holding events because of the recession. Yellow House's revenue fell by 50 percent. She asked her staff a simple question: "What are we going to do to overcome this?"

Noble is committed to being a good employer, surrounded by a good team. Will keeping them updated with the numbers be enough? What factors affect good teamwork? How can Noble motivate her employees to perform well in their jobs?

4 What challenges do managers and employees face in the workplace of the twenty-first century?

OB considers that organizations are made up of levels, moving up from the individual, to the group, to the entire organizational structure. Each level contributes to the

✳ Explore

Exhibit 1-3: Basic OB Model

EXHIBIT 1-3 Basic OB Model

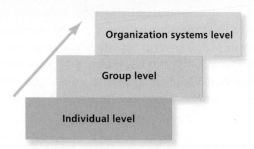

Organization systems level

Group level

Individual level

variety of activities that occur in today's workplace. Exhibit 1-3 presents the three levels of analysis we consider in this text and shows that as we move from the individual level to the organization systems level, we deepen our understanding of behaviour in organizations. The three basic levels are like building blocks: Each level is constructed upon the previous level. Group concepts grow out of the foundation we lay out in the section on individual behaviour. We then overlay structural constraints on the individual and group in order to arrive at OB.

When we look at the different levels in the organization, we recognize that each has challenges that can affect how the levels above and/or below might operate. We consider the challenges at the individual, group, and organizational levels.

Challenges at the Individual Level

At the individual level, managers and employees need to learn how to work with people who may be different from themselves in a variety of dimensions, including personality, perception, values, and attitudes. Individuals also have different levels of job satisfaction and motivation, and these affect how managers manage employees. More organizations expect employees to be empowered and to take on more responsibility than ever before. This expectation puts demands on both managers and employees. Perhaps the greatest issue facing individuals (and organizations) is how to behave ethically in the face of competing demands from different stakeholders.

Individual Differences

People enter groups and organizations with certain characteristics that influence their behaviour, the more obvious of these being personality characteristics, perception, values, and attitudes. These characteristics are essentially intact when an individual joins an organization, and for the most part, there is little that those in the organization can do to alter them. Yet they have a very real impact on behaviour. In this light, we look at perception, personality, values, and attitudes, and their impact on individual behaviour in Chapters 2 and 3.

Job Satisfaction

Employees are increasingly demanding **job satisfaction**, a positive feeling about your job resulting from an evaluation of its characteristics. As we discuss in Chapter 3, overall job satisfaction in the Canadian workplace is somewhat low.[22] The belief that satisfied employees are more productive than dissatisfied employees has been a basic

Does job satisfaction really make a difference?

job satisfaction A positive feeling about one's job resulting from an evaluation of its characteristics.

Microsoft Canada was named Canada's Best Workplace (large employers) in 2011. HR director Carolyn Buccongello, referring to the 2011 annual company-wide survey, said that 95 percent of Microsoft Canada employees reported that they are proud to work there. Results like this indicate strong job satisfaction. Pictured here are president Eric Gales (far right) and several employees volunteering at a local food bank. The company empowers employees to spend up to 40 hours of work time per year contributing to their communities.[23]

assumption among managers for years, though only now has research begun to support it.[24] Ample evidence shows employees who are more satisfied and treated fairly are more willing to engage in the above-and-beyond organizational citizenship behaviour we have said is so vital in the contemporary business environment.[25] Researchers with strong humanistic values argue that satisfaction is a legitimate objective of an organization. They believe that organizations should be responsible for providing employees with jobs that are challenging and intrinsically rewarding. Job satisfaction is also of concern because it is negatively related to absenteeism and turnover, which cost organizations considerable amounts of money annually.

Motivation

A recent survey found that 22 percent of Canadian employees were expressing decreased loyalty to their companies over the previous year, and this increased to 36 percent for employees working in organizations that had laid off employees following the downturn in the economy.[26] Employers are thus facing a demotivated workforce. To address this concern, Chapter 4 discusses the importance of rewards in motivating employees. So when turnover is excessive, or when it involves valuable performers, it can be a disruptive factor that hinders the organization's effectiveness. You may find the discussion of motivation and rewards particularly interesting in *Case Incident—How a UPS Manager Cut Turnover* on page 27, where a manager faces the challenge of motivating different types of employees to reduce turnover.

Empowerment

At the same time that managers are being held responsible for employee satisfaction and happiness, they are also being asked to share more of their power. If you read any popular business magazine nowadays, you will find that managers are often referred to as "coaches," "advisers," "sponsors," or "facilitators" rather than

Are you ready to take on more responsibility at work?

"bosses."[27] In many organizations, employees have become *associates* or *teammates*.[28] The roles of managers and employees have blurred as the responsibilities of employees have grown. Decision making is being pushed down to the operating level, where employees solve work-related problems and are given the freedom to make choices about schedules and procedures.

What is happening is that managers are empowering employees. **Empowerment** means managers are putting employees in charge of what they do. In the process, managers are learning how to give up control, and employees are learning how to take responsibility for their work and make appropriate decisions. The roles for both managers and employees are changing, often without much guidance on how to perform these new roles.

How widespread are these changes in the workplace? While we have no specific Canadian data, a survey by the American Management Association of 1040 executives found that 46 percent of their companies were still using a hierarchical structure, but 31 percent defined their companies as empowered.[29] *OB in the Workplace* looks at how Habañero empowers its employees.

in the **Workplace**
Habañero's Employees Help Set Policies

What do empowered employees do? Steven Fitzgerald, president of Vancouver-based IT firm Habañero Consulting Group, believes in empowering his employees.[30] Employees share human resource duties by mentoring each other, encouraging career development, and making sure everyone understands their jobs.

Fitzgerald knows that an "all work and no play" ethic is not a good way to define the business. As a result, he gives his employees autonomy, telling them they will be "judged on the quality of their work—not the number of hours they put in." Habañero allows telecommuting and flextime, and does not track sick days.

In 2006, Habañero started to grow too quickly, and some of the new hires did not fit into the company culture. Employees complained about the new hires. Together, Fitzgerald and his employees put together a new recruiting process. Now, up to 12 employees interview job candidates, explaining the culture and what the job is like. This new interview process has led to employees who better fit with the organization, and a turnover rate of 1.5 percent in 2010.

More recently, Fitzgerald's employees noted that Habañero's invoicing model, which was based on a target number of billable hours per month, contradicted the company's commitment to work-life balance. The employees worked with management to develop a new model of project-based billing that was more consistent with a truly flexible workplace, while still maintaining profitability. Fitzgerald is pleased with how empowerment has worked for Habañero. He says that knowing what employees want and acting on that knowledge can help you "attract people who are engaged for the right reasons." ●

Throughout this text you will find references to empowerment. We discuss it in terms of power in Chapter 7, and we discuss how leaders contribute to empowerment in Chapter 8.

Behaving Ethically

In an organizational world characterized by cutbacks, expectations of increasing productivity, and tough competition, it's not surprising that many employees feel

empowerment Giving employees responsibility for what they do.

pressured to cut corners, break rules, and engage in other forms of questionable practices. Increasingly they face **ethical dilemmas** and **ethical choices**, in which they are required to identify right and wrong conduct. Should they "blow the whistle" if they uncover illegal activities taking place in their company? Do they follow orders with which they do not personally agree? Do they give an inflated performance evaluation to an employee whom they like, knowing that such an evaluation could save that employee's job? Do they allow themselves to "play politics" to advance their careers?

Ethics starts at the individual level. While the word refers to moral conduct, **ethics** is also the study of moral values or principles that guide our behaviour and inform us whether actions are right or wrong. Ethics helps us "do the right thing," such as not padding expense reports, or not phoning in sick to attend the opening of the latest *Spider-Man* movie.

Individuals as well as organizations can face ethical dilemmas. As we show in Chapter 9, the study of ethics does not come with black and white answers. This chapter's *Ethical Dilemma Exercise* on page 26 asks you to consider whether it is ever appropriate to lie in a business situation. As you may conclude when doing that exercise, many factors need to be considered in determining the ethical thing to do. Those individuals who strive hard to create their own set of ethical values will more often do the right thing. Companies that promote a strong ethical mission, encourage employees to behave with integrity, and provide strong ethical leadership can influence employee decisions to behave ethically.[31]

Throughout this text you will find references to ethical and unethical behaviour. The *Focus on Ethics* vignettes provide thought-provoking illustrations of how various organizations deal with ethics.

Challenges at the Group Level

The behaviour of people in groups is more than the sum total of all the individuals acting in their own way. People's behaviour when they are in a group differs from their behaviour when they are alone. Therefore, the next step in developing an understanding of OB is the study of group behaviour. Chapter 5 lays the foundation for an understanding of the dynamics of group and team behaviour. That chapter discusses how individuals are influenced by the patterns of behaviour they are expected to exhibit, what the team considers to be acceptable standards of behaviour, and how to make teams more effective.

What people-related challenges have you noticed in the workplace?

Chapters 6 and 7 examine some of the more complex issues of interaction: communication, conflict, and negotiation; and power and politics. These two chapters give you an opportunity to think about how communication processes sometimes become complicated because of office politicking and interpersonal and group conflict.

Few people work entirely alone, and some organizations make widespread use of teams. Therefore, most individuals interact with others during the workday. This can lead to a need for greater interpersonal skills. The workplace is also made up of people from a variety of backgrounds. Thus, learning how to work with people from different cultures has become more important. We review some of the challenges that occur at the group level below.

Working with Others

As mentioned earlier, much of an individual's success in any job involves developing good interpersonal skills, or people skills. In fact, The Conference Board of Canada identified the following skills as the foundation for a high-quality workforce: the ability to communicate, manage information, use numbers, think and solve problems,

ethical dilemmas and ethical choices Situations in which individuals are required to define right and wrong conduct.

ethics The study of moral values or principles that guide our behaviour and inform us whether actions are right or wrong.

demonstrate positive attitudes and behaviours, be responsible, be adaptable, learn continuously, work safely, work with others, and participate in projects and tasks.[32] Because many people will work in small and medium-sized firms in the future, Human Resources and Skills Development Canada has noted that additional important skills are team building and priority management.[33]

In Canada's increasingly competitive and demanding workplace, neither managers nor employees can succeed on their technical skills alone. To learn more about the interpersonal skills needed in today's workplace, read *From Concepts to Skills* on pages 28–31.

Why should you care about understanding other people?

Workforce Diversity

The ability to adapt to many different people is one of the most important and broad-based challenges facing organizations. The term we use to describe this challenge is *workforce diversity*. **Workforce diversity** acknowledges a workforce of women and men; a variety of racial and ethnic groups; individuals with a variety of physical or psychological abilities; and people who differ in age and sexual orientation. We discuss workforce diversity issues in Chapter 3.

One of the challenges in Canadian workplaces is the mix of generations—members of the Elder, Baby Boomer, Generation X, Generation Y, and Millennial groups work side by side. Due to their very different life experiences, they bring to the workplace different values and different expectations.

We used to assume that people in organizations who differed from the stereotypical employee would somehow simply fit in. We now know that employees do not set aside their cultural values and lifestyle preferences when they come to work. Organizations therefore try to accommodate diverse groups of people by addressing their

workforce diversity The mix of people in organizations in terms of gender, race, ethnicity, disability, sexual orientation, and age, and demographic characteristics such as education and socio-economic status.

Bombardier Aerospace is a Quebec-based world leader in aircraft manufacturing and was named one of Canada's best diversity employers in 2011 by the *Globe and Mail*. Elisabeth Bussé, director of leadership development and talent management, says, "Increasing diversity is a business strategy: We want our employees to be representative of the community in which we do business." Bombardier was selected for a number of initiatives, including "Women in Leadership." Companies are judged on their diversity and inclusiveness programs for five major employee groups: women; members of visible minorities; people with disabilities; Aboriginal peoples; and lesbian, gay, bisexual, and transgendered/transsexual people.[34]

different lifestyles, family needs, and work styles. We need to keep in mind that what motivates one person may not motivate another. One person may like a straightforward and open style of communication that another finds uncomfortable and threatening. To work effectively with different people, we need to understand how culture shapes them and learn to adapt our interaction style.

The *Focus on Diversity* feature found throughout the text helps create awareness of the diversity issues that arise in organizations. Our first example looks at the ways that Regina-based SGI focuses on the diversity of its employees.

FOCUS ON DIVERSITY

SGI: Top Diversity Employer

How does an organization accommodate its diverse employees? Regina-based Saskatchewan Government Insurance (SGI) must have some clue.[35] The company was named one of Canada's top diversity employers in 2012. Its workforce demonstrates SGI's commitment to diversity: 10 percent of employees are Aboriginal, 5 percent are visible minorities, and 7.5 percent have a disability.

SGI has developed a number of programs to support its workforce. The Aboriginal Advisory Network provides an opportunity for First Nations employees to talk about their own issues and also get career counselling. As the company's website notes the purpose of the network is "to increase the understanding and appreciation of Aboriginal culture and issues."

The company also hosts a diversity celebration each year with "performances from different cultural groups—from Greek traditional dancing to First Nation dancing." This helps employees learn about each other's heritages.

For its 2013 brokers' calendar, SGI invited Canadians to submit photos that reflect the different cultural perspectives found in Canada. According to Toni Ennis, manager of promotions and advertising, "It's about celebrating the multicultural fabric of Canada . . . Our diverse communities give us the unique opportunity to experience, and take pride in, varied cultural identities and backgrounds."

SGI strives to have a workforce that is as diverse as its customers—a goal the company finds makes good business sense. ●

Challenges at the Organizational Level

OB becomes more complex when we move to the organizational level of analysis. Just as groups are not the sum total of individuals, so organizations are not the sum total of individuals and groups. There are many more interacting factors that place constraints on individual and group behaviour. In Chapter 8 we consider how leadership and management affect employee behaviour. In Chapter 9 we discuss decision making and creativity, and then look at the issues of ethics and corporate social responsibility. In Chapter 10 we look at organizational culture, which is generally considered the glue that holds organizations together. We also discuss organizational change in Chapter 10. As we have noted already, and as will become clear throughout the text, change has become a key issue for organizations.

Canadian businesses face many challenges in the twenty-first century. The structure of the workplace is changing. The need to develop effective employees and to manage human resource issues such as absenteeism and turnover is critical. Meanwhile, Canadian businesses face greater competition because of the global economy. Many companies have expanded their operations overseas, which means they have to learn how to manage people from different cultures.

Improving Customer Service

Today, the majority of employees in developed countries work in service jobs, including 78 percent in Canada.[36] In the United States, 80 percent work in service industries. In Australia, the United Kingdom, Germany, and Japan, the percentages are 73, 69, 68, and 65, respectively. Service jobs include technical support representatives, fast-food counter workers, sales clerks, waiters and waitresses, nurses, automobile repair technicians, consultants, credit representatives, financial planners, and flight attendants. The common characteristic of these jobs is substantial interaction with an organization's customers.

Many an organization has failed because its employees failed to please customers. Management needs to create a customer-responsive culture. OB can provide considerable guidance in helping managers create such cultures—in which employees are friendly and courteous, accessible, knowledgeable, prompt in responding to customer needs, and willing to do what's necessary to please the customer.[37]

Richard Branson, CEO of Virgin Group, thinks that "the customer is only right sometimes" more accurately reflects how customers should be treated. Instead, he believes that by recognizing the value of employees, who are the ambassadors of the organization, they will give great customer service.

Stimulating Innovation and Change

Today's successful organizations must foster innovation and master the art of change, or they will become candidates for extinction, like Eatons and Canadian Airlines. Victory will go to the organizations that maintain their flexibility, continually improve their quality, and beat their competition to the marketplace with a constant stream of innovative products and services. Domino's single-handedly brought on the demise of small pizza parlours whose managers thought they could continue doing what they had been doing for years. Domino's started out simply in 1965, and continually innovated as the pizza market became more demanding. In 2010, it overhauled the crust, the sauce, and the toppings because Domino's had come in last in pizza taste tests.

An organization's employees can be the impetus for innovation and change, or they can be a major stumbling block. The challenge for managers is to stimulate their employees' creativity and tolerance for change. The field of OB provides a wealth of ideas and techniques to aid in realizing these goals.

The Use of Temporary (Contingent) Employees

One of the more comprehensive changes taking place in organizations is the addition of temporary, or contingent, employees. Downsizing has eliminated millions of "permanent" jobs, and the number of openings for nonpermanent workers has increased. In 2009, temporary work was responsible for 12.5 percent of paid employment, down from its peak of 13.2 percent in 2005.[38] Eighteen percent of employees were working part-time in June 2011.[39] These include part-timers, on-call workers, short-term hires, temps, day labourers, independent contractors, and leased workers.

Some contingent employees prefer the freedom of a temporary status that permits them to attend school, care for their children, or have the flexibility to travel or pursue other interests. For instance, 35 percent of those working part-time in June 2011 were between the ages of 15 and 24.[40] But many others would prefer to have full-time work if it were available. Because contingent employees lack the security and stability that permanent employees have, they don't always identify with the organization or display the commitment of other employees. Temporary workers typically lack pension plans and have few or no extended health care benefits, such as dental care, prescription plans, and vision care. They are also paid less. For instance, in 2009, temporary employees earned 14 percent less and seasonal and casual employees earned 34 percent less than those who held permanent jobs.[41] Organizations face the challenge of motivating employees who do not feel as connected to the organization as do full-time employees.

Improving Quality and Productivity

Increased competition is forcing managers to reduce costs and, at the same time, improve both productivity and the quality of the products and services their organization offers.

An organization or group is productive if it achieves its goals by transferring inputs (labour and raw materials) to outputs (finished goods or services) at the lowest cost. **Productivity** implies a concern for both **effectiveness** (achieving goals) and **efficiency** (watching costs). The late management expert Peter Drucker stated that *effectiveness* is "doing the right thing," while *efficiency* is "doing things right."[42] A hospital is *effective* when it successfully meets the needs of its patients. It is *efficient* when it can do so at a low cost. If a hospital manages to achieve higher output from its present staff—by reducing the average number of days a patient is confined to a bed, or by increasing the number of staff–patient contacts per day—we say that the hospital has gained productive *efficiency*. Similarly, a student team is effective when it puts together a group project that gets a high mark. It is efficient when all the members manage their time appropriately and are not at one another's throats. Popular measures of organizational efficiency include return on investment, profit per dollar of sales, and output per hour of labour.

When service organizations assess their effectiveness, they must include customer needs and requirements. Why? Because a clear chain of cause and effect runs from employee attitudes and behaviour to customer attitudes and behaviour to a service organization's productivity.[43] Sears has carefully documented this chain.[44] The company's management found that a 5 percent improvement in employee attitudes leads to a 1.3 percent increase in customer satisfaction, which in turn translates into a 0.5 percent improvement in revenue growth. By training employees to improve the employee-customer interaction, Sears was able to improve customer satisfaction by 4 percent over a 12-month period, generating an estimated $200 million in additional revenues.

Developing Effective Employees

One of the major challenges facing organizations in the twenty-first century is how to engage employees effectively so that they are committed to the organization. We use the term **organizational citizenship behaviour (OCB)** to describe discretionary behaviour that is not part of an employee's formal job requirements, but that nevertheless promotes the effective functioning of the organization.[45] Recent research has also looked at expanding the work on OCB to include team behaviour.[46]

Successful organizations need employees who will engage in "good citizenship" behaviours, providing performance that is beyond expectations, such as making constructive statements about their work group and the organization, helping others on their team, volunteering for extra job activities, avoiding unnecessary conflicts, showing care for organizational property, respecting the spirit as well as the letter of rules and regulations, and gracefully tolerating the occasional work-related impositions and nuisances.

Toronto-based BBDO Canada encourages an entrepreneurial spirit as a way of inspiring OCB. The ad agency's president and CEO Gerry Frascione notes that a team leader on the Campbell Soup account overheard a Campbell's representative musing about a program that would launch Campbell's Soup ads when the temperature dipped. "Instead of waiting to get approvals, she acted very entrepreneurially and took it upon herself and made the whole thing happen in one week," says Frascione. "She went back to the client, analyzed the situation, fleshed out the opportunity, came up with an integrated communication plan, came up with a budget, and it was all done within five days."[47]

productivity A performance measure including effectiveness and efficiency.

effectiveness The achievement of goals.

efficiency The ratio of effective work output to the input required to produce the work.

organizational citizenship behaviour (OCB) Discretionary behaviour that is not part of an employee's formal job requirements, but that nevertheless promotes the effective functioning of the organization.

Organizations want and need employees who will do those things that are not in any job description. The evidence indicates that organizations that have such employees outperform those that do not.[48] As a result, OB is concerned with organizational citizenship behaviour.

Helping Employees with Work-Life Balance

Employees are increasingly complaining that the line between work and nonwork time has become blurred, creating personal conflicts and stress.[49] At the same time, however, today's workplace presents opportunities for workers to create and structure their roles.

How do work-life conflicts come about? First, the creation of global organizations means their world never sleeps. On any given day, for instance, thousands of General Electric employees are working somewhere. The need to consult with colleagues or customers 8 or 10 time zones away means that many employees of global firms are "on call" 24 hours a day. Second, communication technology allows employees to do their work at home, in their cars, or on the ski slopes at Whistler—but it also means many feel like they never really get away from the office. Third, organizations are asking employees to be available in off-work hours via cellphones and email.

Employees are increasingly recognizing that work affects their personal lives, and they are not happy about it. Recent studies suggest that employees want jobs that give them flexibility in their work schedules so they can better manage work-life conflicts.[50] In fact, balancing work and life demands now surpasses job security as an employee priority.[51] The Millennial generation of employees (that is, those in their 20s and early 30s) show an even greater concern with balance by referring to it as *life-work balance*.[52] Most college and university students say that attaining a balance between personal life and work is a primary career goal: they want "a life" as well as a job. Organizations that do not help their people achieve work-life balance will find it increasingly difficult to attract and retain the most capable and motivated employees.

Creating a Positive Work Environment

Although competitive pressures on most organizations are stronger than ever, some organizations are trying to realize a competitive advantage by encouraging a positive work environment. For example, Jeff Immelt and Jim McNerney, both disciples of Jack Welch (former CEO of GE), have tried to maintain high performance expectations (a characteristic of GE's culture) while also encouraging a positive work environment in their organizations (GE and Boeing). "In this time of turmoil and cynicism about business, you need to be passionate, positive leaders," Immelt recently told his top managers.

A real growth area in OB research has been **positive organizational scholarship** (also called *positive organizational behaviour*), which studies how organizations develop human strengths, foster vitality and resilience, and unlock potential. Researchers in this area argue that too much of OB research and management practice has been targeted toward identifying what is wrong with organizations and their employees. In response, they try to study what is *good* about organizations.[53] Some key independent variables in positive OB research are engagement, hope, optimism, and resilience in the face of strain.

Positive organizational scholars have studied a concept called "reflected best-self"—asking employees to think about situations in which they were at their "personal best" to understand how to exploit their strengths. The idea is that we all have things at which we are unusually good, yet too often we focus on addressing our limitations and too rarely think about how to exploit our strengths.[54]

Although positive organizational scholarship does not deny the negative (such as critical feedback), it does challenge researchers to look at OB through a new lens and

positive organizational scholarship An area of OB research that concerns how organizations develop human strengths, foster vitality and resilience, and unlock potential.

pushes organizations to think about how to exploit their employees' strengths rather than dwell on their limitations.

Responding to Globalization

In recent years, Canadian businesses have faced tough competition from the United States, Europe, Japan, and even China, as well as from other companies within our borders. To survive, they have had to reduce costs, increase productivity, and improve quality. A number of Canadian companies have found it necessary to merge in order to survive. For instance, Rona, the Boucherville, Quebec-based home improvement store, bought out Lansing, Revy, and Revelstoke in recent years in order to defend its turf against the Atlanta, Georgia-based Home Depot, with the result that in 2012, it was still holding its own against chief rivals Home Depot and Lowes.[55]

Some employers are starting to outsource jobs to other countries, where labour costs are lower. For instance, Toronto-based Dell Canada's technical service lines are handled by technicians working in India. Toronto-based Wall & Associates, a full-service chartered accounting and management consulting firm, outsources document management to Uganda. Employees in Uganda are willing to work for $1 an hour to sort and record receipts. While these wages might seem low, on average, Ugandans make only $1 a day.

Twenty or 30 years ago, national borders protected most firms from foreign competitive pressures. This is no longer the case. Trading blocs such as the North American Free Trade Agreement (NAFTA) and the European Union (EU) have significantly reduced tariffs and barriers to trade, and North America and Europe no longer have a monopoly on highly skilled labour. The Internet has also enabled companies to become more globally connected, by opening up international sales and by increasing the opportunities to carry on business. Even small firms can bid on projects in different countries and compete with larger firms via the Internet.

As multinational corporations develop operations worldwide, as companies develop joint ventures with foreign partners, and as employees increasingly pursue job opportunities across borders, managers and employees must become capable of working with people from different cultures. The changing and global competitive environment means that not only individuals but also organizations have to become increasingly flexible, by learning new skills, new ways of thinking, and new ways of doing business.

OB in Summary

We have discussed the meaning of OB throughout this chapter, and revealed different aspects of what OB covers. The essential points of OB that you should keep in mind as you study this topic are illustrated in Exhibit 1-4.

LESSONS LEARNED

- OB is for everyone.
- OB draws upon a rigorous multidisciplinary research base.

EXHIBIT 1-4 The Fundamentals of OB

- OB considers the multiple levels in an organization: individual, group, and organizational.

- OB is built from the wisdom and research of multiple disciplines, including psychology, sociology, social psychology, and anthropology.

- OB takes a systematic approach to the study of organizational phenomena. It is research-based.

- OB takes a contingency approach to the consideration of organizational phenomena. Recommendations depend on the situation.

Summary and Implications

1 **What is organizational behaviour?** Organizational behaviour (OB) is a field of study that investigates the impact that individuals, groups, and structure have on behaviour within an organization. It uses that knowledge to make organizations work more effectively. Specifically, OB focuses on how to improve productivity, reduce both absenteeism and turnover, and increase employee job satisfaction. OB also helps us understand how people can work together more effectively in the workplace.

OB recognizes differences, helps us see the value of workforce diversity, and calls attention to practices that may need to be changed when managing and working in different countries. It can help improve quality and employee productivity by showing managers how to empower their people, as well as how to design and implement change programs. It offers specific insights to improve people skills.

2 **Isn't organizational behaviour common sense? Or just like psychology?** OB is built on contributions from a number of behavioural disciplines, including psychology, sociology, social psychology, anthropology, and political science.

We all hold generalizations about the behaviour of people. Some of our generalizations may provide valid insights into human behaviour, but many are wrong. If understanding behaviour were simply common sense, we would see fewer problems in the workplace, because managers and employees would know how to behave. OB provides a systematic approach to improving predictions of behaviour that would be made from common sense alone.

3 **How does knowing about organizational behaviour make work and life more understandable?** From a management point of view, knowing OB can help you manage well. Managing people well pays off. It may also lead employees to have greater organizational commitment. From an individual point of view, knowing OB can help you understand why the workplace functions in the way it does. OB can also help you understand how to deal with others if you decide to start your own business.

4 **What challenges do managers and employees face in the workplace of the twenty-first century?** OB considers three levels of analysis—the individual, the group, and the organization—which, combined, help us understand behaviour in organizations. Each level has different challenges. At the individual level, we encounter employees who have different characteristics, and thus we consider how to better understand and make the most of these differences. Because employees have become more cynical about their employers, job satisfaction and motivation have become important issues in today's organizations. Employees are also confronted with the trend toward an empowered workplace. Perhaps the greatest challenge individuals (and organizations) face is how to behave ethically.

At the group level, individuals are increasingly expected to work in teams, which means that they need to do so effectively. Employees are expected to have good interpersonal skills. The workplace is now made up of people from many different backgrounds, requiring a greater ability to understand those different from ourselves.

At the organizational level, Canadian businesses face many challenges in the twenty-first century. They face ongoing competition at home and from US businesses, as well as growing competition from the global marketplace. Productivity is critical. It has become essential to develop effective employees who are committed to the organization. By putting people first, organizations can generate a committed workforce, but taking this approach becomes a challenge for businesses that focus solely on the bottom line. Organizations also have to learn how to be more sensitive to cultural differences, not only because Canada is a multicultural country, but also because competitive companies often develop global alliances or set up plants in foreign countries, where being aware of other cultures becomes a key to success.

OB at Work

for Review

1. Define *organizational behaviour*.

2. What is an organization? Is the family unit an organization? Explain.

3. "Behaviour is generally predictable, so there is no need to formally study OB." Do you agree or disagree with this statement? Why?

4. What does it mean to say OB takes a contingency approach in its analysis of behaviour?

5. What are the three levels of analysis in our OB model? Are they related? If so, how?

6. What are some of the challenges and opportunities that managers face as we move into the twenty-first century?

7. Why is job satisfaction an important consideration for OB?

8. What are effectiveness and efficiency, and how are they related to OB?

for Critical Thinking

1. "OB is for everyone." Build an argument to support this statement.

2. Why do you think the subject of OB might be criticized as being "only common sense," when we would rarely hear such a comment about a course in physics or statistics? Do you think this criticism of OB is fair?

3. On a scale of 1 to 10, measuring the sophistication of a scientific discipline in predicting phenomena, mathematical physics would probably be a 10. Where do you think OB would fall on the scale? Why?

4. Can empowerment lead to greater job satisfaction?

for You

- As you journey through this course in OB, bear in mind that the processes we describe are as relevant to you as an individual as they are to organizations, managers, and employees.

- When you work together with student teams, join a student organization, or volunteer time to a community group, know that your ability to get along with others has an effect on your interactions with the other people in the group and the achievement of the group's goals.

- If you are aware of how your perceptions and personality affect your interactions with others, you can be more careful in forming your initial impression of others.

- By knowing how to motivate others who are working with you, how to communicate effectively, and when to negotiate and compromise, you can get along in a variety of situations that are not necessarily work-related.

OB at work

POINT

Find the Quick Fix to OB Issues

Walk into your nearest major bookstore. You will undoubtedly find a large section of books devoted to management and managing human behaviour. A close look at the titles will find there is certainly no shortage of popular books on topics related to OB. To illustrate the point, consider the following popular book titles that are currently available on the topic of leadership:

- *Killing Cockroaches: And Other Scattered Musings on Leadership* (B&H Publishing, 2009)
- *Leadership Lessons from a Chef: Finding Time to Be Great* (Wiley, 2008)
- *High Altitude Leadership: What the World's Most Forbidding Peaks Teach Us About Success* (Jossey-Bass, 2008)
- *A Pirate Captain's Guide to Leadership* (Lighthouse, 2008)
- *The Verbal Judo Way of Leadership* (Looseleaf, 2007)
- *If Harry Potter Ran General Electric: Leadership Wisdom from the World of Wizards* (Currency/ Doubleday, 2006)
- *The Leadership Secrets of Santa Claus* (Performance Systems, 2004)
- *Leadership Wisdom from the Monk Who Sold His Ferrari* (Hay House, 2003)

Organizations are always looking for leaders; and managers and manager-wannabes are continually looking for ways to improve their leadership skills. Publishers respond to this demand by offering hundreds of titles that claim to provide insights into the subject of leadership. Books like these can provide people with the secrets to leadership that others know about. Moreover, isn't it better to learn about management and leadership from people in the trenches, as opposed to the latest esoteric musings from the "Ivory Tower"? Many of the most important insights we gain from life aren't necessarily the product of careful empirical research studies.

COUNTERPOINT

Beware of the Quick Fix!

We all want to find quick and simple solutions to our complex problems. But here is the bad news: For problems related to OB, quick and simple solutions are often wrong because they fail to consider the diversity among organizations, situations, and individuals. As Einstein said, "Everything should be made as simple as possible, but not simpler."

When it comes to understanding people at work, there are plenty of simplistic ideas and books to promote them. And these books are not just on leadership. Consider three recent bestsellers. *Our Iceberg Is Melting* looks at change through the eyes of a penguin. *Who Moved My Cheese?* is a metaphor about two mice that is meant to convey the benefits of accepting change. And *Whale Done!* proposes that managers can learn a lot about motivating people from techniques used by whale trainers at Sea World in San Diego. Are the "insights" from these books generalizable to people working in hundreds of different countries, in a thousand different organizations, and doing a million different jobs? It's very unlikely.

Popular books on OB often have cute titles and are fun to read, but they can make the job of managing people seem much simpler than it is. Some are based on the authors' opinions rather than substantive research.

OB is a complex subject. Few, if any, simple statements about human behaviour are generalizable to all people in all situations. Should you really try to apply leadership insights you got from a book about Geronimo or Tony Soprano to managing software engineers in the twenty-first century?

Most of the offerings available at your local bookstore tend to be simplistic solutions. To the degree that people buy these books and enthusiastically expect them to provide them with the secrets to effective management, they do a disservice to themselves and those they are trying to manage.

LEARNING ABOUT **YOURSELF** EXERCISE

The Competing Values Framework: Identifying Your Interpersonal Skills

From the list below, identify what you believe to be your strongest skills, and then identify those in which you think your performance is weak. You should identify about 4 strong skills and 4 weak skills.

1. Taking initiative
2. Goal setting ☆
3. Delegating effectively
4. Personal productivity and motivation —
5. Motivating others
6. Time and stress management —
7. Planning
8. Organizing
9. Controlling
10. Receiving and organizing information
11. Evaluating routine information
12. Responding to routine information

13. Understanding yourself and others ☆
14. Interpersonal communication
15. Developing subordinates —
16. Team building —
17. Participative decision making
18. Conflict management
19. Living with change
20. Creative thinking ☆
21. Managing change
22. Building and maintaining a power base
23. Negotiating agreement and commitment ☆
24. Negotiating and selling ideas

Scoring Key:

These skills are based on the Competing Values Framework (pages 28–31), and they appear in detail in Exhibit 1-5 on page 28. Below, you will see how the individual skills relate to various managerial roles. Using the skills you identified as strongest, identify which roles you feel especially prepared for right now. Then, using the skills you identified as weakest, identify areas in which you might want to gain more skill. You should also use this information to determine whether you are currently more internally or externally focused, or oriented more toward flexibility or control.

Director: 1, 2, 3 S
Producer: 4, 5, 6 WW
Coordinator: 7, 8, 9
Monitor: 10, 11, 12

Mentor: 13, 14, 15 SW
Facilitator: 16, 17, 18 W
Innovator: 19, 20, 21 S
Broker: 22, 23, 24 S

After reviewing how your strengths and weaknesses relate to the skills that today's managers and leaders need, as illustrated in Exhibit 1-6 (page 29), you should consider whether you need to develop a broader range of skills.

Source: Created based on material from R. E. Quinn, S. R. Faerman, M. P. Thompson, and M. R. McGrath, *Becoming a Master Manager: A Competency Framework* (New York: John Wiley & Sons, 1990), Chapter 1.

PERSONAL INVENTORY ASSESSMENT

Learn about yourself with the PIA collection of online exercises. Designed to promote self-reflection and engagement, these assessments will enhance your ability to connect with the key concepts of organizational behaviour. Go to MyManagementLab to access the assessments.

OB at work

Form small groups to discuss the following topics, as assigned by your instructor:

1. Consider a group situation in which you have worked. To what extent did the group rely on the technical skills of the group members vs. their interpersonal skills? Which skills seemed most important in helping the group function well?

2. Identify some examples of "worst jobs." What conditions of these jobs made them unpleasant? To what extent were these conditions related to behaviours of individuals?

3. Develop a list of "organizational puzzles," that is, behaviour you have observed in organizations that seemed to make little sense. As the term progresses, see if you can begin to explain these puzzles, using your knowledge of OB.

WORKING WITH OTHERS EXERCISE

Interpersonal Skills in the Workplace

This exercise asks you to consider the skills outlined in the Competing Values Framework on pages 28–31 to develop an understanding of managerial expertise. Steps 1–4 can be completed in 15–20 minutes.

1. Using the skills listed in the *Learning About Yourself Exercise,* identify the 4 skills that you think all managers should have.

2. Identify the 4 skills that you think are least important for managers to have.

3. In groups of 5–7, reach a consensus on the most-needed and least-needed skills identified in steps 1 and 2.

4. Using Exhibit 1-6 on page 29, determine whether your "ideal" managers would have trouble managing in some dimensions of organizational demands.

5. Your instructor will lead a general discussion of your results.

ETHICAL DILEMMA EXERCISE

Lying in Business

Do you think it's ever okay to lie?[56] If you were negotiating for the release of hostages, most people would probably agree that if lying would lead to the hostages' safety, it's okay. What about in business, where the stakes are rarely life or death? Business executives such as Martha Stewart have gone to jail for lying (submitting a false statement to federal investigators). Is misrepresentation or omitting factors okay as long as there is no outright lie?

Consider the negotiation process. A good negotiator never shows all his cards, right? And so omitting certain information is just part of the process. Well, it may surprise you to learn that the law will hold you liable for omitting information if partial disclosure is misleading or if one side has superior information not accessible to the other.

In one case (*Jordan v. Duff and Phelps*), a company (Duff and Phelps) withheld information from an employee (Jordan) about the impending sale of the company. The problem: Jordan was leaving the organization and therefore sold his shares in the company. Ten days later, when the sale of the company became public, those shares became worth much more. Jordan sued his former employer on the grounds that it should have disclosed this information to him. Duff and Phelps countered that it had never lied to Jordan. The US Court of Appeals argued that in such situations, one party cannot take "opportunistic advantage" of the other. In the eyes of the law, sometimes omitting relevant facts can be as bad as lying.

In a business context, is it ever okay to lie? When? Do you think it's fair to fire an employee who lies, no matter what the nature of the lie? Is withholding information for your own advantage the same as lying? Why or why not?

How a UPS Manager Cut Turnover

When Jennifer Shroeger was promoted to district manager for UPS's operation in Buffalo, New York, she faced a serious problem: Turnover was out of control.[57] Part-time employees—who load, unload, and sort packages and who account for half of Buffalo's workforce—were leaving at the rate of 50 percent a year. Cutting this turnover rate became her highest priority.

UPS relies heavily on part-time employees, some of whom eventually become full-time employees. Most of UPS's current executives began as part-timers while attending university, then moved into full-time positions. UPS has always treated its part-timers well, giving them high pay, flexible work hours, full benefits, and substantial financial aid to go back to school, but these pluses did not seem to be enough to keep employees at UPS in Buffalo.

Shroeger developed a comprehensive plan to reduce turnover. It focused on improving hiring, communication, the workplace, and supervisory training.

Shroeger began by modifying the hiring process to screen out people who essentially wanted full-time jobs. She reasoned that unfulfilled expectations were frustrating the hires whose preferences were for full-time work. Given that it typically took new part-timers six years to work up to a full-time job, it made sense to try to identify people who actually preferred part-time work.

Next, Shroeger analyzed the large database of information that UPS had on her district's employees. The data led her to the conclusion that she had five distinct groups working for her—differentiated by age and stages in their careers. And these groups had different needs and interests. In response, Shroeger modified the communication style and motivation techniques she used with each employee to reflect the group to which he or she belonged. For instance, Shroeger found that college students are most interested in building skills that they can apply later in their careers. As long as these employees saw that they

were learning new skills, they were content to keep working at UPS. So Shroeger began offering them Saturday sessions for career-planning discussions.

To further help new employees adjust, she turned some of her best shift supervisors into trainers who provided specific guidance during new hires' first week. Finally, Shroeger expanded training so supervisors had the skills to handle increased empowerment. Because she recognized that her supervisors—most of whom were part-timers themselves—were the ones best equipped to understand the needs of part-time employees, supervisors were taught how to assess difficult management situations, how to communicate in different ways, and how to identify the needs of different people. Supervisors learned to demonstrate interest in their employees as individuals. For instance, they were taught to inquire about employees' hobbies, where they went to school, and the like. Four years later, the attrition rate in Shroeger's district had dropped from 50 percent to 6 percent.

Questions

1. In dollars-and-cents terms, why did Jennifer Shroeger want to reduce turnover?

2. What are the implications from this case for motivating part-time employees?

3. What are the implications from this case for managing in future years when there may be a severe labour shortage?

4. Is it unethical to teach supervisors "to demonstrate interest in their employees as individuals"? Explain.

5. What facts in this case support the argument that OB should be approached from a contingency perspective?

FROM CONCEPTS TO SKILLS

Developing Interpersonal Skills

We note in the chapter that having a broad range of interpersonal skills to draw on makes us more effective organizational participants. So what kinds of interpersonal skills does an individual need in today's workplace?

☀️ Explore

Exhibit 1-5: Competing Values Framework

Robert Quinn, Kim Cameron, and their colleagues have developed a model known as the "Competing Values Framework" that can help us identify some of the most useful skills.[58] They note that the range of issues organizations face can be divided along two dimensions: an internal-external and a flexibility-control focus. This is illustrated in Exhibit 1-5. The internal–external dimension refers to the extent that organizations focus on one of two directions: either inwardly, toward employee needs and concerns and/or production processes and internal systems; or outwardly, toward such factors as the marketplace, government regulations, and the changing social, environmental, and technological conditions of the future. The flexibility–control dimension refers to the competing demands of organizations to stay focused on doing what has been done in the past vs. being more flexible in orientation and outlook.

Because organizations face the competing demands shown in Exhibit 1-5, it becomes obvious that managers and employees need a variety of skills to help them function within the various quadrants at different points. For instance, the skills needed to operate an efficient assembly-line process are not the same as those needed to scan the environment or to create opportunities in anticipation of changes in the environment. Quinn and his colleagues use the term *master manager* to indicate that successful managers learn and apply skills that will help them manage across the range of organizational demands; at some times moving toward flexibility, at others moving toward control, sometimes being more internally focused, sometimes being more externally driven.[59]

EXHIBIT 1-5 Competing Values Framework

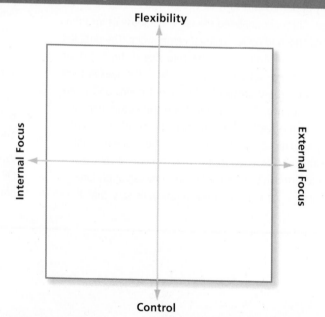

Source: Adapted from *Diagnosing and Changing Organizational Culture: Based on the Competing Values Framework* by K. Cameron and R. E. Quinn. Copyright © 2006, Jossey-Bass. Reproduced with permission of John Wiley & Sons, Inc.

As organizations increasingly cut their layers, reducing the number of managers while also relying more on the use of teams in the workplace, the skills of the master manager apply as well to the employee. In other words, considering the Competing Values Framework, we can see that both managers and individual employees need to learn new skills and new ways of interpreting their organizational contexts. Continuing to use traditional skills and practices that worked in the past is not an option. The growth in self-employment also indicates a need to develop more interpersonal skills, particularly for anyone who goes on to build a business that involves hiring and managing employees.

Exhibit 1-6 outlines the many skills required of today's manager. It gives you an indication of the complex roles that managers and employees fill in the changing workplace. The skills are organized in terms of four major roles: maintaining flexibility, maintaining control, maintaining an external focus, and maintaining an internal focus. The *Learning About Yourself Exercise* on page 25 helps you identify your own strengths and weaknesses in these skill areas so that you can have a better sense of how close you are to becoming a successful manager. For instance, on the flexibility side, organizations want to inspire their employees toward high-performance behaviour. Such behaviour includes looking ahead to the future and imagining possible new directions for the organization. To do these things, employees need to think and act like mentors and facilitators. It is also important to have the skills of innovators and brokers. On the control side, organizations need to set clear goals about productivity expectations, and they have to develop and implement systems to carry out the production process. To be effective on the production side, employees need to have the skills of monitors, coordinators, directors, and producers. The *Working with Others Exercise* on page 26 will help you better

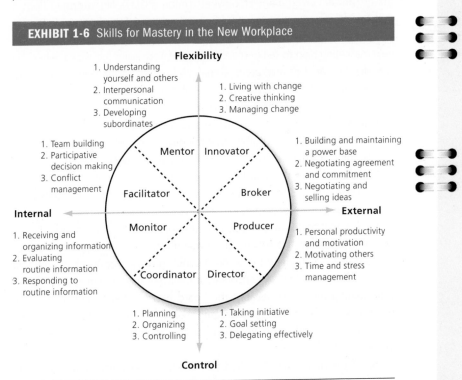

EXHIBIT 1-6 Skills for Mastery in the New Workplace

Source: R. E. Quinn, *Beyond Rational Management* (San Francisco: Jossey-Bass, 1988), p. 86.

understand how closely your views on the ideal skills of managers and leaders match the skills needed to be successful in the broad range of activities that managers and leaders encounter.

At this point, you may wonder whether it is possible for people to learn all of the skills necessary to become a master manager. More important, you may wonder whether we can change our individual style, say from more controlling to more flexible. Here is what Peggy Kent, former chair, president, and CEO of Century Mining Corporation (a mid-tier Canadian gold producer), said about how her managerial style changed from controlling to more flexible over time: "I started out being very dictatorial. Everybody in head office reported to me. I had to learn to trust other executives so we could work out problems together."[60] So, while it is probably true that each of us has a preferred style of operating, it is also the case that we can enhance the skills we have or develop new ones if that is something we choose to do. Learning to work well with others, listening to others, and building trust are skills that are certainly worth trying to master.

Practising Skills

As the father of two young children, Marshall Rogers thought that serving on the board of Marysville Daycare would be a good way to stay in touch with those who cared for his children during the day.[61] But he never dreamed that he would become involved in union-management negotiations with daycare-centre employees.

Late one Sunday evening, in his ninth month as president of the daycare centre, Rogers received a phone call from Grace Ng, a union representative of the Provincial Government Employees' Union (PGEU). Ng informed Rogers that the daycare employees would be unionized the following week. Rogers was stunned to hear this news. Early the next morning, he had to present his new marketing plan to senior management at Techtronix Industries, where he was vice-president of marketing. Somehow he made it through the meeting, wondering why he had not been aware of the employees' unhappiness, and how this action would affect his children.

Following his presentation, Rogers received documentation from the Labour Relations Board indicating that the daycare employees had been working to unionize themselves for more than a year. Rogers immediately contacted Xavier Breslin, the board's vice-president, and together they determined that no one on the board had been aware that the daycare employees were unhappy, let alone prepared to join a union.

Hoping that there was some sort of misunderstanding, Rogers called Emma Reynaud, the Marysville supervisor. Reynaud attended most board meetings, but had never mentioned the union-organizing drive. Yet Reynaud now told Rogers that she had actively encouraged the other daycare employees to consider joining the PGEU because the board had not been interested in the employees' concerns, had not increased their wages sufficiently over the past two years, and had not maintained communication channels between the board and the employees.

All of the board members had full-time jobs elsewhere, and many were upper- and middle-level managers in their own companies. They were used to dealing with unhappy employees in their own workplaces, although none had experienced a union-organizing drive. Like Rogers, they had chosen to serve on the board of Marysville to stay informed about the day-to-day events of the centre. They had not really thought of themselves as the centre's employer, although, as board members, they represented all the parents of children enrolled at Marysville. Their main tasks on the daycare-centre board had been setting fees for the children and wages for the daycare employees. The board members usually saw the staff members several times a week, when they picked up their children, yet the unhappiness represented by the union-organizing drive was surprising to all of them. When they met at an emergency board meeting that evening, they tried to evaluate what had gone wrong at Marysville.

Questions

1. If you were either a board member or a parent, how would you know that the employees taking care of your children were unhappy with their jobs?

2. What might you do if you learned about their unhappiness?

3. What might Rogers have done differently as president of the board?

4. In what ways does this case illustrate that knowledge of OB can be applied beyond your own workplace?

Reinforcing Skills

1. Talk to several managers you know and ask them what skills they think are most important in today's workplace. Ask them to specifically consider the use of teams in their workplaces, and what skills their team members most need to have but are least likely to have. How might you use this information to develop greater interpersonal skills?

2. Talk to several managers you know and ask them what skills they have found to be most important in doing their jobs. Why did they find these skills most important? What advice would they give a would-be manager about skills worth developing?

MyManagementLab Study, practise, and explore real business situations with these helpful resources:

- **Study Plan:** Check your understanding of chapter concepts with self-study quizzes.
- **Online Lesson Presentations:** Study key chapter topics and work through interactive assessments to test your knowledge and master management concepts.
- **Videos:** Learn more about the management practices and strategies of real companies.
- **Simulations:** Practise management decision-making in simulated business environments.

P **I** **A** PERSONAL INVENTORY ASSESSMENT

CHAPTER 2

Perception, Personality, and Emotions

Can a company win best employer in Canada awards *and* be regarded as the worst employer in Canada?

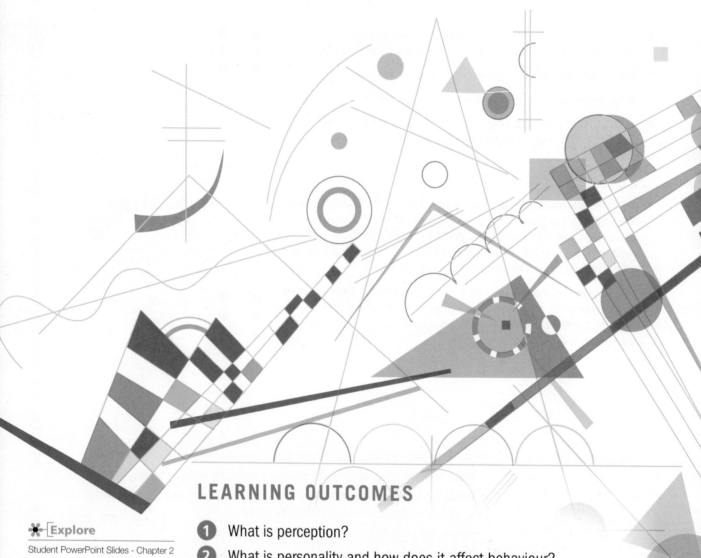

✳ Explore

Student PowerPoint Slides - Chapter 2

LEARNING OUTCOMES

1. What is perception?
2. What is personality and how does it affect behaviour?
3. Can emotions help or get in the way when we are dealing with others?

Walmart Canada.[1] Just the thought of the retailer being in Canada upsets some people. There was strong resistance when Walmart first announced it was coming to Canada in 1994, and a belief that the retailer would somehow destroy the fabric of Canadian society. Almost two decades after its arrival, Mississauga, Ontario-based Walmart Canada serves more than 1 million Canadians each day, employs more than 90 000 Canadians in over 330 stores across Canada, and is Canada's third-largest employer. The company was ranked as one of Canada's best employers on the Hewitt Associates survey of Canada's Best Employers five times between 2001 and 2007. It has also appeared on Waterstone Human Capital's list of Canada's 10 Most Admired Corporate Cultures, most recently in 2009. It was one of Workplace Institute's winners in 2011 for Best Employers Award for 50-Plus Canadians, which it's won several times previously. In presenting the award, Workplace Institute noted, "Wal-Mart has exceptional hiring and recognition programs and a workplace culture that supports diversity." With all of these positive statements about Walmart Canada, customers are not necessarily convinced of Walmart's greatness.

US-based retail giant Target will be opening a number of stores in Canada in 2013 and 2014. Rather than the battle for customers that faced Walmart when it came to Canada, Canadians seem more eager to shop at Target. When asked in a 2011 survey how likely they would be to change their shopping habits once Target opens stores in Canada, 57 percent of Walmart shoppers indicated a willingness to shop at Target. This suggests a specific lack of loyalty by Walmart Canada customers. Less than 20 percent of Canadian Tire, Shoppers Drug Mart, and Costco customers indicated a willingness to shop at Target. How can the perception of Walmart be so negative for some individuals, even though so many people shop there?

All of our behaviour is somewhat shaped by our perceptions, personalities, emotions, and experiences. In this chapter, we consider the role that perception plays in affecting the way we see the world and the people around us. We also consider how personality characteristics affect our attitudes toward people and situations. We then consider how emotions shape many of our work-related behaviours.

THE BIG IDEA

Individual differences can have a large impact on how groups and organizations function.

OB IS FOR EVERYONE

- What causes people to have different perceptions of the same situation?
- Whom do you tend to blame when someone makes a mistake? Ever wonder why?
- Have you ever misjudged a person? Do you know why?
- Can perception really affect outcomes?
- Are people born with their personalities?
- Do you think it is better to be a Type A or a Type B personality?
- Ever wonder why the grocery clerk is always smiling?

LEARNING ABOUT YOURSELF

- Machiavellianism
- Self-Monitoring
- Risk-Taking
- Personality Type

Perception

1 What is perception?

Perception is the process by which individuals select, organize, and interpret their sensory impressions in order to give meaning to their environment. However, what we perceive can be substantially different from objective reality. We often disagree about what is real. As we have seen, Walmart Canada has won many awards, but not every Canadian respects the retailer.

Why is perception important in the study of organizational behaviour (OB)? Simply because people's behaviour is based on their perception of what reality is, not on reality itself. *The world as it is perceived is the world that is behaviourally important.* A 2010 study of political behaviour suggests that once individuals hold particular perceptions, it can be quite difficult to change their minds, even if they are shown contrary evidence.[2]

Factors Influencing Perception

How do we explain that individuals may look at the same thing, yet perceive it differently, and both be right? A number of factors operate to shape and sometimes distort perception. These factors can be found in the *perceiver;* in the object or *target* being perceived; or in the context of the *situation* in which the perception is made. Exhibit 2-1 summarizes the factors influencing perception. This chapter's *Working with Others Exercise* on page 67 will help you understand how your perceptions affect your evaluation of others.

> What causes people to have different perceptions of the same situation?

The Perceiver

When you ("the perceiver") look at a target and attempt to interpret what you see, that interpretation is heavily influenced by your personal characteristics. Characteristics that affect perception include your attitudes, personality, motives, interests, past experiences, and expectations. For instance, if you expect police officers to be authoritative, young people to be lazy, or individuals holding public office to be

Exhibit 2-1: Factors That Influence Perception

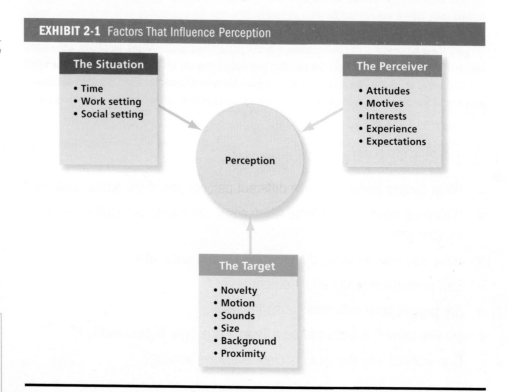

EXHIBIT 2-1 Factors That Influence Perception

The Situation
- Time
- Work setting
- Social setting

The Perceiver
- Attitudes
- Motives
- Interests
- Experience
- Expectations

Perception

The Target
- Novelty
- Motion
- Sounds
- Size
- Background
- Proximity

perception The process by which individuals select, organize, and interpret their sensory impressions in order to give meaning to their environment.

corrupt, you may perceive them as such, regardless of their actual traits. A 2010 study found that one's perceptions of others reveals a lot about the person themselves.[3] People with positive perceptions of others tended to describe themselves (and be described by others) as "enthusiastic, happy, kind-hearted, courteous, emotionally stable and capable." People who had negative perceptions of others were more likely to be narcissistic and engage in antisocial behaviour.

The Target

A target's characteristics can affect what we perceive. Loud people are more likely to be noticed in a group than are quiet ones. So too are extremely attractive or unattractive individuals. Novelty, motion, sound, size, and other attributes of a target shape the way we see it.

Because we don't look at targets in isolation, the relationship of a target to its background influences perception. For instance, we often perceive women, First Nations, Asians, or members of any other group that has clearly distinguishable characteristics as alike in not only physical terms, but other, unrelated ways as well.

The Context

The situation or context is also important. The time at which we see an object or event can influence attention, as can location, light, heat, or any number of situational factors. For example, at a nightclub on Saturday night, you may not notice a young guest "dressed to the nines." Yet that same person so attired for your Monday morning management class would certainly catch your attention (and that of the rest of the class). Neither the perceiver nor the target changed between Saturday night and Monday morning, but the situation is different.

Perceptual Errors

Perceiving and interpreting why others do what they do takes time. As a result, we develop shortcuts to make this task more manageable. These shortcuts are often very helpful—they allow us to make accurate perceptions quickly and provide valid information for making predictions. However, they are not foolproof. They can and do get us into trouble. For instance, when we make a bad first impression on someone, that perception may lead them to treat us poorly or dismiss us as a prospective employee or teammate. Some of the errors that distort the perception process include attribution theory, selective perception, the halo effect, contrast effects, projection, and stereotyping.

Attribution Theory

Attribution theory tries to explain the ways we judge people differently, depending on the cause we attribute to a given behaviour.[4] Basically, the theory suggests that when we observe what seems like atypical behaviour by an individual, we try to make sense of it. We consider whether the individual is responsible for the behaviour (the cause is internal), or whether something outside the individual caused the behaviour (the cause is external). *Internally* caused behaviour is believed to be under the personal control of the individual. *Externally* caused behaviour is believed to result from outside causes; we see the person as having been forced into the behaviour by the situation. For example, if a student is late for class, the instructor might attribute his lateness to partying into the wee hours of the morning and then oversleeping. This would be an internal attribution. But if the instructor assumes that a major automobile accident tied up traffic on the student's regular route to school, that is making an external attribution. In trying to determine whether

Whom do you tend to blame when someone makes a mistake? Ever wonder why?

attribution theory The theory that when we observe what seems to be atypical behaviour by an individual, we attempt to determine whether it is internally or externally caused.

✴ Explore

Exhibit 2-2: Attribution Theory

EXHIBIT 2-2 Attribution Theory

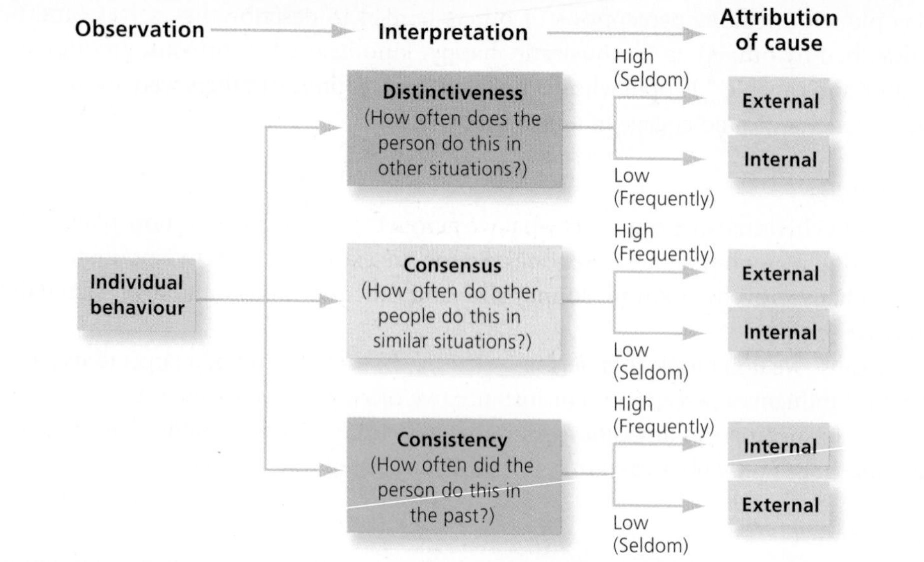

behaviour is internally or externally caused, we rely on three rules about the behaviour: (1) distinctiveness, (2) consensus, and (3) consistency (see Exhibit 2-2). Let's discuss each of these in turn.

Distinctiveness **Distinctiveness** refers to whether an individual acts similarly across a variety of situations. Is the student who arrives late for class today also the one who is always goofing off in team meetings, and not answering urgent emails? What we want to know is whether this behaviour is unusual. If it is, we are likely to give it an external attribution. If it's not, we will probably judge the behaviour to be internal.

Consensus **Consensus** considers how an individual's behaviour compares with that of others in the same situation. If everyone who is faced with a similar situation responds in the same way, we can say the behaviour shows consensus. When consensus is high, an external attribution is given to an individual's behaviour. But if an individual's behaviour is different from everyone else's, you would conclude the cause for that individual's behaviour was internal.

Consistency Finally, an observer looks for **consistency** in a person's actions. Does the person respond the same way over time? If a student is usually on time for class, being 10 minutes late will be perceived differently from the student who is late almost every class.

How Attributions Get Distorted One of the more interesting findings from attribution theory is that there are errors or biases that distort attributions. When we judge the behaviour of other people, we tend to put more emphasis on internal or personal factors and less emphasis on external factors.[5] This **fundamental attribution error** can explain why a sales manager is prone to attribute the poor performance of his or her sales agents to laziness rather than to the innovative product line introduced by a competitor. A 2011 study suggests this same error occurs when we judge leaders to be charismatic, based on limited information.[6] For instance, as CEO of Apple, Steve Jobs gave spellbinding presentations that led him to be considered a charismatic

distinctiveness A behavioural rule that asks whether an individual acts similarly across a variety of situations.

consensus A behavioural rule that asks if everyone faced with a similar situation responds in the same way.

consistency A behavioural rule that asks whether the individual has been acting in the same way over time.

fundamental attribution error The tendency to underestimate the influence of external factors and overestimate the influence of internal factors when making judgments about the behaviour of others.

Have you ever misjudged a person? Do you know why?

EXHIBIT 2-3 Percentage of Individuals Rating Themselves Above Average on Each Attribute

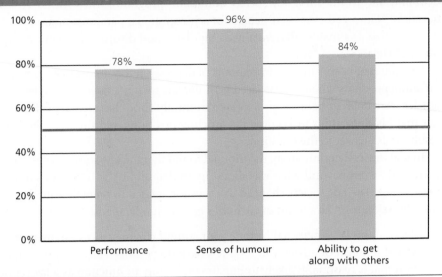

Source: Based on C. Merkle and M. Weber, *True Overconfidence—The Inability of Rational Information Processing to Account for Overconfidence* (March 2009). Available at SSRN: http://ssrn.com/abstract=1373675

visionary. What the audience did not see was "the ten hours of practice Jobs commit[ed] to every ten minute pitch," without which he might have looked less charismatic.[7]

We use **self-serving bias** when we judge ourselves. This means that when we are successful, we are more likely to believe it was because of internal factors, such as ability or effort. When we fail, however, we blame external factors, such as luck. In general, people tend to believe that their own behaviour is more positive than the behaviour of those around them. Research suggests, however, that individuals tend to overestimate their own good behaviour, and underestimate the good behaviour of others.[8] Exhibit 2-3 illustrates this point.

Selective Perception

Because it is impossible for us to absorb everything we see, we engage in **selective perception**. Any characteristic that makes a person, object, or event stand out will increase the probability that we see that characteristic, rather than the whole package of characteristics. This tendency explains why, for example, you are more likely to notice cars like your own.

How does selectivity work as a shortcut in judging other people? Since we cannot absorb all that we see, we take in bits and pieces. But we do not choose randomly; rather, we select according to our interests, background, experience, and attitudes. Selective perception also allows us to speed-read others, but not without the risk of coming to an inaccurate conclusion. Because we see what we want to see, we can make unwarranted conclusions about an ambiguous situation. Selective perception led the Law Society of BC to discriminate against lawyers who suffer from a mental illness, as *Focus on Diversity* shows.

FOCUS ON DIVERSITY

Law Society's Question About Mental Health Challenged

Should employees be required to reveal they have a mental illness? In July 2011, the BC Human Rights Tribunal ruled that the Law Society of BC had discriminated against a lawyer with a mental disability.[9] The lawyer, Peter Mokua Gichuru, was awarded almost $100 000 by the tribunal.

self-serving bias The tendency for individuals to attribute their own successes to internal factors while putting the blame for failures on external factors.

selective perception People's selective interpretation of what they see based on their interests, background, experience, and attitudes.

Gichuru's problems started when he began applying for work as an articling student and had to fill out a law society admission program form with the following question: "Have you ever been treated for schizophrenia, paranoia, or a mood disorder described as a major affective illness, bipolar mood disorder, or manic depressive illness?" He answered "yes."

Gichuru had been suffering from bouts of depression for almost five years and was on antidepressants when he was faced with the law society's question. He felt that his articles were delayed because he answered truthfully about his mental health. He also felt that his difficulties in keeping his articling positions and finding others were a result of his answer to the question.

In making its determination, the tribunal found that the law society, while acting in good faith, went beyond what was necessary to determine the fitness of someone to practise law. The law society changed the question related to mental health history on the admission form as a result of Gichuru's appeal. It now reads:

> Based upon your personal history, your current circumstances or any professional opinion or advice you have received, do you have any existing condition that is reasonably likely to impair your ability to function as a lawyer or articled student? If the answer is "yes" to the question above, please provide a general description of the impairment.

Those who answer "yes" to this new question are followed on a case-by-case basis, but the information is kept confidential and is not disclosed to potential employers. While Gichuru still has some concerns about the use of the information, he testified that it "is a dramatic improvement . . . and that on its face it does not discriminate between so-called physical and mental illnesses." ●

Halo Effect

When we draw a general impression about an individual on the basis of a single characteristic, such as intelligence, likeability, or appearance, a **halo effect** operates. If you are a critic of Prime Minister Stephen Harper, try listing 10 things you admire about him. If you are an admirer, try listing 10 things you dislike about him. No matter

The behaviours that both women and men engage in can affect the perceptions that others have about their ability to become senior managers. A 2010 study found that assertiveness and independence were top qualities to exhibit, and individuals who did not do so were deemed less suited to be CEOs.[10] Those judging the suitability were engaging in selective perception.

halo effect Drawing a general impression of an individual on the basis of a single characteristic.

which group describes you, odds are you won't find this an easy exercise! That is the halo effect: Our general views contaminate our specific ones.

The reality of the halo effect was confirmed in a classic study. Subjects were given a list of traits and asked to evaluate the person to whom those traits applied.[11] When traits such as intelligent, skillful, practical, industrious, determined, and warm were used, the person was judged to be wise, humorous, popular, and imaginative. When cold was substituted for warm, a completely different set of perceptions was obtained, though otherwise the list was identical. Clearly, the subjects were allowing a single trait to influence their overall impression of the person being judged.

Contrast Effects

There is an old saying among entertainers: "Never follow an act that has children or animals in it." Why? Audiences love children and animals so much that you'll look bad in comparison.

This example demonstrates how **contrast effects** can distort perceptions.[12] We do not evaluate a person in isolation. Our reaction to one person is often influenced by other people we have recently encountered.

In a series of job interviews, for instance, interviewers can make distortions in any given candidate's evaluation as a result of his or her place in the interview schedule. The candidate is likely to receive a better evaluation if interviewed after a mediocre applicant, and a worse evaluation if interviewed after a strong applicant.

Projection

It is easy to judge others if we assume that they are similar to us. For instance, if you want challenge and responsibility in your job, you assume that others want the same. Or you are honest and trustworthy, so you take it for granted that other people are equally honest and trustworthy. This tendency to attribute our own characteristics to other people is called **projection**.

People who engage in projection tend to perceive others according to what they themselves are like rather than perceiving others as they really are. Because they always judge people as similar to themselves, when they observe someone who is actually

Aboriginal hip-hop artists, led by Winnipeg's Most (pictured here), have created a coalition against the negative stereotyping of Indigenous rappers by the mainstream media. This initiative is an opportunity for Indigenous hip hop to define itself in a sustainable and healthy manner for the future. Aboriginal musician Jarrett Martineau says that hip hop is popular with Aboriginal youth because it deals with oppression and dispossession and because First Nations culture has a strong tradition of storytelling.[13]

contrast effects　The concept that our reaction to one person is often influenced by other people we have recently encountered.

projection　Attributing one's own characteristics to other people.

like them their perceptions are naturally correct. But when they observe others who are not like them, their perceptions are not so accurate.

Stereotyping

When we judge someone on the basis of our perception of the group to which he or she belongs, we are using the shortcut called **stereotyping**.

We rely on generalizations every day because they help us make decisions quickly. They are a means of simplifying a complex world. It's less difficult to deal with an unmanageable number of stimuli if we use **heuristics** (judgment shortcuts in decision making) or stereotypes. For example, it does make sense to assume that Tre, the new employee from accounting, is going to know something about budgeting, or that Allie from finance will be able to help you figure out a forecasting problem. The problem occurs, of course, when we generalize inaccurately or too much. In organizations, we frequently hear comments that represent stereotypes based on gender, age, race, religion, ethnicity, and even weight:[14] "Women will not relocate for a promotion," "men are not interested in child care," "older workers cannot learn new skills," "Asian immigrants are hard-working and conscientious," "overweight people lack discipline." Stereotypes can be so deeply ingrained and powerful that they influence life-and-death decisions. One study showed that, controlling for a wide array of factors (such as aggravating or mitigating circumstances), the degree to which black defendants in US murder trials looked "stereotypically black" essentially doubled their odds of receiving a death sentence if convicted.[15]

One of the problems of stereotypes is that they *are* widespread and often useful generalizations, despite the fact that they may not contain a shred of truth when applied to a particular person or situation. So we constantly have to check ourselves to make sure we are not unfairly or inaccurately applying a stereotype in our evaluations and decisions. Stereotypes are an example of the warning "The more useful, the more danger from misuse." Stereotypes can lead to strong negative reactions, such as prejudice, which we describe below.

Prejudice **Prejudice** is an unfounded dislike of a person or group based on their belonging to a particular stereotyped group. For instance, an individual may dislike people of a particular religion, or state that she does not want to work with someone of a particular ethnicity. Prejudice can lead to negative consequences in the workplace and, in

Muslim women in Canada often experience discrimination in being hired, or how their co-workers treat them, when they wear a hijab. Co-workers of nurse Sharon Hoosein, shown here, were surprised that she returned to work following her maternity leave. They assumed that because of her religion she would be expected to stay at home to raise children rather than work.

stereotyping Judging someone on the basis of one's perception of the group to which that person belongs.

heuristics Judgment shortcuts in decision making.

prejudice An unfounded dislike of a person or group based on their belonging to a particular stereotyped group.

particular, to discrimination.[16] For instance, an individual of a particular ethnic group might be passed over for a management position because of the belief that employees might not see that person as a good manager. In another instance, an individual in his fifties who is looking for work but cannot find a job may be discriminated against because of the belief that younger workers are more appealing than older workers. Prejudice generally starts with stereotypes and then has negative emotional content added. Prejudice is harmful to the person who is the target of the behaviour. A 2011 study by researchers from the University of Toronto found that Asian women are more likely to take racism than sexism personally and were more negatively affected by racism.[17]

Why Do Perception and Judgment Matter?

People in organizations are always judging one another. Managers must appraise their employees' performances. We evaluate how much effort our co-workers are putting into their jobs. When a new person joins a work team, the other members immediately "size her up." Individuals even make judgments about people's virtues based on whether they exercise, as a study by McMaster University professor Kathleen Martin Ginis showed.[18] In many cases, our judgments have important consequences for the organization. A 2010 study found that in organizations that did not seem to value innovation, employees who wanted to see change were often afraid to speak out, due to fear of negative perceptions from co-workers who valued the status quo.[19] Another 2010 study found that positive employee perceptions of an organization have a positive impact on retention, customer loyalty, and financial outcomes.[20] A 2011 study noted that individuals who misperceive how well they have done on a task (positively or negatively) tended to prepare less and to perform poorly in subsequent tasks.[21]

Can perception really affect outcomes?

Let's briefly look at a few of the most obvious applications of judgment shortcuts in the workplace: employment interviews, performance expectations, and performance evaluations.

Employment Interviews

It's fair to say that few people are hired without an interview. But interviewers make perceptual judgments that are often inaccurate[22] and draw early impressions that quickly become entrenched. Research shows we form impressions of others within a tenth of a second, based on our first glance.[23] If these first impressions are negative, they tend to be more heavily weighted in the interview than if that same information came out later.[24] Most interviewers' decisions change very little after the first 4 or 5 minutes of an interview. As a result, information elicited early in the interview carries greater weight than does information elicited later, and a "good applicant" is probably characterized more by the absence of unfavourable characteristics than by the presence of favourable ones. This chapter's *Ethical Dilemma Exercise* on page 68 illustrates how the perception of people with tattoos affects hiring practices.

Performance Expectations

People attempt to validate their perceptions of reality even when they are faulty.[25] The terms **self-fulfilling prophecy** and *Pygmalion effect* describe how an individual's behaviour is determined by others' expectations. If a manager expects big things from her people, they are not likely to let her down. Similarly, if she expects only minimal performance, they will likely meet those low expectations. Expectations become reality. The self-fulfilling prophecy has been found to affect the performance of students, soldiers, and even accountants.[26]

self-fulfilling prophecy A concept that proposes a person will behave in ways consistent with how he or she is perceived by others.

Performance Evaluations

Performance evaluations very much depend on the perceptual process.[27] An employee's future is closely tied to the appraisal—promotion, pay raises, and continuation of employment are among the most obvious outcomes. Although the appraisal can be objective (for example, a salesperson is appraised on how many dollars of sales he generates in his territory), many jobs are evaluated in subjective terms. Subjective evaluations, though often necessary, are problematic because all the errors we have discussed thus far—selective perception, contrast effects, halo effects, and so on—affect them. Ironically, sometimes performance ratings say as much about the evaluator as they do about the employee!

As you can see, perception plays a large role in how people are evaluated. Personality, which we review below, is another major factor affecting how people relate in the workplace.

Personality

 Walmart faced great outrage from Canadians when it first entered Canada in 1994.[28] Target will arrive in Canada in 2013, taking over more than 130 Zellers locations. Walmart and Target have different personalities. "Target stocks its shelves with low-cost bedspreads, shower curtains, and clothes with bright colors and funky designs. Walmart is for the necessities: cheap Cheerios, laundry detergent, bulk meat, paper plates."

The image of Target is fun, while Walmart's image is frugal. In other words, they have different personalities.

Organizational personalities can be interesting, but even more interesting is the impact of individual personalities on organizational behaviour. Why are some people quiet and passive, while others are loud and aggressive? Are certain personality types better adapted for certain job types? Before we can answer these questions, we need to address a more basic one: What is personality?

What Is Personality?

When we talk of personality we do not mean that a person has charm, a positive attitude toward life, a smiling face, or is a finalist for "Happiest and Friendliest." When psychologists talk of personality, they mean a dynamic concept describing the growth and development of a person's whole psychological system. Gordon Allport produced the most frequently used definition of personality more than 70 years ago. He said personality is "the dynamic organization within the individual of those psychophysical systems that determine his unique adjustments to his environment."[29] For our purposes, you should think of **personality** as the stable patterns of behaviour and consistent internal states that determine how an individual reacts to and interacts with others. It is most often described in terms of measurable traits that a person exhibits.

Measuring Personality

The most important reason managers need to know how to measure personality is that research has shown that personality tests are useful in hiring decisions. Scores on personality tests help managers forecast who is the best fit for a job.[30] Some managers use personality tests to better understand and more effectively manage the people who work for them. The most common means of measuring personality is through self-report surveys, with which individuals evaluate themselves by rating themselves on a series of factors, such as "I worry a lot about the future." Though self-report measures work well when well constructed, one weakness of these measures is that the respondent might lie or practise impression management—that is, the person could "fake it"

personality The stable patterns of behaviour and consistent internal states that determine how an individual reacts to and interacts with others.

on the test to create a good impression. Evidence shows that when people know that their personality scores are going to be used for hiring decisions, they rate themselves as about half a standard deviation more conscientious and emotionally stable than if they are taking the test just to learn more about themselves.[31] Another problem is accuracy. A perfectly good candidate could have just been in a bad mood when the survey was taken.

Observer ratings provide an independent assessment of personality. Here a co-worker or another observer does the rating (sometimes with the subject's knowledge and sometimes without). Though the results of self-reports and observer ratings are strongly correlated, research suggests that observer ratings are a better predictor of success on the job.[32] However, each can tell us something unique about an individual's behaviour in the workplace.

Personality Determinants

An early argument in personality research centred on whether an individual's personality was predetermined at birth, or the result of the individual's interaction with his or her environment. Clearly, there is no simple answer. Personality appears to be a result of both influences. In addition, today we recognize a third factor—the situation. Thus, an adult's personality is now generally considered to be made up of both hereditary and environmental factors, moderated by situational conditions.

Heredity

Heredity refers to those factors that were determined at conception. Physical stature, facial attractiveness, gender, temperament, muscle composition and reflexes, energy level, and biological rhythms are characteristics that are generally considered to be either completely or largely influenced by your parents' biological, physiological, and inherent psychological makeup. The heredity approach argues that the ultimate explanation of an individual's personality is a person's genes.

Are people born with their personalities?

If heredity played little or no part in determining personality, you would expect to find few similarities between identical twins who were separated at birth and raised separately. But researchers who looked at more than 100 sets of separated twins found a lot in common.[33] For almost every behavioural trait, a significant part of the variation between the twins turned out to be associated with genetic factors. For instance, one set of twins, who had been separated for 39 years and raised 70 kilometres apart, were found to drive the same model and colour car, chain-smoke the same brand of cigarette, own dogs with the same name, and regularly vacation within three blocks of each other in a beach community 2000 kilometres away.

Researchers have found that genetics can explain about 50 percent of the personality differences and more than 30 percent of the variation in occupational and leisure interests found in individuals. In other words, blood-related siblings are likely to have more similar personalities, occupations, and leisure interests than unrelated people.

Does personality change over one's lifetime? Most research in this area suggests that while some aspects of our personalities do change over time, the rank orderings do not change very much. For example, people's scores on measures of conscientiousness tend to increase as they get older. However, there are still strong individual differences in conscientiousness, and despite the fact that most of us become more responsible over time, people tend to change by about the same amount, so that the rank order stays roughly the same.[34] For instance, if you are more conscientious than your sibling now, that is likely to be true in 20 years, even though you both should become more conscientious over time. Consistent with the notion that the teenage years are

Source: Peanuts, reprinted by permission of Universal Uclick.

periods of great exploration and change, research has shown that personality is more changeable in adolescence and more stable among adults.[35]

Personality Traits

The early work in the structure of personality revolved around attempts to identify and label enduring characteristics that describe an individual's behaviour. Popular characteristics include shy, aggressive, submissive, lazy, ambitious, loyal, and timid. Those characteristics, when they are exhibited in a large number of situations, are called **personality traits**.[36] The more consistent the characteristic and the more often it occurs in different situations, the more important that trait is in describing the individual.

A number of early research efforts tried to identify the *primary* traits that govern behaviour.[37] However, for the most part, they resulted in long lists of traits that were difficult to generalize from and provided little practical guidance to organizational decision makers. The two exceptions are the Myers-Briggs Type Indicator and the Big Five Personality Model, which are the dominant frameworks used for identifying and classifying personality traits.

Keep in mind that each of us reacts differently to personality traits. This is partially a function of how we perceive those traits. In Exhibit 2-4, you will note that Lucy tells Linus a few things about his personality.

The Myers-Briggs Type Indicator

The **Myers-Briggs Type Indicator (MBTI)** is the most widely used personality-assessment instrument in the world.[38] It's a 100-question personality test that asks people how they usually feel or act in particular situations. On the basis of their answers, individuals are classified as extraverted or introverted (E or I), sensing or intuitive (S or N), thinking or feeling (T or F), and judging or perceiving (J or P). These terms are defined as follows:

- *Extraverted/introverted.* Extraverted individuals are outgoing, sociable, and assertive. Introverts are quiet and shy. E/I measures where we direct our energy when dealing with people and things.

- *Sensing/intuitive.* Sensing types are practical and prefer routine and order. They focus on details. Intuitives rely on unconscious processes and look at the "big picture." This dimension looks at how we process information.

- *Thinking/feeling.* Thinking types use reason and logic to handle problems. Feeling types rely on their personal values and emotions.

- *Judging/perceiving.* Judging types want control and prefer their world to be ordered and structured. Perceiving types are flexible and spontaneous.

personality traits Enduring characteristics that describe an individual's behaviour.

Myers-Briggs Type Indicator (MBTI) A personality test that taps four characteristics and classifies people into 1 of 16 personality types.

These classifications together describe 16 personality types. To illustrate, let's look at three examples:

- *INTJs are visionaries.* They usually have original minds and great drive for their own ideas and purposes. They are skeptical, critical, independent, determined, and often stubborn.

- *ESTJs are organizers.* They are realistic, logical, analytical, decisive, and have a natural head for business or mechanics. They like to organize and run activities.

- *ENTPs are conceptualizers.* They are innovative, individualistic, versatile, and attracted to entrepreneurial ideas. They tend to be resourceful in solving challenging problems, but may neglect routine assignments.

A book profiling 13 contemporary businesspeople who created super-successful firms including Apple Computer, FedEx, Honda Motors, Microsoft, and Sony found that all are intuitive thinkers (NTs).[39] This result is particularly interesting because intuitive thinkers represent only about 5 percent of the population.

The MBTI is widely used by organizations including Apple Computer, AT&T, Citigroup, GE, 3M, Cambridge, Ontario's Fire Department, many hospitals and educational institutions, and even the US Armed Forces. In spite of its popularity, the evidence is mixed as to whether the MBTI is a valid measure of personality—with most of the evidence suggesting that it is not.[40] One problem is that it forces a person into either one type or another (that is, you are either introverted or extraverted). There is no in-between, though people can be both extraverted and introverted to some degree. The best we can say is that the MBTI can be a valuable tool for increasing self-awareness and providing career guidance. But because results tend to be unrelated to job performance, managers probably should not use it as a selection test for job candidates.

The Big Five Personality Model

The MBTI may lack valid supporting evidence, but that cannot be said for the **Big Five Personality Model**. An impressive body of research supports the notion that five basic personality dimensions underlie all others and include most of the significant variations in human personality.[41] The Big Five personality factors are as follows:

- **Extraversion**. This dimension captures a person's comfort level with relationships. Extraverts tend to be gregarious, assertive, and sociable. Introverts tend to be reserved, timid, and quiet.

- **Agreeableness**. This dimension refers to how readily a person will go along with others. Highly agreeable people are cooperative, warm, and trusting. People who score low on agreeableness are cold, disagreeable, and antagonistic.

- **Conscientiousness**. This dimension is a measure of a person's reliability. A highly conscientious person is responsible, organized, dependable, and persistent. Those who score low on this dimension are easily distracted, disorganized, and unreliable.

- **Emotional stability**. This dimension—often labelled by its converse, *neuroticism*—taps into a person's ability to withstand stress. People with positive emotional stability tend to be calm, self-confident, and secure. Those with high negative scores tend to be nervous, anxious, depressed, and insecure.

- **Openness to experience**. The final dimension addresses a person's range of interests and fascination with novelty. Extremely open people are creative, curious, and artistically sensitive. Those at the other end of the openness category are conventional and find comfort in the familiar.

PERSONAL INVENTORY ASSESSMENT

Learn About Yourself
Tolerance of Ambiguity Scale

extraversion A personality factor that describes the degree to which someone is sociable, talkative, and assertive.

agreeableness A personality factor that describes the degree to which someone is good-natured, cooperative, warm, and trusting.

conscientiousness A personality factor that describes the degree to which someone is responsible, dependable, persistent, and achievement-oriented.

emotional stability A personality dimension that characterizes someone as calm, self-confident, secure (positive) vs. nervous, depressed, and insecure (negative).

openness to experience A personality factor that describes the degree to which someone is imaginative, artistically sensitive, and curious.

Explore

Exhibit 2-5: Big Five Personality Factors

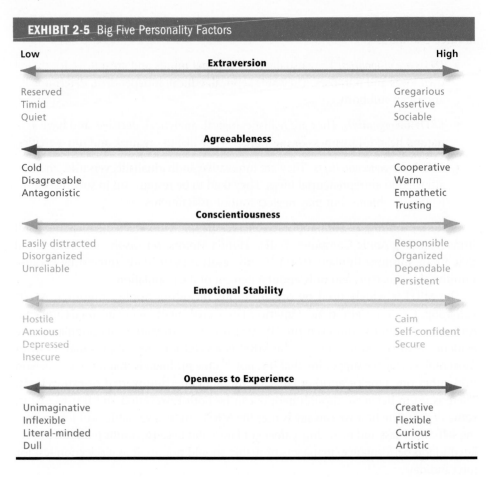

EXHIBIT 2-5 Big Five Personality Factors

Low		High
	Extraversion	
Reserved		Gregarious
Timid		Assertive
Quiet		Sociable
	Agreeableness	
Cold		Cooperative
Disagreeable		Warm
Antagonistic		Empathetic
		Trusting
	Conscientiousness	
Easily distracted		Responsible
Disorganized		Organized
Unreliable		Dependable
		Persistent
	Emotional Stability	
Hostile		Calm
Anxious		Self-confident
Depressed		Secure
Insecure		
	Openness to Experience	
Unimaginative		Creative
Inflexible		Flexible
Literal-minded		Curious
Dull		Artistic

Researchers at the University of Toronto have recently created a "fake proof" personality test to measure these factors.[42] Professor Jordan Peterson, one of the researchers, noted that it is common for people to try to "make themselves look better than they actually are on these questionnaires. . . . This sort of faking can distort the predictive validity of these tests, with significant negative economic consequences. We wanted to develop a measure that could predict real-world performance even in the absence of completely honest responding."[43]

Exhibit 2-5 shows the characteristics for the high and low dimensions of each Big Five personality factor.

Research on the Big Five has found a relationship between the personality dimensions and job performance.[44] As the authors of the most-cited review put it, "The preponderance of evidence shows that individuals who are dependable, reliable, careful, thorough, able to plan, organized, hardworking, persistent, and achievement-oriented tend to have higher job performance in most if not all occupations."[45] In addition, employees who score higher in conscientiousness develop higher levels of job knowledge, probably because highly conscientious people learn more (a review of 138 studies revealed conscientiousness was rather strongly related to grade point average).[46] The higher levels of job knowledge then contribute to higher levels of job performance.[47]

Although conscientiousness is the Big Five trait most consistently related to job performance, the other traits are related to aspects of performance in some situations. All five traits also have other implications for work and for life, as summarized in Exhibit 2-6.

Other Personality Attributes Influencing OB

Although the Big Five traits have proven highly relevant to OB, they don't exhaust the range of traits that can describe someone's personality. Now we will look at other, more specific, attributes that are powerful predictors of behaviour in organizations.

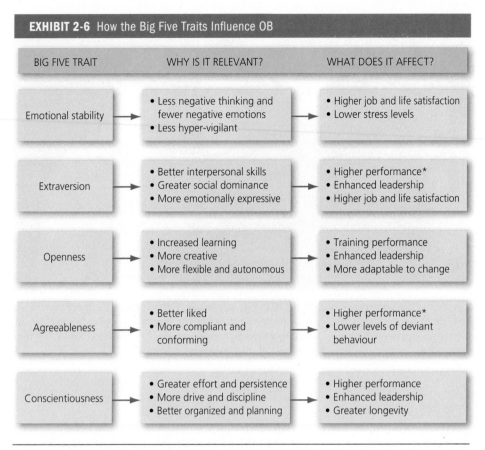

EXHIBIT 2-6 How the Big Five Traits Influence OB

BIG FIVE TRAIT	WHY IS IT RELEVANT?	WHAT DOES IT AFFECT?
Emotional stability	• Less negative thinking and fewer negative emotions • Less hyper-vigilant	• Higher job and life satisfaction • Lower stress levels
Extraversion	• Better interpersonal skills • Greater social dominance • More emotionally expressive	• Higher performance* • Enhanced leadership • Higher job and life satisfaction
Openness	• Increased learning • More creative • More flexible and autonomous	• Training performance • Enhanced leadership • More adaptable to change
Agreeableness	• Better liked • More compliant and conforming	• Higher performance* • Lower levels of deviant behaviour
Conscientiousness	• Greater effort and persistence • More drive and discipline • Better organized and planning	• Higher performance • Enhanced leadership • Greater longevity

*In jobs requiring significant teamwork or frequent interpersonal interactions.

The first relates to one's core self-evaluation. The others are Machiavellianism, narcissism, self-monitoring, propensity for risk-taking, and Type A and B and proactive personalities. If you want to know more about your own personal characteristics, this chapter's *Learning About Yourself Exercises* on pages 62–66 present you with a variety of personality measures to explore.

Indra Nooyi, CEO and chair of PepsiCo, scores high on all personality dimensions of the Big Five Model. She is described as sociable, agreeable, conscientious, emotionally stable, and open to experiences. These personality traits have contributed to Nooyi's high job performance and career success at PepsiCo and are the reason she landed the CEO position.

It is unusual for two people to share the CEO role, but Ronnen Harary (left) and Anton Rabie (right), co-CEOs of Toronto-based toy company Spin Master (pictured with executive vice-president Ben Varadi), like the arrangement. Rabie is an extrovert, while Harary is an introvert. The childhood friends feel their personalities complement each other, making an ideal management team.

Core Self-Evaluation

People who have positive **core self-evaluations** like themselves and see themselves as effective, capable, and in control of their environment. Those with negative core self-evaluations tend to dislike themselves, question their capabilities, and view themselves as powerless over their environment.[48]

People with positive core self-evaluations perform better than others because they set more ambitious goals, are more committed to their goals, and persist longer at attempting to reach these goals. For example, one study of life-insurance agents found that core self-evaluations were critical predictors of performance. In life-insurance sales, 90 percent of sales calls end in rejection, so an agent has to believe in him- or herself to persist. In fact, this study showed that the majority of successful salespersons had positive core self-evaluations.[49] Such people also provide better customer service, are more popular co-workers, and have careers that both begin on better footing and ascend more rapidly over time.[50]

You might wonder whether someone can be too positive. What happens when someone thinks he is capable, but he is actually incompetent? One study of *Fortune* 500 CEOs, for example, showed that many are overconfident, and their perceived infallibility often causes them to make bad decisions.[51] While many people are overconfident, just as many people sell themselves short and are less happy and effective than they could be because of it. If we decide we cannot do something, for example, we won't try, and not doing it only reinforces our self-doubts.

Machiavellianism

The personality characteristic of **machiavellianism** (Mach) is named after Niccolò Machiavelli, who wrote in the sixteenth century on how to gain and use power. An individual high in machiavellianism is highly practical, maintains emotional distance, and believes that ends can justify means. "If it works, use it" is consistent with a high-Mach perspective.

A considerable amount of research has related high- and low-Mach personalities to certain behavioural outcomes.[52] High Machs manipulate more, win more, are persuaded less, and persuade others more than do low Machs.[53] They like their jobs less,

Learn About Yourself
Core Self-Evaluation Scale

core self-evaluation The degree to which an individual likes or dislikes himself or herself, whether the person sees himself or herself as capable and effective, and whether the person feels in control of his or her environment or powerless over the environment.

machiavellianism The degree to which an individual is pragmatic, maintains emotional distance, and believes that ends can justify means.

are more stressed by their work, and engage in more deviant work behaviours.[54] Yet high-Mach outcomes are moderated by situational factors. It has been found that high Machs flourish (1) when they interact face to face with others rather than indirectly; (2) when the situation has a minimum number of rules and regulations, thus allowing latitude for improvisation; and (3) when low Machs get distracted by emotional involvement with details irrelevant to winning.[55]

Should we conclude that high Machs make good employees? That answer depends on the type of job and whether you consider ethical implications in evaluating performance. In jobs that require bargaining skills (such as labour negotiation) or that offer substantial rewards for winning (as in commissioned sales), high Machs will be productive. But if the ends cannot justify the means, if there are absolute standards of behaviour, or if the three situational factors noted in the preceding paragraph are not in evidence, our ability to predict a high Mach's performance will be severely curtailed. If you are interested in determining your level of machiavellianism, you might want to complete *Learning About Yourself Exercise #1* on page 62.

Narcissism

Hans likes to be the centre of attention. He likes to look at himself in the mirror a lot. He has extravagant dreams and seems to consider himself a person of many talents. Hans is a narcissist. The term is from the Greek myth of Narcissus, the story of a man so vain and proud that he fell in love with his own image. In psychology, **narcissism** describes a person who has a grandiose sense of self-importance, requires excessive admiration, has a sense of entitlement, and is arrogant.[56] Are the youth of today narcissistic? Despite claims to that effect, the evidence is unclear. High school seniors in 2006 were more likely than in 1975 to agree they would be "very good" spouses (56 percent of 2006 seniors, compared to 37 percent in 1975), parents (54 percent of 2006 seniors, 36 percent in 1975), and workers (65 percent of 2006 seniors, 49 percent in 1975). On the other hand, scores on the Narcissistic Personality Inventory—the most common measure of narcissism—have not increased since 1982.[57]

Whether it is increasing or not, narcissism can have pretty toxic consequences. A 2011 study found that narcissists were more likely to cheat on exams than others, in part because they did not feel guilty doing so.[58] A study found that while narcissists thought they were *better* leaders than their colleagues, their supervisors actually rated them as *worse* leaders. For example, an executive at Oracle described the company's CEO, Larry Ellison, as follows: "The difference between God and Larry is that God does not believe he is Larry."[59] Because narcissists often want to gain the admiration of others and receive affirmation of their superiority, they tend to "talk down" to those who threaten them, treating others as if they were inferior. Narcissists also tend to be selfish and exploitive, and they often carry the attitude that others exist for their benefit.[60] Studies indicate that narcissists are rated by their bosses as less effective at their jobs than others, particularly when it comes to helping other people.[61] Despite these negative outcomes, one 2011 study found that having two or more narcissists on a team can lead to more creativity.[62] Because narcissists want admiration from their peers, they will attempt to outdo one another, raising the competitiveness within the team.

Self-Monitoring

Self-monitoring refers to an individual's ability to adjust his or her behaviour to external, situational factors.[63] Individuals high in self-monitoring show considerable adaptability in adjusting their behaviour to external situational factors. They are highly sensitive to external cues and can behave differently in different situations. High self-monitors are capable of presenting striking contradictions between their

narcissism The tendency to be arrogant, have a grandiose sense of self-importance, require excessive admiration, and have a sense of entitlement.

self-monitoring A personality trait that measures an individual's ability to adjust behaviour to external, situational factors.

Learn About Yourself
Self-Awareness Assessment

public personae and their private selves. Low self-monitors cannot disguise themselves in the same way. They tend to display their true dispositions and attitudes in every situation. There is high behavioural consistency between who they are and what they do.

Research suggests that high self-monitors tend to pay closer attention to the behaviour of others and are more capable of conforming than are low self-monitors.[64] In addition, high self-monitoring managers tend to be more mobile in their careers and receive more promotions (both internal and cross-organizational) and are more likely to occupy central positions in an organization.[65] Recent research found that self-monitoring is also related to job performance and emerging leaders.[66] Specifically, high self-monitors are more likely to be high performers and more likely to become leaders. To determine whether you are a high or low self-monitor, you might want to complete *Learning About Yourself Exercise #2* on pages 62–63.

Risk-Taking

People differ in their willingness to take chances, a quality that affects how much time and information managers need before they make a decision. In one study, 79 managers worked on simulated exercises that required them to make hiring decisions.[67] High **risk-taking** managers made more rapid decisions and used less information in making their choices than did the low risk-taking managers. Interestingly, the decision accuracy was the same for both groups.

Although previous studies have shown managers in large organizations to be more risk averse than are growth-oriented entrepreneurs who actively manage small businesses, recent findings suggest that managers in large organizations may actually be more willing to take risks than entrepreneurs.[68] The work population as a whole also differs in risk propensity.[69] It makes sense to recognize these differences and even to consider aligning risk-taking propensity with specific job demands. A high risk-taking propensity may lead to more effective performance for a stock trader in a brokerage firm because that type of job demands rapid decision making. On the other hand, a willingness to take risks might prove a major obstacle to an accountant who performs auditing activities. The latter job might be better filled by someone with a low risk-taking propensity. If you are interested in determining where you stand on risk-taking, you might want to complete *Learning About Yourself Exercise #3* on pages 63–65.

Type A and Type B Personalities

Do you know any people who are excessively competitive and always seem to be pushed for time? If you do, it's a good bet that those people have a **Type A personality**. An individual with a Type A personality is "aggressively involved in a chronic, incessant struggle to achieve more and more in less and less time, and, if required to do so, against the opposing efforts of other things or other persons."[70] In North American culture, such characteristics tend to be highly prized and positively associated with ambition and the successful acquisition of material goods.

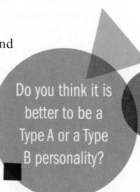

Do you think it is better to be a Type A or a Type B personality?

Type As tend to have the following characteristics:

- Are always moving, walking, and eating rapidly

- Feel impatient with the rate at which most events take place

- Strive to think or do two or more things at once

- Cannot cope with leisure time

risk-taking A person's willingness to take chances or risks.

Type A personality A personality with aggressive involvement in a chronic, incessant struggle to achieve more and more in less and less time and, if necessary, against the opposing efforts of other things or other people.

Personality traits are enduring characteristics that describe an individual's behaviour. British entrepreneur Richard Branson, CEO of Virgin Group, is described as energetic, enthusiastic, charismatic, decisive, ambitious, adaptable, courageous, and industrious. These traits helped Branson build one of the most recognized and respected global brands for products and services in the areas of business travel, entertainment, and lifestyle. In this photo Branson is joined by his daughter Holly during the promotional launch of a new venture—the Marussia Virgin racing partnership with Disney's *Cars 2* film. Identifying personality traits helps organizations select employees and match workers to jobs.

- Are obsessed with numbers, measuring their success in terms of how many or how much of everything they acquire

A person with a **Type B personality** is exactly the opposite of a Type A, "rarely harried by the desire to obtain a wildly increasing number of things or participate in an endless growing series of events in an ever-decreasing amount of time."[71]

Type Bs tend to have the following characteristics:

- Never suffer from a sense of time urgency with its accompanying impatience

- Feel no need to display or discuss either their achievements or accomplishments unless such exposure is demanded by the situation

- Play for fun and relaxation, rather than to exhibit their superiority at any cost

- Can relax without guilt

Type As operate under moderate to high levels of stress. They subject themselves to more or less continuous time pressure, creating a life of deadlines. These characteristics result in some rather specific behavioural outcomes. Type As are fast workers because they emphasize quantity over quality. In managerial positions, Type As demonstrate their competitiveness by working long hours and, not infrequently, making poor decisions because they make them too fast. Stressed Type As are also rarely creative. Because of their concern with quantity and speed, they rely on past experiences when faced with problems. They will not allocate the time that is necessary to develop unique solutions to new problems. They seldom vary in their responses to specific challenges in their environment, and so their behaviour is easier to predict than that of Type Bs.

Type B personality A personality that is described as easy-going, relaxed, and patient.

Are Type As or Type Bs more successful in organizations? Type As do better than Type Bs in job interviews because they are more likely to be judged as having desirable traits such as high drive, competence, aggressiveness, and success motivation.[72] Despite the hard work of Type As, Type Bs are the ones who appear to make it to the top. Great salespeople are usually Type As; senior executives are usually Type Bs.

Why? The answer lies in the tendency of Type As to trade off quality of effort for quantity. Promotions in corporate and professional organizations "usually go to those who are wise rather than to those who are merely hasty, to those who are tactful rather than to those who are hostile, and to those who are creative rather than to those who are merely agile in competitive strife."[73]

If you are interested in determining whether you have a Type A or Type B personality, you might want to complete *Learning About Yourself Exercise #4* on page 65.

Proactive Personality

Did you ever notice that some people actively take the initiative to improve their current circumstances or create new ones? These are proactive personalities.[74] People with a **proactive personality** identify opportunities, show initiative, take action, and persevere until meaningful change occurs. They create positive change in their environment, regardless or even in spite of constraints or obstacles.[75] Not surprisingly, proactives have many desirable behaviours that organizations look for. They are more likely to be seen as leaders and are more likely to act as change agents within the organization.[76]

Other actions of proactives can be positive or negative, depending on the organization and the situation. Proactives are more likely to challenge the status quo or voice their displeasure when situations are not to their liking.[77] If an organization requires people with entrepreneurial initiative, proactives make good candidates; however, these are people who are also more likely to leave an organization to start their own business.[78] As individuals, proactives are more likely to achieve career success.[79] This is because they select, create, and influence work situations in their favour. Proactives are more likely to seek out job and organizational information, develop contacts in high places, engage in career planning, and demonstrate persistence in the face of career obstacles.

Personality and National Culture

The five personality factors identified in the Big Five model appear in almost all cross-cultural studies.[80] These studies have included a wide variety of diverse cultures—such as China, Israel, Germany, Japan, Spain, Nigeria, Norway, Pakistan, and the United States. Differences tend to be in the emphasis on dimensions and whether countries are predominantly individualistic or collectivistic. Chinese managers use the category of conscientiousness more often and agreeableness less often than do US managers. And the Big Five appear to predict a bit better in individualistic than in collectivistic cultures.[81] But there is a surprisingly high amount of agreement, especially among individuals from developed countries. A comprehensive review of studies covering people from what was then the 15-nation European Community found conscientiousness to be a valid predictor of performance across jobs and occupational groups.[82] Studies in the United Stated have found the same to be true.[83] A 2011 review of 200 studies, mainly from Europe and the United States, that examined the relationship between conscientiousness and student performance also showed a strong positive link between the two variables.[84]

One caveat regarding personality tests is that they may be subject to cultural bias when used on samples of people other than those for whom the tests were designed. For instance, on common American personality tests, British people are characterized as "less dominant, achievement-orientated or flexible than Americans, but more

proactive personality A person who identifies opportunities, shows initiative, takes action, and perseveres until meaningful change occurs.

self-controlled."[85] An example of a bias that can appear in such tests is that only 10 percent of British men answer "true" to the statement "I very much like hunting," while 70 percent of American men agree.[86] When these tests are used to select managers, they may result in the selection of individuals who are not as suitable in the British workplace as they would be in the American workplace.

Emotions

Despite the fact that Walmart Canada has won numerous "Best Employer" and "Best Culture" awards, which are based partly on responses of employees, not all Walmart employees agree with those findings.[87] Comments from Walmart employees at RateMyEmployer.ca show a range of emotions from "love it" to "hate it." Over the past 10 years, at least 20 different groups of Walmart employees across the country have tried to unionize. A recent drive in Trail, BC, told fellow employees that unionizing would be "making Walmart an even BETTER place to work." Obviously there are strong feelings about the employer. Could emotions affect how individual employees perceive Walmart?

3 Can emotions help or get in the way when we are dealing with others?

Each of us has a range of personality characteristics, but we also bring with us a range of emotions. Given the obvious role that emotions play in our everyday lives, it might surprise you to learn that, until very recently, the topic of emotions was given little or no attention in the field of OB.[88] Why? We offer two possible explanations.

First is the *myth of rationality*.[89] Until very recently, the protocol of the work world kept a damper on emotions. A well-run organization did not allow employees to express frustration, fear, anger, love, hate, joy, grief, or similar feelings thought to be the antithesis of rationality. Though researchers and managers knew emotions were an inseparable part of everyday life, they tried to create organizations that were emotion-free. Of course, that was not possible.

The second explanation is that many believed emotions of any kind were disruptive.[90] Researchers looked at strong negative emotions—especially anger—that interfered with an employee's ability to work effectively. They rarely viewed emotions as constructive or contributing to enhanced performance.

Certainly some emotions, particularly when exhibited at the wrong time, can reduce employee performance. But employees do bring their emotions with them to work every day, and no study of OB could be complete without considering their role in workplace behaviour.

What Are Emotions and Moods?

Let's look at three terms that are closely intertwined: *affect, emotions,* and *moods.* **Affect** is a generic term that covers a broad range of feelings people experience, including both emotions and moods.[91] **Emotions** are intense feelings that are directed at someone or something.[92] **Moods** are feelings that are less intense than emotions and that lack a contextual stimulus.[93]

Most experts believe emotions are more fleeting than moods.[94] For example, if someone is rude to you, you would likely feel angry. That intense feeling probably comes and goes fairly quickly, maybe even in a matter of seconds. When you are in a bad mood, though, you can feel bad for several hours.

Emotions are reactions to a person (seeing a friend at work may make you feel glad) or an event (dealing with a rude client may make you feel angry). You show your emotions when you are "happy about something, angry at someone, afraid of something."[95] Moods, in contrast, are not usually directed at a person or an event. But emotions can turn into moods when you lose focus on the event or object that started the feeling. And, by the same token, good or bad moods can make you more emotional in response to an event. So when a colleague criticizes how you spoke to a client, you might show emotion (anger) toward a specific object (your colleague). But as the

affect A broad range of feelings that people experience.

emotions Intense feelings that are directed at someone or something.

moods Feelings that tend to be less intense than emotions and that lack a contextual stimulus.

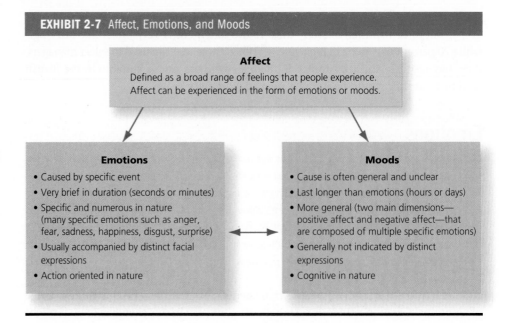

EXHIBIT 2-7 Affect, Emotions, and Moods

Affect

Defined as a broad range of feelings that people experience.
Affect can be experienced in the form of emotions or moods.

Emotions
- Caused by specific event
- Very brief in duration (seconds or minutes)
- Specific and numerous in nature (many specific emotions such as anger, fear, sadness, happiness, disgust, surprise)
- Usually accompanied by distinct facial expressions
- Action oriented in nature

Moods
- Cause is often general and unclear
- Last longer than emotions (hours or days)
- More general (two main dimensions— positive affect and negative affect—that are composed of multiple specific emotions)
- Generally not indicated by distinct expressions
- Cognitive in nature

specific emotion starts to go away, you might just feel generally dispirited. You cannot attribute this feeling to any single event; you are just not your normal self. You might then overreact to other events. This affect state describes a mood. Exhibit 2-7 shows the relationships among affect, emotions, and moods.

First, as the exhibit shows, *affect* is a broad term that encompasses emotions and moods. Second, there are differences between emotions and moods. Some of these differences—that emotions are more likely to be caused by a specific event, and emotions are more fleeting than moods—we just discussed. Other differences are subtler. For example, unlike moods, emotions like anger and disgust tend to be more clearly revealed by facial expressions. Also, some researchers speculate that emotions may be more action oriented—they may lead us to some immediate action—while moods may be more cognitive, meaning they may cause us to think or brood for a while.[96]

Finally, the exhibit shows that emotions and moods are closely connected and can influence each other. Getting your dream job may generate the emotion of joy, which can put you in a good mood for several days. Similarly, if you are in a good or bad mood, it might make you experience a more intense positive or negative emotion than otherwise. In a bad mood, you might blow up in response to a co-worker's comment that would normally have generated only a mild reaction.

Affect, emotions, and moods are separable in theory; in practice the distinction isn't always crystal clear. In some areas, researchers have studied mostly moods, in other areas mainly emotions. So, when we review the OB topics on emotions and moods, you may see more information on emotions in one area and on moods in another. This is simply the state of the research. *OB in the Street* discusses how our perception of emotions can affect our romantic relationships.

in the **STREET**
How Perception Causes Fights in Relationships

What happens if you think your partner is neglecting you?   A 2011 study found that how people perceive the emotions of their romantic partner during a conflict affected their overall view of and reactions to the conflict.[97] The researchers studied the arguments that 105 university students had during an eight-week period. They looked at two types of emotions: "hard" (asserting power) and "soft" (expressing vulnerability). They also looked at two types of perceptions: "perceived threat" (perception that the partner is being hostile, critical, blaming, or controlling); and "perceived neglect" (perception that the partner does not seem committed to or invested in the relationship).

The researchers found that when a person sees his or her partner react with hard emotion, that person perceives a threat to control, power, and status in the relationship. When a person sees his or her partner show little emotion, or less soft emotion than desired, that person perceives partner neglect. The perceived threat and neglect increase the person's own hard and soft emotions.

One of the study's co-authors explained the results as follows: "[W]hat you perceive your partner to be feeling influences different types of thoughts, feelings and reactions in yourself, whether what you perceive is actually correct. . . . If a person perceives the other as angry, they will perceive a threat so they will respond with a hard emotion like anger or blame. Likewise, if a person is perceived to be sad or vulnerable, they will perceive a neglect and will respond [with] either flat or soft [emotions]."[98] ●

Choosing Emotions: Emotional Labour

If you have ever had a job working in retail sales or waiting on tables in a restaurant, you know the importance of projecting a friendly demeanour and smiling. Even though there were days when you did not feel cheerful, you knew management expected you to be upbeat when dealing with customers. So you faked it. Every employee expends physical and mental labour by putting body and mind into the job. But jobs also require **emotional labour**, an employee's expression of organizationally desired emotions during interpersonal transactions at work.[99]

Ever wonder why the grocery clerk is always smiling?

The concept of emotional labour emerged from studies of service jobs. Airlines expect their flight attendants, for instance, to be cheerful; we expect funeral directors to be sad; and we expect doctors to be emotionally neutral. But really, emotional labour is relevant to almost every job. Your managers expect you, for example, to be courteous, not hostile, in interactions with co-workers. The true challenge arises when employees have to project one emotion while simultaneously feeling another.[100] This difference is **emotional dissonance**, and it can take a heavy toll on employees. Bottled-up feelings of frustration, anger, and resentment can eventually lead to emotional exhaustion and burnout.[101] It is because of emotional labour's increasing importance in effective job performance that an understanding of emotion has gained heightened relevance within the field of OB.

Emotional labour creates dilemmas for employees. There are people with whom you have to work that you just do not like. Maybe you consider their personality abrasive. Maybe you know they have said negative things about you behind your back. Regardless, your job requires you to interact with these people on a regular basis. So you are forced to pretend to be friendly.

It can help you, on the job especially, if you separate emotions into *felt* or *displayed emotions*.[102] **Felt emotions** are an individual's actual emotions. In contrast, **displayed emotions** are those that the organization requires employees to show and considers appropriate in a given job. They are not natural; they are learned. "The ritual look of delight on the face of the first runner-up as the [winner] is announced is a product of the display rule that losers should mask their sadness with an expression of joy for the winner."[103] Similarly, most of us know that we are expected to act sad at funerals, regardless of whether we consider the person's death to be a loss, and to pretend to be happy at weddings, even if we do not feel like celebrating.[104]

emotional labour When an employee expresses organizationally desired emotions during interpersonal interactions.

emotional dissonance Inconsistencies between the emotions people feel and the emotions they show.

felt emotions An individual's actual emotions.

displayed emotions Emotions that are organizationally required and considered appropriate in a given job.

Effective managers have learned to be serious when giving an employee a negative performance evaluation and to hide their anger when they have been passed over for promotion. A salesperson who has not learned to smile and appear friendly, regardless of his true feelings at the moment, is not typically going to last long in most sales jobs. How we *experience* an emotion is not always the same as how we *show* it.[105]

Displaying fake emotions requires us to suppress real ones. **Surface acting** is hiding one's inner feelings and hiding emotional expressions in response to display rules. For example, when an employee smiles at a customer even when he does not feel like it, he is surface acting. **Deep acting** is trying to modify one's true inner feelings based on display rules. A health care provider trying to genuinely feel more empathy for her patients is deep acting.[106] Surface acting deals with one's *displayed* emotions, and deep acting deals with one's *felt* emotions. Research shows that surface acting is more stressful to employees than deep acting because it entails faking one's true emotions.[107] Displaying emotions we don't really feel is exhausting, so it is important to give employees who engage in surface displays a chance to relax and recharge. A study that looked at how cheerleading instructors spent their breaks from teaching found those who used their breaks to rest and relax were more effective instructors after their breaks.[108] Instructors who did chores during their breaks were only about as effective after their break as they were before. Though much of the research on emotional labour shows negative consequences for those displaying false positive emotions, a 2011 study suggests that as people age, engaging in positive emotions and attitudes, even when the circumstances warrant otherwise, actually enhances emotional well-being.[109] For further discussion on the costs and benefits of emotional display rules in organizations, read this chapter's *Point/Counterpoint* on page 61 and *Case Incident—The Upside of Anger?* on page 69.

Why Should We Care About Emotions in the Workplace?

Research is increasingly showing that emotions are actually critical to rational thinking.[110] We must have the ability to experience emotions to be rational. Why? Because our emotions provide important information about how we understand the world around us. Would we really want a manager to make a decision about firing an employee without regarding either his or the employee's emotions? The key to good decision making is to employ both thinking *and* feeling in our decisions.

There are a number of other reasons to be concerned about understanding emotions in the workplace.[111] People who know their own emotions and are good at reading others' emotions may be more effective in their jobs. That, in essence, is the theme underlying recent research on emotional intelligence. The entire workplace can be affected by positive or negative workplace emotions, another issue we consider below. One recent study found that when leaders were in a positive mood, individual group members experienced better moods, and groups had a more positive tone. Groups whose leaders had a positive mood also found it easier to coordinate tasks and expended less effort when doing their work.[112]

Emotional Intelligence

Diane Marshall is an office manager. Her awareness of her own and others' emotions is almost zero. She is moody and unable to generate much enthusiasm or interest in her employees. She does not understand why employees get upset with her. She often overreacts to problems and chooses the most ineffectual responses to emotional situations.[113] Diane Marshall has low emotional intelligence. **Emotional intelligence (EI)** is a person's ability to (1) be self-aware (to recognize one's own emotions when one experiences them), (2) detect emotions in others, and (3) manage emotional cues and information. People who know their own emotions and are good at reading emotional cues—for instance, knowing why they are angry and how to express themselves

surface acting Hiding one's inner feelings to display what is expected.

deep acting Trying to modify one's true inner feelings to match what is expected.

emotional intelligence (EI) An assortment of noncognitive skills, capabilities, and competencies that influence a person's ability to succeed in coping with environmental demands and pressures.

without violating norms—are most likely to be effective.[114] One simulation study showed that students who were good at identifying and distinguishing among their feelings were able to make more profitable investment decisions.[115]

A 2011 study on EI reviewed and analyzed most of the previous studies on EI and concluded that EI is strongly and positively correlated with job performance—emotionally intelligent people are better workers.[116] Another illuminating study looked at the successes and failures of 11 American presidents—from Franklin Roosevelt to Bill Clinton. They were evaluated on six qualities—communication, organization, political skill, vision, cognitive style, and emotional intelligence. It was found that the key quality that differentiated the successful (such as Roosevelt, Kennedy, and Reagan) from the unsuccessful (such as Johnson, Carter, and Nixon) was emotional intelligence.[117] Some researchers argue that emotional intelligence is particularly important for leaders.[118]

A recent poll of human resource managers asked the question, How important is it for your workers to demonstrate EI to move up the corporate ladder?[119] Forty percent replied "Very Important." Another 16 percent said "Moderately Important." Irene Taylor, a consultant with Toronto-based Praxis Canada, says her company "has conducted EQ assessments on about 300 Canadian lawyers over the past five years." She also says that demand to get into the company's EI coaching program is high.

EI has been a controversial concept in OB; it has supporters and detractors. In the following sections, we review the arguments for and against the effectiveness of EI in OB. If you are interested in determining your EI, you might want to complete *Learning About Yourself Exercise #5* on page 66. This chapter's *From Concepts to Skills* on pages 70–71 gives you some insight into reading the emotions of others.

The Case for EI

The arguments in favour of EI include its intuitive appeal, the fact that EI predicts criteria that matter, and the idea that EI is biologically based.

Intuitive Appeal There is a lot of intuitive appeal to the EI concept. Almost everyone would agree that it is good to possess street smarts and social intelligence. People who can detect emotions in others, control their own emotions, and handle social interactions well will have a powerful leg up in the business world, so the thinking goes.[120] As just one example, partners in a multinational consulting firm who scored above the median on an EI measure delivered $1.2 million more in business than did the other partners.[121]

EI Predicts Criteria That Matter There is a significant amount of evidence to suggest that a high level of EI means a person will perform well on the job.[122] One study found that EI predicted the performance of employees in a cigarette factory in China.[123] Another study found that being able to recognize emotions in others' facial expressions and to emotionally "eavesdrop" (that is, pick up subtle signals about people's emotions) predicted peer ratings of how valuable those people were to their organization.[124] Finally, professor Stéphane Côté, of the University of Toronto's Rotman School of Management, and his colleagues found in a 2010 study that people who were identified as showing the greatest leadership skills by their peers also had a high level of EI.[125]

EI Is Biologically Based One study has shown that people with damage to the part of the brain that governs emotional processing (lesions in an area of the prefrontal cortex) score significantly lower than others on EI tests. Even though these brain-damaged people scored no lower on standard measures of intelligence than people without similar brain damage, they were still impaired in normal decision making. But they scored significantly lower on EI tests and were impaired in normal decision making, as demonstrated by their poor performance in a card game with monetary rewards. This study suggests that EI is neurologically based in a way that is unrelated to standard measures of intelligence.[126] There is also evidence EI is genetically influenced, further supporting the idea that it measures a real underlying biological factor.[127]

The Case Against EI

For all its supporters, EI has just as many critics. Its critics say that EI is vague and impossible to measure, and they question its validity.

EI Is Too Vague a Concept   To many researchers, it's not clear what EI is. Is it a form of intelligence? Most of us would not think that being self-aware or self-motivated or having empathy is a matter of intellect. Moreover, different researchers often focus on different skills, making it difficult to get a definition of EI. One researcher may study self-discipline, another empathy, another self-awareness. As one reviewer noted, "The concept of EI has now become so broad and the components so variegated that . . . it is no longer even an intelligible concept."[128]

EI Cannot Be Measured   Many critics have raised questions about measuring EI. Because EI is a form of intelligence, they argue, there must be right and wrong answers about it on tests. Some tests do have right and wrong answers, although the validity of some questions is doubtful. One measure asks you to associate particular feelings with specific colours, as if purple always makes us feel cool and not warm. Other measures are self-reported, meaning that there is no right or wrong answer. For example, an EI test question might ask you to respond to the statement "I'm good at 'reading' other people," and have no right or wrong answers. The measures of EI are diverse, and researchers have not subjected them to as much rigorous study as they have measures of personality and general intelligence.[129]

The Validity of EI Is Suspect   Some critics argue that because EI is so closely related to intelligence and personality, once you control for these factors, EI has nothing unique to offer. There is some foundation to this argument. EI appears to be highly correlated with measures of personality, especially emotional stability.[130] If this is true, then the evidence for a biological component to EI is not valid, and biological markers like brain activity and heritability are attributable to other well known and much more researched psychological constructs. But there has not been enough research on whether EI adds insight beyond measures of personality and general intelligence in predicting job performance. Still, EI is wildly popular among consulting firms and in the popular press. One company's promotional materials for an EI measure claimed, "EI accounts for more than 85 percent of star performance in top leaders."[131] To say the least, it's difficult to validate this statement with the research literature.

Weighing the arguments for and against EI, it's still too early to tell whether the concept is useful. It *is* clear, though, that the concept is here to stay.

Negative Workplace Emotions

Negative emotions can lead to a number of deviant workplace behaviours. Anyone who has spent much time in an organization realizes that people often engage in voluntary actions that violate established norms and threaten the organization, its members, or both. These actions are called **employee deviance**.[132] They fall into categories such as production (leaving early, intentionally working slowly); property (stealing, sabotage); political (gossiping, blaming co-workers); and personal aggression (sexual harassment, verbal abuse).[133]

Many of these deviant behaviours can be traced to negative emotions. For instance, envy is an emotion that occurs when you resent someone for having something that

employee deviance Voluntary actions that violate established norms and threaten the organization, its members, or both.

you do not have but strongly desire—such as a better work assignment, larger office, or higher salary.[134] It can lead to malicious deviant behaviours. Envy, for example, has been found to be associated with hostility, "backstabbing," and other forms of political behaviour, as well as with negatively distorting others' successes and positively distorting one's own accomplishments.[135] Angry people look for other people to blame for their bad mood, interpret other people's behaviour as hostile, and have trouble considering others' point of view.[136] It's not hard to see how these thought processes, too, can lead directly to verbal or physical aggression. Evidence suggests that people who feel negative emotions, particularly those who feel angry or hostile, are more likely than others to engage in deviant behaviour at work.[137]

Summary and Implications

1 What is perception? *Perception* is the process by which individuals organize and interpret their impressions to give meaning to their environment. A number of factors operate to shape and sometimes distort perception. The perceiver's attitudes, motives, interests, and past experiences all shape the way he or she sees an event. The target's characteristics also affect what is perceived. Novelty, motion, sounds, size, and other characteristics of a target shape the way it is seen.

2 What is personality and how does it affect behaviour? *Personality* is the stable patterns of behaviour and consistent internal states that determine how an individual reacts to and interacts with others. A review of the personality literature offers general guidelines that can lead to effective job performance. As such, it can improve hiring, transfer, and promotion decisions. Personality attributes give us a framework for predicting behaviour. Personality affects how people react to others and the types of jobs that they may desire. For example, individuals who are shy, introverted, and uncomfortable in social situations would probably make poor salespeople. Individuals who are submissive and conforming might not be effective as advertising "idea" people. Be aware, though, that measuring personality is not an exact science, and as you no doubt learned from the discussion of attribution theory, it is easy to attribute personality characteristics in error.

3 Can emotions help or get in the way when we are dealing with others? *Emotions* are intense feelings that are directed at someone or something. Positive emotions can be motivating for everyone in the workplace. Negative emotions may make it difficult to get along with others. Can managers control the emotions of their colleagues and employees? No. Emotions are a natural part of an individual's makeup. At the same time, managers err if they ignore the emotional elements in OB and assess individual behaviour as if it were completely rational. Managers who understand the role of emotions will significantly improve their ability to explain and predict individual behaviour.

Do emotions affect job performance? Yes. Emotions, especially negative ones, can hinder performance. That is probably why organizations, for the most part, try to remove emotions from the workplace. But emotions can also enhance performance. How? Two ways.[138] First, emotions can increase arousal levels, thus acting as motivators to higher performance. Second, emotional labour recognizes that feelings can be part of a job's required behaviour. So, for instance, the ability to effectively manage emotions in leadership and sales positions may be critical to success in those positions. Research also indicates the importance of emotional intelligence—the assortment of noncognitive skills, capabilities, and competencies that influence a person's ability to succeed in coping with environmental demands and pressures.

SNAPSHOT SUMMARY

1 Perception
Factors Influencing Perception
Perceptual Errors
Why Do Perception and Judgment Matter?

2 Personality
What Is Personality?
Measuring Personality
Personality Determinants
Personality Traits
Other Personality Attributes Influencing OB
Personality and National Culture

3 Emotions
What Are Emotions and Moods?
Choosing Emotions: Emotional Labour
Why Should We Care About Emotions in the Workplace?

✓●—**Practise**
Glossary Flashcards - Chapter 2

—**Listen**
Audio Chapter Summary

for Review

1. Define *perception*.

2. What is attribution theory? What are its implications for explaining behaviour in organizations?

3. What is stereotyping? Give an example of how stereotyping can create perceptual distortion.

4. Give some positive results of using shortcuts when judging others.

5. Describe the factors in the Big Five Personality Model. Which factor shows the greatest value in predicting behaviour?

6. What behavioural predictions might you make if you knew that an employee had (a) a negative core self-evaluation? (b) a low-Mach score? (c) low self-monitoring? (d) a Type A personality?

7. To what extent do people's personalities affect how they are perceived?

8. What is emotional labour and why is it important to understanding OB?

9. What is emotional intelligence and why is it important?

for Critical Thinking

1. How might the differences in experience of students and instructors affect each of their perceptions of classroom behaviour (for example, students' written work and class comments)?

2. An employee does an unsatisfactory job on an assigned project. Explain the attribution process that this person's manager will use to form judgments about this employee's job performance.

3. One day your boss comes in and he is nervous, edgy, and argumentative. The next day he is calm and relaxed. Does this behaviour suggest that personality traits are not consistent from day to day?

4. What, if anything, can managers do to manage emotions? Are there ethical implications in any of these actions? If so, what are they?

5. Give some examples of situations where expressing emotions openly might improve job performance.

for You

■ The discussion of perception might get you thinking about how you view the world. When we perceive someone as a troublemaker, for instance, this may be only a perception and not a real characteristic of the other person. It is always good to question your perceptions, just to be sure that you are not reading something into a situation that is not there.

■ One important thing to consider when looking for a job is whether your personality will fit the organization to which you are applying. For instance, it may be a highly structured organization. If you, by nature, are much less formal, this may not be a good fit for you.

■ Sometimes personalities get in the way when working in groups. You may want to see if you can figure out ways to get personality differences working in favour of group goals.

■ Emotions need not always be suppressed when working with others. While emotions can sometimes hinder performance, positive emotions can motivate you and those around you.

OB *at work*

Display Rules Make Good Business Sense

Organizations today realize that good customer service means good business. After all, who wants to end a shopping trip at the grocery store with a surly cashier? Research clearly shows that organizations that provide good customer service have higher profits than those with poor customer service.[139] An integral part of customer-service training is to set forth display rules to teach employees to interact with customers in a friendly, helpful, professional way—and evidence indicates that such rules work: Having display rules increases the odds that employees will display the emotions expected of them.[140]

As one Starbucks manager says, "What makes Starbucks different is our passion for what we do. We're trying to provide a great experience for people, with a great product. That's what we all care about."[141] Starbucks may have good coffee, but a big part of the company's growth has been the customer experience. For instance, the cashiers are friendly and will get to know you by name if you are a repeat customer.

Asking employees to act friendly is good for them, too. Research shows that employees of organizations that require them to display positive emotions actually feel better as a result.[142] And if someone feels that being asked to smile is bad for him, that person does not belong in the service industry in the first place.

Display Rules Do Not Make Sense

Organizations have no business trying to regulate the emotions of their employees. Companies should not be "the thought police" and force employees to feel and act in ways that serve only organizational needs. Service employees should be professional and courteous, yes, but many companies expect them to take abuse and refrain from defending themselves. That's wrong. As philosopher Jean Paul Sartre wrote, we have a responsibility to be authentic—true to ourselves—and within reasonable limits, organizations have no right to ask us to be otherwise.

Service industries have no justification for teaching their employees to be smiling punching bags. Most customers might even prefer that employees be themselves. Employees should not be openly nasty or hostile, of course, but who appreciates a fake smile? Think about trying on an outfit in a store and the clerk automatically says it looks "absolutely wonderful" when you know it does not and you sense that the clerk is lying. Most customers would rather talk with a "real" person than someone enslaved to an organization's display rules. Furthermore, if an employee does not feel like slapping on an artificial smile, then it's only going to create friction between her and her employer.[143]

Finally, research shows that forcing display rules on employees takes a heavy emotional toll.[144] It's unnatural to expect someone to smile all the time or to passively take abuse from customers, clients, or fellow employees. Organizations can improve their employees' psychological health by encouraging them to be themselves, within reasonable limits.

How Machiavellian Are You?

For each statement, circle the number that most closely resembles your attitude.

Statement	Disagree			Agree	
	A Lot	A Little	Neutral	A Little	A Lot
1. The best way to handle people is to tell them what they want to hear.	1	2	3	4	5
2. When you ask someone to do something for you, it is best to give the real reason for wanting it rather than giving reasons that might carry more weight.	1	2	3	4	5
3. Anyone who completely trusts anyone else is asking for trouble.	1	2	3	4	5
4. It is hard to get ahead without cutting corners here and there.	1	2	3	4	5
5. It is safest to assume that all people have a vicious streak, and it will come out when given a chance.	1	2	3	4	5
6. One should take action only when it is morally right.	1	2	3	4	5
7. Most people are basically good and kind.	1	2	3	4	5
8. There is no excuse for lying to someone else.	1	2	3	4	5
9. Most people more easily forget the death of their fathers than the loss of their property.	1	2	3	4	5
10. Generally speaking, people will not work hard unless they are forced to do so.	1	2	3	4	5

Scoring Key:

To obtain your Mach score, add the number you have checked on questions 1, 3, 4, 5, 9, and 10. For the other 4 questions, reverse the numbers you have checked: 5 becomes 1, 4 is 2, 2 is 4, and 1 is 5. Total your 10 numbers to find your score. The higher your score, the more Machiavellian you are. Among a random sample of American adults, the national average was 25.

Source: R. Christie and F. L. Geis, *Studies in Machiavellianism* (New York: Academic Press, 1970). Reprinted by permission.

Are You a High Self-Monitor?

Indicate the degree to which you think the following statements are true or false by circling the appropriate number. For example, if a statement is always true, circle the 5 next to that statement.

0 = **Certainly, always false**

1 = **Generally false**

2 = **Somewhat false, but with exceptions**

3 = **Somewhat true, but with exceptions**

4 = **Generally true**

5 = **Certainly, always true**

LEARNING ABOUT **YOURSELF** EXERCISE #2 (Continued)

1.	In social situations, I have the ability to alter my behaviour if I feel that something else is called for.	0	1	2	3	4	5
2.	I am often able to read people's true emotions correctly through their eyes.	0	1	2	3	4	5
3.	I have the ability to control the way I come across to people, depending on the impression I wish to give them.	0	1	2	3	4	5
4.	In conversations, I am sensitive to even the slightest change in the facial expression of the person I'm conversing with.	0	1	2	3	4	5
5.	My powers of intuition are quite good when it comes to understanding others' emotions and motives.	0	1	2	3	4	5
6.	I can usually tell when others consider a joke in bad taste, even though they may laugh convincingly.	0	1	2	3	4	5
7.	When I feel that the image I am portraying isn't working, I can readily change it to something that does.	0	1	2	3	4	5
8.	I can usually tell when I've said something inappropriate by reading the listener's eyes.	0	1	2	3	4	5
9.	I have trouble changing my behaviour to suit different people and different situations.	0	1	2	3	4	5
10.	I have found that I can adjust my behaviour to meet the requirements of any situation I find myself in.	0	1	2	3	4	5
11.	If someone is lying to me, I usually know it at once from that person's manner of expression.	0	1	2	3	4	5
12.	Even when it might be to my advantage, I have difficulty putting up a good front.	0	1	2	3	4	5
13.	Once I know what the situation calls for, it's easy for me to regulate my actions accordingly.	0	1	2	3	4	5

Scoring Key:

To obtain your score, add up the numbers circled, except reverse scores for questions 9 and 12. On those, a circled 5 becomes a 0, 4 becomes 1, and so forth. High self-monitors are defined as those with scores of 53 or higher.

Source: R. D. Lennox and R. N. Wolfe, "Revision of the Self-Monitoring Scale," *Journal of Personality and Social Psychology,* June 1984, p. 1361. Copyright © 1984 by the American Psychological Association. Reprinted by permission.

LEARNING ABOUT **YOURSELF** EXERCISE #3

Are You a Risk-Taker?

For each of the following situations, indicate the minimum odds of success you would demand before recommending that one alternative be chosen over another. Try to place yourself in the position of the adviser to the central person in each of the situations.

1. Mr. B, a 45-year-old accountant, has recently been informed by his physician that he has developed a severe heart ailment. The disease will be sufficiently serious to force Mr. B to change many of his strongest life habits— reducing his workload, drastically changing his diet, giving up favourite leisure-time pursuits. The physician suggests that a delicate medical operation could be attempted. If successful, the operation would completely relieve the heart condition. But its success cannot be assured, and in fact the operation might prove fatal.

LEARNING ABOUT **YOURSELF** EXERCISE #3 (Continued)

Imagine that you are advising Mr. B. Listed below are several probabilities or odds that the operation will prove successful. Check the *lowest probability* that you would consider acceptable for the operation to be performed.

_____ Mr. B should not have the operation, no matter what the probabilities.

_____ The chances are 9 in 10 that the operation will be a success.

_____ The chances are 7 in 10 that the operation will be a success.

_____ The chances are 5 in 10 that the operation will be a success.

_____ The chances are 3 in 10 that the operation will be a success.

_____ The chances are 1 in 10 that the operation will be a success.

2. Mr. D is the captain of University X's varsity football team. University X is playing its traditional rival, University Y, in the final game of the season. The game is in its final seconds, and Mr. D's team, University X, is behind in the score. University X has time to make one more play. Mr. D, the captain, must decide on a strategy. Would it be best to try a play that would be almost certain to work and try to settle for a tie score? Or, on the other hand, should he try a more complicated and risky play that would bring victory if it succeeded or defeat if it failed?

Imagine that you are advising Mr. D. Listed below are several probabilities or odds that the risky play will work. Check the *lowest probability* that you would consider acceptable for the risky play to be attempted.

_____ Mr. D should not attempt the risky play, no matter what the probabilities.

_____ The chances are 9 in 10 that the risky play will work.

_____ The chances are 7 in 10 that the risky play will work.

_____ The chances are 5 in 10 that the risky play will work.

_____ The chances are 3 in 10 that the risky play will work.

_____ The chances are 1 in 10 that the risky play will work.

3. Ms. K is a successful businesswoman who has taken part in a number of civic activities of considerable value to the community. Ms. K has been approached by the leaders of her political party as a possible candidate in the next provincial election. Ms. K's party is a minority party in the constituency, though the party has won occasional elections in the past. Ms. K would like to hold political office, but to do so would involve a serious financial sacrifice, since the party does not have enough campaign funds. She would also have to endure the attacks of her political opponents in a heated campaign.

Imagine that you are advising Ms. K. Listed below are several probabilities or odds of Ms. K's winning the election in her constituency. Check the *lowest probability* that you would consider acceptable to make it worthwhile for Ms. K to run for political office.

_____ Ms. K should not run for political office, no matter what the probabilities.

_____ The chances are 9 in 10 that Ms. K will win the election.

_____ The chances are 7 in 10 that Ms. K will win the election.

_____ The chances are 5 in 10 that Ms. K will win the election.

_____ The chances are 3 in 10 that Ms. K will win the election.

_____ The chances are 1 in 10 that Ms. K will win the election.

4. Ms. L, a 30-year-old research physicist, has been given a 5-year appointment by a major university laboratory. As she considers the next 5 years, she realizes that she might work on a difficult long-term problem. If a solution to the problem could be found, it would resolve basic scientific issues in the field and bring high scientific honours. If no solution were found, however, Ms. L would have little to show for her 5 years in the laboratory, and it would be hard for her to get a good job afterward. On the other hand, she could, as most of her professional associates are doing, work on a series of short-term problems for which solutions would be easier to find. Those solutions would be of lesser scientific importance.

Imagine that you are advising Ms. L. Listed below are several probabilities or odds that a solution will be found to the difficult long-term problem that Ms. L has in mind. Check the *lowest probability* that you would consider acceptable to make it worthwhile for Ms. L to work on the more difficult long-term problem.

_____ Ms. L should not choose the long-term, difficult problem, no matter what the probabilities.

_____ The chances are 9 in 10 that Ms. L will solve the long-term problem.

_____ The chances are 7 in 10 that Ms. L will solve the long-term problem.

_____ The chances are 5 in 10 that Ms. L will solve the long-term problem.

_____ The chances are 3 in 10 that Ms. L will solve the long-term problem.

_____ The chances are 1 in 10 that Ms. L will solve the long-term problem.

Scoring Key:

These situations were based on a longer questionnaire. Your results are an indication of your general orientation toward risk rather than a precise measure. To calculate your risk-taking score, add up the chances you were willing to take and divide by 4. (For any of the situations in which you would not take the risk, regardless of the probabilities, give yourself a 10.) The lower your number, the more risk-taking you are.

Source: Adapted from N. Kogan and M. A. Wallach, *Risk Taking: A Study in Cognition and Personality* (New York: Holt, Rinehart and Winston, 1964), pp. 256–261. Reprinted with permission of Wadsworth, a division of Thomson Learning: www.thomsonrights.com. Fax 800-730-2215.

Are You a Type A?

Circle the number on the scale below that best characterizes your behaviour for each trait.

1. Casual about appointments	1	2	3	4	5	6	7	8	Never late
2. Not competitive	1	2	3	4	5	6	7	8	Very competitive
3. Never feel rushed	1	2	3	4	5	6	7	8	Always feel rushed
4. Take things one at a time	1	2	3	4	5	6	7	8	Try to do many things at once
5. Slow doing things	1	2	3	4	5	6	7	8	Fast (eating, walking, etc.)
6. Express feelings	1	2	3	4	5	6	7	8	"Sit on" feelings
7. Many interests	1	2	3	4	5	6	7	8	Few interests outside work

Scoring Key:

Total your score on the 7 questions. Now multiply the total by 3. A total of 120 or more indicates that you are a hard-core Type A. Scores below 90 indicate that you are a hard-core Type B. The following gives you more specifics:

Points	Personality Type
120 or more	A1
106–119	A
100–105	A2
90–99	B1
Less than 90	B

Source: Adapted from *Journal of Chronic Diseases,* Vol. 22, Issue 2, June 1969. R. W. Bortner, "Short Rating Scale as a Potential Measure of Pattern A Behavior," pp. 87–91. Copyright © 1969. With permission from Elsevier.

LEARNING ABOUT **YOURSELF** EXERCISE #5

What's Your EI at Work?

Evaluating the following 25 statements will allow you to rate your social skills and self-awareness, the components of emotional intelligence (EI).

EI, the social equivalent of IQ, is complex, in no small part because it depends on some pretty slippery variables—including your innate compatibility, or lack thereof, with the people who happen to be your co-workers. But if you want to get a rough idea of how your EI stacks up, this quiz will help.

As honestly as you can, estimate how you rate in the eyes of peers, bosses, and subordinates on each of the following traits, on a scale of 1 to 4, with 4 representing strong agreement, and 1 representing strong disagreement.

_____ I usually stay composed, positive, and unflappable even in trying moments.

_____ I can think clearly and stay focused on the task at hand under pressure.

_____ I am able to admit my own mistakes.

_____ I usually or always meet commitments and keep promises.

_____ I hold myself accountable for meeting my goals.

_____ I'm organized and careful in my work.

_____ I regularly seek out fresh ideas from a wide variety of sources.

_____ I'm good at generating new ideas.

_____ I can smoothly handle multiple demands and changing priorities.

_____ I'm result-oriented, with a strong drive to meet my objectives.

_____ I like to set challenging goals and take calculated risks to reach them.

_____ I'm always trying to learn how to improve my performance, including asking advice from people younger than I am.

_____ I readily make sacrifices to meet an important organizational goal.

_____ The company's mission is something I understand and can identify with.

_____ The values of my team—or of our division or department, or the company—influence my decisions and clarify the choices I make.

_____ I actively seek out opportunities to further the overall goals of the organization and enlist others to help me.

_____ I pursue goals beyond what is required or expected of me in my current job.

_____ Obstacles and setbacks may delay me a little, but they don't stop me.

_____ Cutting through red tape and bending outdated rules are sometimes necessary.

_____ I seek fresh perspectives, even if that means trying something totally new.

_____ My impulses or distressing emotions don't often get the best of me at work.

_____ I can change tactics quickly when circumstances change.

_____ Pursuing new information is my best bet for cutting down on uncertainty and finding ways to do things better.

_____ I usually don't attribute setbacks to a personal flaw (mine or someone else's).

_____ I operate from an expectation of success rather than a fear of failure.

Scoring Key:

Total your score. A score below 70 indicates very low EI. EI can be improved. Says Daniel Goleman, author of *Working with Emotional Intelligence,* "Emotional intelligence can be learned, and in fact we are each building it, in varying degrees, throughout life. It's sometimes called maturity. EQ is nothing more or less than a collection of tools that we can sharpen to help ensure our own survival."

Source: A. Fisher, "Success Secret: A High Emotional IQ," *Fortune,* October 26, 1998, p. 298. Reprinted with the permission of Time Warner Inc. Quiz copyright Daniel Goleman.

PERSONAL INVENTORY ASSESSMENT

Tolerance of Ambiguity Scale: Some people are much more tolerant of ambiguity than others, which may impact career preferences. Use this scale to determine your own tolerance of ambiguity.

Core Self-Evaluation Scale: Understanding your own personality can help you select the types of roles that are right for you. Use this scale to learn more about how you view yourself and your confidence levels in specific situations.

Self-Awareness Assessment: This self-assessment is designed to help you gain insight into yourself and efforts you can make to increase your self-awareness.

Emotional Intelligence Assessment: Emotional intelligence can help people communicate more effectively and can assist in the management of conflict. Use this scale to learn more about your personal emotional intelligence.

BREAKOUT GROUP EXERCISES

Form small groups to discuss the following topics, as assigned by your instructor. Each person in the group should first identify 3–5 key personal values.

1. Think back to your perception of this course and your instructor on the first day of class. What factors might have affected your perceptions of what the rest of the term would be like?

2. Describe a situation in which your perception turned out to be wrong. What perceptual errors did you make that might have caused this to happen?

3. Compare your scores on the *Learning About Yourself Exercises* at the end of the chapter. What conclusions could you draw about your group based on these scores?

WORKING WITH OTHERS EXERCISE

Evaluating Your Stereotypes

1. Your instructor will choose 4 volunteers willing to reveal an interesting true-life background fact about themselves. Examples of such background facts are as follows:
   - I can perform various dances, such as polka, rumba, bossa nova, and salsa.
   - I am the youngest of four children, and I attended a Catholic high school.
   - Neither of my parents attended school beyond grade 8.
   - My mother is a homemaker and my father is an author.

2. The instructor will put the 4 facts on the board without revealing to which person each belongs, and the 4 students will remain in the front of the room for the first part of the group discussion below.

3. Students in the class should silently decide which fact belongs to which person.

4. Students should break into groups of about 5 or 6 and try to reach consensus about which fact belongs to which person. Meanwhile, the 4 students can serve as observers to group discussions, listening in on rationales for how students decide to link the facts with the individuals.

5. After 15 minutes of group discussion, several groups will be asked to present their consensus to the class, with justifications.

6. The classroom discussion will focus on perceptions, assumptions, and stereotyping that led to the decisions made.

7. At the end of the discussion, the instructor will reveal which fact belongs to each student.

ETHICAL **DILEMMA** EXERCISE

Hiring Based on Body Art

When Christine Giacomoni applied for a job at the Sherwood Park (Alberta) location of the Real Canadian Superstore, she was wearing a nose stud.[145] She got the job. Six months later, however, she was told that she could no longer wear her small nose stud at work. The company had just recently decided to apply their policy for front-line workers about no nose studs to employees like Giacomoni, who worked in the deli.

The United Food and Commercial Workers (UFCW), Giacomoni's union, grieved this action for her. The complaint ended up in front of a labour arbitrator. The union argued that this company was out of touch with reality. The company argued that nose studs offended customers. They hired Ipsos Reid to survey shoppers, and the results of the poll indicated that "a significant portion" of shoppers would stop shopping at a store that allowed employee facial piercings.

Ultimately, a judge ruled against Real Canadian Superstore's policy. Meanwhile, Giacomoni left to take a job at TELUS, in part because of the store's policy against her piercing. TELUS does not mind that she has a nose stud.

Many employees are aware that tattoos and body piercings can hurt one's chances of being hired. Consider Russell Parrish, 29, who lives near Orlando, Florida, and has dozens of tattoos on his arms, hands, torso, and neck. In searching for a job, Parrish walked into 100 businesses, and in 60 cases, he was refused an application. "I want a career," Parrish says, "I want the same shot as everybody else."

Employers are mixed in their reactions to employees with tattoos or piercings. At Vancouver-based White Spot restaurants, employees cannot have visible tattoos (or pink or blue hair). They are allowed a small, simple nose stud. BC's Starbucks shops don't allow any pierced tongues or visible tattoos. Staff may not wear more than two reasonably sized earrings per ear. At Victoria-based Arq Salons, nearly everyone has a tattoo, "We work in an artistic field," manager Yasmin Morris explains, then adds that staff cannot wear jeans. "We don't want people to look too casual."

A survey of employers revealed that 58 percent indicated that they would be less likely to hire someone with visible tattoos or body piercings. The career centre at the University of Calgary's Haskayne School of Business advises students to "start out understated" when it comes to piercing. "We coach our students to be conservative, and if they do have any facial piercings, we suggest they remove them for the first interview until they find out what the culture's like in the organization," centre director Voula Cocolakis said. "We don't want them to be taken out of the 'yes' pile because of a facial piercing. We want them to interview and compete in the job market based on their qualifications."

In-house policies toward tattoos vary because, legally, employers can do as they wish. As long as the rule is applied equally to everyone (it would not be permissible to allow tattoos on men but not on women, for example), policies against tattoos are perfectly legal. Though not hiring people with tattoos is discrimination, it is not a form of discrimination that is covered by the Canadian Human Rights Act.

Thirty-six percent of those aged 18 to 25 and 40 percent of those aged 26 to 40 have at least one tattoo, whereas only 15 percent of those over 40 do, according to a fall 2006 survey by the Pew Research Center. One study in *American Demographics* suggested that 57 percent of senior citizens viewed visible tattoos as "freakish."

How does the matter of perception explain why some employers ban tattoos while others don't mind them? Is it fair for employers to reject applicants who have tattoos? Is it fair to require employees, if hired, to conceal their tattoos? Should it be illegal to allow tattoos to be a factor at all in the hiring process?

The Upside of Anger?

A researcher doing a case study on emotions in organizations interviewed Laura, a 22-year-old customer-service representative in Australia. The following is a summary of the interview (with some paraphrasing of the interviewer questions):[146]

INTERVIEWER: How would you describe your workplace?

LAURA: Very cold, unproductive, [a] very, umm, cold environment, atmosphere.

INTERVIEWER: What kinds of emotions are prevalent in your organization?

LAURA: Anger, hatred toward other people, other staff members.

INTERVIEWER: So it seems that managers keep employees in line using fear tactics?

LAURA: Yeah. [The General Manager's] favourite saying is, "Nobody's indispensable." So, it's like, "I can't do that because I'll get sacked!"

INTERVIEWER: How do you survive in this situation?

LAURA: You have to cater your emotions to the sort of situation, the specific situation . . . because it's just such a hostile environment, this is sort of the only way you can survive.

INTERVIEWER: Are there emotions you have to hide?

LAURA: Managers don't like you to show your emotions . . . They don't like to show that there is anything wrong or anything emotional in the working environment.

INTERVIEWER: Why do you go along?

LAURA: I feel I have to put on an act because . . . to show your true emotions, especially toward my managers [Laura names two of her senior managers], it would be hatred sometimes. So, you just can't afford to do that because it's your job and you need the money.

INTERVIEWER: Do you ever rebel against this system?

LAURA: You sort of put on a happy face just so you can annoy [the managers]. I find that they don't like people being happy, so you just annoy them by being happy. So, yeah. It just makes you laugh. You just "put it on" just because you know it annoys [management]. It's pretty vindictive and manipulative but you just need to do that.

INTERVIEWER: Do you ever find that this gets to you?

LAURA: I did care in the beginning, and I think it just got me into more trouble. So now I just tell myself, "I don't care." If you tell yourself something for long enough, eventually you believe it. Yeah, so now I just go "Oh well."

INTERVIEWER: Do you intend to keep working here?

LAURA: It's a means to an end now. So every time I go [to work] and every week I just go, "Well, one week down, one week less until I go away." But if I knew that I didn't have this goal, I don't know if I could handle it, or if I would even be there now.

INTERVIEWER: Is there an upside to working here?

LAURA: I'm so much better at telling people off now than I ever used to be. I can put people in place in about three sentences. Like, instead of, before I would walk away from it. But now I just stand there and fight. . . . I don't know if that's a good thing or a bad thing.

Questions

1. Do you think Laura is justified in her responses to her organization's culture? Why or why not?

2. Do you think Laura's strategic use and display of emotions serve to protect her?

3. Assuming that Laura's description is accurate, how would *you* react to the organization's culture?

4. Research shows that acts of co-workers (37 percent) and management (22 percent) cause more negative emotions for employees than do acts of customers (7 percent). What can Laura's company do to change its emotional climate?

FROM CONCEPTS TO SKILLS

Reading Emotions

Understanding another person's felt emotions is very difficult. But we can learn to read others' displayed emotions.[147] We do this by focusing on verbal, nonverbal, and paralanguage cues.

The easiest way to find out what someone is feeling is to ask. Saying something as simple as "Are you okay? What's the problem?" can often provide you with the information to assess an individual's emotional state. But relying on a verbal response has two drawbacks. First, almost all of us conceal our emotions to some extent for privacy and to reflect social expectations. So we might be unwilling to share our true feelings. Second, even if we want to verbally convey our feelings, we may be unable to do so. As we noted earlier, some people have difficulty understanding their own emotions and, hence, are unable to express them verbally. So, at best, verbal responses provide only partial information.

Let's say you are talking with a co-worker. Does the fact that his back is rigid, his teeth are clenched, and his facial muscles tight tell you something about his emotional state? It probably should. Facial expressions, gestures, body movements, and physical distance are nonverbal cues that can provide additional insights into what a person is feeling. The facial expressions shown in Exhibit 2-8, for instance, are a window into a person's feelings. Notice the difference in facial features: the height of the cheeks, the raising or lowering of the brow, the turn of the mouth, the positioning of the lips, and the configuration of muscles around the eyes. Even something as subtle as the distance someone chooses to put between him- or herself and you can convey how much intimacy, aggressiveness, repugnance, or withdrawal that person feels.

Explore

Exhibit 2-8: Facial Expressions and Emotions

EXHIBIT 2-8 Facial Expressions and Emotions

Each picture portrays a different emotion. Try to identify them before looking at the answers.

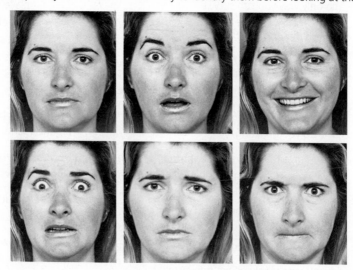

Top, left to right: neutral, surprise, happiness. Bottom: fear, sadness, anger.

Source: Paul Ekman, PhD/Paul Eckman Group, LLC.

When you speak with someone, you may notice a sharp change in the tone of her voice and the speed at which she speaks. You are tapping into the third source of information on a person's emotions—paralanguage. This is communication that goes beyond the specific spoken words. It includes pitch, amplitude, rate, and voice quality of speech. Paralanguage reminds us that people convey their feelings not only in what they say, but also in how they say it.

Practising Skills

Part A. Form groups of 2. Each person is to spend a couple of minutes thinking of a time in the past when she or he was emotional about something. Examples might include being upset with a parent, sibling, or friend; being excited or disappointed about an academic or athletic achievement; being angry with someone over an insult or slight; being disgusted by something someone has said or done; or being happy because of something good that happened. Do not share this event with the other person in your group.

Part B. Now you will conduct 2 role plays. Each will be an interview. In the first, 1 person will play the interviewer and the other will play the job applicant. The job is for a summer management internship with a large retail chain. Each role play will last no longer than 10 minutes. The interviewer is to conduct a normal job interview, except you are to continually rethink the emotional episode you envisioned in part A. Try hard to convey this emotion while, at the same time, being professional in interviewing the job applicant.

Part C. Now reverse positions for the second role play. The interviewer becomes the job applicant and vice versa. The new interviewer will conduct a normal job interview, except that he or she will continually rethink the emotional episode chosen in part A.

Part D. Spend 10 minutes analyzing the interview, with specific attention focused on these questions: What emotion(s) do you think the other person was conveying? What cues did you pick up? How accurate were you in reading those cues?

Reinforcing Skills

1. Watch the actors in an emotion-laden film, such as *Death of a Salesman* or *12 Angry Men,* for clues to the emotions they are exhibiting. Try to determine the various emotions projected and explain how you arrived at your conclusion.

2. Spend a day specifically looking for emotional cues in the people with whom you interact. Did this improve communication?

MyManagementLab Study, practise, and explore real business situations with these helpful resources:

- **Study Plan:** Check your understanding of chapter concepts with self-study quizzes.
- **Online Lesson Presentations:** Study key chapter topics and work through interactive assessments to test your knowledge and master management concepts.
- **Videos:** Learn more about the management practices and strategies of real companies.
- **Simulations:** Practise management decision-making in simulated business environments.

P I A PERSONAL INVENTORY ASSESSMENT

CHAPTER 3

Values, Attitudes, and Their Effects in the Workplace

At SaskGaming, diversity is valued and respected. How does this affect the company's workplace?

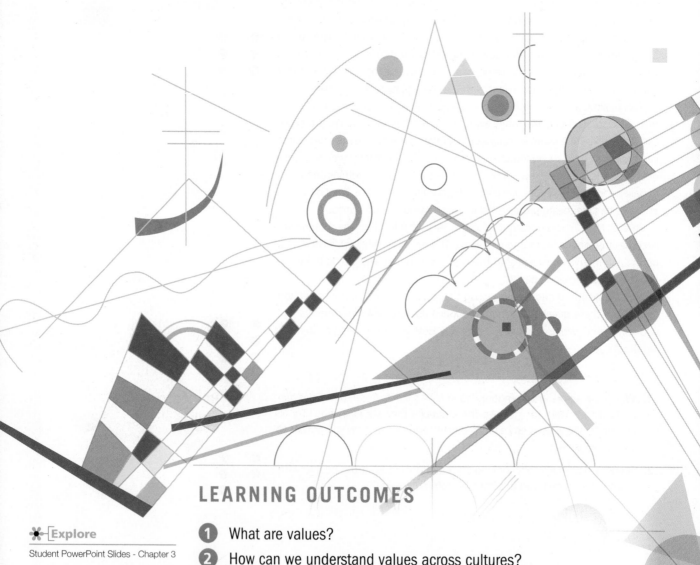

LEARNING OUTCOMES

✳ Explore

Student PowerPoint Slides - Chapter 3

1. What are values?
2. How can we understand values across cultures?
3. Are there unique Canadian values?
4. What are attitudes and why are they important?

Regina-based SaskGaming, which operates two casinos (Casino Regina and Casino Moose Jaw), faces an interesting perception problem.[1] Not everyone thinks that gambling is okay, and a number of studies show the negative impact of gambling. Still, gambling is legal, and SaskGaming is committed to being a good employer. In fact, it was named one of Canada's Top 100 Employers in both 2008 and 2009, one of Saskatchewan's Top 10 Employers for the third year in a row in 2009, and one of Canada's Best Diversity Employers in 2010.

SaskGaming lists its four organizational values on its website: respect, integrity, passion, and innovation. These values operate under the company's mandate: to "offer casino entertainment in a socially responsible manner, generating quality employment, economic benefit to the community and profit for Saskatchewan people in partnership with First Nations."

Generally, we expect that an organization's values, like those of an individual, will be reflected in corresponding behaviour and attitudes. If a company stated that it valued workforce diversity, and yet no behaviour followed from that statement, we would question whether that value was really so important to the company. However, in SaskGaming's case, the company backs up its value statements with concrete policies and actions to show support for its values. Does having strong values make for a better workplace?

In this chapter, we look more carefully at how values influence behaviour and consider the relationship between values and attitudes. We then consider two specific issues that arise from our discussion of values and attitudes: job satisfaction and organizational commitment.

THE BIG IDEA

Values and attitudes affect behaviour and can have a big impact on how much people are committed to and engaged in their jobs.

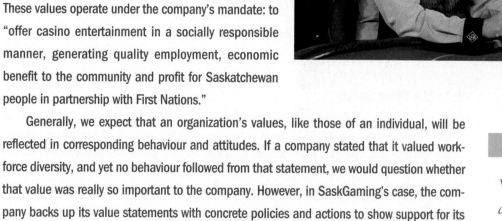

OB IS FOR EVERYONE

- How do countries differ in their values?
- Are Gen-Ys really different from their elders?
- What can you learn about OB from Aboriginal culture?
- What would you need to know to set up a business in Asia?

LEARNING ABOUT YOURSELF

- Values

Values

1 What are values?

Is capital punishment right or wrong? How about employment equity guidelines in hiring? If a person likes power, is that good or bad? The answers to these questions are value-laden. Some might argue, for example, that capital punishment is right because it is a suitable punishment for crimes such as murder. However, others might argue just as strongly that no government has the right to take anyone's life.

Values represent basic convictions that "a specific mode of conduct or end-state of existence is personally or socially preferable to an opposite or converse mode of conduct or end-state of existence."[2] They contain a judgmental element in that they carry an individual's ideas as to what is right, good, or desirable. Values have both content and intensity attributes. The content attribute says a mode of conduct or end-state of existence is *important*. The intensity attribute specifies *how important* it is. When we rank an individual's values in terms of their intensity, we obtain that person's **value system**. All of us have a hierarchy of values that forms our value system, and these influence our attitudes and behaviour.[3]

Values tend to be relatively stable and enduring.[4] Most of our values are formed in our early years—with input from parents, teachers, friends, and others. As children, we are told that certain behaviours or outcomes are always desirable or always undesirable. There are few grey areas. It is this absolute or "black-or-white" learning of values that more or less ensures their stability and endurance.

We examine two frameworks for understanding values: Milton Rokeach's terminal and instrumental values, and Kent Hodgson's general moral principles.

Rokeach Value Survey

Milton Rokeach created the Rokeach Value Survey (RVS), which consists of two sets of values, each containing 18 individual value items.[5] One set, called **terminal values**, refers to desirable end-states of existence. These are the goals that individuals would like to achieve during their lifetime. They include

- A comfortable life (a prosperous life)
- An exciting life (a stimulating, active life)
- A sense of accomplishment (lasting contribution)
- Equality (brotherhood, equal opportunity for all)
- Inner harmony (freedom from inner conflict)
- Happiness (contentedness)[6]

The other set, called **instrumental values**, refers to preferable ways of behaving, or means for achieving the terminal values. They include

- Ambitious (hard-working, aspiring)
- Broad-minded (open-minded)
- Capable (competent, effective)
- Courageous (standing up for your beliefs)
- Imaginative (daring, creative)
- Honest (sincere, truthful)[7]

values Basic convictions that a specific mode of conduct or end-state of existence is personally or socially preferable to an opposite or converse mode of conduct or end-state of existence.

value system A hierarchy based on a ranking of an individual's values in terms of their intensity.

terminal values Goals that individuals would like to achieve during their lifetime.

instrumental values Preferable ways of behaving.

Several studies confirm that RVS values vary among groups.[8] People in the same occupations or categories (corporate managers, union members, parents, students) tend to hold similar values. One study compared corporate executives, members of the steelworkers' union, and members of a community activist group. Although there

EXHIBIT 3-1 Value Ranking of Executives, Union Members, and Activists (Top Five Only)

EXECUTIVES		UNION MEMBERS		ACTIVISTS	
Terminal	Instrumental	Terminal	Instrumental	Terminal	Instrumental
1. Self-respect	1. Honest	1. Family security	1. Responsible	1. Equality	1. Honest
2. Family security	2. Responsible	2. Freedom	2. Honest	2. A world of peace	2. Helpful
3. Freedom	3. Capable	3. Happiness	3. Courageous	3. Family security	3. Courageous
4. A sense of accomplishment	4. Ambitious	4. Self-respect	4. Independent	4. Self-respect	4. Responsible
5. Happiness	5. Independent	5. Mature love	5. Capable	5. Freedom	5. Capable

Source: Based on W. C. Frederick and J. Weber, "The Values of Corporate Managers and Their Critics: An Empirical Description and Normative Implications," in *Business Ethics: Research Issues and Empirical Studies*, ed. W. C. Frederick and L. E. Preston (Greenwich, CT: JAI Press, 1990), pp. 123–144.

was a good deal of overlap among the three groups,[9] there were also some very significant differences (see Exhibit 3-1). The activists ranked "equality" as their most important terminal value; executives and union members ranked this value 12 and 13, respectively. Activists ranked "helpful" as their second-highest instrumental value. The other two groups both ranked it 14. Because executives, union members, and activists all have a vested interest in what corporations do, these differences can create serious conflicts when these groups have to reach agreement on the organization's economic and social policies.[10]

Explore

Exhibit 3-1: Value Ranking Executives, Union Members, and Activists (Top Five Only)

Hodgson's General Moral Principles

Ethics is the study of moral values or principles that guide our behaviour and inform us whether actions are right or wrong. Thus, ethical values are related to moral judgments about right and wrong.

In recent years, there has been concern that individuals are not grounded in moral values. It is believed that this lack of moral roots has resulted in a number of business scandals, such as those at WorldCom, Enron, Hollinger International, and in the sponsorship scandal of the Canadian government. We discuss the issue of ethics further in Chapter 9.

Management consultant Kent Hodgson has identified seven general moral principles that individuals should follow when making decisions about behaviour. He calls these "the Magnificent Seven" and suggests that they are universal values that managers should use to make *principled, appropriate,* and *defensible* decisions.[11] They are presented in *OB in Action—The Magnificent Seven Principles*. With these principles in mind, *OB in the Street* considers whether management was right to fire employees who participated in the Stanley Cup riots in Vancouver.

in the STREET
Stanley Cup Rioting Leads to Employee Firing

Should an ethical lapse in your nightlife affect your day job? After the Vancouver Canucks lost in Game 7 of the Stanley Cup finals in 2011, riots broke out throughout Vancouver's downtown core.[12] Many of the rioters were young men and women in their teens and early 20s. Many Vancouverites were appalled at the rioting, the looting, the fires, and the attacks on police and firefighters.

ethics The study of moral values or principles that guide our behaviour and inform us whether actions are right or wrong.

in **Action**
The Magnificent Seven Principles

→ *Dignity of human life.* The lives of **people are to be respected**.

→ *Autonomy.* All persons are **intrinsically valuable** and have the **right to self-determination**.

→ *Honesty.* **The truth should be told** to those who have a right to know it.

→ *Loyalty.* **Promises, contracts,** and **commitments** should be **honoured**.

→ *Fairness.* **People should be treated justly.**

→ *Humaneness.* Our **actions ought to accomplish good**, and we should **avoid doing evil**.

→ *The common good.* Actions should accomplish **the greatest good for the greatest number** of people.[13]

Many of the rioters boasted about their behaviour on Facebook, and even posted pictures of their activities. Others were shown in videos taken at the scene and then posted to YouTube and other social media sites. As perpetrators were identified, law-abiding citizens started calling for justice—customers and clients complained to companies where some of these individuals were employed.

One young woman, a part-time receptionist at a downtown Vancouver Toyota dealership, lost her job because she was seen gleefully stealing clothing in a video clip taken at the scene. One young man, who apparently did not engage in the riots, provided status updates on Facebook live from the scene; his comments applauding the riots included "awesome" and "vancouver needed remodeling anyway. . . ." He was fired. His employer, Delta, BC-based RiteTech, was listed on his Facebook page and received more than 100 emails and 20 phone calls complaining about the 21-year-old's postings.

Employees did these activities outside their work time and may not have expected their employers to respond so harshly. Managers, on the other hand, found that the rioters' actions could negatively affect their business and harm other employees, and may have considered their response to be in the best interest of the common good. ●

Assessing Cultural Values

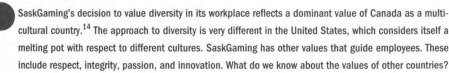

② How can we understand values across cultures?

SaskGaming's decision to value diversity in its workplace reflects a dominant value of Canada as a multicultural country.[14] The approach to diversity is very different in the United States, which considers itself a melting pot with respect to different cultures. SaskGaming has other values that guide employees. These include respect, integrity, passion, and innovation. What do we know about the values of other countries? What values make Canada unique?

In Chapter 1, we noted that managers have to become capable of working with people from different cultures. Thus it is important to understand how values differ across cultures.

Hofstede's Framework for Assessing Cultures

One of the most widely referenced approaches for analyzing variations among cultures was done in the late 1970s by Geert Hofstede.[15] He surveyed more than 116 000 IBM employees in 40 countries about their work-related values and found that managers and employees vary on five value dimensions of national culture:

How do countries differ in their values?

• *Power distance.* **Power distance** describes the degree to which people in a country accept that power in institutions and organizations is distributed unequally. A high rating on power distance means that large inequalities of power and wealth exist and are tolerated in the culture, as in a class or caste system that discourages upward mobility of its citizens. A low power distance rating characterizes societies that stress equality and opportunity.

power distance A national culture attribute that describes the extent to which a society accepts that power in institutions and organizations is distributed unequally.

- *Individualism vs. collectivism.* **Individualism** is the degree to which people prefer to act as individuals rather than as members of groups and believe in individual rights above all else. **Collectivism** emphasizes a tight social framework in which people expect others in groups of which they are a part to look after them and protect them.

- *Masculinity vs. femininity.* Hofstede's construct of **masculinity** is the degree to which the culture favours traditional masculine roles, such as achievement, power, and control, as opposed to viewing men and women as equals. A high masculinity rating indicates the culture has separate roles for men and women, with men dominating the society. A high **femininity** rating means the culture sees little differentiation between male and female roles and treats women as the equals of men in all respects.

- *Uncertainty avoidance.* The degree to which people in a country prefer structured over unstructured situations defines their **uncertainty avoidance**. In cultures that score high on uncertainty avoidance, people have an increased level of anxiety about uncertainty and ambiguity, and use laws and controls to reduce uncertainty. Cultures low on uncertainty avoidance are more accepting of ambiguity and are less rule-oriented, take more risks, and more readily accept change.

- *Long-term vs. short-term orientation.* This recent addition to Hofstede's typology measures a society's long-term devotion to traditional values. People in a culture with **long-term orientation** look to the future and value thrift, persistence, and tradition. In a culture with **short-term orientation**, people value the here and now; they accept change more readily and don't see commitments as impediments to change.

  More recently, Hofstede added a sixth dimension to his typology based on studies he has conducted over the past 10 years:[16]

- *Indulgence vs. restraint.* This newest addition to Hofstede's typology measures society's devotion (or lack thereof) to indulgence. Cultures that emphasize **indulgence** encourage "relatively free gratification of basic and natural human desires related to enjoying life."[17] Those that favour **restraint** emphasize the need to control the gratification of needs.

How do different countries score on Hofstede's dimensions? Exhibit 3-2 shows the ratings for the countries for which data are available. For example, power distance is higher in Malaysia and Slovak Republic than in any other countries. Canada is tied with the Netherlands as one of the top five individualistic countries in the world, falling just behind the United States, Australia, and Great Britain. Canada also tends to be short term in orientation and is low in power distance (people in Canada tend not to accept built-in class differences among people). Canada is also relatively low on uncertainty avoidance, meaning that most adults are relatively tolerant of uncertainty and ambiguity. Canada scores relatively high on masculinity (meaning that most people emphasize traditional gender roles) in comparison with countries such as Denmark, Finland, Norway, and Sweden, although its score is lower than that of the United States.

You will notice regional differences. Western and Northern nations such as Canada and the Netherlands tend to be more individualistic. Poorer countries such as Mexico and the Philippines tend to be higher on power distance. South American nations tend to be higher than other countries on uncertainty avoidance, and Asian countries tend to have a long-term orientation. North and South America tend to show more indulgence, as does Western Europe. Restraint is characteristic of Eastern Europe, Asia, and the predominantly Muslim countries.

Hofstede's cultural dimensions have been enormously influential on OB researchers and managers. Nevertheless, his research has been criticized. First, Hofstede's

individualism A national culture attribute that describes the degree to which people prefer to act as individuals rather than as members of groups.

collectivism A national culture attribute that describes a tight social framework in which people expect others in groups of which they are a part to look after them and protect them.

masculinity A national culture attribute that describes the extent to which the culture favours traditional masculine work roles of achievement, power, and control. Societal values are characterized by assertiveness and materialism.

femininity A national culture attribute that sees little differentiation between male and female roles; women are treated as the equals of men in all respects.

uncertainty avoidance A national culture attribute that describes the extent to which a society feels threatened by uncertain and ambiguous situations and tries to avoid them.

long-term orientation A national culture attribute that emphasizes the future, thrift, and persistence.

short-term orientation A national culture attribute that emphasizes the past and present, respect for tradition, and fulfillment of social obligations.

indulgence A national culture attribute that emphasizes the gratification of basic needs and desires to enjoy life.

restraint A national culture attribute that emphasizes the importance of controlling the gratification of needs.

EXHIBIT 3-2 Hofstede's Cultural Values by Nation

Country	Power Distance Index	Individualism Index	Masculinity Index	Uncertainty Avoidance Index	Long-Term Orientation Index
Argentina	49	46	56	86	20
Australia	36	90	61	51	21
Austria	11	55	79	70	60
Belgium	65	75	54	94	82
Brazil	69	38	49	76	44
Canada	39	80	52	48	36
Canada French	54	73	45	60	na
Chile	63	23	28	86	31
China	80	20	66	30	87
Colombia	67	13	64	80	13
Costa Rica	35	15	21	86	na
Czech Republic	57	58	57	74	70
Denmark	18	74	16	23	35
Ecuador	78	8	63	67	na
El Salvador	66	19	40	94	20
Finland	33	63	26	59	38
France	68	71	43	86	63
Germany	35	67	66	65	83
Great Britain	35	89	66	35	51
Greece	60	35	57	112	45
Guatemala	95	6	37	101	na
Hong Kong	68	25	57	29	61
India	77	48	56	40	51
Indonesia	78	14	46	48	62
Iran	58	41	43	59	14
Ireland	28	70	68	35	24
Israel	13	54	47	81	38
Italy	50	76	70	75	61
Jamaica	45	39	68	13	na
Japan	54	46	95	92	88
Korea (South)	60	18	39	85	100
Malaysia	104	26	50	36	41
Mexico	81	30	69	82	24
Netherlands	38	80	14	53	67
New Zealand	22	79	58	49	33
Norway	31	69	8	50	35
Pakistan	55	14	50	70	50
Panama	95	11	44	86	na
Peru	64	16	42	87	25
Philippines	94	32	64	44	27
Poland	68	60	64	93	38
Portugal	63	27	31	104	28
Singapore	74	20	48	8	72
Slovak Republic	104	52	110	51	77
South Africa (white)	49	65	83	49	na
Spain	57	51	42	86	48
Sweden	31	71	5	29	53
Switzerland	34	68	70	58	74
Taiwan	58	17	45	69	93
Thailand	64	20	34	64	32
Turkey	66	37	45	85	46
United States	40	91	62	46	26
Uruguay	61	36	38	100	26
Venezuela	81	12	73	76	16
Vietnam	70	20	40	30	57

Scores range from 0 = extremely low on dimension to 100 = extremely high.

Source: Geert Hofstede, Gert Jan Hofstede, Michael Minkov, *Cultures and Organizations, Software of the Mind,* Third Revised Edition, McGrawHill 2010, ISBN 0-07-166418-1. By permission of the author.

original work is nearly 40 years old and was based on a single company (IBM). So people question its relevance today. However, the work was updated and reaffirmed by a Canadian researcher at the Chinese University of Hong Kong (Michael Bond), who conducted research on values in 22 countries on 5 continents during the 1980s.[18] Between 1990 and 2002, the work was updated again by Hofstede and his colleagues with six major studies that each included a minimum of 14 countries.[19] These more recent studies used a variety of subjects: elites; employees and managers of corporations other than IBM; airline pilots; consumers; and civil servants. Hofstede notes that the more recent studies are consistent with the results of his original study. Second, few researchers have read the details of Hofstede's methodology closely and are therefore unaware of the many decisions and judgment calls he had to make (for example, reducing the number of cultural values to just five). Some results are unexpected. For example, Japan, which is often considered a highly collectivistic nation, is considered only average on collectivism under Hofstede's dimensions.[20] Despite these concerns, many of which Hofstede refutes,[21] he has been one of the most widely cited social scientists ever, and his framework has left a lasting mark on OB.

The GLOBE Framework for Assessing Cultures

Begun in 1993, the Global Leadership and Organizational Behavior Effectiveness (GLOBE) research program is an ongoing cross-cultural investigation of leadership and national culture. Using data from 825 organizations in 62 countries, the GLOBE team identified nine dimensions on which national cultures differ.[22] Some—such as power distance, individualism/collectivism, uncertainty avoidance, gender differentiation (similar to masculinity vs. femininity), and future orientation (similar to long-term vs. short-term orientation)—resemble the Hofstede dimensions. The main difference is that the GLOBE framework added dimensions, such as humane orientation (the degree to which a society rewards individuals for being altruistic, generous, and kind to others) and performance orientation (the degree to which a society encourages and rewards group members for performance improvement and excellence).

Which framework is better? That is hard to say, and each has its adherents. We give more emphasis to Hofstede's dimensions here because they have stood the test of time and the GLOBE study confirmed them. However, researchers continue to debate the differences between these frameworks, and future studies may, in time, favour the more nuanced perspective of the GLOBE study.[23]

In this chapter's *Working with Others Exercise* on page 100, you have the opportunity to compare the cultural values of two countries and determine how differences might affect group behaviour. The *Ethical Dilemma Exercise* on page 101 asks you to consider when something is a gift and when it is a bribe. Different cultures take different approaches to this question.

Values in the Canadian Workplace

Studies have shown that when individual values align with organizational values, the results are positive. Individuals who have an accurate understanding of the job requirements and the organization's values adjust better to their jobs and have greater levels of satisfaction and organizational commitment.[24] In addition, shared values between the employee and the organization lead to more positive work attitudes,[25] lower turnover,[26] and greater productivity.[27]

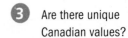 Are there unique Canadian values?

Individual and organizational values do not always align. Moreover, within organizations, individuals can have very different values. Two major factors lead to a potential clash of values in the workplace: generational differences and cultural differences. *OB in the Workplace* considers the difficulties the nonprofit sector has had in retaining younger people and minorities.

in the WORKPLACE
The Nonprofit Sector Looks to Diversify Its Workforce

How can the nonprofit sector attract and keep younger and diverse employees? Ottawa-based HR Council for the Nonprofit Sector (HR Council) wants to change the face of the nonprofit sector, which, far from being diverse, is dominated by Caucasians (89 percent of employees) and Baby Boomers (39 percent of employees are 45 or older).[28] As the Baby Boomers retire from the nonprofit sector, efforts are underway to increase the number of younger and diverse employees in the sector's labour force.

Avnish Mehta joined the board of directors of the HR Council to get involved in its diversity project. "I'm a visible minority, but I'm a born-and-raised Calgarian . . . and I thought I would be able to bring a little bit of a different flair to the way that things are being built," says Mehta. "My goal is to be able to lend the voice of young people in this sector, to show there are people who are motivated," he adds.

As a member of the HR Council's diversity project, Mehta is trying to find ways to recruit more diverse employees. The project found that first-year turnover rates for new immigrants and visible minorities were higher than for other groups.

Tanara Pickard, a project manager for the HR Council, said that part of the problem for immigrants and minorities relates to "cultural differences in workplace etiquette." As well, there is the question of values. "What we were finding is that because the not-for-profit sector is so values-driven, rather than focused on cost and the bottom line, they're looking for people to have a good fit within their organization," Pickard says.

Mehta suggests that nonprofits may need to consider changing their organizational structure to be more inclusive. "Maybe some of the [organizational] structures that we've relied on for such a long time are maybe not the best ones for motivating us [minorities] to stick around." ●

Let's look at the findings and implications of generational and cultural differences in Canada.

Generational Differences

Research suggests that generational differences exist in the workplace among the Baby Boomers (born between the mid-1940s and the mid-1960s), the Generation Xers (born between the mid-1960s and the late 1970s), and the Generation Ys (born between 1979 through 1994).[29] Gen-Xers are squeezed in the workplace between the much larger Baby Boomer and Gen-Y groups. With Generation Y starting to climb the ladder in organizations, while Boomers are continuing to hold on to their jobs rather than retire, the impact of having these two large generations—one younger and one older—in the workplace is gaining attention. Bear in mind that our discussion of these generations presents broad generalizations, and you should certainly avoid stereotyping individuals on the basis of these generalizations. There are individual differences in values. For instance, there is no law that says a Baby Boomer cannot think like someone from Generation Y. Despite these limitations, values do change over generations.[30] We can gain some useful insights from analyzing values this way to understand how others might view things differently from ourselves, even when they are exposed to the same situation. In this chapter's *Learning About Yourself Exercise* on page 99, you have the opportunity to examine some of the things that you value.

Robert Dutton, president and CEO of Boucherville, Quebec-based Rona, started working at the company under a grandfather, and then later found himself working with fellow Baby Boomers. Recently he has realized that Generation Y is starting to make up a larger portion of Rona's dealers, and finds that it has changed his life to "have the chance to work with young people—to share ideas with them, their thoughts, their vision for the future."[31] Dutton started the group Young Rona Business Leaders to help develop the talent that will be the future of Rona.

Baby Boomers

Baby Boomers (called *Boomers* for short) are a large cohort born after World War II, when veterans returned to their families and times were good. Boomers entered the workforce from the mid-1960s through the mid-1980s. They brought with them a large measure of the "hippie ethic" and distrust of authority. But they placed a great deal of emphasis on achievement and material success. They work hard and want to enjoy the fruits of their labours. They are pragmatists who believe ends can justify means. Boomers see the organizations that employ them merely as vehicles for their careers. Terminal values such as a sense of accomplishment and social recognition rank high with them.

Generation X

The lives of Gen-Xers (Generation Xers) have been shaped by globalization, two-career parents, MTV, AIDS, and computers. They value flexibility, life options, and the achievement of job satisfaction. Family and relationships are very important to this cohort. Gen-Xers are skeptical, particularly of authority. They also enjoy team-oriented work. In search of balance in their lives, Gen-Xers are less willing to make personal sacrifices for the sake of their employer than previous generations were. On the Rokeach Value Survey, they rate high on the terminal values of true friendship, happiness, and pleasure.

Are Gen-Ys really different from their elders?

Generation Y

The most recent entrants to the workforce, Generation Y (also called *Millennials, Netters, Nexters,* and *Generation Nexters*), grew up during prosperous times. They have high

When Sean Durfy, CEO of Calgary-based WestJet, announced in March 2011 that he was stepping down from the position, he said it was for "family reasons." While that has often been code for "being let go," in Durfy's case it was more likely the truth. His wife had been ill for four years, and the couple has young children. Instead, there was talk that Durfy's announcement was the start of what might be expected from other Generation Xers, who "work to live rather than live to work." Baby Boomers were expected to sacrifice one's family to climb the corporate ladder. But this may no longer be true of younger generations.

expectations and seek meaning in their work. Gen-Ys have life goals more oriented toward becoming rich (81 percent) and famous (51 percent) than do Generation Xers (62 percent and 29 percent, respectively), but they also see themselves as socially responsible. Gen-Ys are at ease with diversity and are the first generation to take technology for granted. More than other generations, they tend to be questioning, electronically networked, and entrepreneurial. At the same time, some have described Gen-Ys as entitled and needy. They grew up with parents who watched (and praised) their every move. One employer said, "This is the most high-maintenance workforce in the history of the world. The good news is they're also going to be the most high-performing."[32] Bruce Tulgan, author of *Not Everyone Gets a Trophy: How to Manage Generation Y*, suggests that managers need to give Gen-Ys extra direction, encouragement, and feedback to keep them focused and loyal.[33]

The Generations Meet in the Workplace

An understanding that individuals' values differ but tend to reflect the societal values of the period in which they grew up can be a valuable aid in explaining and predicting behaviour. Baby Boomers currently dominate the workplace, but their years of being in charge are limited. In 2013, half of them will be at least 55 and 18 percent will be over 60.[34] Recent research suggests that Baby Boomers and Generation Y have a significant amount in common in their views toward the workplace, and that this might have profound effects on the organization of the workplace in the future.[35] Members of these two generations, much more than those from Generation X, want more flexible workplaces, more opportunity for time off to explore themselves, and more work-life balance. Generation Y will certainly change the face of the workplace in significant ways. Its members have mastered a communication and information system that many of their parents have yet to understand. In Chapter 4, we discuss further motivational differences between the Baby Boomers and Gen-Ys.

Cultural Differences

Canada is a multicultural country. One in five Canadians is an immigrant, according to the 2006 Census.[36] In 2006, 46 percent of Metropolitan Toronto's population, 40 percent of Vancouver's population, and 21 percent of Montreal's population were made up of immigrants.[37] The 2006 Census found that 20.1 percent of Canada's population spoke neither of the country's two official languages as their first language. In Vancouver and Toronto, this rate was 41 percent and 44 percent, respectively, so considerably more than one-third of the population of those two cities does not speak either English or French as a first language.[38] Of those who speak other languages, 16 percent speak Chinese (mainly Mandarin or Cantonese). The other dominant languages in Canada are Italian (in fourth place), followed by German, Punjabi, and Spanish.[39] These figures indicate the very different cultures that are part of the Canadian fabric of life.

Though we live in a multicultural society, there are some tensions among people from different races and ethnic groups. For instance, a Statistics Canada survey on ethnic diversity found that while most Canadians (93 percent) say they have never or rarely experienced unfair treatment because of their ethnicity or culture, 20 percent of visible minorities reported having been unfairly treated sometimes or often.[40]

Canadians often define themselves as "not Americans" and point out differences in the values of the two countries. Ipsos Reid recently conducted a national survey of Americans and Canadians, ages 18 to 34, and found a number of differences between the two countries' young adults. Both groups rated health care, education, and employment as their top concerns. "When we compare the lifestyles of young adults in the United States and Canada, one could describe the Americans as more 'traditional' and more 'domestic' in their values and focus, whereas Canadians are more of the 'free-spirit' type," said Samantha McAra, senior research manager with Ipsos Reid.[41] Exhibit 3-3 shows some of the other differences between Canadian and American young adults.

PERSONAL INVENTORY ASSESSMENT

Learn About Yourself
Intercultural Sensitivity Scale

EXHIBIT 3-3 Differences between Canadian and American Young Adults, 18 to 34		
	Canada	**United States**
Text messages per week (sent and received)	78.7	129.6
Online social media	Facebook: 81% had a profile MySpace: 23% had registered a profile	Facebook: 57% had registered a profile MySpace: 54% had registered a profile
Married	25%	39%
Domestic partnerships	18%	7%
Own a home	35%	45%
Employed on a full- or part-time basis or self-employed	62%	64%
Some post-secondary education	76%	68%
Actively participate in a recycling program	88%	72%
Use public transportation once a week or more often	33%	20%
Favourite sport	NHL hockey (58%)	NFL football (57%)

Source: Based on Ipsos Reid, *A Check-up on the Habits and Values of North America's Young Adults (Part 1)* (Calgary: Ipsos Reid, 2009), http://www.ipsos-na.com/news-polls/pressrelease.aspx?id=4532

In his book *Fire and Ice*, pollster Michael Adams finds that there is a growing dissimilarity between Canadian and American values. The two groups differ in 41 of the 56 values that Adams examined. For 24 values the gap actually widened between 1992 and 2000, indicating that Canadians' social values are growing more distinct from those of Americans.[42] Adams suggests that the September 11, 2001, attacks have affected the personality of Americans. He finds Americans are more accepting of patriarchy and hierarchy these days, and he concludes that it is "the supposedly bold, individualistic Americans who are the nodding conformists, and the supposedly shy, deferential and law-abiding Canadians who are most likely to assert their personal autonomy and political agency."[43]

In what follows, we identify a number of cultural values that influence workplace behaviour in Canada. Be aware that these are generalizations, and it would be a mistake to assume that everyone coming from the same cultural background acts similarly. Rather, these overviews are meant to encourage you to think about cultural differences and similarities so that you can better understand people's behaviour.

Francophone and Anglophone Values

Quebec is generally seen as culturally, linguistically, politically, and legally distinct from the rest of Canada.[44] French, not English, is the dominant language in Quebec, and Roman Catholicism, not Protestantism, is the dominant religion. Unlike the rest of Canada, where the law is based on English common law principles, Quebec's legal system is based on the French civil code. From time to time, Quebec separatists threaten

Understanding differences in values across cultures helps explain the behaviour of employees from different countries. According to Hofstede's framework for assessing cultures, China, like all Asian nations, ranks high in long-term orientation. China also ranks high in power distance, where the inequality of power and wealth within the country is accepted by citizens as part of their cultural heritage. Ranking low in individualism, China has a strong collectivistic culture that fosters relationships where everyone takes responsibility for group members. Using these and other ratings can help organizations considering doing business in China to predict the behaviour of employees shown here at a glassware factory.

that the province will leave Canada. Thus, it is important for managers and employees in Canadian firms to be aware of some of the potential cultural differences when managing in francophone environments compared with anglophone environments.

A number of studies have shown that English-speaking Canadians and French-speaking Canadians have distinctive value priorities. In general, Canadian anglophone managers are seen to be more individualistic than Canadian francophone managers,[45] although more recent research finds greater similarity between anglophone and francophone middle managers in terms of their individualistic-collectivistic orientation.[46] Francophones have also been shown to be more concerned about the interpersonal aspects of the workplace than task competence.[47] They have also been found to be more committed to their work organizations.[48] Earlier studies suggested that anglophones took more risks,[49] but more recent studies have found that this point has become less true and that French-speaking Canadians had the highest values for "reducing or avoiding ambiguity and uncertainty at work."[50]

Canadian anglophone business people have been found to use a more cooperative negotiating style when dealing with one another, compared with Canadian francophone business people.[51] However, Canadian francophones are more likely than Canadian anglophones to use a more cooperative approach during cross-cultural negotiations.[52] Other studies indicate that anglophone managers tend to value autonomy and intrinsic job values, such as achievement, and thus are more achievement-oriented, while francophone managers tend to value affiliation and extrinsic job values, such as technical supervision.[53] A recent study conducted at the University of Ottawa and Laval University suggests that some of the differences reported in previous research may be decreasing.[54] Another study suggests that anglophones and francophones are not very different personality-wise.[55] Yet another study indicates that French Canadians have become more like English Canadians in valuing autonomy and self-fulfillment.[56] These studies are consistent with a recent study that suggests there are few differences between francophones and anglophones.[57]

Professor Carolyn Egri of the business school at Simon Fraser University led a cross-cultural study on the attitudes of managers toward different influence strategies.[58] The study found that Canadian anglophone and francophone managers tend to favour somewhat different influence strategies. Specifically, Canadian anglophone managers consider behaviour that is beneficial to the organization first and foremost as more acceptable than do Canadian francophone managers. By contrast, Canadian francophone managers favour behaviour that is beneficial to their own interests first. They also consider the following behaviours more acceptable than do Canadian anglophone managers: "destructive legal behaviours" (what the authors term a "get out of my way or get trampled" approach) and "destructive illegal behaviours" (what the authors term a "burn, pillage and plunder" approach). The study also found that Mexican managers score higher than Canadian francophone managers on their acceptance of destructive behaviours. Both American and Canadian anglophone managers consider destructive behaviours to be less acceptable. The results of this study suggest that Canadian francophone managers might serve as a bridge between Mexican managers at one end and American and Canadian anglophone managers on the other because of their level of acceptance of the different influence styles studied. The study's authors concluded that Canadian francophones would do well in "joint ventures, business negotiations, and other organizational interactions that involve members of more divergent cultural groups. For example, a national Canadian firm may find it strategically advantageous to utilize Canadian francophones in negotiating business contracts with Mexican firms."[59]

Despite some cultural and lifestyle value differences, both francophone and anglophone managers today have been exposed to similar types of organizational theories during their post-secondary school training, which might also influence their outlook as managers. Thus we would not expect to find large differences in the way that firms in francophone Canada are managed compared with those in the rest of Canada. Throughout this text, you will see a number of examples of Quebec-based businesses that support this conclusion.

Aboriginal Values

Entrepreneurial activity among Canada's Aboriginal peoples has been increasing at the same time that there are more partnerships and alliances between Aboriginal and non-Aboriginal businesses. Because of these business interactions, it is important to examine the types of differences we might observe in how each culture manages its businesses. For instance, sustainability is an important value in Aboriginal logging companies. Chilanko Forks, BC-based Tsi Del Del, a logging company, received the 2011 Aboriginal Forest Products Business Leadership Award because of the substantial amount of revenues the company put into education.[60] For every cubic metre harvested, the Alexis Creek First Nations–owned company puts 50 cents into a post-secondary educational fund. The fund is used to train the next generation of loggers. Andrew Gage, vice-president of the Forest Products Association of Canada, says that it's a wise investment for the company. "You are not going to find a group of people that are more committed to sustainable harvesting. They share those values that our industry has been trying to get to for the last decade or so."[61]

> What can you learn about OB from Aboriginal culture?

"Aboriginal values are usually perceived (by non-Aboriginals) as an impediment to economic development and organizational effectiveness."[62] These values include reluctance to compete, a time orientation different from the Western one, and an emphasis on consensus decision making.[63] Aboriginal people do not necessarily agree that these values are business impediments, however.

Specifically, although Canadian businesses and government have historically assumed that "non-Native people must teach Native people how to run their own organizations," the First Nations of Canada are not convinced.[64] They believe that traditional culture, values, and languages can help build a self-sustaining economy. Moreover, they believe that their cultural values may actually be a positive force in conducting business.[65]

In recent years, Canadian businesses facing Native land claims have met some difficulties in trying to accommodate demands for appropriate land use. In some cases, *accommodation* can mean less logging or mining by businesses until land claims are worked out. In order to achieve better communication between businesses and Native leaders, Cliff Hickey and David Natcher, two anthropologists from the University of Alberta, collaborated with the Little Red River Cree Nation in northern Alberta to develop a new model for forestry operations on First Nations land.[66] The anthropologists sought to balance the Native community's traditional lifestyle with the economic concerns of forestry operations. *OB in Action—Ground Rules for Developing Business Partnerships with Aboriginal People* outlines several of Hickey and Natcher's recommended ground rules, which they say could be used in oil and gas developments as well. Johnson Sewepagaham, chief of the Little Red River Cree, said his community would use these recommendations to resolve difficulties on treaty

in **ACTION**
Ground Rules for Developing Business Partnerships with Aboriginal People

→ Modify management operations to **reduce negative impact on wildlife species**.

→ Modify operations to **ensure community access** to lands and resources.

→ **Protect** all those **areas identified by community members** as having biological, cultural, and historical significance.

→ **Recognize and protect Aboriginal and treaty rights** to hunting, fishing, trapping, and gathering activities.

→ **Increase** forest-based **economic opportunities** for community members.

→ **Increase** the **involvement of community members** in decision making.[67]

lands for which Vernon, BC-based Tolko Industries and Vancouver-based Ainsworth jointly hold forest tenure. The two companies presented their General Development Plan to the Cree in fall 2008.[68] In 2009, the Cree were effective in persuading Tolko to revise its tree harvesting activities in a way that recognizes and respects the First Nations' ecological and cultural needs.[69]

Lindsay Redpath of Athabasca University has noted that Aboriginal cultures are more collectivist in orientation than are non-Aboriginal cultures in Canada and the United States.[70] Aboriginal organizations are much more likely to reflect and advance the goals of the community. There is also a greater sense of family within the workplace, with greater affiliation and loyalty. Power distance in Aboriginal cultures is smaller than in non-Aboriginal cultures of Canada and the United States, and there is an emphasis on consensual decision making. Aboriginal cultures are lower on uncertainty avoidance than non-Aboriginal cultures in Canada and the United States. Aboriginal organizations and cultures tend to have fewer rules and regulations. Each of these differences suggests that businesses created by Aboriginal people will differ from non-Aboriginal businesses, and both research and anecdotal evidence support this view.[71] For instance, Richard Prokopanko, director of government relations for Montreal-based Alcan, says that a move from handling issues in a generally legalistic, contract-oriented manner to valuing more dialogue and collaboration has helped ease some of the tension that had built up over 48 years between Alcan and First Nations people.[72]

Asian Values

The largest visible minority group in Canada are the Chinese. Over 1 million people of this group live in Canada and represent 26 percent of the country's visible minority population.[73] The Chinese in this country are a diverse group; they come from different countries (for example, China, Hong Kong, Malaysia), speak different languages, and practise different religions. The Chinese are only one part of the entire influence of the entire East and Southeast Asian population that influences Canadian society. It's predicted that by 2017, almost one-half of all visible minorities in Canada will come from two groups, South Asian and Chinese, and that these groups will be represented in almost equal numbers.[74] As well, many Canadian organizations, particularly those in British Columbia, conduct significant business with Asian firms. Asian cultures differ from Canadian culture on many of the GLOBE dimensions discussed earlier. For instance, Asian cultures tend to exhibit greater power distance and greater collectivism. These differences in values can affect individual interactions.

What would you need to know to set up a business in Asia?

Professor Rosalie Tung of Simon Fraser University and her student Irene Yeung examined the importance of *guanxi* (personal connections with the appropriate authorities or individuals) for a sample of North American, European, and Hong Kong firms doing business with companies in mainland China.[75] They suggest that their findings are also relevant in understanding how to develop relationships with firms from Japan, South Korea, and Hong Kong.

"*Guanxi* refers to the establishment of a connection between two independent individuals to enable a bilateral flow of personal or social transactions. Both parties must derive benefits from the transaction to ensure the continuation of such a relationship."[76] *Guanxi* relations are based on reciprocation, unlike Western networked relationships, which may be characterized more by self-interest. *Guanxi* relationships are meant to be long term and enduring, in contrast with the immediate gains sometimes expected in Western relationships. *Guanxi* also relies less on institutional law, and more on personal power and authority, than do Western relationships. Finally, *guanxi* relations are governed more by the notion of shame (that is, external pressures on performance), while Western relations often rely on guilt (that is, internal pressures on performance) to maintain agreements. *Guanxi* is seen as extremely important for business success in China—more than such factors as right location, price, or strategy, or product differentiation and quality. For Western firms wanting to do business with Asian firms, an understanding of *guanxi* and an effort to build relationships are important strategic advantages.

Our discussion about differences in cross-cultural values should suggest to you that understanding other cultures matters. When Canadian firms develop operations across Canada, south of the border, or overseas, employees need to understand other cultures in order to work more effectively and get along with others.

PERSONAL INVENTORY ASSESSMENT

Learn About Yourself
Multicultural Awareness Scale

   4   What are attitudes and why are they important?

Attitudes

Despite recognition over the years as a good employer, the employees at SaskGaming's Casino Regina went on strike for almost two months in June and July 2010.[77] The employees had been without a collective agreement since May 2009.

Fran Mohr, spokesperson for the Public Service Alliance of Canada (PSAC), which represents the striking employees, was relieved to see the strike end. "We are happy it's finally over. I feel like a lot of weight has been lifted off my shoulders," said Mohr. "It's a big thing having 400 people walking a picket line day after day. It's a really good feeling to be going back. It feels like we've been gone a long time."

Though the casino had to run much shorter hours, public attitude seemed to favour the employees during the course of the strike. Those on the picket line received frequent donations of food and money. Mohr, a cashier at the casino, said the public understood why the employees went on strike. "We love what we do and no one wants to go on strike, but at some point you have to stand up for yourself. We have our families to consider and I think our clientele really respects that." The attitudes of the striking employees toward their employer were considerably negative before the strike began and became stronger as the strike progressed. So how do employees' attitudes get formed, and can they really be changed?

Attitudes are evaluative statements—either positive or negative—about objects, people, or events. They reflect how we feel about something. When I say, "I like my job," I am expressing my attitude about work.

Specific attitudes tend to predict specific behaviours, whereas general attitudes tend to predict general behaviours. For instance, asking an employee about her intention to stay with an organization for the next six months is likely to better predict turnover for that person than asking her how satisfied she is with her job. On the other hand, overall job satisfaction would better predict a general behaviour, such as whether the employee is engaged in her work or motivated to contribute to her organization.[78]

In organizations, attitudes are important because they affect job behaviour.[79] Employees may believe, for example, that supervisors, auditors, managers, and time-and-motion engineers are all conspiring to make them work harder for the same or less money. This may then lead to a negative attitude toward management when an employee is asked to stay late and help on a special project.

Employees may also be negatively affected by the attitudes of their co-workers or clients. *From Concepts to Skills* on pages 102–103 looks at whether it's possible to change someone's attitude, and how that might happen in the workplace.

A person can have thousands of attitudes, but OB focuses our attention on a limited number of work-related attitudes.[80] Below we consider four important attitudes that affect organizational performance: job satisfaction, organizational commitment, job involvement, and employee engagement.

Job Satisfaction

Our definition of **job satisfaction**—a positive feeling about a job resulting from an evaluation of its characteristics—is clearly broad.[81] A 2011 survey conducted by

attitudes Positive or negative feelings about objects, people, or events.

job satisfaction A positive feeling about a job resulting from an evaluation of its characteristics.

Mercer found that Canadians are not all that satisfied: 36 percent said they were thinking about leaving their employers and another 20 percent were ambivalent about staying or going.[82]

What Causes Job Satisfaction?

Think about the best job you have ever had. What made it so? Chances are you liked the work you did and the people with whom you worked. Interesting jobs that provide training, variety, independence, and control satisfy most employees.[83] There is also a strong correspondence between how well people enjoy the social context of their workplace and how satisfied they are overall. Interdependence, feedback, social support, and interaction with co-workers outside the workplace are strongly related to job satisfaction even after accounting for characteristics of the work itself.[84]

You have probably noticed that pay comes up often when people discuss job satisfaction. For people who are poor (for example, living below the poverty line) or who live in poor countries, pay does correlate with job satisfaction and overall happiness. But once an individual reaches a level of comfortable living (in Canada, that occurs at about $40 000 a year, depending on the region and family size), the relationship between pay and job satisfaction virtually disappears. People who earn $80 000 are, on average, no happier with their jobs than those who earn close to $40 000.[85] High-paying jobs have average satisfaction levels no higher than those that pay much less. One researcher even found no significant difference when he compared the overall well-being of the richest people on the *Forbes* 400 list with that of Maasai herders in East Africa.[86] *Case Incident—Thinking Your Way to a Better Job* on page 101 considers the effect state of mind has on a person's job satisfaction.

Money does motivate people, as we will discover in Chapter 4. But what motivates us is not necessarily the same as what makes us happy. A recent poll found that entering first-year university students rated becoming "very well off financially" first on a list of 19 goals, ahead of choices such as helping others, raising a family, or becoming proficient in an academic pursuit. Maybe your goal isn't to be happy. But if it is, money is probably not going to do much to get you there.[87]

Job satisfaction is not just about job conditions. Personality also plays a role. Research has shown that people who have positive **core self-evaluations**—who

When asked "On a scale of 1 (not at all) to 7 (completely) how satisfied are you with your life?" *Forbes* magazine's "richest Americans" averaged 5.8 and an East African Maasai tribe, who engage in traditional herding and lead nomadic lives, averaged 5.7. The results of this study suggest that money does not buy life satisfaction.[88]

core self-evaluation Bottom-line conclusions individuals have about their capabilities, competence, and worth as a person.

believe in their inner worth and basic competence—are more satisfied with their jobs than those with negative core self-evaluations. Not only do they see their work as fulfilling and challenging, they are more likely to gravitate toward challenging jobs in the first place. Those with negative core self-evaluations set less ambitious goals and are more likely to give up when confronting difficulties. Thus, they are more likely to be stuck in boring, repetitive jobs than those with positive core self-evaluations.[89]

So what are the consequences of job satisfaction? We examine this question below.

Job Satisfaction and Productivity

The idea that "happy workers are productive workers" developed in the 1930s and 1940s, largely as a result the Hawthorne studies at Western Electric. Based on those conclusions, managers focused on working conditions and the work environment to make employees happier. Then, in the 1980s, an influential review of the research suggested that the relationship between job satisfaction and job performance was not particularly high. The authors of that review even labelled it "illusory."[90]

More recently, a review of more than 300 studies corrected some errors in that earlier review and found the correlation between job satisfaction and job performance to be moderately strong, even across international contexts. This conclusion also appears to be generalizable across international contexts. The correlation is higher for complex jobs that provide employees with more discretion to act on their attitudes.[91] A review of 16 studies that assessed job performance and satisfaction over time also linked job satisfaction to job performance[92] and suggested the relationship mostly works one way: Satisfaction was a likely cause of better performance, but higher performance was not a cause of higher job satisfaction.

We cannot be entirely sure, however, whether satisfaction causes productivity or productivity causes satisfaction.[93] In other words, if you do a good job, you

eBay's young employees rank their employer as one of the best places to work for Millennials. The company's culture of fun, casual dress, and flexible work schedules that provide for a work-life balance appeal to Generation-Y employees like those shown here at eBay's offices in San Jose, California. Young employees say that eBay managers give them job responsibility quickly, generous recognition for their achievements, and learning opportunities to advance their careers. They also admire eBay's "Social Venture" initiatives such as WorldofGood.com, eBay Giving Works, and MicroPlace that make a positive difference in the lives of people throughout the world.

intrinsically feel good about it. In addition, your higher productivity should increase your recognition, your pay level, and your likelihood of promotion. Cumulatively, these rewards, in turn, increase your level of satisfaction with the job. Most likely, satisfaction can lead to high levels of performance for some people, while for others, high performance is satisfying. *Point/Counterpoint* on page 98 further explores the debate on whether job satisfaction is created by the situation or by an individual's characteristics.

As we move from the individual to the organizational level, we also find support for the satisfaction-performance relationship.[94] When we gather satisfaction and productivity data for the organization as a whole, we find organizations with more satisfied employees tend to be more effective than organizations with less satisfied employees.

Job Satisfaction and Organizational Citizenship Behaviour

In Chapter 1, we defined **organizational citizenship behaviour (OCB)** as discretionary behaviour that is not part of an employee's formal job requirements and is not usually rewarded, but that nevertheless promotes the effective functioning of the organization.[95] Individuals who are high in OCB will go beyond their usual job duties, providing performance that is beyond expectations. Examples of such behaviour include helping colleagues with their workloads, taking only limited breaks, and alerting others to work-related problems.[96] More recently OCB has been associated with the following workplace behaviours: "altruism, conscientiousness, loyalty, civic virtue, voice, functional participation, sportsmanship, courtesy, and advocacy participation."[97] Organizational citizenship is important, as it can help the organization function more efficiently and more effectively.[98] Recent work by York University professors Sabrina Salamon and Yuval Deutsch suggest that OCB may be a way for individuals to signal to managers and co-workers abilities that might not be immediately observable.[99]

It seems logical to assume that job satisfaction should be a major determinant of an employee's OCB.[100] Satisfied employees would seem more likely to talk positively about an organization, help others, and go beyond the normal expectations in their jobs.[101] They might go beyond the call of duty because they want to reciprocate their positive experiences. Consistent with this thinking, evidence suggests job satisfaction is moderately correlated with OCBs; people who are more satisfied with their jobs are more likely to engage in OCBs.[102] Why? Fairness perceptions help explain the relationship.[103] Those who feel their co-workers support them are more likely to engage in helpful behaviours, whereas those who have antagonistic relationships with co-workers are less likely to do so.[104]

Job Satisfaction and Customer Satisfaction

As we noted in Chapter 1, employees in service jobs often interact with customers. Since managers of service organizations should be concerned with pleasing those customers, it is reasonable to ask: Is employee satisfaction related to positive customer outcomes? For front-line employees who have regular contact with customers, the answer is yes. Satisfied employees increase customer satisfaction and loyalty.[105]

Why? In service organizations, customer retention and defection are highly dependent on how front-line employees deal with customers. Satisfied employees are more likely to be friendly, upbeat, and responsive—which customers appreciate. Because satisfied employees are less prone to turnover, customers are more likely to encounter familiar faces and receive experienced service. These qualities build customer satisfaction and loyalty. In addition, the relationship seems to apply in reverse: Dissatisfied customers can increase an employee's job dissatisfaction. Employees who interact with rude, thoughtless, or unreasonably demanding customers report lower job satisfaction.[106]

organizational citizenship behaviour (OCB) Discretionary behaviour that is not part of an employee's formal job requirements, but that nevertheless promotes the effective functioning of the organization.

How Employees Can Express Dissatisfaction

Job dissatisfaction and antagonistic relationships with co-workers predict a variety of behaviours organizations find undesirable, including unionization attempts, substance abuse, stealing at work, undue socializing, and tardiness. Researchers argue that these behaviours are indicators of a broader syndrome called *deviant behaviour in the workplace* (or *employee withdrawal*).[107] If employees don't like their work environment, they will respond somehow, though it is not always easy to forecast exactly *how*. One worker might quit. Another might use work time to surf the Internet or take work supplies home for personal use. In short, workers who don't like their jobs "get even" in various ways—and because those ways can be quite creative, controlling only one behaviour, such as with an absence control policy, leaves the root cause untouched. To effectively control the undesirable consequences of job dissatisfaction, employers should attack the source of the problem—the dissatisfaction—rather than try to control the different responses.

Exhibit 3-4 presents a model—the exit-voice-loyalty-neglect framework—that can be used to examine individual responses to dissatisfaction along two dimensions: whether they are constructive or destructive and whether they are active or passive. Four types of behaviour result:[108]

- **Exit**. Actively attempting to leave the organization, including looking for a new position as well as resigning. This is a destructive action from the point of view of the organization.

- **Voice**. Actively and constructively trying to improve conditions, including suggesting improvements, discussing problems with superiors, and some forms of union activity.

- **Loyalty**. Passively but optimistically waiting for conditions to improve, including speaking up for the organization in the face of external criticism and trusting the organization and its management to do the right thing.

exit Dissatisfaction expressed by actively attempting to leave the organization.

voice Dissatisfaction expressed by actively and constructively attempting to improve conditions.

loyalty Dissatisfaction expressed by passively waiting for conditions to improve.

Service organizations know that whether customers are satisfied and loyal depends on how front-line employees deal with customers. Singapore Airlines has earned a reputation among world travellers for outstanding customer service. The airline's "putting people first" philosophy applies to both its employees and customers. In recruiting flight attendants, the airline selects people who are warm, hospitable, and happy to serve others. Through extensive training, Singapore Airlines moulds recruits into attendants focused on complete customer satisfaction.

EXHIBIT 3-4 Responses to Job Dissatisfaction

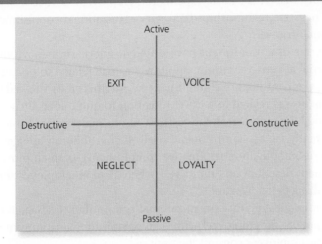

Source: "When Bureaucrats Get the Blues: Responses to Dissatisfaction Among Federal Employees" by Caryl Rusbult, David Lowery. *Journal of Applied Social Psychology 15*, no. 1, p. 83. Copyright © 1985, John Wiley and Sons. http://onlinelibrary.wiley.com/doi/10.1111/jasp.1985.15.issue-1/issuetoc

- **Neglect**. Passively allowing conditions to worsen, including chronic absenteeism or lateness, reduced effort, and increased error rate.

Exit and neglect behaviours reflect employee choices of lowered productivity, absenteeism, and turnover in the face of dissatisfaction. But this model also presents constructive behaviours such as voice and loyalty that allow individuals to tolerate unpleasant situations or to work toward satisfactory working conditions. It helps us understand situations, such as those we sometimes find among unionized workers, where low job satisfaction is coupled with low turnover.[109] Union members often express dissatisfaction through the grievance procedure or through formal contract negotiations. These voice mechanisms allow them to continue in their jobs while convincing themselves that they are acting to improve the situation.

Organizational Commitment

In **organizational commitment** an employee identifies with a particular organization and its goals, and wishes to remain a member.[110]

Professor John Meyer at the University of Western Ontario and his colleagues have identified and developed measures for three types of commitment:[111]

- **Affective commitment**. An individual's emotional attachment to the organization and a belief in its values. For example, a PetSmart employee may be affectively committed to the company because of its involvement with animals.

- **Normative commitment**. The obligation an individual feels to staying with the organization for moral or ethical reasons. An employee spearheading a new initiative may remain with an employer because she feels she would "leave the employer in the lurch" if she left.

- **Continuance commitment**. An individual's perceived economic value of remaining with an organization. An employee may be committed to an employer because she is paid well and feels it would hurt her family to quit.

A positive relationship appears to exist between organizational commitment and job productivity, but it is a modest one.[112] A review of 27 studies suggested that the

neglect Dissatisfaction expressed by passively allowing conditions to worsen.

organizational commitment A state in which an employee identifies with a particular organization and its goals, and wishes to maintain membership in the organization.

affective commitment An individual's emotional attachment to and identification with an organization, and a belief in its values.

normative commitment The obligation an individual feels to stay with an organization.

continuance commitment An individual's calculation to stay with an organization based on the perceived costs of leaving the organization.

relationship between commitment and performance is strongest for new employees, and considerably weaker for more experienced employees.[113] The research evidence demonstrates negative relationships between organizational commitment and both absenteeism and turnover.[114]

Different forms of commitment have different effects on behaviour. One study found managerial affective commitment more strongly related to organizational performance than was continuance commitment.[115] Another study showed that continuance commitment was related to a lower intention to quit but an increased tendency to be absent and lower job performance. These results make sense in that continuance commitment really isn't a commitment at all. Rather than an allegiance (affective commitment) or an obligation (normative commitment) to an employer, a continuance commitment describes an employee "tethered" to an employer simply because there isn't anything better available.[116]

How can companies increase organizational commitment? Research on a number of companies known for employees with high organizational commitment identified five reasons why employees commit themselves:[117]

- They are proud of [the company's] aspirations, accomplishments, and legacy; they share its values.

- They know what each person is expected to do, how performance is measured, and why it matters.

- They are in control of their own destinies; they savour the high-risk, high-reward work environment.

- They are recognized mostly for the quality of their individual performance.

- They have fun and enjoy the supportive and highly interactive environment.

These findings suggest a variety of ways for organizations to increase the commitment of employees. Earlier in the chapter we discussed the role of satisfaction

A major focus of Nissan Motor Company's Diversity Development Office in Japan is helping female employees develop their careers. Nissan provides women such as the assembly-line workers shown here with one-on-one counselling services of career advisers and training programs to develop applicable skills. Women can also visit Nissan's corporate intranet to read interviews with "role models," women who have made substantial contributions to the company. Nissan believes that hiring more women and supporting their careers will contribute to the company's competitive edge.

on organizational citizenship behaviour (OCB). We should also note that when individuals have high organizational commitment, they are likely to engage in more OCB.

Job Involvement

Related to job satisfaction is **job involvement**,[118] which measures the degree to which people identify psychologically with their job and consider their perceived performance level important to self-worth.[119] Employees with a high level of job involvement strongly identify with and really care about the kind of work they do. Another closely related concept is **psychological empowerment**, employees' beliefs in the degree to which they influence their work environment, their competence, the meaningfulness of their job, and their perceived autonomy.[120] High levels of both job involvement and psychological empowerment are positively related to organizational citizenship and job performance.[121] High job involvement is also related to reduced absences and lower resignation rates.[122]

Employee Engagement

A new concept that comes out of the work on job involvement is **employee engagement**, an individual's involvement with, satisfaction with, and enthusiasm for the work he or she does. For example, we might ask employees about the availability of resources and the opportunities to learn new skills, whether they feel their work is important and meaningful, and whether their interactions with co-workers and supervisors are rewarding.[123] Highly engaged employees have a passion for their work and feel a deep connection to their company; disengaged employees have essentially "checked out"—putting time but not energy or attention into their work. Calgary-based Vista Projects, an engineering procurement and construction management firm, consults with its employees for engagement ideas. Doing so has resulted in education initiatives, opportunities for company ownership, and time off for religious holidays.[124] To encourage engagement, the president of Charlottetown, PEI-based Holland College visits the college's 24 sites routinely to give employees an opportunity to raise concerns.

A study of nearly 8000 business units in 36 companies found that those whose employees had high average levels of engagement had higher levels of customer satisfaction, were more productive, had higher profits, and had lower levels of turnover and accidents than at other companies.[125] Toronto-based Molson Coors Canada found that engaged employees were five times less likely to have safety incidents, and when one did occur, it was much less serious and less costly for the engaged employee than for a disengaged one ($63 per incident vs. $392).

Such promising findings have earned employee engagement a following in many business organizations and management consulting firms. However, the concept is relatively new and still generates active debate about its usefulness. One review of the literature concluded that the meaning of the term is ambiguous for both practitioners and academics,[126] while another reviewer called engagement "an umbrella term for whatever one wants it to be."[127] Still, a 2011 study that draws from the best current research to create a model of work engagement suggests that there is a lot of promise to this concept.[128]

Organizations will likely continue using employee engagement, and it will remain a subject of research. The ambiguity surrounding it arises from its newness and may also, ironically, reflect its popularity. Engagement is a very general concept, perhaps broad enough to capture the intersection of the other variables we have discussed. In other words, it may be what these attitudes have in common.

PERSONAL INVENTORY ASSESSMENT

Learn About Yourself
Effective Empowerment and Engagement

PERSONAL INVENTORY ASSESSMENT

Learn About Yourself
Flourishing Scale

LESSONS LEARNED

- Values represent basic convictions about what is important, right, and good.
- Attitudes tend to predict behaviours.
- Job satisfaction leads to better performance.

job involvement The degree to which a person identifies with a job, actively participates in it, and considers performance important to self-worth.

psychological empowerment Employees' belief in the degree to which they affect their work environment, their competence, the meaningfulness of their job, and their perceived autonomy in their work.

employee engagement An individual's involvement with, satisfaction with, and enthusiasm for the work he or she does.

Summary and Implications

1 **What are values?** Values guide how we make decisions about and evaluations of behaviours and events. They represent basic convictions about what is important, right, and good to the individual. Although they do not have a direct impact on behaviour, values strongly influence a person's attitudes. So knowledge of an individual's values can provide insight into his or her attitudes.

2 **How can we understand values across cultures?** Geert Hofstede found that managers and employees vary on five value dimensions of national culture: power distance, individualism vs. collectivism, masculinity vs. femininity, uncertainty avoidance, and long-term vs. short-term orientation. His insights were expanded by the GLOBE research program, an ongoing cross-cultural investigation of leadership and national culture.

3 **Are there unique Canadian values?** Recent research suggests that Canadian values tend to be affected by generational and cultural differences. The three dominant age groups of adults in the Canadian workplace are the Baby Boomers (born between the mid-1940s and mid-1960s), the Generation Xers (born between the mid-1960s and the late 1970s), and the Generation Ys (born between 1979 through 1994). Canada is a multicultural country, and there are a number of groups that contribute to its diverse values, such as Aboriginal people, French Canadians, and various immigrant groups. Canadian values differ from American values and those of its other trading partners in a variety of ways.

4 **What are attitudes and why are they important?** *Attitudes* are positive or negative feelings about objects, people, or events. Attitudes affect the way people respond to situations. When I say "I like my job," I am expressing my attitude to work and I am likely to be more committed in my behaviour than if my attitude was one of not liking my job. A person can have thousands of attitudes, but OB focuses our attention on a limited number of job-related attitudes. These job-related attitudes tap positive or negative evaluations that employees hold about aspects of their work environment. Most of the research in OB has been concerned with four attitudes: job satisfaction, organizational commitment, job involvement, and employee engagement.

for Review

1. Describe the five value dimensions of national culture proposed by Geert Hofstede.

2. Compare Aboriginal and non-Aboriginal values.

3. How might differences in generational values affect the workplace?

4. Describe the profile of Generation-Y employees.

5. What might explain low levels of employee job satisfaction in recent years?

6. Are satisfied employees productive employees? Explain your answer.

7. What is the relationship between job satisfaction and absenteeism? Job satisfaction and turnover? Which is the stronger relationship?

8. Contrast exit, voice, loyalty, and neglect as employee responses to job satisfaction.

for Critical Thinking

1. "Thirty-five years ago, young employees we hired were ambitious, conscientious, hard-working, and honest. Today's young employees don't have the same values." Do you agree or disagree with this manager's comments? Support your position.

2. Do you think there might be any positive and significant relationship between the possession of certain personal values and successful career progression in organizations such as Merrill Lynch, the Canadian Union of Postal Workers (CUPW), and the City of Regina's police department? Discuss.

3. "Managers should do everything they can to enhance the job satisfaction of their employees." Do you agree or disagree? Support your position.

4. When employees are asked whether they would again choose the same work or whether they would want their children to follow in their footsteps, fewer than half typically answer "yes." What, if anything, do you think this implies about employee job satisfaction?

for You

- You will encounter many people who have values different from yours in the classroom, in various kinds of activities in which you participate, as well as in the workplace. You should try to understand value differences and to figure out ways to work positively with people who are different from you.

- Though we often try to generalize about people's values based on either their generation or their culture, not all people in a group hold the same values. Be prepared to look beyond the group characteristics to understand the person.

- The variety of possible responses to dissatisfaction (exit, voice, loyalty, neglect) gives you alternatives to consider when you are feeling dissatisfied with a situation. Neglect may be an easy way to respond, but consider whether voice might be more effective.

OB at work

POINT

COUNTERPOINT

Managers Create Job Satisfaction

A review of the evidence has identified four factors conducive to high levels of employee job satisfaction: mentally challenging work, equitable rewards, supportive working conditions, and supportive colleagues.[129] Management is able to control each of these factors.

Mentally challenging work. Generally, people prefer jobs that give them opportunities to use their skills and abilities and offer a variety of tasks, freedom, and feedback on how well they are doing. These characteristics make work mentally challenging.

Equitable rewards. Employees want pay systems that they perceive as just, unambiguous, and in line with their expectations. When they see pay as fair—based on job demands, individual skill level, and community pay standards—satisfaction is likely to result.

Supportive working conditions. Employees want their work environments to be safe and personally comfortable and to facilitate their doing a good job. Most employees prefer working relatively close to home, in clean and up-to-date facilities, with adequate tools and equipment.

Supportive colleagues. People get more out of work than merely money or tangible achievements. Work also fills the need for social interaction. Not surprisingly, therefore, friendly and supportive co-workers lead to increased job satisfaction. The boss's behaviour is also a major factor; employee satisfaction is increased when the immediate supervisor is understanding and friendly, offers praise for good performance, listens to employees' opinions, and shows a personal interest in employees.

Satisfaction Is Individually Determined

The notion that managers and organizations can control the level of employee job satisfaction is inherently attractive. It fits nicely with the view that managers directly influence organizational processes and outcomes. Unfortunately a growing body of evidence challenges this idea. The most recent findings indicate that job satisfaction is largely genetically determined.[130]

Whether people are happy is essentially determined by gene structure. Approximately 50 to 80 percent of people's differences in happiness, or subjective well-being, has been found to be attributable to their different genes. Identical twins, for example, tend to have very similar careers, report similar levels of job satisfaction, and change jobs at similar rates.

Analysis of satisfaction data for a selected sample of individuals over a 50-year period found that individual results were stable over time, even when subjects changed employers and occupations. This and other research suggests that an individual's disposition toward life—positive or negative—is established by his or her genetic makeup, holds over time, and influences disposition toward work.

Given these findings, most managers can do little to influence employee satisfaction. Despite their manipulating job characteristics, working conditions, and rewards, people will inevitably return to their own "set point." A bonus may temporarily increase the satisfaction level of a negatively disposed employee, but it is unlikely to sustain it. Sooner or later, a dissatisfied employee will find new fault with the job.

The only place managers will have any significant influence is in the selection process. If managers want satisfied employees, they need to screen out negative people who derive little satisfaction from their jobs, irrespective of work conditions.

LEARNING ABOUT **YOURSELF** EXERCISE

What Do You Value?

There are 16 items in the list below. Rate how important each one is to you on a scale of 0 (not important) to 100 (very important). Write a number between 0 and 100 on the line to the left of each item.

Not Important				Somewhat Important					Very Important	
0	10	20	30	40	50	60	70	80	90	100

_____ **1.** An enjoyable, satisfying job.

_____ **2.** A high-paying job.

_____ **3.** A good marriage.

_____ **4.** Meeting new people; social events.

_____ **5.** Involvement in community activities.

_____ **6.** My religion.

_____ **7.** Exercising, playing sports.

_____ **8.** Intellectual development.

_____ **9.** A career with challenging opportunities.

_____ **10.** Nice cars, clothes, home, and so on.

_____ **11.** Spending time with family.

_____ **12.** Having several close friends.

_____ **13.** Volunteer work for nonprofit organizations, such as the Canadian Cancer Society.

_____ **14.** Meditation, quiet time to think, pray, and so on.

_____ **15.** A healthy, balanced diet.

_____ **16.** Educational reading, television, self-improvement programs, and so on.

Scoring Key:

Transfer the numbers for each of the 16 items to the appropriate column; then add up the 2 numbers in each column.

	Professional	Financial	Family	Social
	1. _____	2. _____	3. _____	4. _____
	9. _____	10. _____	11. _____	12. _____
Totals	_____	_____	_____	_____
	Community	**Spiritual**	**Physical**	**Intellectual**
	5. _____	6. _____	7. _____	8. _____
	13. _____	14. _____	15. _____	16. _____
Totals	_____	_____	_____	_____

The higher the total in any value dimension, the higher the importance you place on that value set. The closer the numbers are in all 8 dimensions, the more well rounded you are.

Source: R. N. Lussier, *Human Relations in Organizations: A Skill Building Approach,* 2nd ed. (Homewood, IL: Richard D. Irwin, 1993). Reprinted by permission of the McGraw-Hill Companies, Inc.

OB at work

Intercultural Sensitivity Scale: Cultural sensitivity can minimize conflict and tension in the workplace. Use this scale to better understand how culturally sensitive you are. Sensitivity levels can be improved with education, contact with other cultures, and effort.

Multicultural Awareness Scale: Understanding other cultures is especially important in Canadian workplaces, since the Canadian workforce is extremely diverse. Use this scale to see how well you understand other cultures and their business practices.

Effective Empowerment and Engagement: Some engagement and empowerment techniques are more effective than others. Use this scale to see how your approach measures up, and to get some ideas for improvement.

Flourishing Scale: Flourishing is an indicator of well-being connected to engagement, job satisfaction, and life satisfaction. Use this scale to get a sense of your current level of well-being.

BREAKOUT **GROUP** EXERCISES

Form small groups to discuss the following topics, as assigned by your instructor. Each person in the group should first identify 3 to 5 key personal values.

1. Identify the extent to which values overlap in your group.

2. Try to uncover with your group members the source of some of your key values (for example, parents, peer group, teachers, church).

3. What kind of workplace would be most suitable for the values that you hold most closely?

WORKING WITH OTHERS EXERCISE

Understanding Cultural Values

Objective   To compare the cultural values of two countries, and determine how differences might affect group behaviour.

Time   Approximately 30 minutes.

Procedure

1. Break into groups of 5 or 6.

2. Pretend that you are a group of students working on a project. Half of you are from Canada and hold typically "Canadian" cultural values; the other half are from the country assigned and hold that country's cultural values.

3. Consider the values of power distance, individualism/collectivism, and uncertainty avoidance, and discuss the differences between Canadian cultural values and the values of the country assigned to you. (Refer to Exhibit 3-2 on page 78 to identify the values of your assigned country.)

4. Answer the following questions:
   What challenges might you expect in working together?
   What steps could be taken to work together more effectively?

ETHICAL **DILEMMA** EXERCISE

Is It a Bribe or a Gift?

The Corruption of Foreign Public Officials Act prohibits Canadian firms from making payments to foreign government officials with the aim of gaining or maintaining business.[131] But payments are acceptable if they don't violate local laws. For instance, payments to officers working for foreign corporations are legal. Many countries don't have such legal guidelines.

Bribery is a common way of doing business in many underdeveloped countries. Government jobs there often don't pay very well, so it's tempting for officials to supplement their income with bribes. In addition, in many countries, the penalties for demanding and receiving bribes are few or nonexistent.

You are a Canadian who works for a large European multinational computer manufacturer. You are currently working to sell a $5 million system to a government agency in Nigeria. The Nigerian official who heads up the team that will decide who gets this contract has asked you for a payment of $20 000. He says this payment will not guarantee you get the order, but without it he cannot be very encouraging. Your company's policy is very flexible on the issue of "gifts" to facilitate sales. Your boss says that it's okay to pay the $20 000, but only if you can be relatively assured of the order.

You are not sure what you should do. The Nigerian official has told you specifically that any payment to him is not to be mentioned to anyone else on the Nigerian team. You know for certain that three other companies are also negotiating, but it's unconfirmed whether two of those companies have turned down the payment request.

What would you do?

CASE INCIDENT

Thinking Your Way to a Better Job

You have probably been dissatisfied with a job at one time or another in your life.[132] When faced with a dissatisfying job, researchers and job holders alike usually think about how to increase job satisfaction: Ask for more pay, take control over your work, change your schedule, minimize contact with a toxic co-worker, or even change jobs. While each of these remedies may be appropriate in certain situations, increasingly researchers are uncovering an interesting truth about job satisfaction: It is as much a state of mind as a function of job conditions.

Here, we are not talking about the dispositional source of job satisfaction. It's true that some people have trouble finding any job satisfying, whereas others cannot be brought down by even the most onerous of jobs. However, by state of mind, we mean changeable, easily implemented ways of thinking that can affect your job satisfaction. In case you think we have gone the way of self-help gurus Deepak Chopra and Wayne Dyer, think again. There is some solid, albeit fairly preliminary, evidence supporting the idea that our views of our job and life can be significantly impacted by changing the way we think.

One main area where this "state of mind" research might help you change the way you think about your job (or life) is in gratitude. Researchers have found that when people are asked to make short lists of things for which they are grateful, they report being happier, and the increased happiness seems to last well beyond the moments when people made the list.

Indeed, gratitude may explain why, when the economy is in bad shape, people actually become more satisfied with their jobs. One survey revealed that, from 2007 to 2008, when the economy slid into recession, the percentage of people reporting that they were "very satisfied" with their jobs increased to a whopping 38 percent (from 28 percent to 38 percent). When we see other people suffering, particularly those we see as similar to ourselves, it often leads us to realize that, as bad as things may seem, they can always be worse. As *Wall Street Journal* columnist Jeffrey Zaslow wrote, "People who still have jobs are finding reasons to be appreciative."

Questions

1. So, right now, make a short list of things about your job and life for which you are grateful. After having done that, do you feel more positively about your job and your life?

2. Now try doing this every day for a week. Do you think this exercise might make a difference in how you feel about your job and your life?

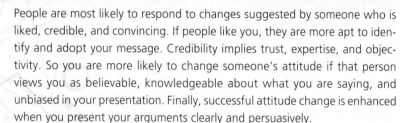

FROM CONCEPTS TO SKILLS

Changing Attitudes

Can you change unfavourable employee attitudes? Sometimes! It depends on who you are, the strength of the employee's attitude, the magnitude of the change, and the technique you choose to try to change the attitude.

People are most likely to respond to changes suggested by someone who is liked, credible, and convincing. If people like you, they are more apt to identify and adopt your message. Credibility implies trust, expertise, and objectivity. So you are more likely to change someone's attitude if that person views you as believable, knowledgeable about what you are saying, and unbiased in your presentation. Finally, successful attitude change is enhanced when you present your arguments clearly and persuasively.

It's easier to change a person's attitude if he or she is not strongly committed to it. Conversely, the stronger the belief in the attitude, the harder it is to change it. Also, attitudes that have been expressed publicly are more difficult to change because doing so requires admitting having made a mistake.

It's also easier to change attitudes when the change required is not very significant. To get a person to accept a new attitude that varies greatly from his or her current position requires more effort. It may also threaten other deeply held attitudes.

All attitude-change techniques are not equally effective across situations. Oral persuasion techniques are most effective when you use a positive, tactful tone; present strong evidence to support your position; tailor your argument to the listener; use logic; and support your evidence by appealing to the person's fears, frustrations, and other emotions. But people are more likely to embrace change when they can experience it. The use of training sessions in which employees share and personalize experiences, and practise new behaviours, can be powerful stimulants for change. Consistent with self-perception theory, changes in behaviour can lead to changes in attitudes.

Practising Skills

Form groups of 2. Person A is to choose any topic that he or she feels strongly about and state his or her position on the topic in 30 words or less. Person B's task will be to try to change Person A's attitude on this topic. Person B will have 10 minutes to make his or her case. When the time is up, the roles are reversed. Person B picks the topic and Person A has 10 minutes to try to change Person B's attitude.

Potential topics (you can choose *either* side of a topic) include the following: politics; the economy; world events; social practices; or specific management issues, such as that organizations should require all employees to undergo regular drug testing, there is no such thing as organizational loyalty any more, the customer is always right, and layoffs are an indication of management failures.

Questions

1. Were you successful in changing the other person's attitude? Why or why not?

2. Was the other person successful in changing your attitude? Why or why not?

3. What conclusions can you draw about changing the attitudes of yourself and others?

Reinforcing Skills

1. Try to convince a friend or relative to go with you to see a movie or play that you know he or she does not want to see.

2. Try to convince a friend or relative to try a different brand of toothpaste.

MyManagementLab

Study, practise, and explore real business situations with these helpful resources:

- **Study Plan:** Check your understanding of chapter concepts with self-study quizzes.
- **Online Lesson Presentations:** Study key chapter topics and work through interactive assessments to test your knowledge and master management concepts.
- **Videos:** Learn more about the management practices and strategies of real companies.
- **Simulations:** Practise management decision-making in simulated business environments.

P I A PERSONAL INVENTORY ASSESSMENT

OB on the Edge

Stress @Work

Long-haul truck driving is not an easy job. Drivers face heavy traffic, demanding schedules, challenges accessing healthy food, and fatigue. Surrey, BC-based Coastal Pacific Xpress (CPx) looks after its drivers and, for this, won an Award of Excellence from the British Columbia Medical Association in June 2011.[1] The award specifically noted CPx's "Focus on Fitness Friday," where drivers and staff get healthy meals and snacks, and are encouraged to exercise by walking. All employees have free access to pedometers, and CPx donates $2 to charity for every 1000 steps recorded on its pedometers on Focus on Fitness Fridays.

Employees are also encouraged to track their heart rate, Body Mass Index, weight, oxygen saturation levels, and other vital signs using on-site Life-Clinic kiosks. Laurie Forbes, vice-president of administration, notes that "healthy drivers cope better with stress, have less downtime due to illness, are better-rested and safer drivers."

Being sensitive to workplace stress is putting increased responsibilities on managers. When Janie Toivanen was diagnosed with severe depression, she approached her employer, Vancouver-based Electronic Arts (EA) Canada, to request indefinite stress leave.[2] Instead, just days later, she was fired. After working there for six years, she "felt like she had been thrown away." Toivanen thought EA cared about its employees, and could not believe it would not do anything to help her as she struggled to overcome her illness. She subsequently filed a complaint with the BC Human Rights Tribunal and was awarded, among other things, $20 000 for injury to her dignity, feelings, and self-respect and $19 744 in severance pay.

Are We Overstressed?

Stress appears to be a major factor in the lives of many Canadians. A 2010 survey conducted by Statistics Canada found that Canadians experience a great deal of stress, with those from Quebec topping the list.[3] The survey also found that women were more stressed than men. The inset *Stressed Quite a Lot, 2010* reports the findings.

The impact of stress on the Canadian economy is huge, costing an estimated $33 billion a year in lost productivity, and considerably more than that in medical costs. To address these costs, Prime Minister Stephen Harper announced the creation of the Mental Health Commission of Canada in 2007. At the launch of the commission, Harper noted that mental health disorders are "now the fastest-growing category of disability insurance claims in Canada."[4]

Shannon Wagner, a clinical psychologist and a specialist in workplace stress research at the University of Northern British Columbia, notes that changes in the nature of jobs may be increasing the levels of stress in the workplace. While many jobs are not as physically demanding, they are often more mentally demanding. "A lot of people now are identifying techno-stress and the 24/7 workday, which we didn't have even 10 or 15 years ago, this feeling of being constantly plugged in, of checking email 500 times a day."[5]

An additional problem is that employees are increasingly asked to donate labour to their employers, according to professor Linda Duxbury of Carleton University's Sprott School of Business and Professor Chris Higgins of the Richard Ivey School of Business at the University of Western Ontario. Their survey of 31 571 Canadians found that in the previous month half of them had worked an extra 2.5 days of unpaid overtime, and more than half had donated 3.5 days of working at home to catch up.[6] Canadians are frequently reporting that they want more balance in their work and family lives.[7]

Jobs and Stress Levels

How do jobs rate in terms of stress? The inset *The Most and Least Stressful Jobs* on page 106 shows how selected occupations ranked in an evaluation of 250 jobs. Among the criteria used in the rankings were overtime, quotas, deadlines, competitiveness, physical demands, environmental conditions, hazards encountered, initiative required, stamina required, win-lose situations, and working in the public eye.

Stress is not something that can be ignored in the workplace. A recent poll by Ipsos Reid found that 66 percent of the CEOs surveyed said that "stress, burnout or other physical and mental health issues" have a negative effect on productivity.[8] A study conducted in 15 developed countries found that individuals who report that they are stressed in their jobs are 25 percent more likely to quit and 25 percent more likely to miss days of work.[9] Canadian, French, and Swedish employees reported the highest stress levels. In Canada, 41 percent of employees noted that they "often" or "always" experience stress at work, while only 31 percent of employees in Denmark and Switzerland reported stress levels this high. "In the wake of years of fiscal downsizing, workers across all sectors are working harder and longer than ever while trying to balance family responsibilities," said Scott Morris, former head of the Vancouver-based consulting firm Priority Management Systems.[10] Daniel Ondrack, a professor at the Rotman

Stressed Quite a Lot, 2010 (Percent)

Canada	Male	Females
Newfoundland and Labrador	**22.0**	**24.9**
Prince Edward Island	16.6	14.6
Nova Scotia	12.4*	14.3
New Brunswick	17.0	21.1
Quebec	18.6	21.9
Ontario	24.0	29.5
Manitoba	22.2	25.1
Saskatchewan	17.7	23.3
Alberta	19.1	19.5
British Columbia	21.2	23.1
Yukon	23.0	22.6
Northwest Territories	15.7	20.4
Nunavut	14.9	19.0*
	18.7*	17.7*

*Use with caution.

Note: Population aged 15 and older who reported experiencing quite a lot or extreme stress most days of their lives.

Source: From "Perceived life stress, quite a lot, by sex, by province and territory," Statistics Canada's Summary Tables, http://www40.statcan.ca/l01/cst01/health107b-eng.htm, July 14, 2011

OB on the **EDGE**

School of Management at the University of Toronto, notes that "one of the major reasons for absenteeism is the logistical problems workers face in just getting to work, including transporting children to school and finding daycare. Single parents, especially female, have to juggle all the daycare and family responsibilities, and that makes it extremely difficult for people to keep up with work demands."[11]

What Is Stress?

Stress is a dynamic condition in which an individual is confronted with an opportunity, demand, or resource related to what the individual desires and for which the outcome is perceived to be both uncertain and important.[12] This is a complicated definition. Let's look at its components more closely.

Stress is not necessarily bad in and of itself. Although stress is typically discussed in a negative context, it also has a positive value.[13] Consider, for example, the superior performance that an athlete or stage performer gives in "clutch" situations. Such individuals often use stress positively to rise to the occasion and perform at or near their maximum. Similarly, many professionals see the pressures of heavy workloads and deadlines as positive challenges that enhance the quality of their work and the satisfaction they get from their job. In short, some stress can be good, and some can be bad.

Recently, researchers have argued that *challenge stressors*—or stressors associated with workload, pressure to complete tasks, and time urgency—operate quite differently from *hindrance stressors*—or stressors that keep you from reaching your goals (red tape, office politics, confusion over job responsibilities). Although research has just started to accumulate, early evidence suggests that chal-

The Most and Least Stressful Jobs

How do jobs rate in terms of stress? According to *Health* magazine, the top 10 most and least stressful jobs are as follows.[14]

Ten Most Stressful Jobs
1. Inner-city high school teacher
2. Police officer
3. Miner
4. Air traffic controller
5. Medical intern
6. Stockbroker
7. Journalist
8. Customer-service/complaint worker
9. Secretary
10. Waiter

Ten Least Stressful Jobs
1. Forester
2. Bookbinder
3. Telephone line worker
4. Toolmaker
5. Millwright
6. Repairperson
7. Civil engineer
8. Therapist
9. Natural scientist
10. Sales representative

lenge stressors produce less strain than hindrance stressors.[15] Role ambiguity, role conflict, role overload, job insecurity, environmental uncertainty, and situational constraints were all consistently negatively related to job performance.[16] Evidence also suggests that challenge stress improves job performance in a supportive work environment, whereas hindrance stress reduces job performance in all work environments.[17] It appears that employees who have a stronger affective commitment to their organization can transfer psychological stress into greater focus and higher sales performance, whereas employees with low levels of commitment perform worse under stress.[18]

More typically, stress is associated with *demands* and *resources*. Demands are responsibilities, pressures, obligations, and even uncertainties that individuals face in the workplace. Resources are things within an individual's control that can be used to resolve the demands. For example, when you take a test, you feel stress because you confront opportunities and performance pressures. To the

extent that you can apply resources to the demands on you—such as being prepared for the exam—you will feel less stress.

Under the demands-resources perspective, having resources to cope with stress is just as important in offsetting it as demands are in increasing it.[19]

Causes of Stress

The workplace provides a variety of stressors:[20]

- *Environmental factors.* Uncertainty is the biggest reason people have trouble coping with organizational changes.[21] Two types of environmental uncertainty are economic and technological. Changes in the business cycle create *economic uncertainties*. When the economy is contracting, for example, people become increasingly anxious about their job security. Because new innovations can make an employee's skills and experience obsolete in a very short time, computers, robotics, automation, and similar forms of *technological change* are a threat to many people and cause them stress.

106

- *Organizational factors.* There is no shortage of factors within an organization that can cause stress. Pressures to avoid errors or complete tasks in a limited time, work overload, a demanding and insensitive boss, and unpleasant co-workers are a few examples. We have categorized these factors around task, role, and interpersonal demands.[22]

  - *Task demands* relate to a person's job. They include the design of the individual's job (autonomy, task variety, degree of automation), working conditions, and the physical work layout. Assembly lines can put pressure on people when they perceive the line's speed to be excessive. Working in an overcrowded room or in a visible location where noise and interruptions are constant can increase anxiety and stress.[23] As customer service grows ever more important, emotional labour becomes a source of stress.[24] Do you think you could put on a happy face when you are having a bad day?

  - *Role demands* relate to pressures placed on a person as a function of the particular role he or she plays in the organization.

  - *Interpersonal demands* are pressures created by other employees. Lack of social support from colleagues and poor interpersonal relationships can cause stress, especially among employees with a high social need. A rapidly growing body of research has also shown that negative co-worker and supervisor behaviours, including fights, bullying, incivility, racial harassment, and sexual harassment, are especially strongly related to stress at work.[25]

- *Personal factors.* The typical individual works about 40 to 50 hours a week. But the experiences and problems that people encounter in the other 120-plus nonwork hours can spill over to the job. Our final category, then, encompasses factors in the employee's personal life: family issues, personal economic problems, and personality characteristics.

  - National surveys consistently show that people hold *family* and personal relationships dear. Marital difficulties, the breaking off of a relationship, caring for elderly parents, and discipline troubles with children create stress employees often cannot leave at the front door when they arrive at work.[26]

  - Regardless of income level—people who make $100 000 per year seem to have as much trouble handling their finances as those who earn $20 000—some people are poor money managers or have wants that exceed their earning capacity. The *economic* problems of overextended financial resources create stress and take attention away from work.

  - Studies in three diverse organizations found that participants who reported stress symptoms before beginning a job accounted for most of the variance in stress symptoms reported nine months later.[27] The researchers concluded that some people may have an inherent tendency to accentuate negative aspects of the world in general. If this is true, then stress symptoms expressed on the job may actually originate in the person's *personality*.

When we review stressors individually, it's easy to overlook that stress is an additive phenomenon—it builds up.[28] Each new and persistent stressor adds to an individual's stress level. A single stressor may seem relatively unimportant in and of itself, but if it is added to an already high level of stress, it can be "the straw that breaks the camel's back."

Consequences of Stress

Stress manifests itself in a number of ways, such as high blood pressure, ulcers, irritability, difficulty in making routine decisions, loss of appetite, accident proneness, and the like. These symptoms can be placed under three general categories: physiological, psychological, and behavioural symptoms.[30]

- *Physiological symptoms.* Most early research concerned with stress was directed at physiological symptoms because most researchers in this area were specialists in the

FACT**BOX**

- About 8% of full-time employees in Canada missed work in any given week for personal reasons in 2010.

- The average employee missed 8 days of work in 2000, compared with 9.1 days in 2010, which means that about 100 million work-days were lost in 2010 due to absenteeism.

- In 2008, 21.2% of males and 23.4% of females aged 15 or older reported that most days were "quite a bit or extremely stressful."

- 24% of employed Canadians did not take all of their vacation days in 2009, giving back an average of 2.03 days of unused vacation time.[29]

health and medical sciences. Their work led to the conclusion that stress could create changes in metabolism, increase heart and breathing rates, increase blood pressure, cause headaches, and induce heart attacks. Because symptoms are complex and difficult to measure objectively, researchers concluded there were few, if any, consistent relationships.[31] More recently, some evidence suggests stress may have harmful physiological effects. One study linked stressful job demands to increased susceptibility to upper respiratory illnesses and poor immune system functioning, especially for individuals with low self-efficacy.[32] Furthermore, stress hits workers at all ages, and it is not unusual for employees in their 20s, 30s, and 40s to suffer long-term disabilities, claiming illnesses that are either psychiatric (such as depression) or more difficult to diagnose (such as chronic fatigue syndrome or fibromyalgia, a musculoskeletal discomfort). The increase in disability claims may be the result of downsizing taking its toll on the psyches of those in the workforce.[33]

- *Psychological symptoms.* Job dissatisfaction is "the simplest and most obvious psychological effect" of stress.[34] But stress also shows itself in other psychological states—for instance, tension, anxiety, irritability, boredom, and procrastination.

The evidence indicates that when people are placed in jobs that make multiple and conflicting demands or in which there is a lack of clarity as to the person's duties, authority, and responsibilities, both stress and dissatisfaction increase.[35] Similarly, the less control people have over the pace

of their work, the greater the stress and dissatisfaction. Although more research is needed to clarify the relationship, jobs providing a low level of variety, significance, autonomy, feedback, and identity create stress and reduce satisfaction and involvement in the job.[36]

- *Behavioural symptoms.* Behaviourally related stress symptoms include changes in productivity, absence, and turnover, as well as changes in eating habits, increased smoking or consumption of alcohol, rapid speech, fidgeting, and sleep disorders. More recently, stress has been linked to aggression and violence in the workplace.

Why Do Individuals Differ in Their Experience of Stress?

Some people thrive on stressful situations, while others are overwhelmed by them. What differentiates people in terms of their ability to handle stress? What individual difference variables moderate the relationship between *potential* stressors and *experienced* stress? At least four variables—perception, job experience, social support, and personality—are relevant.

- *Perception.* Individuals react in response to their *perception* of reality rather than to reality itself. Perception, therefore, moderates the relationship between a potential stress condition and an employee's reaction to it. Layoffs may cause one person to fear losing his job, while another sees an opportunity to get a large severance allowance and start her own business.[37] So stress potential does not lie in objective conditions; instead it lies in an employee's interpretation of those conditions.

- *Job experience.* Experience on the job tends to be negatively related to work stress. Two explanations have been offered.[38] First is selective withdrawal. Voluntary turnover is more probable among people who experience more stress. Therefore, people who remain with the organization longer are those with more stress-resistant traits or those who are more resistant to the stress characteristics of their organization. Second, people eventually develop coping mechanisms to deal with stress. Because this takes time, senior members of the organization are more likely to be fully adapted and should experience less stress.

- *Social support.* Collegial relationships with co-workers or supervisors can buffer the impact of stress.[39] Social support helps ease the negative effects of even high-strain jobs. Outside the job, involvement with family, friends, and community can provide the support if it is missing at work.

- *Personality.* Personality affects not only the degree to which people experience stress but also how they cope with it. Perhaps the most widely studied personality trait in stress is *Type A personality*, discussed in Chapter 2. Type A—particularly that aspect that manifests itself in hostility and anger—is associated with increased levels of stress and risk for heart disease.[40] People who are quick to anger, maintain a persistently hostile outlook, and project a cynical mistrust of others are at increased risk of experiencing stress in situations. Stressed Type As recover from stressful situations slower than Type B personalities, which suggests Type A individuals tend to have higher rates of death associ-

ated with hypertension, coronary heart disease, and coronary artery disease.[41]

How Do We Manage Stress?

Below we discuss ways that individuals can manage stress, and what programs organizations use to help employees manage stress.

Individual Approaches

An employee can take personal responsibility for reducing his or her stress level. Individual strategies that have proven effective include time management techniques, physical exercise, relaxation techniques, and a close social support network.

- *Time management.* Many people manage their time poorly. The well-organized employee, like the well-organized student, can often accomplish twice as much as the person who is poorly organized. So understanding and using basic time management principles can help individuals cope better with tensions created by job demands.[42] A few of the more well-known time management principles are (1) making daily lists of activities to be accomplished; (2) prioritizing activities by importance and urgency; (3) scheduling activities according to the priorities set; and (4) knowing your daily productivity cycle and handling the most demanding parts of your job during the high part of your cycle, when you are most alert and productive.[43]

- *Physical activity.* Physicians have recommended noncompetitive physical exercise, such as aerobics, walking, jogging, swimming, and riding a bicycle, as a way to deal with excessive stress levels. These forms of physical exercise increase heart capacity, lower at-rest heart rate, provide a mental diversion from work pressures, and slow the physical and mental effects of aging.[44]

- *Relaxation techniques.* Individuals can teach themselves to reduce tension through relaxation techniques such as meditation, hypnosis, and biofeedback. The objective is to reach a state of deep relaxation, in which you feel somewhat detached from the immediate environment and from body sensations.[45] Deep relaxation for 15 or 20 minutes a day releases tension and provides a pronounced sense of peacefulness, as well as significant changes in heart rate, blood pressure, and other physiological factors.

- *Building social supports.* Having friends, family, or colleagues to talk to provides an outlet when stress levels become excessive. Expanding your social support network provides you with someone to listen to your problems and to offer a more objective perspective on the situation.

The inset *Tips for Reducing Stress* offers additional ideas for managing stress.

Organizational Approaches

Employees who work at Montreal-based Ericsson Canada, a global telecommunications supplier, have access to a comprehensive wellness program. They can engage in activities that address their intellectual, emotional, social, physical, and spiritual well-being. "The program has really evolved over the years," says Louise Leonhardt, manager of human resources. "We've found it helps people balance their life, just like the on-site daycare does."[47]

Employees who work at Toronto-based BCS Group, a publishing, advertising, and public relations agency, receive biweekly shiatsu massages, paid for by the company. The company spends about $700 a month for the massages, equivalent to the amount it used to spend providing coffee to the employees. "It's in my company's best interest to have my employees be healthy," says Caroline Tapp-McDougall, BCS Group publisher.[48]

Tips for Reducing Stress

- At least two or three times a week, spend time with supportive friends or family.
- Ask for support when you are under pressure. This is a sign of health, not weakness.
- If you have spiritual or religious beliefs, increase or maintain your involvement.
- Use a variety of methods to reduce stress. Consider exercise, nutrition, hobbies, positive thinking, and relaxation techniques such as meditation or yoga.[46]

Most firms that have introduced wellness programs have found significant benefits. Health Canada reports that businesses get back $3.39 for each corporate dollar they invest in wellness initiatives. For individuals with three to five risk factors (such as high cholesterol, being overweight, or smoking) the return was $2.04 for each dollar spent.[49] The savings come about because there is less turnover, greater productivity, and reduced medical claims.[50] While many Canadian businesses report having wellness initiatives, only 24 percent have "fully implemented wellness strategies" (which includes multi-year goals and an evaluation of results), according to a 2010 survey.[51]

So what can organizations do to reduce employee stress? In general, strategies to reduce stress include improved processes for choosing employees, placement of employees in appropriate jobs, realistic goal setting, designing jobs with employee needs and skills in mind, increased employee involvement, improved organizational communication, offering employee sabbaticals, and, as mentioned, establishment of corporate wellness programs.

Certain jobs are more stressful than others, but individuals also differ in their response to stress situations. We know, for example, that individuals with little experience or an external locus of control tend to be more prone to stress. Selection and placement decisions should take these facts into consideration. Although management should not restrict hiring to only experienced individuals with an internal locus of control, such individuals may adapt better to high-stress jobs and perform those jobs more effectively.

Individuals perform better when they have specific and challenging goals and receive feedback on how well they are progressing toward them.[53] Goals can reduce stress as well as provide motivation.[54] Specific goals that are perceived as attainable clarify performance expectations. Additionally, goal feedback reduces uncertainties as to actual job performance. The result is less employee frustration, role ambiguity, and stress.

Redesigning jobs to give employees more responsibility, more meaningful work, more autonomy, and increased feedback can reduce stress because these factors give the employee greater control over work

activities and lessen dependence on others. Of course, not all employees want jobs with increased responsibility. The right design for employees with a low need for growth might be less responsibility and increased specialization. If individuals prefer structure and routine, more structured jobs should also reduce uncertainties and stress levels.

Role stress is detrimental to a large extent because employees feel uncertain about goals, expectations, how they will be evaluated, and the like. By giving these employees a voice in the decisions that directly affect their job performance, management can increase employee control and reduce role stress. So managers should consider *increasing employee involvement* in decision making.[55]

Increasing formal organizational communication with employees reduces uncertainty by lessening role ambiguity and role conflict. Given the importance that perceptions play in moderating the stress-response relationship, management can also use effective communication as a means to shape employee perceptions. Remember that what employees categorize as demands, threats, or opportunities are merely interpretations, and those interpretations can be affected by the symbols and actions communicated by management.

Some employees need an occasional escape from the frenetic pace of their work. In recent years, companies such as Charles Schwab, DuPont, L.L.Bean, Nike, and 3Com have begun to provide extended voluntary leaves.[56] These *sabbaticals*—ranging in length from a few weeks to several months—allow employees to travel, relax, or pursue personal projects that consume time beyond normal vacation weeks. Proponents say that these sabbaticals can revive and rejuvenate workers who might be headed for burnout.

Toward Less Stressful Work

- Avoid high-stress jobs—such as stockbroker, customer service/complaint worker, police officer, waiter, medical intern, secretary, and air traffic controller—unless you are confident in your ability to handle stress.

- If you do experience stress at work, try to find a job that has plenty of control (so you can decide how to perform your work) and supportive co-workers.

- Lack of money is the top stressor reported by people under age 30, so pursue a career that pays you well but does not have a high degree of stress.[52]

Our final suggestion is to offer organizationally supported wellness programs. These typically provide workshops to help people quit smoking, control alcohol use, lose weight, eat better, and develop a regular exercise program; they focus on the employee's total physical and mental condition.[57] A study of 36 programs designed to reduce stress (including wellness programs) showed that interventions to help employees reframe stressful situations and use active coping strategies led to an appreciable reduction in stress levels.[58] Most wellness programs assume that employees need to take personal responsibility for their physical and mental health and that the organization is merely a means to that end. The inset *Toward Less Stressful Work* offers additional ideas.

RESEARCH EXERCISES

1. Look for data on stress levels in other countries. How do these data compare with the Canadian data presented above? Are the sources of stress the same in different countries? What might you conclude about how stress affects people in different cultures?

2. Find out what three Canadian organizations in three different industries have done to help employees manage stress. Are there common themes in these programs? Did you find any unusual programs? To what extent are these programs tailored to the needs of the employees in those industries?

YOUR PERSPECTIVE

1. Think of all the technical avenues enabling employees to be connected 24/7 to the workplace:

F A C E O F F

When organizations provide on-site daycare facilities, they are filling a needed role in parents' lives, and making it easier for parents to attend to their job demands rather than worry about child-care arrangements.

When employees expect organizations to provide child care, they are shifting their responsibilities to their employers, rather than keeping their family needs and concerns private. Moreover, it is unfair to offer child-care benefits when not all employees have children.

email, texting, company web pages. A generation ago, most employees could go home after a day at work and not be "on call." What are the positive benefits of this change? What are the downsides? As an employee facing the demand to "stay connected" to your workplace, how would you try to maintain a balance in your life?

2. How much responsibility should individuals take for managing their own stress? To what extent should organizations become involved in the personal lives of their employees when trying to help them manage stress? What are the pros and cons for whether employees or organizations take responsibility for managing stress?

WANT TO KNOW MORE?

If you are wondering how stressed you are, go to **www.heartandstroke.ca** and click on "Health Information," "Heart Disease," and then "Other Resources for Heart Disease" to take a stress test. The site also offers tips on reducing stress.

CHAPTER 4

Motivating Self and Others

Figure skater Patrick Chan is a two-time and reigning world champion in figure skating and has set three world records. How has motivation influenced his impressive performance?

PART 2
STRIVING FOR
PERFORMANCE

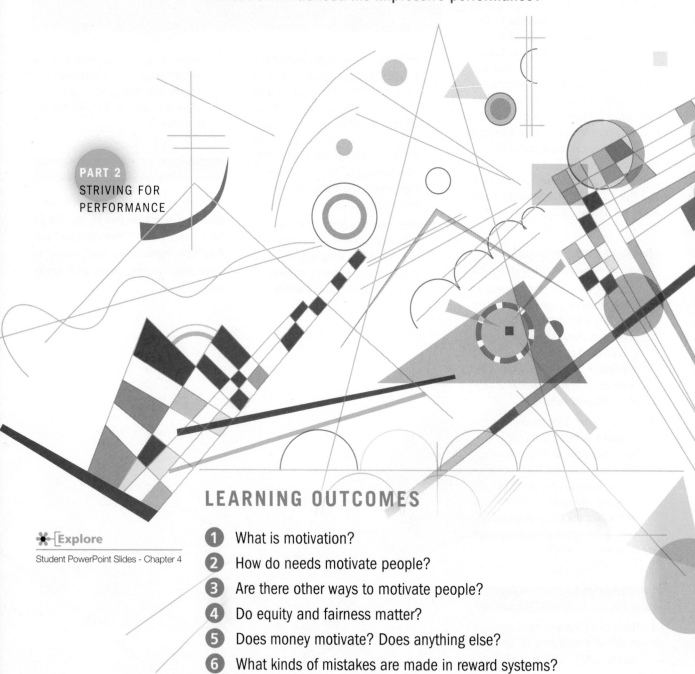

✳️-Explore

Student PowerPoint Slides - Chapter 4

LEARNING OUTCOMES

1. What is motivation?
2. How do needs motivate people?
3. Are there other ways to motivate people?
4. Do equity and fairness matter?
5. Does money motivate? Does anything else?
6. What kinds of mistakes are made in reward systems?

Patrick Chan, currently Canada's number one male figure skater, is motivated.[1] After placing a disappointing fifth in the Vancouver 2010 Winter Olympics, despite skating a personal best in the free skate program, he had to make a decision. Chan had to either introduce the very challenging quadruple jump (the hallmark of elite skaters such as Kurt Browning) into his routines or continue to hope that a quadruple was not necessary for champion skaters.

Chan took the loss in the Olympics with grace. "I think after overcoming the Olympics and not doing your best, that's the biggest challenge and that's the Mount Everest of athletes. I think now I can go to Worlds in March [2010] and say, you know, this is a walk in the park."

In preparing for the World Figure Skating Championships, Chan had to consider the impact of figure skating's judging system. At one time, the perfect score was 6.0, although it was not quite clear how that score was achieved. Under the new system introduced in 2004, every element—"from jumps to spins to the step sequences in between—[has] an assigned value." Judges then add or subtract points based on how well the skater executes each element.

Chan won a gold medal at the 2010 Grand Prix Finals in Beijing. Then at the 2011 Moscow Worlds, he not only won gold but also set three world records in doing so. At the end of 2011, Chan had won his second consecutive gold in the Grand Prix Finals held in Quebec City. In January 2012, he had won his fifth national title. By the spring of the same year, he won his second Worlds title in Nice, France. So what made Chan's loss at the 2010 Olympics motivational rather than make him want to quit skating completely?

In this chapter, we examine the subject of motivation and rewards. We look at what motivation is, key motivation theories, and how motivation theories and reward systems can be used effectively in the workplace.

THE BIG IDEA

Successfully motivating individuals requires identifying their needs and making it possible for them to achieve their needs.

OB IS FOR EVERYONE

- Are managers manipulating employees when they link rewards to productivity? Is this ethical?
- Why are some managers better than others at motivating people?
- How important is fairness to you?
- What can you do if you think your salary is unfair?
- When might job redesign be an appropriate motivational tool?
- Ever wonder why employees do some strange things?
- Are rewards overrated?

LEARNING ABOUT YOURSELF

- Motivation

What Is Motivation?

 1 What is motivation?

We define **motivation** as the process that accounts for an individual's intensity, direction, and persistence of effort toward reaching a goal.[2]

The three key elements in our definition are intensity, direction, and persistence. *Intensity* describes how hard a person tries. This is the element most of us focus on when we talk about motivation. However, high intensity is unlikely to lead to favourable job-performance outcomes unless the effort is channelled in a *direction* that is beneficial. Therefore, we consider the quality of effort as well as its intensity. Finally, the effort requires *persistence*. This measures how long a person can maintain effort. Motivated individuals stay with a task long enough to achieve their goal.

Many people incorrectly view motivation as a personal trait—that is, some have it and others do not. Along these lines, Douglas McGregor has proposed two distinct views of human beings. **Theory X**, which is basically negative, suggests that employees dislike work, will try to avoid it, and must be coerced, controlled, or threatened with punishment to achieve goals. **Theory Y**, which is basically positive, suggests that employees like work, are creative, seek responsibility, and will exercise self-direction and self-control if they are committed to the goals.[3]

Our knowledge of motivation tells us that neither of these theories fully accounts for employee behaviour. What we know is that motivation is the result of the interaction of the individual and the situation. Certainly, individuals differ in their basic motivational drives. But the same employee who is quickly bored when pulling the lever on a drill press may enthusiastically pull a slot machine lever in Casino Windsor for hours on end. You may read *The Hunger Games* at one sitting, yet find it difficult to concentrate on a textbook for more than 20 minutes. It's not necessarily you—it's the situation. So as we analyze the concept of motivation, keep in mind that the level of motivation varies both *among* individuals and *within* individuals at different times.

You should also realize that what motivates individuals will also vary among individuals and situations. Motivation theorists talk about **intrinsic motivators** and **extrinsic motivators**. Extrinsic motivators come from outside the person and include such things as pay, bonuses, and other tangible rewards. Intrinsic motivators come from a person's internal desire to do something, motivated by such things as interest, challenge, and personal satisfaction. Individuals are intrinsically motivated when they genuinely care about their work, look for better ways to do it, and are energized and fulfilled by doing it well.[4] The rewards the individual gets from intrinsic motivation come from the work itself, rather than from external factors such as increases in pay or compliments from the boss.

Are individuals primarily intrinsically or extrinsically motivated? Theory X suggests that people are almost exclusively driven by extrinsic motivators. However, Theory Y suggests that people are more intrinsically motivated. This view is consistent with that of Alfie Kohn, author of *Punished by Rewards*, who suggests that it's only necessary to provide the right environment, and people will be motivated.[5] We discuss his ideas further later in the chapter.

Intrinsic and extrinsic motivation may reflect the situation, however, rather than individual personalities. For example, suppose your mother has asked you to take her to a meeting an hour away and then drop off your twin brother somewhere else. You may be willing to drive her, without any thought of compensation, because it will make you feel nice to do something for her. That is intrinsic motivation. But if you have a love-hate relationship with your brother, you may insist that he buy you lunch for helping out. Lunch would then be an extrinsic motivator—something that came from outside yourself and motivated you to do the task. Later in the chapter, we review the evidence regarding the significance of extrinsic vs. intrinsic motivators, and also examine how to increase intrinsic motivation.

PERSONAL INVENTORY ASSESSMENT

Learn About Yourself
Work Motivation Indicator

motivation The intensity, direction, and persistence of effort a person shows in reaching a goal.

Theory X The assumption that employees dislike work, will attempt to avoid it, and must be coerced, controlled, or threatened with punishment to achieve goals.

Theory Y The assumption that employees like work, are creative, seek responsibility, and will exercise self-direction and self-control if they are committed to the goals.

intrinsic motivators A person's internal desire to do something due to such things as interest, challenge, and personal satisfaction.

extrinsic motivators Motivation that comes from outside the person and includes such things as pay, bonuses, and other tangible rewards.

Needs Theories of Motivation

Theories of motivation generally fall into two categories: needs theories and process theories. *Needs theories* describe the types of needs that must be met in order to motivate individuals. *Process theories* help us understand the actual ways in which we and others can be motivated. There are a variety of needs theories, including Maslow's hierarchy of needs, Alderfer's ERG theory,[6] Herzberg's motivation-hygiene theory (sometimes called the *two-factor theory*), and McClelland's theory of needs.[7] We briefly review these needs theories and their basic properties.

Needs theories are widely criticized for not standing up to scientific review. However, you should know them because (1) they represent a foundation from which contemporary theories have grown, and (2) practising managers still regularly use these theories and their terminology in explaining employee motivation.

2 How do needs motivate people?

Maslow's Hierarchy of Needs Theory

It is probably safe to say that the best-known theory of motivation is Abraham Maslow's **hierarchy of needs theory**.[8] Maslow hypothesized that within every human being there exists a hierarchy of five needs:

- *Physiological.* Includes hunger, thirst, shelter, sex, and other bodily needs.
- *Safety.* Includes security and protection from physical and emotional harm.
- *Social.* Includes affection, belongingness, acceptance, and friendship.
- *Esteem.* Includes internal esteem factors such as self-respect, autonomy, and achievement; and external esteem factors such as status, recognition, and attention.
- *Self-actualization.* Includes growth, achieving one's potential, and self-fulfillment. This is the drive to become what one is capable of becoming.

Although no need is ever fully met, a substantially satisfied need no longer motivates. Thus, as each of these needs becomes substantially satisfied, the next need becomes dominant. This is what Maslow means by moving up the steps of the hierarchy. So if you want to motivate someone, according to Maslow, you need to understand what level of the hierarchy that person is currently on and focus on satisfying the needs at or above that level. Exhibit 4-1 identifies Maslow's hierarchy of needs on the left, and then illustrates how these needs are applied in the workplace.[9]

Maslow separated the five needs into higher and lower orders. Physiological and safety needs were **lower-order needs**, and social, esteem, and **self-actualization** were **higher-order needs**. The differentiation between the two orders was made on the premise that higher-order needs are satisfied internally (within the person), whereas lower-order needs are mainly satisfied externally (by such things as pay, union contracts, and tenure).

Maslow's needs theory continues to receive wide recognition, particularly among practising managers. It is intuitively logical and easy to understand, even though there is little research supporting the theory. Maslow himself provided no empirical evidence, and there is little evidence that need structures are organized along the dimensions proposed by Maslow, that unsatisfied needs motivate, or that a satisfied need activates movement to a new need level.[10] One 2011 study differs in its findings, however. Using data from 123 countries, the study found that Maslow's needs are universally related to individual happiness, but that the order of need fulfillment had little bearing on life satisfaction and enjoyment. Lower-order needs were related to positive life evaluation, while higher-order needs were linked to enjoying life. The researchers concluded that the findings overall supported Maslow's theory.[11]

hierarchy of needs theory A hierarchy of five needs—physiological, safety, social, esteem, and self-actualization—in which, as each need is substantially satisfied, the next need becomes dominant.

lower-order needs Needs that are satisfied externally, such as physiological and safety needs.

self-actualization The drive to become what a person is capable of becoming.

higher-order needs Needs that are satisfied internally, such as social, esteem, and self-actualization needs.

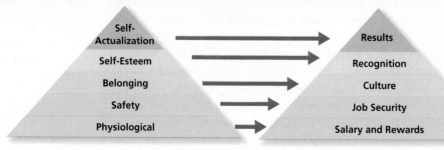

Source: *How Great Companies Get Their Mojo from Maslow* by Chip Conley and Tony Hsieh. Copyright © 2007, Jossey-Bass. Reprinted with permission of John Wiley & Sons, Inc.

ERG Theory

Clayton Alderfer has reworked Maslow's hierarchy of needs to align it more closely with the empirical research. His revised need hierarchy is called **ERG theory**.[12]

Alderfer argued that there are three groups of core needs—*existence* (similar to Maslow's physiological and safety needs), *relatedness* (similar to Maslow's social needs), and *growth* (similar to Maslow's esteem needs and self-actualization). Unlike Maslow, Alderfer did not assume that these needs existed in a rigid hierarchy. An individual could focus on all three need categories simultaneously. Despite these differences, empirical research has not been any more supportive of ERG theory than it has of Maslow's theory.[13]

Motivation-Hygiene Theory

Psychologist Frederick Herzberg proposed the **motivation-hygiene theory** (also called the *two-factor theory*).[14] Believing that an individual's relationship to work is basic and that attitude toward this work can very well determine success or failure, Herzberg investigated the question, "What do people want from their jobs?" He asked people to describe, in detail, situations in which they felt exceptionally good or bad about their jobs. He then tabulated and categorized the response. Exhibit 4-2 illustrates factors affecting job attitudes, as reported in 12 investigations conducted by Herzberg.

Herzberg concluded that the replies people gave when they felt good about their jobs significantly differed from when they felt bad. As shown in Exhibit 4-2, intrinsic factors, such as achievement, recognition, the work itself, responsibility, advancement, and growth, seem to be related to job satisfaction. Respondents who felt good about their work tended to attribute these characteristics to themselves. On the other hand, dissatisfied respondents tended to cite extrinsic factors, such as company policy and administration, supervision, interpersonal relations, and work conditions.

According to Herzberg, the data suggest that the opposite of satisfaction is not dissatisfaction, as was traditionally believed. Removing dissatisfying characteristics from a job does not necessarily make the job satisfying. As illustrated in Exhibit 4-3, Herzberg proposes that his findings indicate the existence of a dual continuum: the opposite of "Satisfaction" is "No Satisfaction," and the opposite of "Dissatisfaction" is "No Dissatisfaction."

Herzberg explained that the factors leading to job satisfaction (motivators) are separate and distinct from those that lead to job dissatisfaction (**hygiene factors**). Therefore, managers who seek to eliminate factors that create job dissatisfaction may bring about peace but not necessarily motivation. They will be placating rather than motivating their employees. As a result, Herzberg characterized conditions such as quality

ERG theory A revised need hierarchy theory that emphasizes the core needs of existence, relatedness, and growth.

motivation-hygiene theory A theory that relates intrinsic factors to job satisfaction and associates extrinsic factors with dissatisfaction. Also called the *two-factor theory*.

hygiene factors Factors—such as company policy and administration, supervision, and salary—that, when adequate in a job, placate employees. When these factors are adequate, people will not be dissatisfied.

EXHIBIT 4-2 Comparison of Satisfiers and Dissatisfiers

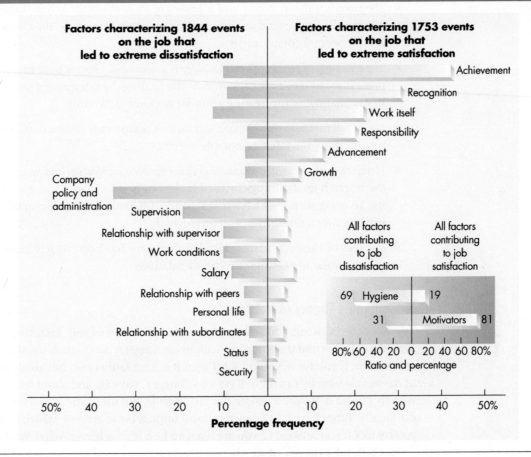

of supervision, pay, company policies, physical working conditions, relationships with others, and job security as hygiene factors. When they are adequate, people will not be dissatisfied; but neither will they be satisfied. If we want to motivate people in their jobs, Herzberg suggested emphasizing factors associated with the work itself or with outcomes directly derived from it, such as promotional opportunities, personal growth opportunities, recognition, responsibility, and achievement. These are the characteristics people find intrinsically rewarding.

✳ Explore

Exhibit 4-2: Comparison of Satisfiers and Dissatisfiers

EXHIBIT 4-3 Contrasting Views of Satisfaction and Dissatisfaction

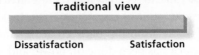

Traditional view

Dissatisfaction   Satisfaction

Herzberg's view

Hygiene Factors

Dissatisfaction   No Dissatisfaction

Motivators

No Satisfaction   Satisfaction

✳ Explore

Exhibit 4-3: Contrasting Views of Satisfaction and Dissatisfaction

The motivation-hygiene theory is not without its critics, who suggest the following:[15]

- *The procedure that Herzberg used is limited by its methodology.* When things are going well, people tend to take credit themselves. Contrarily, they blame failure on the external environment.

- *The reliability of Herzberg's methodology is questionable.* Raters have to make interpretations, so they may contaminate the findings by interpreting one response in one manner while treating a similar response differently.

- *No overall measure of satisfaction was used.* A person may dislike part of their job, yet still think the job is acceptable overall.

- *Herzberg assumed that a relationship exists between satisfaction and productivity.* But the research methodology he used looked only at satisfaction, not at productivity. To make such research relevant, one must assume that a strong relationship exists between satisfaction and productivity.[16]

Regardless of these criticisms, Herzberg's theory has been widely read, and few managers are unfamiliar with his recommendations.

McClelland's Theory of Needs

You have one beanbag, and five targets are set up in front of you. Each target is farther away than the last and thus more difficult to hit. Target A is a cinch. It sits almost within arm's reach. If you hit it, you get $2. Target B is a bit farther out, but about 80 percent of the people who try can hit it. It pays $4. Target C pays $8, and about half the people who try can hit it. Very few people can hit Target D, but the payoff is $16 for those who do. Finally, Target E pays $32, but it's almost impossible to achieve. Which target would you try for? If you selected C, you are likely to be a high achiever. Why? Read on.

McClelland's theory of needs was developed by David McClelland and his associates.[17] The theory focuses on three needs, defined as follows:

- **Need for achievement (nAch).** The drive to excel, to achieve in relation to a set of standards, to strive to succeed.

- **Need for power (nPow).** The need to make others behave in a way that they would not have behaved otherwise.

- **Need for affiliation (nAff).** The desire for friendly and close interpersonal relationships.

Of the three needs, McClelland and subsequent researchers focused most of their attention on nAch. High achievers perform best when they perceive their probability of success as 0.5—that is, a 50-50 chance of success.[18] They dislike gambling with high odds because they get no achievement satisfaction from success that comes by pure chance. Similarly, they dislike low odds (high probability of success) because then there is no challenge to their skills. They like to set goals that require stretching themselves a little.

Relying on an extensive amount of research, we can make some reasonably well-supported predictions of the relationship between achievement need and job performance. Although less research has been done on power and affiliation needs, findings are consistent there, too. First, when jobs have a high degree of personal responsibility, feedback, and an intermediate degree of risk, high achievers are strongly motivated. They are successful in entrepreneurial activities such as running their own businesses, for example, and managing self-contained units within large organizations.[19] Second, a high need to achieve does not necessarily make someone a good manager, especially in large organizations. People with a high achievement need are interested in how well they do personally and not in influencing others to do well. High-nAch salespeople do not necessarily make good sales managers, and the good general manager in a large

McClelland's theory of needs Achievement, power, and affiliation are three important needs that help explain motivation.

need for achievement (nAch) The drive to excel, to achieve in relation to a set of standards, to strive to succeed.

need for power (nPow) The need to make others behave in a way that they would not have behaved otherwise.

need for affiliation (nAff) The desire for friendly and close interpersonal relationships.

organization does not typically have a high need to achieve.[20] Third, needs for affiliation and power tend to be closely related to managerial success. The best managers are high in their need for power and low in their need for affiliation.[21] In fact, a high power motive may be a requirement for managerial effectiveness.[22]

McClelland's theory has had the best research support of the different needs theories. Unfortunately, it has less practical effect than the others. Because McClelland argued that the three needs are subconscious—meaning we may be high on them but not know it—measuring them is not easy. In the most common approach, a trained expert presents pictures to individuals, asks them to tell a story about each, and then scores their responses in terms of the three needs. However, the process is time consuming and expensive, and few organizations have been willing to invest time and resources in measuring McClelland's concept.

Anne Sweeney, co-chair of Disney Media Networks and president of Disney/ABC Television Group, is a high achiever. Sweeney's Disney/ABC Television Group was the first media company to feature television content on new platforms, such as the iPod and iPad. More recently, she was instrumental in Disney's becoming an equity partner in Hulu.com. Sweeney's unofficial motto is "create what's next."

Summarizing Needs Theories

The needs theories we've just reviewed all propose a similar idea: Individuals have needs that, when unsatisfied, will result in motivation. For instance, if you have a need to be praised, you may work harder at your task in order to receive recognition from your manager or other co-workers. Similarly, if you need money and you are asked to do something, within reason, that offers money as a reward, you will be motivated to complete that task.

Where needs theories differ is in the types of needs they consider, and whether they propose a hierarchy of needs (where some needs have to be satisfied before others) or simply a list of needs. Exhibit 4-4 illustrates the relationship of the four needs theories that we discussed, and Exhibit 4-5 indicates whether the theory proposes a hierarchy of needs, and the contribution of and empirical support for each theory.

What can we conclude from needs theories? We can safely say that individuals have needs and that they can be highly motivated to achieve those needs. The types of needs, and their importance, vary by individual, and probably vary over time for the same individual as well. When rewarding individuals, you should consider their specific needs. Some employees may be struggling to make ends meet, while others are looking for more opportunities to reach self-actualization. Individual needs also change over time, depending on one's stage in life. Obviously, in a workplace it would be difficult to design a reward structure that could completely take into account the specific needs of each employee. To better understand what might motivate you in the workplace, look at this chapter's *Learning About Yourself Exercise* on page 151.

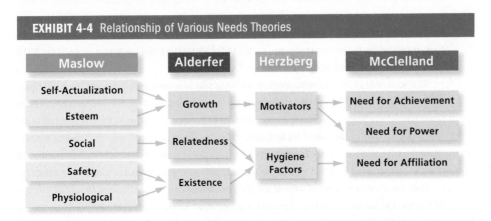

EXHIBIT 4-4 Relationship of Various Needs Theories

 Explore

Exhibit 4-4: Relationship of Various Needs Theories

EXHIBIT 4-5 Summarizing the Various Needs Theories

Theory	Maslow	Alderfer	Herzberg	McClelland
Is there a hierarchy of needs?	The theory argues that lower-order needs must be satisfied before one progresses to higher-order needs.	More than one need can be important at the same time. If a higher-order need is not being met, the desire to satisfy a lower-level need increases.	Hygiene factors must be met if a person is not to be dissatisfied. They will not lead to satisfaction, however. Motivators lead to satisfaction.	People vary in the types of needs they have. Their motivation and how well they perform in a work situation are related to whether they have a need for achievement, power, or affiliation.
What is the theory's impact/ contribution?	The theory enjoys wide recognition among practising managers. Most managers are familiar with it.	The theory is seen as a more valid version of the need hierarchy. It tells us that achievers will be motivated by jobs that offer personal responsibility, feedback, and moderate risks.	The popularity of giving employees greater responsibility for planning and controlling their work can be attributed to this theory (see, for instance, the job characteristics model in Chapter 5). It shows that more than one need may operate at the same time.	The theory tells us that high-need achievers do not necessarily make good managers, since high achievers are more interested in how they do personally.
What empirical support/ criticisms exist?	Research has not validated the hierarchical nature of needs. However, a 2011 study found that the needs are universally related to individual happiness.	It ignores situational variables.	It is not really a theory of motivation: It assumes a link between satisfaction and productivity that was not measured or demonstrated.	It has mixed empirical support, but the theory is consistent with our knowledge of individual differences among people. Good empirical support exists on needs achievement in particular.

Explore

Exhibit 4-5: Summarizing the Various Needs Theories

 Are there other ways to motivate people?

Process Theories of Motivation

After finishing fifth at the Vancouver 2010 Winter Olympics, Patrick Chan had to work on improving his performance.[23] A year later, Chan placed first at the 2011 World Figure Skating Championships in Moscow (which included a quadruple jump), winning his first World Title, and breaking records in doing so. His short program score broke the record previously held by former Olympic champion Evgeni Plushenko. His total score beat the former record of Japan's Daisuke Takahashi (who won the bronze medal in the 2010 Olympics) by more than 16 points.

What motivated Chan's dramatic improvement in the year between the Olympics and the World Figure Skating Championships? Chan acknowledges that the disappointing experience at the Olympics made him "push himself and improve in order to capture the world's top spot." But winning his first Worlds title did not make Chan feel at ease about his next competition. He knows he has to keep practising to improve. "It's funny but I didn't feel totally satisfied with my free [skate] in Moscow. I felt that I wasn't as connected to the Phantom [of the Opera] as I am to this new program which gives me goose bumps when I skate it."

Chan is motivated by a mix of intrinsic and extrinsic motivation. Like any talented athlete, he wants to be number one. But he also gets joy out of skating well. What makes someone like Patrick Chan show up at the skating rink, day after day, practising his routines?

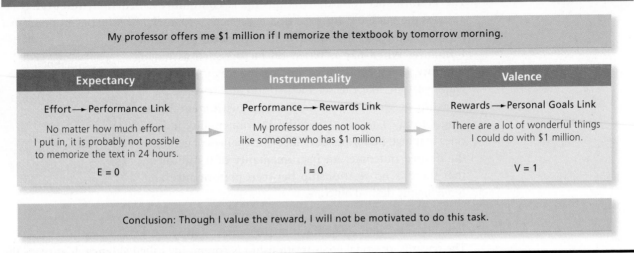

EXHIBIT 4-6 How Does Expectancy Theory Work?

My professor offers me $1 million if I memorize the textbook by tomorrow morning.

Expectancy	Instrumentality	Valence
Effort → Performance Link	Performance → Rewards Link	Rewards → Personal Goals Link
No matter how much effort I put in, it is probably not possible to memorize the text in 24 hours.	My professor does not look like someone who has $1 million.	There are a lot of wonderful things I could do with $1 million.
E = 0	I = 0	V = 1

Conclusion: Though I value the reward, I will not be motivated to do this task.

Process theories go beyond individual needs and focus on the broader picture of *how* one motivates one's self and others. Process theories include *expectancy theory, goal-setting theory* (and its application, management by objectives), and *self-efficacy theory*.

Explore

Exhibit 4-6: How Does Expectancy Theory Work?

Expectancy Theory

Currently, one of the most widely accepted explanations of motivation is Victor Vroom's **expectancy theory**.[24]

From a practical perspective, expectancy theory says that employees will be motivated to exert a high level of effort when they believe the following:

- That the effort will lead to good performance
- That good performance will lead to organizational rewards, such as a bonus, a salary increase, or a promotion
- That the rewards will satisfy employees' personal goals

The theory focuses on the three relationships (expectancy, instrumentality, and valence) illustrated in Exhibit 4-6 and described below. This exhibit also provides an example of how you might apply the theory.

Effort-Performance Relationship

The effort-performance relationship is commonly called **expectancy**. It answers the question: *If I give a maximum effort, will it be recognized in my performance appraisal?* For many employees, the answer is "no." Why? Their skill level may be deficient, which means that no matter how hard they try, they are not likely to be high performers. The organization's performance appraisal system may be designed to assess nonperformance factors such as loyalty, initiative, or courage, which means more effort will not necessarily result in a higher evaluation. Another possibility is that employees, rightly or wrongly, perceive the boss does not like them. As a result, they expect to get a poor appraisal, regardless of level of effort. These examples suggest one possible source of low motivation is employees' belief that, no matter how hard they work, the likelihood of getting a good performance appraisal is low. Expectancy can be expressed as a probability, and ranges from 0 to 1.

The *Point/Counterpoint* discussion on page 150 further examines whether praise motivates or demotivates.

expectancy theory The theory that individuals act on their evaluation of whether their effort will lead to good performance, whether good performance will be followed by a given outcome, and whether that outcome is attractive.

expectancy The belief that effort is related to performance.

Performance–Rewards Relationship

The performance–rewards relationship is commonly called **instrumentality**. It answers the question: *If I get a good performance appraisal, will it lead to organizational rewards?* Many organizations reward a lot of things besides performance. When pay is based on factors such as having seniority, being cooperative, or "kissing up" to the boss, employees are likely to see the performance-reward relationship as weak and demotivating. Instrumentality ranges from −1 to +1. A negative instrumentality indicates that high performance reduces the chances of getting the desired outcome. An instrumentality of 0 indicates that there is no relationship between performance and receiving the desired outcome.

> Are managers manipulating employees when they link rewards to productivity? Is this ethical?

Rewards–Personal Goals Relationship

The rewards–personal goals relationship is commonly called **valence**. It answers the question: *If I'm rewarded, are the rewards attractive to me?* The employee works hard in the hope of getting a promotion but gets a pay raise instead. Or the employee wants a more interesting and challenging job but receives only a few words of praise. Or the employee puts in extra effort to be relocated to the Paris office but instead is transferred to Singapore. It's important to tailor rewards to individual employee needs. Unfortunately, many managers are limited in the rewards they can distribute, which makes it difficult to personalize rewards. Moreover, some managers incorrectly assume that all employees want the same thing. They overlook the motivational effects of differentiating rewards. In either case, employee motivation may be lower because the specific need the employee has is not being met through the reward structure. Valence ranges from −1 (very undesirable reward) to +1 (very desirable reward).

> Why are some managers better than others at motivating people?

Golfers such as Hamilton, Ontario's Alena Sharp, who won the 25th Canadian Women's PGA Championship in September 2011, illustrate the effectiveness of the expectancy theory of motivation, where rewards are tied to effort and outcome. Players on the LPGA tour are paid strictly according to their performance, unlike members of professional sports teams. Sharp's first LPGA Tour victory came in 2004. As Sharp has put more effort into her play, she has been increasing her earnings. In 2010, she earned $163 000 compared with $97 000 in 2006.[25]

instrumentality The belief that performance is related to rewards.

valence The value or importance an individual places on a reward.

EXHIBIT 4-7 Steps to Increasing Motivation, Using Expectancy Theory

Improving Expectancy	Improving Instrumentality	Improving Valence
Improve the ability of the individual to perform.	Increase the individual's belief that performance will lead to reward.	Make sure that the reward is meaningful to the individual.
• Make sure employees have skills for the task. • Provide training. • Assign reasonable tasks and goals.	• Observe and recognize performance. • Deliver rewards as promised. • Indicate to employees how previous good performance led to greater rewards.	• Ask employees what rewards they value. • Give rewards that are valued.

Expectancy Theory in the Workplace

Does expectancy theory work? Although it has its critics,[26] most of the research evidence supports the theory.[27] Research in cross-cultural settings has also indicated support for expectancy theory.[28]

Exhibit 4-7 shows how managers can increase the motivation of employees, using insights from expectancy theory.

Goal-Setting Theory

You have heard the phrase a number of times: "Just do your best. That's all anyone can ask." But what does "do your best" mean? Do we ever know if we have achieved that vague goal? Might you have done better in your high school English class if your parents had said, "You should strive for 75 percent or higher on all your work in English" instead of "do your best"?

The research on **goal-setting theory** by Edwin Locke and his colleague, professor Gary Latham at the University of Toronto, shows that intentions to work toward a **goal** are a major source of work motivation.[29] Goals tell an employee what needs to be done and how much effort will need to be expended.[30]

Hasso Plattner, co-founder of the German software firm SAP, motivates employees by setting stretch goals. Plattner set a shockingly optimistic goal of 15 percent annual growth for SAP's software licence revenues. Employees responded by achieving an even higher growth rate of 18 percent. Plattner set another stretch goal by announcing a bonus plan that would pay $381 million to hundreds of managers and key employees if they could double the company's market capitalization, from a starting point of $57 billion, by the end of 2010. For Plattner, setting stretch goals is a way to inject entrepreneurial energy into the 40-year-old company.

Goal-setting theory has an impressive base of research support.[31] But as a manager, how do you put the theory into action? That is often left up to the individual manager or leader. Some managers explicitly set aggressive performance targets—what General Electric called "stretch goals." For example, some CEOs, such as Procter & Gamble's A. G. Laffey and SAP's Hasso Plattner, are known for the demanding performance goals they set. The problem with leaving it up to the individual manager is that, in many cases, managers do not set goals. A recent survey revealed that when asked whether their job had clearly defined goals, only a minority of employees agreed.[32]

A more systematic way to implement goal setting is through a **management by objectives (MBO)** program.[33] In MBO, managers and employees jointly set performance goals that are tangible, verifiable, and measurable; progress on goals is periodically reviewed, and rewards are allocated on the basis of this progress.

A relatively new way of using goal setting in the workplace is by creating a Results-Only Work Environment (ROWE). In this type of environment, employees focus only on achieving results and manage their time accordingly, as this *OB in the Workplace* describes.

goal-setting theory A theory that says that specific and difficult goals, with feedback, lead to higher performance.

goal What an individual is trying to accomplish.

management by objectives (MBO) An approach to goal setting in which specific measurable goals are jointly set by managers and employees; progress on goals is periodically reviewed, and rewards are allocated on the basis of this progress.

in the **WORKPLACE**
Results-Only Work Environments

Can a focus only on results change the federal government? Peter Hadwen, an Ottawa-based consultant, is trying to change the face of the federal government.[34] He thinks employees would be more productive if government departments were turned into Results-Only Work Environments (ROWEs). Employees would not be working to the clock, worrying about meetings, or being in the office at all. Employees could organize their time any way they wish, as long as they achieve the work results expected of them.

Though Hadwen has consulted for such government bureaucracies as Transport Canada, the Department of Fisheries and Oceans, and the Treasury Board Secretariat for a number of years, selling their managers on ROWE is not easy. "There's always a bit of skepticism regarding the ability to measure results," he says. "But with enough effort and discussion, we can get past that. Especially when dealing with organizations that are transaction focused, and which have a defined process and manner of doing things."

Best Buy, Netflix, and IBM have all turned to ROWE to make their workplaces happier and more efficient. The idea was created by two former employees of Best Buy, Cali Ressler and Jody Thompson, who wrote the book *Why Work Sucks and How to Fix It* to describe ROWE. The system makes employees more accountable, and leads to greater work-life balance. "People have a feeling that they are less beholden to a clock than they are to a work result on their own time. As such, it leads to less stress and a better morale," Hadwen says.

Though the federal government has been slow to implement ROWE, Waterloo, Ontario-based MKS, which produces life-cycle management software, has picked up on the idea of ROWE to evaluate its employees. Because the organization operates globally (97 percent of its revenue comes from outside Canada), everyone is encouraged to work when, where, and how they want to, including odd hours, as long as they get the job done. ●

ROWE is effective because it encourages intrinsic motivation. Employees working under ROWE have more autonomy, they work on things that really matter, and they feel that the work they do actually makes a difference.[35]

How Does Goal Setting Motivate?
According to Locke, goal setting motivates in four ways (see Exhibit 4-8):[36]

- *Goals direct attention.* Goals indicate where individuals should direct their efforts when they are choosing among things to do. For instance, recognizing that an important assignment is due in a few days, goal setting may encourage you to say no when friends invite you to a movie this evening.

- *Goals regulate effort.* Goals suggest how much effort an individual should put into a given task. For instance, if earning a high mark in accounting is more important to you than earning a high mark in organizational behaviour, you will likely put more effort into studying accounting.

- *Goals increase persistence.* Persistence represents the effort spent on a task over time. When people keep goals in mind, they will work hard on them, even in the face of obstacles.

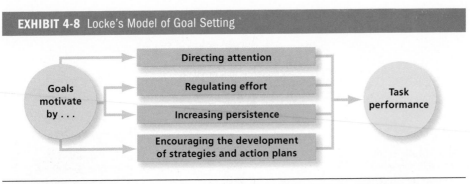

EXHIBIT 4-8 Locke's Model of Goal Setting

Source: Adapted from E. A. Locke and G. P. Latham, *A Theory of Goal Setting and Task Performance* (Englewood Cliffs, NJ: Prentice Hall, 1980). Reprinted by permission of Edwin A. Locke.

- *Goals encourage the development of strategies and action plans.* Once goals are set, individuals can develop plans for achieving those goals. For instance, a goal to become more fit may include plans to join a gym, work out with friends, and change eating habits.

In order for goals to be effective, they should be "SMART." SMART stands for

- **S**pecific: Individuals know exactly what is to be achieved.
- **M**easurable: The goals proposed can be tracked and reviewed.
- **A**ttainable: The goals, even if difficult, are reasonable and achievable.
- **R**esults-oriented: The goals should support the vision of the organization.
- **T**ime-bound: The goals are to be achieved within a stated time.

From Concepts to Skills on pages 156–157 gives further ideas on how to effectively engage in goal setting.

Although goal setting has positive outcomes, some goals may be *too* effective.[37] When learning something is important, goals related to performance may cause people to become too focused on outcomes and ignore changing conditions. In this case, a goal to learn and generate alternative solutions will be more effective than a goal to perform. Some authors have also argued that goals can lead employees to be too focused on a single standard to the exclusion of all others. Consider the narrow focus on short-term stock prices in many businesses—so much attention to this one standard for performance may have led organizations to ignore long-term success, and even to engage in such unethical behaviour as accounting fraud or excessively risky investments. Of course it is possible for organizations to establish goals for ethical performance. Despite differences of opinion, most researchers do agree that goals are powerful in shaping behaviour. Managers should make sure they are actually aligned with the company's objectives.

Goal-setting theory is consistent with expectancy theory. The goals can be considered the effort-performance link—in other words, the goals determine what must be done. Feedback can be considered the performance-rewards relationship, where the individual's efforts are recognized. Finally, the implication of goal setting is that the achievement of the goals will result in intrinsic satisfaction (and may of course be linked to external rewards).

Self-Efficacy Theory

Self-efficacy refers to an individual's belief that he or she is capable of performing a task.[38] The higher your self-efficacy, the more confidence you have in your ability to succeed in a task. So, in difficult situations, people with low self-efficacy are more

self-efficacy An individual's belief that he or she is capable of performing a task.

✱⌐Explore

Exhibit 4-9: Joint Effects of Goals and
Self-Efficacy on Performance

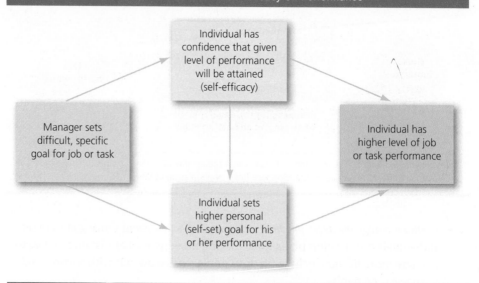

EXHIBIT 4-9 Joint Effects of Goals and Self-Efficacy on Performance

Source: Based on E. A. Locke and G. P. Latham, "Building a Practically Useful Theory of Goal Setting and Task Motivation: A 35-Year Odyssey," *American Psychologist,* September 2002, pp. 705–717.

likely to lessen their effort or give up altogether, while those with high self-efficacy will try harder to master the challenge.[39] In addition, individuals high in self-efficacy seem to respond to negative feedback with increased effort and motivation, while those low in self-efficacy are likely to lessen their effort when given negative feedback.[40] How can managers help their employees achieve high levels of self-efficacy? By bringing together goal-setting theory and self-efficacy theory (also known as *social cognitive theory* or *social learning theory*).

Goal-setting theory and self-efficacy theory don't compete with one another; rather, they complement each other. As Exhibit 4-9 shows, when a manager sets difficult goals for employees, this leads employees to have a higher level of self-efficacy, and also leads them to set higher goals for their own performance. Why? Research shows that setting difficult goals for people communicates your confidence in them. For example, imagine that your boss sets a higher goal for you. How would you interpret this? As long as you did not feel you were being picked on, you would probably think, "Well, I guess my boss thinks I'm capable of performing better than others." This sets in motion a psychological process in which you are more confident in yourself (higher self-efficacy) and you set higher personal goals, causing you to perform better both in the workplace and outside it.

Responses to the Reward System

4 Do equity and fairness matter?

After the new judging system for figure skating and ice dancing was put into place in 2004, Skate Canada immediately had analysts review how points would be allocated for figure skating, and Canadian skaters were instructed on how to make best use of the system.[41]

"We were fortunate with how well-educated our federation made us about the system," said Jeff Buttle, who won a silver medal for Canada at the 2005 World Figure Skating Championships in Moscow after finishing 15th under the old system in 2003. "We sat down right from the beginning of that first season and talked about what we needed to be focusing on to maximize our scores."

Still, the new system was not without controversy. While it allows gifted "total" skaters—like Jeff Buttle, Patrick Chan, and Joannie Rochette—to earn high scores on overall skating skills rather than focusing on jumps, the scoring is still somewhat subjective. This subjectivity causes frustration for the skaters. At the 2009 World Championships in Los Angeles, the Canadian team was surprised when Brian Joubert of

France beat Patrick Chan, who is well regarded for "footwork, transitions and overall skating skills." As Buttle pointed out, "Joubert may be a better jumper in the sense that he can do the quad, but people who don't even watch skating could easily see the difference in quality between Patrick and Brian." Outcomes like this can make the system seem unfair, with individuals giving the best performances not getting the highest marks. When individuals encounter unfairness in reward systems, how do they respond?

To a large extent, motivation theories are about rewards. The theories suggest that individuals have needs and will exert effort to have those needs met. The needs theories specifically identify those needs. Goal-setting and expectancy theories portray processes by which individuals act and then receive desirable rewards (intrinsic or extrinsic) for their behaviour.

Three additional process theories ask us to consider how individuals respond to rewards. *Equity theory* suggests that individuals evaluate and interpret rewards. *Fair process* goes one step further, suggesting that employees are sensitive to a variety of fairness issues in the workplace that extend beyond the reward system but also affect employee motivation. *Cognitive evaluation theory* examines how individuals respond to the introduction of extrinsic rewards for intrinsically satisfying activities.

Equity Theory

Equity theory suggests that employees compare their job inputs (that is, effort, experience, education, competence, creativity) and outcomes (that is, salary levels, raises, recognition, challenging assignments, working conditions) with those of others. We perceive what we get from a job situation (the outcomes mentioned above) in relation to what we put into it (the inputs mentioned above), and then we compare our outcome-input ratio with the outcome-input ratio of relevant others. (This idea is illustrated in Exhibit 4-10.) If we perceive our ratio to be equal to that of the relevant others with whom we compare ourselves, a state of equity is said to exist. We perceive our situation as fair and justice prevails. When we see ourselves as underrewarded, the tension creates anger; when we see ourselves as overrewarded, it

How important is fairness to you?

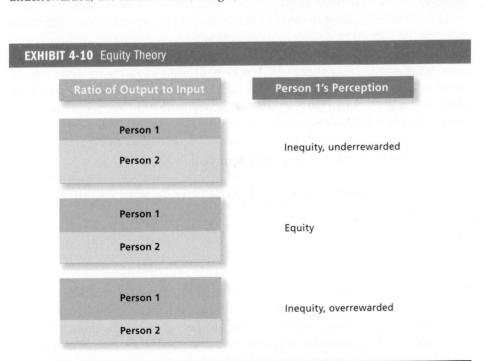

EXHIBIT 4-10 Equity Theory

Ratio of Output to Input	Person 1's Perception
Person 1 / Person 2	Inequity, underrewarded
Person 1 / Person 2	Equity
Person 1 / Person 2	Inequity, overrewarded

Explore
Exhibit 4-10: Equity Theory

equity theory Individuals compare their job inputs and outcomes with those of others and then respond so as to eliminate any inequities.

creates guilt. J. Stacy Adams has proposed that this negative state of tension provides the motivation to do something to correct it.[42]

Imagine that you wrote a case analysis for your marketing professor and spent 18 hours researching and writing it. Your classmate spent 6 hours doing her analysis. Each of you received a mark of 75 percent. It is likely that you would perceive this as unfair, as you worked considerably harder (i.e., exerted more effort) than your class-mate. Thus, according to equity theory, you might be inclined to spend considerably less time on your next assignment for your marketing professor.

What Happens When We Feel Treated Inequitably?

Based on equity theory, employees who perceive an inequity will make one of six choices.[43]

- *Change their inputs* (exert less effort if underpaid, or more if overpaid; for example, Patrick Chan decided to practise even harder to place first in subsequent competitions).

- *Change their outcomes* (individuals paid on a piece-rate basis can increase their pay by producing a higher quantity of units of lower quality).

- *Adjust perceptions of self* ("I used to think I worked at a moderate pace, but now I realize I work a lot harder than everyone else.")

- *Adjust perceptions of others* ("Mike's job isn't as desirable as I thought.")

- *Choose a different referent* ("I may not make as much as my brother-in-law, but I'm doing a lot better than my Dad did when he was my age.")

- *Leave the field* (quit the job).

What can you do if you think your salary is unfair?

RESEARCH FINDINGS: Inequitable Pay

Some of these propositions have been supported, but others have not.[44] First, inequities created by overpayment do not seem to have a significant impact on behaviour in most work situations. Apparently, people have a great deal more tolerance of overpayment inequities than of underpayment inequities, or are better able to rationalize them. It's pretty damaging to a theory when half the equation (how people respond to overreward) falls apart. Second, not all people are equity sensitive.[45] A small part of the working population actually prefers outcome-input ratios less than the referent comparisons. Predictions from equity theory are not likely to be very accurate with these "benevolent types." Note too that while most research on equity theory has focused on pay, employees seem to look for equity in the distribution of other organizational rewards. High-status job titles and large and lavishly furnished offices may function as outcomes for some employees in their equity equation.[46]

Fair Process and Treatment

distributive justice The perceived fairness of the amount and allocation of rewards among individuals.

organizational justice An overall perception of what is fair in the workplace, composed of distributive, procedural, and interactional justice.

Recent research has expanded the meaning of equity, or fairness.[47] Historically, equity theory focused on **distributive justice**, or the perceived fairness of the *amount* and *allocation* of rewards among individuals. But, increasingly, equity is thought of from the standpoint of **organizational justice**, or the overall larger perception of what is fair in the workplace. Employees perceive their organizations as just when they believe the outcomes they have received and the way they received them are fair.[48] One key element of organizational justice is an individual's *perception* of justice. In other words, fairness or equity can be subjective, residing in our perception. What one person sees as unfair, another may see as perfectly appropriate. In general, people have an egocentric, or self-serving, bias. They see allocations or procedure favouring themselves as fair.[49] In a recent poll, 61 percent of respondents said they are paying their fair share of taxes, but an almost equal number (54 percent) felt the system as a whole is unfair, saying some people skirt it.[50]

Beyond its focus on perceptions of fairness, the other key element of organizational justice is the view that justice is multidimensional. How much we get paid relative to what we think we should be paid (distributive justice) is obviously important. But, according to researchers, *how* we get paid is just as important. Thus, people also care about **procedural justice**—the perceived fairness of the *process* used to determine the distribution of rewards.[51] Two key elements of procedural justice are process control and explanations. *Process control* is the opportunity to present your point of view about desired outcomes to decision makers. *Explanations* are clear reasons management gives for the outcome. Thus, for employees to see a process as fair, they need to feel they have some control over the outcome and that they were given an adequate explanation about why the outcome occurred. It's also important that a manager is *consistent* (across people and over time), is *unbiased*, makes decisions based on *accurate information*, and is *open to appeals*.[52] Exhibit 4-11 shows a model of organizational justice.

A recent addition to research on organizational justice is **interactional justice**, an individual's perception of the degree to which she is treated with dignity, concern, and respect. When people are treated in an unjust manner (at least in their own eyes), they respond by retaliating (for example, badmouthing a supervisor).[53] Because people intimately connect interactional justice or injustice to the person who communicates the information (usually one's supervisor), we would expect perceptions of injustice to be more closely related to one's supervisor. Generally, that is what the evidence suggests.[54]

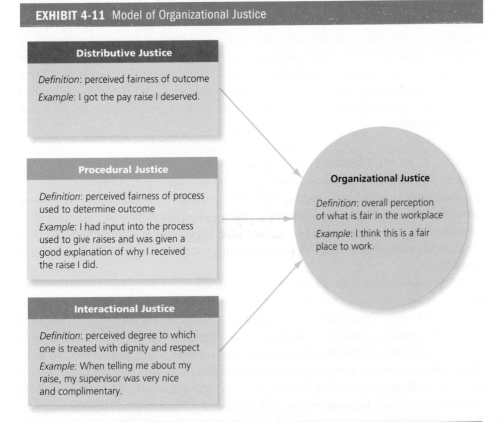

EXHIBIT 4-11 Model of Organizational Justice

Exhibit 4-11: Model of Organizational Justice

procedural justice The perceived fairness of the process used to determine the distribution of rewards.

interactional justice The perceived quality of the interpersonal treatment received from a manager.

Of these three forms of organizational justice, distributive justice is most strongly related to organizational commitment satisfaction with outcomes such as pay. Procedural justice relates most strongly to job satisfaction, employee trust, withdrawal from the organization, job performance, and organizational citizenship behaviour. There is less evidence on how interactional justice affects employee behaviour.[55]

Managers can help foster employees' perceptions of fairness. First, they should realize that employees are especially sensitive to unfairness in procedures when bad news has to be communicated (that is, when distributive justice is low). Thus, it's especially important to openly share information about how allocation decisions are made, follow consistent and unbiased procedures, and engage in similar practices to increase the perception of procedural justice. Second, when addressing perceived injustices, managers need to focus their actions on the source of the problem. Professor Daniel Skarlicki of the Sauder School of Business at the University of British Columbia has found that it is when unfavourable outcomes are combined with unfair procedures or poor interpersonal treatment that resentment and retaliation (for example, theft, badmouthing, and sabotage) are most likely.[56] *Case Incident—Bullying Bosses* on page 155 describes what could happen to the motivation and behaviour of employees who have bullies for bosses.

Learn About Yourself
Workplace Discipline Indicator

Self-Determination Theory

"It's strange," said Marcia. "I started work at the Humane Society as a volunteer. I put in fifteen hours a week helping people adopt pets. And I loved coming to work. Then, three months ago, they hired me full-time at eleven dollars an hour. I'm doing the same work I did before. But I'm not finding it near as much fun."

Does Marcia's reaction seem counterintuitive? There is an explanation for it. It's called **self-determination theory**, which proposes that people prefer to feel they have control over their actions, so anything that makes a previously enjoyed task feel more like an obligation than a freely chosen activity will undermine motivation.[57] Much research on self-determination theory in OB has focused on **cognitive evaluation theory**, which hypothesizes that extrinsic rewards will reduce intrinsic interest in a task. When people are paid for work, it feels less like something they *want* to do and more like something they *have* to do. Self-determination theory also proposes that in addition to being driven by a need for autonomy, people seek ways to achieve competence and positive connections to others. A large number of studies support self-determination theory.[58] As we will show, its major implications relate to work rewards.

Extrinsic vs. Intrinsic Rewards

Historically, motivation theorists have generally assumed that intrinsic motivators are independent of extrinsic motivators. That is, the stimulation of one would not affect the other. But cognitive evaluation theory suggests otherwise. It argues that when extrinsic rewards are used by organizations as payoffs for superior performance, the intrinsic rewards, which are derived from individuals doing what they like to do, are reduced.

When organizations use extrinsic rewards as payoffs for superior performance, employees feel less like they are doing a good job because of their own intrinsic desire to excel and more like they are doing a good job because that is what the organization wants. Eliminating extrinsic rewards can also shift from an external to an internal explanation of an individual's perception of why she works on a task. If you are reading a novel a week because your contemporary literature instructor requires you to, you can attribute your reading behaviour to an external source. If you stop reading novels the moment the course ends, this is more evidence that your behaviour was due to an external source. However, if you find yourself continuing to read a novel a

self-determination theory A theory of motivation that is concerned with the beneficial effects of intrinsic motivation and the harmful effects of extrinsic motivation.

cognitive evaluation theory Offering extrinsic rewards (for example, pay) for work effort that was previously rewarding intrinsically will tend to decrease the overall level of a person's motivation.

week when the course ends, your natural inclination is to say, "I must enjoy reading novels, because I'm still reading one a week!"

Recent studies examining how extrinsic rewards increased motivation for some creative tasks suggest we might need to place cognitive evaluation theory's predictions in a broader context.[59] Goal setting is more effective in improving motivation, for instance, when we provide rewards for achieving the goals. The original authors of self-determination theory acknowledge that extrinsic rewards such as verbal praise and feedback about competence can improve even intrinsic motivation under specific circumstances. Deadlines and specific work standards do, too, if people believe they are in control of their behaviour.[60] This is consistent with the central theme of self-determination theory: Rewards and deadlines diminish motivation if people see them as coercive.

What does self-determination theory suggest for providing rewards? Consider two situations. If a senior sales representative really enjoys selling and making the deal, a commission indicates she has been doing a good job at this valued task. The reward will increase her sense of competence by providing feedback that could improve intrinsic motivation. On the other hand, if a computer programmer values writing code because she likes to solve problems, a reward for working to an externally imposed standard she does not accept could feel coercive, and her intrinsic motivation would suffer. She would be less interested in the task and might reduce her effort.

Increasing Intrinsic Motivation

Our discussion of motivation theories and our discussion of how to apply motivation theories in the workplace focuses mainly on improving extrinsic motivation. Professor Kenneth Thomas of the Naval Postgraduate School in Monterey, California, has developed a model of intrinsic motivation that draws from the job characteristics model and cognitive evaluation theory.[61] He identifies four key rewards that increase an individual's intrinsic motivation:

- *Sense of choice.* The opportunity to select what one will do and perform the way one thinks best. Individuals can use their own judgment to carry out the task.

- *Sense of competence.* The feeling of accomplishment for doing a good job. People are more likely to feel a sense of accomplishment when they carry out challenging tasks.

- *Sense of meaningfulness.* The opportunity to pursue worthwhile tasks. Individuals feel good about what they are doing and believe that what they are doing matters.

- *Sense of progress.* The feeling of accomplishment that one is making progress on a task, and that it is moving forward. Individuals feel that they are spending their time wisely in doing their jobs.

Thomas also identified four sets of behaviours managers can use to create intrinsic rewards for their employees:

- *Leading for choice.* Empowering employees and delegating tasks

- *Leading for competence.* Supporting and coaching employees

- *Leading for meaningfulness.* Inspiring employees and modelling desired behaviours

- *Leading for progress.* Monitoring and rewarding employees

Exhibit 4-12 presents the building blocks that increase the likelihood that intrinsic rewards are motivational.

EXHIBIT 4-12 Building Blocks for Intrinsic Rewards

Leading for Choice	Leading for Competence
• Delegated authority • Trust in workers • Security (no punishment) for honest mistakes • A clear purpose • Information	• Knowledge • Positive feedback • Skill recognition • Challenge • High, noncomparative standards
Leading for Meaningfulness	**Leading for Progress**
• A noncynical climate • Clearly identified passions • An exciting vision • Relevant task purposes • Whole tasks	• A collaborative climate • Milestones • Celebrations • Access to customers • Measurement of improvement

Source: Reprinted with permission of the publisher. From *Intrinsic Motivation at Work: Building Energy and Commitment.* Copyright © K. Thomas. 1997. Berrett-Koehler Publishers Inc., San Francisco, CA. All rights reserved. www.bkconnection.com.

From Theory to Practice: Creating a Motivating Workplace

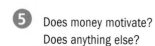 **5** Does money motivate? Does anything else?

Organizations use specific incentives to motivate individuals, teams, and the entire organization to achieve organizational goals such as productivity, reduced turnover, and leadership effectiveness. They can also redesign jobs to create more motivating workplaces. Before examining the different approaches used to motivate employees, we will consider the role of money in motivation.

The Role of Money

Despite the importance of money in attracting and retaining employees, and rewarding and recognizing them, little attention has been given to individual differences in people's feelings about money.[62] With respect to job satisfaction, one 2010 study found that pay level was only moderately correlated, and concluded that a person could be satisfied with his or her pay level, and still not have job satisfaction.[63] A 2011 study concluded that "money leads to autonomy but it does not add to well-being or happiness."[64] Supporting this idea, recent research suggests that money is not the sole motivator for Generation Y and Baby Boomer employees. Both generations find having "a great team, challenging assignments, a range of new experiences, and explicit performance evaluation and recognition" as important as money.[65] Exhibit 4-13 illustrates the key differences and similarities of what the two generations value in addition to money.

A number of studies suggest that there are personality traits and demographic factors that correlate with an individual's attitude toward money.[66] People who highly value money score higher on "attributes like sensation seeking, competitiveness, materialism, and control." People who desire money score higher on self-esteem, need for achievement, and Type A personality measures. Men seem to value money more than women, who value recognition for doing a good job more.[67]

What these findings suggest is that when organizations develop reward programs, they need to consider very carefully the importance to the individual of the specific

EXHIBIT 4-13 What Baby Boomers and Generation Y Value as Much as Compensation

Baby Boomers	Generation Y
High-quality colleagues	High-quality colleagues
An intellectually stimulating workplace	Flexible work arrangements
Autonomy regarding work tasks	Prospects for advancement
Flexible work arrangements	Recognition from one's company or boss
Access to new experiences and challenges	A steady rate of advancement and promotion
Giving back to the world through work	Access to new experiences and challenges
Recognition from one's company or boss	

Source: S. A. Hewlett, L. Sherbin, and K. Sumberg, "How Gen Y & Boomers Will Reshape Your Agenda," *Harvard Business Review*, July/August 2009, p. 76.

rewards offered. The *Ethical Dilemma Exercise* on page 154 gives you an intriguing look at the amount of money needed to motivate some Canadian CEOs.

Employee Recognition: Showing People That They Matter

A few years ago, 1500 employees were surveyed in a variety of work settings to find out what they considered to be the most powerful workplace motivator. Their response? Recognition, recognition, and more recognition![68]

Expectancy theory tells us that a key component of motivation is the link between performance and reward (that is, having your behaviour recognized). Employee recognition programs cover a wide spectrum of activities. They range from a spontaneous and private "thank you" on up to widely publicized formal programs in which specific types of behaviour are encouraged and the procedures for attaining recognition are clearly identified.[69] Some research suggests financial incentives may be more motivating in the short term, but in the long run it's nonfinancial incentives that are motivating.[70]

Toronto-based software developer RL Solutions developed a formal program for employees to recognize co-workers who go above and beyond in working with clients or in other aspects of their work. Those recognized by their co-workers receive cash and/or other rewards. Employees are also recognized with bonuses when they refer good job candidates to the company.[71] Brian Scudamore, CEO of Vancouver-based 1-800-GOT-JUNK? understands the importance of showing employees that they are appreciated. "I believe that the best way to engage someone is with heartfelt thanks. We have created a culture of peer recognition, and 'thank yous' have become contagious. Whether it's a card, kudos at the huddle or basic one-on-one thanks, gratitude goes a long way toward building team engagement, loyalty and, of course, happiness."[72] Scudamore says that actions like these keep the company growing, and employees having fun.

A recent survey of Canadian firms found that 34 percent of companies recognize individual or group achievements with cash or merchandise.[73] Other ways of recognizing performance include sending employees personal thank-you notes or emails for good performance, putting employees on prestigious committees, sending employees for training, and giving an employee an assistant for a day to help clear backlogs. Recognition and praise, however, need to be meaningful.[74]

Employee recognition may reduce turnover in organizations, particularly that of good employees. When executives were asked the reasons why employees left for jobs with other companies, 34 percent said it was due to lack of recognition and praise, compared with 29 percent who mentioned low compensation, 13 percent who mentioned limited authority, and 8 percent who cited personality problems.[75]

Variable-Pay Programs and Improving Productivity

Despite the fact that not everyone values money, a large body of research suggests that pay is far more motivational than some motivation theorists such as Maslow and Herzberg suggest.[76] Consistent with this research, managers generally look at ways to manipulate pay to improve performance by considering a variety of incentive schemes. Some of these are individually based, some are team-based, and some reward all members of the organization for working together toward productivity goals. The rewards used are all forms of **variable-pay programs**. What differentiates these forms of compensation from more traditional programs is that they do not pay a person only for time on the job or seniority. Instead, a portion of an employee's pay is based on some individual and/or organizational measure of performance. Earnings therefore fluctuate up and down with the measure of performance,[77] as Jason Easton, corporate communications manager at Toronto-based GM Canada, explains: "In any given year the variable pay can actually be zero, below the target or above the target, depending on how the company has performed."[78] GM Canada gave performance-based bonuses to its salaried employees in 2011, generating discontent among union employees who had no such provision in their collective agreement.[79]

Variable-pay programs have long been used to compensate salespeople and executives. Recently they have begun to be applied to other employees. An international survey by Hewitt Associates of large organizations in 46 countries found that more than 80 percent offered variable pay in 2010. In Canada, 9.6 percent of the payroll, on average, goes to variable pay.[80]

Variable-pay programs can be applied at individual, team, and company-wide levels, making it possible to link rewards to the appropriate level of performance. Below, we briefly describe some examples of incentives at these different levels of the organization.

Individual-Based Incentives

Piece-Rate Wages   The **piece-rate pay plan** has long been popular as a means for compensating production employees by paying a fixed sum for each unit of production completed. A pure piece-rate plan provides no base salary and pays the employee only for what he or she produces. People who work at baseball parks selling peanuts and soft drinks frequently are paid this way. At a rate of 25 cents for every bag of peanuts sold, they make $50 if they sell 200 bags during a game, and $10 if they sell only 40 bags. The Vancouver Canucks' four best players were well paid for the 2011–2012 season: The Sedin twins were paid $6.1 million, Roberto Luongo was paid $5.3 million, and Ryan Kesler earned $5 million, regardless of how many games they helped their team win.[81] Would it be better to pay each of them a fixed amount for each win? It seems unlikely they would accept such a deal, and it may cause unanticipated consequences as well (such as cheating). So, although incentives are motivating and relevant for some jobs, it is unrealistic to think they can constitute the only piece of some employees' pay.

Merit-Based Pay   **Merit-based pay plans** pay for individual performance based on performance appraisal ratings. Most large organizations have merit-based pay plans, especially for salaried employees. IBM Canada's merit pay plan, for example, provides increases to employees' base salary based on their annual performance evaluation. Since the 1990s, when the economy stumbled badly, an increasing number of Japanese companies have abandoned seniority-based pay in favour of merit-based pay. Koichi Yanashita of Takeda Chemical Industries commented, "The merit-based salary system is an important means to achieve goals set by the company's top management, not just a way to change wages."[82]

The thinking behind merit pay is that people who are high performers should be given bigger raises. For merit pay to be effective, however, individuals need to perceive

variable-pay programs Reward programs in which a portion of an employee's pay is based on some individual and/or organizational measure of performance.

piece-rate pay plan An individual-based incentive plan in which employees are paid a fixed sum for each unit of production completed.

merit-based pay plan An individual-based incentive plan based on performance appraisal ratings.

a strong relationship between their performance and the rewards they receive.[83] Unfortunately, the evidence suggests that this is not the case.[84]

Despite the intuitive appeal of paying for performance, merit-based pay plans have several limitations. One is that they are typically based on an annual performance appraisal and thus are only as valid as the performance ratings. Another limitation is that the pay raise pool fluctuates based on economic or other conditions that have little to do with an individual employee's performance. One year, a colleague at a top university who performed very well in teaching and research was given a pay raise of $300. Why? Because the budget for pay raises was very small. Yet that is hardly pay for performance. Unions typically resist merit-based pay plans and prefer seniority-based pay, where all employees get the same raises.

Finally, merit pay systems may result in gender and racial discrimination in pay. A 2010 study found that when organizations have merit-based cultures, managers tend to favour male employees over female employees, with men getting larger monetary rewards. The researchers conclude that there may be "unrecognized risks behind certain organizational efforts used to reward merit."[85]

Bonuses   An annual **bonus** is a significant component of total compensation for many jobs.[86] Bonuses reward employees for recent performance rather than historical performance and are one-time rewards rather than ongoing entitlements. They are used by such companies as Ontario Hydro Energy, the Bank of Montreal, and Molson Coors Brewing Company. The incentive effects of performance bonuses should be higher because, rather than paying for performance that may have occurred years ago (and was rolled into their base pay), bonuses reward only recent performance. Moreover, when times are bad, firms can cut bonuses to reduce compensation costs. Steel company Nucor, for example, guarantees its employees only about $10 per hour, but bonuses can be substantial. In 2006, the average Nucor employee made roughly $91 000. When the recession hit, bonuses were cut dramatically: In 2009, total pay had dropped 40 percent.[87]

Bonuses are not free from organizational politics (which we discuss in Chapter 7), and they can sometimes result in negative behaviour. When using bonuses, managers

Using employee performance software, convenience store retailer 7-Eleven measures the efforts of store managers and employees at 8800 North American stores. The company ties employee compensation to performance outcomes based on 7-Eleven's five fundamental strategic initiatives—product assortment, value, quality, service, and cleanliness—as well as meeting goals set for new products. Many other companies reward simply on sales, which does not capture the full range of value-added services that employees provide.

bonus An individual-based incentive plan that rewards employees for recent performance rather than historical performance.

should be mindful of potential unexpected behaviours that may arise when employees try to ensure that they will receive bonuses.

Group-Based Incentives

Gainsharing **Gainsharing** is a formula-based group incentive plan that uses improvements in group productivity from one period to another to determine the total amount of money to be shared.[88] The productivity savings can be divided between the company and employees in any number of ways, but 50-50 is fairly typical. Approximately 45 percent of *Fortune* 1000 firms have implemented gainsharing plans.[89]

Gainsharing differs from profit-sharing, discussed below, in that it ties rewards to productivity gains rather than profits. Employees in a gainsharing plan can receive incentive awards even when the organization is not profitable. Because the benefits accrue to groups of workers, high-performing workers pressure weaker performers to work harder, improving performance for the group as a whole.[90] Delta, BC-based Avcorp Industries, and governments, such as Ontario's Kingston Township and Town of Ajax, have introduced gainsharing. It has been found to improve productivity in a majority of cases and often has a positive impact on employee attitudes.[91]

Organizational-Based Incentives

There are two major forms of organizational-based pay-for-performance programs: profit-sharing and stock option plans, including employee stock ownership plans.

Profit-Sharing Plans A **profit-sharing plan** is an organization-wide plan in which the employer shares profits with employees based on a predetermined formula. The plan can distribute direct cash outlays or stock options. Though senior executives are most likely to be rewarded through profit-sharing plans, employees at any level can be recipients. Burlington, Ontario-based O.C. Tanner Canada pays all of its employees bonuses based on profits, twice a year.

Profit-sharing plans do not necessarily focus employees on the future, because employees and managers look for ways to cut costs today without considering longer-term organizational needs. They also tend to ignore factors such as customer service and employee development, which may not be seen as directly linked to profits. Employees can see inconsistent rewards in such a plan. Gregg Saretsky, WestJet's former CEO, worried about the flatness of the company's stock price compared with how it soared after the company's initial public offering in 1999. With 84 percent owning shares, most WestJet employees' compensation is affected by stock prices. However, pay is not the only motivator at WestJet. "You have to have fun and feel you can make a contribution and drive a difference. WestJetters have that in spades," says Saretsky.[92] Vancouver-based 1-800-GOT-JUNK? made no payment in 2007 when the company used its profits to invest in international expansion. Tania Hall, senior PR manager, acknowledged that the lack of a reward cheque could "test employee staying power. This is an opportunity to grow and be part of shaping the future, and you're either in or not."[93]

Three Canadian studies by Professor Richard J. Long of the University of Saskatchewan's College of Commerce show that a profit-sharing plan is most effective in workplaces where there is more involvement by employees, more teamwork, and a managerial philosophy that encourages participation.[94] Employees working under profit-sharing plans have a greater feeling of psychological ownership.[95]

Employee Stock Ownership Plans and Stock Options An **employee stock ownership plan (ESOP)**[96] is a company-established benefit plan in which employees acquire stock as part of their benefits. Stock options give employees the right to buy stocks in the company at a later date for a guaranteed price. In either case, the idea is that employees will be more likely to think about the consequences of their behaviour on the bottom line if they own part of the company.

gainsharing A group-based incentive plan in which improvements in group productivity determine the total amount of money to be shared.

profit-sharing plan An organization-wide plan in which the employer shares profits with employees based on a predetermined formula.

employee stock ownership plan (ESOP) A company-established benefit plan in which employees acquire stock as part of their benefits.

Canadian companies lag far behind the United States in the use of ESOPs because Canada's tax environment is less conducive to such plans. Nevertheless, Edmonton-based PCL Constructors has been owned by its employees since 1977, with 80 percent of employees owning shares. Ross Grieve, the company's president and CEO, says that ownership "elevates [the employees'] commitment to the organization."[97] Toronto-based I Love Rewards and Edmonton-based Cybertech are other examples of companies that have employee stock ownership programs.

RESEARCH FINDINGS: ESOPs

The research on ESOPs indicates that while they increase employee satisfaction,[98] their impact on performance is less clear. For instance, one study compared 45 companies with ESOPs against 238 companies without ESOPs.[99] Companies with ESOPs outperformed those without, both in terms of employment and sales growth. Other studies on companies with ESOPs have shown disappointing results.[100] More important, ESOPs can sometimes focus employees on trying to increase short-term stock prices while not worrying about the impact of their behaviour on the long-term effectiveness of the organization.

ESOPs have the potential to increase employee job satisfaction and work motivation. For this potential to be realized, employees need to psychologically experience ownership.[101] In addition to their financial stake in the company, they need to be kept regularly informed on the status of the business, and have the opportunity to exercise influence over it to achieve significant improvements in the organization's performance.[102]

ESOPs for top management can reduce unethical behaviour. CEOs are more likely to manipulate firm earnings reports to make themselves look good in the short run when they don't have an ownership share, even though this manipulation will eventually lead to lower stock prices. However, when CEOs own a large value of stock, they report earnings accurately because they don't want the negative consequences of declining stock prices.[103]

RESEARCH FINDINGS: Variable-Pay Programs

Do variable-pay programs increase motivation and productivity? The answer is a qualified "yes." Studies generally support the idea that organizations with profit-sharing plans have higher levels of profitability than those without them.[104] Similarly, gainsharing has been found to improve productivity in a majority of cases, and often has a positive impact on employee attitudes.[105] Another study found that although piece-rate pay-for-performance plans stimulated higher levels of productivity, this positive effect was not observed for risk-averse employees. Thus, American economist Ed Lazear generally seems right when he says, "Workers respond to prices just as economic theory predicts. Claims by sociologists and others that monetizing incentives may actually reduce output are unambiguously refuted by the data."[106] However, that does not mean everyone responds positively to variable-pay programs.[107]

Teamwork and unions present distinct challenges to pay-for-performance programs.

Teamwork   Incentive pay, especially when it is awarded to individuals, can have a negative effect on group cohesiveness and productivity, and in some cases may not offer significant benefits to a company.[108] For example, Montreal-based National

Bank of Canada offered a $5 employee bonus for every time employees referred clients for loans, mutual funds, or other bank products. But the bonus so upset employees that the plan was abandoned after just three months.[109] Tellers complained that the bonus caused colleagues to compete against one another. Meanwhile, the bank could not determine whether the referrals actually generated new business.

If an organization wants a group of individuals to function as a "team" (which we define in Chapter 5), emphasis needs to be placed on team-based rewards rather than individual rewards. We will discuss the nature of team-based rewards in Chapter 5.

Unions   Organized labour is, in general, cool to the idea of pay for performance. Andrew Jackson, director of the Social and Economic Policy Department at the Canadian Labour Congress, explains that "it hurts co-operation in the workplace. It can lead to competition between workers, speeding up the pace of work. It's a bad thing if it creates a stressful work environment where older workers can't keep up."[110] Pay for performance can also be problematic if work is speeded up to such unfair levels that employees can injure themselves. Still, not all unions oppose pay for performance, and the benefits and drawbacks of such incentive plans must be carefully considered before they are introduced.

Motivating Beyond Productivity

In recent years, organizations have been paying for performance on bases other than strict productivity. Compensation experts Patricia Zingheim and Jay Schuster note the following activities that merit additional compensation:[111]

- *Commissions beyond sales.* Commissions might be determined by customer satisfaction and/or sales team outcomes, such as meeting revenue or profit targets.

- *Leadership effectiveness.* Rewards can be determined by employee satisfaction or measures of how the manager handles his or her employees.

- *New goals.* Rewards go to all employees who contribute to specific organizational goals, such as customer satisfaction, cycle time, or quality measures.

- *Knowledge workers in teams.* Rewards are linked to the performance of knowledge workers and/or professional employees who work on teams.

- *Competency and/or skills.* Rewards are based on employees' abstract knowledge or competencies—for example, knowledge of technology, the international business context, customer service, or social skills.

Exhibit 4-14 compares the strengths and weaknesses of variable-pay programs, team-based rewards, and skill-based pay programs. **Skill-based pay** is based on how many skills an employee has or how many jobs he or she can do.

While rewarding individuals for something other than performance may make sense in some instances, not everyone agrees that these rewards are fair. *OB in the Street* questions whether athletic scholarships should be given for athletic skills only, with little concern for academic merit or financial need.

in the STREET
Scholarships for Jocks: Skills or Smarts?

Should university athletes be awarded money just for their athletic abilities? Jack Drover, athletic director at Mount Allison University in Sackville, New Brunswick, thinks not.[112] He objects to student-athlete awards that are often offered because of what coaches and teams need rather than what the individual student needs.

skill-based pay Pay based on how many skills an employee has or how many jobs he or she can do.

EXHIBIT 4-14 Comparing Various Pay Programs

Approach	Strengths	Weaknesses
Variable pay	• Motivates for performance. • Cost-effective. • Clearly links organizational goals and individual rewards.	• Individuals do not always have control over factors that affect productivity. • Earnings vary from year to year. • Can cause unhealthy competition among employees.
Team-based rewards	• Encourages individuals to work together effectively. • Promotes goal of team-based work.	• Difficult to evaluate team performance sometimes. • Equity problems could arise if all members paid equally.
Skill-based pay	• Increases the skill levels of employees. • Increases the flexibility of the workforce. • Can reduce the number of employees needed.	• Employers may end up paying for unneeded skills. • Employees may not be able to learn some skills, and thus feel demotivated.

Many university presidents react negatively to schools using financial rewards to recruit athletes. Some high school athletes can get full-tuition scholarships to university, even though they have not achieved high marks in school. While not every university finds this problematic, others feel awarding scholarships that do not recognize academic achievement or financial need is "an affront to the values of higher education."

Schools across the country interpret the rules for scholarships differently, which may affect the quality of school sports teams. Universities in Ontario (which rarely give athletic scholarships to first-year students) have had particular difficulty competing with schools across the country. For example, since 1995 only four football teams in Ontario have won the Vanier Cup: the Ottawa Gee Gees (2000) and the Wilfrid Laurier Golden Hawks (2005), the Queen's Golden Gaels (2009), and the McMaster Marauders (2011); the University of Ottawa is one of the few schools in the province that gives many athletic scholarships. In contrast, the Saint Mary's Huskies of Halifax, Nova Scotia, have been in the Vanier Cup final five times since 1999, winning twice. Rivals claim that a reason for the team's successes is its "plentiful" athletic scholarships.[113]

Some members of Canadian Interuniversity Sport (CIS) suggest that schools should be allowed to make their own decisions, including giving "full ride" scholarships, which would cover more than just tuition. With this model, CIS members would face a cap on how much money could be awarded for scholarships, and the money could be allocated across many athletes, or a few stars. However, CIS members could not decide on this approach to scholarships and "tuition only" scholarships remain in place. ●

Designing Motivating Jobs

Either as an alternative or a supplement to various reward programs, managers can consider redesigning jobs to make them more motivating. OB researchers Richard Hackman from Harvard University and Greg Oldham from the University of Illinois explored the nature of good jobs through their **job characteristics model (JCM)**.[114] The JCM identifies five core job dimensions and their relationship to personal and work outcomes. Building on Herzberg's motivation-hygiene theory, the JCM focuses on the *content* of jobs rather than the *context* of jobs and can be considered as a way of motivating employees and increasing job satisfaction.

When might job redesign be an appropriate motivational tool?

job characteristics model (JCM) A model that identifies five core job dimensions and their relationship to personal and work outcomes.

EXHIBIT 4-15	Examples of High and Low Job Characteristics
Skill Variety	
High variety	The owner-operator of a garage who does electrical repair, rebuilds engines, does body work, and interacts with customers
Low variety	A body shop worker who sprays paint eight hours a day
Task Identity	
High identity	A cabinet maker who designs a piece of furniture, selects the wood, builds the object, and finishes it to perfection
Low identity	A worker in a furniture factory who operates a lathe solely to make table legs
Task Significance	
High significance	Nursing the sick in a hospital intensive care unit
Low significance	Sweeping hospital floors
Autonomy	
High autonomy	A telephone installer who schedules his or her own work for the day, makes visits without supervision, and decides on the most effective techniques for a particular installation
Low autonomy	A telephone operator who must handle calls as they come according to a routine, highly specified procedure
Feedback	
High feedback	An electronics factory worker who assembles a radio and then tests it to determine if it operates properly
Low feedback	An electronics factory worker who assembles a radio and then routes it to a quality control inspector who tests it for proper operation and makes needed adjustments

Source: G. Johns, *Organizational Behavior: Understanding and Managing Life at Work,* 4th ed. Copyright © 1997. Adapted by permission of Pearson Education, Inc., Upper Saddle River, NJ.

job enrichment The vertical expansion of jobs, which increases the degree to which employees control the planning, execution, and evaluation of their work.

skill variety The degree to which the job requires a variety of different activities.

task identity The degree to which the job requires completion of a whole and identifiable piece of work.

task significance The degree to which the job has a substantial impact on the lives or work of other people.

autonomy The degree to which the job provides substantial freedom, independence, and discretion to the individual in scheduling the work and determining the procedures to be used in carrying it out.

feedback The degree to which individuals obtain direct and clear information about the effectiveness of their performance.

Job enrichment, an application of the JCM, refers to the vertical expansion of jobs. It increases the degree to which employees control the planning, execution, and evaluation of their work. An enriched job organizes tasks to allow the employee to do a complete activity, increases the employee's freedom and independence, increases responsibility, and provides feedback so individuals can assess and correct their own performance.[115]

Core Job Dimensions

According to the JCM, any job can be described in terms of five core job dimensions:

- **Skill variety**. The degree to which the job requires a variety of different activities so the employee can use a number of different skills and talents.

- **Task identity**. The degree to which the job requires completion of a whole and identifiable piece of work.

- **Task significance**. The degree to which the job has a substantial impact on the lives or work of other people.

- **Autonomy**. The degree to which the job provides substantial freedom, independence, and discretion to the individual in scheduling the work and determining the procedures to be used in carrying it out.

- **Feedback**. The degree to which carrying out the work activities required by the job results in the individual's obtaining direct and clear information about the effectiveness of his or her performance.

Jobs can be rated as high or low on these dimensions. Examples of jobs with high and low ratings appear in Exhibit 4-15.

EXHIBIT 4-16 The Job Characteristics Model

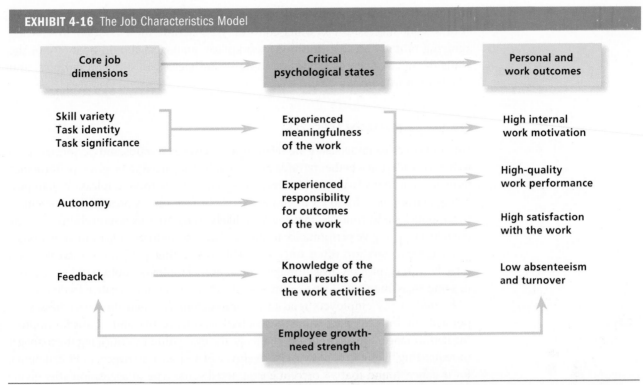

Source: J. RICHARD HACKMAN & GREG R. OLDHAM, WORK REDESIGN, 1st Edition, © 1980. Reprinted by permission of Pearson Education, Inc., Upper Saddle River, NJ.

Critical Psychological States

The JCM, presented in Exhibit 4-16, links the five core job dimensions to three critical psychological states:[116]

- *Experienced meaningfulness of the work.* The model predicts that if an employee's task is meaningful, the employee will view the job as important, valuable, and worthwhile. (Notice how in Exhibit 4-16 skill variety, task identity, and task significance combine to create meaningful work.)

- *Experienced responsibility for outcomes of the work.* Employees feel a sense of personal responsibility for results when their jobs give them greater autonomy.

- *Knowledge of the actual results of the work activities.* Feedback helps employees know whether they are performing effectively. The feedback can come from managers, clients, co-workers, or the nature of the task itself.

The model suggests that the more employees experience meaningfulness, responsibility, and knowledge of the actual results, the greater their motivation, performance, and satisfaction, and the lower their absenteeism and likelihood of leaving the organization.[117] As Exhibit 4-16 shows, the links between the core job dimensions and the outcomes are moderated or adjusted by the strength of the individual's growth need—in other words, the employee's desire for self-esteem and self-actualization. This means, for example, that not every employee will respond favourably to a job with skill variety, task identity, task significance, autonomy, or feedback. Those with high self-esteem and self-actualization needs will respond more favourably than others with different needs.

Caveat Emptor: Apply Motivation Theories Wisely

Applying motivation theories without giving performance feedback makes little sense. Second, when managers are not careful, they can send the wrong signals by how they use rewards. Third, rewards may not always be necessary. Finally, while

 What kinds of mistakes are made in reward systems?

motivation theories generally work well in Canada and the United States, they do not always work successfully in other cultures. We examine these issues below. When applying motivation theories in the workplace, managers should be aware of the kinds of signals rewards send, how rewards are viewed in different cultures, and whether rewards are essential.

Provide Performance Feedback

For employees to understand the relationship between rewards and performance, as well as considering whether rewards are equitable, they need to be given performance feedback. For many managers, however, few activities are more unpleasant than providing performance feedback to employees.[118] In fact, unless pressured by organizational policies and controls, managers are likely to ignore this responsibility.[119] Why the reluctance to give performance feedback? There seem to be at least three reasons.

First, managers are often uncomfortable discussing performance weaknesses directly with employees. Even though almost every employee could stand to improve in some areas, managers fear a confrontation when presenting negative feedback.

Second, many employees tend to become defensive when their weaknesses are pointed out. Instead of accepting the feedback as constructive and a basis for improving performance, some employees challenge the evaluation by criticizing the manager or redirecting blame to someone else. A survey of 151 area managers in Philadelphia, for instance, found that 98 percent encountered some type of aggression after giving employees negative appraisals.[120]

Finally, employees tend to have an inflated assessment of their own performance. Statistically speaking, half of all employees must be below-average performers. But the evidence indicates that the average employee's estimate of his or her own performance level generally falls around the 75th percentile.[121] So even when managers are providing good news, employees are likely to perceive it as not good enough.

The solution to the performance feedback problem is not to ignore it, but to train managers to conduct constructive feedback sessions. An effective review—one in which the employee perceives the appraisal as fair, the manager as sincere, and the climate as constructive—can result in the employee's leaving the interview in an upbeat mood, informed about the performance areas needing improvement, and determined to correct the deficiencies.[122] In addition, the performance review should be designed more as a counselling activity than a judgment process. This can best be accomplished by allowing the review to evolve out of the employee's own self-evaluation. For more tips on performance feedback, see *OB in Action—Giving More Effective Feedback.*

OB in ACTION
Giving More Effective Feedback

Managers can use the following tips to give more effective feedback:

→ Relate feedback to existing performance **goals** and clear **expectations**.
→ Give **specific** feedback tied to observable behaviour or measurable results.
→ Channel feedback toward **key result areas**.
→ Give feedback as **soon** as possible.
→ Give positive feedback for **improvement**, not just final results.
→ Focus feedback on **performance**, not personalities.
→ Base feedback on **accurate** and **credible** information.[123]

Beware the Signals That Rewards Send

Perhaps more often than we would like, organizations engage in what has been called "the folly of rewarding A, while hoping for B"[124]; in other words, hoping employees will engage in one type of behaviour, while managers reward for another type.

Expectancy theory suggests that individuals will generally perform in ways that raise the probability of receiving

Ever wonder why employees do some strange things?

the rewards offered. By focusing on test scores (easy to measure) rather than learning (harder to measure), administrators in the Atlanta, Georgia, school district encouraged teachers to change students' answers on tests, as *OB in the Workplace* shows.

OB in the WORKPLACE
Bonuses Lead to Cheating

How far will teachers go to comply with the law? The United States' No Child Left Behind Act expects school districts to adhere to strict standards regarding test scores and failure rates for children. Schools that do not comply with the standards receive less funding.

A number of teachers in the Atlanta public school district faced serious allegations in summer 2011, after investigators uncovered the "largest-ever cheating scandal" in the United States.[125] A total of 178 teachers were named in the investigators' report, and 82 confessed to test cheating.

For the previous several years, teachers were belittled or told that "Walmart was hiring" if their students' scores were low, and some were fired. For some, the pressure to perform became too much. At one school, teachers gathered together to change the answers on the tests before the tests were scanned and scored, apparently with the approval of administrators. Trying to explain this kind of behaviour, one teacher said, "It is not that the teachers are bad people and want to do it. It is that they are scared."

While teachers feared for their jobs, the schools were receiving thousands of dollars from the federal government because of improved test scores. The former superintendent of the Atlanta school district, Beverly Hall, received bonuses of tens of thousands of dollars because of the higher test scores in the district. In other words, the federal government, by linking bonuses to improved test scores, may have helped create the cheating scandal, particularly in an underfunded school district. ●

Exhibit 4-17 provides further examples of common management reward follies. Research suggests that there are three major obstacles to ending these follies:[126]

- *Individuals are unable to break out of old ways of thinking about reward and recognition practices.* Management often emphasizes quantifiable behaviours to the exclusion of nonquantifiable behaviours; management is sometimes reluctant to change the existing performance system; and employees sometimes have an entitlement mentality (that is, they do not want to change because they are comfortable with the current system for rewards).

- *Organizations often do not look at the big picture of their performance system.* Consequently, rewards are allocated at subunit levels, with the result that units often compete against each other.

- *Both management and shareholders often focus on short-term results.* They do not reward employees for longer-range planning.

Organizations would do well to ensure that they do not send the wrong message when offering rewards. When organizations outline an organizational objective of "team performance," for example, but reward each employee according to individual productivity, this does not send a message that teams are valued. When a retailer tells commissioned employees that they are responsible for monitoring and replacing stock as necessary, those employees will nevertheless concentrate on making sales.

EXHIBIT 4-17 Management Reward Follies

We hope for . . .	But we reward . . .
Teamwork and collaboration	The best team members
Innovative thinking and risk-taking	Proven methods and not making mistakes
Development of people skills	Technical achievements and accomplishments
Employee involvement and empowerment	Tight control over operations and resources
High achievement	Another year's effort
Long-term growth; environmental responsibility	Quarterly earnings
Commitment to total quality	Shipping on schedule, even with defects
Candour; surfacing bad news early	Reporting good news, whether it's true or not; agreeing with the manager, whether or not (s)he's right

Sources: Constructed from S. Kerr, "On the Folly of Rewarding A, While Hoping for B," *Academy of Management Executive* 9, no. 1 (1995), pp. 7–14; and "More on the Folly," *Academy of Management Executive* 9, no. 1 (1995), pp. 15–16. Copyright © Academy of Management, 1990.

Employees motivated by the promise of rewards will do those things that earn them the rewards they value.

Gordon Nixon, president and CEO of the Royal Bank of Canada, highlights changes RBC made to be sure it was rewarding the right things: "We constantly reinforce the values of the organization and ensure it is living up to those values by the way we respect people, the way we compensate and promote people, the way we recognize [them]. We changed our review process to ensure there is alignment with respect to values and culture—that there is alignment between our values and how people are recognized and rewarded."[127]

Can We Just Eliminate Rewards?

Alfie Kohn, in his book *Punished by Rewards,* argues that "the desire to do something, much less to do it well, simply cannot be imposed; in this sense, it is a mistake to talk about motivating other people. All we can do is set up certain conditions that will maximize the probability of their developing an interest in what they are doing and remove the conditions that function as constraints."[128]

Based on his research and consulting experience, Kohn proposes actions that organizations can take to create a motivating work environment.[129]

Are rewards overrated?

Abolish Incentive Pay   Paying people generously and fairly makes sure they do not feel exploited and takes pay off their minds. As a result, employees will be more able to focus on the goals of the organization rather than have their paycheque as their main goal.

Re-evaluate Evaluation   Instead of making performance appraisals look and feel like a punitive effort—who gets raises, who gets promoted, who is told he or she is performing poorly—structure the performance evaluation system more like a two-way conversation to trade ideas and questions. The discussion of performance should not be tied to compensation. "Providing feedback that employees can use to do a better job ought never to be confused or combined with controlling them by offering (or withholding) rewards."[130]

Create the Conditions for Authentic Motivation   A noted economist recently summarized the evidence about pay for productivity as follows: "Changing the way workers are *treated* may boost productivity more than changing the way they are *paid*."[131] There is some consensus about what the conditions for creating authentic motivation might be: helping employees rather than putting them under surveillance; listening to employee concerns and thinking about problems from their viewpoint; and providing plenty of feedback so they know what they have done right and what they need to improve.[132]

Encourage Collaboration   People are more likely to perform better in well-functioning groups where they can get feedback and learn from one another.[133] Therefore, it is important to provide the necessary supports to create well-functioning teams.

Enhance Content   People are generally the most motivated when their jobs give them an opportunity to learn new skills, provide variety in the tasks that are performed, and enable them to demonstrate competence. Some of this can be fostered by carefully matching people to their jobs, and by giving them the opportunity to try new jobs. It's also possible to increase the meaningfulness of many jobs.

But what about jobs that do not seem inherently interesting? One psychologist suggests that in cases where the jobs are fundamentally unappealing, the manager might acknowledge frankly that the task is not fun, give a meaningful rationale for why it must be done, and then give people as much choice as possible in how the task is completed.[134] One sociologist studying a group of garbage collectors in San Francisco discovered that they were quite satisfied with their work.[135] Their satisfaction came from the way the work and the company were organized: Relationships among the crew were important, the tasks and routes were varied to provided interest, and the company was set up as a cooperative, so that each employee owned a share of the company and thus felt "pride of ownership."

Provide Choice   "We are most likely to become enthusiastic about what we are doing— and all else being equal, to do it well—when we are free to make decisions about the way we carry out a task."[136] Extrinsic rewards (and punishments) actually remove choice, because they focus us on rewards, rather than on tasks or goals. Research suggests that burnout, dissatisfaction, absenteeism, stress, and coronary heart disease are related to situations where individuals did not have enough control over their work.[137] By *choice* we do not mean lack of management, but rather involving people in the decisions that are to be made. A number of case studies indicate that participative management, when it includes full participation by everyone, is successful.[138]

It would be difficult for many organizations to implement these ideas immediately and expect that they would work. Managers would need to relinquish control and take on the job of coach. Employees would need to believe that their participation and input mattered. Nevertheless, these actions, when implemented, can lead to quite a different workplace than what we often see. Moreover, Kohn suggests that sometimes it's not the type or amount of rewards that makes a difference as much as whether the work itself is intrinsically interesting.

Motivation Theories Are Culture-Bound

Reward strategies that have been used successfully in Canada and the United States do not always work successfully in other cultures. Take, for instance, a study comparing sales representatives at a large electronics company in the United States with one in

Japan. The study found that while Rolex watches, expensive dinners, and fancy vacations were valued rewards for star performers in the United States, taking the whole sales team bowling was more appreciated in Japan. The study's authors found that "being a member of a successful team with shared goals and values, rather than financial rewards, is what drives Japanese sales representatives to succeed."[139]

Why do our motivation theories perform less well when we look at their use in countries beyond Canada and the United States? Most current motivation theories were developed in the United States and so take US cultural norms for granted.[140] That may account for why Canada and the United States, which have more individualistic cultures, rely more heavily on extrinsic motivating factors than some other countries.[141] Japanese and German firms rarely make use of individual work incentives because their cultures are more collectivist.[142]

Many of the social-psychological theories of motivation rely heavily on the idea of motivating the individual through individual rewards. Thus they emphasize, particularly in an organizational context, the meaning of "pay" and give little attention to the informal rewards that come from group norms and prestige from peers.[143] Exhibit 4-18 presents a quick summary of the cultural differences in motivation observed by a number of studies.

Motivation theories also assume that needs are similar across societies. For instance, according to Maslow's hierarchy of needs, people start at the physiological level and then move progressively up the hierarchy in this order: physiological, safety, social, esteem, and self-actualization. This hierarchy, if it applies at all, aligns well with American culture and reasonably well with Canadian culture. However, in countries such as Austria, Denmark, and Germany, where uncertainty avoidance characteristics are strong, security needs would be at the top of the needs hierarchy. Countries that score high on humane orientation characteristics—Indonesia, Egypt, and Malaysia—would have social needs on top.[144] We would predict, for instance, that group work will motivate employees more when the country's culture scores high on the humane orientation criterion.

Equity theory has gained a relatively strong following in Canada and the United States. That is no surprise, since North American reward systems assume that employees are highly sensitive to equity in the granting of rewards and expect pay to be tied closely to performance. However, recent evidence suggests that in collectivistic cultures, especially in the former socialist countries of Central and Eastern Europe, employees expect rewards to reflect their individual needs as well as their performance.[145]

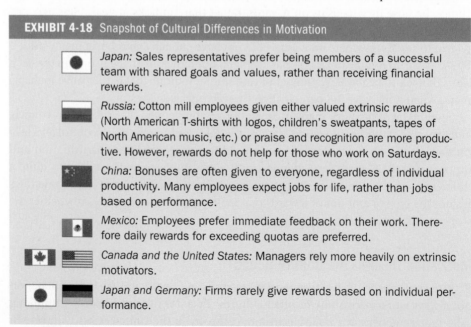

EXHIBIT 4-18 Snapshot of Cultural Differences in Motivation

Japan: Sales representatives prefer being members of a successful team with shared goals and values, rather than receiving financial rewards.

Russia: Cotton mill employees given either valued extrinsic rewards (North American T-shirts with logos, children's sweatpants, tapes of North American music, etc.) or praise and recognition are more productive. However, rewards do not help for those who work on Saturdays.

China: Bonuses are often given to everyone, regardless of individual productivity. Many employees expect jobs for life, rather than jobs based on performance.

Mexico: Employees prefer immediate feedback on their work. Therefore daily rewards for exceeding quotas are preferred.

Canada and the United States: Managers rely more heavily on extrinsic motivators.

Japan and Germany: Firms rarely give rewards based on individual performance.

Moreover, consistent with a legacy of Communism and centrally planned economies, employees show an entitlement attitude—they expect outcomes to be *greater* than their inputs.[146] These findings suggest that Canadian- and US-style pay practices may need modification, especially in Russia and former Communist countries, in order to be perceived as fair by employees.

These international findings indicate that it is important to consider the internal norms of a country when developing an incentive plan rather than simply import a plan that works well in Canada and the United States.

Putting It All Together

While it is always dangerous to synthesize a large number of complex ideas into a few simple guidelines, the following suggestions summarize the essence of what we know about motivating employees in organizations:

- *Recognize individual differences.* Employees have different needs and should not be treated alike. Managers should spend the time necessary to understand what is important to each employee and then align goals, level of involvement, and rewards with individual needs. This chapter's *Working with Others Exercise* on pages 152–153 gives you an opportunity to understand the different needs of a diverse workforce.

- *Use goals and feedback.* Employees should have hard, specific goals, as well as feedback on how well they are faring in pursuit of those goals.

- *Allow employees to participate in decisions that affect them.* Employees can contribute to a number of decisions that affect them: setting work goals, choosing their own benefits packages, solving productivity and quality problems, and the like. This can increase employee productivity, commitment to work goals, motivation, and job satisfaction.

- *When giving rewards, be sure that they are clearly related to the performance desired.* It is important that employees perceive a clear link between rewards and the type of performance expected. How closely rewards are *actually* correlated to performance criteria is less important than the *perception* of this relationship. If individuals perceive that there is little relation between the performance desired and the rewards they receive, the results will be low performance, a decrease in job satisfaction, and an increase in turnover and absenteeism.

- *Check the system for equity.* Employees should be able to perceive rewards as matching the inputs they bring to the job. At a simplistic level, this means that experience, skills, abilities, effort, and other obvious inputs should explain differences in performance and, hence, pay, job assignments, and other obvious rewards.

Summary and Implications

1 What is motivation? Motivation is the process that accounts for an individual's intensity, direction, and persistence of effort toward reaching a goal. *Intensity* is concerned with how hard a person tries. This is the element most of us focus on when we talk about motivation. However, high intensity is unlikely to lead to good job performance unless the effort is channelled in a useful *direction*. Finally, the effort requires *persistence*.

2 How do needs motivate people? All needs theories of motivation, including Maslow's hierarchy of needs, Alderfer's ERG theory, Herzberg's motivation-hygiene theory (sometimes called the *two-factor theory*), and McClelland's theory of needs, propose a similar idea: Individuals have needs that when unsatisfied

P I A
PERSONAL INVENTORY ASSESSMENT

Learn About Yourself
Diagnosing Poor Performance and Enhancing Motivation

LESSONS LEARNED

- Recognize individual differences.
- Goals and feedback help motivate individuals.
- Rewards signal what is important to the employer (or leader).

SNAPSHOT SUMMARY

1 What Is Motivation?

2 Needs Theories of Motivation
Maslow's Hierarchy of Needs Theory
ERG Theory
Motivation-Hygiene Theory
McClelland's Theory of Needs
Summarizing Needs Theories

will result in motivation. Needs theories suggest that motivation will be high to the degree that the rewards individuals receive for high performance satisfy their dominant needs.

3 Are there other ways to motivate people? Process theories focus on the broader picture of how someone can set about motivating another individual. Process theories include expectancy theory, goal-setting theory (and its application, management by objectives), and self-efficacy theory. Expectancy theory says that an employee will be motivated to exert a high level of effort when he or she believes (1) that the effort will lead to good performance; (2) that good performance will lead to organizational rewards, such as a bonus, a salary increase, or a promotion; and (3) that the rewards will satisfy his or her personal goals. Goal-setting theory suggests that intentions to work toward a goal are a major source of work motivation. That is, goals tell an employee what needs to be done and how much effort will need to be expended. Specific goals increase performance; difficult goals, when accepted, result in higher performance than do easy goals; and feedback leads to higher performance than does nonfeedback. Achieving goals can be affected by one's self-efficacy, which refers to an individual's belief that he or she is capable of performing a task. The higher one's self-efficacy, the more confidence a person has about succeeding in a task.

4 Do equity and fairness matter? Individuals look for fairness in the reward system. Rewards should be perceived by employees as related to the inputs they bring to the job. At a simplistic level, this means that experience, skills, abilities, effort, and other obvious inputs should explain differences in performance and, hence, pay, job assignments, and other obvious rewards.

5 Does money motivate? Does anything else? The most commonly used reward in organizations is money. Despite the importance of money in attracting and retaining employees, and rewarding and recognizing them, little attention has been given to individual differences in people's feelings about money. Some studies indicate that money is not employees' top priority. When organizations want to reward individuals for specific high performance, they often turn to employee recognition programs. Recognizing an employee's superior performance often costs little or no money. When organizations want to improve productivity, they often use variable-pay programs. With these programs, a portion of an employee's pay is based on some individual and/or organizational measure of performance. Managers can enrich jobs following the job characteristics model. The model tells us that jobs that offer skill variety, task identity, task significance, autonomy, and feedback tend to be more motivating for employees.

6 What kinds of mistakes are made in reward systems? Individuals are responsive to the signals sent out by organizations, and if they determine that some activities are not valued, they may not engage in them, even when the firm expects them to do so. Rewards should be linked to the type of performance expected. Rewards are also culture-bound. Individuals respond to rewards in general and specific rewards differently, depending upon what culture they come from. Finally, rewards are not always necessary. In the right context, individuals often motivate themselves intrinsically and can achieve quite high levels of performance doing so. We also know that giving rewards for things that were previously done for intrinsic motivation will decrease motivation.

OB at Work

for Review

1. Define motivation. What are its key elements?

2. What are the implications of Theories X and Y for motivation practices?

3. Identify the variables in expectancy theory.

4. Describe the four ways in which goal setting motivates.

5. Explain cognitive evaluation theory. How applicable is it to management practice?

6. What are the pluses and minuses of variable-pay programs from an employee's viewpoint? From management's viewpoint?

7. What is an ESOP? How might it positively influence employee motivation?

8. Define the five core dimensions in the JCM.

9. Describe three jobs that score high on the JCM. Describe three jobs that score low.

10. What can firms do to create more motivating environments for their employees?

for Critical Thinking

1. Identify three activities you really enjoy (for example, playing tennis, reading a novel, going shopping). Next, identify three activities you really dislike (for example, visiting the dentist, cleaning the house, following a low-fat diet). Using expectancy theory, analyze each of your answers to assess why some activities stimulate your effort while others do not.

2. Identify five different bases by which organizations can compensate employees. Based on your knowledge and experience, is performance the basis most used in practice? Discuss.

3. "Employee recognition may be motivational for the moment, but it doesn't have any staying power. Why? Because employees can't take recognition to Roots or The Bay!" Do you agree or disagree? Discuss.

4. "Performance can't be measured, so any effort to link pay with performance is a fantasy. Differences in performance are often caused by the system, which means the organization ends up rewarding the circumstances. It's the same thing as rewarding the weather forecaster for a pleasant day." Do you agree or disagree with this statement? Support your position.

5. This text argues for recognizing individual differences. It also suggests paying attention to the needs of members of diverse groups. Does this view contradict the principles of equity theory? Discuss.

for You

- To motivate yourself to finish a particularly long and dry chapter in a textbook, plan a snack break. Or buy yourself a new CD once that major accounting assignment is finished.

- The people you interact with appreciate recognition. Consider including a brief note on a nice card to show thanks for a job well done. Or you might send a bouquet of flowers. Sometimes just sending a pleasant, thankful email is enough to make a person feel valued. All of these things are easy enough to do and appreciated greatly by the recipient.

- Be aware of the kinds of things that motivate you, so you can choose jobs and activities that suit you better.

POINT

COUNTERPOINT

Praise Motivates!

Some of the most memorable, and meaningful, words we have ever heard have probably been words of praise.[147] Genuine compliments mean a lot to people—and can go a long way toward inspiring the best performance. Numerous research studies show that students who receive praise from their teachers are more motivated, and often this motivation lasts well after the praise is given. Too often we assume that simple words mean little, but most of us yearn for genuine praise from people in a position to evaluate us.

Companies are starting to learn this lesson. Walt Disney, Lands' End, and Hallmark have worked to use praise as a work reward to motivate employees. The Container Store estimates that 1 of its 4000 employees receives praise every 20 seconds. A recent research study of two retail stores suggested managers who praise their employees get higher performance out of them.

Praise is important even to long-term relationships. The Gottman Institute, a relationship research and training firm in Seattle, says its research suggests the happiest marriages are those in which couples make five times as many positive statements to and about each other as negative ones.

Finally, a recent neuropsychology study found that praise activated the same part of the human brain as material rewards, which points to another benefit to praise: It may be just as motivating as money and, best of all, it's free.

Praise Is Highly Overrated

Sure, in theory it's nice to receive compliments, but in practice praise has some real pitfalls. First, a lot of praise is not genuine, and false praise breeds narcissism. Researcher Jean Twenge says scores on narcissism have risen steadily since 1982, and lavishing praise may be the culprit. If told we are wonderful time after time, we start to believe it even when we are not.

Second, praise is paradoxical—if we tell everyone they are special, soon it means nothing to those who do achieve something terrific. In the animated film *The Incredibles,* a superhero's mom tells her son "Everyone's special!" His reply: "Which is another way of saying no one is."

Third, praise can be manipulative. A study of hairdressers found those who complimented their customers earned significantly higher tips. So praise often means the "praiser" wants something from the "praisee."

Fourth, some of the most motivating people are difficult to please. Think of Jack Welch, former CEO of GE, or A. G. Lafley, ex-CEO of Procter & Gamble. They are known for being difficult to please, which means most people will work harder to meet their expectations. When you dish out kudos for an employee who merely shows up, you have sent a message that simply showing up is enough.

Often what people really need is a gentle kick in the pants. As Steve Smolinsky of the Wharton School at the University of Pennsylvania says, "You have to tell students, 'It's not as good as you can do. . . . You can do better.'"

One management consultant says, "People want to know how they're doing. Don't sugarcoat it. Just give them the damn data."

What Motivates You?

Circle the number that most closely agrees with how you feel. Consider your answers in the context of your current job or a past work experience.

	Strongly Disagree			Strongly Agree	
1. I try very hard to improve on my past performance at work.	1	2	3	4	5
2. I enjoy competition and winning.	1	2	3	4	5
3. I often find myself talking to those around me about nonwork matters.	1	2	3	4	5
4. I enjoy a difficult challenge.	1	2	3	4	5
5. I enjoy being in charge.	1	2	3	4	5
6. I want to be liked by others.	1	2	3	4	5
7. I want to know how I am progressing as I complete tasks.	1	2	3	4	5
8. I confront people who do things I disagree with.	1	2	3	4	5
9. I tend to build close relationships with co-workers.	1	2	3	4	5
10. I enjoy setting and achieving realistic goals.	1	2	3	4	5
11. I enjoy influencing other people to get my way.	1	2	3	4	5
12. I enjoy belonging to groups and organizations.	1	2	3	4	5
13. I enjoy the satisfaction of completing a difficult task.	1	2	3	4	5
14. I often work to gain more control over the events around me.	1	2	3	4	5
15. I enjoy working with others more than working alone.	1	2	3	4	5

Scoring Key:

To determine your dominant needs—and what motivates you—place the number 1 through 5 that represents your score for each statement next to the number for that statement.

Achievement	Power	Affiliation
1. _____	2. _____	3. _____
4. _____	5. _____	6. _____
7. _____	8. _____	9. _____
10. _____	11. _____	12. _____
13. _____	14. _____	15. _____
Totals: _____	_____	_____

Add up the total of each column. The sum of the numbers in each column will be between 5 and 25 points. The column with the highest score tells you your dominant need.

Sources: Based on R. Steers and D. Braunstein, "A Behaviorally Based Measure of Manifest Needs in Work Settings," *Journal of Vocational Behavior,* October 1976, p. 254; and R. N. Lussier, *Human Relations in Organizations: A Skill Building Approach* (Homewood, IL: Richard D. Irwin, 1990), p. 120.

OB at work

PERSONAL INVENTORY ASSESSMENT

Work Motivation Indicator: Motivation levels can be situational depending on whether you consider your occupation a job, a career, or a calling. Use this scale to see how your current occupation ranks.

Workplace Discipline Indicator: Not all forms of discipline are effective. This instrument helps you identify areas in which you may struggle when disciplining subordinates.

Diagnosing Poor Performance and Enhancing Motivation: Correcting poor performance is a key management responsibility. This instrument helps you assess your abilities in this area.

BREAKOUT GROUP EXERCISES

Form small groups to discuss the following topics, as assigned by your instructor:

1. One of the members of your team continually arrives late for meetings and does not turn drafts of assignments in on time. Choose one of the available theories and indicate how the theory explains the member's current behaviour and how the theory could be used to motivate the group member to perform more responsibly.

2. You are unhappy with the performance of one of your instructors and would like to encourage the instructor to present livelier classes. Choose one of the available theories and indicate how the theory explains the instructor's current behaviour. How could you as a student use the theory to motivate the instructor to present livelier classes?

3. Harvard University recently changed its grading policy to recommend to instructors that the average course mark should be a B. This was the result of a study showing that more than 50 percent of students were receiving an A or A– for coursework. Harvard students are often referred to as "the best and the brightest," and they pay $36 000 (US) per academic year for their education, so they expect high grades. Discuss the impact of this change in policy on the motivation of Harvard students to study harder.

WORKING WITH OTHERS EXERCISE

Rewards for a Diverse Workforce

Purpose To learn about the different needs of a diverse workforce.[148]

Time Approximately 40 minutes.

Directions Divide the class into groups of approximately 6 students. Each group is assigned 1 of the following people and is to determine the best benefits package for that person.

- Lise is 28 years old. She is a divorced mother of 3 children, aged 3, 5, and 7. She is the department head. She earns $37 000 a year in her job and receives another $3600 a year in child support from her ex-husband.

- Ethel is a 72-year-old widow. She works 25 hours a week to supplement her $8000 annual pension. Including her hourly wage of $7.75, she earns $18 075 a year.

- John is a 34-year-old black male born in Trinidad who is now a Canadian resident. He is married and the father of two small children. John attends college at night and is within a year of earning his bachelor's degree. His salary is $24 000 a year. His wife is an attorney and earns approximately $54 000 a year.

- Sanjay is a 26-year-old physically impaired Indo-Canadian male. He is single and has a master's degree in education. Sanjay is paralyzed and confined to a wheelchair as a result of a car accident. He earns $29 000 a year.

- Wei Mei is a single 22-year-old immigrant. Born and raised in China, she came to Canada only three months ago. Wei Mei's English needs considerable improvement. She earns $18 000 a year.

- Mike is a 16-year-old white male in his 2nd year of high school. He works 15 hours a week after school and during vacations. He earns $7.75 an hour, or approximately $6045 a year.

WORKING WITH OTHERS EXERCISE (Continued)

Background

Our 6 participants work for a company that has recently installed a flexible benefits program. Instead of the traditional "one benefits package fits all," the company is allocating an additional 25 percent of each employee's annual pay to be used for discretionary benefits. Those benefits and their annual costs are listed on the next page.

Benefit Yearly Cost

Extended medical care (for services such as private hospital room, eyeglasses, and dental care that are not provided by the province's health insurance plan) for employee:

Plan A (No deductible and pays 90%)	$3000
Plan B ($200 deductible and pays 80%)	$2000
Plan C ($1000 deductible and pays 70%)	$ 500

Extended medical care for dependants (same deductibles and percentages as above):

Plan A	$2000
Plan B	$1500
Plan C	$ 500
Supplementary dental plan	$ 500

Life insurance:

Plan A ($25 000 coverage)	$ 500
Plan B ($50 000 coverage)	$1000
Plan C ($100 000 coverage)	$2000
Plan D ($250 000 coverage)	$3000
Mental health plan	$ 500
Prepaid legal assistance	$ 300
Vacation	2% of annual pay for each week, up to 6 weeks a year
Pension at retirement equal to approximately 50% of final annual earnings	$1500
Four-day workweek during the three summer months	4% of annual pay (available only to full-time employees)
Daycare services (after company contribution)	
for all of an employee's children, regardless of number	$2000
Company-provided transportation to and from work	$ 750
University tuition reimbursement	$1000
Language class tuition reimbursement	$ 500

The Task

1. Each group has 15 minutes to develop a flexible benefits package that consumes 25 percent (and no more!) of its character's pay.

2. After completing step 1, each group appoints a spokesperson who describes to the entire class the benefits package the group has arrived at for its character.

3. The entire class then discusses the results. How did the needs, concerns, and problems of each participant influence the group's decision? What do the results suggest for trying to motivate a diverse workforce?

ETHICAL **DILEMMA** EXERCISE

Are CEOs Paid Too Much?

Critics have described the astronomical pay packages given to Canadian and American CEOs as "rampant greed."[149] In 2010, the average total compensation (salary, bonus, share units, stock options, etc.) of Canada's 100 best-paid CEOs was $6 million, an increase of 13 percent over 2009.[150] This was more than 135 times what the average full-time Canadian employee earned in 2010 ($44 365.88).[151]

How do you explain such large pay packages for CEOs? Some say this represents a classic economic response to a situation in which the demand is great for high-quality top-executive talent, and the supply is low. Other arguments in favour of paying executives millions a year are the need to compensate people for the tremendous responsibilities and stress that go with such jobs; the motivating potential that seven- and eight-figure annual incomes provide to senior executives and those who might aspire to be; and the influence of senior executives on the company's bottom line.

Critics of executive pay practices in Canada and the United States argue that CEOs choose board members whom they can count on to support ever-increasing pay for top management. If board members fail to "play along," they risk losing their positions, their fees, and the prestige and power inherent in board membership.

In addition, it is not clear that executive compensation is tied to firm performance. For instance, KPMG found in one survey that for 40 percent of the respondents, there was no correlation between the size of the bonus and how poorly or well the company fared. Consider the data in Exhibit 4-19, which illustrates the disconnect that can sometimes happen between CEO compensation and firm performance. *National Post Business* writers calculate a "Bang for the Buck" formula that can be used to determine which CEOs were overpaid (or underpaid), based on their company's performance between 2010 and 2011.

Is high compensation of CEOs a problem? If so, does the blame for the problem lie with CEOs or with the shareholders and boards that knowingly allow the practice? Are Canadian and American CEOs greedy? Are these CEOs acting unethically? Should their pay reflect more closely some multiple of their employees' wages? What do you think?

EXHIBIT 4-19 2011 Compensation of Canada's "Most Overpaid" CEOs*

CEO	Was Paid (2-Yr Avg.)	Should Have Been Paid	Amount Overpaid
1. Peter Marrone Yamana Gold Inc. Toronto, Ontario	$10 950 000	$ 643 000	$10 307 000
2. J. Michael Pearson Valeant Pharmaceuticals Intl, Inc. Mississauga, Ontario	$ 8 726 000	$ 1 745 000	$ 6 981 000
3. Scott Saxberg Crescent Point Energy Corp. Calgary, Alberta	$ 9 042 000	$ 1 808 000	$ 7 234 000
4. Jochen Tilk Inmet Mining Corp. Toronto, Ontario	$ 3 617 000	$ 1 194 000	$ 2 423 000
5. Ian Delaney Sherritt International Corp. Toronto, Ontario	$ 3 835 000	$ 1 342 000	$ 2 493 000

National Post Business calculated a "Bang for the Buck" formula to derive the amount overpaid, taking into account CEO performance variables.

Source: Based on information in "CEO Scorecard," http://www.financialpost.com/executive/ceo/scorecard/index.html; and "Guide to Using the CEO Scorecard," *Financial Post Magazine*, November 1, 2011.

Bullying Bosses

"It got to where I was twitching, literally, on the way into work," states Carrie Clark, a 52-year-old retired teacher and administrator.[152] After enduring 10 months of repeated insults and mistreatment from her supervisor, she finally quit her job. "I had to take care of my health."

Although many individuals recall bullies from their elementary school days, some are realizing that bullies can exist in the workplace as well. And these bullies do not just pick on the weakest in the group; rather, any subordinate in their path may fall prey to their torment, according to Dr. Gary Namie, director of the Workplace Bullying and Trauma Institute. Dr. Namie further says workplace bullies are not limited to men—women are at least as likely to be bullies. However, gender discrepancies are found in victims of bullying, as women are more likely to be targets.

What motivates a boss to be a bully? Dr. Harvey Hornstein, a retired professor from Teachers College at Columbia University, suggests that supervisors may use bullying as a means to subdue a subordinate who poses a threat to the supervisor's status. In addition, supervisors may bully individuals to vent frustrations. Many times, however, the sheer desire to wield power may be the primary reason for bullying.

What is the impact of bullying on employee motivation and behaviour? Surprisingly, even though victims of workplace bullies may feel less motivated to go to work every day, it does not appear that they discontinue performing their required job duties. However, it does appear that victims of bullies are less motivated to perform extra-role or citizenship behaviours. Helping others, speaking positively about the organization, and going beyond the call of duty are behaviours that are reduced as a result of bullying. According to Dr. Bennett Tepper of the University of North Carolina, fear may be the reason that many employees continue to perform their job duties. And not all individuals reduce their citizenship behaviours. Some continue to engage in extra-role behaviours to make themselves look better than their colleagues.

What should you do if your boss is bullying you? Don't necessarily expect help from co-workers. As Emelise Aleandri, an actress and producer from New York who left her job after being bullied, stated, "Some people were afraid to do anything. But others didn't mind what was happening at all, because they wanted my job." Moreover, according to Dr. Michelle Duffy of the University of Kentucky, co-workers often blame victims of bullying in order to resolve their guilt. "They do this by wondering whether maybe the person deserved the treatment, that he or she has been annoying or lazy, they did something to earn it," states Dr. Duffy. One example of an employee who observed this phenomenon first-hand is Sherry Hamby, who was frequently verbally abused by her boss and then eventually fired. She stated, "This was a man who insulted me, who insulted my family, who would lay into me while everyone else in the office just sat there and let it happen. The people in my office eventually started blaming me."

What can a bullied employee do? Dr. Hornstein suggests that employees try to ignore the insults and respond only to the substance of the bully's gripe. "Stick with the substance, not the process, and often it won't escalate," he states. Of course, that is easier said than done.

Questions

1. What aspects of motivation might workplace bullying reduce? For example, are there likely to be effects on an employee's self-efficacy? If so, what might those effects be?

2. If you were a victim of workplace bullying, what steps would you take to try to reduce its occurrence? What strategies would be most effective? What strategies might be ineffective? What would you do if one of your colleagues were a victim of an abusive supervisor?

3. What factors do you believe contribute to workplace bullying? Are bullies a product of the situation, or do they have flawed personalities? What situations and what personality factors might contribute to the presence of bullies?

OB at work

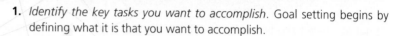

FROM CONCEPTS TO SKILLS

Setting Goals

You can be more effective at setting goals if you use the following eight suggestions.[153]

1. *Identify the key tasks you want to accomplish.* Goal setting begins by defining what it is that you want to accomplish.

2. *Establish specific and challenging goals for each key task.* Identify the level of performance you want to accomplish for each task. Specify the targets toward which you will work.

3. *Specify the deadlines for each goal.* Putting deadlines on each goal reduces ambiguity. Deadlines, however, should not be set arbitrarily. Rather, they need to be realistic, given the tasks to be completed.

4. *Allow the employee to participate actively.* When employees participate in goal setting, they are more likely to accept the goals. However, it must be sincere participation. That is, employees must perceive that you are truly seeking their input, not just going through the motions.

5. *Prioritize goals.* When you have more than one goal, it's important to rank the goals in order of importance. The purpose of prioritizing is to encourage you to take action and expend effort on each goal in proportion to its importance.

6. *Rate goals for difficulty and importance.* Goal setting should not encourage people to choose easy goals. Instead, goals should be rated for their difficulty and importance. When goals are rated, individuals can be given credit for trying to reach difficult goals, even if they don't fully achieve them.

7. *Build in feedback mechanisms to assess goal progress.* Feedback lets you know whether your level of effort is sufficient to attain the goal. Set deadlines for when you will evaluate how you are performing. You should review your progress frequently.

8. *Link rewards to goal attainment.* Sometimes we get discouraged when working toward our goals. Link rewards to the achievement of goals to help motivate you.

Practising Skills

Tammie Arnold worked her way through college while holding down a part-time job bagging groceries at the Food Town supermarket chain. She liked working in the food industry, and when she graduated she accepted a position with Food Town as a management trainee. Over the next three years, Arnold gained experience in the grocery store industry and in operating a large supermarket. About a year ago, Arnold received a promotion to store manager at one of the chain's locations. One of the things she has liked about Food Town is that it gives store managers a great deal of autonomy in running their stores. The company provides very general guidelines to its managers. Top management is concerned with the bottom line; for the most part, how the store manager gets there is up to him or her. Now that Arnold is finally a store manager, she wants to use goal setting to motivate her employees. She likes the idea that everyone should have clear goals to work toward and then be evaluated against those goals.

The store employs 70 people, although except for the managers, most work only 20 to 30 hours per week. There are 6 people reporting to Arnold: an assistant manager; a weekend manager; and grocery, produce, meat, and bakery managers. The only highly skilled jobs belong to the butchers, who have strict training and regulatory guidelines. Other less-skilled jobs include cashier, shelf stocker, maintenance employee, and grocery bagger.

Arnold has come to you for advice on how to design a goal-setting program for her store. Specifically describe how she should go about setting goals in her new position. Include examples of goals for the jobs of butcher, cashier, and bakery manager.

Reinforcing Skills

1. Set personal and academic goals you want to achieve by the end of this term. Prioritize and rate them for difficulty.

2. Where do you want to be in five years? Do you have specific five-year goals? Establish three goals you want to achieve in five years. Make sure these goals are specific, challenging, and measurable.

MyManagementLab   Study, practise, and explore real business situations with these helpful resources:

- **Study Plan:** Check your understanding of chapter concepts with self-study quizzes.
- **Online Lesson Presentations:** Study key chapter topics and work through interactive assessments to test your knowledge and master management concepts.
- **Videos:** Learn more about the management practices and strategies of real companies.
- **Simulations:** Practise management decision-making in simulated business environments.

P I A PERSONAL INVENTORY ASSESSMENT

CHAPTER 5

Working in Teams

How can a team come together and rehearse a new performance in just a few short months?

✳ Explore

Student PowerPoint Slides - Chapter 5

LEARNING OUTCOMES

1. What are teams and groups?
2. Do groups and teams go through stages while they work?
3. How do we create effective teams?
4. How do virtual teams work?
5. Are teams always the answer?

Quebec-based Cirque du Soleil is recognized worldwide for the many creative shows it has produced since its start in 1984.[1] The company has 5000 employees, with 2000 of them located at its headquarters in Montreal. Its employees represent "more than 50 nationalities and speak 25 different languages," which could present challenges in developing a spirit of teamwork.

Teamwork, however, is what Cirque du Soleil does best. According to Lyn Heward, the company's director of creation, "no matter what your product is . . . your results lie in having a passionate strong team of people. People are the driving force. I think because the Cirque's product is the sum total of people, it's a little more evident." Heward notes the importance of building trust so that everyone can work together interdependently. Guy Laliberté, the founder and majority owner of Cirque, emphasizes that the whole is much bigger than the sum of the parts, as each individual employee is "but a quarter note in a grand symphony."

Cirque assesses 60 to 70 new candidates a year, trying to find individuals who will add to the many talented employees on board. Candidates are evaluated on a number of dimensions, but team skills are important. Specifically, recruiters evaluate whether individuals can effectively work in teams to solve problems and whether they generously share ideas with others.

For teams to excel, a number of conditions need to be met. Effective teams need wise leadership, a variety of resources, and a way to solve problems. Team members need to be dedicated, and they need to build trust. In this chapter, we examine why teams have become so popular in the workplace, how groups and teams develop, how to create effective teams, how virtual teams work, and when a team is your best option to get work done.

THE BIG IDEA

Effective teams don't simply happen. They require attention to process, team composition, and rewards.

OB IS FOR EVERYONE

- Ever wonder what causes flurries of activity in groups?
- Should individuals be paid for their "teamwork" or their individual performance?
- Why do some teams seem to get along better than others?
- Why don't some team members pull their weight?

LEARNING ABOUT YOURSELF

- Building and Leading a Team

What are teams and groups?

Teams vs. Groups: What's the Difference?

There is some debate about whether groups and teams are really separate concepts, or whether the two terms can be used interchangeably. We think that there is a subtle difference between the terms. A **group** is two or more people with a common relationship. Thus a group could be co-workers or people meeting for lunch or standing at the bus stop. Unlike teams, groups don't necessarily engage in collective work that requires interdependent effort.

A **team** is "a small number of people with complementary skills who are committed to a common purpose, performance goals, and approach for which they hold themselves mutually accountable."[2] Groups become teams when they meet the following conditions:[3]

- Team members share *leadership*.
- Both individuals and the team as a whole share *accountability* for the work of the team.
- The team develops its own *purpose* or *mission*.
- The team works on *problem solving* continuously, rather than just at scheduled meeting times.
- The team's measure of *effectiveness* is the team's outcomes and goals, not individual outcomes and goals.

Thus while not all groups are teams, all teams can be considered groups. Much of what we discuss in this chapter applies equally well to both. We will offer some suggestions on creating effective teams later in the chapter. This chapter's *Point/Counterpoint* on page 184 discusses whether sports teams are good models for helping us understand how teams function in the workplace.

Why Have Teams Become So Popular?

How do we explain the current popularity of teams? As organizations have restructured themselves to compete more effectively and efficiently, they have turned to

At the Louis Vuitton factory in Ducey, France, all employees work in problem-solving teams, with each team focusing on one product at a time. Team members are encouraged to suggest improvements in manufacturing work methods and processes as well as product quality. When a team was asked to make a test run on a prototype of a new handbag, team members discovered that decorative studs were causing the bag's zipper to bunch up. The team alerted managers, who had technicians move the studs away from the zipper, which solved the problem.

group Two or more people with a common relationship.

team A small number of people who work closely together toward a common objective and are accountable to one another.

teams as a better way to use employee talents. Management has found that teams are more flexible and responsive to changing events than are traditional departments or other forms of permanent groupings. Teams have the capability to quickly assemble, deploy, refocus, and disband. Teams also can be more motivational. Recall from the job characteristics model in Chapter 4 that having greater task identity is one way of increasing motivation. Teams allow for greater task identity, with team members working on tasks together.

Do teams work? The evidence suggests that teams typically outperform individuals when the tasks being done require multiple skills, judgment, and experience.[4] However, teams are not necessarily appropriate in every situation. Are teams truly effective? What conditions affect their potential? How do team members work together? These are some of the questions we'll answer in this chapter.

Stages of Group and Team Development

 As Cirque du Soleil's creative team and cast prepared for the October 2011 opening of *Michael Jackson: The Immortal World Tour*, they faced a number of questions. Would the show capture the magic of Michael Jackson? What was the show's writer and director, Jamie King, going to be like? Who would fill some of the key roles in the show? What would it be like to produce a show unlike any other that Cirque had done in the past? Could the team all work well together? To build a successful team that produces a high-quality, creative performance, Cirque's cast members had to go through several stages. So what stages do teams go through as they develop?

2 Do groups and teams go through stages while they work?

While we make a distinction between groups and teams, the stages of development they go through are similar. In this section, we discuss two models of group development. The five-stage model describes the standardized sequence of stages groups pass through. The punctuated-equilibrium model describes the pattern of development specific to temporary groups with deadlines. These models can be applied equally to groups and teams.

The Five-Stage Model

From the mid-1960s, it was believed that groups passed through a standard sequence of five stages.[5] As shown in Exhibit 5-1, these five stages have been labelled *forming, storming, norming, performing,* and *adjourning*. Although we now know that not all groups pass through these stages in a linear fashion, the five-stage model of group development can still help in addressing any anxieties you might have about working in groups and teams. The model shows how individuals move from being independent to working interdependently with group members.

- *Stage I: Forming.* Think about the first time you met with a new team. Do you remember how some people seemed silent and others felt confused about the task you were to accomplish? Those feelings arise during the first stage of group development, known as **forming**. Forming is characterized by a great deal of uncertainty about the team's purpose, structure, and leadership. Members are "testing the waters" to determine what types of behaviour are acceptable. This stage is complete when members have begun to think of themselves as part of a team.

- *Stage II: Storming.* Do you remember how some people in your team just did not seem to get along, and sometimes power struggles even emerged? These reactions are typical of the **storming** stage, which is one of intragroup conflict. Members accept the existence of the team, but resist the constraints that the team imposes on individuality. Furthermore, there is conflict over who will control the team. When this stage is complete, a relatively clear hierarchy of leadership will emerge within the team.

forming The first stage in group development, characterized by much uncertainty.

storming The second stage in group development, characterized by intragroup conflict.

EXHIBIT 5-1 Stages of Group Development and Accompanying Issues

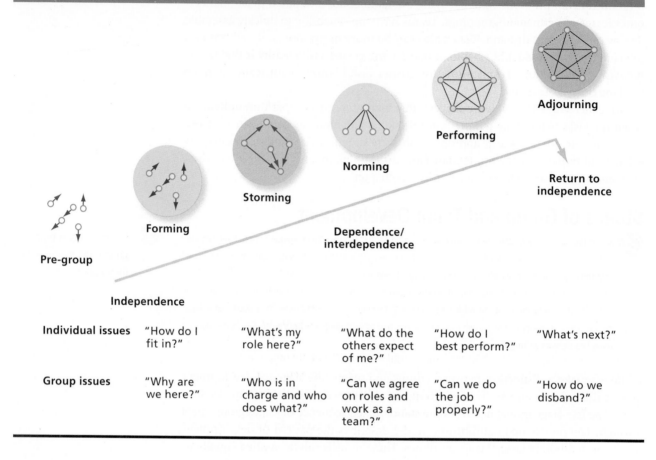

	Forming	Storming	Norming	Performing	Adjourning
Individual issues	"How do I fit in?"	"What's my role here?"	"What do the others expect of me?"	"How do I best perform?"	"What's next?"
Group issues	"Why are we here?"	"Who is in charge and who does what?"	"Can we agree on roles and work as a team?"	"Can we do the job properly?"	"How do we disband?"

Explore

Exhibit 5-1: Stages of Group Development and Accompanying Issues

norms Acceptable standards of behaviour within a group that are shared by its members.

norming The third stage in group development, characterized by close relationships and cohesiveness.

performing The fourth stage in group development, when the group is fully functional.

Some teams never really emerge from the storming stage, or they move back and forth through storming and the other stages. A team that remains forever planted in the storming stage may have less ability to complete the task because of all the interpersonal problems.

- *Stage III: Norming.* Many teams resolve the interpersonal conflict and reach the third stage, in which close relationships develop and the team demonstrates cohesiveness. There is now a strong sense of team identity and camaraderie. The team develops **norms**, acceptable standards of behaviour that are shared by its members. All teams have established norms that tell members what they ought and ought not to do under certain circumstances. When agreed to and accepted by the team, norms act as a means of influencing the behaviour of team members with a minimum of external controls. This **norming** stage is complete when the team structure solidifies and the team has assimilated a common set of expectations about what defines correct member behaviour.

- *Stage IV: Performing.* Next, and you may have noticed this in some of your own team interactions, some teams just seem to come together well and start to do their work. This fourth stage, when significant task progress is being made, is called **performing**. The structure at this point is fully functional and accepted. Team energy has moved from getting to know and understand one another to performing the task at hand.

- *Stage V: Adjourning.* For permanent work groups and teams, performing is the last stage in their development. However, for temporary committees, teams, task forces, and similar groups that have a limited task to perform, there is an **adjourning** stage. In this stage, the group prepares to split up. High task performance is no longer the group's top priority. Instead, attention is directed toward wrapping up activities. Group members' responses vary at this stage. Some members are upbeat, basking in the group's accomplishments. Others may be depressed over the loss of camaraderie and friendships gained during the work group's life.

Putting the Five-Stage Model into Perspective

Many interpreters of the five-stage model have assumed that a group becomes more effective as it progresses through the first four stages. This assumption may be generally true, but what makes a group effective is more complex than this model acknowledges. Under some conditions, high levels of conflict lead to high group performance, as long as the conflict is directed toward the task and not toward group members. So we might expect to find situations in which groups in Stage II outperform those in Stage III or Stage IV. Similarly, groups don't always proceed clearly from one stage to the next. Sometimes, in fact, several stages go on simultaneously, as when groups are storming and performing at the same time. Groups even occasionally move backwards to previous stages. Therefore, you should not assume that all groups follow the five-stage process precisely, or that Stage IV is always the most preferable.

The five-stage model ignores organizational context.[6] For instance, a study of a cockpit crew in an airliner found that, within 10 minutes, three strangers assigned to fly together for the first time had become a high-performing team. How could a team come together so quickly? The answer lies in the strong organizational context surrounding the tasks of the cockpit crew. This context provided the rules, task definitions, information, and resources needed for the team to perform. They did not need to develop plans, assign roles, determine and allocate resources, resolve conflicts, and set norms the way the five-stage model predicts.

The Punctuated-Equilibrium Model

Temporary groups with deadlines don't seem to follow the previous model. Studies indicate that temporary groups with deadlines have their own unique sequence of action (or inaction):[7]

Ever wonder what causes flurries of activity in groups?

- The first meeting sets the group's direction.

- The first phase of group activity is one of inertia.

- A transition takes place at the end of the first phase, which occurs exactly when the group has used up half its allotted time.

- The transition initiates major changes.

- A second phase of inertia follows the transition.

- The group's last meeting is characterized by high levels of productive activity.

This pattern is called the *punctuated-equilibrium model*, developed by Professor Connie Gersick, a Visiting Scholar at the Yale University School of Management, and is shown in Exhibit 5-2.[8] It is important for you to understand these shifts in group behaviour. If you are ever in a group that is not working well or has got off to a slow start, knowing about these shifts can help you think of ways to get the group to move to a more productive phase.

adjourning The final stage in group development for temporary groups, where attention is directed toward wrapping up activities rather than task performance.

✱ Explore

Exhibit 5-2: The Punctuated Equilibrium Model

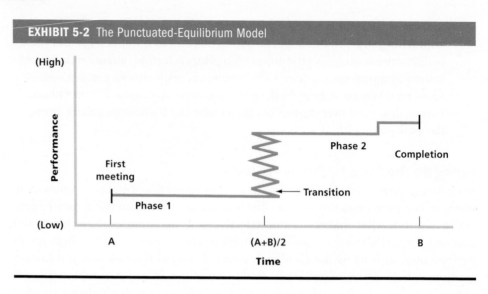

EXHIBIT 5-2 The Punctuated-Equilibrium Model

Phase 1

As both a team member and possibly a team leader, you need to recognize that the first meeting sets the team's direction. A framework of behavioural patterns and assumptions through which the team will approach its project emerges in this first meeting. These lasting patterns can appear as early as the first few seconds of the team's life.

Once set, the team's direction becomes accepted and is unlikely to be re-examined throughout the first half of the team's life. This is a period of inertia—that is, the team tends to stand still or become locked into a fixed course of action. Even if it gains new insights that challenge initial patterns and assumptions, the team is incapable of acting on these new insights in Phase 1. You may recognize that in some teams, during the early period of trying to get things accomplished, no one really did his or her assigned tasks. You may also recognize this phase as one in which everyone carries out the tasks, but not in a very coordinated fashion. Thus, the team is performing at a relatively low state. This does not necessarily mean that it is doing nothing at all, however.

Phase 2

At some point, the team moves out of the inertia stage and recognizes that work needs to get completed. One of the more interesting discoveries made in these studies was that each team experienced its transition at the same point in its calendar—precisely halfway between its first meeting and its official deadline. The similarity occurred despite the fact that some teams spent as little as an hour on their projects, while others spent six months. It was as if the teams universally experienced a mid-life crisis at this point. The midpoint appears to work like an alarm clock, heightening members' awareness that their time is limited and that they need to "get moving." When you work on your next team project, you might want to examine when your team starts to "get moving."

This transition ends Phase 1 and is characterized by a concentrated burst of changes, dropping of old patterns, and adoption of new perspectives. The transition sets a revised direction for Phase 2, which is a new equilibrium or period of inertia. In this phase, the team executes plans created during the transition period. The team's last meeting is characterized by a final burst of activity to finish its work. There have been a number of studies that support the basic premise of punctuated equilibrium, though not all of them found that the transition in the team occurred exactly at the midpoint.[9]

Applying the Punctuated-Equilibrium Model

We can use this model to describe typical experiences of student teams created for doing group term projects. At the first meeting, a basic timetable is established. Members size up one another. They agree they have nine weeks to complete their project. The instructor's requirements are discussed and debated. From that point, the group meets regularly to carry out its activities. About four or five weeks into the project, however, problems are confronted. Criticism begins to be taken seriously. Discussion becomes more open. The group reassesses where it has been and aggressively moves to make necessary changes. If the right changes are made, the next four or five weeks find the group developing a first-rate project. The group's last meeting, which will probably occur just before the project is due, lasts longer than the others. In it, all final issues are discussed and details resolved.

In summary, the punctuated-equilibrium model characterizes deadline-oriented teams as exhibiting long periods of inertia, interspersed with brief revolutionary changes triggered primarily by their members' awareness of time and deadlines. To use the terminology of the five-stage model, the group begins by combining the *forming* and *norming* stages, then goes through a period of *low performing*, followed by *storming*, then a period of *high performing*, and, finally, *adjourning*.

Several researchers have suggested that the five-stage and punctuated-equilibrium models are at odds with each other.[10] However, it makes more sense to view the models as complementary: The five-stage model considers the interpersonal process of the group, while the punctuated-equilibrium model considers the time challenges that the group faces.[11]

Creating Effective Teams

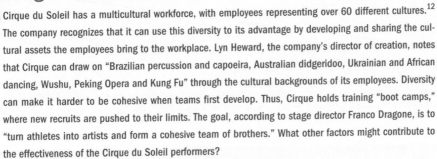

Cirque du Soleil has a multicultural workforce, with employees representing over 60 different cultures.[12] The company recognizes that it can use this diversity to its advantage by developing and sharing the cultural assets the employees bring to the workplace. Lyn Heward, the company's director of creation, notes that Cirque can draw on "Brazilian percussion and capoeira, Australian didgeridoo, Ukrainian and African dancing, Wushu, Peking Opera and Kung Fu" through the cultural backgrounds of its employees. Diversity can make it harder to be cohesive when teams first develop. Thus, Cirque holds training "boot camps," where new recruits are pushed to their limits. The goal, according to stage director Franco Dragone, is to "turn athletes into artists and form a cohesive team of brothers." What other factors might contribute to the effectiveness of the Cirque du Soleil performers?

3 How do we create effective teams?

When we consider team effectiveness, we refer to such objective measures as the team's productivity, managers' ratings of the team's performance, and aggregate measures of member satisfaction. Some of the considerations necessary to create effective teams are outlined next. However, we are also interested in team process. Exhibit 5-3 provides a checklist of the characteristics of an effective team.

There is no shortage of efforts that try to identify the factors that lead to team effectiveness.[13] However, studies have taken what was once a "veritable laundry list of characteristics"[14] and organized them into a relatively focused model with four general categories summarized in Exhibit 5-4:[15]

- Resources and other contextual influences that make teams effective

- Team composition

- Work design

- Team process (those things that go on in the team that influence how effective the team is)

Becoming a team player is not easy, as *OB in the Street* demonstrates.

EXHIBIT 5-3 Characteristics of an Effective Team

1. Clear purpose	The vision, mission, goal, or task of the team has been defined and is now accepted by everyone. There is an action plan.
2. Informality	The climate tends to be informal, comfortable, and relaxed. There are no obvious tensions or signs of boredom.
3. Participation	There is much discussion, and everyone is encouraged to participate.
4. Listening	The members use effective listening techniques such as questioning, paraphrasing, and summarizing to get out ideas.
5. Civilized disagreement	There is disagreement, but the team is comfortable with this and shows no signs of avoiding, smoothing over, or suppressing conflict.
6. Consensus decisions	For important decisions, the goal is substantial but not necessarily unanimous agreement through open discussion of everyone's ideas, avoidance of formal voting, or easy compromises.
7. Open communication	Team members feel free to express their feelings on the tasks as well as on the group's operation. There are few hidden agendas. Communication takes place outside of meetings.
8. Clear rules and work assignments	There are clear expectations about the roles played by each team member. When action is taken, clear assignments are made, accepted, and carried out. Work is distributed among team members.
9. Shared leadership	While the team has a formal leader, leadership functions shift from time to time depending on the circumstances, the needs of the group, and the skills of the members. The formal leader models the appropriate behaviour and helps establish positive norms.
10. External relations	The team spends time developing key outside relationships, mobilizing resources, and building credibility with important players in other parts of the organization.
11. Style diversity	The team has a broad spectrum of team-player types including members who emphasize attention to task, goal setting, focus on process, and questions about how the team is functioning.
12. Self-assessment	Periodically, the team stops to examine how well it is functioning and what may be interfering with its effectiveness.

Source: G. M. Parker, *Team Players and Teamwork: The New Competitive Business Strategy* (San Francisco: Jossey-Bass, 1990), Table 2, p. 33. Copyright © 1990 by Jossey-Bass Inc., Publishers. Reprinted by permission of John Wiley & Sons, Inc.

Explore

Exhibit 5-2: The Punctuated Equilibrium Model

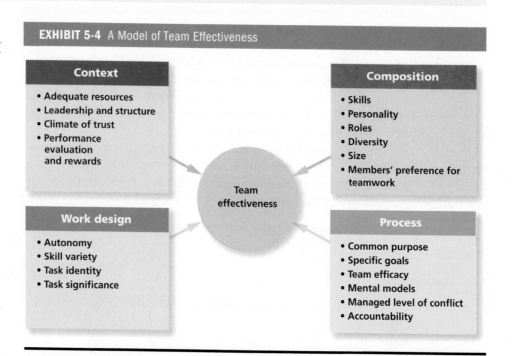

EXHIBIT 5-4 A Model of Team Effectiveness

Context
- Adequate resources
- Leadership and structure
- Climate of trust
- Performance evaluation and rewards

Composition
- Skills
- Personality
- Roles
- Diversity
- Size
- Members' preference for teamwork

Work design
- Autonomy
- Skill variety
- Task identity
- Task significance

Process
- Common purpose
- Specific goals
- Team efficacy
- Mental models
- Managed level of conflict
- Accountability

Team effectiveness

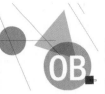

in the STREET
Top Skeleton Racer Finds Teamwork a Real Challenge

Is being a team player all that tough? Jeff Pain spent much of the 2000s trying his best not to be a team player, even though he was part of the Canadian men's skeleton team (a skeleton sled is a one-person racing toboggan).[16] Much of Pain's negativity toward teamwork was directed at team member Duff Gibson, his rival for over five years. "When Duff started skeleton [in 1999], I had a difficult time with my team dynamics because I felt that I knew a lot more than the people I was sliding with," says Pain. "I didn't want to share information with them and I carried that mistaken belief right up to [2004]. That was probably my and Duff's worst year."[17]

In summer 2004, Pain, Gibson, and fellow team member Paul Boehm decided to work together to share information about the tracks they were competing on, and then tried to help each other out.

Pain and Gibson improved their times and reached the highest level in international standings. Pain admits that learning how to be more of a team player has helped him improve in a sport that he was thinking of quitting because of his unhappiness with other team members. "I really insulated myself, and that didn't create a good environment for me or the team," Pain says.[18] At the 2006 Olympics, the two teammates wound up taking the top spots in skeleton racing: Gibson won gold, and Pain won silver. ●

Keep in mind two caveats as you review the issues that lead to effective teams:

- First, teams differ in form and structure. Since the model we present attempts to generalize across all varieties of teams, you need to be careful not to rigidly apply the model's predictions to all teams.[19] The model should be used as a guide, not as an inflexible prescription.

- Second, the model assumes that it's already been determined that teamwork is preferable over individual work. Creating "effective" teams in situations in which individuals can do the job better is equivalent to solving the wrong problem perfectly.

OB in Action—Harming Your Team presents actions that can make a team ineffective. You might want to evaluate your own team experiences against this checklist to give you some idea of how well your team is functioning or to understand what might be causing problems for your team. Then consider the factors that lead to more effective teams below. For an applied look at the process of building an effective team, see the *Working with Others Exercise* on pages 186–187, which asks you to build a paper tower with teammates and then analyze how the team performed.

Context

Teams can require a great deal of maintenance to function properly. They need management support as well as an organizational structure that supports teamwork. The four

in ACTION
Harming Your Team

→ **Refuse to share** issues and concerns. Team members refuse to share information and engage in silence, avoidance, and meetings behind closed doors where not all members are included.

→ **Depend** too much **on the leader**. Members rely too much on the leader and don't carry out their responsibilities.

→ **Fail to follow through** on decisions. Teams do not take action after decision making, showing that the needs of the team have low priority, or members are not committed to the decisions that were made.

→ **Hide conflict**. Team members don't reveal that they have a difference of opinion, and this causes tension.

→ **Fail at conflict resolution**. Infighting, put-downs, and attempts to hurt other members damage the team.

→ **Form subgroups**. The team breaks up into smaller groups that put their needs ahead of the team as a whole.[20]

Kerri Molinaro, president of Burlington, Ontario-based IKEA Canada, believes that teams are the best way to bring employees together. IKEA's leadership style is informal, and the company values people who are humble and trustworthy. This also makes them good team members.

contextual factors that appear to be most significantly related to team performance are adequate resources, effective leadership, a climate of trust, and a performance evaluation and reward system that reflects team contributions.

Adequate Resources

All work teams rely on resources outside the team to sustain them. A scarcity of resources directly reduces the ability of a team to perform its job effectively. As one set of researchers concluded after looking at 13 factors potentially related to team performance, "perhaps one of the most important characteristics of an effective work group is the support the group receives from the organization."[21] This support includes technology, adequate staffing, administrative assistance, encouragement, and timely information. Teams must receive the necessary support from management and the larger organization if they are going to succeed in achieving their goals.

Leadership and Structure

Leadership plays a crucial role in the development and success of teams. Professor Richard Hackman of Harvard University, who is a leading expert on teams, suggests that the role of team leader involves the following:[22]

- Creating a real team rather than a team in name only

- Setting a clear and meaningful direction for the team's work

- Making sure that the team structure will support its working effectively

- Ensuring that the team operates within a supportive organizational context

- Providing expert coaching

There are some practical problems that must be resolved when a team first starts working together. Team members must agree on who is to do what and ensure that all members contribute equally in sharing the workload. The team also needs to determine how schedules will be set, what skills need to be developed, how the team will resolve conflicts, and how the team will make and modify decisions. Agreeing on the specifics of work and how they fit together to integrate individual skills requires team leadership and structure. This, incidentally, can be provided directly by management or by the team members themselves. Although you might think there is no role for leaders in self-managed teams, that could not be further from the truth. It is true that, in self-managed teams, team members absorb many of the duties typically assumed by managers. However, a manager's job becomes managing *outside* (rather than inside) the team.

Leadership is especially important in **multi-team systems**—where different teams need to coordinate their efforts to produce a desired outcome. In such systems, leaders need to empower teams by delegating responsibility to them, and they need to play the role of facilitator, making sure the teams are coordinating their efforts so that they work together rather than against one another.[23] The *Learning About Yourself Exercise* on pages 185–186 will help you evaluate how suited you are to building and leading a team.

Recent research suggests that women may make better team leaders than men. "The more women participating equally in a project, the better the outcome," suggests professor Jennifer Berdahl of the Rotman School of Management at the University of Toronto.[24] Berdahl's research, which looked at 169 students enrolled in her organizational behaviour courses, found that in predominantly female teams, women shared leadership roles and were more egalitarian in how they worked. Male-led teams,

multi-team systems Systems in which different teams need to coordinate their efforts to produce a desired outcome.

whether they were predominantly male groups or mixed-gender groups, received poorer grades on their projects than teams where women shared leadership roles. Berdahl gives this advice to students: "In a creative project team, it's really important to ensure there is equal opportunity for participation."[25]

Sometimes teams need coaches more than they need leaders. Though workplace teams often report that they receive little coaching compared with leadership,[26] productivity-related coaching may help teams perform more effectively. In particular, coaching may be best at three particular stages in the team's history: "at the beginning for effort-related (motivational) interventions, near the midpoint for strategy-related (consultative) interventions, and at the end of a task cycle for (educational) interventions that address knowledge and skill."[27]

Teams don't always need a leader. For instance, the evidence indicates that self-managed work teams often perform better than teams with formally appointed leaders.[28] Leaders can also obstruct high performance when they interfere with self-managed teams.[29] On self-managed teams, team members absorb many of the duties typically assumed by managers.

Climate of Trust

Members of effective teams trust one another. For team members to achieve a climate of trust, they must feel that the team is capable of getting the task done, and they must believe that "the team will not harm the individual or his or her interests."[30] Interpersonal trust among team members facilitates cooperation, reduces the need to monitor one another's behaviour, and bonds members around the belief that others on the team will not take advantage of them. Team members are more likely to take risks and expose vulnerabilities when they believe they can trust others on their team. *OB in Action—Building Trust* shows the dimensions that underlie the concept of trust.

Team members must also trust their leaders.[31] Trust in leadership is important in that it allows the team to be willing to accept and commit to their leader's goals and decisions. Management at Mississauga, Ontario-based Flynn Canada invests in employees to help them become good team players. The company also helps employees build trust in one another, so that they can work effectively. Employees are encouraged to take pride in their work and successful outcomes. They are also encouraged to be open with one another. "Personally, what attracted me to Flynn is that it's got scale and horsepower but it has a heart and soul; it's not just another corporate entity. We are authentic in our interactions with each other. What you see is what you get," says Gerard Montocchio, vice-president of human resources.[32]

OB in ACTION
Building Trust

The following actions, in order of importance, help build one's trustworthiness.

→ **Integrity**—built through **honesty** and **truthfulness**.

→ **Competence**—demonstrated by technical and interpersonal **knowledge** and **skills**.

→ **Consistency**—shown by **reliability**, **predictability**, and **good judgment** in handling situations.

→ **Loyalty**—one's willingness to **protect** and **stand up** for another person.

→ **Openness**—one's willingness to **share ideas** and **information** freely.[33]

Performance Evaluation and Rewards

How do you get team members to be both individually and jointly accountable? The traditional individually oriented evaluation must be modified to reflect team performance.[34]

Individual performance evaluations, fixed hourly wages, individual incentives, and the like are not consistent with the development of high-performance teams. So in addition to evaluating and rewarding employees for their individual contributions, management should consider group-based appraisals, profit sharing, gainsharing, small-group incentives, and other system modifications that

Should individuals be paid for their "teamwork" or their individual performance?

will reinforce team effort and commitment. Managers need to carefully consider the balance between paying on the basis of group performance[35] and the level of trust among team members. Recent research found that when team members did not trust their colleagues' ability, honesty, and dependability, they preferred individual-based rewards rather than team-based rewards. Even when trust improved over time from working together, there was still a preference for individual-based rewards, suggesting that "teams must have a very high level of trust for members to truly embrace group-based pay."[36]

One additional consideration when deciding whether and how to reward team members is the effect of pay dispersion on team performance. Research by Nancy Langton, your Vancouver-based author, shows that when there is a large discrepancy in wages among group members, collaboration is lowered.[37] A study of baseball players' salaries also found that teams in which players were paid more similarly often outperformed teams with highly paid "stars" and lowly paid "scrubs."[38]

Composition

This category includes variables that relate to how teams should be staffed. In this section, we address the skills, personality, and roles of team members, the diversity and size of the team, and members' preference for teamwork.

> Why do some teams seem to get along better than others?

Skills

To perform effectively, a team requires three different types of skills:

1. It needs people with *technical expertise*.

2. It needs people with the *problem-solving* and *decision-making* skills to be able to identify problems, generate alternatives, evaluate those alternatives, and make competent choices.

3. It needs people with good listening, feedback, conflict resolution, and other *interpersonal skills*.[39]

No team can achieve its performance potential without developing all three types of skills. The right mix is crucial. Too much of one at the expense of others will result in lower team performance. But teams don't need to have all the complementary skills in place at the beginning. It's not uncommon for one or more members to take responsibility to learn the skills in which the group is deficient, thereby allowing the team to reach its full potential. Exhibit 5-5 identifies some important teamwork skills that help teams function well.

Personality

Teams have different needs, and people should be selected for the team on the basis of their personalities and preferences, as well as the team's needs for diversity and specific roles. We demonstrated in Chapter 2 that personality has a significant influence on individual employee behaviour. Personality also influences team behaviour.

Many of the dimensions identified in the Big Five Personality Model have been shown to be relevant to team effectiveness. A recent review of the literature suggested that three of the Big Five traits are especially important for team performance.[40] Specifically, teams that rate higher on mean levels of conscientiousness and openness to experience tend to perform better. Moreover, a 2011 study found that the level of team member agreeableness also matters: Teams did worse when they had one or more highly disagreeable members.[41] Perhaps one bad apple *can* spoil the whole bunch!

EXHIBIT 5-5 Teamwork Skills

Orients Team to Problem-Solving Situation	Assists the team in arriving at a common understanding of the situation or problem. Determines the important elements of a problem situation. Seeks out relevant data related to the situation or problem.
Organizes and Manages Team Performance	Helps team establish specific, challenging, and accepted team goals. Monitors, evaluates, and provides feedback on team performance. Identifies alternative strategies or reallocates resources to address feedback on team performance.
Promotes a Positive Team Environment	Assists in creating and reinforcing norms of tolerance, respect, and excellence. Recognizes and praises other team members' efforts. Helps and supports other team members. Models desirable team member behaviour.
Facilitates and Manages Task Conflict	Encourages desirable and discourages undesirable team conflict. Recognizes the type and source of conflict confronting the team and implements an appropriate resolution strategy. Employs "win-win" negotiation strategies to resolve team conflicts.
Appropriately Promotes Perspective	Defends stated preferences, argues for a particular point of view, and withstands pressure to change position for another that is not supported by logical or knowledge-based arguments. Changes or modifies position if a defensible argument is made by another team member. Projects courtesy and friendliness to others while arguing position.

Source: G. Chen, L. M. Donahue, and R. J. Klimoski, "Training Undergraduates to Work in Organizational Teams," *Academy of Management Learning & Education* 3, no. 1 (March 2004), p. 40. Copyright © Academy of Management, 2002.

Explore

Exhibit 5-5: Teamwork Skills

British Chief Inspector of Nuclear Installations Mike Weightman is the leader of an 18-member global team created by the International Atomic Energy Commission to study the Fukushima nuclear power station accident triggered by the 2011 earthquake in Japan. This high-ability team with members from 12 countries includes experts with experience across a wide range of nuclear specialties. Team members apply their technical expertise, problem-solving, and decision-making skills, as well as interpersonal skills to their mission of identifying lessons learned from the accident that can help improve nuclear safety around the world. Here, Weightman (left) shakes hands with the Fukushima plant chief after the team inspected the crippled nuclear power plant.

Research has also provided us with a good idea about why these personality traits are important to teams. Conscientious people are valuable in teams because they are good at backing up other team members, and they are also good at sensing when that support is truly needed. Open team members communicate better with one another and throw out more ideas, which leads teams composed of open people to be more creative and innovative.[42]

Roles

Teams have different needs, and members should be selected to ensure all the various **roles** are filled. A study of 778 major league baseball teams over a 21-year period highlights the importance of assigning roles appropriately.[43] As you might expect, teams with more experienced and skilled members performed better. However, the experience and skill of those in core roles who handle more of the workflow of the team, and who are central to all work processes (in this case, pitchers and catchers), were especially vital. In other words, put your most able, experienced, and conscientious workers in the most central roles in a team.

Within almost any group, two sets of role relationships need to be considered: task-oriented roles and maintenance roles. **Task-oriented roles** are performed by group members to ensure that the tasks of the group are accomplished. These roles include initiators, information seekers, information providers, elaborators, summarizers, and consensus makers. **Maintenance roles** are carried out to ensure that group members maintain good relations. These roles include harmonizers, compromisers, gatekeepers, and encouragers.

Effective teams maintain some balance between task orientation and maintenance of relations. Exhibit 5-6 identifies a number of task-oriented and maintenance behaviours in the key roles that you might find in a team.

On many teams, there are individuals who will be flexible enough to play multiple roles and/or complete one another's tasks. This is an obvious plus to a team because it greatly improves its adaptability and makes it less reliant on any single member.[44] Selecting members who themselves value flexibility, and then cross-training them to be able to do one another's jobs, should lead to a higher level of team performance over time.

Occasionally within teams, you will see people take on **individual roles** that are not productive for keeping the team on task. When this happens, the individual is demonstrating more concern for himself or herself than the team as a whole.

Most roles, whether in the workplace or in our personal lives, are governed by **role expectations**, that is, how others believe a person should act in a given situation. **Role conflict** exists when an individual finds that complying with one role requirement may make it more difficult to comply with another.[45] At the extreme, it can include situations in which two or more role expectations are mutually contradictory!

Diversity

Group diversity refers to the presence of a heterogeneous mix of individuals within a group.[46] Individuals can be different not only in functional characteristics (jobs, positions, expertise, or work experiences) but also in demographic or cultural characteristics (age, race, sex, and citizenship). Many of us hold the optimistic view that diversity should be a good thing—diverse teams should benefit from differing perspectives and do better. Two meta-analytic reviews of the research literature show, however, that demographic diversity is essentially unrelated to team performance overall.[47] One qualifier is that gender and ethnic diversity have more negative effects in occupations dominated by white or male employees, but in more demographically balanced occupations, diversity is less of a problem. Diversity in function and expertise are positively related to group performance, but these effects are quite small and depend on the situation.

One of the pervasive challenges with teams is that while diversity may have real potential benefits, a team is deeply focused on commonly held information. But to

role A set of expected behaviours of a person in a given position in a social unit.

task-oriented roles Roles performed by group members to ensure that the tasks of the group are carried out.

maintenance roles Roles performed by group members to maintain good relations within the group.

individual roles Roles performed by group members that are not productive for keeping the team on task.

role expectations How others believe a person should act in a given situation.

role conflict A situation in which an individual finds that complying with one role requirement may make it more difficult to comply with another.

group diversity The presence of a heterogeneous mix of individuals within a group.

EXHIBIT 5-6 Roles Required for Effective Team Functioning

	Function	Description	Example
Roles that build task accomplishment	*Initiating*	Stating the goal or problem, making proposals about how to work on it, setting time limits.	"Let's set up an agenda for discussing each of the problems we have to consider."
	Seeking information and opinions	Asking group members for specific factual information related to the task or problem, or for their opinions about it.	"What do you think would be the best approach to this, Jack?"
	Providing information and opinions	Sharing information or opinions related to the task or problems.	"I worked on a similar problem last year and found . . ."
	Clarifying	Helping one another understand ideas and suggestions that come up in the group.	"What you mean, Sue, is that we could . . ."
	Elaborating	Building on one another's ideas and suggestions.	"Building on Don's idea, I think we could . . ."
	Summarizing	Reviewing the points covered by the group and the different ideas stated so that decisions can be based on full information.	Appointing a recorder to take notes on a blackboard.
	Consensus testing	Providing periodic testing on whether the group is nearing a decision or needs to continue discussion.	"Is the group ready to decide about this?"
Roles that build and maintain a team	*Harmonizing*	Mediating conflict among other members, reconciling disagreements, relieving tensions.	"Don, I don't think you and Sue really see the question that differently."
	Compromising	Admitting error at times of group conflict.	"Well, I'd be willing to change if you provided some help on ..."
	Gatekeeping	Making sure all members have a chance to express their ideas and feelings and preventing members from being interrupted.	"Sue, we haven't heard from you on this issue."
	Encouraging	Helping a group member make his or her point. Establishing a climate of acceptance in the group.	"I think what you started to say is important, Jack. Please continue."

Source: From Ancona / Kochan / Scully / Van Maanen. Managing for the Future, 1E. c 1996 South-Western, a part of Cengage Learning, Inc. Reproduced by permission. www.cengage.com/permissions

realize their creative potential, diverse teams need to focus not on their similarities but on their differences. Some evidence suggests that when team members believe others have more expertise, they will work to support those members, leading to higher levels of effectiveness.[48] The key is for members of diverse teams to communicate what they uniquely know and also what they don't know. Proper leadership can also improve the performance of diverse teams. When leaders provide an inspirational common goal for members with varying types of education and knowledge, teams are very creative. When leaders don't provide such goals, diverse teams fail to take advantage of their unique skills and are actually *less* creative than teams with homogeneous skills.

Explore

Exhibit 5-6: Roles Required for Effective Team Functioning

Size

Generally speaking, the most effective teams have five to nine members. And experts suggest using the smallest number of people who can do the task. Unfortunately, there is a tendency for managers to make teams too large. While a minimum of four or five members may be necessary to develop a diversity of views and skills, managers seem to seriously underestimate how coordination problems can dramatically increase as team members are added. When teams have excess members, cohesiveness and mutual accountability decline, social loafing increases, and more and more people do less talking compared with others. So in designing effective teams, managers should try to keep the number of members at less than 10. If a work unit is larger and you want a team effort, consider breaking the unit into subteams. An uneven number of members in a team provides a mechanism to break ties and resolve conflicts, while an even number of members may foster the need to create more consensus.

Size and Social Loafing   One of the most important findings related to the size of a team has been labelled **social loafing**. Social loafing is the tendency of individuals to expend less effort when working collectively than when working individually.[49] It directly challenges the logic that the productivity of the team as a whole should at least equal the sum of the productivity of each individual in that team. Research looking at teams working on a rope-pulling task showed that the larger the team, the less individual effort expended.[50] One person pulling on a rope alone exerted an average of 63 kilograms of force. In groups of three, per-person force dropped to 53 kilograms. And in groups of eight, it fell to only 31 kilograms per person. Other research supports these findings.[51] More may be better in the sense that the total productivity of a group of four is greater than that of one or two people, but the individual productivity of each group member declines.

Why don't some team members pull their weight?

What causes this social loafing effect? It may be due to a belief that others in the team are not carrying their fair share. If you view others as lazy or inept, you can re-establish equity by reducing your effort. Another explanation is the dispersion of responsibility. Because the results of the team cannot be attributed to any single

Employees in Taigu County, China, are collecting harvest grapes for the production of red wine. In collectivistic societies such as China, employees perform better in a group than when working alone and they are less likely to engage in social loafing. Unlike individualistic cultures like Canada and the United States, where people are dominated by self-interest, the Chinese are motivated by in-group goals.

social loafing The tendency of individuals to expend less effort when working collectively than when working individually.

person, the relationship between an individual's input and the team's output is clouded. In such situations, individuals may be tempted to become "free riders" and coast on the team's efforts. In other words, there will be a reduction in efficiency when individuals believe that their contribution cannot be measured. To reduce social loafing, teams should not be larger than necessary and individuals should be held accountable for their actions. You might also consider the ideas presented on dealing with shirkers in this chapter's *Ethical Dilemma Exercise* on page 187.

Members' Preference for Teamwork

Not every employee is a team player. Given the option, many employees will "select themselves out" of team participation. When people who would prefer to work alone are required to team up, there is a direct threat to the team's morale.[52] This suggests that, when selecting team members, individual preferences should be considered, as well as abilities, personalities, and skills. High-performing teams are likely to be composed of people who prefer working as part of a team. *Case Incident—Toyota's Team Culture* on pages 187–188 discusses how the auto manufacturer hires employees who are more likely to be good team members.

Work Design

Effective teams need to work together and take collective responsibility to complete significant tasks. They must be more than a "team-in-name-only."[53] The work design category includes variables such as freedom and autonomy, the opportunity to use a variety of skills and talents, the ability to complete a whole and identifiable task or product, and the participation in a task or project that has a substantial impact on others. The evidence indicates that these characteristics enhance member motivation and increase team effectiveness.[54] These work design characteristics motivate teams because they increase members' sense of responsibility for and ownership of the work, and because they make the work more interesting to perform.[55] These recommendations are consistent with the job characteristics model we presented in Chapter 4.

Process

Process variables make up the final component of team effectiveness. The process category includes member commitment to a common purpose; establishment of specific goals; team efficacy; shared mental models; a managed level of conflict; and a system of accountability. These variables will be especially important in larger teams, and in teams that are highly interdependent.[56]

Why are processes important to team effectiveness? We learned from social loafing that $1 + 1 + 1$ does not necessarily add up to 3. When each member's contribution is not clearly visible, individuals tend to decrease their effort. Social loafing, in other words, illustrates a process loss from using teams. But teams should create outputs greater than the sum of their inputs, as when a diverse group develops creative alternatives. Exhibit 5-7 illustrates how group processes can have an impact on a group's actual effectiveness.[57] Scientists often work in teams because they can draw on the diverse skills of various individuals to produce more meaningful research than could

EXHIBIT 5-7 Effects of Group Processes

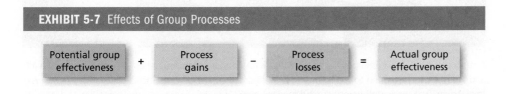

be generated by all the researchers working independently—that is, they produce positive synergy, and their process gains exceed their process losses.

Common Purpose

Effective teams begin by analyzing the team's mission, developing goals to achieve that mission, and creating strategies for achieving the goals. Teams that establish a clear sense of what needs to be done and how consistently perform better.[58]

Members of successful teams put a tremendous amount of time and effort into discussing, shaping, and agreeing on a purpose that belongs to them both collectively and individually. This common purpose, when accepted by the team, becomes the equivalent of what celestial navigation is to a ship's captain—it provides direction and guidance under any and all conditions. Like a ship following the wrong course, teams that don't have good planning skills are doomed; perfectly executing the wrong plan is a lost cause.[59] Effective teams also show **reflexivity**, meaning that they reflect on and adjust their master plan when necessary. A team has to have a good plan, but it also has to be willing and able to adapt when conditions call for it.[60]

Specific Goals

Successful teams translate their common purpose into specific, measurable, and realistic performance goals. Just as we demonstrated in Chapter 4 how goals lead individuals to higher performance, so goals also energize teams. Specific goals facilitate clear communication and also help teams maintain their focus on achieving results.

Consistent with the research on individual goals, team goals should be challenging. Difficult goals have been found to raise team performance on those criteria for which they are set. So, for instance, goals for quantity tend to raise quantity, goals for speed tend to raise speed, goals for accuracy tend to raise accuracy, and so on.[61]

Team Efficacy

Effective teams have confidence in themselves. They believe they can succeed. We call this *team efficacy*.[62] Teams that have been successful raise their beliefs about future success which, in turn, motivates them to work harder.

A study of 23 National Basketball Association teams found that "shared experience"—tenure on the team and time on court—tended to reduce turnover and boost win-loss performance significantly. Why do you think teams that stay together longer tend to play better?

reflexivity A characteristic of effective teams, allowing them to reflect on and adjust their master plan when necessary.

EXHIBIT 5-8 Relationship among Team Cohesiveness, Performance Norms, and Productivity

Explore

Exhibit 5-8: Relationship among Team Cohesiveness, Performance Norms, and Productivity

Cohesiveness

Performance Norms		High	Low
	High	High productivity	Moderate productivity
	Low	Low productivity	Moderate to low productivity

One of the factors that helps teams build their efficacy is **cohesiveness**—the degree to which members are attracted to one another and are motivated to stay on the team.[63] Though teams differ in their cohesiveness, it is important because it has been found to be related to the team's productivity.[64]

Studies consistently show that the relation between cohesiveness and productivity depends on the performance-related norms established by the group.[65] If performance-related norms are high (for example, high output, quality work, cooperation with individuals outside the group), a cohesive group will be more productive than a less cohesive group. If cohesiveness is high and performance norms are low, productivity will be low. If cohesiveness is low and performance norms are high, productivity increases—but less than in the high cohesiveness–high norms situation. Where cohesiveness and performance-related norms are both low, productivity will tend to fall into the low-to-moderate range. These conclusions are summarized in Exhibit 5-8. *OB in Action—Creating a Team Charter* provides a way for teams to develop productivity norms when the team first forms.

Most studies of cohesiveness focus on *socio-emotional cohesiveness*, the "sense of togetherness that develops when individuals derive emotional satisfaction from group participation."[66] There is also *instrumental cohesiveness*: the "sense of togetherness that develops when group members are mutually dependent on one another because they believe they could not achieve the group's goal by acting separately." Teams need to achieve a balance of these two types of cohesiveness to function well. *OB in Action—Increasing Group Cohesiveness* indicates how to increase both socio-emotional and instrumental cohesiveness.

What, if anything, can management do to increase team efficacy? Two possible options are helping the team to achieve small successes and skill training. Small successes build team confidence. As a team develops an increasingly stronger performance record, it also increases the collective belief that future efforts will lead to success. In addition, managers should consider providing training to improve members' technical and interpersonal skills. The greater the abilities of team members, the greater the likelihood that the team will develop confidence and the capability to deliver on that confidence.

Mental Models

Effective teams have accurate and common **mental models**—knowledge and beliefs (a "psychological map") about how the work gets done. If team members have the

PERSONAL INVENTORY ASSESSMENT

Learn About Yourself
Diagnosing the Need for Team Building

OB in ACTION
Creating a Team Charter

When you form a new team, you may want to develop a team charter, so that everyone agrees on the basic norms for group performance. Consider including answers to the following in your charter:

→ What are team members' **names and contact information** (phone, email)?

→ How will **communication** among team members take place (phone, email)?

→ What will the **team ground rules** be (where and when to meet, attendance expectations, workload expectations)?

→ How will **decisions** be made (consensus, majority vote, leader rules)?

→ What **potential conflicts** may arise within the team? Among team members?

→ How will **conflicts be resolved** by the group?[67]

PERSONAL INVENTORY ASSESSMENT

Learn About Yourself
Positive Practices Survey

cohesiveness The degree to which team members are attracted to one another and are motivated to stay on the team.

mental models Team members' knowledge and beliefs about how the work gets done by the team.

OB in **ACTION**
Increasing Group Cohesiveness

To increase socio-emotional cohesiveness:

→ Keep the group relatively **small**.

→ Strive for a **favourable public image** to increase the status and prestige of belonging.

→ Encourage **interaction** and **cooperation**.

→ Emphasize members' **common characteristics** and interests.

→ **Point out environmental threats** (e.g., competitors' achievements) to rally the group.

To increase instrumental cohesiveness:

→ Regularly update and **clarify the group's goal(s)**.

→ Give every group member a **vital "piece of the action."**

→ Channel each group member's special talents toward the **common goal(s)**.

→ **Recognize** and equitably reinforce **every member's contributions**.

→ Frequently remind group members they **need one another** to get the job done.[68]

wrong mental models, which is particularly likely to happen with teams under acute stress, their performance suffers.[69] For example, in the Iraq war, many military leaders said they underestimated the power of the insurgency and the infighting among Iraqi religious sects. The similarity of team members' mental models matters, too. If team members have different ideas about how to do things, the teams will fight over how to do things rather than focus on what needs to be done.[70]

Managed Level of Conflict

Conflict on a team is not necessarily bad. Though relationship conflicts—those based on interpersonal incompatibilities, tension, and animosity toward others—are almost always dysfunctional, teams that are completely void of conflict are likely to be less effective, with the members becoming withdrawn and only superficially harmonious.[71] On teams performing nonroutine activities, disagreements among members about task content (called *task conflicts*) stimulate discussion, promote critical assessment of problems and options, and can lead to better team decisions. The way conflicts are resolved can also make the difference between effective and ineffective teams. Effective teams resolved conflicts by explicitly discussing the issues, whereas ineffective teams had conflicts focused more on personalities and the way things were said.[72]

Kathleen Eisenhardt of the Stanford Graduate School of Business and her colleagues studied top management teams in technology-based companies to understand how they manage conflict.[73] Their research identified six tactics that helped the teams successfully manage the interpersonal conflict that can accompany group interactions. These are presented in *OB in Action—Reducing Team Conflict*. By handling the interpersonal conflict well, the teams were able to achieve their goals without letting conflict get in the way.

Groups need mechanisms by which they can manage the conflict, however.[74] From the research reported above, we could conclude that sharing information and goals, and striving to be open and get along, are helpful strategies for negotiating our way through the maze of conflict. A sense of humour, and a willingness to understand the points of others without insisting that everyone agree on all points, are also important. Group members should try to focus on the issues rather than on personalities, and strive to achieve fairness and equity in the group process.

Accountability

Successful teams make members individually and jointly accountable for the team's purpose, goals, and approach.[75] They clearly define what they are individually responsible for and what they are jointly responsible for. This reduces the ability for individuals to engage in social loafing. *From Concepts to Skills* on pages 188–189 discusses how to conduct effective team meetings.

OB in **ACTION**
Reducing Team Conflict

→ Work with **more, rather than less, information**, and debate on the basis of **facts**.

→ Develop **multiple alternatives** to enrich the level of debate.

→ Develop commonly agreed-upon **goals**.

→ Use **humour** when making tough decisions.

→ Maintain a **balanced power** structure.

→ Resolve issues **without forcing consensus**.[76]

Twenty-First Century Teamwork: Virtual Teams

When we think of teams, we often picture face-to-face interactions. **Virtual teams**, however, seldom interact face-to-face, and they use computer technology to tie together physically separated members in order to achieve a common goal.[77] They enable people to collaborate online—using communication links such as wide-area networks, videoconferencing, and email—whether team members are only a room away or continents apart. Virtual teams are so pervasive, and technology has advanced so far, that it's probably a bit of a misnomer to call these teams "virtual." Nearly all teams today do at least some of their work remotely.

Virtual teams can suffer from the limited social contact of team members. This can lead to bonding problems, which the research on teams suggests is important for team performance. A meta-analysis of 27 studies of virtual teams questioned whether members of virtual teams ever bond in the traditional sense.[78] Lack of bonding can lead to slower and less accurate performance than is the case for face-to-face teams.

Virtual teams can also suffer from the absence of *paraverbal* and *nonverbal* cues in their communications. In face-to-face conversation, people use paraverbal (tone of voice, inflection, voice volume) and nonverbal (eye movement, facial expression, hand gestures, and other body language) cues to provide increased meaning. In virtual communications, team members are not able to duplicate the normal give-and-take of face-to-face discussion. As a result, virtual team members often have less social rapport and are more at risk of misunderstanding one another.

Virtual Teams and Trust

There has been some concern that, because virtual teams lack face-to-face interaction, it may be more difficult to build trust among individuals. However, two studies that examined how virtual teams work on projects indicate that virtual teams can develop close interaction and trust; these qualities simply evolve differently than in face-to-face groups.[79] In face-to-face groups, trust comes from direct interaction, over time. In virtual teams, trust is either established at the outset or it generally does not develop. The researchers found that initial electronic messages set the tone for how interactions occur throughout the entire project. In one team, for instance, when the appointed leader sent an introductory message that had a distrustful tone, the team suffered low morale and poor performance throughout the duration of the project. The researchers suggest that virtual teams should start with an electronic "courtship," where members provide some personal information. Then the teams should assign clear roles to members, helping members to identify with one another. Finally, the researchers noted that teams whose members had a positive attitude (eagerness, enthusiasm, and intense action orientation in messages) did considerably better than teams that had one or more pessimists among them.

Creating Virtual Workspaces

It is obvious that virtual teams must rely on technology to communicate. But what is the best way to do this? Team members can be overwhelmed with email, drowning in messages to the point of failing to read them. To better understand the problem, one study looked at 54 teams from 26 companies operating in a wide variety of industries.[80] The researchers found that 83 percent of the teams studied used virtual workspaces (also known as *virtual meeting rooms*) to communicate. The virtual workspace is a team website on a company's intranet designed to help remind team members of their "decisions, rationales, and commitments." The virtual workspace can have "walls" or links to information about each person, and discussion forums with topic threads that cover important issues and problems. The discussion forums can also serve as places to post work-in-progress to get feedback. Exhibit 5-9 shows an example of a virtual workspace for a project at Shell.

4 How do virtual teams work?

virtual teams Teams that seldom interact face-to-face and use computer technology to tie together physically dispersed members in order to achieve a common goal.

EXHIBIT 5-9 An Illustration of a Virtual Workspace

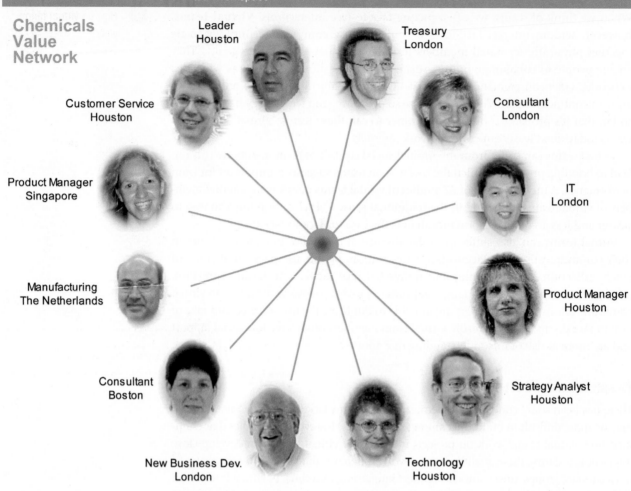

Chemicals
Value
Network

Leader
Houston

Treasury
London

Consultant
London

Customer Service
Houston

IT
London

Product Manager
Singapore

Product Manager
Houston

Manufacturing
The Netherlands

Consultant
Boston

Strategy Analyst
Houston

New Business Dev.
London

Technology
Houston

Source: Reprinted by permission of Shell Chemical LP.

For virtual teams to be effective, management should ensure that (1) trust is established among team members (one inflammatory remark in a team member email can severely undermine team trust); (2) team progress is monitored closely (so the team does not lose sight of its goals and no team member "disappears"); and (3) the efforts and products of the virtual team are publicized throughout the organization (so the team does not become invisible).[81] For more tips on improving the way virtual teams function, see *OB in Action—Managing Virtual Teams.*

Beware! Teams Are Not Always the Answer

5 Are teams always the answer?

Despite considerable success in the use of teams, they are not necessarily appropriate in all situations, as Exhibit 5-10 suggests. Teamwork takes more time and often more resources than individual work. Teams have greater communication demands, conflicts to be managed, and meetings to be run. So the benefits of using teams have to exceed the costs, and that is not always the case.[82] A study by Statistics Canada found that the introduction of teamwork lowered turnover in the service industries, for both high- and low-skilled employees. However, manufacturing companies experienced higher turnover if they introduced teamwork and formal teamwork training, compared with not doing so (15.8 percent vs. 10.7 percent).[83]

How do you know if the work of your group would be better done in teams? It has been suggested that three tests be applied to see if a team fits the situation:[84]

- *Can the work be done better by more than one person?* Simple tasks that don't require diverse input are probably better left to individuals.

- *Does the work create a common purpose or set of goals for the people in the group that is more than the sum of individual goals?* For instance, the service departments of many new-car dealers have introduced teams that link customer service personnel, mechanics, parts specialists, and sales representatives. Such teams can better manage collective responsibility for ensuring that customers' needs are properly met.

- *Are the members of the group interdependent?* Teams make sense where there is interdependence between tasks—where the success of the whole depends on the success of each one *and* the success of each one depends on the success of the others. Soccer, for instance, is an obvious *team* sport because of the interdependence of the players. Swim teams, by contrast, except for relays, are not really teams, but groups of individuals whose total performance is merely the sum of the individual performances. They are groups of individuals performing individually, whose total performance is merely the aggregate summation of their individual performances.

EXHIBIT 5-10

GROUP WRITING

Source: Dilbert reprinted by permission of Universal Uclick.

Explore

Exhibit 5-10

OB in **ACTION**
Managing Virtual Teams

Establishing trust and commitment, encouraging communication, and assessing team members pose tremendous challenges for virtual team managers. Here are a few tips to make the process easier:

→ Establish **regular times** for group interaction.
→ Set up **firm rules** for communication.
→ Use **visual forms of communication** where possible.
→ **Copy the good points of face-to-face teams**. For example, allow time for informal chitchat and socializing, and celebrate achievements.
→ **Give and receive feedback** and offer assistance on a regular basis. Be persistent with people who are not communicating with you or one another.
→ Agree on **standard technology** so all team members can work together easily.
→ Consider using **360-degree feedback** to better understand and evaluate team members. This type of feedback comes from the full circle of daily contacts that an employee might have, including supervisors, peers, subordinates, and clients.
→ Provide a **virtual workspace** via an intranet, website, or bulletin board.
→ Note which employees **effectively use email** to build team rapport.
→ **Smooth the way for the next assignment** if membership on the team, or the team itself, is not permanent.
→ **Be available** to employees, but don't wait for them to seek you out.
→ Encourage **informal, off-line conversation** between team members.[85]

LESSONS LEARNED

- A good team will achieve balance between individual needs and team needs.
- To create effective teams, members should be rewarded for engaging in team behaviour rather than individual behaviour.
- Teams should not be created for tasks that could be better done by individuals.

Summary and Implications

1 **What are teams and groups?**   Groups and teams differ. The output of a group is simply the sum of individual efforts. A team, because of the close collaboration among members, produces output that is greater than the sum of individual efforts.

2 **Do groups and teams go through stages while they work?**   Two different models illustrate how teams and groups develop. The first, the five-stage model, describes the standard sequence of stages groups pass through: forming, storming, norming, performing, and adjourning. Through these stages, group members learn how to settle conflicts and develop norms, which enable them to perform. The second, the punctuated-equilibrium model, describes the pattern of development specific to temporary groups with deadlines. In this model, the group shows two great periods of activity. The first peak in activity takes place after the midpoint of the project, a time in which the team performs at a higher level than it did previously. The second peak in activity takes place right before the project comes due.

3 **How do we create effective teams?**   For teams to be effective, careful consideration must be given to resources, the team's composition, work design, and process variables. The four contextual factors that appear to be most significantly related to team performance are the presence of adequate resources, effective leadership, a climate of trust, and a performance evaluation and reward system that reflects team contributions. Effective teams are neither too large nor too small—typically they range in size from five to nine people. They have members who fill role demands, are flexible, and who prefer to be part of a group. Teams will be more effective if members have freedom and autonomy to do their tasks and believe that the task will have a substantial impact on others. Finally, effective teams have members committed to a common purpose and specific team goals.

4 **How do virtual teams work?**   Virtual teams can do many of the same things face-to-face teams can, but they have more challenges, especially when it comes to team-member bonding and building trust. To help build understanding among teammates, members should provide some personal information early on, and they should also be clear on one another's roles from the outset. Researchers have found that virtual teams with members who have positive attitudes do better than teams with pessimistic members. Often, virtual teams communicate, discuss ideas, post work-in-progress, and exchange feedback through a virtual workspace via an intranet, website, or bulletin board.

5 **Are teams always the answer?**   Teams are not necessarily appropriate in every situation. How do you know if the work of your group would be better done in teams? It's been suggested that three tests be applied to see if a team fits the situation: (1) Can the work be done better by more than one person? (2) Does the work create a common purpose or set of goals for the people in the group that is more than the sum of individual goals? and (3) Are the members of the group interdependent? This third test asks whether the success of the whole depends on the success of each one *and* the success of each one depends on the success of the others.

OB at Work

for Review

1. How can teams increase employee motivation?

2. Describe the five-stage model of group development.

3. Describe the punctuated-equilibrium model of group development.

4. What are the characteristics of an effective team?

5. How can team members harm their team?

6. What is the difference between task-oriented roles and maintenance roles?

7. What are the effects of team size on performance?

8. How can a team minimize social loafing?

9. Contrast virtual and face-to-face teams.

10. What conditions favour creating a team, rather than letting an individual perform a given task?

for Critical Thinking

1. How could you use the punctuated-equilibrium model to better understand team behaviour?

2. Have you experienced social loafing as a team member? What did you do to prevent this problem?

3. Would you prefer to work alone or as part of a team? Why? How do you think your answer compares with that of others in your class?

4. What effect, if any, do you think workforce diversity has on a team's performance and satisfaction?

for You

■ Know that you will be asked to work on teams and groups both during your post-secondary years and later on in life, so understanding how teams work is an important skill to have.

■ Think about the roles that you play on teams. Teams need task-oriented people to get the job done, but they also need maintenance-oriented people who help keep people working together and feeling committed to the team.

■ Help your team set specific, measurable, realistic goals, as this leads to more successful outcomes.

POINT

Sports Teams Are Good Models for Workplace Teams

Studies from hockey, football, soccer, basketball, and baseball have found a number of elements in successful sports teams that can be applied to successful work teams.[86]

Goals foster team cohesion. A study of basketball teams found that while those that set team goals and those that did not had similar levels of cohesion when the season began, those with goals were more cohesive at the end of the season.

Successful teams score early wins. Early successes build teammates' faith in themselves and their capacity as a team. For instance, research on hockey teams of relatively equal ability found that 72 percent of the time the team that was ahead at the end of the first period went on to win the game. So managers should provide teams with early tasks that are simple and provide "easy wins."

Successful teams avoid losing streaks. A couple of failures can lead to a downward spiral if a team becomes demoralized and believes it is helpless to end its losing streak. Managers need to instill the confidence in team members that they can turn things around when they encounter setbacks.

Practice makes perfect. Successful sports teams execute on game day but learn from their mistakes in practice. A wise manager carves out time and space in which work teams can experiment and learn.

Successful teams use halftime breaks. The best coaches in basketball and football use halftime during a game to reassess what is working and what is not. Managers of work teams should build in similar assessments at about the halfway point in a team project to evaluate how the team can improve.

Being slightly behind can be motivating. A recent study of 6572 NCAA basketball games revealed that the team slightly behind at halftime won more games than it lost. Teams that are slightly ahead may suffer from "victory disease" by relaxing and trying not to lose, whereas those slightly behind may be more motivated.

Winning teams have a stable membership. Studies of professional basketball teams have found that the more stable a team's membership, the more likely the team is to win. The more time teammates have together, the more able they are to anticipate one another's moves and the clearer they are about one another's roles.

COUNTERPOINT

Sports Teams Are Not the Model for All Teams

There are flaws in using sports as a model for developing effective work teams. Here are five caveats.

All sports teams are not alike. In baseball, for instance, there is little interaction among teammates. Rarely are more than two or three players directly involved in a play. The performance of the team is largely the sum of the performance of its individual players. In contrast, basketball has much more interdependence among players: Team members are densely clustered and must switch from offence to defence at a moment's notice. The performance of the team is more than the sum of its individual players. So when using sports teams as a model for work teams, be sure you are making the correct comparison.

Work teams are more varied and complex. In an athletic league, the design of the task, the design of the team, and the team's context vary relatively little from team to team. But these variables can differ greatly between work teams. As a result, coaching plays a much more significant part in a sports team's performance than a work team's. Performance of work teams is a function of getting the team's structural and design variables right. Managers of work teams should focus more on getting the team set up for success than on coaching.

A lot of employees cannot relate to sports metaphors. Not everyone on work teams is conversant with sports. Team members from different cultures also may not know the sports metaphors you are using. Moreover, different cultures view the team metaphor differently. In Latin America, the work team is considered a family. "Families are involved in all parts of your life, and are expected to celebrate with you socially. Your involvement in your sports team is more limited. Less caretaking, more competitive."[87]

Work team outcomes are not easily defined in terms of wins and losses. Sports teams usually measure success in terms of wins and losses. Success is rarely as clear or black and white for work teams.

Sports team metaphors oversimplify. Sports team metaphors simplify a complicated world. While such shortcuts hold an intuitive appeal, we also have to recognize that rather than expanding our minds to the full range of possibilities, sports metaphors reduce and simplify—not something to recommend to the enlightened manager.

How Good Am I at Building and Leading a Team?

Use the following rating scale to respond to the 18 questions on building and leading an effective team:

Strongly Disagree	Disagree	Slightly Disagree	Slightly Agree	Agree	Strongly Agree
1	2	3	4	5	6

1. I am knowledgeable about the different stages of development that teams can go through in their life cycles.   1 2 3 4 5 6

2. When a team forms, I make certain that all team members are introduced to one another at the outset.   1 2 3 4 5 6

3. When the team first comes together, I provide directions, answer team members' questions, and clarify goals, expectations, and procedures.   1 2 3 4 5 6

4. I help team members establish a foundation of trust among themselves and between themselves and me.   1 2 3 4 5 6

5. I ensure that standards of excellence, not mediocrity or mere acceptability, characterize the team's work.   1 2 3 4 5 6

6. I provide a great deal of feedback to team members regarding their performance.   1 2 3 4 5 6

7. I encourage team members to balance individual autonomy with interdependence among other team members.   1 2 3 4 5 6

8. I help team members become at least as committed to the success of the team as to their own personal success.   1 2 3 4 5 6

9. I help team members learn to play roles that assist the team in accomplishing its tasks, as well as building strong interpersonal relationships.   1 2 3 4 5 6

10. I articulate a clear, exciting, passionate vision of what the team can achieve.   1 2 3 4 5 6

11. I help team members become committed to the team vision.   1 2 3 4 5 6

12. I encourage a win-win philosophy in the team; that is, when one member wins, every member wins.   1 2 3 4 5 6

13. I help the team avoid making the group's survival more important than accomplishing its goal.   1 2 3 4 5 6

14. I use formal process-management procedures to help the group become faster, more efficient, and more productive, and to prevent errors.   1 2 3 4 5 6

15. I encourage team members to represent the team's vision, goals, and accomplishments to outsiders.   1 2 3 4 5 6

16. I diagnose and capitalize on the team's core competence.   1 2 3 4 5 6

17. I encourage the team to achieve dramatic breakthrough innovations, as well as small continuous improvements.   1 2 3 4 5 6

18. I help the team work toward preventing mistakes, not just correcting them after the fact.   1 2 3 4 5 6

Scoring Key:

This instrument assesses team development behaviours in five areas: diagnosing team development (items 1, 16); managing the forming stage (items 2–4); managing the storming stage (items 10–12, 14, 15); managing the norming stage (items 6–9, 13); and managing the performing stage (items 5, 17, 18). Add up your score. Your total score will range between 18 and 108.

OB at work

LEARNING ABOUT **YOURSELF** EXERCISE (Continued)

Based on a norm group of 500 business students, the following can help estimate where you are relative to others:

95 or above = You are in the top quartile of being able to build and lead a team

72–94 = You are in the second quartile

60–71 = You are in the third quartile

Below 60 = You are in the bottom quartile

Source: Adapted from D. A. Whetten and K. S. Cameron, *Developing Management Skills,* 3rd ed. © 1995, pp. 534–535. Adapted by permission of Pearson Education, Inc., Upper Saddle River, NJ.

PERSONAL INVENTORY ASSESSMENT

Team Development Behaviours: This self-assessment is designed to help you better understand the contributions you make to building effective teams and teamwork.

Diagnosing the Need for Team Building: Team cohesion is important for optimal team functioning. Use this scale to determine if team-building activities would benefit your group.

Positive Practices Survey: This diagnostic instrument helps you identify the behaviours that are typical of the very highest performing teams and organizations.

BREAKOUT **GROUP** EXERCISES

Form small groups to discuss the following topics, as assigned by your instructor:

1. One of the members of your team continually arrives late for meetings and does not turn drafts of assignments in on time. In general, this group member is engaging in social loafing. What can the members of your group do to reduce social loafing?

2. Consider a team with which you have worked. Using the information in Exhibit 5-6 on page 173, consider whether there were more task-oriented or maintenance-oriented roles in the group. What impact did this have on the group's performance?

3. Identify 4 or 5 norms that a team could put into place near the beginning of its life to help it function better over time.

WORKING WITH OTHERS EXERCISE

The Paper Tower Exercise

Step 1   Each group will receive 20 index cards, 12 paper clips, and 2 marking pens. Groups have 10 minutes to plan a paper tower that will be judged on the basis of 3 criteria: height, stability, and beauty. No physical work (building) is allowed during this planning period.

Step 2   Each group has 15 minutes for the actual construction of the paper tower.

Step 3   Each tower will be identified by a number assigned by your instructor. Each student is to individually examine all the paper towers. Your group is then to come to a consensus as to which tower is the winner (5 minutes). A spokesperson from your group should report its decision and the criteria the group used in reaching it.

Step 4   In your small groups, discuss the following questions (your instructor may choose to have you discuss only a subset of these questions):

    a. What percentage of the plan did each member of your group contribute, on average?

    b. Did your group have a leader? Why or why not?

WORKING WITH OTHERS EXERCISE (Continued)

c. How did the group generally respond to the ideas that were expressed during the planning period?

d. To what extent did your group follow the five-stage model of group development?

e. List specific behaviours exhibited during the planning and building sessions that you felt were helpful to the group. Explain why you found them helpful.

f. List specific behaviours exhibited during the planning and building sessions that you felt were dysfunctional to the group. Explain why you found them dysfunctional.

Source: This exercise is based on *The Paper Tower Exercise: Experiencing Leadership and Group Dynamics*, by Phillip L. Hunsaker and Johanna S. Hunsaker, unpublished manuscript. A brief description is included in "Exchange," *Organizational Behavior Teaching Journal* 4, no. 2 (1979), p. 49. Reprinted by permission of the authors. The materials list was suggested by Professor Sally Maitlis, Sauder School of Business, University of British Columbia.

ETHICAL DILEMMA EXERCISE

Dealing with Shirkers

We have noted that one of the most common problems in groups is social loafing, which means group members contribute less than if they were working on their own. We might call such individuals "shirkers"—those who are contributing far less than other group members.

Most of us have experienced social loafing, or shirking, in groups. And we may even admit to times when we shirked ourselves. We discussed earlier in the chapter some ways of discouraging social loafing, such as limiting group size, holding individuals responsible for their contributions, and setting group goals. While these tactics may be effective, in our experience, many students simply work around shirkers. "We just did it ourselves—it was easier that way," says one group member.

Consider the following questions for dealing with shirking in groups:

1. If group members end up "working around" shirkers, do you think this information should be communicated to the instructor so that this individual's contribution to the project is judged more fairly? If so, does the group have an ethical responsibility to communicate this to the shirking group member? If not, isn't the shirking group member unfairly reaping the rewards of a "free ride"?

2. Do you think confronting the shirking group member is justified? Does this depend on the skills of the shirker (whether he or she is capable of doing good-quality work)?

3. Social loafing has been found to be higher in Western, more individualist nations than in other countries. Do you think this means we should tolerate shirking on the part of North American workers to a greater degree than if it occurred with someone from Asia?

CASE INCIDENT

Toyota's Team Culture

Many companies proudly promote their team culture. At Toyota, the promotion seems sincere.[88]

Teamwork is one of Toyota's core values, along with trust, continuous improvement, long-term thinking, standardization, innovation, and problem solving. The firm's value statement says the following: "To ensure the success of our company, each team member has the responsibility to work together, and communicate honestly, share ideas, and ensure team member understanding."

So how does Toyota's culture reflect its emphasis on teamwork?

First, although individualism is a prominent value in Western culture, it is deemphasized at Toyota. In its place is an emphasis on systems, in which people and products are seen as intertwined value streams and people are trained to be problem solvers so as to make the product system leaner and better.

Second, before hiring, Toyota tests candidates to ensure they are not only competent and technically skilled but also oriented toward teamwork—able to trust their team, be comfortable solving problems collaboratively, and motivated to achieve collective outcomes.

OB at work

CASE INCIDENT (Continued)

Third, and not surprisingly, Toyota structures its work around teams. Every Toyota employee knows the adage "All of us are smarter than any of us." Teams are used not only in the production process but also at every level and in every function: in sales and marketing, in finance, in engineering, in design, and at the executive level.

Fourth, Toyota considers the team to be the power centre of the organization. The leader serves the team, not the other way around. When asked whether he would feature himself in advertisements the way other automakers had (most famously, "Dr. Z," Daimler's CEO Dieter Zetsche), Toyota USA's CEO, Yuki Funo, said, "No. We want to show everybody in the company. The heroes. Not one single person."

Questions

1. Do you think Toyota has succeeded because of its team-oriented culture, or do you think it would have succeeded without it?

2. Do you think you would be comfortable working in Toyota's culture? Why or why not?

3. In response to the recession and the firm's first-ever quarterly loss, Toyota's managers accepted a 10 percent pay cut in 2009 to avoid employee layoffs. Do you think such a response is a good means of promoting camaraderie? What are the risks in such a plan?

4. Recently, DCH Group, a company comprising 33 auto dealerships, decided to adapt Toyota's culture to its own, particularly its emphasis on teamwork. DCH's CEO, Susan Scarola, said, "Trying to bring it down to day-to-day operations is tough. It was not something that everybody immediately embraced, even at the senior level." Do you think the culture will work in what is typically the dog-eat-dog world of auto dealerships? Why or why not?

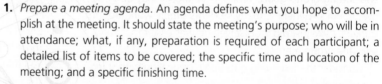

FROM CONCEPTS TO SKILLS

Conducting a Team Meeting

Team meetings have a reputation for inefficiency. For instance, noted Canadian-born economist John Kenneth Galbraith has said, "Meetings are indispensable when you don't want to do anything."

When you are responsible for conducting a meeting, what can you do to make it more efficient and effective? Follow these 12 steps:[89]

1. *Prepare a meeting agenda.* An agenda defines what you hope to accomplish at the meeting. It should state the meeting's purpose; who will be in attendance; what, if any, preparation is required of each participant; a detailed list of items to be covered; the specific time and location of the meeting; and a specific finishing time.

2. *Distribute the agenda in advance.* Participants should have the agenda far enough in advance that they can adequately prepare for the meeting.

3. *Consult with participants before the meeting.* An unprepared participant cannot contribute to his or her full potential. It is your responsibility to ensure that members are prepared, so check with them ahead of time.

4. *Get participants to go over the agenda.* The first thing to do at the meeting is to have participants review the agenda, make any changes, and then approve the final agenda.

5. *Establish specific time limits.* Meetings should begin on time and have a specific time for completion. It is your responsibility to specify these times and to hold to them.

6. *Maintain focused discussion.* It is your responsibility to give direction to the discussion; to keep it focused on the issues; and to minimize interruptions, disruptions, and irrelevant comments.

7. *Encourage and support participation of all members.* To maximize the effectiveness of problem-oriented meetings, each participant must be encouraged to contribute. Quiet or reserved personalities need to be drawn out so their ideas can be heard.

8. *Maintain a balanced style*. The effective group leader pushes when necessary and is passive when need be.
9. *Encourage the clash of ideas*. You need to encourage different points of view, critical thinking, and constructive disagreement.
10. *Discourage the clash of personalities*. An effective meeting is characterized by the critical assessment of ideas, not attacks on people. When running a meeting, you must quickly intercede to stop personal attacks or other forms of verbal insult.
11. *Be an effective listener*. You need to listen with intensity, empathy, and objectivity, and do whatever is necessary to get the full intended meaning from each participant's comments.
12. *Bring proper closure*. You should close a meeting by summarizing the group's accomplishments; clarifying what actions, if any, need to follow the meeting; and allocating follow-up assignments. If any decisions are made, you also need to determine who will be responsible for communicating and implementing them.

Practising Skills

Jameel Saumur is the leader of a five-member project team that has been assigned the task of moving his engineering firm into the booming area of high-speed intercity rail construction. Saumur and his team members have been researching the field, identifying specific business opportunities, negotiating alliances with equipment vendors, and evaluating high-speed rail experts and consultants from around the world. Throughout the process, Tonya Eckler, a highly qualified and respected engineer, has challenged a number of things Saumur has said during team meetings and in the workplace. For example, at a meeting two weeks ago, Saumur presented the team with a list of 10 possible high-speed rail projects and started evaluating the company's ability to compete for them. Eckler contradicted virtually all of Saumur's comments, questioned his statistics, and was quite pessimistic about the possibility of getting contracts on these projects. After this latest display of displeasure, two other group members, Bryan Worth and Maggie Ames, are complaining that Eckler's actions are damaging the team's effectiveness. Eckler was originally assigned to the team for her unique expertise and insight. If you had to advise this team, what suggestions would you make to get the team on the right track to achieve its fullest potential?

Reinforcing Skills

1. Interview three managers from different organizations. Ask them about their experiences in managing teams. Have each describe teams that they thought were effective and why they succeeded. Have each also describe teams that they thought were ineffective and the reasons that might have caused this.
2. Contrast a team you have been in in which members trusted one another with another team you have been in in which members lacked trust in one another. How did the conditions in each team develop? What were the consequences in terms of interaction patterns and performance?

CHAPTER 6

Communication, Conflict, and Negotiation

How can a nonprofit organization better use communication to convince its community to invest more in girls' hockey?

PART 3
INTERACTING
EFFECTIVELY

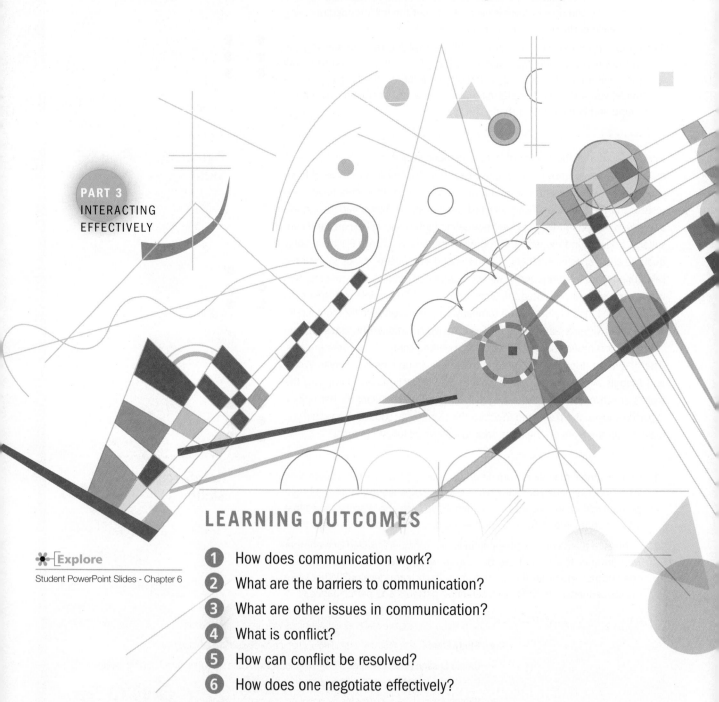

✴ Explore

Student PowerPoint Slides - Chapter 6

LEARNING OUTCOMES

1. How does communication work?
2. What are the barriers to communication?
3. What are other issues in communication?
4. What is conflict?
5. How can conflict be resolved?
6. How does one negotiate effectively?

Ted Reeve Arena, one of 48 community arenas owned by the city of Toronto, is run by a volunteer board that decides how to allocate ice time to hockey leagues in the community.[1] Players and coaches from the Toronto Leaside Girls Hockey Association (TLGHA) felt they received limited access to the arena, especially compared with some other leagues. This was costing the Association an average of $200 000 in fees to rent ice time elsewhere. In the fall of 2009, TLGHA decided to fight back and launched an extensive communication campaign to let the community know about its concerns. The main goal was to force the City of Toronto to enforce its ice allocation policy at all publicly owned arenas.

In developing its communication campaign, the TLGHA carefully considered its target audience: the city's then mayor David Miller; members of Toronto city council; the TLGHA players and their families and fans; and the news media. The intent was to communicate effectively with these different groups to gain their support.

In this chapter we explore the foundations of communication and then consider the effects of communication on conflict and negotiation.

THE BIG IDEA

Real communication requires feedback (both giving it and seeking it). Resolving conflicts and engaging in successful negotiations requires understanding your objectives and the objectives of the other party.

OB IS FOR EVERYONE

- What information should be sent by which communication channel?
- Does body language really make a difference?
- How can you communicate better when you are stressed out?
- Ever notice that communicating via email can lead to misunderstandings?
- What factors hinder cross-cultural communication?
- Is conflict always bad?
- Should you try to win at any cost when you bargain?

LEARNING ABOUT YOURSELF

- Conflict Handling

① How does
   communication work?

The Communication Process

Individuals spend nearly 70 percent of their waking hours communicating—writing, reading, speaking, listening—which means that they have many opportunities in which to engage in poor communication. Communication is an important consideration for organizations and individuals alike. Communication is a foundation for many things that happen among groups and within the workplace—from motivating, to providing information, to controlling behaviour, to expressing emotion. Good communication skills are very important to your career success. A recent study of recruiters found that they rated communication skills as *the* most important characteristic of an ideal job candidate.[2]

No group can exist without **communication**, which is the transfer and understanding of a message between two or more people. Communication can be thought of as a process, or flow, as shown in Exhibit 6-1. The *sender* initiates a message by encoding a thought. The *message* is the actual physical product of the sender's *encoding*. When we speak, the speech is the message. When we write, the writing is the message. When we gesture, the movements of our arms and the expressions on our faces are the message. The *channel* is the medium through which the message travels. The sender selects it, determining whether to use a formal or informal channel. **Formal channels** are established by the organization and transmit messages related to the professional activities of members. They traditionally follow the authority chain within the organization. Other forms of messages, such as personal or social, follow **informal channels**, which are spontaneous and emerge as a response to individual choices.[3] The *receiver* is the person(s) to whom the message is directed, who must first translate the symbols into understandable form. This step is the *decoding* of the message. *Noise* represents communication barriers that distort the clarity of the message, such as perceptual problems, information overload, semantic difficulties, or cultural differences. The final link in the communication process is a feedback loop. *Feedback* is the check on how successful we have been in transferring our messages as originally intended. It determines whether understanding has been achieved.

The model indicates that communication is both an interactive and iterative process. The sender has to keep in mind the receiver (or audience), and in finalizing the communication may decide to revisit decisions about the message, the encoding, and/or the feedback.

> What information should be sent by which communication channel?

⚹ Explore

Exhibit 6-1: The Communication
Process Model

communication The transfer and
understanding of a message between
two or more people.

formal channels Communication
channels established by an organization to transmit messages related to
the professional activities of
members.

informal channels Communication
channels that are created spontane-
ously and that emerge as responses
to individual choices.

channel The medium through which
a message travels.

Choosing a Channel

The **channel** is the medium through which a message travels. It is selected by the source, who must determine which

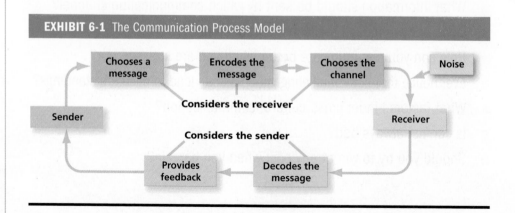

EXHIBIT 6-1 The Communication Process Model

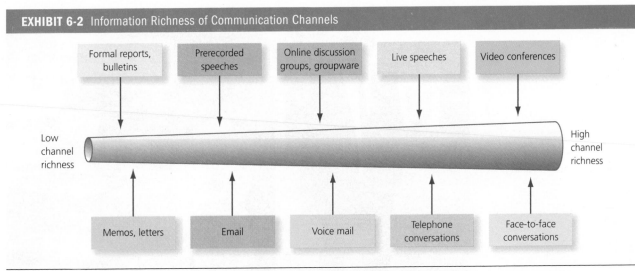

EXHIBIT 6-2 Information Richness of Communication Channels

Source: From Daft. *Organizational Behavior*, 1E. © 2001 South-Western, a part of Cengage Learning, Inc. Reproduced by permission. www.cengage.com/permissions.

channel is formal and which one is informal. Examples of channels include formal memos, voice mail, email, and meetings. Choosing a poor channel, or one with a high noise level, can distort communication.

Why do people choose one channel of communication over another; for instance, a phone call instead of a face-to-face talk? One answer might be anxiety! An estimated 5 to 20 percent of the population suffers from debilitating **communication apprehension**, or anxiety, which is undue tension and anxiety about oral communication, written communication, or both.[4] We all know people who dread speaking in front of a group, but some people may find it extremely difficult to talk with others face to face or become extremely anxious when they have to use the telephone. As a result, they may rely on memos, letters, or email to convey messages when a phone call would not only be faster but also more appropriate.

But what about the 80 to 95 percent of the population who don't suffer from this problem? Is there any general insight we might be able to provide regarding choice of communication channel? The answer is a qualified "yes." A model of media richness has been developed to explain channel selection among managers.[5]

Research has found that channels differ in their capacity to convey information. Some are rich in that they have the ability to (1) handle multiple cues at the same time, (2) allow rapid feedback, and (3) be very personal. Others are lean in that they score low on these three factors. As Exhibit 6-2 illustrates, face-to-face conversation scores highest in terms of **channel richness** because it provides for the maximum amount of information to be transmitted during a communication episode. That is, it offers multiple information cues (words, postures, facial expressions, gestures, intonations), immediate feedback (both verbal and nonverbal), and the personal touch of "being there." Impersonal written media such as formal reports and bulletins rate lowest in richness. Mississauga, Ontario-based Phonak Canada, a manufacturer of advanced hearing systems, holds monthly town-hall meetings for all staff. The firm shares information, introduces new employees, and recognizes notable achievements. It provides an opportunity to make sure that everyone in the company is on the same page.[6]

Two students were suspended from class for choosing YouTube, a very rich channel, to distribute their message. Their actions also raised concerns about privacy in the classroom, as *Focus on Ethics* reveals.

 Explore

Exhibit 6-2: Information Richness of Communication Channels

communication apprehension Undue tension and anxiety about oral communication, written communication, or both.

channel richness The amount of information that can be transmitted during a communication episode.

According to Rob Sobey, president of Lawtons Drugs, a memo never motivates. It can thank and compliment, but in a true crisis, you need to hold a town hall meeting to communicate seminal information. Use of a rich communication channel to communicate a nonroutine message is more likely to be successful.

FOCUS ON ETHICS

YouTube's Darker Side

Is it okay for students to post a teacher's outburst on YouTube? Two grade 9 students from École Secondaire Mont-Bleu in Gatineau, Quebec, were suspended from school after teachers discovered a video the students had posted on YouTube.[7] One of the students provoked the teacher during class time while the other secretly taped the scene for about 50 minutes with a compact digital camera.

The students, who have academic problems, were in a special-education class. The teacher had 33 years of experience and specialized in teaching students with learning disabilities. After the incident, the teacher went on sick leave, and his union said, "He is so embarrassed that he may never return to class."

There was no apparent explanation for why the students decided to provoke and then film the teacher. Other students have said that "the teacher was good at helping them improve their grades."

"I think students are just trying to embarrass the teachers they don't like," school board president Jocelyn Blondin said. "In the future, students will have to keep their cellphones in their pockets and use them outside of class," she predicted shortly after the incident.

Teachers and school boards are trying to determine strategies for handling these kinds of events in classrooms. The Gatineau school no longer allows personal electronic devices in the classroom. In Ontario, changes to the Safe Schools Act made in 2007 state that students who engage in online bullying are to be suspended from classes. ●

The choice of one channel over another depends on whether the message is routine or nonroutine. Routine messages tend to be straightforward and have a minimum of ambiguity. Nonroutine messages are likely to be complicated and have the potential for misunderstandings. Individuals can communicate routine messages efficiently through channels that are lower in richness. However, they can communicate nonroutine messages more effectively by selecting rich channels. Evidence indicates that high-performing managers tend to be more media-sensitive than low-performing managers.[8] In other words, they are better able to match appropriate media richness with the ambiguity involved in the communication. Rob Sobey, president of the Dartmouth, Nova Scotia-based Lawtons Drugs chain, knows that memos don't help in a crisis when staff morale needs boosting. "A memo never motivates. A memo can thank and compliment, but you need the town hall meeting [in a true crisis]. You have to put yourself out there in the flesh."[9]

One study found that managers preferred delivering bad news (layoffs, promotion denials, and negative feedback) via email, and that the messages were delivered more accurately this way. However, sending negative information through email is generally not recommended. One of the co-authors of the study noted that "offering negative comments face-to-face is often taken as a sign that the news is important and the deliverer cares about the recipient."[10] It appears that a CEO's use of a channel relatively low in richness (email) to convey a nonroutine and complex message did a lot of harm to his company, as this *OB in the Workplace* shows.

in the WORKPLACE
Some Emails Should Be Left Unsent

Is email the best way to communicate sensitive messages? Neal L. Patterson, CEO at medical software maker Cerner Corp., likes email.[11] Maybe too much so. Upset with his staff's work ethic, he sent a seething email to his firm's 400 managers. Here are some of its highlights:

> Hell will freeze over before this CEO implements ANOTHER EMPLOYEE benefit in this Culture. . . . We are getting less than 40 hours of work from a large number of our Kansas City-based employees. The parking lot is sparsely used at 8 a.m.; likewise at 5 p.m. As managers—you either do not know what your EMPLOYEES are doing; or YOU do not CARE. . . . You have a problem and you will fix it or I will replace you. . . . What you are doing, as managers, with this company makes me SICK.

Patterson's email suggested managers schedule meetings at 7:00 a.m., 6:00 p.m., and Saturday mornings; promised a staff reduction of 5 percent and the institution of a time-clock system; and announced his intention to charge unapproved absences to employees' vacation time.

Within hours, copies of the email had made their way onto a Yahoo! website. And within 3 days, Cerner's stock price had plummeted 22 percent. Although we can wonder whether such harsh criticism should be communicated at all, one thing is clear: Patterson erred by selecting the wrong channel for his message. Such an emotional and sensitive message might have been better received in a face-to-face meeting. ●

The media richness model is consistent with organizational trends and practices of the past decade. It is not just coincidence that more and more senior managers have been using meetings to facilitate communication and regularly leaving the isolated sanctuary of their executive offices to manage by walking around. These executives are relying on richer channels of communication to transmit the more ambiguous messages they need to convey. The past decade has been characterized by organizations closing facilities, imposing large layoffs, restructuring, merging, consolidating, and introducing new products and services at an accelerated pace—all nonroutine messages high in ambiguity and requiring the use of channels that can convey a large amount of information. It is not surprising, therefore, to see the most effective managers expanding their use of rich channels.

Barriers to Effective Communication

 2 What are the barriers to communication?

When the Toronto Leaside Girls Hockey Association (TLGHA) decided to launch its campaign to get more ice time, it faced significant challenges.[12] There were sexist attitudes toward girls' and women's hockey to overcome. As Ward 30 councillor Paula Fletcher noted, the anti-female attitudes were "left over from the past" and "need[ed] to change. It's just shocking that in this day and age, girls' hockey is being treated so poorly."

Because of such difficulties, the communication team for TLGHA had to consider the best way to deliver the message of change. Approaching the volunteer-run boards of the arenas appeared to be a good strategy, as the problem was a city-wide issue. Therefore, the association threatened to launch a human-rights complaint against the city in a letter sent to the mayor. What factors would the communication team have considered to ensure their concerns were heard?

PERSONAL INVENTORY ASSESSMENT

Learn About Yourself
Communicating Supportively

A number of factors have been identified as barriers to communication. This section presents the most prominent ones.

Filtering

Filtering occurs when a sender manipulates information so that the receiver will view it more favourably. For example, when a manager tells a senior executive what the manager thinks the executive wants to hear, the manager is filtering information. The more vertical levels in the organization's hierarchy, the more opportunities there are for filtering. But some filtering will occur wherever there are status differences. Factors such as fear of conveying bad news and the desire to please the boss often lead employees to tell their superiors what they think they want to hear, thus distorting upward communications.

Selective Perception

Receivers in the communication process selectively see and hear based on their needs, motivations, experience, background, and other personal characteristics. Receivers also project their interests and expectations into communications as they decode them. For example, the employment interviewer who believes that young people are more interested in spending time on leisure and social activities than working extra hours to further their careers is likely to be influenced by that stereotype when interviewing young job applicants. As we discussed in Chapter 2, we don't see reality; rather, we interpret what we see and call it "reality." A 2011 study found that people perceived that they communicated better with people with whom they were close (friends and partners) than with strangers. However, in ambiguous conversations, it turned out that their ability to communicate with close friends was no better than their ability to communicate with strangers.[13]

Defensiveness

When people feel that they are being threatened, they tend to react in ways that reduce their ability to achieve mutual understanding. That is, they become defensive—engaging in behaviours such as verbally attacking others, making sarcastic remarks, being overly judgmental, and questioning others' motives. So when individuals interpret another's message as threatening, they often respond in ways that hinder effective communication.

Emotions

You may interpret the same message differently when you are angry or distraught than when you are happy. Extreme emotions such as jubilation or depression are most likely to hinder effective communication. In such instances, we are most prone to disregard our rational and objective thinking processes and substitute emotional judgments.

filtering A sender's manipulation of information so that it will be seen more favourably by the receiver.

Information Overload

Individuals have a finite capacity for processing data. When the information we have to work with exceeds our ability to process it, the result is **information overload**. With emails, phone calls, text messages, meetings, and the need to keep current in one's field, more and more employees are suffering from too much information. The information can be distracting as well. A recent study of employees who have tracking software on their computers found that they clicked on their email program more than 50 times in the course of a day, and used instant messaging 77 times. The study also found that on average, employees visited 40 websites during the workday.[14]

What happens when individuals have more information than they can sort out and use? They tend to select out, ignore, pass over, or forget information. Or they may put off further processing until the overload situation is over. Regardless, the result is lost information and less effective communication.

Language

Even when we are communicating in the same language, words mean different things to different people. Age and context are two of the biggest factors that influence such differences.

When Michael Schiller, a business consultant, was talking with his 15-year-old daughter about where she was going with her friends, he told her, "You need to recognize your ARAs and measure against them." Schiller said that in response, his daughter "looked at him like he was from outer space." (For the record, *ARA* stands for accountability, responsibility, and authority.) Those new to corporate lingo may find acronyms such as *ARA*, words such as *skeds* (schedules), and phrases such as *bake your noodle* (provide a service) bewildering, in the same way parents may be mystified by teen slang.[15]

In short, our use of language is far from uniform. If we knew how each of us modified the language, we could minimize communication difficulties, but we usually don't know. Senders tend to assume that the words and terms they use mean the same to the receiver as to them.

Call-centre operators at Convergys Corp. in New Delhi, India, speak English in serving their customers from North America and the United Kingdom. But even though the operators and customers speak a common language, communication barriers exist because of differences in the countries' cultures and language accents. To overcome these barriers, the operators receive training in North American and British pop culture so they can make small talk and are taught to speak with Western accents so they can be more easily understood by the calling clients.

information overload The state of having more information than one can process.

Silence

It's easy to ignore silence or lack of communication, precisely because it is defined by the absence of information. However, research suggests silence and withholding communication are both common and problematic.[16] One survey found over 85 percent of managers reported remaining silent about at least one issue of significant concern.[17] Employee silence means managers lack information about ongoing operational problems. Moreover, silence regarding discrimination, harassment, corruption, and misconduct means top management cannot take action to eliminate this behaviour. Finally, employees who are silent about important issues may also experience psychological stress.

A study looking at the human factors that caused airline accidents found that pilots who had "take charge" attitudes with their crews were more likely to make wrong decisions than pilots who were more inclusive and consulted with their crews before deciding what to do.[18] It was the communication style of the pilot that affected the crew's behaviour. Crew members were not willing to intervene, even when they had necessary information, when they regularly worked under "decisive" pilots. That kind of silence can be fatal. In his book *Outliers*, Malcolm Gladwell noted, "The kinds of errors that cause plane crashes are invariably errors of teamwork and communication. One pilot knows something important and somehow doesn't tell the other pilot."[19]

Silence is less likely where minority opinions are treated with respect, work group identification is high, and high procedural justice prevails.[20] Practically, this means managers must make sure they behave in a supportive manner when employees voice divergent opinions or express concerns, and they must take these concerns under advisement. One act of ignoring or belittling an employee for expressing concerns may well lead the employee to withhold important information in the future.

Professors Craig Pinder of the Peter B. Gustavson School of Business at the University of Victoria and Karen Harlos of the Desautels Faculty of Management at McGill University have noted that silence generally has often been thought to represent *inaction* or *nonbehaviour*, much as we saw with the airline pilots. But silence is not necessarily inaction, nor a failure to communicate. Silence can, in fact, be a powerful form of communication.[21] It can mean a person is thinking or contemplating a response to a question. It can mean a person is anxious and fearful of speaking. It can signal agreement, dissent, frustration, or anger.

Failing to pay close attention to the silent portion of a conversation can result in missing a vital part of the message. Astute communicators watch for gaps, pauses, and hesitations. They hear and interpret silence. They treat pauses, for instance, as analogous to a flashing yellow light at an intersection—they pay attention to what comes next. Is the person thinking, deciding how to frame an answer? Is the person suffering from communication apprehension? Sometimes the real message in a communication is buried in the silence.

Nonverbal Communication

Every time we deliver a verbal message, we also impart a nonverbal message.[22] Sometimes the nonverbal component may stand alone. Anyone who has ever paid a visit to a singles bar or a nightclub is aware that communication need not be verbal to convey a message. A glance, a stare, a smile, a frown, a provocative body movement—they all convey meaning. This example illustrates that no discussion of communication would be complete without considering **nonverbal communication**. This type of communication includes body movements, facial expressions, and the physical distance between the sender and receiver.

Does body language really make a difference?

nonverbal communication Messages conveyed through body movements, facial expressions, and the physical distance between the sender and receiver.

It has been argued that every body movement has a meaning and that no movement is accidental.[23] Through body language, we can say such things as, "Help me, I'm confused," or "Leave me alone, I'm really angry." Rarely do we send our messages consciously. We act out our state of being with nonverbal body language, even if we are not aware of doing so. We lift one eyebrow for disbelief. We rub our noses for puzzlement. We clasp our arms to isolate ourselves or to protect ourselves. We shrug our shoulders for indifference, wink one eye for intimacy, tap our fingers for impatience, slap our forehead for forgetfulness.[24]

The two most important messages that body language conveys are (1) the extent to which an individual likes another and is interested in his or her views and (2) the relative perceived status between a sender and receiver.[25] For instance, we are more likely to position ourselves closer to people we like and to touch them more often. Similarly, if you feel that you are of higher status than another, you are more likely to display body movements—such as crossed legs or a slouched seated position—that reflect a casual and relaxed manner.[26]

While we may disagree with the specific meaning of certain movements (and different cultures may interpret specific body movements differently), body language adds to and often complicates verbal communication. For instance, if you read the transcript of a meeting, you don't grasp the impact of what was said in the same way you would if you had been there or had seen the meeting on video. Why? There is no record of nonverbal communication. The *intonations,* or emphasis, given to words or phrases is missing.

The *facial expression* of a person also conveys meaning. A snarling face says something different from a smile. Facial expressions, along with intonations, can show arrogance, aggressiveness, fear, shyness, and other characteristics that would never be communicated if you read a transcript of the meeting.

The way individuals space themselves in terms of *physical distance,* commonly called **proxemics**, also has meaning. What is considered proper spacing is largely dependent on cultural norms. For instance, studies have shown that those from "contact" cultures (for example, Arabs, Latin Americans, southern Europeans) are more comfortable with body closeness and touch than those from "noncontact" cultures (for example, Asians, North Americans, northern Europeans).[27] These differences can lead to confusion. If someone stands closer to you than expected according to your cultural norms, you may interpret the action as an expression of aggressiveness or sexual interest. However, if the person stands farther away than you expect, you might think he or she is displeased with you or uninterested. Someone whose cultural norms differ from yours might be very surprised by your interpretation.

It's important for the receiver to be alert to these nonverbal aspects of communication. You should look for nonverbal cues, as well as listen to the literal meaning of a sender's words. In particular, you should be aware of contradictions between the messages. The manager may say that she is free to talk to you about that raise you have been seeking, but you may see nonverbal signals (such as looking at her watch) that suggest this is not the time to discuss the subject. It's not uncommon for people to express one emotion verbally and another nonverbally. These contradictions often suggest that actions speak louder (and more accurately) than words.

We should also monitor body language with some care. For instance, while it is often thought that people who cross their arms in front of their chest are showing resistance to a message, individuals might also do this if they are feeling cold, regardless of their reaction to a message.

How can you communicate better when you are stressed out?

Stress

One of the most difficult times to communicate properly is when one is under stress. One consultant has identified

proxemics The study of physical space in interpersonal relationships.

several tips for communicating under stress. These tips are also appropriate for encouraging less stressful communication.[28]

- *Speak clearly.* Be direct about what you want to say, and avoid hiding behind words. For instance, as difficult as it might be to say "You did not receive the position," the listener is better able to process the information when it is spoken that directly.

- *Be aware of the nonverbal part of communicating.* Tone, facial expression, and body language send signals that may or may not be consistent with your message. In a stressful situation, it is best to speak in a neutral manner.

- *Think carefully about how you state things.* In many situations, it is better to be restrained so that you don't offend your listener. For instance, when you threaten someone if they don't do exactly what you want ("I insist on speaking to your manager this minute"), you simply escalate the situation. It is better to state what you want calmly, so that you can be heard accurately.

Current Issues in Communication

3 What are other issues in communication?

How organizations communicate with their employees plays an important role in whether the employees actually hear the message. How have electronic communications changed the way people communicate with one another in organizations? Why do men and women often have difficulty communicating with each other? How can individuals improve their cross-cultural communication? We address each of these issues below.

Electronic Communications

An indispensable—and in about 71 percent of cases, the primary—medium of communication in today's organizations is electronic. Electronic communications—which include email, instant messaging, text messaging, social networking sites, and blogs—make it possible for you to work, even if you are away from your workstation.

Email

Email is now so pervasive that it's hard to imagine life without it. As a communication tool, email has a long list of benefits. Email messages can be quickly written, edited, and stored. They can be distributed to one person or thousands with a click of a mouse. They can be read, in their entirety, at the convenience of the recipient. And the cost of sending formal email messages to employees is a fraction of the cost of printing, duplicating, and distributing a comparable letter or brochure.[29]

Ever notice that communicating via email can lead to misunderstandings?

Email, of course, is not without drawbacks. Email has added considerably to the number of hours worked per week, according to a study by Christina Cavanagh, former professor of management communications at the Richard Ivey School of Business, University of Western Ontario.[30] One researcher suggests that knowledge workers devote about 28 percent of their day to email.[31] Over one-third of the survey respondents said they had trouble handling all of their email, and only 43 percent thought that email increased efficiency at work. The increase in the volume of corporate email seems to have slowed due to a rise in the use of instant messages and social networks,[32] but the volume of junk mail shows no let-up.[33] Canadians divert 42 percent of their email directly to junk mail folders, according to an Ipsos Reid study. There may be some relief in sight, however. Bill C-28, which passed in December 2010, is set to come into effect by 2013. It bans commercial emails (such as those soliciting clients) sent to individuals without their prior consent.

The following are some of the most significant limitations of email and what organizations should do to reduce or eliminate these problems:

- *Misinterpreting the message.* It's true that we often misinterpret verbal messages, but the potential for misinterpretation with email is even greater. One research team found that we can accurately decode an email's intent and tone only 50 percent of the time, yet most of us vastly overestimate our ability to send and interpret clear messages. If you are sending an important message, be sure to reread it for clarity. Moreover, if you are upset about the presumed tone of someone else's message, keep in mind that you may be misinterpreting it.[34]

- *Communicating negative messages.* When companies have negative information to communicate, managers need to think carefully. Email may not be the best way to communicate the message. When RadioShack decided to lay off 400 employees, it was widely criticized for doing it via email. Employees need to be careful communicating negative messages via email, too. Justen Deal, 22, wrote an email critical of some strategic decisions made by his employer, pharmaceutical giant Kaiser Permanente. In the email, he criticized the "misleadership" of Kaiser CEO George Halvorson and questioned the financing of several information technology projects. Within hours, Deal's computer was seized; he was later fired.[35]

- *Time-consuming nature of email.* An estimated 100 trillion emails are sent every year, of which approximately 20 percent are non-spam messages.[36] Someone has to answer all those non-spam messages, and delete all the spam messages! According to one consulting group, the average person receives about 45 emails a day, while corporate users send or receive about 170 emails a day. A survey of Canadian managers revealed 58 percent spent 2 to 4 hours per day reading and responding to emails. The average worker checks his or her email 50 times a day. Some people, such as venture capitalist and Dallas Mavericks owner Mark Cuban, receive more than 1000 messages a day (Cuban says 10 percent are of the "I want" variety). Although you probably don't receive that many, most of us have trouble keeping up with all the email we receive, especially as we advance in our career. Experts suggest the following strategies:
  - *Do not check email in the morning.* Take care of important tasks before getting ensnared in emails. Otherwise, you may never get to those tasks.
  - *Check email in batches.* Don't check email continually throughout the day. Some experts suggest twice a day. "You wouldn't want to do a new load of laundry every time you have a dirty pair of socks," says one expert.
  - *Unsubscribe.* Stop newsletters and other subscriptions you don't really need.
  - *Stop sending email.* The best way to receive lots of email is to send lots of email, so send less. Shorter emails garner shorter responses. "A well-written message can and should be as concise as possible," says one expert.
  - *Declare email bankruptcy.* Some people, like recording artist Moby and venture capitalist Fred Wilson, become so overwhelmed by email they declare "email bankruptcy." They wipe out their entire inbox and start over.

    Although some of these steps may not work for you, keep in mind that email can be less productive than it seems: We often seem busy but get less accomplished through email than we might think.[37]

- *Email emotions.* We tend to think of email as a sort of sterile, faceless form of communication. Some researchers say the lack of visual and vocal cues means emotionally positive messages, such as those including praise, will be seen as more emotionally neutral than the sender intended.[38] But, as you no doubt know, emails are often highly emotional. One CEO said, "I've seen people not talk to each other, turf wars break out and people quit their jobs as a result of

EXHIBIT 6-3 Showing Emotions in Email

Email need not be emotion-free. Over the years, email users have developed a way of displaying text, as well as a set of symbols (*emoticons*) for expressing emotions. For instance, the use of all caps (as in THIS PROJECT NEEDS YOUR IMMEDIATE ATTEN-TION!) is the email equivalent of shouting. The following highlights some emoticons:

:)	Smile	:-e	Disappointed
<g>	Grin	:-@	Scream
:(	Frown	:-0	Yell
;)	Wink	:-D	Shock or surprise
:-[	Really sad face	:'(	Crying

emails." Email tends to make senders feel free to write things they would never be comfortable saying in person. Facial expressions tend to temper our emotional expressions, but in email, there is no other face to look at, and so many of us fire away. An increasingly common way of communicating emotions in email is with emoticons (see Exhibit 6-3). For example, Yahoo!'s email software allows users to pick from 75 graphical emoticons. Although emoticons used to be considered for personal use only, adults are increasingly using them in business emails. Still, some see them as too informal for business use.

If you find yourself angry or upset as you write an email, save it as a draft, and look at it again once you are on a more even keel. When others send flaming messages, remain calm and try not to respond in kind. And, as hard as it might sometimes be, try to see the flaming message from the other party's point of view. That in itself may calm your nerves.[39] *Case Incident—Dianna Abdala* on page 225 considers the limitations of communicating by email.

- *Privacy concerns.* There are two privacy issues with email. First, you need to be aware that your emails may be, and often are, monitored. Also, you cannot always trust that the recipient of your email will keep it confidential. For these reasons, you should not write anything you would not want made public. Second, you need to exercise caution in forwarding email from your company's email account to a personal, or "public" (for example, Gmail, Yahoo!, MSN), email account. These accounts often are not as secure as corporate accounts, so when you forward a company email to them, you may be violating your organization's policy or unintentionally disclosing confidential data. Many employers hire vendors to sift through emails, using software to catch not only the obvious keywords ("insider trading") but also the vague ("that thing we talked about") or guilt ridden ("regret"). One survey found that nearly 40 percent of companies have employees whose only job is to read other employees' email. You are being watched—so be careful what you email![40]

Focus on Ethics illustrates that employees cannot assume that their email is private.

FOCUS ON ETHICS

Your Email Can Get You Fired

Should your email be safe from your manager's eyes? A recent poll conducted by Environics found that 35 percent of Canadians say they have sent emails from their work-based email address that they worry could come back to hurt them.[41] Even so, about the same percentage of employees believe their employers probably check on email accounts, and 52 percent think their employer has the right to do so. Moreover, 30 percent of Canadians know someone who has been disciplined because of an email sent at work.

While a City of Toronto employee was merely disciplined after sending "inappropriate" pictures using a city computer, Fred Jones (not his real name) was fired from a Canadian company for forwarding dirty jokes to his clients.[42] Until this incident, Jones had been a high-performing employee who sold network computers for his company. Jones thought that he was only sending the jokes to clients who liked them, and assumed that the clients would tell him if they did not want to receive the jokes. Instead, a client complained to the company about receiving the dirty jokes. After an investigation, the company fired Jones. Jones is still puzzled about being fired. He views his email as private; to him, emailing jokes is the same as telling them at the water cooler.

Jones was not aware that under current law, employee information, including email, is not necessarily private. Most federal employees, provincial public sector employees, and employees working for federally regulated industries are covered by the federal Privacy Act and Access to Information Act, in place since 1985. Many private sector employees are not covered by privacy legislation, however. ●

Ann Cavoukian, Information and Privacy Commissioner of Ontario, notes that "employees deserve to be treated like adults and companies should limit surveillance to rare instances, such as when there is suspicion of criminal activity or harassment."[43] She suggests that employers use respect and courtesy when dealing with employees' email, and she likens email to office phone calls, which generally are not monitored by the employer. It is clearly important, in any event, that employees be aware of their companies' policies on email.

Instant Messaging and Text Messaging

Instant messaging (IM) and text messaging (TM), which have been popular among teens for more than a decade, are now being used in business.[44]

The growth of IM and TM has been spectacular. In 2002, Canadians sent 174 million text messages, while the estimate for 2011 is 72.6 billion, a staggering increase.[45] More people are using IM than email as their primary communication tool at work.[46]

IM and TM represent fast and inexpensive means for managers to stay in touch with employees and for employees to stay in touch with one another. In an increasing number of cases, this is not a luxury, it is a business imperative.

Despite the advantages of IM and TM, email is still probably a better device for conveying long messages that need to be saved. IM is preferable for one- or two-line messages that would just clutter up an email inbox. On the downside, some IM/TM users find the technology intrusive and distracting. Its continual presence can make it hard for employees to concentrate and stay focused. For example, a survey of managers revealed that in 86 percent of meetings, at least some participants checked TM, and another survey revealed 20 percent of managers report having been reprimanded for using wireless devices during meetings.[47] Finally, because instant messages can be intercepted easily, many organizations are concerned about the security of IM/TM.[48]

One other point: It's important to not let the informality of text messaging ("omg! r u serious? brb") spill over into business emails. Many prefer to keep business communication relatively formal. A survey of employers revealed that 58 percent rate grammar, spelling, and punctuation as "very important" in email messages.[49] By making sure your professional communications are, well, professional, you will show yourself to be mature and serious. Avoid jargon and slang, use formal titles, use formal email addresses for yourself (lose that partyanimal@yahoo.com address), and take care to make your message concise and well written. That does not mean, of course, that you have to give up TM or IM; you just need to maintain the boundaries between how you communicate with your friends and how you communicate professionally.

Toronto-based Upverter was started by three friends (left to right) Zak Homuth, Stephen Hamer, and Michael Woodworth (shown here at the Maker Faire, an event that showcases grassroots innovation). The three, all trained as electrical engineers, wanted to create a network for online collaboration for hardware designers. They launched a "crowd-sourced library of parts and design tools," and the company took off quickly after they demonstrated the service at DemoFall 2011 in Santa Clara, California.

Social Networking

Nowhere has communication been more transformed than in social networking. You are probably familiar with and perhaps a user of social networking platforms such as Facebook. LinkedIn, XING, and ZoomInfo are all professional websites that allow users to set up lists of contacts and do everything from casually "pinging" them with updates to hosting chat rooms for all or some of the users' contacts. Some companies, such as IBM, have their own social networks. IBM is selling its BluePages tool to companies and individual users. Microsoft is doing the same thing with its SharePoint tool.

To get the most out of social networks and avoid irritating your contacts, use them for high-value items only—not as an everyday or even every-week tool. Remember that a prospective employer might check your Facebook entry. Some entrepreneurs have developed software that mines such websites for companies (or individuals) that want to check up on a job applicant (or potential date). So keep in mind that what you post may be read by people other than your intended contacts.[50] Employees have been disciplined for Facebook postings, as this *OB in the Workplace* shows.

 **in the WORKPLACE**
An RCMP Officer's Facebook Posts Land Him in Trouble

What was he thinking? A 26-year-old RCMP officer based in Nanaimo, BC, ended up under investigation for comments he posted on Facebook, including "Night shift and St. Paddy's Day, can't wait to drop kick all the drunk idiots" and "Bar watch shift tonight, I'm gonna catch me a ginger."[51] The officer, who has not been named, thought he was just joking among friends. He also blamed it on the stress of his job. "I've got a stressful job and the way I deal with it is I use humour. It's obviously pretty stupid to post that stuff on there. I didn't intend it to go out in the public."

The BC RCMP detachments received social media guidelines in the weeks before the officer's Facebook account came under scrutiny.

RCMP E Division senior media relations officer Rob Vermeulen noted, "You're accountable on and off duty. If there's a lesson we can already learn, for police officers and everyone else, there's no reasonable expectation of privacy of stuff we post to the Internet." ●

Blogs

Peter Aceto, CEO of Toronto-based Tangerine (formerly ING Direct Canada) is a big fan of the **blog (web log)**, a website about a single person or company that is usually updated daily. He encourages his employees to have blogs and has one himself. Aceto allows readers to post comments and rate his blog entries.

Obviously, Aceto is not the only fan of blogs. Experts estimate that more than 112 million blogs and more than 350 million blog entries are now read daily.[52] While most blogs are written by individuals, many organizations and organizational leaders have blogs that speak for the organization.

OB in the Street considers employers' responses to blogging.

in the **STREET**
When a Personal Blog Becomes a Workplace Issue

Should blog entries about work be a concern for employers? Andrew McDonald landed an internship with the television channel Comedy Central, and on his first day at work, he started a blog.[53] His supervisors asked him to change various things about the blog, essentially removing all specific references to Comedy Central. Kelly Kreth was fired from her job as a marketing director for blogging about her co-workers. So was Jessa Werner, who later said, "I came to the realization that I probably shouldn't have been blogging about work."

Although some companies have policies in place governing the content of blogs, many don't. Many bloggers think their personal blogs are outside their employer's purview, and 39 percent of individual bloggers say they have posted comments that could be construed as harmful to their company's reputation.

If someone else in a company happens to read a blog entry, there is nothing to keep him or her from sharing that information with others, and the employee could be dismissed as a result. Some companies may not fire an employee over any blog entry short of one that broke the law. But most organizations are unlikely to be so forgiving of any blog entry that might cast a negative light on them. In short, if you are going to have a personal blog, maintain a strict work-personal "firewall." ●

As a variant of blogs (which are generally either personal or company-owned), Twitter is a service that allows users to post "micro-blog" entries about any topic, including work. Many organizational leaders send Twitter messages ("tweets"), but they can come from any employee about any work topic, leaving organizations with less control over the communication of important or sensitive information. While many CEOs worry about the use of Twitter, Peter Aceto posts to Twitter at least five times a day. One of his tweets in September 2012 informed his over 5900 Twitter followers about the results of his son's sports team. Aceto uses social media because "I felt my personal involvement in being transparent would be important for our brand."[54] A 2012 study found that only 3.8 percent of CEOs at *Fortune* 500 companies have Twitter accounts, while over 70 percent have no social media presence at all.[55]

blog (web log) A website where entries are written, and generally displayed in reverse chronological order, about news, events, and personal diary entries.

Communication Barriers between Women and Men

Research by Deborah Tannen provides us with important insights into differences in the conversation styles of men and women.[56] In particular, Tannen has been able to explain why gender often creates oral communication barriers. Her research does not suggest that *all* men or *all* women behave the same way in their communication, but she illustrates some important generalizations.

The essence of Tannen's research is that men use talk to emphasize status, while women use it to create connection. According to Tannen, women speak and hear a language of connection and intimacy, while men speak and hear a language of status and independence. So, for many men, conversations are primarily a way to preserve independence and maintain status in a hierarchical social order. For many women, however, conversations are negotiations for closeness in which people try to seek and give confirmation and support. The following examples will illustrate Tannen's thesis.

Men often complain that women talk on and on about their problems. Women criticize men for not listening. What is happening is that when men hear a problem, they often assert their desire for independence and control by offering solutions. Many women, on the other hand, view telling a problem as a means to promote closeness. The women present the problem to gain support and connection, not to get the male's advice. Mutual understanding, as sought by women, is symmetrical. But giving advice is asymmetrical—it sets up the (male) advice giver as more knowledgeable, more reasonable, and more in control; this contributes to distancing men and women in their efforts to communicate.

Men often criticize women for seeming to apologize all the time. Men tend to see the phrase "I'm sorry" as a weakness because they interpret the phrase to mean the woman is accepting blame. However, women typically use "I'm sorry" to express empathy: "I know you must feel bad about this. I probably would too in the same position."

While Tannen has received wide acknowledgment of her work, some suggest that it is anecdotal and/or based on faulty research. Goldsmith and Fulfs argue that men and women have more similarities than differences as communicators, although they acknowledge that when communication difficulties do appear, it is appealing to attribute them to gender.[57] Despite this, Nancy Langton, your Vancouver-based author, has noted, based on evidence from role plays, that men and women make requests for raises differently, and men are more likely to state that men were more effective at making requests, while women are more likely to indicate that it was women who handled the interaction more favourably.[58]

Cross-Cultural Communication

Effective communication is difficult under the best of conditions. Cross-cultural factors clearly create the potential for increased communication problems.

What factors hinder cross-cultural communication?

Cultural Barriers to Communication

One author has identified four specific problems related to language difficulties in cross-cultural communications.[59] First, there are *barriers caused by semantics*. As we have noted previously, words mean different things to different people. This is particularly true for people from different national cultures. Some words, for instance, don't translate between cultures. For instance, the new capitalists in Russia may have difficulty communicating with their English-speaking counterparts because English terms such as *efficiency*, *free market*, and *regulation* cannot be translated directly into Russian.

Second, there are *barriers caused by word connotations*. Words imply different things in different languages. The Japanese word *hai* translates as "yes," but its connotation may be "yes, I am listening," rather than "yes, I agree." Western executives may be hampered in their negotiations if they don't understand this connotation.

Third are *barriers caused by tone differences.* In some cultures language is formal, and in others it's informal. In some cultures, the tone changes depending on the context: People speak differently at home, in social situations, and at work. Using a personal, informal style in a situation where a more formal style is expected can be embarrassing and offensive.

Fourth, there are *barriers caused by differences in perceptions.* People who speak different languages actually view the world in different ways. The Inuit perceive snow differently because they have many words for it. They also perceive "no" differently from English speakers because the Inuit have no such word in their vocabulary.

A Guide to Overcoming Cross-Cultural Difficulties

When communicating with people from a different culture, what can you do to reduce misperceptions, misinterpretations, and misevaluations? Following these four rules can be helpful:[60]

- *Assume differences until similarity is proven.* Most of us assume that others are more similar to us than they actually are. But people from different countries often are very different from us. So you are far less likely to make an error if you assume that others are different from you rather than assuming similarity until difference is proven.

- *Emphasize description rather than interpretation or evaluation.* Interpreting or evaluating what someone has said or done, in contrast with describing, is based more on the observer's culture and background than on the observed situation. As a result, delay judgment until you have had sufficient time to observe and interpret the situation from the differing viewpoints of all the cultures involved.

- *Be empathetic.* Before sending a message, put yourself in the recipient's shoes. What are his or her values, experiences, and frames of reference? What do you know about his or her education, upbringing, and background that can give you added insight? Try to see the other person as he or she really is.

Globalization has changed the way Toyota Motor Corporation provides employees with the information they need for decision making. In the past, Toyota transferred employee knowledge on the job from generation to generation through "tacit understanding," a common communication method used in the conformist and subdued Japanese culture. Today, however, as a global organization, Toyota transfers knowledge of its production methods to overseas employees by bringing them to its training centre in Japan, shown here, to teach them production methods by using how-to manuals, practice drills, and lectures.

- *Treat your interpretations as a working hypothesis.* Once you have developed an explanation for a new situation or think you empathize with someone from a foreign culture, treat your interpretation as a hypothesis that needs further testing rather than as a certainty. Carefully assess the feedback provided by recipients to see if it confirms your hypothesis. For important decisions or communiqués, you can also check with other foreign and home-country colleagues to ensure that your interpretations are on target.

How Communication Breakdown Leads to Conflict

4 What is conflict?

Several common themes underlie most definitions of conflict.[61] Conflict must be *perceived* by the parties to it; if no one is aware of a conflict, it is generally agreed that no conflict exists. Conflict also involves opposition or incompatibility and some form of interaction between the parties.[62] These factors set the conditions that determine the beginning point of the conflict process. We can define **conflict**, then, as a process that begins when one party perceives that another party has negatively affected, or is about to negatively affect, something that the first party cares about.[63]

This definition is deliberately broad. It describes that point in any ongoing activity when an interaction "crosses over" to become an interparty conflict. It encompasses the wide range of conflicts that people experience in groups and organizations—incompatibility of goals, differences over interpretations of facts, disagreements based on behavioural expectations, and the like. Finally, our definition is flexible enough to cover the full range of conflict levels—from subtle forms of disagreement to overt and violent acts.

Conflict has positive sides and negative sides, which we will discuss further when we cover functional and dysfunctional conflict. For more on this debate, refer to the *Point/Counterpoint* discussion on page 221.

Functional vs. Dysfunctional Conflict

The general view on conflict is that not all conflict is bad.[64] Some conflicts support the goals of the group and improve its performance; these are **functional**, or constructive, forms of conflict. But there are conflicts that hinder group performance; these are **dysfunctional**, or destructive, forms of conflict. The criterion that differentiates functional from dysfunctional conflict is group performance. If a group is unable to achieve its goals because of conflict, then the conflict is dysfunctional.

Exhibit 6-4 provides a way of visualizing conflict behaviour. All conflicts exist somewhere along this continuum. At the lower part of the continuum, we have conflicts characterized by subtle, indirect, and highly controlled forms of tension. An illustration might be a student politely objecting to a point the instructor has just made in class. Conflict intensities escalate as they move upward along the continuum,

conflict A process that begins when one party perceives that another party has negatively affected, or is about to negatively affect, something that the first party cares about.

functional conflict Conflict that supports the goals of the group and improves its performance.

dysfunctional conflict Conflict that hinders group performance.

cognitive conflict Conflict that is task-oriented and related to differences in perspectives and judgments.

affective conflict Conflict that is emotional and aimed at a person rather than an issue.

RESEARCH FINDINGS: Conflict

Research on conflict has yet to clearly identify those situations in which conflict is more likely to be constructive than destructive. However, there is growing evidence that the source of the conflict is a significant factor determining functionality.[65] **Cognitive conflict**, which is task-oriented and occurs because of differences in perspectives and judgments, can often result in identifying potential solutions to problems. Thus it would be regarded as functional conflict. **Affective conflict**, which is emotional and aimed at a person rather than an issue, tends to be dysfunctional conflict.

EXHIBIT 6-4 Conflict Intensity Continuum

Annihilatory conflict — Overt efforts to destroy the other party

— Aggressive physical attacks

— Threats and ultimatums

— Assertive verbal attacks

— Overt questioning or challenging of others

— Minor disagreements or misunderstandings

No conflict

Sources: Based on S. P. Robbins, *Managing Organizational Conflict: A Nontraditional Approach* (Upper Saddle River, NJ: Prentice Hall, 1974), pp. 93–97; and F. Glasl, "The Process of Conflict Escalation and the Roles of Third Parties," in *Conflict Management and Industrial Relations*, ed. G. B. J. Bomers and R. Peterson (Boston: Kluwer-Nijhoff, 1982), pp. 119–140.

until they become highly destructive. Strikes and lockouts, riots, and wars clearly fall into this upper range. For the most part, you should assume that conflicts that reach the upper ranges of the continuum are almost always dysfunctional. Functional conflicts are typically confined to the lower range of the continuum.

One study of 53 teams found that cognitive conflict, because it generates more alternatives, led to better decisions, more acceptance of the decisions, and ownership of the decisions. Teams experiencing affective conflict, where members had personality incompatibilities and disputes, showed poorer decisions and lower levels of acceptance of the decisions.[66] It also appears that the friction and interpersonal hostilities inherent in affective conflicts increase personality clashes and decrease mutual understanding, which hinders the completion of organizational tasks. Unfortunately, managers spend a lot of effort resolving personality conflicts among staff members; one survey indicated this task consumes 18 percent of their time.[67]

Because conflict can involve our emotions in a variety of ways, it can also lead to stress. You may want to refer to the *OB on the Edge—Stress at Work* on pages 104–111 to get some ideas on how to manage the stress that might arise from conflicts you experience.

Conflict Resolution

Conflict in the workplace can affect the effectiveness of individuals, teams, and the entire organization.[68] One study found that 20 percent of managers' time is spent managing conflict.[69]

Once conflict arises, what can be done to resolve it? The way a conflict is defined goes a long way toward establishing the sort of outcomes that might settle it. For instance, if I define our salary disagreement as a zero-sum or *win-lose situation*—that is, if you get the increase in pay you want, there will be just that amount less for me—I am going to be far less willing to look for mutual solutions than if I frame the conflict as a potential *win-win situation*. So individual attitudes toward a conflict are important, because attitudes typically define the set of possible settlements.

5 How can conflict be resolved?

Is conflict always bad?

PIA
PERSONAL INVENTORY ASSESSMENT

Learn About Yourself
Strategies for Handling Conflict

Conflict Management Strategies

Conflict researchers often use dual concern theory to describe people's conflict management strategies. Dual concern theory considers how one's degree of *cooperativeness* (the degree to which one tries to satisfy the other person's concerns) and *assertiveness* (the degree to which one tries to satisfy one's own concerns) determine how a conflict is handled.[70] The five conflict-handling strategies identified by the theory are as follows:[71]

- *Forcing.* Imposing one's will on the other party.

- *Problem solving.* Trying to reach an agreement that satisfies both one's own and the other party's aspirations as much as possible.

- *Avoiding.* Ignoring or minimizing the importance of the issues creating the conflict.

- *Yielding.* Accepting and incorporating the will of the other party.

- *Compromising.* Balancing concern for oneself with concern for the other party in order to reach a solution.

Forcing is a win-lose solution, as is yielding, while problem solving seeks a win-win solution. Avoiding conflict and pretending it does not exist and compromising, so that neither person gets what they want, can yield lose-lose solutions. Exhibit 6-5 illustrates these five strategies, along with specific actions that one might take when using them.

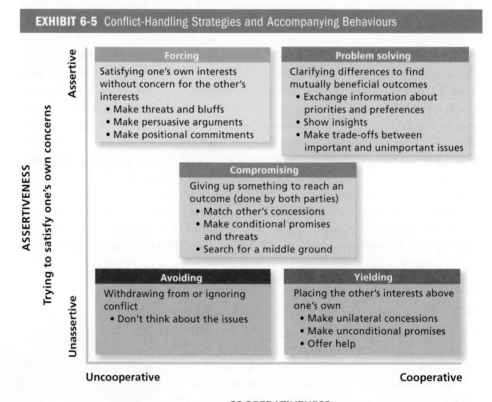

EXHIBIT 6-5 Conflict-Handling Strategies and Accompanying Behaviours

Sources: Based on K. W. Thomas, "Conflict and Negotiation Processes in Organizations," in *Handbook of Industrial and Organizational Psychology,* vol. 3, 2nd ed., ed. M. D. Dunnette and L. M. Hough (Palo Alto, CA: Consulting Psychologists Press, 1992), p. 668; C. K. W. De Dreu, A. Evers, B. Beersma, E. S. Kluwer, and A. Nauta, "A Theory-Based Measure of Conflict Management Strategies in the Workplace," *Journal of Organizational Behavior* 22, no. 6 (September 2001), pp. 645–668; and D. G. Pruitt and J. Rubin, *Social Conflict: Escalation, Stalemate and Settlement* (New York: Random House, 1986).

Choosing a particular strategy for resolving conflict depends on a variety of factors. Research shows that while people may choose among the strategies, they have an underlying disposition to handle conflicts in certain ways.[72] In addition, some situations call for particular strategies. For instance, when a small child insists on trying to run into the street, a parent may need a forcing strategy to restrain the child. Co-workers who are having a conflict over setting deadlines to complete a project on time may decide that problem solving is the best strategy to use.

This chapter's *Learning About Yourself Exercise* on page 222 gives you the opportunity to discover your preferred conflict-handling strategy. As well, *OB in Action—Choosing Strategies to Deal with Conflicts* indicates the situations in which each strategy is best used.

What Can Individuals Do to Manage Conflict?

There are a number of conflict resolution techniques that individuals can use to try to defuse conflict inside and outside the workplace. These include the following:[73]

- *Problem solving.* Requesting a face-to-face meeting to identify the problem and resolve it through open discussion.

- *Developing overarching goals.* Creating a shared goal that requires both parties to work together and motivates them to do so.

- *Smoothing.* Playing down differences while emphasizing common interests with the other party.

- *Compromising.* Agreeing with the other party that each will give up something of value to reach an accord.

- *Avoidance.* Withdrawing from, or suppressing, the conflict.

The choice of technique may depend on how serious the issue is to you, whether you take a win-win or a win-lose approach, and your preferred conflict management style.

When the conflict is specifically work-related, there are additional techniques that might be used:

- *Expansion of resources.* The scarcity of a resource—say, money, promotion opportunities, office space—can create conflict. Expansion of the resource can create a win-win solution.

- *Authoritative command.* Management can use its formal authority to resolve the conflict and then communicate its desires to the parties involved.

- *Altering the human variable.* Behavioural change techniques such as human relations training can alter attitudes and behaviours that cause conflict.

- *Altering the structural variables.* The formal organization structure and the interaction patterns of conflicting parties can be changed through job redesign, transfers, creation of coordinating positions, and the like.

in **ACTION**
Choosing Strategies to Deal with Conflicts

Forcing
→ In **emergencies**
→ On **important** but unpopular **issues**
→ On **vital issues** when you know you are right
→ Against **people who take advantage** of noncompetitive behaviour

Problem solving
→ If both sets of concerns are **too important to be compromised**
→ To **merge different perspectives**
→ To **gain commitment** through a consensus
→ To **mend a relationship**

Avoiding
→ When an issue is **trivial**
→ When your **concerns will not be met**
→ When potential **disruption outweighs the benefits** of resolution
→ To let people **cool down** and regain perspective

Yielding
→ When you find **you are wrong**
→ To show your **reasonableness**
→ When **issues are more important to others** than to yourself
→ To **build social credits** for later issues
→ When **harmony and stability** are especially important

Compromising
→ When **goals are important but not worth more assertive approaches**
→ When opponents are committed to **mutually exclusive goals**
→ To achieve **temporary settlements** to complex issues
→ To arrive at **expedient solutions** under time pressure.[74]

in ACTION
Handling Personality Conflicts

Tips for employees having a personality conflict

→ **Communicate directly** with the other person to resolve the perceived conflict (emphasize problem solving and common objectives, not personalities).

→ **Avoid dragging** co-workers into the conflict.

→ If dysfunctional conflict persists, **seek help** from direct supervisors or human resource specialists.

Tips for third-party observers of a personality conflict

→ **Do not take sides** in someone else's personality conflict.

→ **Suggest the parties work things out** themselves in a constructive and positive way.

→ If dysfunctional conflict persists, **refer the problem to the parties' direct supervisors**.

Tips for managers whose employees are having a personality conflict

→ **Investigate and document** conflict.

→ If appropriate, **take corrective action** (e.g., feedback or behaviour shaping).

→ If necessary, **attempt informal dispute resolution**.

→ **Refer difficult conflicts** to human resource specialists or hired counsellors for formal resolution attempts and other interventions.[78]

Resolving Personality Conflicts

Personality conflicts are an everyday occurrence in the workplace. A 2011 study found that Canadian supervisors spend about 16 percent of their time handling disputes among employees.[75] A variety of factors leads to personality conflicts at work, including the following:[76]

- Misunderstandings based on age, race, or cultural differences

- Intolerance, prejudice, discrimination, or bigotry

- Perceived inequities

- Misunderstandings, rumours, or falsehoods about an individual or group

- Blaming for mistakes or mishaps (finger-pointing)

Personality conflicts can result in lowered productivity when people find it difficult to work together. The individuals experiencing the conflict may seek sympathy from other members of the work group, causing co-workers to take sides. The ideal solution would be for the two people in conflict to work it out between themselves, without involving others, but this does not always happen. However, it is not always possible for people to talk things out, and it may be a Western cultural bias to expect that individuals should generally be able to do so.[77] *OB in Action—Handling Personality Conflicts* suggests ways of dealing with personality conflicts in the workplace.

Negotiation

6 How does one negotiate effectively?

When parties are potentially in conflict, they may choose to negotiate a resolution. Negotiation occurs in the interactions of almost everyone in groups and organizations: Labour bargains with management; managers negotiate with employees, peers, and senior management; salespeople negotiate with customers; purchasing agents negotiate with suppliers; employees agree to answer a colleague's phone for a few minutes in exchange for some past or future benefit. In today's team-based organizations, negotiation skills become critical so that teams can work together effectively.

We define **negotiation** as a process in which two or more parties try to agree on the exchange rate for goods or services they are trading.[79] Note that we use the terms *negotiation* and *bargaining* interchangeably.

Within a negotiation, one should be aware that individuals have *issues*, *positions*, and *interests*. *Issues* are items that are specifically placed on the bargaining table for discussion. *Positions* are the individual's stand on the issues. For instance, salary may be an issue for discussion. The salary you hope to receive is your position. Finally, *interests* are the underlying concerns that are affected by the negotiation resolution. For instance, the reason that you might want a six-figure salary is that you are trying to buy a house in Vancouver, and a pay increase is your only hope of being able to make mortgage payments.

negotiation A process in which two or more parties exchange goods or services and try to agree upon the exchange rate for them.

Bargaining Characteristic	Distributive Bargaining	Integrative Bargaining
EXHIBIT 6-6 Distributive vs. Integrative Bargaining		
Available resources	Fixed amount of resources to be divided	Variable amount of resources to be divided
Primary motivations	I win, you lose	I win, you win
Primary interests	Opposed to each other	Convergent or congruent with each other
Focus of relationships	Short-term	Long-term

Source: Based on R. J. Lewicki and J. A. Litterer, *Negotiation* (Homewood, IL: Irwin, 1985), p. 280.

Negotiators who recognize the underlying interests of themselves and the other party may have more flexibility in achieving a resolution. For instance, in the example just given, an employer who offers you a mortgage at a lower rate than the bank does, or who provides you with an interest-free loan that can be used against the mortgage, may be able to address your underlying interests without actually meeting your salary position. You may be satisfied with this alternative, if you understand what your interest is.

Interest-based bargaining enabled the Information Services Corporation (ISC) to sign a mutually beneficial three-year contract with the Saskatchewan Government and General Employees' Union (SGEU) Local 2214 in May 2010, after nine days of bargaining. The agreement provided for wage and pension increases plus greater dental plan benefits for employees and efficiencies in recruitment and leaves for the Government.[80] ISC Union Chairperson Barb Wright called the result "a true testament to the interest-based bargaining process."[81]

Bargaining Strategies

There are two general approaches to negotiation—*distributive bargaining* and *integrative bargaining*.[82] These are compared in Exhibit 6-6.

Distributive Bargaining

Distributive bargaining is a negotiating strategy that operates under zero-sum (win-lose) conditions. That is, any gain I make is at your expense, and vice versa. You see a used car advertised for sale online. It appears to be just what you have been looking to buy. You go out to see the car. It's great, and you want it. The owner tells you the asking price. You don't want to pay that much. The two of you then negotiate over the price. Every dollar you can get the seller to cut from the car's price is a dollar you save, and every dollar more the seller can get from you comes at your expense.

Should you try to win at any cost when you bargain?

So the essence of distributive bargaining is negotiating over who gets what share of a fixed pie. By **fixed pie**, we mean a set amount of goods or services to be divided up. When the pie is fixed, or parties believe it is, they tend to bargain distributively.

A party engaged in distributive bargaining focuses on trying to get the opponent to agree to a specific target point, or to get as close to it as possible. Examples of such tactics are persuading your opponent of the impossibility of reaching his or her target point and the advisability of accepting a settlement near yours; arguing that your target is fair, while your opponent's is not; and trying to get your opponent to feel emotionally generous toward you and thus accept an outcome close to your target point.

distributive bargaining Negotiation that seeks to divide up a fixed amount of resources; a win-lose solution.

fixed pie The belief that there is only a set amount of goods or services to be divided up between the parties.

When engaged in distributive bargaining, one of the best things you can do is to make the first offer, and to make it an aggressive one. Research consistently shows that the best negotiators are those who make the first offer and whose initial offer has very favourable terms. Why is this so? One reason is that making the first offer shows power; research shows that individuals in power are much more likely to make initial offers, speak first at meetings, and thereby gain the advantage. Another reason is the anchoring bias (the tendency for people to fixate on initial information). Once that anchoring point is set, people fail to adequately adjust it based on subsequent information. A savvy negotiator sets an anchor with the initial offer, and scores of negotiation studies show that such anchors greatly favour the person who sets them.[83] What happens more often than not is that we ask for less than what we could have gotten. This might not always be a bad strategy.

OB in the Street shows that in the context of eBay auctions, however, sellers who start with a low price on an item can end up getting a higher selling price.

in the STREET
A Low Anchor Value Can Reap Higher Returns on eBay

Should a seller use a high or a low starting bid in an eBay auction? In their analysis of auction results on eBay, a group of researchers found that *lower* starting bids generated higher final prices.[84] As just one example, Nikon digital cameras with ridiculously low starting bids (one penny) sold for an average of $312, whereas those with higher starting prices went for an average of $204.

What explains such a counterintuitive result? The researchers found that low starting bids attract more bidders, and this increased traffic generates more competing bidders, so in the end the price is higher. Although this may seem irrational, negotiation and bidding behaviour are not always rational, and as you have probably experienced first-hand, once you start bidding for something, you want to win, forgetting that for many auctions the one with the highest bid is often the loser (the so-called winner's curse).

If you are thinking of participating in an auction, consider the following two points. First, some buyers think sealed-bid auctions—where bidders submit a single bid in a concealed fashion—present an opportunity to get a "steal" because a price war cannot develop among bidders. However, evidence routinely indicates that sealed-bid auctions are bad for the winning bidder (and thus good for the seller) because the winning bid is higher than would otherwise be the case. Second, buyers sometimes think jumping bids—placing a bid higher than the auctioneer is asking—is a smart strategy because it drives away competing bidders early in the game. Again, this is a myth. Evidence indicates bid jumping is good at causing other bidders to follow suit, thus increasing the value of the winning bid. ●

Another distributive bargaining tactic is revealing a deadline. Negotiators who reveal deadlines speed concessions from their negotiating counterparts, making them reconsider their position. And even though negotiators don't *think* this tactic works, in reality, negotiators who reveal deadlines do better.[85]

integrative bargaining Negotiation that seeks one or more settlements that can create a win-win solution.

Integrative Bargaining

In contrast to distributive bargaining, **integrative bargaining** operates under the assumption that there exists one or more settlements that can create a win-win solution.

In terms of intraorganizational behaviour, all things being equal, integrative bargaining is preferable to distributive bargaining. Why? Because the former builds long-term relationships and makes working together in the future easier. It bonds negotiators and allows both sides to leave the bargaining table feeling that they have achieved a victory. For instance, in union-management negotiations, both sides might sit down to figure out other ways to reduce costs within an organization so that it is possible to have greater wage increases. Distributive bargaining, on the other hand, leaves one party a loser. It tends to build animosities and deepen divisions when people must work together on an ongoing basis.

Research shows that over repeated bargaining episodes, when the "losing" party feels positive about the negotiation outcome, the party is much more likely to bargain cooperatively in subsequent negotiations. This points to the important advantage of integrative negotiations: Even when you "win," you want your opponent to feel positively about the negotiation.[86]

How to Negotiate

Exhibit 6-7 provides a simplified model of the negotiation process. It views negotiation as made up of five steps: (1) developing a strategy; (2) defining ground rules; (3) clarification and justification; (4) bargaining and problem solving; and (5) closure and implementation.

Developing a Strategy

Before you start negotiating, you need to do your homework. What is the nature of the conflict? What is the history leading up to this negotiation? Who is involved and what are their perceptions of the conflict? What do you want from the negotiation?

EXHIBIT 6-7 The Negotiation Process

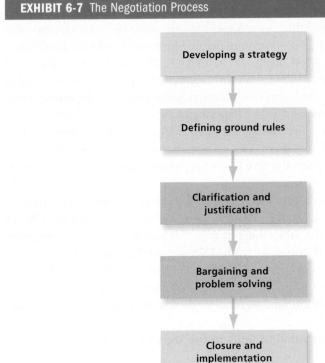

Source: This model is based on R. J. Lewicki, "Bargaining and Negotiation," *Exchange: The Organizational Behavior Teaching Journal* 6, no. 2 (1981), pp. 39–40.

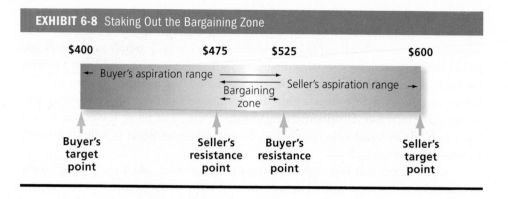

EXHIBIT 6-8 Staking Out the Bargaining Zone

What are *your* goals? It often helps to put your goals in writing and develop a range of outcomes—from "most hopeful" to "minimally acceptable"—to keep your attention focused.

You also want to prepare an assessment of what you think are the other party's goals. What are they likely to ask for? How entrenched are they likely to be in their position? What intangible or hidden interests may be important to them? On what terms might they be willing to settle? When you can anticipate your opponent's position, you are better equipped to counter arguments with the facts and figures that support your position. You want to be sure, however, that the information that you consider regarding your opponent is relevant to the negotiation. A 2011 study found that too much of the wrong kinds of information can make for worse bargaining outcomes. In some cases the person with extraneous information stopped looking for mutually beneficial outcomes earlier than those who did not have this information.[87]

In determining goals, parties are well advised to consider their "target and resistance" points, as well as their *best alternative to a negotiated agreement* (**BATNA**).[88] The buyer and the seller represent two negotiators. Each has a *target point* that defines what he or she would like to achieve. Each also has a *resistance point*, which marks the lowest outcome that is acceptable—the point below which each would break off negotiations rather than accept a less favourable settlement. The area between these two points makes up each negotiator's aspiration range. As long as there is some overlap between the buyer's and seller's aspiration ranges, there exists a **bargaining zone** where each side's aspirations can be met. Referring to Exhibit 6-8, if the buyer's resistance point is $450 and the seller's resistance point is $500, then the two may not be able to reach agreement because there is no overlap in their aspiration ranges. Recent research suggests that having an attractive BATNA is particularly powerful to a negotiator when the bargaining zone is small.[89]

One's BATNA represents the alternative that an individual will face if negotiations fail. Therefore, as part of your strategy, you should determine not only your BATNA but also some estimate of the other side's as well.[90] If you go into your negotiation having a good idea of what the other party's BATNA is, even if you are not able to meet theirs, you might be able to get them to change it. Think carefully about what the other side is willing to give up. People who underestimate their opponent's willingness to give on key issues before the negotiation even starts end up with lower outcomes from a negotiation.[91]

You can practise your negotiating skills in the *Working with Others Exercise* on pages 223–224.

Defining Ground Rules

Once you have done your planning and developed a strategy, you are ready to begin defining the ground rules and procedures with the other party over the negotiation

BATNA The *best alternative to a negotiated agreement*; the outcome an individual faces if negotiations fail.

bargaining zone The zone between each party's resistance point, assuming that there is overlap in this range.

Hockey teams, including the Vancouver Canucks and the LA Kings, were locked out by National Hockey League owners after their collective agreement expired on September 15, 2012. One of the key issues the owners and players could not come to agreement on was the share of revenues that should go to players. The owners felt the 57 percent share that went to players in 2010–2011 should be reduced. The players and the owners were so far apart on what each wanted in the new collective agreement that the dispute led to an impasse soon after the lockout.

itself. Who will do the negotiating? Where will it take place? What time constraints, if any, will apply? To what issues will negotiation be limited? Will there be a specific procedure to follow if an impasse is reached? During this phase, the parties will also exchange their initial proposals or demands. *From Concepts to Skills* on pages 226–227 directly addresses some of the actions you should take to improve the likelihood that you can achieve a good agreement.

Clarification and Justification

When initial positions have been exchanged, both you and the other party will explain, amplify, clarify, bolster, and justify your original demands. This part of the process need not be confrontational. Rather, it is an opportunity for educating and informing each other on the issues, why they are important, and how each arrived at their initial demands. This is the point at which you might want to provide the other party with any documentation that helps support your position. The *Ethical Dilemma Exercise* on page 224 considers whether it is ever appropriate to lie during negotiations.

Bargaining and Problem Solving

The essence of the negotiation process is the actual give and take in trying to hash out an agreement. It is here that concessions will undoubtedly need to be made by both parties. A 2011 study found that those who used competing and collaborating (essentially a combination of forcing and problem solving conflict resolution styles discussed earlier in the chapter) as part of their strategy to gain a higher starting salary were more successful (and received higher increases) than those who used

OB in ACTION
Tips for Getting to Yes

R. Fisher and W. Ury present four principles for win-win negotiations in their book *Getting to Yes*:

→ **Separate** the **people from** the **problem**. Work on the issues at hand, rather than getting involved in personality issues between the parties.

→ Focus on **interests, not positions**. Try to identify what each person needs or wants, rather than coming up with an unmovable position.

→ Look for ways to achieve **mutual gains**. Rather than focusing on one "right" solution for your position, brainstorm for solutions that will satisfy the needs of both parties.

→ Use **objective criteria** to achieve a fair solution. Try to focus on fair standards, such as market value, expert opinion, norms, or laws to help guide decision making.[92]

- Just because something is said, it does not mean that it was heard.
- Communication is rarely "objective." Both the sender's and receiver's reality affects the framing and understanding of the message.
- Information overload is a serious problem for most individuals.
- A medium level of conflict often results in higher productivity than an absence of conflict.
- Negotiators should identify their BATNA (*b*est *a*lternative *t*o *n*egotiated *a*greement).
- In relationships with long-term consequences, it is best to use a win-win strategy in bargaining.

SNAPSHOT SUMMARY

1 The Communication Process
   Choosing a Channel

2 Barriers to Effective Communication
   Filtering
   Selective Perception
   Defensiveness
   Emotions
   Information Overload
   Language
   Silence
   Nonverbal Communication
   Stress

3 Current Issues in Communication
   Electronic Communications
   Communication Barriers between Women and Men
   Cross-Cultural Communication

compromising and accommodating strategies.[93] The study looked at the influence of individual differences and negotiation strategies on starting salary outcomes based on a sample of 149 newly hired employees in various industry settings. Results indicated that those who chose to negotiate increased their starting salaries by an average of $5000. Individuals who negotiated by using competing and collaborating strategies, characterized by an open discussion of one's positions, issues, and perspectives, further increased their salaries as compared with those who used compromising and accommodating strategies. Individual differences, including risk aversion and integrative attitudes, played a significant role in predicting whether individuals negotiated, and if so, what strategies they used.

OB in Action—Tips for Getting to Yes on page 217 gives you further ideas on how to make negotiating work for you, based on the popular book *Getting to Yes*.[94]

Closure and Implementation

The final step in the negotiation process is formalizing the agreement that has been worked out and developing procedures that are necessary for implementation and monitoring. For major negotiations—which would include everything from labour-management negotiations, to bargaining over lease terms, to buying real estate, to negotiating a job offer for a senior management position—this will require hammering out the specifics in a formal contract. In most cases, however, closure of the negotiation process is nothing more formal than a handshake.

Summary and Implications

1 **How does communication work?**   Findings in this chapter suggest that the goal of perfect communication is unattainable. Yet there is evidence that demonstrates a positive relationship between effective communication and employee productivity.[95] Therefore, choosing the correct channel, being a good listener, and using feedback well may make for more effective communication.

2 **What are the barriers to communication?**   Human beings will always be subject to errors in communication because of filtering, selective perception, defensiveness, emotions, information overload, and language. What is said may not be what is heard. Nonverbal cues help provide a clearer picture of what someone is trying to say. Silence can be an important communication clue, and failing to pay attention to silence can result in missing some or all of a message. Good communicators hear and interpret silence. Whatever the sender's expectations, the decoded message in the mind of the receiver represents his or her reality. This "reality" will determine the individual's reactions, including performance, motivation, and degree of satisfaction in the workplace.

3 **What are other issues in communication?**   The big topics in communication are electronic communications, gender differences in communication, and cross-cultural differences in communication. As we saw in this chapter, email, among other electronic communications, can cause more stress and can be misused; thus, it is not always the most effective means of communication. We can make some generalizations about differences in the conversational style of men and women; men are more likely to use talk to emphasize status, while women use talk to create connection. We noted that there are a variety of barriers when communicating with someone from a different culture and that it is best to assume differences until similarity is proven, emphasize description rather than *interpretation* or *evaluation*, practise empathy, and treat your interpretations as a working hypothesis.

4 **What is conflict?** Conflict occurs when one person perceives that another person's actions will have a negative effect on something the first party cares about. Many people automatically assume that all conflict is bad. However, conflict can be either functional (constructive) or dysfunctional (destructive) to the performance of a group or unit. An optimal level of conflict encourages communication, prevents stagnation, stimulates creativity, allows tensions to be released, and plants the seeds of change, yet not so much as to be disruptive or to deter activities.

5 **How can conflict be resolved?** The way a conflict is defined goes a long way toward establishing the sort of outcomes that might settle it. One can work toward a *win-lose solution* or a *win-win solution*. Conflict management strategies are determined by the extent to which one wants to cooperate with another party, and the extent to which one asserts his or her own concerns.

6 **How does one negotiate effectively?** Negotiation is a process in which two or more parties try to agree on the exchange rate for goods or services they are trading. Negotiation is an ongoing activity in groups and organizations. Distributive bargaining can resolve disputes, but it often negatively affects one or more negotiators' satisfaction because it is focused on the short term and because it is confrontational. Integrative bargaining, by contrast, tends to provide outcomes that satisfy all parties and build lasting relationships.

for Review

1. Describe the communication process and identify its key components. Give an example of how this process operates with both oral and written messages.

2. Contrast encoding and decoding.

3. What does the phrase "sometimes the real message in a communication is buried in the silence" mean?

4. What is nonverbal communication? Does it aid or hinder verbal communication?

5. What are the advantages and disadvantages of email? Of instant messaging?

6. What are the managerial implications from the research contrasting male and female communication styles?

7. List four specific problems related to language difficulties in cross-cultural communication.

8. What is the difference between functional and dysfunctional conflict? What determines functionality?

9. What defines the bargaining zone in distributive bargaining?

10. How can you improve your negotiating effectiveness?

for Critical Thinking

1. "Ineffective communication is the fault of the sender." Do you agree or disagree? Discuss.

2. Using the concept of channel richness, give examples of messages best conveyed by email, in face-to-face communication, and on the company bulletin board.

3. Why do you think so many people are poor listeners?

4. Assume that one of your co-workers must negotiate a contract with someone from China. What problems might he or she face? If the co-worker were to ask you for advice, what suggestions would you make to help facilitate an agreement?

5. From your own experience, describe a situation you were involved in where the conflict was dysfunctional. Describe another example, from your experience, where the conflict was functional. Would the other parties in the conflicts agree with your assessment of what is functional or dysfunctional?

for You

- If you are having difficulty communicating with someone, you might consider that both you and the other person are contributing something to that breakdown. This tends to be true even if you are inclined to believe that the other person is the party more responsible for the breakdown.

- Often either selective perception or defensiveness gets in the way of communication. As you work in your groups on student projects, you may want to observe communication flows more critically to help you understand ways that communication can be improved and dysfunctional conflict avoided.

- It may seem easier, but avoiding conflict does not necessarily have a more positive outcome than working with someone to resolve the conflict.

- Trying to achieve a win-win solution in a conflict situation tends to lead to better relationships and greater trust.

Conflict Is Good for an Organization

Let's briefly review how stimulating conflict can provide benefits to the organization:[96]

- *Conflict is a means by which to bring about radical change.* It is an effective device by which management can drastically change the existing power structure, current interaction patterns, and entrenched attitudes. If there is no conflict, it means the real problems are not being addressed.

- *Conflict facilitates group cohesiveness.* While conflict increases hostility between groups, external threats tend to cause a group to pull together as a unit. Conflict with another group brings together those within each group. Such intragroup cohesion is a critical resource that groups draw on in good and especially in bad times.

- *Conflict improves group and organizational effectiveness.* Groups or organizations devoid of conflict are likely to suffer from apathy, stagnation, groupthink, and other debilitating diseases. In fact, more organizations probably fail because they have *too little* conflict, not because they have too much. Stagnation is the biggest threat to organizations, but since it occurs slowly its ill effects often go unnoticed until it's too late. Conflict can break complacency—though most of us don't like conflict, it often is the last best hope of saving an organization.

- *Conflict brings about a slightly higher, more constructive level of tension.* Constructive levels of tension improve the chances of solving the conflicts in a way that is satisfactory to all parties concerned. When the level of tension is very low, the parties may not be sufficiently motivated to do something about a conflict.

All Conflicts Are Dysfunctional!

It may be true that conflict is an inherent part of any group or organization. It may not be possible to eliminate it completely. However, just because conflicts exist is no reason to worship them. All conflicts are dysfunctional, and it is one of management's major responsibilities to keep conflict intensity as low as humanly possible. A few points support this case:

- *The negative consequences from conflict can be devastating.* The list of negatives associated with conflict is impressive. The most obvious are increased turnover, decreased employee satisfaction, inefficiencies between work units, sabotage, labour grievances and strikes, and physical aggression. One study estimated that managing conflict at work costs the average employer nearly 450 days of management time a year.[97]

- *Effective managers build teamwork.* A good manager builds a coordinated team. Conflict works against such an objective. A successful work group is like a successful sports team: Each member knows his or her role and supports his or her teammates. When a team works well, the whole becomes greater than the sum of the parts. Management creates teamwork by minimizing internal conflicts and facilitating internal coordination.

- *Competition is good for an organization, but conflict is not.* Competition and conflict should not be confused with each other. *Conflict* is behaviour directed against another party, whereas *competition* is behaviour aimed at obtaining a goal without interference from another party. Competition is healthy; it is the source of organizational vitality. Conflict, on the other hand, is destructive.

- *Conflict is avoidable.* It may be true that conflict is inevitable when an organization is in a downward spiral, but the goal of good leadership and effective management is to avoid the spiral to begin with.

OB *at work*

What Is Your Primary Conflict-Handling Style?

Indicate how often you rely on each of the following tactics by circling the number you feel is most appropriate. When I have a conflict at work, I do the following:

	Not at All			Very Much	
1. I give in to the wishes of the other party.	1	2	3	4	5
2. I try to realize a middle-of-the-road solution.	1	2	3	4	5
3. I push my own point of view.	1	2	3	4	5
4. I examine issues until I find a solution that really satisfies me and the other party.	1	2	3	4	5
5. I avoid a confrontation about our differences.	1	2	3	4	5
6. I concur with the other party.	1	2	3	4	5
7. I emphasize that we have to find a compromise solution.	1	2	3	4	5
8. I search for gains.	1	2	3	4	5
9. I stand for my own and the other party's goals and interests.	1	2	3	4	5
10. I avoid differences of opinion as much as possible.	1	2	3	4	5
11. I try to accommodate the other party.	1	2	3	4	5
12. I insist we both give in a little.	1	2	3	4	5
13. I fight for a good outcome for myself.	1	2	3	4	5
14. I examine ideas from both sides to find a mutually optimal solution.	1	2	3	4	5
15. I try to make differences loom less large.	1	2	3	4	5
16. I adapt to the other party's goals and interests.	1	2	3	4	5
17. I strive whenever possible toward a 50-50 compromise.	1	2	3	4	5
18. I do everything to win.	1	2	3	4	5
19. I work out a solution that serves my own as well as the other party's interests as well as possible.	1	2	3	4	5
20. I try to avoid a confrontation with the other party.	1	2	3	4	5

Scoring Key:

To determine your primary conflict-handling strategy, place the number 1 through 5 that represents your score for each statement next to the number for that statement. Then add up the columns.

Yielding	Compromising	Forcing	Problem solving	Avoiding
1. _____	2. _____	3. _____	4. _____	5. _____
6. _____	7. _____	8. _____	9. _____	10. _____
11. _____	12. _____	13. _____	14. _____	15. _____
16. _____	17. _____	18. _____	19. _____	20. _____
Totals _____	_____	_____	_____	_____

Your primary conflict-handling style is the category with the highest total. Your fallback intention is the category with the second-highest total.

Source: C. K. W. De Dreu, A. Evers, B. Beersma, E. S. Kluwer, and A. Nauta, "A Theory-Based Measure of Conflict Management Strategies in the Workplace," *Journal of Organizational Behavior* 22, no. 6 (September 2001), pp. 645–668. Copyright © John Wiley & Sons Limited. Reproduced with permission.

PERSONAL INVENTORY ASSESSMENT

Communication Styles: Different people tend to prefer different interpersonal communication styles. Use this scale to determine your communication style, and then think about how variations in style may impact communication effectiveness.

Communicating Supportively: Supportive communication is a skill that must be practised. Use this scale to find out how well you do at supportive communication now, and get some ideas for future improvement.

Strategies for Handling Conflict: Different people tend to rely on different strategies for handling conflict. Use this scale to determine your preferred strategy. Is there an alternative strategy that may be more effective in workplace situations?

Managing Interpersonal Conflict: This self-assessment is designed to help you better understand your preferred approaches to managing interpersonal conflict.

BREAKOUT **GROUP** EXERCISES

Form small groups to discuss the following topics, as assigned by your instructor:

1. Describe a situation in which you ignored someone. What impact did it have on that person's subsequent communication behaviours?

2. What differences have you observed in the ways that men and women communicate?

3. You and 2 other students carpool to school every day. The driver has recently taken to playing a new radio station quite loudly. You don't like the music, or the loudness. Using one of the conflict-handling strategies outlined in Exhibit 6-5 on page 210, indicate how you might go about resolving this conflict. Identify a number of BATNAs (*best alternative to a negotiated agreement*) available to you, and then decide whether you should continue carpooling.

WORKING WITH OTHERS EXERCISE

A Negotiation Role Play

This role play is designed to help you develop your negotiating skills. The class is to break into pairs. One person will play the role of Terry, the department supervisor. The other person will play Dale, Terry's boss.

The Situation: Terry and Dale work for hockey-equipment manufacturer Bauer. Terry supervises a research laboratory. Dale is the manager of research and development (R & D). Terry and Dale are former skaters who have worked for Bauer for more than 6 years. Dale has been Terry's boss for 2 years.

One of Terry's employees has greatly impressed Terry. This employee is Lisa Roland. Lisa was hired 11 months ago. She is 24 years old and holds a master's degree in mechanical engineering. Her entry-level salary was $52 500 a year. She was told by Terry that, in accordance with corporation policy, she would receive an initial performance evaluation at 6 months and a comprehensive review after 1 year. Based on her performance record, Lisa was told she could expect a salary adjustment at the time of the 1-year evaluation.

Terry's evaluation of Lisa after 6 months was very positive. Terry commented on the long hours Lisa was working, her cooperative spirit, the fact that others in the lab enjoyed working with her, and her immediate positive impact on the project to which she had been assigned. Now that Lisa's first anniversary is coming up, Terry has again reviewed Lisa's performance. Terry thinks Lisa may be the best new person the R & D group has ever hired. After only a year, Terry has ranked Lisa as the number 3 performer in a department of 11.

Salaries in the department vary greatly. Terry, for instance, has a basic salary of $93 800, plus eligibility for a bonus that might add another $7000 to $11 000 a year. The salary range of the 11 department members is $42 500 to $79 000. The lowest salary is a recent hire with a bachelor's degree in physics. The two people that Terry has rated above Lisa earn base salaries of $73 800 and $78 900. They are both 27 years old and have been at Bauer for 3 and 4 years, respectively. The median salary in Terry's department is $65 300.

WORKING WITH **OTHERS** EXERCISE (Continued)

Terry's Role: You want to give Lisa a big raise. While she is young, she has proven to be an excellent addition to the department. You don't want to lose her. More important, she knows in general what other people in the department are earning, and she thinks she is underpaid. The company typically gives 1-year raises of 5 percent, although 10 percent is not unusual and 20 to 30 percent increases have been approved on occasion. You would like to get Lisa as large an increase as Dale will approve.

Dale's Role: All your supervisors typically try to squeeze you for as much money as they can for their people. You understand this because you did the same thing when you were a supervisor, but your boss wants to keep a lid on costs. He wants you to keep raises for recent hires generally in the range of 5 to 8 percent. In fact, he has sent a memo to all managers and supervisors stating this objective. However, your boss is also very concerned with equity and paying people what they are worth. You feel assured that he will support any salary recommendation you make, as long as it can be justified. Your goal, consistent with cost reduction, is to keep salary increases as low as possible.

The Negotiation: Terry has a meeting scheduled with Dale to discuss Lisa's performance review and salary adjustment. In your role of either Dale or Terry, take a couple of minutes to think through the facts in this exercise and to prepare a strategy. Determine what your target and resistance points are and what your BATNA is. Then you have up to 15 minutes to conduct your negotiation. When your negotiation is complete, the class will compare the various strategies used and the outcomes that resulted.

ETHICAL **DILEMMA** EXERCISE

Is It Unethical to Lie and Deceive During Negotiations?

The topic of lying as it relates to negotiation is important because, for many people, there is no such thing as lying when it comes to negotiating.[98]

It has been said that the whole notion of negotiation is built on ethical quicksand: To succeed, you must deceive.[99] Is this true? Apparently a lot of people think so. For instance, one study found that 28 percent of negotiators lied about a common interest issue during negotiations, while another study found that 100 percent of negotiators either failed to reveal a problem or actively lied about it during negotiations if they were not directly asked about the issue.

Is it possible for someone to maintain high ethical standards and, at the same time, deal with the daily need to negotiate with bosses, peers, staff, people from other organizations, friends, and even relatives?

We can probably agree that bald-faced lies during negotiation are wrong. At least most ethicists would probably agree. The universal dilemma surrounds the little lies—the omissions, evasions, and concealments that are often necessary to best an opponent.

During negotiations, when is a lie a lie? Is exaggerating benefits, downplaying negatives, ignoring flaws, or saying "I don't know" when in reality you do know considered lying? Is declaring that "this is my final offer and it's non-negotiable" (even when you are posturing) a lie? Is pretending to bend over backward to make meaningful concessions lying? Rather than being unethical practices, the use of these "lies" is considered by many as indicators that a negotiator is strong, smart, and savvy.

When are evasiveness and deception out of bounds? Is it naive to be completely honest and bare your soul during negotiations? Or are the rules of negotiations unique: Is any tactic that will improve your chance of winning acceptable?

CASE INCIDENT

Dianna Abdala

Consider the case of Dianna Abdala.[100] In 2005, Abdala was a recent graduate of Suffolk University's law school. She passed the bar exam and was offered a job at a law firm started by William Korman, a former state prosecutor.

The following is a summary of their email communications:

—————Original Message—————
From: Dianna Abdala
Sent: Friday, February 03, 2006 9:23 p.m.
To: William A. Korman
Subject: Thank you

Dear Attorney Korman,

At this time, I am writing to inform you that I will not be accepting your offer. After careful consideration, I have come to the conclusion that the pay you are offering would neither fulfill me nor support the lifestyle I am living in light of the work I would be doing for you. I have decided instead to work for myself, and reap 100 percent of the benefits that I sew [*sic*].
Thank you for the interviews.

Dianna L. Abdala, Esq.

—————Original Message—————
From: William A. Korman
To: Dianna Abdala
Sent: Monday, February 06, 2006 12:15 p.m.
Subject: RE: Thank you

Dianna- -

Given that you had two interviews, were offered and accepted the job (indeed, you had a definite start date), I am surprised that you chose an e-mail and a 9:30 p.m. voice-mail message to convey this information to me. It smacks of immaturity and is quite unprofessional. Indeed, I did rely upon your acceptance by ordering stationary [*sic*] and business cards with your name, reformatting a computer, and setting up both internal and external e-mails for you here at the office. While I do not quarrel with your reasoning, I am extremely disappointed in the way this played out. I sincerely wish you the best of luck in your future endeavors.
Will Korman

—————Original Message—————
From: Dianna Abdala
Sent: Monday, February 06, 2006 4:01 p.m.
To: William A. Korman
Subject: Re: Thank you

A real lawyer would have put the contract into writing and not exercised any such reliance until he did so.
Again, thank you.

—————Original Message—————
From: William A. Korman
To: Dianna Abdala
Sent: Monday, February 06, 2006 4:18 p.m.
Subject: RE: Thank you

Thank you for the refresher course on contracts. This is not a bar exam question. You need to realize that this is a very small legal community, especially the criminal defense bar. Do you really want to start pissing off more experienced lawyers at this early stage of your career?

—————Original Message—————
From: Dianna Abdala
To: William A. Korman
Sent: Monday, February 06, 2006 4:28 p.m.
Subject: Re: Thank you
bla bla bla

After this email exchange, Korman forwarded the correspondence to several colleagues, and it quickly spread.

Questions

1. With whom do you side here—Abdala or Korman?

2. What mistakes do you think each party made?

3. Do you think this exchange will damage Abdala's career? Korman's firm?

4. What does this exchange tell you about the limitations of email?

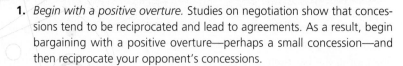

FROM CONCEPTS TO SKILLS

Negotiating

Once you have taken the time to assess your own goals, to consider the other party's goals and interests, and to develop a strategy, you are ready to begin actual negotiations. The following five suggestions should improve your negotiating skills:[101]

1. *Begin with a positive overture.* Studies on negotiation show that concessions tend to be reciprocated and lead to agreements. As a result, begin bargaining with a positive overture—perhaps a small concession—and then reciprocate your opponent's concessions.

2. *Address problems, not personalities.* Concentrate on the negotiation issues, not on the personal characteristics of your opponent. When negotiations get tough, avoid the tendency to attack your opponent. It's your opponent's ideas or position that you disagree with, not him or her personally. Separate the people from the problem, and don't personalize differences.

3. *Pay little attention to initial offers.* Treat an initial offer as merely a point of departure. Everyone has to have an initial position. These initial offers tend to be extreme and idealistic. Treat them as such.

4. *Emphasize win-win solutions.* Inexperienced negotiators often assume that their gain must come at the expense of the other party. As noted with integrative bargaining, that need not be the case. There are often win-win solutions. But assuming a zero-sum game means missed opportunities for trade-offs that could benefit both sides. So if conditions are supportive, look for an integrative solution. Frame options in terms of your opponent's interests, and look for solutions that can allow your opponent, as well as yourself, to declare a victory.

5. *Create an open and trusting climate.* Skilled negotiators are better listeners, ask more questions, focus their arguments more directly, are less defensive, and have learned to avoid words and phrases that can irritate an opponent (for example, "generous offer," "fair price," "reasonable arrangement"). In other words, they are better at creating the open and trusting climate necessary for reaching an integrative settlement.

Practising Skills

As marketing director for Done Right, a regional home-repair chain, you have come up with a plan you believe has significant potential for future sales. Your plan involves a customer information service designed to help people make their homes more environmentally sensitive. Then, based on homeowners' assessments of their homes' environmental impact, your firm will be prepared to help them deal with problems or concerns they may uncover. You are really excited about the competitive potential of this new service. You envision pamphlets, in-store appearances by environmental experts, as well as contests for consumers and school kids. After several weeks of preparations, you make your pitch to your boss, Nick Castro. You point out how the market for environmentally sensitive products is growing and how this growing demand represents the perfect opportunity for Done Right. Nick seems impressed by your presentation, but he has expressed one major concern: He thinks your workload is already too heavy. He does not see how you are going to have enough time to start this new service and still be able to look after all of your other assigned marketing duties. You really want to start the new service. What strategy will you follow in your negotiation with Nick?

Reinforcing Skills

1. Negotiate with a team member or work colleague to handle a small section of work that you are not going to be able to get done in time for an important deadline.

2. The next time you purchase a relatively expensive item (such as an automobile, apartment lease, appliance, jewellery), attempt to negotiate a better price and gain some concessions such as an extended warranty, smaller down payment, maintenance services, or the like.

MyManagementLab

Study, practise, and explore real business situations with these helpful resources:

- **Study Plan:** Check your understanding of chapter concepts with self-study quizzes.
- **Online Lesson Presentations:** Study key chapter topics and work through interactive assessments to test your knowledge and master management concepts.
- **Videos:** Learn more about the management practices and strategies of real companies.
- **Simulations:** Practise management decision-making in simulated business environments.

P I A PERSONAL INVENTORY ASSESSMENT

CHAPTER 7
Power and Politics

What led franchise owners to file a class action suit against Tim Hortons? Power and politics tell much of the story.

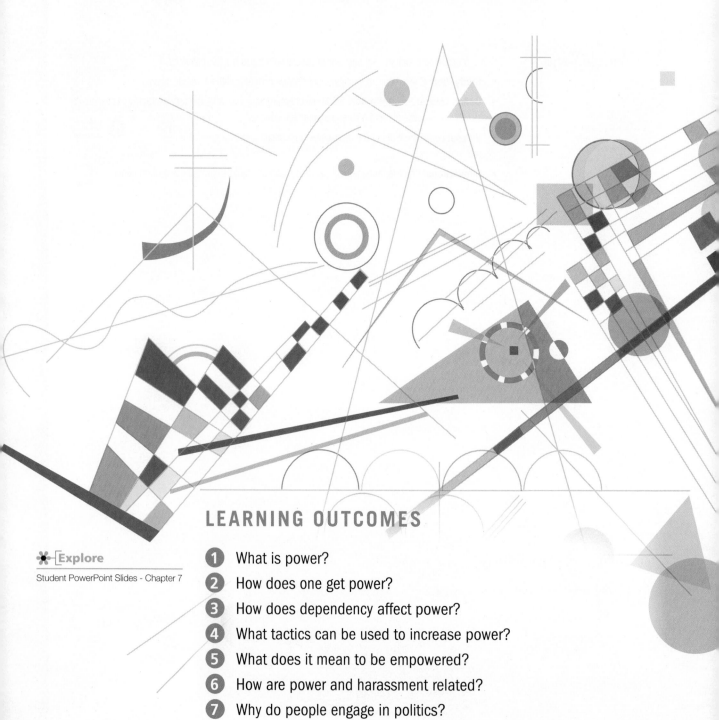

✳ Explore

Student PowerPoint Slides - Chapter 7

LEARNING OUTCOMES

1. What is power?
2. How does one get power?
3. How does dependency affect power?
4. What tactics can be used to increase power?
5. What does it mean to be empowered?
6. How are power and harassment related?
7. Why do people engage in politics?

Arch and Anne Jollymore are not happy with Tim Hortons' senior management.[1] The couple, who own several Tim Hortons franchises, brought a class action lawsuit against the company that was heard in August 2011. They argued that the company's management forced changes in the production of donuts and other baked goods that enriched management and shareholders at the expense of the franchise owners.

One of the key complaints is the move to using "flash frozen" baked goods in the coffee shops in 2002. Before then, each Tim Hortons store had its own baker, who made all the baked goods from scratch, and baked them on the premises. The move has made donut production more expensive.

The franchise owners who signed on to the lawsuit complain bitterly about what they see as the company's abuse of power. An email sent to Roland Walton, head of Tim Hortons' Canadian operations, shortly after the lawsuit was launched, explained the power differential between management and franchisees: "[T]he feeling is that [the company's] attitude is 'We're still the best game in town, if you don't like it or aren't happy, there is a waiting list to get stores.'"

A major theme throughout this chapter is that power and politics are a natural process in any group or organization. Although you might have heard the saying "Power corrupts, and absolute power corrupts absolutely," power is not always bad. Understanding how to use power and politics effectively makes organizational life more manageable, because it can help you gain the support you need to do your job effectively.

THE BIG IDEA

Power is not necessarily a zero-sum game. Sharing power may in fact increase everyone's power.

OB IS FOR EVERYONE

- Have you ever wondered how you might increase your power?
- What do you need to be truly empowered?
- Why do some people seem to engage in politics more than others?
- In what situations does impression management work best?

LEARNING ABOUT YOURSELF

- Political Skills

A Definition of Power

1   What is power?

Power refers to a capacity that A has to influence the behaviour of B, so that B acts in accordance with A's wishes.[2] This definition implies that there is a *potential* for power if someone is dependent on another. But one can have power and not impose it.

Probably the most important aspect of power is that it is a function of **dependency**. The more that B depends on A, the more power A has in the relationship. Dependence, in turn, is based on the alternatives that B perceives and the importance that B places on the alternative(s) that A controls. A person can have power over you only if he or she controls something you desire. If you are attending college or university on funds totally provided by your parents, you probably recognize the power that your parents hold over you. You are dependent on them for financial support. But once you are out of school, have a job, and are making a good income, your parents' power is reduced significantly. Who among us, though, has not known or heard of the rich relative who is able to control a large number of family members merely through the implicit or explicit threat of "writing them out of the will"?

Within larger organizations, the information technology (IT) group often has considerable power, because everyone, right up to the CEO, is dependent on this group to keep computers and networks running. Since few people have the technical expertise to do so, IT personnel end up being viewed as irreplaceable. This gives them a lot of power within the organization.

Power makes people uncomfortable.[3] People who have power deny it, people who want it try not to look like they are seeking it, and those who are good at getting it are secretive about how they do so.[4] Commenting on a recent study, one researcher noted, "A person's sense of power is an extremely pervasive feeling in everyday life."[5]

Part of the discomfort about power may have to do with how people perceive those in power. A 2011 study found that people who behave rudely—putting their feet up on a chair, ordering a meal brusquely—were believed by those watching this behaviour to be more likely to "get to make decisions" and able to "get people to listen to what [they] say" than people who behave politely. The researchers concluded that "norm violators are perceived as having the capacity to act as they please."[6] As a result, they seem more powerful. A 2010 study found that people who have power judged others much more negatively for speeding, dodging taxes, and keeping a stolen bike than if they engaged in this behaviour themselves. The researchers found that those who had legitimate power were even more likely to indulge in moral hypocrisy than those who did not feel personally entitled to their power.[7]

Power should not be considered a bad thing, however. "Power, if used appropriately, should actually be a positive influence in your organization," says Professor Patricia Bradshaw of the Schulich School of Business at York University. "Having more power doesn't necessarily turn you into a Machiavellian monster. It can help your team and your organization achieve its goals and increase its potential."[8] The positive benefits of power (and politics) have also been explored by professor Tom Lawrence of SFU Business (at Simon Fraser University) and his colleagues.[9]

A major theme of this chapter is that power and political behaviour are natural processes in any group or organization. By learning how power works in organizations, you will be better able to use your knowledge to become a more effective manager.

2   How does one get power?

Bases of Power

Where does power come from? What is it that gives an individual or a group influence over others? The answer to these questions was developed by social scientists John French and Bertrand Raven, who first presented a five-category classification scheme of sources or bases of power: coercive, reward, legitimate, expert, and referent.[10] They subsequently added information power to that schema (see Exhibit 7-1).[11]

power A capacity that A has to influence the behaviour of B, so that B acts in accordance with A's wishes.

dependency B's relationship to A when A possesses something that B needs.

EXHIBIT 7-1 Measuring Bases of Power

✳—Explore

Exhibit 7-1: Measuring Bases of Power

Does a person have one or more of the six bases of power? These descriptions help identify the person's power base.

Power Base	Statement
Coercive	The person can make things difficult for people, and you want to avoid getting him or her angry.
Reward	The person is able to give special benefits or rewards to people, and you find it advantageous to trade favours with him or her.
Legitimate	The person has the right, considering his or her position and your job responsibilities, to expect you to comply with legitimate requests.
Expert	The person has the experience and knowledge to earn your respect, and you defer to his or her judgment in some matters.
Referent	You like the person and enjoy doing things for him or her.
Information	The person has data or knowledge that you need.

Source: Adapted from G. Yukl and C. M. Falbe, "Importance of Different Power Sources in Downward and Lateral Relations," *Journal of Applied Psychology*, June 1991, p. 417.

Coercive Power

Coercive power is defined by French and Raven as dependent on fear of the negative results that might occur if one fails to comply. It rests on the application, or the threat of the application, of physical sanctions such as the infliction of pain, the generation of frustration through restriction of movement, or the controlling by force of basic physiological or safety needs.

At the organizational level, A has coercive power over B if A can dismiss, suspend, or demote B, assuming that B values his or her job. Similarly, if A can assign B work activities that B finds unpleasant or treat B in a manner that B finds embarrassing, A possesses coercive power over B.

Reward Power

The opposite of coercive power is **reward power**. People will go along with the wishes or directives of another if doing so produces positive benefits; therefore, one who can distribute rewards that others view as valuable will have power over those others. These rewards can be either financial—such as controlling pay rates, raises, and bonuses—or nonfinancial, including offering recognition, promotions, interesting work assignments, friendly colleagues, important information, and preferred work shifts or sales territories.[12]

As with coercive power, you don't have to be a manager to be able to exert influence through rewards. Rewards such as friendliness, acceptance, and praise are available to everyone in an organization. To the degree that an individual seeks such rewards, your ability to give or withhold them gives you power over that individual.

Legitimate Power

In formal groups and organizations, probably the most frequent access to one or more of the bases of power is through a person's structural position. This is called **legitimate power**. It represents the power a person receives as a result of his or her position in the formal hierarchy of an organization.

coercive power Power that is based on fear.

reward power Power that achieves compliance based on the ability to distribute rewards that others view as valuable.

legitimate power Power that a person receives as a result of his or her position in the formal hierarchy of an organization.

In India, Naina Lal Kidwai is a powerful woman in the banking industry. She derives her power as managing director and vice chairman of HSBC Securities and Capital Markets, a group within the Hongkong and Shanghai Banking Corporation. Kidwai's formal power is based on her position at the bank.

Legitimate power is broader than the power to coerce and reward. Specifically, it includes acceptance by members of an organization of the authority of a position. We associate power so closely with the concept of hierarchy that just drawing longer lines in an organization chart leads people to infer that the leaders are especially powerful, and when a powerful executive is described, people tend to put the person at a higher position when drawing an organization chart.[13] When school principals, bank presidents, or generals speak (assuming that their directives are viewed as within the authority of their positions), teachers, tellers, and privates listen and usually comply. You will note in Exhibit 7-2 that one of the men in the meeting identifies himself as the rule maker, which means that he has legitimate power.

Expert Power

Expert power is influence based on expertise, special skills, or knowledge. Expertise has become one of the most powerful sources of influence as the world has become more technologically oriented. While it is generally acknowledged that physicians have expertise and hence expert power—most of us follow the advice that our doctors give us—you should also recognize that computer specialists, tax accountants, economists, and other specialists can have power as a result of their expertise. Young people may find they have increased power in the workplace these

EXHIBIT 7-2

"I was just going to say 'Well, I don't make the rules.' But, of course, I _do_ make the rules."

expert power Influence based on special skills or knowledge.

Source: © Leo Cullum/ The New Yorker Collection/ www.cartoonbank.com

days because of the technical knowledge and expertise that their Baby Boomer managers may not have.

Referent Power

Referent power develops out of admiration of another and a desire to be like that person. Sometimes teachers and coaches have referent power because of our admiration of them. Referent power explains why celebrities are paid millions of dollars to endorse products in commercials. Mississauga, Ontario-based Alexis Life Sciences uses endorsements from Don Cherry of *Hockey Night in Canada* and popular athletes such as Alexandre Bilodeau, Clara Hughes, and Joannie Rochette to convince people to buy COLD-FX, its cold and flu product. Similarly, Nike Canada uses sports celebrities, such as Montreal Canadiens defenceman P. K. Subban, to promote its products.

Information Power

Information power comes from access to and control over information. People in an organization who have data or knowledge that others need can make those others dependent on them. Managers, for instance, because of their access to privileged sales, cost, salary, profit, and similar data, can use this information to control and shape subordinates' behaviour. Similarly, departments that possess information that is critical to a company's performance in times of high uncertainty—for example, the legal department when a firm faces a major lawsuit or the human resource department during critical labour negotiations—will gain increased power in their organizations until those uncertainties are resolved. Withholding information can result in poor-quality performance by those who need the information.[14] The *Working with Others Exercise* on pages 252–253 gives you the opportunity to explore the effectiveness of different bases of power in changing someone's behaviour.

Evaluating the Bases of Power

Generally, people will respond in one of three ways when faced with the people who use the bases of power described above:

- *Commitment.* The person is enthusiastic about the request and shows initiative and persistence in carrying it out.

- *Compliance.* The person goes along with the request grudgingly, puts in minimal effort, and takes little initiative in carrying out the request.

- *Resistance.* The person is opposed to the request and tries to avoid it with such tactics as refusing, stalling, or arguing about it.[15]

A review of the research on the effectiveness of these forms of power finds that they differ in their impact on a person's performance.[16] Exhibit 7-3 summarizes some of this research. Coercive power leads to resistance from individuals, decreased satisfaction, and increased mistrust. Reward power results in compliance if the rewards are consistent with what individuals want as rewards, something the *Ethical Dilemma Exercise* on page 254 shows clearly. Legitimate power also results in compliance, but it does not generally result in increased commitment. In other words, legitimate power does not inspire individuals to act beyond the basic level. Expert and referent powers are the most likely to lead to commitment from individuals. Research shows that deadline pressures increase group members' reliance on individuals with expert and information power.[17] Ironically, the least effective bases of power for improving commitment—coercive, reward, and legitimate—are the ones most often used by managers, perhaps because they are the easiest to introduce.[18]

referent power Influence based on possession by an individual of desirable resources or personal traits.

information power Power that comes from access to and control over information.

EXHIBIT 7-3 Continuum of Responses to Power

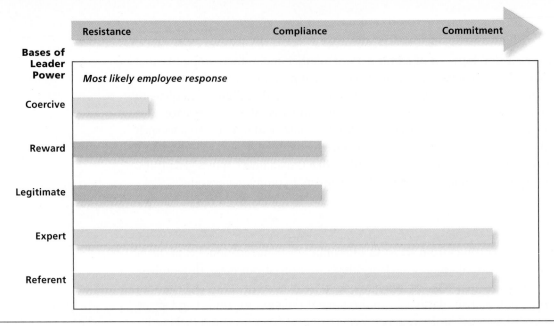

Source: R. M. Steers and J. S. Black, *Organizational Behavior,* 5th ed. (New York: HarperCollins, 1994), p. 487. Reprinted by permission of Pearson Education Inc., Upper Saddle River, New Jersey.

Exhibit 7-3: Continuum of Responses to Power

 How does dependency affect power?

Dependency: The Key to Power

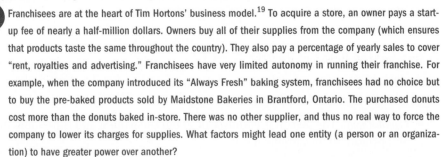

Franchisees are at the heart of Tim Hortons' business model.[19] To acquire a store, an owner pays a start-up fee of nearly a half-million dollars. Owners buy all of their supplies from the company (which ensures that products taste the same throughout the country). They also pay a percentage of yearly sales to cover "rent, royalties and advertising." Franchisees have very limited autonomy in running their franchise. For example, when the company introduced its "Always Fresh" baking system, franchisees had no choice but to buy the pre-baked products sold by Maidstone Bakeries in Brantford, Ontario. The purchased donuts cost more than the donuts baked in-store. There was no other supplier, and thus no real way to force the company to lower its charges for supplies. What factors might lead one entity (a person or an organization) to have greater power over another?

In this section, we show how an understanding of dependency is central to furthering your understanding of power itself.

The General Dependency Postulate

Let's begin with a general postulate: *The greater B's dependency on A, the greater the power A has over B.* When you possess anything that others require but that you alone control, you make them dependent upon you and therefore you gain power over them.[20] Another way to frame dependency is to think about a relationship in terms of "who needs whom?" The person who has the most need is the one most dependent on the relationship.[21]

Dependency is inversely proportional to the alternative sources of supply. If something is plentiful, possession of it will not increase your power. If everyone is intelligent, intelligence gives no special advantage. Similarly, in the circles of the super rich, money does not result in power. But if you can create a monopoly by controlling information, prestige, or anything that others crave, they become dependent on you. Alternatively, the more options you have, the less power you place in the hands of others.

This explains, for example, why most organizations develop multiple suppliers rather than give their business to only one.

What Creates Dependency?

Dependency is increased when the resource you control is important, scarce, and cannot be substituted.[22]

Importance

If nobody wants what you have, there is no dependency. To create dependency, the thing(s) you control must be perceived as important. In some organizations, people who control the budget have a great deal of importance. In other organizations, those who possess the knowledge to keep technology working smoothly are viewed as important. What is important is situational. It varies among organizations and undoubtedly also varies over time within any given organization.

Scarcity

As noted previously, if something is plentiful, possession of it will not increase your power. A resource must be perceived as scarce to create dependency.

Scarcity can help explain how low-ranking employees gain power if they have important knowledge not available to high-ranking employees. Possession of a scarce resource—in this case, important knowledge—makes those who don't have it dependent on those who do. Thus, an individual might refuse to show others how to do a job, or might refuse to share information, thereby increasing his or her importance.

Nonsubstitutability

The fewer substitutes for a resource, the more power comes from control over that resource. During his tenure as CEO, the common belief at Apple Computer, for example, was that Steve Jobs was not replaceable. His passing in October 2011 meant that Apple had to contend with replacing the company's charismatic figurehead (inevitably, new CEO Tim Cook has been scrutinized not only for his ability to manage Apple but also for how he compares with Jobs). The unanswered question at the time of his death was whether Apple could continue to be innovative and edgy without Jobs at the helm. In another example, when a union goes on strike and management is not permitted to replace the striking employees, the union has considerable control over the organization's ability to carry out its tasks.

People are often able to ask for special rewards (higher pay or better assignments) because they have skills that others do not.

Because Xerox Corporation has staked its future on development and innovation, Sophie Vanderbroek is in a position of power at Xerox. As the company's chief technology officer, she manages Xerox's 4000 scientists and engineers at the company's global research centres. The group's mission is "to pioneer high-impact technologies that enable us to lead in our core markets and to create future markets for Xerox." Xerox depends on Vanderbroek to make that mission a reality.

Influence Tactics

 Tim Hortons' management used a number of influence tactics to persuade its franchisees to adopt the "Always Fresh" baking system in their stores.[23] Management started with a taste test at the 2000 annual convention, an inspirational appeal that convinced some of the franchisees that the taste was much better. Management then used rational persuasion to convince owners that the increased cost was worth the gain in convenience. Under the in-house baking system, franchise owners were paying about 5 to 9 cents to make one donut. According to some franchisees, they were told that the new process would result in donuts that cost about 11.5 cents to produce. "We all knew that that was more than we were paying to bake

 What tactics can be used to increase power?

in-house, but we all felt the same," Ottawa franchisee Greg Gilson said. "The convenience of it would be worth the offset of the three to four cents." Thus, management further influenced the decisions of the franchisees by emphasizing convenience. However, when the final cost turned out to be about 18 cents per donut, head office used its legitimate power to require the owners to buy the "flash frozen" donuts from Maidstone Bakeries. So how and why do influence tactics work?

How do individuals translate their bases of power into specific, desired actions? Research indicates that people use common tactics to influence outcomes.[24] One study identifies the nine **influence tactics** managers and employees use to increase their power:[25]

> Have you ever wondered how you might increase your power?

1. *Rational persuasion.* Using facts and data to make a logical or rational presentation of ideas.

2. *Inspirational appeals.* Appealing to values, ideals, and goals when making a request.

3. *Consultation.* Getting others involved to support one's objectives.

4. *Ingratiation.* Using flattery, creating goodwill, and being friendly prior to making a request.

5. *Personal appeals.* Appealing to loyalty and friendship when asking for something.

6. *Exchange.* Offering favours or benefits in exchange for support.

7. *Coalitions.* Getting the support of other people to provide backing when making a request.

8. *Pressure.* Using demands, threats, and reminders to get someone to do something.

9. *Legitimacy.* Claiming the authority or right to make a request, or showing that it supports organizational goals or policies.

Some tactics are more effective than others. Rational persuasion, inspirational appeals, and consultation tend to be the most effective, especially when the audience is highly interested in the outcomes of a decision process. Pressure tends to frequently backfire and is typically the least effective of the nine tactics.[26] You can also increase your chance of success by using more than one type of tactic at the same time or sequentially, as long as your choices are compatible.[27] For instance, using both ingratiation and legitimacy can lessen the negative reactions that might come from appearing to "dictate" outcomes, but only when the audience does not really care about the outcomes of a decision process or the policy is routine.[28]

The effectiveness of some influence tactics depends on the direction of influence.[29] Studies have found that rational persuasion is the only tactic that is effective across organizational levels. Inspirational appeals work best as a downward-influencing tactic with subordinates. When pressure works, it's generally only to achieve downward influence. The use of personal appeals and coalitions is most effective with lateral influence attempts. In addition to the direction of influence, a number of other factors have been found to affect which tactics work best. These include the sequencing of tactics, a person's skill in using the tactic, and the culture of the organization.

You are more likely to be effective if you begin with "softer" tactics that rely on personal power such as personal and inspirational appeals, rational persuasion, and consultation. If these fail, you can move to "harder" tactics (which emphasize formal power and involve greater costs and risks), such as exchange, coalitions, and pressure.[30] Interestingly, it has been found that using a single soft tactic is more effective than using a single hard tactic, and that combining two soft tactics or a soft tactic and

Learn About Yourself
Gaining Power and Influence

Learn About Yourself
Using Influence Strategies

influence tactics Ways that individuals translate power bases into specific actions.

rational persuasion is more effective than any single tactic or a combination of hard tactics.[31] The effectiveness of tactics depends on the audience.[32] People especially likely to comply with soft power tactics tend to be more reflective, are intrinsically motivated, have high self-esteem, and have greater desire for control. People especially likely to comply with hard power tactics are more action oriented and extrinsically motivated and are more focused on getting along with others than with getting their own way.

Empowerment: Giving Power to Employees

Thus far our discussion has implied that—to some extent, at least—power is most likely to rest in the hands of managers, to be used as part of their interaction with employees. However, in today's workplace, there is a movement toward sharing more power with employees by putting them in teams and also by making them responsible for some of the decisions regarding their jobs. For instance, at Vancouver-based iQmetrix Software Development, employees are part of a results-only workplace, where they are encouraged to make their own decisions.[33] Organizational specialists refer to this increasing responsibility as *empowerment*.

Definition of Empowerment

The definition of **empowerment** that we use here refers to the freedom and the ability of employees to make decisions and commitments.[34] Unfortunately, neither managers nor researchers can agree on the definition of empowerment. One study found that executives were split about 50-50 in their definition.[35] One group of executives "believed that empowerment was about delegating decision making within a set of clear boundaries." Empowerment would start at the top, specific goals and tasks would

5 What does it mean to be empowered?

PERSONAL INVENTORY ASSESSMENT

Learn About Yourself
Personal Empowerment Assessment

WestJet has an empowerment culture. As Sean Durfy, WestJet's former president and CEO, notes: "If you empower people to do the right things, then they will. If you align the interests of the people with the interests of the company, it's very powerful. That's what we do." WestJet's empowerment culture is admired by others as well. In 2011, the company was named one of "Canada's Most Admired Corporate Cultures for Western Canada" by Waterstone Human Capital. Two years earlier, WestJet was named to Waterstone Human Capital's Inaugural Hall of Fame after having placed on its "Canada's 10 Most Admired Corporate Cultures" list four times in a row, including three times in a row at number one.

empowerment The freedom and the ability of employees to make decisions and commitments.

be assigned, responsibility would be delegated, and people would be held accountable for their results. The other group believed that empowerment was "a process of risk taking and personal growth." This type of empowerment starts at the bottom, with considering the employees' needs, showing them what empowered behaviour looks like, building teams, encouraging risk-taking, and demonstrating trust in employees' ability to perform.

Empowerment in the Workplace

One difficulty with empowerment is that managers often give lip service to the idea,[36] with organizations telling employees that they have decision-making responsibility but not giving them the authority to carry out their decisions. This leads to a great deal of cynicism in many workplaces, particularly when "empowered" employees are micromanaged. Professor Marylène Gagné of Concordia's John Molson School of Business notes that "For example, in some cultures, bosses can't ask the opinion of subordinates, because it makes them appear weak. So managers in these environments have to find other ways to make people feel autonomous. There is no simple recipe."[37] For an employee to be fully empowered, he or she needs access to the information required to make decisions; rewards for acting in appropriate, responsible ways; and the authority to make the necessary decisions. Empowerment means that employees understand how their jobs fit into the organization and that they are able to make decisions regarding job action in light of the organization's purpose and mission.

What do you need to be truly empowered?

In some cases, employees don't want to be empowered, and having more power can even make them ill. A study carried out by Professor Jia Lin Xie, of the University of Toronto's Rotman School of Management, and colleagues found that when people are put in charge at work but don't have the confidence to handle their responsibilities, they can become ill.[38] Specifically, people who blame themselves when things go wrong are more likely to suffer colds and infections if they have high levels of control at work. This finding by Professor Xie and her colleagues was somewhat unexpected, as some have hypothesized that greater control at work would lead to less stress. The study showed, instead, that the impact of empowerment depended on personality and job factors. Those who had control, but did not blame themselves when things went wrong, suffered less stress, even if the job was demanding.

When employees are empowered, it means that they are expected to act, at least in a small way, as owners of the company, rather than just as employees. Ownership is not necessary in the financial sense, but in terms of identifying with the goals and mission of the organization. For employees to be empowered, however, and have an ownership mentality, four conditions need to be met, according to Professor Dan Ondrack at the Rotman School of Management:

- There must be a clear definition of the values and mission of the company.

- The company must help employees gain the relevant skills.

- Employees need to be supported in their decision making and not criticized when they try to do something extraordinary.

- Employees need to be recognized for their efforts.[39]

Exhibit 7-4 outlines what two researchers discovered in studying the characteristics of empowered employees.

EXHIBIT 7-4 Characteristics of Empowered People

Robert E. Quinn and Gretchen M. Spreitzer, in their research on the characteristics of empowered people (through both in-depth interviews and survey analysis), found four characteristics that most empowered people have in common:

- Empowered people have a sense of *self-determination* (this means that they are free to choose how to do their work; they are not micromanaged).

- Empowered people have a sense of *meaning* (they feel that their work is important to them; they care about what they are doing).

- Empowered people have a sense of *competence* (this means that they are confident about their ability to do their work well; they know they can perform).

- Empowered people have a sense of *impact* (this means that people believe they can have influence on their work unit; others listen to their ideas).

Source: R. E. Quinn and G. M. Spreitzer, "The Road to Empowerment: Seven Questions Every Leader Should Consider," *Organizational Dynamics,* Autumn 1997, p. 41, with permission from Elsevier.

The Abuse of Power: Harassment in the Workplace

People who engage in harassment in the workplace are typically abusing their power positions. The manager-employee relationship best characterizes an unequal power relationship, where position power gives the managers the capacity to reward and coerce. Managers give employees their assignments, evaluate their performance, make recommendations for salary adjustments and promotions, and even decide whether employees retain their jobs. These decisions give managers power. Since employees want favourable performance reviews, salary increases, and the like, it is clear that managers control the resources that most employees consider important and scarce.

Although co-workers don't have position power, they can have influence and use it to harass peers. In fact, although co-workers appear to engage in somewhat less severe forms of harassment than do managers, co-workers are the most frequent perpetrators of harassment, particularly sexual harassment, in organizations. How do co-workers exercise power? Most often they provide or withhold information, cooperation, and support.

Some categories of harassment have long been illegal in Canada, including those based on race, religion, and national origin, as well as sexual harassment. Unfortunately, some types of harassment that occur in the workplace are not deemed illegal, even if they create problems for employees and managers. We focus here on two types of harassment that have received considerable attention in the press: workplace bullying and sexual harassment.

6 How are power and harassment related?

Workplace Bullying

Many of us are aware, anecdotally if not personally, of managers who harass employees, demanding overtime without pay or excessive work performance. Further, some of the recent stories of workplace violence have reportedly been the result of an employee's feeling intimidated at work. In research conducted in the private and public sector in southern Saskatchewan, Céleste Brotheridge, a professor at the Université du Québec à Montréal, found that bullying was rather prevalent in the workplace. Forty percent of the respondents noted that they had experienced one or more forms of bullying weekly in the past six months. Ten percent experienced bullying at a much greater level: five or more incidents a week. Brotheridge notes that bullying has a negative effect on the workplace: "Given bullying's [negative] effects on employee health, it is reason for concern."[40]

There is no clear definition of workplace bullying, and Marilyn Noble, a Fredericton-based adult educator, remarks that in some instances there can be a fine line between managing and bullying. However, recent research suggests that bosses who feel inadequate or overwhelmed are more likely to bully.[41] As one of the study's co-authors explained: "The combination of having a high-power role and fearing that one is not up to the task . . . causes power holders to lash out."[42]

The effects of bullying can be devastating. Professors Sandy Hershcovis of the University of Manitoba and Julian Barling of Queen's University found that the consequences of bullying were more harmful to its victims than those who suffered sexual harassment. Bullied employees more often quit their jobs, were less satisfied with their jobs, and had more difficult relationships with their supervisors.[43]

Quebec introduced the first anti-bullying labour legislation in North America on June 1, 2004. The legislation defines psychological harassment as "any vexatious behaviour in the form of repeated and hostile or unwanted conduct, verbal comments, actions or gestures that affect an employee's dignity or psychological or physical integrity and that results in a harmful work environment for the employee."[44] Under the Quebec law, bullying allegations will be sent to mediation, where the accuser and the accused will work with an independent third party to try to resolve the problem. If mediation fails, employers who have allowed psychological harassment can be fined up to $10 000 and ordered to pay financial damages to the victim. Other provinces have followed Quebec's lead, with British Columbia the most recent province to pass workplace bullying legislation, in July 2012. Saskatchewan did so in 2007, Ontario in 2009, and Manitoba in 2011.[45]

Sexual Harassment

Sexual harassment is wrong. It can also be costly to employers. Just ask executives at the RCMP, Walmart, the World Bank, and the United Nations.[46] The Supreme Court of Canada defines **sexual harassment** as unwelcome behaviour of a sexual nature in the workplace that negatively affects the work environment or leads to adverse job-related consequences for the employee.[47] Despite the legal framework for defining sexual harassment, there continues to be disagreement as to what *specifically* constitutes sexual harassment. Sexual harassment includes unwanted physical touching, recurring requests for dates when it is made clear the person is not interested, and coercive threats that a person will lose her or his job if she or he refuses a sexual proposition. The problems of interpreting sexual harassment often surface around some of its more subtle forms—unwanted looks or comments, off-colour jokes, sexual artifacts such as nude calendars in the workplace, sexual innuendo, or misinterpretations of where the line between "being friendly" ends and "harassment" begins. Most studies confirm that the concept of power is central to understanding sexual harassment.[48] It's about an individual controlling or threatening another individual. This seems to be true whether the harassment comes from a manager, a co-worker, or even an employee.

Because of power inequities, sexual harassment by one's manager typically creates the greatest difficulty for the person being harassed. If there are no witnesses, it is the manager's word against the employee's word. Are there others whom this manager has harassed, and if so, will they come forward? Because of the manager's control over resources, many of those who are harassed are afraid of speaking out for fear of retaliation by the manager.

Workplaces are not the only place where sexual harassment occurs. While nonconsensual sex between professors and students is rape and subject to criminal charges, it is harder to evaluate apparently consensual relationships that occur outside the classroom. There is some argument over whether truly consensual sex is ever possible between students and professors. In an effort to underscore the power discrepancy and

sexual harassment Unwelcome behaviour of a sexual nature in the workplace that negatively affects the work environment or leads to adverse job-related consequences for the employee.

potential for abuse of it by professors, in 2009 Yale University implemented a policy forbidding romantic relationships between professors and their undergraduate students as well.[49] Deputy Provost Charles Long explained the university's decision: "I think we have a responsibility to protect students from behavior that is damaging to them and to the objectives for their being here." Most universities have been unwilling to adopt such an extreme stance, and it's not clear that in Canada such a policy would stand up in the Courts. Carleton University does not prohibit relationships between individuals in authority and those who are not, but does include the following statement in its sexual harassment policy: "No individual in a position of authority is permitted to grade or supervise the performance of any student, or evaluate an employee or a colleague, with whom they are sexually involved or have been within the past five years."[50]

One recent study found that nearly two-thirds of university students experience some type of sexual harassment, but most of these incidents go unreported.[51] However, much of this harassment comes from student-on-student incidents. Matt Abbott, a student at the University of New Brunswick, says that "certain aspects of sexual violence are almost normal within the dating culture in campus communities." A University of British Columbia student, Anoushka Ratnarajah, notes that "'the line' with respect to sexual harassment and the issue of consent are still fuzzy for many students."[52]

A recent review of the literature shows the damage caused by sexual harassment. As you would expect, individuals who are sexually harassed report more negative job attitudes (lower job satisfaction, diminished organizational commitment) as a result. This review also revealed that sexual harassment undermines the victims' mental and physical health. However, sexual harassment also negatively affects the group in which the victim works, lowering its level of productivity. The authors of this study conclude that sexual harassment "is significantly and substantively associated with a host of harms."[53]

In concluding this discussion, we would like to point out that sexual harassment is about power. It is about an individual controlling or threatening another individual. It is wrong. Moreover, it is illegal. You can understand how sexual harassment surfaces in organizations if you analyze it in power terms. We should also point out that sexual harassment is not something done only by men to women. There have been several cases of males reporting sexual harassment by male managers.[54] While there have been no media reports of women sexually harassing either men or women in Canada, under the framework of the law, it is certainly feasible.

Politics: Power in Action

Archibald Jollymore was a senior executive at Tim Hortons before he retired and became the owner of a franchise in Burlington, Ontario.[55] His cousin is Ron Joyce, co-founder of Tim Hortons. Joyce sold the company to Wendy's in 1995 and regrets doing so. There is speculation that Joyce is the financial backer behind the lawsuit, although neither Joyce nor Jollymore confirms this. Joyce does not like the direction the company has taken under his successor, Paul D. House, and is vocal in his complaints about the executive team. With respect to the "Always Fresh" donuts, Joyce said publicly, "This is not a philosophy that I would have embraced if I still owned the company." Thus, politics, rather than money, may be part of the reason behind the lawsuit.

The lawsuit has also pitted franchise operators against one another. Some claim that they lost money with the "Always Fresh" baking system, while others suggest that it was "a welcome transition." Some franchisees even launched a website to encourage others to stand up against the lawsuit. "How comfortable are you sharing your profitability with the media?" the website asks. "Do we want the press reporting about the Tim Hortons' brand in a negative way?" In other words, the franchise owners are forming coalitions to either foster or hinder the lawsuit, depending on their perspective on the matter. Why is politics so prevalent in organizations? Is it merely a fact of life?

 Why do people engage in politics?

When people get together in groups, power will be exerted. People want to carve out niches from which to exert influence, to earn rewards, and to advance their careers.[56] When employees in organizations convert their power into action, we describe them as engaged in politics. Those with good political skills have the ability to use their bases of power effectively.[57] Below we cover the types of political activity people use to try to influence others as well as impression management. Political skills are not confined to adults, of course. Even young children are quite adept at waging careful, deliberate campaigns to wear their parents down, so that they can get things that they want.

Definition of Political Behaviour

There has been no shortage of definitions for organizational politics. One clever definition of *politics* comes from Tom Jakobek, Toronto's former budget chief, who said, "In politics, you may have to go from A to C to D to E to F to G and then to B."[58]

For our purposes, we will define **political behaviour** in organizations as those activities that are outside one's formal role (that is, not part of one's specific job duties), and that influence, or try to influence, the distribution of advantages and disadvantages within the organization.[59]

This definition encompasses key elements from what most people mean when they talk about organizational politics. Political behaviour is *outside* one's specified job requirements. The behaviour attempts to use one's *bases of power*. Our definition also encompasses efforts to influence the goals, criteria, or processes used for decision making when we state that politics is concerned with "the distribution of advantages and disadvantages within the organization." Our definition is broad enough to include such varied political behaviours as joining a coalition, whistle-blowing, spreading rumours, withholding key information from decision makers, leaking confidential information about organizational activities to the media, exchanging favours with others in the organization for mutual benefit, and lobbying on behalf of or against a particular individual or decision alternative. Exhibit 7-5 provides a quick measure to help you assess how political your workplace is.

Now that you have learned a bit about political behaviour, you may want to assess your own political behaviour in our *Learning About Yourself Exercise* on page 251.

Political behaviour is not confined to just individual hopes and goals. Politics might also be used to achieve organizational goals.[60] For instance, if a CEO wants to change the way employees are paid, say from salaries to commissions, this might not be a popular choice to the employees. While it might make good organizational sense to make this change (perhaps the CEO believes this will increase productivity), simply imposing the change through the use of power (go along with this or you're fired) might not be very popular. Instead, the CEO may try to pitch the reasons for the change to sympathetic managers and employees, trying to get them to understand the necessity for the change. Burnaby, BC-based TELUS used a direct approach with its employees after four and a half years of unsuccessful bargaining with union leaders. Management became frustrated with the impasse and explained their wage and benefit offer directly to employees in the hopes of getting the employees to side with management rather than their union leaders. The union was outraged by this behaviour, and it took several more months for union members and management to finally complete a new collective agreement in fall 2005.

The Reality of Politics

Why, you may wonder, must politics exist? Isn't it possible for an organization to be politics-free? It's *possible*, but most unlikely. Organizations are made up of individuals and groups with different values, goals, and interests.[61] This sets up the potential for conflict over resources. The allocation of departmental budgets, space, project

political behaviour Those activities that influence, or attempt to influence, the distribution of advantages and disadvantages within the organization.

EXHIBIT 7-5 A Quick Measure of How Political Your Workplace Is	

How political is your workplace? Answer the 12 questions using the following scale:

SD = Strongly disagree
D = Disagree
U = Uncertain
A = Agree
SA = Strongly agree

1. Managers often use the selection system to hire only people who can help them in their future. _____

2. The rules and policies concerning promotion and pay are fair; it's how managers carry out the policies that is unfair and self-serving. _____

3. The performance ratings people receive from their managers reflect more of the managers' "own agenda" than the actual performance of the employee. _____

4. Although a lot of what my manager does around here appears to be directed at helping employees, it's actually intended to protect my manager. _____

5. There are cliques or "in-groups" that hinder effectiveness around here. _____

6. My co-workers help themselves, not others. _____

7. I have seen people deliberately distort information requested by others for purposes of personal gain, either by withholding it or by selectively reporting it. _____

8. If co-workers offer to lend some assistance, it is because they expect to get something out of it. _____

9. Favouritism rather than merit determines who gets ahead around here. _____

10. You can usually get what you want around here if you know the right person to ask. _____

11. Overall, the rules and policies concerning promotion and pay are specific and well-defined. _____

12. Pay and promotion policies are generally clearly communicated in this organization. _____

This questionnaire taps the three salient dimensions that have been found to be related to perceptions of politics: manager behaviour; co-worker behaviour; and organizational policies and practices. To calculate your score for items 1–10, give yourself 1 point for Strongly disagree; 2 points for Disagree; and so forth (through 5 points for Strongly agree). For items 11 and 12, reverse the score (that is, 1 point for Strongly agree, etc.). Sum up the total: The higher the total score, the greater the degree of perceived organizational politics.

Source: G. R. Ferris, D. D. Frink, D. P. S. Bhawuk, J. Zhou, and D. C. Gilmore, "Reactions of Diverse Groups to Politics in the Workplace," *Journal of Management* 22, no. 1 (1996), pp. 32–33. Reprinted by permission of SAGE Publications.

responsibilities, and bonuses are the kind of resource issues about which organizational members will disagree.

Resources in organizations are also limited, which often turns potential conflict into real conflict. If resources were abundant, then all the various constituencies within the organization could satisfy their goals. Because they are limited, not everyone's interests can be provided for. Moreover, whether true or not, gains by one individual or group are often *perceived* as being at the expense of others within the organization. These forces create competition among members for the organization's limited resources.

Maybe the most important factor behind politics within organizations is the realization that most of the "facts" that are used to allocate the limited resources are open to interpretation. What, for instance, is *good* performance? What is an *adequate* improvement? What constitutes an *unsatisfactory* job? It is in this large and ambiguous middle ground of organizational life—where the facts *do not* speak for themselves—that politics flourish.

When American figure skater Johnny Weir's low scores were announced at the men's 2010 Olympic Figure Skating finals, almost the entire crowd booed the judges in the Vancouver stadium. Some thought that the judges were engaging in politics to send a message to him that his style of artistic skating was not "masculine" enough for the sport.

Finally, because most decisions must be made in a climate of ambiguity—where facts are rarely fully objective and thus are open to interpretation—people within organizations will use whatever influence they can to taint the facts to support their goals and interests. That, of course, creates the activities we call *politicking*. For more about how one engages in politicking, see *From Concepts to Skills* on pages 256–257.

Therefore, to answer the earlier question of whether it is possible for an organization to be politics-free, we can say "yes"—but only if all the members of that organization hold the same goals and interests, organizational resources are not scarce, and performance outcomes are completely clear and objective. However, that does not describe the organizational world that most of us live in!

RESEARCH FINDINGS: Politicking

Our earlier discussion focused on the favourable outcomes for individuals who have who successfully engage in politicking. But for most people—who have modest political skills or are unwilling to play the politics game—outcomes tend to be mainly negative.[62] There is, for instance, very strong evidence indicating that perceptions of organizational politics are negatively related to job satisfaction.[63] The perception of politics also tends to increase job anxiety and stress. This seems to be because of the belief that, by not engaging in politics, a person may be losing ground to others who are active politickers, or, conversely, because of the additional pressures individuals feel of having entered into and competing in the political arena.[64] Not surprisingly, when politicking becomes too much to handle, it can lead employees to quit.[65] Finally, there is preliminary evidence suggesting that politics leads to self-reported declines in employee performance.[66] Perceived organizational politics appears to have a demotivating effect on individuals, and thus leads to decreased performance levels.

Types of Political Activity

Within organizations, we can find a variety of political activities in which people engage. These include the following:[67]

- *Attacking or blaming others.* Used when trying to avoid responsibility for failure.

- *Using information.* Withholding or distorting information, particularly to hide negative information.

- *Managing impressions.* Bringing positive attention to oneself or taking credit for the positive accomplishments of others.

- *Building support for ideas.* Making sure that others will support one's ideas before they are presented.

- *Praising others.* Making important people feel good.

- *Building coalitions.* Joining with other people to create a powerful group.

- *Associating with influential people.* Building support networks.

- *Creating obligations.* Doing favours for others so they will owe you favours later.

Individuals will use these political activities for different purposes. Some of these activities are more likely to be used to defend one's position (such as attacking or blaming others), while other activities are meant to enhance one's image (such as building support for ideas and managing impressions).

Why do some people seem to engage in politics more than others?

Impression Management

The process by which individuals attempt to control the impression others form of them is called **impression management**.[68] Being perceived positively by others should have benefits for people in organizations. It might, for instance, help them initially to get the jobs they want in an organization and, once hired, to get favourable evaluations, superior salary increases, and more rapid promotions. In a political context, it might help bring more advantages their way. *Case Incident—Dressing for Success* on page 255 looks at impression management through the company dress code.

In what situations does impression management work best?

Impression management does not imply that the impressions people convey are necessarily false (although, of course, they sometimes are).[69] Some activities may be done with great sincerity. For instance, you may *actually* believe that ads contribute little to sales in your region or that you are the key to the tripling of your division's sales. However, if the image claimed is false, you may be discredited.[70] The impression manager must be cautious not to be perceived as insincere or manipulative.[71] This chapter's *Point/Counterpoint* on page 250 considers the ethics of managing impressions.

RESEARCH FINDINGS: Impression Management Techniques

Most of the studies undertaken to test the effectiveness of impression management techniques have related it to two criteria: interview success and performance evaluations. Let's consider each of these.

impression management The process by which individuals attempt to control the impression others form of them.

The evidence indicates that most job applicants use impression management techniques in interviews[72] and that, when impression management behaviour is used, it works.[73] In one study, for instance, interviewers felt that applicants for a position as a customer-service representative who used impression management techniques performed better in the interview, and they seemed somewhat more inclined to hire these people.[74] Moreover, when the researchers considered applicants' credentials, they concluded that it was the impression management techniques alone that influenced the interviewers. That is, it did not seem to matter if applicants were well or poorly qualified. If they used impression management techniques, they did better in the interview.

Research indicates that some impression management techniques work better than others in an interview. Researchers have compared applicants who used techniques that focused on promoting one's accomplishments (called *self-promotion*) to applicants who used techniques that focused on complimenting the interviewer and finding areas of agreement (referred to as *ingratiation*). In general, applicants appear to use self-promotion more than ingratiation.[75] What is more, self-promotion tactics may be more important to interviewing success. Applicants who work to create an appearance of competence by enhancing their accomplishments, taking credit for successes, and explaining away failures do better in interviews. These effects reach beyond the interview: Applicants who use more self-promotion tactics also seem to get more follow-up job-site visits, even after adjusting for grade-point average, gender, and job type. Ingratiation also works well in interviews, meaning that applicants who compliment the interviewer, agree with his or her opinions, and emphasize areas of fit do better than those who do not.[76]

In terms of performance ratings, the picture is quite different. Ingratiation is positively related to performance ratings, meaning that those who ingratiate with their supervisors get higher performance evaluations. However, self-promotion appears to backfire: Those who self-promote actually seem to receive *lower* performance evaluations.[77] There is an important qualifier to this general result. It appears that individuals high in political skill are able to translate impression management into higher performance appraisals, whereas those lower in political skill are more likely to be hurt by their attempts at impression management.[78]

What explains these results? If you think about them, they make sense. Ingratiating always works because everyone—both interviewers and supervisors—likes to be treated nicely. However, self-promotion may work only in interviews and backfire on the job because, whereas the interviewer has little idea whether you are blowing smoke about your accomplishments, the supervisor knows because it's his or her job to observe you. Thus, if you are going to self-promote, remember that what works in an interview will not always work once you are on the job.

Making Office Politics Work

One thing to be aware of is that extreme office politics can have a negative effect on employees. Researchers have found that organizational politics is associated with less organizational commitment,[79] lower job satisfaction,[80] and decreased job performance.[81] Individuals who experience greater organizational politics are more likely to report higher levels of job anxiety,[82] and they are more likely to consider leaving the organization.[83]

Is there an effective way to engage in office politics that is less likely to be disruptive or negative? We discussed different negotiation strategies in Chapter 6, including a *win-lose* strategy, which means that if I win, you lose, and a *win-win* strategy, which means creating situations in which both of us can win. *Fast Company*, a business magazine, identifies several rules that may help you make your way through the office politics maze:[84]

- *Nobody wins unless everybody wins.* The most successful proposals look for ways to acknowledge, if not include, the interests of others. This requires building support for your ideas across the organization. "Real political skill isn't about campaign tactics," says Lou DiNatale, a veteran political consultant at the University of Massachusetts. "It's about pulling people toward your ideas and then pushing those ideas through to other people." When ideas are packaged to look as if they are best for the organization as a whole and will help others, it is harder for others to counteract your proposal.

- *Don't just ask for opinions—change them.* It is helpful to find out what people think and then, if necessary, set out to change their opinions so that they can see what you want to do. It is also important to seek out the opinions of those you don't know well, or who are less likely to agree with you. Gathering together people who always support you is often not enough to build an effective coalition.

- *Everyone expects to be paid back.* In organizations, as in life, we develop personal relationships with those around us. It is those personal relationships that affect much of the behaviour in organizations. By building good relationships with colleagues, supporting them in their endeavours, and showing appreciation for what they accomplish, you are building a foundation of support for your own ideas.

- *Success can create opposition.* As part of the office politics, success can be viewed as a *win-lose* strategy, which we identified above. Some people may feel that your success comes at their expense. So, for instance, your higher profile may mean that a project of theirs will be received less favourably. You have to be prepared to deal with this opposition.

Summary and Implications

1 What is power?   *Power* refers to a capacity that A has to influence the behaviour of B, so that B acts in accordance with A's wishes.

2 How does one get power?   There are six bases or sources of power: coercive, reward, legitimate, expert, referent, and information. These forms of power differ in their ability to improve a person's performance. *Coercive power* tends to result in negative performance responses from individuals; it decreases satisfaction, increases mistrust, and creates fear. *Reward power* may improve performance, but it can also lead to unethical behaviour. *Legitimate power* does not have a negative effect, but does not generally stimulate employees to improve their attitudes or performance, and it does not generally result in increased commitment. Ironically, the least effective bases of power—coercive, legitimate, and reward—are the ones most likely to be used by managers, perhaps because they are the easiest to implement. By contrast, effective leaders use *expert* and/or *referent power*; these forms of power are not derived from the person's position. *Information power* comes from access to and control over information and can be used in both positive (sharing) and negative (withholding) ways in the organization.

3 How does dependency affect power?   To maximize your power, you will want to increase others' dependence on you. You can, for instance, increase your power in relation to your employer by developing knowledge or a skill that he or she needs and for which there is no ready substitute. However, you will not be alone in trying to build your bases of power. Others, particularly employees and peers, will seek to make you dependent on them. While you try to maximize others' dependence on you, you will be trying to minimize your dependence on others. Of course, others you work with will be trying to do the same. The result is a continual struggle for power.

LESSONS LEARNED

- Effective leaders use expert and/or referent power.
- To maximize your power, increase others' dependence on you.
- Politics is inevitable; managing politics well is a skill.

SNAPSHOT SUMMARY

1 A Definition of Power

2 Bases of Power
Coercive Power
Reward Power
Legitimate Power
Expert Power
Referent Power
Information Power
Evaluating the Bases of Power

3 Dependency: The Key to Power
The General Dependency Postulate
What Creates Dependency?

4 **What tactics can be used to increase power?** One particular study identified nine tactics, or strategies, that managers and employees use to increase their power: rational persuasion, inspirational appeals, consultation, ingratiation, personal appeals, exchange, coalitions, pressure, and legitimacy.[85]

5 **What does it mean to be empowered?** *Empowerment* refers to the freedom and the ability of employees to make decisions and commitments. There is a lot of positive press on empowerment. However, much of the talk of empowerment in organizations does not result in employees being empowered. Some managers don't fully understand how to go about empowering their employees, and others find it difficult to share their power with employees. As well, some employees have little or no interest in being empowered, and empowerment is not something that works well in every culture.

6 **How are power and harassment related?** People who engage in harassment in the workplace are typically abusing their power position. Harassment can come in many forms, from gross abuse of power toward anyone of lower rank, to abuse of individuals because of their personal characteristics, such as race, religion, national origin, and gender.

7 **Why do people engage in politics?** People use politics to influence others to help them achieve their personal objectives. Whenever people get together in groups, power will be exerted. People also use impression management to influence people. Impression management is the process by which individuals attempt to control the impression others form of them. Though politics is a natural occurrence in organizations, when it is carried to an extreme it can damage relationships among individuals.

1. What is power? How do you get it?

2. Contrast the bases of power and influence tactics.

3. How might people respond to the different bases of power that someone might use?

4. Which of the six bases of power lie with the individual? Which are derived from the organization?

5. Define the general dependency postulate.

6. What creates dependency? Give an applied example.

7. Identify the range of empowerment that might be available to employees.

8. Define *sexual harassment.* Who is most likely to harass an employee: a boss, a co-worker, or a subordinate? Explain.

9. How are power and politics related?

10. Define *political behaviour.* Why is politics a fact of life in organizations?

1. Based on the information presented in this chapter, if you were a recent graduate entering a new job, what would you do to maximize your power and accelerate your career progress?

2. "Politics isn't inherently bad. It is merely a way to get things accomplished within organizations." Do you agree or disagree? Defend your position.

3. You are a sales representative for an international software company. After four excellent years, sales in your territory are off 30 percent this year. Describe three impression management techniques you might use to convince your manager that your sales record is better than one could have expected under the circumstances.

4. Which impression management techniques have you used? What ethical implications, if any, are there in using impression management?

5. "Sexual harassment should not be tolerated in the workplace." "Workplace romances are a natural occurrence in organizations." Are both of these statements true? Can they be reconciled?

■ There are a variety of ways to increase your power in an organization. As an example, you could acquire more knowledge about a situation and then use that information to negotiate a bonus with your employer. Even if you don't get the bonus, the knowledge may help you in other ways.

■ To increase your power, consider how dependent others are on you. Dependency is affected by your importance, substitutability, and scarcity options. If you have needed skills that no one else has, you will have more power.

■ You can develop political skills. Remembering to take time to join in an office birthday celebration for someone is part of developing the skill of working with others effectively.

POINT

COUNTERPOINT

Managing Impressions Is Unethical

Managing impressions is wrong for both ethical and practical reasons.

First, managing impressions is just another name for lying. Don't we have a responsibility, both to ourselves and to others, to present ourselves as we really are? Australian philosopher Tony Coady wrote, "Dishonesty has always been perceived in our culture, and in all cultures but the most bizarre, as a central human vice." Immanuel Kant's categorical imperative asks us to consider the following: If you want to know whether telling a lie on a particular occasion is justifiable, you must try to imagine what would happen if everyone were to lie. Surely, you would agree that a world in which no one lies is preferable to one in which lying is common, because in such a world we could never trust anyone. Thus, we should try to present the truth as best we can. Impression management goes against this virtue.

Practically speaking, impression management generally backfires in the long run. Remember Sir Walter Scott's quote, "Oh what a tangled web we weave, when first we practise to deceive!" Once we start to distort the facts, where do we stop? Dr. Philip Baker, former dean of the Faculty of Medicine at the University of Alberta, wanted to give the 2011 graduating class a memorable speech at their graduation dinner. Unfortunately, he didn't write his own speech, but mostly reused a speech given by Dr. Atul Gawande at Stanford University in 2010.[86] When the truth came out, Baker had to resign as Dean.

People are most satisfied with their jobs when their values match the culture of the organizations. If either side misrepresents itself in the interview process, then odds are people will not fit in the organizations they choose. What is the benefit in this?

This does not imply that a person should not put his or her best foot forward. But that means exhibiting qualities that are good no matter the context—being friendly, being positive and self-confident, being qualified and competent, while still being honest.

There Is Nothing Wrong with Managing Impressions

Let's be real here. Everybody fudges to some degree in the process of applying for a job. If you really told the interviewer what your greatest weakness or worst mistake was, you would never get hired. What if you answered, "I find it hard to get up in the morning and get to work"?

These sorts of "white lies" are expected and act as a kind of social lubricant. If we really knew what people were thinking, we would go crazy. Moreover, you can quote all the philosophy you want, but sometimes it's necessary to lie. You mean you would not lie to save the life of a family member? It's naive to think we can live in a world without lying.

Sometimes a bit of deception is necessary to get a job. I know a gay applicant who was rejected from a job he really wanted because he told the interviewer he had written two articles for gay magazines. What if he had told the interviewer a little lie? Would harm really have been done? At least he would have a job.

As another example, when an interviewer asks you what you earned on your previous job, that information will be used against you, to pay you a salary lower than you deserve. Is it wrong to boost your salary a bit? Or would it be better to disclose your actual salary and be taken advantage of?

The same goes for complimenting interviewers, agreeing with their opinions, and so forth. If an interviewer tells you, "We believe in community involvement," are you supposed to tell the interviewer you have never volunteered for anything?

Of course, you can go too far. We are not advocating that people totally fabricate their backgrounds. What we are talking about here is a reasonable amount of enhancement. If we can help ourselves without doing any real harm, then impression management is not the same as lying and actually is something we should teach others.

How Political Are You?

To determine your political tendencies, please review the following statements. Check the answer that best represents your behaviour or belief, even if that particular behaviour or belief is not present all the time.

	True	False
1. You should make others feel important through an open appreciation of their ideas and work.	_____	_____
2. Because people tend to judge you when they first meet you, always try to make a good first impression.	_____	_____
3. Try to let others do most of the talking, be sympathetic to their problems, and resist telling people that they are totally wrong.	_____	_____
4. Praise the good traits of the people you meet, and always give people an opportunity to save face if they are wrong or make a mistake.	_____	_____
5. Spreading false rumours, planting misleading information, and backstabbing are necessary, if somewhat unpleasant, methods of dealing with your enemies.	_____	_____
6. Sometimes it is necessary to make promises that you know you will not or cannot keep.	_____	_____
7. It is important to get along with everybody, even with those who are generally recognized as windbags, abrasive, or constant complainers.	_____	_____
8. It is vital to do favours for others so that you can call in these IOUs at times when they will do you the most good.	_____	_____
9. Be willing to compromise, particularly on issues that are minor to you but major to others.	_____	_____
10. On controversial issues, it is important to delay or avoid your involvement if possible.	_____	_____

Scoring Key:

According to the author of this instrument, a complete organizational politician will answer "true" to all 10 questions. Organizational politicians with fundamental ethical standards will answer "false" to questions 5 and 6, which deal with deliberate lies and uncharitable behaviour. Individuals who regard manipulation, incomplete disclosure, and self-serving behaviour as unacceptable will answer "false" to all or almost all of the questions.

Source: J. F. Byrnes, "The Political Behavior Inventory." Reprinted by permission of Dr. Joseph F. Byrnes, Bentley College, Waltham, Massachusetts.

PERSONAL INVENTORY ASSESSMENT

Gaining Power and Influence: Power and influence can be gained in many ways, but most people have a preferred style or tactic. Use this scale to determine your preferred power and influence tactics. Are there alternative tactics that may be more effective?

Using Influence Strategies: The ability to influence others is a key component of effective social interaction. This self assessment helps you identify your preferred approach to exercising influence.

Personal Empowerment Assessment: This self-assessment helps you better understand the extent to which you are empowered in a particular role.

BREAKOUT **GROUP** EXERCISES

Form small groups to discuss the following topics, as assigned by your instructor:

1. Describe an incident in which you tried to use political behaviour in order to get something you wanted. What influence tactics did you use?

2. In thinking about the incident described above, were your influence tactics effective? Why?

3. Describe an incident in which you saw someone engaging in politics. What was your reaction to observing the political behaviour? Under what circumstances do you think political behaviour is appropriate?

WORKING WITH **OTHERS** EXERCISE

Understanding Bases of Power

Step 1: Your instructor will divide the class into groups of about 5 or 6 (making sure there are at least 5 groups).[87] Each group will be assigned 1 of the following bases of power: (1) coercive, (2) reward, (3) legitimate, (4) expert, (5) referent, (6) information. Refer to your text for discussion of these terms.

Step 2: Each group is to develop a role play that highlights the use of the power assigned. The role play should be developed using the following scenario:

> You are the leader of a group that is trying to develop a website for a new client. One of your group members, who was assigned the task of researching and analyzing the websites of your client's competition, has twice failed to bring the analysis to scheduled meetings, even though the member knew the assignment was due. Consequently, your group is falling behind in getting the website developed. As leader of the group, you have decided to speak with this team member and to use your specific brand of power to influence the individual's behaviour.

Step 3: Each group should select 1 person to play the group leader and another to play the member who has not done the assignment. You have 10 minutes to prepare an influence plan.

Step 4: Each group will conduct its role play. In the event of multiple groups being assigned the same power base, 1 of the groups may be asked to volunteer. While you are watching the other groups' role plays, try to put yourself in the place of the person being influenced to see whether that type of influence would cause you to change your behaviour.

Immediately after each role play, while the next one is being set up, you should pretend that you were the person being influenced, and then record your reaction using the questionnaire below. To do this, take out a sheet of paper and tear it into 5 (or 6) pieces. At the top of each piece of paper, write the type of influence that was used. Then write the letters *A, B, C,* and *D* in a column, and indicate which number on the scale (see below) reflects the influence attempt.

WORKING WITH **OTHERS** EXERCISE (Continued)

Reaction to Influence Questionnaire

For each role play, think of yourself being on the receiving end of the influence attempt described and record your own reaction.

Type of power used _____

A. As a result of the influence attempt, I will . . .

definitely not comply   1   2   3   4   5   **definitely comply**

B. Any change that does come about will be . . .

temporary   1   2   3   4   5   **long-lasting**

C. My own personal reaction is . . .

resistant   1   2   3   4   5   **accepting**

D. As a result of this influence attempt, my relationship with my group leader will probably be . . .

worse   1   2   3   4   5   **better**

Step 5: For each influence type, 1 member of each group will take the pieces of paper from group members and calculate the average group score for each of the 4 questions. For efficiency, this should be done while the role plays are being conducted.

Step 6: Your instructor will collect the summaries from each group, and then lead a discussion based on these results.

Step 7: Discussion.

    1. Which kind of influence is most likely to result immediately in the desired behaviour?

    2. Which will have the longest-lasting effects?

    3. What effect will using a particular base of power have on the ongoing relationship?

    4. Which form of power will others find most acceptable? Least acceptable? Why?

    5. Are there some situations in which a particular type of influence strategy might be more effective than others?

Swapping Personal Favours?

Jack Grubman was a powerful man on Wall Street.[88] As a star analyst of telecom companies for the Salomon Smith Barney unit of Citigroup, his recommendations carried a lot of weight with investors.

For years, Grubman had been negative about the stock of AT&T. But then he upgraded his opinion on the stock. According to email evidence, it appears that Grubman's decision to upgrade AT&T was not based on the stock's fundamentals. There were other factors involved.

At the time, his boss at Citigroup, Sanford Weill, was in the midst of a power struggle with co-CEO John Reed to become the single head of the company. Meanwhile, Salomon was looking for additional business to increase its revenues. Getting investment banking business fees from AT&T would be a big plus toward improving revenues. Salomon's efforts at getting that AT&T business would definitely be improved if Grubman would upgrade his opinion on the stock. Furthermore, Weill sought Grubman's upgrade to win favour with AT&T CEO Michael Armstrong, who sat on Citigroup's board. Weill wanted Armstrong's backing in his efforts to oust Reed.

Grubman had his own concerns. Although he was earning tens of millions a year in his job, he was a man of modest background. He was the son of a city employee. He wanted the best for his twin daughters, which included entry to an exclusive nursery school—a school that a year earlier had reportedly turned down Madonna's daughter. Weill made a call on Grubman's behalf to the school and pledged a $1 million donation from Citigroup.

At approximately the same time, Weill also asked Grubman to "take a fresh look" at his neutral rating on AT&T.

Shortly after being asked to review his rating, Grubman turned positive, raised his rating, and AT&T awarded Salomon an investment-banking job worth nearly $45 million.

Did Sanford Weill do anything unethical? How about Jack Grubman? What do you think?

CASE INCIDENT

Dressing for Success

Jennifer Cohen thought she had a good grip on her company's dress code. She was wrong.[89]

Cohen works for a marketing firm. Before a meeting, an older colleague pulled 24-year-old Cohen aside and told her that she was dressing inappropriately by wearing Bermuda shorts and sleeveless tops. Cohen was stunned by the rebuke. "Each generation seems to have a different idea of what is acceptable in the workplace," she said. "In this case, I was highly offended."

What offended Cohen even more was what came next: Cohen was not allowed to attend the meeting because her attire was deemed inappropriate.

Cohen's employer is not alone. Although many employers have "casual" days at work, the number of employers who are enforcing more formal dress codes has increased, according to a survey of employers by the Society for Human Resource Management. Heading into Summer 2011, Renfrew County, near Ottawa, updated its dress code to prevent government employees from wearing flip-flops.

Ironically, as more employers enforce more formal dress codes, other employers known for their formality are going the other way. IBM, which once had a dress code of business suits with white shirts, has thrown out dress codes altogether. IBM researcher Dan Gruhl typically goes to work at IBM's San Jose, California, office in flip-flops and shorts. "Having a relaxed environment encourages you to think more openly," he says. Although not going quite as far as IBM, other traditional employers, such as Ford, General Motors, and Procter & Gamble, have relaxed dress codes. At Toronto-based Google Canada, an even simpler code is in place: Employees must wear clothes.

Still, for every Google, there are more companies that have tightened the rules. Even the National Basketball Association (NBA) has adopted an off-court dress code for its players. As for Cohen, she still bristles at the dress code. "When you're comfortable, you don't worry," she says. "You focus on your work."

Questions

1. Do you think Cohen had a right to be offended? Why or why not?

2. In explaining why she was offended, Cohen argued, "People my age are taught to express themselves, and saying something negative about someone's fashion is saying something negative about them." Do you agree with Cohen?

3. Does an employer have an unfettered right to set a company's dress code? Why or why not?

4. How far would you go to conform to an organization's dress code? If your boss dressed in a relatively formal manner, would you feel compelled to dress in a like manner to manage impressions?

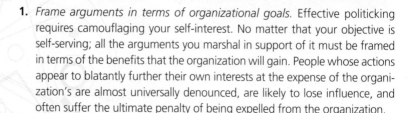

FROM CONCEPTS TO SKILLS

Politicking

Forget, for a moment, the ethics of politicking and any negative impressions you may have of people who engage in organizational politics.[90] If you wanted to be more politically adept in your organization, what could you do? The following eight suggestions are likely to improve your political effectiveness.

1. *Frame arguments in terms of organizational goals.* Effective politicking requires camouflaging your self-interest. No matter that your objective is self-serving; all the arguments you marshal in support of it must be framed in terms of the benefits that the organization will gain. People whose actions appear to blatantly further their own interests at the expense of the organization's are almost universally denounced, are likely to lose influence, and often suffer the ultimate penalty of being expelled from the organization.

2. *Develop the right image.* If you know your organization's culture, you understand what the organization wants and values from its employees—in terms of dress; associates to cultivate, and those to avoid; whether to appear risk-taking or risk-aversive; the preferred leadership style; the importance placed on getting along well with others; and so forth. Then you are equipped to project the appropriate image. Because the assessment of your performance is not a fully objective process, both style and substance must be addressed.

3. *Gain control of organizational resources.* The control of organizational resources that are scarce and important is a source of power. Knowledge and expertise are particularly effective resources to control. They make you more valuable to the organization and therefore more likely to gain security, advancement, and a receptive audience for your ideas.

4. *Make yourself appear indispensable.* Because we are dealing with appearances rather than objective facts, you can enhance your power by appearing to be indispensable. That is, you don't have to really be indispensable as long as key people in the organization believe that you are. If the organization's prime decision makers believe there is no ready substitute for what you are giving the organization, they are likely to go to great lengths to ensure that your desires are satisfied.

5. *Be visible.* Because performance evaluation has a substantial subjective component, it is important that your manager and those in power in the organization be made aware of your contribution. If you are fortunate enough to have a job that brings your accomplishments to the attention of others, it may not be necessary to take direct measures to increase your visibility. But your job may require you to handle activities that are low in visibility, or your specific contribution may be indistinguishable because you are part of a team endeavour. In such cases—without appearing to toot your own horn or create the image of a braggart—you will want to call attention to yourself by highlighting your successes in routine reports, having satisfied customers relay their appreciation to senior executives in your organization, being seen at social functions, being active in your professional associations, developing powerful allies who speak positively about your accomplishments, and similar tactics. Of course, the skilled politician actively and successfully lobbies to get those projects that will increase his or her visibility.

6. *Develop powerful allies.* It helps to have powerful people in your camp. Cultivate contacts with potentially influential people above you, at your own level, and in the lower ranks. They can provide you with important information that may not be available through normal channels. There will be times, too, when decisions will be made in favour of those with the greatest support. Having powerful allies can provide you with a coalition of support if and when you need it.

7. *Avoid "tainted" members.* In almost every organization, there are fringe members whose status is questionable. Their performance and/or loyalty is suspect. Keep your distance from such individuals. Given the reality that effectiveness has a large subjective component, your own effectiveness might be called into question if you are perceived as too closely associated with tainted members.

8. *Support your manager.* Your immediate future is in the hands of your current manager. Since he or she evaluates your performance, you will typically want to do whatever is necessary to have your manager on your side. You should make every effort to help your manager succeed, make her look good, support her if she is under siege, and spend the time to find out what criteria she will be using to assess your effectiveness. Don't undermine your manager, and don't speak negatively of her to others.

Practising Skills

You used to be the star marketing manager for Hilton Electronics Corporation. But for the past year, you have been outpaced again and again by Sean, a new manager in the design department who has been accomplishing everything expected of him and more. Meanwhile, your best efforts to do your job well have been sabotaged and undercut by Maria—your and Sean's manager. For example, before last year's international consumer electronics show, Maria moved $30 000 from your budget to Sean's. Despite your best efforts, your marketing team could not complete all the marketing materials normally developed to showcase all of your organization's new products at this important industry show. Also, Maria has chipped away at your staff and budget ever since. Although you have been able to meet most of your goals with fewer staff and less budget, Maria has continued to slice away resources from your group. Just last week, she eliminated two positions in your team of eight marketing specialists to make room for a new designer and some extra equipment for Sean. Maria is clearly taking away your resources while giving Sean whatever he wants and more. You think it's time to do something or soon you will not have any team or resources left. What do you need to do to make sure your division has the resources to survive and grow?

Reinforcing Skills

1. Keep a one-week journal of your behaviour describing incidents when you tried to influence others around you. Assess each incident by asking: Were you successful at these attempts to influence them? Why or why not? What could you have done differently?

2. Outline a specific action plan, based on concepts in this module, that would improve your career progression in the organization in which you currently work or an organization in which you think you would like to be employed.

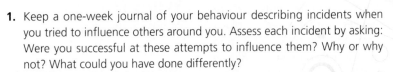

MyManagementLab — Study, practise, and explore real business situations with these helpful resources:

- **Study Plan:** Check your understanding of chapter concepts with self-study quizzes.
- **Online Lesson Presentations:** Study key chapter topics and work through interactive assessments to test your knowledge and master management concepts.
- **Videos:** Learn more about the management practices and strategies of real companies.
- **Simulations:** Practise management decision-making in simulated business environments.

OB on the Edge

The Toxic Workplace

It's not unusual to find employees acting badly in today's workplace, but it is sometimes unusual to find managers doing something about it. BC Lions coach Wally Buono fired team leader and quarterback Casey Printers on October 13, 2010. Two days earlier, in a game against the Winnipeg Blue Bombers, Printers had thrown down his helmet angrily when teammate O'Neill Wilson missed Printers' pass. The fumble led to a game-changing interception and touchdown by the Bombers. As the game ended, Printers lashed out at Wilson in front of live TV cameras, something his coach found highly inappropriate.

"What happened in the fourth quarter was an embarrassment to all of us," Buono said. "The BC Lions, as an organization, [doesn't] condone that type of behaviour. We've worked hard for many, many years to build the reputation of an organization that has dignity and has class and has discipline, and in the fourth quarter there was none of that."[1] Centre Angus Reid, one of Printers' teammates, explained why Buono's action made sense: "I think the real issue is when you have a guy that's paid to be your leader [Printers], and he's the one who ends up causing post-game problems—and I'm putting the performance aside—

I think that's when you have to say, well, we can't have this guy as our leader anymore."[2]

What Is Happening in Our Workplaces?

Workplaces today are receiving highly critical reviews, being called everything from "uncivil" to "toxic."

Lynne Anderson and Christine Pearson, two management professors from St. Joseph's University and the University of North Carolina, respectively, note that "historians may view the dawn of the twenty-first century as a time of thoughtless acts and rudeness:

258

We tailgate, even in the slow lane; we dial wrong numbers and then slam the receiver on the innocent respondent; we break appointments with nonchalance."[3] The workplace has often been seen as one of the places where civility still ruled, with co-workers treating one another with a mixture of formality and friendliness, distance and politeness. However, with downsizing, re-engineering, budget cuts, pressures for increased productivity, autocratic work environments, and the use of part-time employees, there has been an increase in "uncivil and aggressive workplace behaviours."[4]

What does civility in the workplace mean? A simple definition of workplace civility is behaviour "involving politeness and regard for others in the workplace, within workplace norms for respect."[5] Workplace incivility, then, "involves acting with disregard for others in the workplace, in violation of workplace norms for respect."[6] Of course, different workplaces will have different norms for what determines mutual respect. For instance, in most restaurants, if the staff were rude to you when you were there for dinner, you would be annoyed, and perhaps even complain to the manager. However, at The Elbow Room in downtown Vancouver, if customers complain they are in a hurry, manager Patrick Savoie might well say, "If you're in a hurry, you should have gone to McDonald's."[7] Such a comeback is acceptable to the diners at The Elbow Room, because rudeness is its trademark.

Most work environments are not expected to be characterized by such rudeness. However, this has been changing in recent years. Robert Warren, a University of Manitoba marketing professor, notes that "simple courtesy has gone by the board."[8]

Instead, we see workplaces characterized by workplace bullying, "the repeated, health-harming mistreatment of one or more persons (the

targets) by one or more perpetrators that takes one or more of the following forms: verbal abuse; offensive conduct/behaviours (including nonverbal) which are threatening, humiliating, or intimidating; and work interference—sabotage—which prevents work from getting done."[9]

What Do We Know About Workplace Bullying?

The WBI-Zogby survey is the largest scientific study of bullying in the United States. A recent large study on bullying found the following:[10]

- Most bullies are bosses (72 percent).

- 60 percent of bullies are men.

- 57 percent of targets are women.

- Bullying is four times more prevalent than illegal forms of harassment.

- 62 percent of employers ignore or worsen the problem.

FACT**BOX**

What happens when employees experience rudeness in the workplace?

- "48% decreased their work effort,

- 47% decreased their time at work,

- 38% decreased their work quality,

- 66% said their performance declined,

- 80% lost work time worrying about the incident,

- 63% lost time avoiding the offender, and

- 78% said their commitment to the organization declined."[11]

- 45 percent of targets suffer stress-related health problems.

- 40 percent of bullied individuals never tell their employers.

- Only 3 percent of bullied people file lawsuits.

The evidence suggests that rudeness, bullying, and violence are all on the rise. The victims of these negative behaviours are not just the ones who suffer, however.[12] Witnesses to bullying also suffer.[13]

While rudeness is on the rise, professor André Roberge at Laval University suggests that some of the rudeness is generational. He finds that "young clerks often lack both knowledge and civility. Employers are having to train young people in simple manners because that is not being done at home."[14] Professor Warren backs this up: "One of the biggest complaints I hear from businesses when I go to talk about graduates is the lack of interpersonal skills."[15]

Workplace Violence

Recently, researchers have suggested that incivility may be the beginning of more negative behaviours in the workplace, including aggression and violence.[16]

Dave Burns chose a deadly way to exhibit the anger he had stored up after being suspended from his job for inappropriate jokes and poor behaviour.[17] He shot and killed a parts manager and injured another employee on March 10, 2010, at the Great West Chrysler dealership in Edmonton, before turning the gun on himself. According to witnesses, Burns did not get along with the two men who were shot. "He wasn't interested in taking hostages," the witness tearfully said. "He never said a word. It wasn't a cry for help. This was about anger and vengeance, plain and simple."

OB on the EDGE

Workplace violence, according to the International Labour Organization (ILO), includes

any incident in which a person is abused, threatened or assaulted in circumstances relating to [his or her] work. These behaviours would originate from customers or co-workers at any level of the organization. This definition would include all forms of harassment, bullying, intimidation, physical threats, assaults, robbery and other intrusive behaviour.[18]

No Canadian statistics on anger at work are available, although 53 percent of women and 47 percent of men reported experiencing workplace violence in 2004. About 17 percent of the incidents where violent victimization occurred happened in the workplace.[19] Studies show that anger pervades the US workplace. Between 1992 and 2006, there was an average of 800 workplace killings each year.[20] A Gallup poll conducted in the United States found that 25 percent of the working adults surveyed felt like screaming or shouting because of job stress, 14 percent had considered hitting a co-worker, and 10 percent worry about colleagues becoming violent. Almost half of American workers experienced yelling and verbal abuse on the job in 2008, and about 2.5 percent report that they have pushed, slapped, or hit someone at work.[21] Twenty employees are murdered each week in the United States.[22]

Canadian workplaces are not murder-free, however. Between 2001 and 2005, an average of 14 employees were killed each year while "on-the-job."[23] Most of these workplace incidents were carried out by male spouses and partners of female employees. Surprisingly, Canada scores higher than the United States on workplace violence. In an ILO study involving 130 000 workers in 32 countries, Argentina was ranked

the most violent. Romania was second, France third, and Canada fourth. The United States placed ninth.[24]

Sixty-four percent of union representatives who were surveyed reported an increase in workplace aggression, based on their review of incident reports, grievance files, and other solid evidence.[25] To understand the seriousness of this situation, consider that one-quarter of Nova Scotia teachers surveyed reported that they faced physical violence at work during the 2009–2010 school year.[26]

What Causes Incivility (and Worse) in the Workplace?

If employers and employees are acting with less civility toward each other, what is causing this to happen?

Managers and employees often have different views of the employee's role in the organization. Jeffrey Pfeffer, a professor of organizational behaviour at the Graduate School of Business at Stanford University, notes that many companies don't really value their employees: "Most managers, if they're being honest with themselves, will admit it: When they look at their people, they see costs, they see salaries, they see benefits, they see overhead. Very few companies look at their people and see assets."[27]

Most employees, however, like to think that they are assets to their organization. The realization that they are simply costs and not valued members of an organization can cause frustration for employees.

In addition, "employers' excessive demands and top-down style of management are contributing to the rise of 'work rage,'" claims Gerry Smith, vice-president of organizational health and training at Toronto-based Shepell•fgi and author of *Work Rage*.[28] He cites

demands coming from a variety of sources: "overtime, downsizing, rapid technological changes, company restructuring and difficulty balancing the demands of job and home."[29] Smith worries about the consequences of these demands: "If you push people too hard, set unrealistic expectations and cut back their benefits, they're going to strike back."[30]

Smith's work supports the findings of studies that report the most common cause of anger and bullying is the actions of supervisors or managers.[31] Other common causes of anger identified by the researchers include lack of productivity by co-workers and others; tight deadlines; heavy workload; interaction with the public; and bad treatment. The inset *Do You Have a Bad Boss?* describes some of the bad behaviour of bosses.

A 2011 study found that how managers deal with displays of anger at work can do much to defuse tensions. Co-workers want to see the manager take some responsibility for a fellow employee's anger, rather than disciplining the employee, if the manager or the working conditions are the source of the anger.[32]

The Psychological Contract

Some researchers have looked at this frustration in terms of a breakdown of the psychological contract formed between employees and employers.

An employer and employee begin to develop psychological contracts as they are first introduced to each other in the hiring process.[33] These contracts continue over time as the employer and the employee come to understand each other's expectations about the amounts and quality of work to be performed and the types of rewards to be given. For instance, when an employee is continually asked to work late and/or be available at all hours through

Do You Have a Bad Boss?

You know you have a bad boss if he or she . . . (percent reporting bosses who did this)[34]

- . . . fails to keep promises (39%)
- . . . fails to give credit when due (37%)
- . . . gave you the "silent treatment" at least once in the past year (31%)
- . . . makes negative comments about you behind your back to other employees or managers (25%)
- . . . invades your personal privacy (24%)
- . . . blames others to cover up mistakes or to minimize their own embarrassment (23%)

FACTBOX

Percentage of employees who say their managers

- make inappropriate comments—74%
- show favouritism—70%
- are unwilling to follow due process—63%
- treat employees with disrespect—62%
- bully or intimidate—57%[35]

pagers and email, the employee may assume that doing so will result in greater rewards or faster promotion down the line. The employer may have had no such intention, and may even be thinking that the employee should be grateful simply to have a job. Later, when the employee does not get expected (though never promised) rewards, he or she is disappointed.

Sandra Robinson, an organizational behaviour professor at the Sauder School of Business at the University of British Columbia, and her colleagues have found that when a psychological contract is violated (perceptually or actually), the relationship between the employee and the employer is damaged. The result can be a loss of trust.[36] The breakdown in trust can cause employees to be less ready to accept decisions or obey rules.[37] The erosion of trust can also lead employees to take revenge on the employer. So they don't carry out their end of a task. Or they refuse to pass on messages. They engage in any number of subtle and not-so-subtle behaviours that affect the way work gets done—or prevents work from getting done.

Recent research on the psychological contract suggests that violations of implicit or explicit promises may not be necessary to affect employee intentions to stay with the organization and/or engage in citizenship behaviours. Professors Samantha Montes and David Zweig of the Rotman School of Management found that employees expect decent pay, developmental opportunities, and support (whether or not employers promise to deliver such); and when they don't receive those things, their behaviour toward the organization becomes negative.[38]

The Toxic Organization

Pfeffer suggests that companies have become "toxic places to work."[39] He notes that companies, particularly in Silicon Valley, ask their employees to sign contracts on the first day of work indicating the employee's understanding that the company has the right to

How to Deal with a Toxic Boss

- *Empathize, and don't take it personally.* It's difficult, but if you try to understand your boss's perspective, it may help you cope more effectively.
- *Draw a line.* When behaviour is inappropriate or abusive, stand up for yourself. At some point, no job is worth being harassed or abused.
- *Don't sabotage or be vindictive.* If you take revenge, you become part of the problem.
- *Be patient and take notes.* You may find it useful to have notes at your disposal should the boss shine the spotlight on you.[40]

fire at will and for any reason. Some employers also ask their employees to choose between having a life and having a career. Pfeffer relates a joke people used to tell about Microsoft: "We offer flexible time—you can work any 18 hours you want."[41] This kind of attitude can be toxic to employees, though this does not imply that Microsoft is a toxic employer. The inset *How to Deal with a Toxic Boss* gives tips, should you find yourself in that situation.

What does it mean to be a toxic organization? The inset *What Does a Toxic Organization Look Like?* describes one. The late professor Peter Frost of the Sauder School of Business at the University of British Columbia noted that there will always be pain in organizations, but that sometimes it becomes so intense or prolonged that conditions within the organization begin to break down. In other words, the situation becomes toxic. This is not dissimilar to what the liver or kidneys do when toxins become too intense in a human body.[42]

What causes organizations to be toxic? Like Pfeffer, professors Frost and Robinson identify a number of factors. Downsizing and organizational change are two main factors, particularly in recent years. Sometimes organizations experience unexpected events—such as the sudden death of a key manager, an

unwise move by senior management, strong competition from a start-up company—that lead to toxicity. Other organizations are toxic throughout their system due to policies and practices that create distress. Such factors as unreasonable stretch goals or performance targets, or unrelenting internal competition, can create toxicity. There are also toxic managers who lead through insensitivity, vindictiveness, and failure to take responsibility, or they are control freaks or are unethical.

What Are the Effects of Incivility and Toxicity in the Workplace?

In general, researchers have found that the effects of workplace anger are sometimes subtle: a hostile work environment and the tendency to do only enough work to get by.[44]

Those who feel chronic anger in the workplace are more likely to report "feelings of betrayal by the organization, decreased feelings of loyalty, a decreased sense that respondent values and the organization's values are similar, a decreased sense that the employer treated the respondent with dignity and respect, and a decreased sense that employers had fulfilled promises made to respondents."[45] So do these feelings make a difference?

Apparently so. Researchers have found that those who felt angry with their employers were less likely to put forth their best effort, more likely to be competitive toward other employees, and less likely to suggest "a quicker and better way to do their job."[46] All of these actions tend to decrease the productivity possible in the workplace.

It's not just those who work for an organization who are affected by incivility and toxicity. Poor service, from indifference to rudeness to outright hostility, characterizes many transactions in Canadian businesses. "Across the country, better business bureaus, provincial government consumer-help agencies and media ombudsmen report a lengthening litany of complaints about contractors, car dealers, repair shops, moving companies, airlines and department stores."[47] This suggests that customers and clients may well be feeling the impact of internal workplace dynamics.

The Toxin Handler

Employees of toxic organizations suffer pain from their experiences in a toxic environment. In some organizations, mechanisms, often informal, are set up to deal with the results of toxicity.

Frost and Robinson identified a special role that some employees play in trying to relieve the toxicity within an organization: the toxin handler. This person tries to mitigate the pain by softening the blow of downsizing, or change, or the behaviour of the toxic leader. Essentially, the toxin handler helps others around him or her deal with the strains of the organization by counselling, advising, shielding employees from the wrath of angry managers, reinterpreting the managers' messages to make them less harsh, etcetera.

So who takes on this role? Certainly no organization to date has a line on its organizational chart for "the toxin handler." Often the role emerges as part of

What Does a Toxic Organization Look Like?

Toxic organizations have the following characteristics:[43]

- inability to achieve operation goals and commitments
- problem-solving processes driven by fear with few good decisions
- poor internal communication
- huge amounts of waste that result from poor decisions, and lots of rework
- interpersonal relationships driven by manipulative and self-centred agendas

an individual's position in an organization; for instance, a manager in the human resource department may take on this role. In many cases, however, handlers are pulled into the role "bit by bit—by their colleagues, who turn to them because they are trustworthy, calm, kind and nonjudgmental."[48]

Frost and Robinson, in profiling these individuals, suggest that toxin handlers are predisposed to say yes, have a high tolerance for pain, have a surplus of empathy, and when they notice people in pain, have a need to make the situation right. But these are not individuals who thrive simply on dealing with the emotional needs of others. Quoting one of the managers in their study, Frost and Robinson cite the full range of activities of most toxin handlers: "These people are usually relentless in their drive to accomplish organizational targets and rarely lose focus on business issues. Managing emotional pain is one of their means."[49]

The inset *How Toxin Handlers Alleviate Organizational Pain* identifies the many tasks that toxin handlers take on in an organization. Frost and Robinson suggest that these tasks will

FACEOFF

Manners are an over-romanticized concept. The big issue is not that employees need to be concerned about their manners. Rather, employers should be paying better wages.

The Golden Rule, "Do unto others as you would have others do unto you," should still have a role in today's workplace. Being nice pays off.

probably need to be handled forever, and they recommend that organizations take steps to actively support people performing this role.

RESEARCH EXERCISES

1. Look for data on violence and anger in the workplace in other countries. How do these data compare with the Canadian and American data presented here? What might you conclude about how violence and anger in the workplace are expressed in different cultures?

2. Identify three Canadian organizations that are trying to foster better and/or less toxic environments for their employees. What kind of effect

is this having on the organizations' bottom lines?

YOUR PERSPECTIVE

1. Is it reasonable to suggest, as some researchers have, that young people today have not learned to be civil to others or do not place a high priority on doing so? Do you see this as one of the causes of incivility in the workplace?

2. What should be done about managers who create toxicity in the workplace while being rewarded because they achieve bottom-line results? Should bottom-line results justify their behaviour?

WANT TO KNOW MORE?

If you would like to read more on this topic, see Linnda Durré, *Surviving the Toxic Workplace* (New York: McGraw Hill, 2010); Peter Frost, *Toxic Emotions at Work* (Cambridge, MA: Harvard Business School Press, 2003); and K. Macklem, "The Toxic Workplace: A Poisoned Work Environment Can Wreak Havoc on a Company's Culture and Its Employees," *Macleans.ca*, January 31, 2005. You can find the latter article at **www.macleans.ca/article.jsp?content= 20050131_99562_99562**.

How Toxin Handlers Alleviate Organizational Pain

- They listen empathetically.
- They suggest solutions.
- They work behind the scenes to prevent pain.
- They carry the confidences of others.
- They reframe difficult messages.[50]

CHAPTER 8

Leadership

Lieutenant Colonel Maryse Carmichael leads Canada's Snowbirds, the country's top military aerobatic team. In her role, she faces many exciting challenges, including finding new ways to capture the hearts and minds of a nation. So what does it take to lead at an elite level?

PART 4
SHARING THE
ORGANIZATIONAL
VISION

✳ Explore

Student PowerPoint Slides - Chapter 8

LEARNING OUTCOMES

① What is the difference between a manager and a leader?

② Are there specific traits, behaviours, and situations that affect how one leads?

③ How does a leader lead with vision?

④ Are there leadership roles for nonmanagers?

⑤ What are some of the contemporary issues in leadership?

Leadership in a team setting is something that Lieutenant Colonel Maryse Carmichael knows a lot about.[1] Since May 2010 she has been the Commanding Officer (CO) of the 431 Air Demonstration Squadron, better known as Canada's Snowbirds. Carmichael is responsible for 14 pilots and 71 ground employees, and she knows the importance of maintaining strong relationships with her staff. In fact, it was the military's desire to promote strong relationships that led to the creation of her position.

Previously, the squadron's CO had always been a Major and a flying member of the demonstration team. With so many staff on the ground, however, it became hard to manage personnel effectively while on the road. The Canadian Forces created a new CO role at the Lieutenant Colonel level, responsible for administration and command of the fleet, maintenance, and personnel. Carmichael's two decades of experience with the Canadian Air Force in a number of flying and non-flying roles made her a natural choice for the newly defined position. She entered the job having established the trust and respect of both pilots and ground personnel, since she had proven herself in both areas.

Carmichael believes that working with the Snowbirds provides an opportunity for leadership at two levels. "For me it is about looking at the overall operations of the entire squadron and the future of the squadron." But it is also about a broader kind of leadership. "We demonstrate to the Canadian public the skills, professionalism, and teamwork of the Canadian Forces." For Carmichael, it is not enough to inspire her own team; she seeks to inspire an entire nation.

In this chapter, we review leadership studies to determine what makes an effective leader. We consider factors that affect one's ability to lead and examine inspirational leadership and self-management. Finally, we discuss contemporary issues in leadership.

THE BIG IDEA

Knowing how to lead well does not come naturally. Effective leadership requires an understanding of how to inspire individuals to achieve common goals.

OB IS FOR EVERYONE

- Have you ever wondered if there was one *right* way to lead?
- Is a leader always necessary?
- Can anyone be a leader?
- How do you manage yourself?

LEARNING ABOUT YOURSELF
- Self-Management

Management	Leadership

Management	Leadership
1. Engages in day-to-day caretaker activities: Maintains and allocates resources	Formulates long-term objectives for reforming the system: Plans strategy and tactics
2. Exhibits supervisory behaviour: Acts to make others maintain standard job behaviour	Exhibits leading behaviour: Acts to bring about change in others congruent with long-term objectives
3. Administers subsystems within organizations	Innovates for the entire organization
4. Asks how and when to engage in standard practice	Asks what and why to change standard practice
5. Acts within established culture of the organization	Creates vision and meaning for the organization
6. Uses transactional influence: Induces compliance in manifest behaviour using rewards, sanctions, and formal authority	Uses transformational influence: Induces change in values, attitudes, and behaviour using personal examples and expertise
7. Relies on control strategies to get things done by subordinates	Uses empowering strategies to make followers internalize values
8. Status quo supporter and stabilizer	Status quo challenger and change creator

Source: Copyright 1998, Canadian Psychological Association. Permission granted for use of material.

 Explore

Exhibit 8-1: Distinguishing Leadership from Management

 ① What is the difference between a manager and a leader?

Are Managers and Leaders the Same?

Leadership and *management* are two terms that are often confused. What is the difference between them?

John Kotter of the Harvard Business School argues that "managers promote stability while leaders press for change and only organizations that embrace both sides of the contradiction can survive in turbulent times."[2]

Professor Rabindra Kanungo at McGill University sees a growing consensus emerging "among management scholars that the concept of 'leadership' must be distinguished from the concept of 'supervision/management.'"[3] Exhibit 8-1 illustrates Kanungo's distinctions between management and leadership. Leaders establish direction by developing a vision of the future; then they align people by communicating this vision and inspiring them to overcome hurdles. In other words, leaders need to develop followers. Managers implement the vision and strategy provided by leaders, coordinate and staff the organization, and handle day-to-day problems. Organizations need strong leadership *and* strong management for optimal effectiveness.

In our discussion of leadership, we will focus on two major tasks of those who lead in organizations: managing those around them to get the day-to-day tasks done (leadership as supervision) and inspiring others to do the extraordinary (leadership as vision). It will become clear that successful leaders rely on a variety of interpersonal skills in order to encourage others to perform at their best. It will also become clear that, no matter the place in the hierarchy, from CEO to team leader, a variety of individuals can be called on to perform leadership roles.

Leadership as Supervision

② Are there specific traits, behaviours, and situations that affect how one leads?

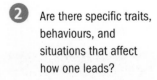 Lt.-Col. Maryse Carmichael served as a Snowbird pilot from early 2000 until late 2001, at which point she received a promotion to an Executive Officer role, followed by relocation to the air force base at Bagotville, Quebec.[4] She says that returning to the Snowbirds as Commanding Officer has given her a new perspective on leadership: "This time around it is really about the entire squadron, about leading the men and women of 431 Squadron to accomplish our mission every day. So it has a broader focus this time."

Her focus on the big picture makes sense in more ways than one. Military jobs are unique in that roles and responsibilities are highly formalized and defined in great detail, and the level of compliance with policies and procedures is extremely high. Penalties for non-compliance are also highly formalized and follow standardized procedures. This helps senior officers maintain a strong focus on strategic decision making rather than on acting as supervisors, since lower level employees have full information and very little ambiguity about managing their day-to-day tasks. So, what makes an effective leader?

In this section we discuss theories of leadership that were developed before 1980. These early theories focused on the supervisory nature of leadership—that is, how leaders managed the day-to-day functioning of employees. The three general types of theories that emerged were (1) trait theories, which propose that leaders have a particular set of traits that makes them different from nonleaders; (2) behavioural theories, which propose that particular behaviours make for better leaders; and (3) contingency theories, which propose that the situation has an effect on leaders. When you think about these theories, remember that although they have been considered "theories of leadership," they rely on an older understanding of what "leadership" means, and they do not convey Kanungo's distinction between leadership and supervision.

Trait Theories: Are Leaders Different from Others?

Have you ever wondered whether there is some fundamental personality difference that makes some people "born leaders"? **Trait theories of leadership** focus on personal qualities and characteristics. We recognize leaders like South Africa's Nelson Mandela, Virgin Group CEO Richard Branson, and Apple co-founder Steve Jobs as *charismatic, enthusiastic,* and *courageous.* Trait theory emerged in the hope that if it were possible to identify the traits of leaders, it would be easier to select people to fill leadership roles. Being able to select good leaders is important because not all people know how to be good leaders, as *Focus on Research* shows.

Focus on Research

Bad Bosses Everywhere

Doesn't leadership come naturally? Although much is expected of leaders, what is surprising is how rarely they seem to meet the most basic definitions of effectiveness. A recent study of 700 employees revealed that many believe their supervisors don't give credit when it's due, gossip about them behind their backs, and don't keep their word.[5] The situation is so bad that for many employees, the study's lead author says, "They don't leave their company, they leave their boss."

Key findings of the study are as follows:

- 39 percent said their supervisor failed to keep promises.
- 37 percent said their supervisor failed to give credit when due.
- 31 percent said their supervisor gave them the "silent treatment" in the past year.
- 27 percent said their supervisor made negative comments about them to other employees or managers.
- 24 percent said their supervisor invaded their privacy.
- 23 percent said their supervisor blames others to cover up mistakes or minimize embarrassment.

Why do companies promote such people into leadership positions? One reason may be the Peter Principle. When people are promoted into one job (say, as a supervisor or coach) based on how well they did another (say, salesperson or player), that assumes that the skills of one role are the same as the other. The only time such people stop being promoted is when they reach their level of incompetence. Judging from the results of this study, that level of leadership incompetence is reached all too often.

trait theories of leadership
Theories that consider personal qualities and characteristics that differentiate leaders from nonleaders.

A 2010 study found that lack of respect for a leader by employees—for instance, when employees feel that the leader is not the best person for the job—has a significant impact on whether employees will follow that leader. The researchers found that simply naming someone "the leader" did not by itself create effective leadership.[6] ●

Research efforts at isolating leadership traits resulted in a number of dead ends. For instance, a review in the late 1960s of 20 studies identified nearly 80 leadership traits, but only 5 of these traits were common to 4 or more of the investigations.[7] By the 1990s, after numerous studies and analyses, about the best thing that could be said was that most "leaders are not like other people," but the particular traits that were isolated varied a great deal from review to review.[8] It was a pretty confusing state of affairs.

A breakthrough, of sorts, came when researchers began organizing traits around the Big Five Personality Model (see Chapter 2).[9] Most of the dozens of traits in various leadership reviews fit under one of the Big Five (ambition and energy are part of extraversion, for instance), giving strong support to traits as predictors of leadership.

A comprehensive review of the leadership literature, when organized around the Big Five, found extraversion to be the most important trait of effective leaders[10] but more strongly related to leader emergence than to leader effectiveness. Sociable and dominant people are more likely to assert themselves in group situations but leaders need to make sure they are not too assertive—one study found that leaders who scored very high on assertiveness were less effective than those who scored moderately high.[11]

Unlike agreeableness and emotional stability, conscientiousness and openness to experience also showed strong and consistent relationships to leadership, though not quite as strong as extraversion. Overall, the trait approach does have something to offer. Leaders who like being around people and are able to assert themselves (extraverted), are disciplined and keep commitments they make (conscientious), and are creative and flexible (open) do have an advantage when it comes to leadership, suggesting that good leaders do have key traits in common.

One reason is that conscientiousness and extraversion are positively related to leaders' self-efficacy, which explained most of the variance in subordinates' ratings of leader performance.[12] People are more likely to follow someone who is confident that she is going in the right direction.

Another trait that may indicate effective leadership is emotional intelligence (EI), discussed in Chapter 2. Advocates of EI argue that without it, a person can have outstanding training, a highly analytical mind, a compelling vision, and an endless supply of terrific ideas but still not make a great leader. This may be especially true as individuals move up in an organization.[13] Why is EI so critical to effective leadership? A core component of EI is empathy. Empathetic leaders can sense others' needs, listen to what followers say (and don't say), and read the reactions of others. As one leader noted, "The caring part of empathy, especially for the people with whom you work, is what inspires people to stay with a leader when the going gets rough. The mere fact that someone cares is more often than not rewarded with loyalty."[14]

The link between EI and leadership effectiveness is still much less investigated than other traits. One reviewer noted, "Speculating about the practical utility of the EI construct might be premature. Despite such warnings, EI is being viewed as a panacea for many organizational malaises with recent suggestions that EI is essential for leadership effectiveness."[15] But until more rigorous evidence accumulates, we cannot be confident about the connection.

Based on the latest findings, we offer two conclusions. First, traits can predict leadership. Twenty years ago, the evidence suggested otherwise. But this was probably because of the lack of a valid framework for classifying and organizing traits. The Big Five seem to have fixed that. Second, traits do a better job at predicting the emergence of leaders and the appearance of leadership than in actually distinguishing between *effective* and *ineffective* leaders.[16] The fact that an individual exhibits the traits and others consider that person to be a leader does not necessarily mean that the leader is successful at getting his or her group to achieve its goals.

This chapter's *Point/Counterpoint* on page 293 raises further issues on whether leaders are born or made. *Case Incident—Moving from Colleague to Supervisor* on page 297 helps you think about the challenges one faces when moving from being a co-worker to taking on leadership responsibilities.

Behavioural Theories: Do Leaders Behave in Particular Ways?

The failures of early trait studies led researchers in the late 1940s through the 1960s to go in a different direction. They wondered whether there was something unique in the way that effective leaders behave. Trait research provides a basis for *selecting* the right people for leadership. In contrast, behavioural theories implied we could *train* people to be leaders. Many argued that **behavioural theories of leadership** had advantages over trait theories.

Sally Jewell, CEO of Recreational Equipment, Inc. (REI), is an employee-oriented leader. During her tenure as CEO, Jewell has turned a struggling company into one with record sales. But she credits REI's success to the work of employees, stating that she does not believe in "hero CEOs." Jewell respects each employee's contribution to the company and includes in her leadership people who are very different from herself. Described as a leader high in consideration, she listens to employees' ideas and empowers them in performing their jobs.

The Ohio State Studies

The most comprehensive and replicated behavioural theories resulted from the Ohio State Studies in the late 1940s,[17] which sought to identify independent dimensions of leader behaviour. Beginning with more than a thousand dimensions, the studies narrowed the list to two that substantially accounted for most of the leadership behaviour described by employees. Researchers called these *initiating structure* and *consideration*.[18] **Initiating structure** is the extent to which a leader is likely to define and structure his or her role and those of employees in order to attain goals; it includes behaviour that tries to organize work, work relationships, and goals. A leader high in initiating structure is someone who "assigns group members to particular tasks," "expects workers to maintain definite standards of performance," and "emphasizes the meeting of deadlines."

Consideration is the extent to which a leader's job relationships are characterized by mutual trust, respect for employees' ideas, and regard for their feelings. A leader high in consideration helps employees with personal problems, is friendly and approachable, treats all employees as equals, and expresses appreciation and support. In a recent survey, when asked to indicate the factors that most motivated them at work, 66 percent of employees mentioned appreciation.[19]

The Michigan Studies

Leadership studies at the University of Michigan's Survey Research Center had similar objectives: to locate behavioural characteristics of leaders that appeared related to performance effectiveness.[20] The Michigan group also came up with two behavioural dimensions: the **employee-oriented leaders** emphasized interpersonal relations by taking a personal interest in the needs of employees and accepting individual differences among them; the **production-oriented leaders** emphasized the technical or task aspects of the job—focused on accomplishing the group's task. These dimensions are closely related to the Ohio State dimensions. Employee-oriented leadership is similar to consideration, and production-oriented leadership is similar to initiating structure. In fact, most leadership researchers use the terms synonymously.[21]

At one time, the results of testing behavioural theories were thought to be disappointing. One 1992 review concluded, "Overall, the research based on a two-factor conceptualization of leadership behavior has added little to our knowledge about

behavioural theories of leadership Theories that propose that specific behaviours differentiate leaders from nonleaders.

initiating structure The extent to which a leader is likely to define and structure his or her role and the roles of employees in order to attain goals.

consideration The extent to which a leader is likely to have job relationships characterized by mutual trust, respect for employees' ideas, and regard for their feelings.

employee-oriented leader A leader who emphasizes interpersonal relations.

production-oriented leader A leader who emphasizes the technical or task aspects of the job.

effective leadership."[22] However, a more recent review of 160 studies found the followers of leaders high in consideration were more satisfied with their jobs, were more motivated, and had more respect for their leader. Initiating structure was more strongly related to higher levels of group and organization productivity and more positive performance evaluations.

RESEARCH **FINDINGS:** Behavioural Theories of Leadership

While the results of the behavioural studies have been somewhat mixed,[23] a careful evaluation of the situations that leaders face provides some insights into when leaders should be production-oriented and when they should be people-oriented:[24]

- When subordinates experience a lot of pressure because of deadlines or unclear tasks, leaders who are people-oriented will increase employee satisfaction and performance.
- When the task is interesting or satisfying, there is less need for leaders to be people-oriented.
- When it's clear how to perform the task and what the goals are, leaders who are people-oriented will increase employee satisfaction, while those who are task-oriented will increase dissatisfaction.
- When people do not know what to do or individuals do not have the knowledge or skills to do the job, it's more important for leaders to be production-oriented than people-oriented.

The followers of leaders who are high on people orientation are more satisfied with their jobs, more motivated, and also have more respect for their leaders. Leaders who are high in task orientation show higher levels of group and organization productivity and receive more positive performance evaluations.

Contingency Theories: Does the Situation Matter?

As research on leadership developed, it became clear that predicting leadership success was more complex than simply isolating a few traits or preferable behaviours. Starting in the 1960s, leadership theories began to examine the situational factors that affect a leader's ability to act. This research pointed out that not all leaders can lead in every situation.[25]

Situational, or contingency, theories of leadership try to isolate critical situational factors that affect leadership effectiveness. The theories consider the degree of structure in the task being performed, the quality of leader-member relations; the leader's position power; the clarity of the employee's role; group norms; information availability; employee acceptance of the leader's decisions; and employee maturity.[26]

Have you ever wondered if there was one *right* way to lead?

We consider four situational theories below: the Fiedler contingency model, Hersey and Blanchard's Situational Leadership®, path-goal theory, and substitutes for leadership. All of these theories focus on the relationship of the leader to followers, and there is broad support for the idea that this relationship is important.[27]

situational, or contingency, theories Theories that propose that leadership effectiveness is dependent on the situation.

Fiedler Contingency Model

The first comprehensive contingency model for leadership was developed by Fred Fiedler.[28] The **Fiedler contingency model** proposes that effective group performance depends on the proper match between the leader's style and the degree to which the situation gives the leader control.

Fiedler created the *least preferred co-worker (LPC)* questionnaire to determine whether individuals were mainly interested in good personal relations with co-workers, and thus *relationship-oriented,* or mainly interested in productivity, and thus *task-oriented.* Fiedler assumed that an individual's leadership style is fixed. Therefore, if a situation requires a task-oriented leader and the person in that leadership position is relationship-oriented, either the situation has to be modified or the leader must be removed and replaced for optimum effectiveness to be achieved.

After assessing an individual's basic leadership style through an LPC questionnaire, the next step is to match the leader with the situation. Fiedler identified three contingency dimensions that determine the situation a leader faces. That situation will then affect the leader's effectiveness:

- *Leader-member relations.* The degree of confidence, trust, and respect members have for their leader.

- *Task structure.* The degree to which the job assignments are procedurized (that is, structured or unstructured).

- *Position power.* The degree of influence a leader has over power variables such as hiring, firing, discipline, promotions, and salary increases.

The next step is to evaluate the situation in terms of these three variables. Fiedler stated that the better the leader-member relations, the more highly structured the job, and the stronger the position power, the more control the leader has. A very favourable situation (in which the leader has a great deal of control) might include a payroll manager who is well respected and whose employees have confidence in her (good leader-member relations); activities to be done—such as wage computation, cheque writing, and report filing—that are specific and clear (high task structure); and provision of considerable freedom to reward and punish employees (strong position power). An unfavourable situation might be that of the disliked chairperson of a volunteer United Way fundraising team. In this job, the leader has very little control.

Fiedler suggested that task-oriented leaders perform best in situations of high and low control, while relationship-oriented leaders perform best in moderate control situations.[29] In a high-control situation, a leader can "get away" with task orientation, because the relationships are good and followers are easily influenced.[30] In a low-control situation (which is marked by poor relations, ill-defined tasks, and low influence), task orientation may be the only thing that makes it possible to get something done. In a moderate-control situation, the leader's relationship orientation may smooth the way to getting things done.

How would you apply Fiedler's findings? You would match leaders with the type of situation—in terms of leader-member relationships, task structure, and position power—for which they were best suited. Because Fiedler views an individual's leadership style as fixed, there are only two ways to improve leader effectiveness.

First, you can change the leader to fit the situation—as a baseball manager puts a right- or left-handed pitcher into the game depending on the hitter. If a group situation rates highly unfavourable but is currently led by a relationship-oriented manager, the group's performance could be improved under a manager who is task-oriented. The second alternative is to change the situation to fit the leader, by restructuring tasks or increasing or decreasing the leader's power to control factors such as salary increases, promotions, and disciplinary actions.

Fiedler contingency model A leadership theory that proposes that effective group performance depends on the proper match between the leader's style and the degree to which the situation gives the leader control.

Explore

Exhibit 8-2: Hersey and Blanchard's
Situational Leadership

EXHIBIT 8-2 Hersey and Blanchard's Situational Leadership®

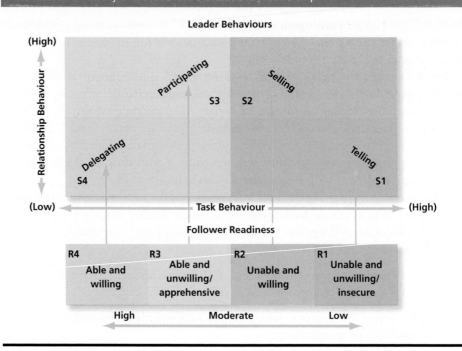

Fiedler's theory has been found to be more difficult to apply in the workplace than some of the other contingency theories we review.[31]

Hersey and Blanchard's Situational Leadership®

Paul Hersey and Ken Blanchard's **Situational Leadership® (SL)**—has been incorporated into the leadership training of more than 700 of the *Fortune* 1000 companies, and more than a million managers a year from a wide variety of organizations are being taught its basic elements.[32]

SL says successful leadership is achieved by selecting the right leadership style contingent on the followers' *readiness,* or the extent to which they are willing and able to accomplish a specific task. A leader should choose one of four behaviours depending on follower readiness. This idea is illustrated in Exhibit 8-2.

If followers are *unable* and *unwilling* to do a task, the leader needs to give clear and specific directions; if they are *unable* and *willing,* the leader needs to display high task orientation to compensate for followers' lack of ability and high relationship orientation to get them to "buy into" the leader's desires. If followers are *able* and *unwilling,* the leader needs to use a supportive and participative style; if they are both *able* and *willing,* the leader does not need to do much.

SL has intuitive appeal. It acknowledges the importance of followers and builds on the logic that leaders can compensate for their limited ability and motivation. Yet research efforts to test and support the theory have generally been disappointing.[33] Why? Possible explanations include internal ambiguities and inconsistencies in the model itself as well as problems with research methodology in tests. So despite its intuitive appeal and wide popularity, any endorsement must be cautious for now.

Path-Goal Theory

Developed by University of Toronto professor Martin Evans in the late 1960s and later expanded on by Robert House (formerly at the University of Toronto, but now at the Wharton School of Business at the University of Pennsylvania), **path-goal theory** extracts elements from the Ohio State leadership research on initiating structure and

Situational Leadership® (SL) A leadership theory that proposes that effective leaders adapt their leadership style according to how willing and able a follower is to perform tasks.

path-goal theory A leadership theory that says it is the leader's job to assist followers in attaining their goals and to provide the necessary direction and/or support to ensure that their individual goals are compatible with the overall goals of the group or organization.

consideration and the expectancy theory of motivation (discussed in Chapter 4).[34] It says that it is the leader's job to provide followers with the information, support, or other resources necessary to achieve their goals. (The term *path-goal* implies effective leaders clarify followers' paths to their work goals and make the journey easier by reducing roadblocks.)

According to this theory, leaders should follow three guidelines to be effective:[35]

- *Determine the outcomes subordinates want.* These might include good pay, job security, interesting work, and the autonomy to do one's job.

- *Reward individuals with their desired outcomes* when they perform well.

- *Let individuals know what they need to do to receive rewards* (that is, the path to the goal), remove any barriers that would prevent a high level of performance, and express confidence that individuals have the ability to perform well.

Path-goal theory identifies four leadership behaviours that might be used in different situations to motivate individuals:

- The *directive leader* lets followers know what is expected of them, schedules work to be done, and gives specific guidance as to how to accomplish tasks. This closely parallels the Ohio State dimension of initiating structure. This behaviour is best used when individuals have difficulty doing tasks or the tasks are ambiguous. It would not be very helpful when used with individuals who are already highly motivated, have the skills and abilities to do the task, and understand the requirements of the task.

- The *supportive leader* is friendly and shows concern for the needs of followers. This is essentially synonymous with the Ohio State dimension of consideration. This behaviour is often recommended when individuals are under stress or otherwise show that they need to be supported.

- The *participative leader* consults with followers and uses their suggestions before making a decision. This behaviour is most appropriate when individuals need to buy in to decisions.

- The *achievement-oriented leader* sets challenging goals and expects followers to perform at their highest level. This behaviour works well with individuals who like challenges and are highly motivated. It would be less effective with less capable individuals or those who are highly stressed from overwork.

As Exhibit 8-3 illustrates, path-goal theory proposes two types of contingency variables that affect the leadership behaviour–outcome relationship: environmental variables that are outside the control of the employee and variables that are part of the personal characteristics of the employee. House assumes that leaders are flexible and can display any or all of these behaviours, depending on the situation. Some situations may in fact need more than one style from the leader. The theory proposes that employee performance and satisfaction are likely to be positively influenced when the leader compensates for things lacking in either the employee or the work setting. However, the leader who spends time explaining tasks when those tasks are already clear or when the employee has the ability and experience to handle them without interference is likely to be ineffective because the employee will see such directive behaviour as redundant or even insulting. Research generally supports path-goal theory.[36]

One of the dangers of any theory of situational leadership is the assumption that the behaviour of a leader should adjust to meet followers' needs. It may be that a leader acts on employees' perceived needs rather than their real needs. Recall from Chapter 2 that "perceptions are reality." A 2010 study found that "if managers view followers positively—that they are good citizens, industrious, enthusiastic—they will treat their employees positively. If they think of their employees negatively—that they

Learn About Yourself
Leadership Style Indicator

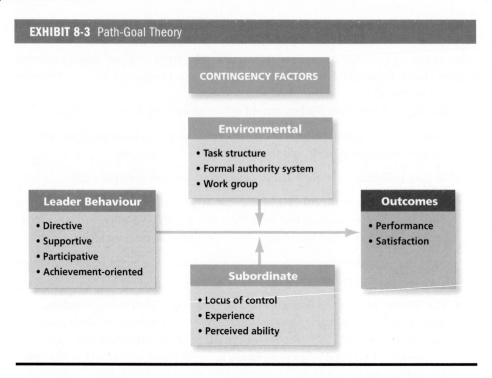

EXHIBIT 8-3 Path-Goal Theory

CONTINGENCY FACTORS

Environmental
- Task structure
- Formal authority system
- Work group

Leader Behaviour
- Directive
- Supportive
- Participative
- Achievement-oriented

Subordinate
- Locus of control
- Experience
- Perceived ability

Outcomes
- Performance
- Satisfaction

are conforming, insubordinate and incompetent—they will treat them that way."[37] By extension, managers may not adopt the appropriate situational leadership behaviour if they have incorrect perceptions of their employees and their needs.

Substitutes for Leadership

The previous three theories argue that leaders are needed, but that leaders should consider the situation in determining the style of leadership to adopt. However, numerous studies collectively demonstrate that, in many situations, leaders' actions are irrelevant. Experience and training are among the *substitutes* that can replace the need for a leader's support or ability to create structure. Organizational characteristics such as explicit formalized goals, rigid rules and procedures, and cohesive work groups can also replace formal leadership, while indifference to organizational rewards can neutralize its effects. *Neutralizers* make it impossible for leader behaviour to make any difference to follower outcomes. These are shown in Exhibit 8-4.[38]

Is a leader always necessary?

This observation should not be too surprising. After all, we have introduced a number of variables—such as attitudes, personality, ability, and group norms—that affect employee performance and satisfaction. It's simplistic to think employees are guided to goal accomplishments solely by the actions of their leader. Leadership is simply another independent variable in our overall OB model.

There are many possible substitutes for and neutralizers of many different types of leader behaviours across many different situations. Moreover, sometimes the difference between substitutes and neutralizers is fuzzy. If I am working on a task that is intrinsically enjoyable, theory predicts that leadership will be less important because the task itself provides enough motivation. But does that mean intrinsically enjoyable tasks neutralize leadership effects, or substitute for them, or both? Another problem is that while substitutes for leadership (such as employee characteristics, the nature of the task, and so forth) matter to performance, that does not necessarily mean that leadership does not matter to performance.[39]

EXHIBIT 8-4 Substitutes and Neutralizers for Leadership

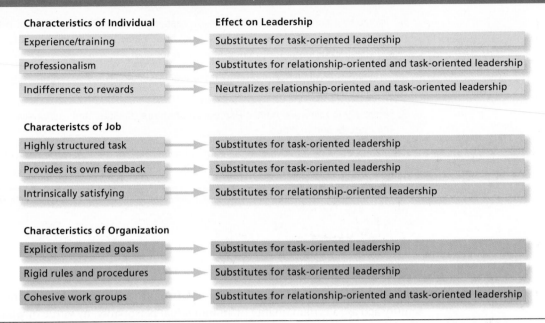

Characteristics of Individual	Effect on Leadership
Experience/training	Substitutes for task-oriented leadership
Professionalism	Substitutes for relationship-oriented and task-oriented leadership
Indifference to rewards	Neutralizes relationship-oriented and task-oriented leadership

Characteristcs of Job	
Highly structured task	Substitutes for task-oriented leadership
Provides its own feedback	Substitutes for task-oriented leadership
Intrinsically satisfying	Substitutes for relationship-oriented leadership

Characteristics of Organization	
Explicit formalized goals	Substitutes for task-oriented leadership
Rigid rules and procedures	Substitutes for task-oriented leadership
Cohesive work groups	Substitutes for relationship-oriented and task-oriented leadership

Source: Based on S. Kerr and J. M. Jermier, "Substitutes for Leadership: Their Meaning and Measurement," *Organizational Behavior and Human Performance,* December 1978, p. 378.

Inspirational Leadership

 Lt.-Col. Maryse Carmichael's leadership role extends out into the community, where the Snowbirds are a source of inspiration and wonder (not to mention an important tool used for recruitment purposes).[40] "If I can influence not only young girls but boys to follow their passion then that's great," Carmichael says. That is why she ensures that new candidates for pilot jobs are not screened solely on the basis on flying ability. "Teamwork is so important," she adds, noting that to a large degree teamwork is what defines the Snowbirds. But the desire and ability to engage with communities and do public relations work is critical too. After all, for many Canadians, the Snowbirds are the face of the military. "People often hear about Canadian Forces in Afghanistan but you rarely get to meet them. We get to meet Canadians on a daily basis." She vividly remembers her own first experience seeing the Snowbirds at a show in Beauport, Quebec, when she was five years old. "It's sometimes hard to quantify what we do," she says. "How can you explain that we motivate young people to dream?" What does it take to be an inspiring leader?

3 How does a leader lead with vision?

The leadership theories we have discussed above ignore the importance of the leader as a communicator who inspires others to act beyond their immediate self-interests. In this section, we present two contemporary leadership theories with a common theme. They view leaders as individuals who inspire followers through their words, ideas, and behaviours. These theories are charismatic leadership and transformational leadership.

Charismatic Leadership

The following individuals are frequently cited as being charismatic leaders: Frank Stronach of Aurora, Ontario-based Magna International; Mogens Smed, CEO of Calgary-based DIRTT (Doing It Right This Time); Pierre Trudeau, the late prime minister; René Lévesque, the late Quebec premier; Lucien Bouchard, former Bloc Québécois leader; Michaëlle Jean, former Governor General; and Craig Kielburger, who founded Kids Can Free the Children as a teenager. So what do they have in common?

EXHIBIT 8-5 Key Characteristics of Charismatic Leaders

1. *Vision and articulation.* Has a vision—expressed as an idealized goal—that proposes a future better than the status quo; and is able to clarify the importance of the vision in terms that are understandable to others.

2. *Personal risk.* Willing to take on high personal risk, incur high costs, and engage in self-sacrifice to achieve the vision.

3. *Sensitivity to followers' needs.* Perceptive of others' abilities and responsive to their needs and feelings.

4. *Unconventional behaviour.* Engages in behaviours that are perceived as novel and counter to norms.

Source: Based on J. A. Conger and R. N. Kanungo, *Charismatic Leadership in Organizations* (Thousand Oaks, CA: Sage, 1998), p. 94.

What Is Charismatic Leadership?

Max Weber, a sociologist, defined *charisma* (from the Greek for "gift") more than a century ago as "a certain quality of an individual personality, by virtue of which he or she is set apart from ordinary people and treated as endowed with supernatural, superhuman, or at least specifically exceptional powers or qualities. These are not accessible to the ordinary person and are regarded as of divine origin or as exemplary, and on the basis of them the individual concerned is treated as a leader."[41] Weber argued that **charismatic leadership** was one of several ideal types of authority.

The first researcher to consider charismatic leadership in terms of OB was Robert House. According to House's **charismatic leadership theory**, followers attribute heroic or extraordinary leadership abilities to certain behaviours they observe in leaders.[42] A number of studies have attempted to identify the characteristics of the charismatic leader and have documented four: they have a vision, they are willing to take personal risks to achieve that vision, they are sensitive to followers' needs, and they exhibit behaviours that are out of the ordinary (see Exhibit 8-5).[43]

How Charismatic Leaders Influence Followers

How do charismatic leaders actually influence followers? The evidence suggests a four-step process.[44] It begins by the leader articulating an appealing **vision**, a long-term strategy for how to attain a goal by linking the present with a better future for the organization. Desirable visions fit the times and circumstances and reflect the uniqueness of the organization. Steve Jobs championed the iPod, noting, "It's as Apple as anything Apple has ever done." People in the organization must also believe the vision is challenging yet attainable. The creation of the iPod achieved Apple's goal of offering groundbreaking and easy-to-use technology.

Second, a vision is incomplete without an accompanying **vision statement**, a formal articulation of an organization's vision or mission. Charismatic leaders may use vision statements to imprint on followers an overarching goal and purpose. They then communicate high performance expectations and express confidence that followers can attain them. This enhances follower self-esteem and self-confidence.

Next, through words and actions, the leader conveys a new set of values and sets an example for followers to imitate. One study of Israeli bank employees showed, for example, that charismatic leaders were more effective because their employees personally identified with them.[45] Charismatic leaders also set a tone of cooperation and mutual support. A study of 115 government employees found they had a stronger sense of personal belonging at work when they had charismatic leaders, increasing their willingness to engage in helping and compliance-oriented behaviour.[46]

charismatic leadership Leadership that critically examines the status quo with a view to developing and articulating future strategic goals or vision for the organization, and then leading organizational members to achieve these goals through empowering strategies.

charismatic leadership theory A leadership theory that states that followers attribute heroic or extraordinary leadership abilities to certain behaviours they observe in leaders.

vision A long-term strategy for attaining a goal or goals.

vision statement A formal articulation of an organization's vision or mission.

Finally, the charismatic leader engages in emotion-inducing and often unconventional behaviour to demonstrate courage and convictions about the vision. Followers "catch" the emotions their leader is conveying.[47]

What are examples of visions? The late Steve Jobs' vision of elegance in design influenced how all of Apple's products were built. Facebook founder and CEO Mark Zuckerberg's vision for his company is to have it be a one-stop place for everyone's communication needs, including text messaging.

RESEARCH FINDINGS: Charismatic Leadership

Research shows impressive correlations between charismatic leadership and high performance and satisfaction among followers.[48] People working for charismatic leaders are motivated to exert extra work effort and, because they like and respect their leader, express greater satisfaction. It also appears that organizations with charismatic CEOs are more profitable. And charismatic professors enjoy higher course evaluations.[49]

However, charisma may not always be generalizable; its effectiveness may depend on the situation. Charisma appears to be most successful when the follower's task has an ideological component or when the environment involves a high degree of stress and uncertainty.[50] Even in laboratory studies, when people are psychologically aroused, they are more likely to respond to charismatic leaders.[51] This may explain why charismatic leaders tend to surface in politics, religion, wartime, or a business firm that is in its infancy or facing a life-threatening crisis.

People are especially receptive to charismatic leadership when they sense a crisis, when they are under stress, or when they fear for their lives. More generally, some people's personalities are especially susceptible to charismatic leadership.[52] Consider self-esteem. If a person lacks self-esteem and questions his or her self-worth, that person is more likely to absorb a leader's direction rather than establish his or her own way of leading or thinking.

The creative vision of Steve Jobs, Apple's charismatic co-founder, was to make state-of-the-art technology that is easy for people to use. As Apple CEO, Jobs inspired, motivated, and led employees to develop products such as Macintosh computers, iPod music players, iPads, and iPhones. "The iPhone is like having your life in your pocket," said Jobs. In October 2011, Jobs passed away, and Apple employees and others paid tribute to him as the ultimate consumer-electronics visionary.

A 2010 study found that it is possible for a person to learn how to communicate charismatically, which would then lead that person to be perceived more as a leader. People who are perceived to be charismatic show empathy, enthusiasm, and self-confidence; have good speaking and listening skills; and make eye contact.[53] To learn more about how to be charismatic yourself, see the *Working with Others Exercise* on page 295.

The Dark Side of Charismatic Leadership

When organizations are in need of great change, charismatic leaders are often able to inspire their followers to meet the challenges of change. Be aware that a charismatic leader may become a liability to an organization once the crisis is over and the need for dramatic change subsides.[54] Why? Because then the charismatic leader's overwhelming self-confidence can be a liability. He or she is unable to listen to others, becomes uncomfortable when challenged by aggressive employees, and begins to hold an unjustifiable belief in his or her "rightness" on issues. Some would argue that Stephane Dion's behaviour after the Liberal party lost 19 seats in the 2008 federal election, first refusing to step down, and then trying to form a coalition government shortly thereafter, would fit this description.

Many have argued that the financial scandals and large losses experienced by investors in North America, including the ponzi scheme created by Bernie Madoff and the near bankruptcy of the Caisse de dépôt et placement du Québec because of the "audacious investment strategies" of Henri-Paul Rousseau, point to some of the dangers of charismatic leadership.[55]

Charismatic leadership, by its very nature, silences criticism. Thus, employees follow the lead of their visionary CEOs unquestioningly. Professor David Leighton, of the Richard Ivey School of Business at the University of Western Ontario, notes that even boards of directors and auditors are reluctant to challenge these CEOs. He finds that Canada's "more balanced culture" is less likely to turn CEOs into heroes.[56]

A study of 29 companies that went from good to great (their cumulative stock returns were all at least three times better than the general stock market over 15 years) found that a key difference in successful charismatic leaders may be the *absence* of being ego-driven.[57] Although the leaders of these firms were fiercely ambitious and driven, their ambition was directed toward their company rather than themselves. They took responsibility for mistakes and poor results but gave credit for successes to other people. These individuals are called level 5 leaders because they have four basic leadership qualities—individual capability, team skills, managerial competence, and the ability to stimulate others to high performance—plus a fifth quality: a paradoxical blend of personal humility and professional will. **Level 5 leaders** channel their ego needs away from themselves and into the goal of building a great company while getting little notoriety in the business press.

Transformational Leadership

A stream of research has focused on differentiating transformational from transactional leaders.[58] The Ohio and Michigan State studies, the Fiedler contingency model, and path-goal theory describe **transactional leaders**—those who guide their followers toward established goals by clarifying role and task requirements. **Transformational leaders** inspire followers to transcend their self-interests for the good of the organization, and can have an extraordinary effect on their followers.[59] Andrea Jung at Avon, Richard Branson of the Virgin Group, and Jim McNerney of Boeing are all examples of transformational leaders. They pay attention to the concerns and developmental needs of individual followers; they change followers' awareness of issues by helping them to look at old problems in new ways; and they excite and inspire followers to put out extra effort to achieve group goals. Exhibit 8-6 briefly identifies and defines the characteristics that differentiate these two types of leaders.

level 5 leaders Leaders who are fiercely ambitious and driven, but their ambition is directed toward their company rather than themselves.

transactional leaders Leaders who guide or motivate their followers in the direction of established goals by clarifying role and task requirements.

transformational leaders Leaders who inspire followers to go beyond their own self-interests for the good of the organization and have a profound and extraordinary effect on followers.

EXHIBIT 8-6 Characteristics of Transactional and Transformational Leaders

Transactional Leader

Contingent reward: Contracts exchange of rewards for effort, promises rewards for good performance, recognizes accomplishments.

Management by exception (active): Watches and searches for deviations from rules and standards, takes corrective action.

Management by exception (passive): Intervenes only if standards are not met.

Laissez-faire: Abdicates responsibilities, avoids making decisions.

Transformational Leader

Idealized influence: Provides vision and sense of mission, instills pride, gains respect and trust.

Inspirational motivation: Communicates high expectations, uses symbols to focus efforts, expresses important purposes in simple ways.

Intellectual stimulation: Promotes intelligence, rationality, and careful problem solving.

Individualized consideration: Gives personal attention, treats each employee individually, coaches, advises.

Source: Reprinted from B. M. Bass, "From Transactional to Transformational Leadership: Learning to Share the Vision," *Organizational Dynamics,* Winter 1990, p. 22, with permission from Elsevier.

Transactional and transformational leadership are not opposing approaches to getting things done.[60] They complement each other, though they are not equally important. Transformational leadership *builds on* transactional leadership and produces levels of follower effort and performance that go beyond what transactional leadership alone can do. But the reverse isn't true. So if you are a good transactional leader but do not have transformational qualities, you'll likely only be a mediocre leader. The best leaders are transactional *and* transformational.

✴ Explore

Exhibit 8-6: Characteristics of Transactional and Transformational Leaders

Full Range of Leadership Model

Exhibit 8-7 shows the full range of leadership model. The lower three styles represent aspects of transactional leadership. Laissez-faire is the most passive and therefore the least effective of the leader behaviours.[61] Management by exception—active or passive—is slightly better than laissez-faire, but it's still considered ineffective. Management by exception leaders tend to be available only when there is a problem, which is often too late. Contingent reward leadership can be an effective style of leadership, but will not get employees to go above and beyond the call of duty.

Only with the four remaining leadership styles—all aspects of transformational leadership—are leaders able to motivate followers to perform above expectations and transcend their own self-interest for the sake of the organization. Individualized consideration, intellectual stimulation, inspirational motivation, and idealized influence all result in extra effort from employees, higher productivity, higher morale and satisfaction, higher organizational effectiveness, lower turnover, lower absenteeism, and greater organizational adaptability. Based on this model, leaders are generally most effective when they regularly use each of the four transformational behaviours.

How Transformational Leadership Works

Transformational leaders are more effective because they themselves are more creative and also because they encourage those who follow them to be creative, too.[62] In companies with transformational leaders, there is greater decentralization of responsibility, managers have more propensity to take risks, and compensation plans are geared toward long-term results, all of which facilitate corporate entrepreneurship.[63]

Companies with transformational leaders also show greater agreement among top managers about the organization's goals, which yields superior organizational

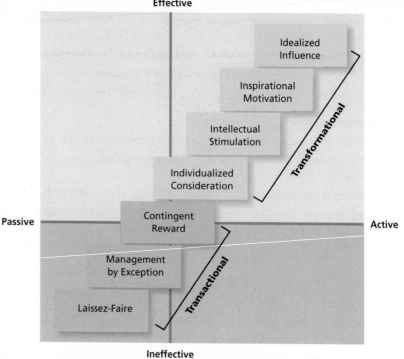

EXHIBIT 8-7 Full Range of Leadership Model

performance.[64] Similar results, showing that transformational leaders improve performance by building consensus among group members, have been demonstrated in the Israeli military.[65] Transformational leaders are able to increase follower self-efficacy, giving the group a "can do" spirit.[66] Followers of transformational leaders are more likely to pursue ambitious goals, be familiar with and agree on the strategic goals of the organization, and believe that the goals they are pursuing are personally important.[67]

Research has shown that vision explains part of the effect of transformational leadership. One study found that vision was even more important than a charismatic (effusive, dynamic, lively) communication style in explaining the success of entrepreneurial firms.[68] Finally, transformational leadership also engenders commitment on the part of followers and instills in them a greater sense of trust in the leader.[69]

RESEARCH FINDINGS: Transformational Leadership

Transformational leadership has been impressively supported at various job levels and in disparate occupations (school principals, marine commanders, ministers, presidents of MBA associations, military cadets, union shop stewards, schoolteachers, sales reps). One recent study of R & D firms found that teams whose project leaders scored high on transformational leadership produced better-quality products as judged one year later and were more profitable five years later.[70] A review of 87 studies testing transformational leadership found that it was related to the motivation and satisfaction of followers and to the higher performance and perceived effectiveness of leaders.[71]

Transformational leadership is not equally effective in all situations, however. It has a greater impact on the bottom line in smaller, privately held firms than in more complicated organizations.[72] The personal nature of transformational leadership may be most effective when leaders can directly interact with the workforce and make decisions than when they report to an external board of directors or deal with a complex bureaucratic structure. Another study showed transformational leaders were more effective in improving group potency in teams higher in power distance and collectivism.[73] Where group members are highly individualistic and don't readily cede decision-making authority, transformational leadership might not have much impact.

Transformational leadership theory is not perfect. There are concerns about whether contingent reward leadership is strictly a characteristic of transactional leaders only. And contrary to the full range of leadership model, the 4 *I*'s in transformational leadership are not always superior in effectiveness to transactional leadership (contingent reward leadership sometimes works as well as transformational leadership).

In summary, transformational leadership is more strongly correlated than transactional leadership with lower turnover rates, higher productivity, lower employee stress and burnout, and higher employee satisfaction.[74] Like charisma, it can be learned. One study of Canadian bank managers found that branches managed by those who underwent transformational leadership training performed significantly better than branches whose managers did not receive training. Other studies show similar results.[75]

Transformational Leadership vs. Charismatic Leadership

There is some debate about whether transformational leadership and charismatic leadership are the same. Researcher Robert House considers them synonymous, calling the differences "modest" and "minor." McGill University professor Rabindra Kanungo agrees.[76] However, one researcher who disagrees says, "The purely charismatic [leader] may want followers to adopt the charismatic's world view and go no further; the transformational leader will attempt to instill in followers the ability to question not only established views but eventually those established by the leader."[77] Although many researchers believe that transformational leadership is broader than charismatic leadership, a leader who scores high on transformational leadership is also likely to score high on charisma. Therefore, in practice, they may be roughly equivalent. Would you be able to be a charismatic leader? We give you tips in this chapter's *From Concepts to Skills* on pages 298–299.

Contemplary Leadership Roles

 The military may be a surprising place to find self-directed leadership, given the rigid formality of the hierarchy and role definitions.[78] However, senior leaders still find ways to create opportunities to take initiative. For example, retired Snowbird Dan Dempsey notes that historic Snowbird team pictures were scattered about the base but not organized or protected in a systematic way. With the support of base command, Dempsey started a museum in the squadron, eventually collecting enough material to fill a book. "I was able to find, through a vast myriad of collections, a whole bunch of old-timers and pioneers who started the air-show industry in Canada and adapt their personal accounts." By enabling this self-directed project, the Snowbird team ended up with both a museum and a book that continue to help them address public relations and community engagement goals. What can formal leaders do to help foster self-directed leadership among employees?

4 Are there leadership roles for nonmanagers?

Can anyone be a leader?

Transformational leadership theory focuses on heroic leaders, leaders at the top echelons of the organization, and also on individuals rather than teams. However, the notion of "leader at the top" does not adequately reflect what is happening in some workplaces today, where there

N. R. Narayana Murthy is one of the founders of Infosys in Bangalore, India. He has served the firm as chairman and chief mentor of the board, where he has shared his experiences, knowledge, and lessons learned while building Infosys for over three decades into a company with 142 000 employees globally and annual sales of over $6 billion. In August 2011, Mr. Murthy retired from Infosys and is currently Chairman Emeritus of the company. He is shown here with Infosys employees at the company's Bangalore campus, which is also its corporate headquarters.

Learn About Yourself
Personal Assessment of
Management Skills

is less hierarchy and more connections, both inside and outside of the organization. There is a need for more "distributed leadership." In this form, leadership is "distributed across many players, both within and across organizations, up and down the hierarchy, wherever information, expertise, vision, and new ways of working together reside."[79]

The following sections aim to explain how leadership can be spread throughout the organization through mentoring, self-leadership, team leadership, online leadership, and leading without authority. Even if you are not a manager or someone thinking about leadership in a corporate situation, this discussion offers important insights into how you can take on a leadership role in an organization.

Mentoring

Many leaders take responsibility for developing future leaders through mentoring relationships. A **mentor** is a senior employee who sponsors and supports a less-experienced employee (a protégé). The mentoring role includes coaching, counselling, and sponsorship to help their protégés develop skills, to provide support and help bolster protégés' self-confidence, and to lobby so that protégés get good assignments, promotions, and salary increases.[80] Successful mentors are good teachers. They present ideas clearly, listen well, and empathize with protégés' problems.

Traditional informal mentoring relationships develop when leaders identify a less experienced, lower-level employee who appears to have potential for future development.[81] The protégé will often be tested with a particularly challenging assignment. If he or she performs acceptably, the mentor will develop the relationship, informally showing the protégé how the organization *really* works outside its formal structures and procedures. Protégés can also learn how the mentor has navigated early career issues or led effectively and how to work through problems with minimal stress.

Why would a leader want to be a mentor?[82] Many feel they have something to share with the younger generation and want to provide a legacy. Mentoring provides unfiltered access to the attitudes of lower-ranking employees and protégés can be an excellent source of early warning signals that identify potential organizational problems.

Are all employees in an organization equally likely to participate in a mentoring relationship? Unfortunately no.[83] The evidence indicates that minorities and women are less likely to be chosen as protégés than are white males. Mentors tend to select protégés who are similar to themselves in criteria such as background, education, gender, race, ethnicity, and religion. "People naturally move to mentor and can more easily communicate with those with whom they most closely identify."[84] Senior male managers may also select male protégés to minimize problems such as sexual attraction or gossip.

In a twist to the typical mentoring-down idea, Procter & Gamble introduced a Mentoring Up program to help senior managers become more aware of what female managers can contribute to the organization. In its program, mid-level female managers mentor senior-level male executives. The program has led to fewer departures of female managers and has exposed women to top decision makers.[85]

mentor A senior employee who sponsors and supports a less-experienced employee.

Coaching

A number of organizations have introduced coaching, which is different from mentoring. "Mentoring, at its best, involves a longer term relationship in which there is an emotional attachment between mentor and protégé."[86] By contrast, coaching is often more task-oriented and short term. Coaching is used by senior and middle managers in particular, although other managers use coaching as part of their leadership style. A good coach

- Emphasizes self-development and self-discovery of the person being coached
- Offers the person being coached constructive feedback on how to improve
- Meets regularly with the person being coached
- Is a good listener
- Challenges the person being coached to perform
- Sets realistic standards for the person being coached to achieve.[87]

Self-Leadership (or Self-Management)

A growing trend in organizations is the focus on self-leadership, or self-management, where individuals and teams set goals, plan and implement tasks, evaluate performance, solve their own problems, and motivate themselves.[88] (Recall our discussion of self-managed teams in Chapter 5.)

Reduced levels of supervision; offices in the home; teamwork; and growth in service and professional employment have increased the demand for self-leadership. Self-management can also be a substitute or neutralizer for leadership from others.

Despite the lack of studies of self-management techniques in organizational settings, self-management strategies have been shown to be successful in nonorganizational settings.[89] Those who practise self-management look for opportunities to be more effective in the workplace and improve their career success and provide their own sense of reward and feedback after carrying out their tasks. Moreover, self-reinforced behaviour is often maintained at a higher rate than behaviour that is externally regulated.[90] *OB in Action—Engaging in Self-Leadership* indicates ways in which you can practise effective self-leadership.

How do leaders create self-leaders? The following approaches have been suggested:[91]

- *Model self-leadership.* Practise self-observation, setting challenging personal goals, self-direction, and self-reinforcement. Then display these behaviours, and encourage others to rehearse and then produce them.
- *Encourage employees to create self-set goals.* Support employees in developing quantitative, specific goals; having such goals is the most important part of self-leadership.
- *Encourage the use of self-rewards to strengthen and increase desirable behaviours.* By contrast, limit self-punishment only to occasions when the employee has been dishonest or destructive.
- *Create positive thought patterns.* Encourage employees to use mental imagery and self-talk to further stimulate self-motivation.

How do you manage yourself?

OB in ACTION
Engaging in Self-Leadership

To engage in effective self-leadership:[92]

- **Think horizontally, not vertically.** Vertical relationships in the organization matter, but peers can become trusted colleagues and have a great impact on your work.
- Focus on **influence, not control.** Work with your colleagues, not for them. Be collaborative and share credit.
- **Create opportunities**, do not wait for them. Rather than look for the right time, be more action-oriented.

- *Create a climate of self-leadership.* Redesign the work to increase the natural rewards of a job and focus on these naturally rewarding features of work to increase motivation.

- *Encourage constructive self-criticism.* Encourage individuals to be critical of their own performance to find ways to improve.

The underlying assumptions behind self-leadership are that people are responsible, capable, and able to exercise initiative without the external constraints of bosses, rules, or regulations. Given the proper support, individuals can monitor and control their own behaviour. The *Learning About Yourself Exercise* on page 294 provides further examples of how to engage in self-leadership.

Team Leadership

Leadership is increasingly taking place within a team context. As teams grow in popularity, the role of the leader in guiding team members takes on more importance.[93] Also, because of its more collaborative nature, the role of team leader differs from the traditional leadership role performed by front-line supervisors.

Many leaders are not equipped to handle the move to team leader. As one prominent consultant noted, "Even the most capable managers have trouble making the transition because all the command-and-control type things they were encouraged to do before are no longer appropriate. There's no reason to have any skill or sense of this."[94] This same consultant estimated that "probably 15 percent of managers are natural team leaders; another 15 percent could never lead a team because it runs counter to their personality. [They are unable to put aside their dominating style for the good of the team.] Then there's that huge group in the middle: team leadership doesn't come naturally to them, but they can learn it."[95]

Effective team leaders need to build commitment and confidence, remove obstacles, create opportunities, and be part of the team.[96] They have to learn skills such as the patience to share information, the willingness to trust others, the ability to give up authority, and an understanding of when to intervene. New team leaders may try to retain too much control at a time when team members need more autonomy, or they may abandon their teams at times when the teams need support and help.[97]

Exhibit 8-8 gives a lighthearted look at what it means to be a team leader.

EXHIBIT 8-8

Source: Dilbert, reprinted by permission of Universal Uclick.

Roles of Team Leaders

A recent study of 20 organizations that reorganized themselves around teams found certain common responsibilities that all leaders had to assume. These included coaching, facilitating, handling disciplinary problems, reviewing team/individual performance, training, and communicating.[98] Many of these responsibilities apply to managers in general. A more meaningful way to describe the team leader's job is to focus on two priorities: managing the team's relations with outsiders and facilitating the team process.[99] We have divided these priorities into four specific roles that team leaders play:

- *Liaisons with outsiders.* Outsiders include upper management, other internal teams, customers, and suppliers. The leader represents the team to other constituencies, secures needed resources, clarifies others' expectations of the team, gathers information from the outside, and shares this information with team members.

- *Troubleshooters.* When the team has problems and asks for assistance, team leaders sit in on meetings and try to help resolve the problems. This rarely relates to technical or operational issues because the team members typically know more about the tasks being done than does the team leader. The leader contributes by asking penetrating questions, by helping the team discuss problems, and by getting needed resources from external constituencies. For instance, when a team in an aerospace firm found itself short-handed, its team leader took responsibility for getting more staff. He presented the team's case to upper management and got the approval through the company's human resource department.

- *Conflict managers.* When disagreements surface, team leaders help process the conflict. What is the source of the conflict? Who is involved? What are the issues? What resolution options are available? What are the advantages and disadvantages of each? By getting team members to address questions such as these, the leader minimizes the disruptive aspects of intrateam conflicts.

- *Coaches.* They clarify expectations and roles, teach, offer support, cheerlead, and do whatever else is necessary to help team members improve their work performance.

Online Leadership

How do you lead people who are physically separated from you and with whom you communicate electronically? This question has received minimal attention from organizational behaviour researchers.[100] But today's managers and their employees are increasingly being linked by networks rather than geographical proximity. Obvious examples include managers who regularly use email to communicate with their staff, managers who oversee virtual projects or teams, and managers whose teleworking employees are linked to the office by an Internet connection.

Electronic communication is a powerful channel that can build and enhance leadership effectiveness. But when misused, it can undermine much of what a leader has achieved through verbal communication. In face-to-face communications, harsh *words* can be softened by nonverbal action. A smile and comforting gestures, for instance, can lessen the blow behind strong words like *disappointed, unsatisfactory, inadequate,* or *below expectations.* That nonverbal component does not exist with online interactions. The *structure* of words in a digital communication has the power to motivate or demotivate the receiver. We propose that online leaders have to think carefully about what actions they want their digital messages to initiate.

Jane Howell at the Richard Ivey School of Business, University of Western Ontario, and one of her students, Kate Hall-Merenda, considered the issues of leading from a distance.[101] They noted that physical distance has the potential to create many problems, with team members feeling isolated, forgotten, and perhaps not cared about. It may result in lowered productivity. Their study of 109 business leaders and 371 followers in a large financial institution found that physical distance makes it more difficult to develop high-quality relationships.

Howell and Hall-Merenda suggest that some of the same characteristics of transformational leaders are appropriate for long-distance managing. In particular, they emphasize the need to articulate a compelling vision and to communicate that vision in an inspiring way. Encouraging employees to think about ways to strive toward that vision is another important task of the leader.

Online leaders confront unique challenges, the greatest of which appears to be developing and maintaining trust. **Identification-based trust**, based on a mutual understanding of each other's intentions and appreciation of others' wants and desires, is particularly difficult to achieve without face-to-face interaction.[102] Online negotiations can also be hindered because parties express lower levels of trust.[103] It's not clear whether it's even possible for employees to identify with or trust leaders with whom they only communicate electronically.[104]

This discussion leads us to the tentative conclusion that, for an increasing number of managers, good leadership skills may include the abilities to communicate support, trust, and inspiration through keyboarded words and accurately read emotions in others' messages. In electronic communication, writing skills are likely to become an extension of interpersonal skills.

Leading without Authority

Can you lead, even if you do not have the authority (or formal appointment) to be a leader? For instance, what if you wanted to convince the dean to introduce more relevant business courses, or you wanted to convince the president of the company where you work to use more environmentally friendly strategies in dealing with waste? How do you effectively lead in a student group, when everyone is a peer?

Leadership at the grassroots level in organizations does happen. Rosabeth Moss Kanter, in her book *The Change Masters*,[105] discusses examples of employees who saw something that needed changing and took on the responsibility to do so. Employees were more likely to do this when organizations permitted initiative at all levels of the organization, rather than making it a tool of senior executives only.

Leading without authority means exhibiting leadership behaviour even though you do not have a formal position or title. Neither Martin Luther King Jr. nor Nelson Mandela operated from a position of authority, yet each was able to inspire many to follow him in the quest for social justice. The workplace can be an opportunity for leading without authority as well. As Ronald Heifetz of Harvard's Kennedy School of Government notes, "Leadership means taking responsibility for hard problems beyond anyone's expectations."[106] It also means not waiting for the coach's call.[107]

What are the benefits of leading without authority? Heifetz has identified three:[108]

- *Latitude for creative deviance.* It's easier to raise harder questions and look for less traditional solutions when a person is not locked into the trappings that go with authority.

- *Issue focus.* Individuals can focus on a single issue, rather than be concerned with the myriad issues that those in authority face.

- *Front-line information.* An individual is closer to the detailed experiences of some of the stakeholders and thus, more information is available.

Not all organizations support this type of leadership, and some have been known to actively suppress it. Still, you may want to reflect on the possibility of engaging in

identification-based trust Trust based on a mutual understanding of each other's intentions and appreciation of each other's wants and desires.

leadership behaviour because you see a need, rather than because you are required to act.

Contemporary Issues in Leadership

 When Lt.-Col. Maryse Carmichael watched her first air show at age five, she was inspired to fly planes herself one day.[109] At the time, however, becoming a Snowbird pilot seemed like an impossible dream. Females in the Canadian military were barred from pilot training until the mid-1980s. It is therefore not surprising that she is the first female Commanding Officer in the group's 41 year history.

Despite being the first female CO of her squadron, Carmichael downplays gender, finding team familiarity and fit to be more important to her acceptance as a leader. "At my level perhaps it is a new thing to have a woman as a CO," she says, "but for me it's been my entire career working with these people. I don't see anything different." She also takes equal joy in the thought of inspiring young boys and girls and is quick to point out that she is not the first female flight squadron leader in the military, only the most visible. In fact Carmichael sees the Snowbirds' show as an equalizing force in communities. "That is the beauty . . . if you are looking up at the display you wouldn't know if it is a man or a woman flying. All that matters is that you can do the job." Does gender impact leadership style?

 5 What are some of the contemporary issues in leadership?

What is authentic leadership? Is there a moral dimension to leadership? Do men and women rely on different leadership styles, and if so, is one style inherently superior to the other? In this section, we briefly address these contemporary issues in leadership.

Authentic Leadership

Authentic leaders know who they are, know what they believe in and value, and act on those values and beliefs openly and candidly. Their followers consider them to be ethical people. The primary quality produced by authentic leadership is trust. Authentic leaders share information, encourage open communication, and stick to their ideals. The result: People come to have faith in leaders.

Because the concept is so recent, there has been little research on authentic leadership.[110] However, it's a promising way to think about ethics and trust in leadership because it focuses on the moral aspects of being a leader. Transformational or charismatic leaders can have a vision and communicate it persuasively, but sometimes the vision is wrong (as in the case of Hitler), or the leader is more concerned with his own needs or pleasures, as in the case of business leader Bernie Madoff (ex-chair of Bernard L. Madoff Investment Securities).[111]

Moral Leadership

Only recently have ethicists and leadership researchers begun to consider the ethical implications in leadership.[112] Why now? One reason may be the growing interest in ethics throughout the field of management. Another reason may be that, these days, it seems that ethical lapses by business leaders are never absent from the headlines. Another may be the discovery that many past leaders—such as Martin Luther King Jr., and John F. Kennedy—suffered ethical shortcomings. Some companies, like Boeing, are tying executive compensation to ethics to reinforce the idea that, in CEO Jim McNerney's words, "there's no compromise between doing things the right way and performance."[113]

Ethics and leadership intersect in a number of ways. Transformational leaders have been described as encouraging moral virtue when they try to change the attitudes and behaviours of followers.[114] Charisma, too, has an ethical component. Unethical leaders use their charisma to enhance power over followers, directed toward self-serving ends. Ethical leaders use it in a socially constructive way to serve others.[115] Leaders who treat their followers with fairness, especially by providing honest, frequent, and

PERSONAL INVENTORY ASSESSMENT

Learn About Yourself
Ethical Leadership Assessment

authentic leaders Leaders who know who they are, know what they believe in and value, and act on these values and beliefs openly and candidly. Their followers would consider them to be ethical people.

accurate information, are seen as more effective.[116] Because top executives set the moral tone for an organization, they need to set high ethical standards, demonstrate those standards through their own behaviour, and encourage and reward integrity in others while avoiding abuses of power such as giving themselves large raises and bonuses while seeking to cut costs by laying off long-time employees.

Leadership is not value-free. In assessing its effectiveness we need to address the *means* that a leader uses in trying to achieve goals, as well as the content of those goals. Scholars have tried to integrate ethical and charismatic leadership by advancing the idea of **socialized charismatic leadership**—leadership that conveys other-centred (not self-centred) values by leaders who model ethical conduct.[117] Socialized charismatic leaders are able to bring employee values in line with their own values through their words and actions.[118]

One researcher suggests that there are four cornerstones to a "moral foundation of leadership":[119]

- *Truth telling.* Leaders who tell the truth as they see it allow for a mutual, fair exchange to occur.

- *Promise keeping.* Leaders need to be careful about the commitments they make, and then careful to keep those commitments.

- *Fairness.* Leaders who are equitable ensure that followers get their fair share for their contributions to the organization.

- *Respect for the individual.* Leaders who tell the truth, keep promises, and are fair show respect for followers. Respect means treating people with dignity.

Moral leadership comes from within the individual, and in general means treating people well and with respect. This chapter's *Ethical Dilemma Exercise* on page 296 raises some provocative issues about whether we should consider just the ends toward which a leader strives, or the means as well.

Gender: Do Men and Women Lead Differently?

In 2011, women made up 47.3 percent of the labour force in Canada, but they held only 37.9 percent of managerial roles, and 28.9 percent of the senior management roles. Women held 14.5 percent of the board seats and 17.7 percent of the highest corporate titles—CEO, chief financial officer, or chief operating officer—of the *Financial Post* 500.[120]

Do men and women lead differently? An extensive review of the literature suggests two conclusions.[121] First, most recent evidence suggests that there is a great deal of overlap between males and females in their leadership styles. Second, what differences there are seem to be that women fall back on a more democratic leadership style while men feel more comfortable with a directive style.

A recent review of 45 organizations found female leaders were more transformational than males. The authors concluded, "These data attest to the ability of women to perform very well in leadership roles in contemporary organizations."[122] However, women who demonstrate stereotypical male behaviours (self-confidence, assertiveness, and dominance) can face "backlash" at work for not fitting the female stereotype for behaviour. A 2011 study found that "women who displayed male characteristics and self-monitored their behaviour were more likely to be promoted than those who did not self-monitor."[123] One of the authors of the study explained: "Working women face a real dilemma: if they are seen to behave in a stereotypically male way, they may damage their chances of promotion, even though these traits are synonymous with successful managers. These findings suggest if these women learn how to self-monitor their behavior, they have a better chance of promotion."[124]

socialized charismatic leadership A leadership concept that states that leaders model ethical conduct and convey values that are other-centred rather than self-centred.

Despite the previous conclusion, studies indicate some differences in the inherent leadership styles of women and men. A recent Conference Board of Canada study found that "women are particularly strong in managing interpersonal relationships and their approach is more consensual."[125] Other studies have shown that women tend to adopt a style of shared leadership. They encourage participation, share power and information, and try to enhance followers' self-worth. They prefer to lead through inclusion and rely on their charisma, expertise, contacts, and interpersonal skills to influence others. Men, on the other hand, are more likely to use a directive command-and-control style. They rely on the formal authority of their position for their influence base.

Bill Young created Toronto-based Social Capital Partners to help businesses hire the hard to employ: youths, single mothers, Aboriginal people, new immigrants, and those with disabilities or problems with substance abuse. His goal is to help people who are struggling get back into the economic mainstream.

Although it's interesting to see how men's and women's leadership styles differ, a more important question is whether they differ in effectiveness. Although some researchers have shown that men and women tend to be equally effective as leaders,[126] an increasing number of studies have shown that women executives, when rated by their peers, employees, and bosses, score higher than their male counterparts in a wide variety of measures, including getting extra effort from subordinates and overall effectiveness in leading. Subordinates also report more satisfaction with the leadership given by women.[127] A 2011 study of over 7000 men and women in leadership positions found that women scored higher than men in 12 of the 16 competencies that are considered part of outstanding leadership.[128] Exhibit 8-9 summarizes the results of the study.

We know that there is no one best style for all situations. Instead, which leadership style is effective will depend on the situation. So even if men and women differ in their leadership styles, we should not assume that one is always preferable to the other. In today's organizations, flexibility, teamwork, trust, and information sharing are replacing rigid structures, competitive individualism, control, and secrecy. The best leaders listen, motivate, and provide support to their people.

George Cooke, CEO of Toronto-based Dominion of Canada General Insurance, believes in promoting women to senior positions. He is noteworthy for this: Dominion is well above the national average in the percentage of women who have made it to the executive ranks of Canada's top companies: 54 percent of senior management (VP and up) are female and 78 percent of officers are female.

EXHIBIT 8-9 The Top 16 Competencies Top Leaders Exemplify Most

	Male Mean Percentile	Female Mean Percentile	T value
Takes Initiative	48	56	–11.58
Practices Self-Development	48	55	–9.45
Displays High Integrity and Honesty	48	55	–9.28
Drives for Results	48	54	–8.84
Develops Others	48	54	–7.94
Inspires and Motivates Others	49	54	–7.53
Builds Relationships	49	54	–7.15
Collaboration and Teamwork	49	53	–6.14
Establishes Stretch Goals	49	53	–5.41
Champions Change	49	53	–4.48
Solves Problems and Analyzes Issues	50	52	–2.53
Communicates Powerfully and Prolifically	50	52	–2.47
Connects the Group to the Outside World	50	51	–0.78
Innovates	50	51	–0.76
Technical or Professional Expertise	50	51	–0.11
Develops Strategic Perspective	51	49	2.79

J. Zenger and J. Folkman, "Are Women Better Leaders than Men?" *HBR Blog Network*, March 15, 2012, http://blogs.hbr.org/cs/2012/03/a_study_in_leadership_women_do.html

LESSONS LEARNED

- Leaders provide vision and strategy; managers implement that vision and strategy.
- Leaders need to have a vision, they need to communicate that vision, and they must have followers.
- Leaders need to adjust their behaviours, depending on the situation and the needs of employees.

Summary and Implications

1 **What is the difference between a manager and a leader?** Managers promote stability, while leaders press for change. Leaders provide vision and strategy; managers implement that vision and strategy, coordinate and staff the organization, and handle day-to-day problems.

2 **Are there specific traits, behaviours, and situations that affect how one leads?** Early leadership theories were concerned with supervision and sought to find out if there were ways to identify leaders. Trait theories examined whether any traits were universal among leaders. While there are some common traits, leaders are more different than the same in terms of traits. Emotional intelligence is one of the few traits that has been found to be extremely important for leadership success. Other research has tried to discover whether some behaviours create better leaders than others. The findings were mixed, suggesting that leaders need to be both task-oriented and people-oriented. The mixed findings led researchers to contingency theories that consider the effect of the situations in which leadership is applied. This research tells us that leaders need to adjust their behaviours depending on the situation and the needs of employees. Contingency theories were an important contribution to the study of leadership.

3 **How does a leader lead with vision?** The more recent approaches to leadership move away from the supervisory tasks of leaders and focus on vision-setting activities. These theories try to explain how certain leaders can achieve extraordinary performance levels from their followers, and they stress symbolic and emotionally appealing leadership behaviours. These leaders, known as *charismatic* or *transformational leaders,* inspire followers to go beyond their own self-interests for the good of the organization.

④ Are there leadership roles for nonmanagers?   There are several approaches to being a leader even if one does not have a formal position of leadership. Mentoring is one way to be an informal leader. Mentors sponsor and support less-experienced employees, coaching and counselling them about their jobs. With self-leadership, individuals and teams set goals, plan and implement tasks, evaluate performance, solve their own problems, and motivate themselves. The supervisor plays a much reduced role. A person can also act as an informal leader on a team. Providing leadership online to telecommuting and physically distant employees is another leadership role available to many people. Leadership demands are different when one does not have the opportunity for face-to-face interaction. For an increasing number of leaders, good interpersonal skills may include the ability to communicate support and leadership through written words on a computer screen and to read emotions in others' messages. Leading without authority means exhibiting leadership behaviour even though you do not have a formal position or title that might encourage others to obey.

⑤ What are some of the contemporary issues in leadership?   One leadership challenge today is how to be an authentic leader. Authentic leaders know who they are, know what they believe in and value, and act on those values and beliefs openly and candidly. Leaders also face the demand to be moral in their leadership. Moral leadership comes from within the individual, and, in general, means treating people well and with respect. Another hot issue in leadership is the question of whether men and women use different leadership styles, and, if that is the case, whether one style is inherently superior to the other. The literature suggests two conclusions. First, the similarities between men and women tend to outweigh the differences. Second, what differences there are seem to relate to women's falling back on a more democratic leadership style and men's feeling more comfortable with a directive style.

SNAPSHOT SUMMARY

④ Contemporary Leadership Roles
Mentoring
Self-Leadership (or Self-Management)
Team Leadership
Online Leadership
Leading without Authority

⑤ Contemporary Issues in Leadership
Authentic Leadership
Moral Leadership
Gender: Do Men and Women Lead Differently?

✓● **Practise**
Glossary Flashcards - Chapter 8

((●● **Listen**
Audio Chapter Summary

OB at Work

for Review

1. Trace the development of leadership research.

2. Describe the strengths and weaknesses of trait theories of leadership.

3. What do behavioural theories imply about leadership?

4. What are the contingency variables in path-goal theory?

5. When might leaders be irrelevant?

6. What characteristics define an effective follower?

7. What are the differences between transactional and transformational leaders?

8. Describe the strengths and weaknesses of a charismatic leader.

9. What is moral leadership?

10. Why do you think effective female and male managers often exhibit similar traits and behaviours?

for Critical Thinking

1. Reconcile path-goal theory and substitutes for leadership.

2. What kind of activities could a full-time college or university student pursue that might lead to the perception that he or she is a charismatic leader? In pursuing those activities, what might the student do to enhance this perception?

3. Based on the low representation of women in upper management, to what extent do you think that organizations should actively promote women into the senior ranks of management?

4. Is there an ethical problem if leaders focus more on looking like leaders than actually being leaders? Discuss.

5. "Leaders make a real difference in an organization's performance." Build an argument in support of this statement. Then build an argument against this statement.

for You

- It is easy to imagine that theories of leadership are more important to those who are leaders or who plan in the near future to become leaders. However, leadership opportunities occur throughout an organization. You have no doubt seen student leaders who did not necessarily have any formal authority be extremely successful.

- Leaders are not born. They learn how to lead by paying attention to situations and what needs to be done.

- There is no one best way to lead. It is important to consider the situation and the needs of the people who will be led.

- Sometimes no leader is needed—the individuals in the group simply work well enough together that each takes turns at leadership without appointing a formal leader.

POINT

COUNTERPOINT

Leaders Are Born

In North America, people are socialized to believe they can be whoever they want to be—and that includes being a leader.[129] While that makes for a nice children's tale (think *The Little Engine That Could*—"I think I can, I think I can"), life is not always wrapped in pretty little packages, and this is one example. Being an effective leader has more to do with what you are born with than what you do with what you have.

That leaders are born, not made, is not a new idea. Victorian-era historian Thomas Carlyle wrote, "History is nothing but the biography of a few great men." Although today we should modify this to include women, his point still rings true: Great leaders are what make teams, companies, and even countries great. Can anyone disagree that people like Lester Pearson and Pierre Trudeau were gifted political leaders? Or that Joan of Arc and George Patton were brilliant and courageous military leaders?

Or that Henry Ford, Jack Welch, Steve Jobs, and Rupert Murdoch are, or were, gifted business leaders? As one reviewer of the literature put it, "Leaders are not like other people." These leaders are great leaders because they have the right stuff—stuff the rest of us don't have, or have in lesser quantities.

If you are not yet convinced, a recent study of several hundred identical twins separated at birth found an amazing correlation in their ascendance into leadership roles. These twins were raised in totally different environments—some rich, some poor, some by educated parents, others by relatively uneducated parents, some in cities, others in small towns. But despite their different environments, each pair of twins had striking similarities in terms of whether they became leaders.

Other research has found that shared environment—being raised in the same household, for example—has very little influence on leadership emergence. Despite what we might like to believe, the evidence is clear: A substantial part of leadership is a product of our genes. If we have the right stuff, we are destined to be effective leaders. If we have the wrong stuff, we are unlikely to excel in that role. Leadership cannot be for everyone, and we make a mistake in thinking that everyone is equally capable of being a good leader.

Leaders Are Made

Of course, personal qualities and characteristics matter to leadership, as they do to most other behaviours.[130] But the real key is what you do with what you have.

First, if great leadership were merely the possession of a few key traits—say, intelligence and personality—we could simply give people a test and select the most intelligent, extraverted, and conscientious people to be leaders. But that would be a disaster. Leadership is much too complex to be reduced to a simple formula of traits. As smart as Larry Page of Google is, there are smarter and more extraverted people out there—thousands of them. That is not the essence of what makes him, or political or military leaders, great. It is a combination of factors—upbringing, early business experiences, learning from failure, and driving ambition. Second, great leaders tell us that the key to their leadership success is not the characteristics they had at birth, but what they learned along the way.

Take Warren Buffett, admired not only for his investing prowess but also as a leader and boss. Being a great leader, according to Buffett, is a matter of acquiring the right habits. "The chains of habit are too light to be noticed until they are too heavy to be broken," he says. Buffett argues that characteristics or habits such as intelligence, trustworthiness, and integrity are the most important to leadership—and at least the latter two can be developed. He says, "You need integrity, intelligence, and energy to succeed. Integrity is totally a matter of choice—and it is habit-forming."

Finally, this focus on "great men and great women" is not very productive. People need to believe in something, and one of those things is that they can improve themselves. Who would want to think we were just some accumulation of genetic markers and our entire life was just a stage in which our genes played themselves out? People like the optimistic story of *The Little Engine That Could* because we have a choice to think positively (we can become good leaders) or negatively (leaders are predetermined), and it's better to be positive.

LEARNING ABOUT **YOURSELF** EXERCISE

Are You a Self-Manager?

To determine your self-management initiative, rate each of the following items, from 1 ("Never Do This") to 7 ("Always Do This").

	Never Do This						Always Do This

Planning

1. I plan out my day before beginning to work.	1	2	3	4	5	6	7
2. I try to schedule my work in advance.	1	2	3	4	5	6	7
3. I plan my career carefully.	1	2	3	4	5	6	7
4. I come to work early to plan my day.	1	2	3	4	5	6	7
5. I use lists and agendas to structure my workday.	1	2	3	4	5	6	7
6. I set specific job goals on a regular basis.	1	2	3	4	5	6	7
7. I set daily goals for myself.	1	2	3	4	5	6	7
8. I try to manage my time.	1	2	3	4	5	6	7

Access management

1. I control the access subordinates have to me in order to get my work done.	1	2	3	4	5	6	7
2. I use a special place at work where I can work uninterrupted.	1	2	3	4	5	6	7
3. I hold my telephone calls when I need to get things done.	1	2	3	4	5	6	7

Catch-up activities

1. I come in early or stay late at work to prevent distractions from interfering with my work.	1	2	3	4	5	6	7
2. I take my work home with me to make sure it gets done.	1	2	3	4	5	6	7
3. I come in on my days off to catch up on my work.	1	2	3	4	5	6	7

Emotions management

1. I have learned to manage my aggressiveness with my subordinates.	1	2	3	4	5	6	7
2. My facial expression and conversational tone are important in dealing with subordinates.	1	2	3	4	5	6	7
3. It's important for me to maintain a "professional" manager-subordinate relationship.	1	2	3	4	5	6	7
4. I try to keep my emotions under control.	1	2	3	4	5	6	7

Scoring Key:

Higher scores mean a higher degree of self-management. For the overall scale, scores of 100 or higher represent high scores. For each area, the following represent high scores: planning, scores of 48 or higher; access management, scores of 18 or higher; catch-up activities, scores of 18 or higher; and emotions management, scores of 24 or higher.

Source: M. Castaneda, T. A. Kolenko, and R. J. Aldag, "Self-Management Perceptions and Practices: A Structural Equations Analysis," *Journal of Organizational Behavior* 20, 1999. Table 4, pp. 114–115. Copyright © John Wiley & Sons, Inc. Reproduced with permission.

PERSONAL INVENTORY ASSESSMENT

Leadership Style Indicator: While leadership styles will often need to vary based on the situation, most people have a preference for one style or another. Use this scale to assess your personal leadership style preference.

Personal Assessment of Management Skills: This instrument is designed to assess your proficiency in the use of important personal and interpersonal skills that are relevant for managers.

Ethical Leadership Assessment: Since leaders set the tone for the entire organization, it's especially important that they engage in ethical behaviours. Use this scale to assess your ethical perspective on leadership roles.

BREAKOUT GROUP EXERCISES

Form small groups to discuss the following topics, as assigned by your instructor:

1. Identify an example of someone you think of as a good leader (currently or in the past). What traits did he or she have? How did these traits differ from someone you identify as a bad leader?

2. Identify a situation in which you were in a leadership position (in a group, in the workplace, within your family, etc.). To what extent were you able to use a contingency approach to leadership? What made that easier or more difficult for you?

3. When you have worked in student groups, how frequently have leaders emerged in the group? What difficulties occur when leaders are leading peers? Are there ways to overcome these difficulties?

WORKING WITH OTHERS EXERCISE

Being Charismatic

From Concepts to Skills on pages 298–299 suggests how to become charismatic. In this exercise, you will use that information to practise projecting charisma.[131]

1. The class should break into pairs.

2. Student A's task is to "lead" Student B through a new-student orientation to your college or university. The orientation should last about 10 to 15 minutes. Assume Student B is new to your college or university and is unfamiliar with the campus. Student A should try to project himself or herself as charismatic.

3. Roles now reverse and Student B's task is to "lead" Student A in a 10- to 15-minute program on how to study more effectively for college or university exams. Take a few minutes to think about what has worked well for you, and assume that Student A is a new student interested in improving his or her study habits. This time, Student B should try to project himself or herself as charismatic.

4. When both role plays are complete, each pair should assess how well it did in projecting charisma and how it might improve.

ETHICAL **DILEMMA** EXERCISE

Do the Ends Justify the Means?

Whole Foods, a fast-growing chain of upscale grocery stores with stores in Vancouver, West Vancouver, Toronto, and Oakville, a few in London, England, as well as a large number in the United States, has long been a Wall Street favourite.[132] It regularly appears on *Fortune*'s list of 100 Best Companies to Work For (it was #32 in 2012) and has spawned its share of competitors, including Fresh Market and Wild Oats.

Given that most industry analysts see a bright future for upscale organic markets like Whole Foods, it's no surprise they have attracted their share of investor blogs. One prominent blogger, "Rahodeb," consistently extolled the virtues of Whole Foods stock and derided Wild Oats. Rahodeb predicted Wild Oats would eventually be forced into bankruptcy and the Whole Foods stock price would grow at an annual rate of 18 percent. Rahodeb's Yahoo! Finance blog entries were widely read because he seemed to have special insights into the industry and into Whole Foods in particular.

Would it surprise you to learn that Rahodeb was exposed in 2007 as Whole Foods co-founder and CEO John Mackey? ("Rahodeb" is an anagram of "Deborah," the name of Mackey's wife.) What is more, while Rahodeb was talking down Wild Oats stock, Whole Foods was in the process of acquiring Wild Oats, and deriding the target may have made the acquisition easier and cheaper. Because the companies often have stores in the same cities, the Federal Trade Commission (FTC) attempted to block the acquisition and was responsible for "outing" Mackey. In March 2009, Whole Foods agreed to sell 31 of the Wild Oats stores it had acquired, drop use of the Wild Oats name, and undertake other actions that nullified the benefits of the acquisition.

Mackey lamented the debacle—*not* his secret blogging but the Wild Oats acquisition. He said, "We would be better off today if we hadn't done this deal—taking on all this debt right before the economy collapsed." By 2008, Mackey was blogging again, under his real name. His posts are neither as frequent nor as interesting as Rahodeb's.

Do you think it is unethical for a company leader like Mackey to pose as an investor, talking up his or her company's stock price while talking down his competitor's? Should leaders be judged solely on their end achievements? Or do the means they choose also reflect on their leadership qualities? Would Mackey's behaviour affect your willingness to work for or invest in Whole Foods? Is it impossible for leaders to be ethical and successful?

CASE INCIDENT

Moving from Colleague to Supervisor

Cheryl Kahn, Rob Carstons, and Linda McGee have something in common.[133] They all were promoted within their organizations into management positions. As well, each found the transition a challenge.

Kahn was promoted to director of catering for the Glazier Group of restaurants. With the promotion, she realized that things would never be the same again. No longer would she be able to participate in water-cooler gossip or shrug off an employee's chronic lateness. She says she found her new role to be daunting. "At first I was like a bulldozer knocking everyone over, and that was not well received. I was saying, 'It's my way or the highway.' And was forgetting that my friends were also in transition." She admits that this style alienated just about everyone with whom she worked.

Carstons, a technical manager at IBM, talks about the uncertainty he felt after being promoted to a manager from a junior programmer. "It was a little bit challenging to be suddenly giving directives to peers, when just the day before you were one of them. You try to be careful not to offend anyone. It's strange walking into a room and the whole conversation changes. People don't want to be as open with you when you become the boss."

McGee is now president of Medex Insurance Services. She started as a customer-service representative with the company, then leapfrogged over colleagues in a series of promotions. Her fast rise created problems. Colleagues would say, "'Oh, here comes the big cheese now.' God only knows what they talked about behind my back."

Questions

1. A lot of new managers err in selecting the right leadership style when they move into management. Why do you think this happens?

2. If new managers don't know what leadership style to use, what does this say about leadership and leadership training?

3. Which leadership theories, if any, could help new leaders deal with this transition?

4. Do you think it's easier or harder to be promoted internally into a formal leadership position than to come into it as an outsider? Explain.

FROM CONCEPTS TO SKILLS

Practising to Be Charismatic

In order to be charismatic in your leadership style, you need to engage in the following behaviours:[134]

1. *Project a powerful, confident, and dynamic presence.* This has both verbal and nonverbal components. Use a captivating and engaging tone of voice. Convey confidence. Talk directly to people, maintain direct eye contact, and hold your body posture in a way that says you are sure of yourself. Speak clearly, avoid stammering, and avoid sprinkling your sentences with noncontent phrases such as "ahhh" and "you know."

2. *Articulate an overarching goal.* You need to share a vision for the future, develop an unconventional way of achieving the vision, and have the ability to communicate the vision to others.

   The vision is a clear statement of where you want to go and how you are going to get there. You need to persuade others that the achievement of this vision is in their self-interest.

   You need to look for fresh and radically different approaches to problems. The road to achieving your vision should be seen as novel but also appropriate to the context.

   Charismatic individuals not only have a vision; they are also able to get others to buy into it. The real power of Martin Luther King Jr. was not that he had a dream but that he could articulate it in terms that made it accessible to millions.

3. *Communicate high performance expectations and confidence in others' ability to meet these expectations.* You need to demonstrate your confidence in people by stating ambitious goals for them individually and as a group. You then convey absolute belief that they will achieve their expectations.

4. *Be sensitive to the needs of followers.* Charismatic leaders get to know their followers individually. You need to understand their individual needs and develop intensely personal relationships with each. This is done by encouraging them to express their points of view, being approachable, genuinely listening to and caring about their concerns, and asking questions so that followers can learn what is really important to them.

Practising Skills

You recently graduated from college with your degree in business administration. You have spent the past two summers working at London Mutual Insurance (LMI), filling in as an intern on a number of different jobs while employees took their vacations. You have received and accepted an offer to join LMI full time as supervisor of the policy-renewal department.

LMI is a large insurance company. In the headquarters office alone, where you will be working, there are more than 1500 employees. The company believes strongly in the personal development of its employees. This translates into a philosophy, emanating from the top executive offices, of trust and respect for all LMI employees. The company is also regularly at the top of most lists of "best companies to work for," largely because of its progressive work/life programs and strong commitment to minimizing layoffs.

In your new job, you will direct the activities of 18 policy-renewal clerks. Their jobs require little training and are highly routine. A clerk's responsibility is to ensure that renewal notices are sent on current policies, to tabulate any changes in premiums, to advise the sales division if a policy is to be cancelled as a result of nonresponse to renewal notices, and to answer questions and solve problems related to renewals.

The people in your work group range in age from 19 to 62, with a median age of 25. For the most part, they are high school graduates with little previous working experience. They earn between $1850 and $2400 a month. You will be replacing a long-time LMI employee, Jan Allison. Jan is retiring after 37 years with LMI, the past 14 spent as a policy-renewal supervisor. Because you spent a few weeks in Jan's group last summer, you are familiar with Jan's style and are acquainted with most of the department members. But people don't know you very well and are suspicious of the fact that you are fresh out of university and have little experience in the department. And the reality is that you got this job because management wanted someone with a post-secondary degree to oversee the department.

Your most vocal critic is Lillian Lantz. Lillian is well into her 50s, has been a policy-renewal clerk for over 12 years, and—as the person who has worked the longest in the department—carries a lot of weight with group members. It will be very hard to lead this department without Lillian's support.

Using your knowledge of leadership concepts, which leadership style would you choose and why?

Reinforcing Skills

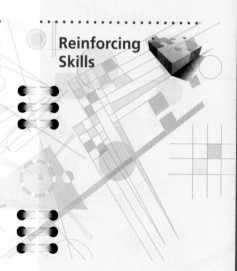

1. Think of a group or team to which you currently belong or of which you have been a part. What type of leadership style did the leader of this group appear to exhibit? Give some specific examples of the types of leadership behaviours he or she used. Evaluate the leadership style. Was it appropriate for the group? Why or why not? What would you have done differently? Why?

2. Observe two sports teams (either college or professional—one that you consider successful and the other unsuccessful). What leadership styles appear to be used in these teams? Give some specific examples of the types of leadership behaviours you observe. How would you evaluate the leadership style? Was it appropriate for the team? Why or why not? To what degree do you think leadership style influenced the team's outcomes?

MyManagementLab   Study, practise, and explore real business situations with these helpful resources:

- **Study Plan:** Check your understanding of chapter concepts with self-study quizzes.
- **Online Lesson Presentations:** Study key chapter topics and work through interactive assessments to test your knowledge and master management concepts.
- **Videos:** Learn more about the management practices and strategies of real companies.
- **Simulations:** Practise management decision-making in simulated business environments.

P I A PERSONAL INVENTORY ASSESSMENT

CHAPTER 9

Decision Making, Creativity, and Ethics

A coffee roasting company in BC's interior may seem remote from the workers on coffee plantations in South America. But its co-owners wanted their business to make a difference. Can committing to selling only fair trade coffee be a successful strategy?

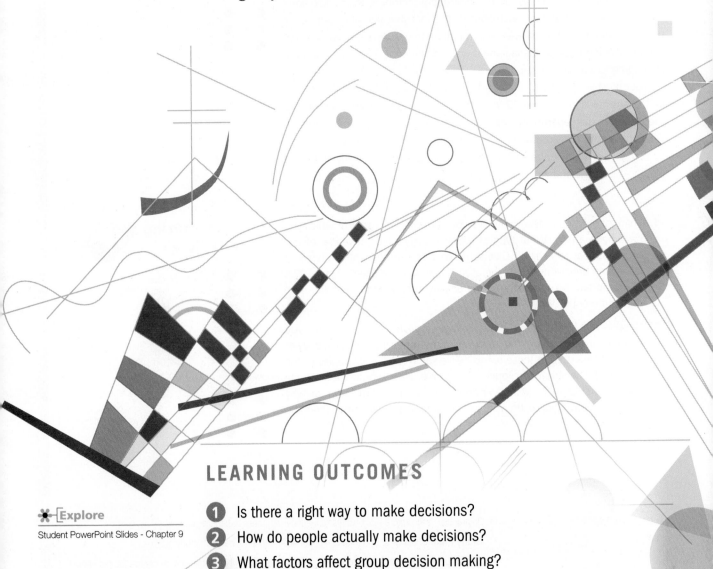

✳️ Explore

Student PowerPoint Slides - Chapter 9

LEARNING OUTCOMES

1. Is there a right way to make decisions?
2. How do people actually make decisions?
3. What factors affect group decision making?
4. How can we get more creative decisions?
5. What is ethics, and how can it be used for better decision making?
6. What is corporate social responsibility?

Elana Rosenfeld and Leo Johnson are the founders and owners of Invermere, BC-based Kicking Horse Coffee Company, the top organic fair trade coffee company in Canada.[1] The decision to create a fair trade coffee company reflects the values the two have toward their employees and the farmer co-ops in Mexico, Nicaragua, Peru, and other countries from which they buy their coffee. When the two travel to the coffee plantations for weeks at a time, they rely on their employees to keep everything running smoothly back in BC.

"Knowing we can leave the shop in good hands allows us to develop a personal relationship with local suppliers," Rosenfeld says. "In turn, we can report back to our employees and customers on how fair trade coffee makes a real difference to the lives of those who were often exploited. That message encourages further support for the company's mission and products."

Rosenfeld and Johnson started roasting coffee in their garage in 1996, with their small children in tow. Two years later they were one of the first companies to join TransFair Canada (now known as Fairtrade Canada), an organization that encourages Canadian organizations to make choices that would improve the working conditions of farmers and workers in the developing world. By 2003 Kicking Horse Coffee made the decision to purchase and roast only 100 percent certified organic coffee beans.

In this chapter, we describe how decisions in organizations are made, as well as how creativity is linked to decision making. We also look at the ethical and socially responsible aspects of decision making as part of our discussion. Decision making affects people at all levels of the organization, and it is engaged in by both individuals and groups. Therefore, we also consider the special characteristics of group decision making.

THE BIG IDEA

Decision making can be improved through systematic thinking and an awareness of common biases.

OB IS FOR EVERYONE

- Do people really consider every alternative when making a decision?
- Is it okay to use intuition when making decisions?
- Why is it that we sometimes make bad decisions?
- Why are some people more creative than others?
- Why do some people make more ethical decisions than others?

LEARNING ABOUT YOURSELF

- Decision-Making Style

How Should Decisions Be Made?

① Is there a right way to make decisions?

A **decision** is the choice made from two or more alternatives. Decision making occurs as a reaction to a problem or an opportunity. A **problem** is a discrepancy between some current state of affairs and some desired state, requiring consideration of alternative courses of action.[2] An **opportunity** occurs when something unplanned happens, giving rise to thoughts about new ways of proceeding.

Whenever any of us make a decision, we have a process that we go through to help us arrive at that decision. Some of us take a very rational approach, with specific steps by which we analyze parts of the decision, others rely on intuition, and some just decide to put two or more alternatives into a hat and pull one out.

Knowing how to make decisions is an important part of everyday life. Below we consider various decision-making models that apply to both individual and group choices. (Later in the chapter, we discuss special aspects of group decision making.) We start with the *rational model*, which describes decision making in the ideal world, a situation that rarely exists. We then look at alternatives to the rational model and how decisions actually get made.

The Rational Decision-Making Process

The **rational** decision maker makes consistent, high-quality choices within specified constraints.[3] These choices are made following a six-step **rational decision-making model**.[4]

The Rational Model

The six steps in the rational decision-making model are presented in Exhibit 9-1.

First, the decision maker must *define the problem*. If you calculate your monthly expenses and find you are spending $50 more than your monthly earnings, you have defined a problem. Many poor decisions can be traced to the decision maker overlooking a problem or defining the wrong problem.

✳ Explore

Exhibit 9-1: Steps in the Rational Decision-Making Model

decision The choice made from two or more alternatives.

problem A discrepancy between some current state of affairs and some desired state.

opportunity An occasion that gives rise to thoughts about new ways of proceeding.

rational Refers to choices that are consistent and value-maximizing within specified constraints.

rational decision-making model A six-step decision-making model that describes how individuals should behave in order to maximize some outcome.

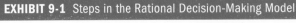

EXHIBIT 9-1 Steps in the Rational Decision-Making Model

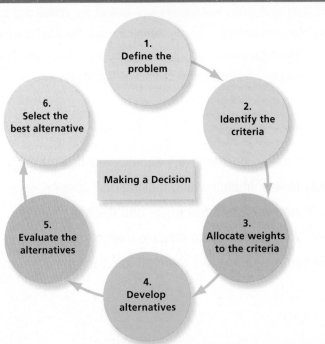

1. Define the problem
2. Identify the criteria
3. Allocate weights to the criteria
4. Develop alternatives
5. Evaluate the alternatives
6. Select the best alternative

Making a Decision

The decision maker then needs to *identify the criteria* that are relevant to making the decision. This step brings the decision maker's interests, values, and similar personal preferences into the process, because not all individuals will consider the same factors relevant for any particular decision.

To understand the types of criteria that might be used to make a decision, consider the many sponsorship requests the Toronto-based Canadian Imperial Bank of Commerce (CIBC) receives each year. When it makes a decision about whether to support a request, the bank takes into account a number of criteria. Specifically, to be eligible for funding, a request must

- Be aligned to youth, education or health

- Be for a Canadian organization, using funds in Canada

- Be for a registered charity with a Canada Revenue Agency Charitable Registration Number or a non-profit organization

- Have a record of achievement or potential for success in line with [CIBC's] overall goals

- Address a community need and provide direct impact to the community served

- Include planned outcomes, supported by a measurement and evaluation process

- Have audited financial statements for the organization, sound financial practices and a sustainable funding model[5]

During his 10-year tenure as CEO of Symantec, John Thompson made a decision in reaction to the problem of an explosion of Internet viruses. Thompson, now chairman of the board of directors, said, "About every 15 to 18 months, there's a new form of attack that makes old technologies less effective." So he decided to acquire 13 companies that specialize in products such as personal firewalls, intrusion detection, and early warning systems that protect everything from corporate intranets to consumer email inboxes.

If the sponsorship request does not meet these criteria, it is not funded.

Because the criteria identified are rarely all equal in importance, the third step requires the decision maker to *allocate weights to the criteria*.

The fourth step requires the decision maker to *develop alternatives* that could succeed in resolving the problem.

The decision maker then critically *evaluates the alternatives*, using the previously established criteria and weights.

Finally, the decision maker *selects the best alternative* by evaluating each alternative against the weighted criteria and selecting the alternative with the highest total score.

Assumptions of the Model

The rational decision-making model we just described contains a number of assumptions.[6] Let's briefly outline those assumptions.

- *Problem clarity.* The problem is clear and unambiguous and complete information is available.

- *Known options.* It is assumed that the decision maker can identify all relevant criteria, all workable alternatives, and their consequences.

- *Clear preferences.* The criteria and alternatives can be ranked and weighted to reflect their importance.

- *Constant preferences.* The specific decision criteria are constant and the weights assigned to them are stable over time.

- *No time or cost constraints.* The decision maker can obtain full information about criteria and alternatives because there are no time or cost constraints.

- *Maximum payoff.* The decision maker will choose the alternative that yields the highest perceived value.

How Do Individuals Actually Make Decisions?

2 How do people actually make decisions?

In 1996, when Elana Rosenfeld and Leo Johnson were just getting their Kicking Horse Coffee Company started, they had one goal: "get everyone to drink good coffee."[7] Obviously, people differ as to what they perceive good coffee to be. Some like Tim Hortons the best. Others enjoy Starbucks. Fans of one company complain about the coffee of the other. Rosenfeld felt she knew what really good coffee was, and it started with fair trade beans. When she first began educating her customers about her product, they thought she meant "free trade." To change customer perceptions, Rosenfeld said they "did a good job of marketing and explaining it on our packaging." They also knew that some people thought good coffee meant Italian coffee, which Kicking Horse does not sell. So they created fun names for the coffee, such as *454 Horse Power* and *Hoodoo Jo* to appeal to a broader number of consumers. What sorts of perceptual biases might affect the decisions people make?

Do decision makers actually follow the rational model? Do they carefully assess problems, identify all relevant criteria, use their creativity to identify all workable alternatives, and painstakingly evaluate every alternative to find an optimizing choice? When decision makers are faced with a simple problem and few alternative courses of action, and when the cost of searching out and evaluating alternatives is low, the rational model provides a fairly accurate description of the decision process.[8] However, such situations are the exception. Most decisions in the real world do not follow the rational model. People are usually content to find an acceptable or reasonable solution to their problem rather than an optimal one. Choices tend to be confined to the problem symptom and to the current alternative. As one expert in decision making has concluded: "Most significant decisions are made by judgment, rather than by a defined prescriptive model."[9] What is more, people are remarkably unaware of making suboptimal decisions.[10]

In the following sections, we identify areas where the reality of decision making conflicts with the rational model.[11] None of these ways of making decisions should be considered *irrational*; they simply depart from the rational model and occur when information is unavailable or too costly to collect.

Bounded Rationality in Considering Alternatives

When you considered which college or university to attend, did you look at every possible alternative? Did you carefully identify all the criteria that were important to your decision? Did you evaluate each alternative against the criteria in order to find the school that is best for you? The answer to these questions is probably "no." But don't feel bad, because few people select their educational institution this way.

It's difficult for individuals to identify and consider every possible alternative available to them. Realistically speaking, people are limited by their ability to interpret, process, and act on information. This is called **bounded rationality**.[12]

Do people really consider every alternative when making a decision?

How does bounded rationality work for the typical individual? Once we have identified a problem, we begin to search for criteria and alternatives. But the list of criteria is likely to be far from exhaustive. We identify a limited list of the most obvious choices, which usually represent familiar criteria and tried-and-true solutions. Next, we begin reviewing them, but our review will not be comprehensive. Instead, we focus on alternatives that differ only in a relatively small degree from the choice currently in effect. Following familiar and well-worn paths, we review alternatives only until we identify one that is "good enough"—that meets an acceptable level of performance. That ends our search. So the solution represents a **satisficing** choice—the first *acceptable* one we encounter—rather than an optimal one. In practice, this might mean

bounded rationality Limitations on a person's ability to interpret, process, and act on information.

satisfice To provide a solution that is both satisfactory and sufficient.

that rather than interview 10 job candidates for a position and then make a hiring decision, a manager interviews one at a time until someone that is "good enough" is found. This process of satisficing is not always a bad idea—using a simple process may frequently be more sensible than the traditional rational decision-making model.[13]

Intuition

Perhaps the least rational way of making decisions is to rely on intuition. **Intuitive decision making** is a nonconscious process created from distilled experience.[14] Its defining qualities are that it occurs outside conscious thought; it relies on holistic associations, or links between disparate pieces of information; it's fast; and it's affectively charged, meaning that it usually engages the emotions.[15]

Is it okay to use intuition when making decisions?

Intuition is not rational, but that does not necessarily make it wrong. Nor does it always operate in opposition to rational analysis; rather, the two can complement each other. Intuition can be a powerful force in decision making. But intuition is not superstition, or the product of some magical or paranormal sixth sense. As one recent review noted, "Intuition is a highly complex and highly developed form of reasoning that is based on years of experience and learning."[16] *OB in the Street* shows how intuition applies to grand master chess players.

in the STREET
Intuition Comes to the Chess Board

Can intuition really help you win a chess game? Apparently so.[17] Novice chess players and grand masters were shown an actual, but unfamiliar, chess game with about 25 pieces on the board. After 5 or 10 seconds, the pieces were removed, and each subject was asked to reconstruct the pieces by position. On average, the grand master could put 23 or 24 pieces in their correct squares, while the novice was able to replace only 6. Then the exercise was changed. This time, the pieces were placed randomly on the board. Again, the novice got only about 6 correct, but so did the grand master! The second exercise demonstrated that the grand master did not have a better memory than the novice. What the grand master *did* have was the ability, based on the experience of having played thousands of chess games, to recognize patterns and clusters of pieces that occur on chessboards in the course of games. Studies also show that chess professionals can play 50 or more games simultaneously, making decisions in seconds, and exhibit only a moderately lower level of skill than when playing one game under tournament conditions, where decisions take half an hour or longer. The expert's experience allows him or her to recognize the pattern in a situation and draw on previously learned information associated with that pattern to arrive at a decision quickly. The result is that the intuitive decision maker can decide rapidly based on what appears to be very limited information. ●

As the example of the chess players shows, those who use intuition effectively often rely on their experiences to help guide and assess their intuitions. For most of the twentieth century, experts believed that decision makers' use of intuition was irrational or ineffective. That is no longer the case.[18] We now recognize that rational analysis has been overemphasized and that, in certain instances, relying on intuition can improve decision making.[19] But, we cannot rely on it too much. Because it is so

intuitive decision making A nonconscious decision-making process created out of a person's many experiences.

unquantifiable, it's hard to know when our hunches are right or wrong. A 2010 study that examined people's ability to "use their gut" to make decisions found that not everyone's gut is reliable. For some people, the physiological feelings that one associates with intuition works, but for others it does not.[20] The key is not to either abandon or rely solely on intuition, but to supplement it with evidence and good judgment.

Judgment Shortcuts

Decision makers engage in bounded rationality, but they also allow systematic biases and errors to creep into their judgments.[21] To minimize effort and avoid difficult trade-offs, people tend to rely too heavily on experience, impulses, gut feelings, and convenient rules of thumb. In many instances, these shortcuts are helpful. However, they can lead to distortions of rationality, as *OB in the Street* shows.

Why is it that we sometimes make bad decisions?

in the STREET
Penalty Kick Decisions

Should you stand still or leap into action? This is the classic question facing a goalie in a faceoff against a midfielder for a penalty kick.[22] Ofer H. Azar, a lecturer in the School of Management at Ben-Gurion University in Israel, finds that goalies often make the wrong decision.

Why? The goalie tries to anticipate where the ball will go after the kick. There is only a split second to do anything after the kick, so anticipating and acting seem like a good decision.

Azar became interested in studying goalie behaviour after realizing that the "incentives are huge" for the goalie to get it right. "Goalkeepers face penalty kicks regularly, so they are not only high-motivated decision makers, but also very experienced ones," he explains. That said, 80 percent of penalty kicks score, so goalies are in a difficult situation at that instant when the kick goes off.

Azar's study found that goalies rarely stayed in the centre of the net as the ball was fired (just 6.3 percent of the time). But staying in the centre is actually the best strategy. Goalies halted penalty kicks when staying in the centre 33.3 percent of the time. They were successful only 14.2 percent of the time when they moved left and only 12.6 percent of the time when they moved right.

Azar argues that the results show that there is a "bias for action," explaining that goalies think they will feel worse if they do *nothing* and miss, than if they do *something* and miss. This bias then clouds their judgment, encouraging them to move to one side or the other, rather than just staying in the centre, where the odds are actually more in their favour. ●

For more on the "bias for action" debate, see this chapter's *Point/Counterpoint* on page 327.

In what follows, we discuss some of the most common judgment shortcuts to alert you to mistakes that are often made when making decisions.

Overconfidence Bias

It's been said that "no problem in judgment and decision making is more prevalent and more potentially catastrophic than overconfidence."[23]

When we are given factual questions and asked to judge the probability that our answers are correct, we tend to be far too optimistic. This is known as **overconfidence bias**. When people say they are 65 to 70 percent confident that they are right, they are actually correct only about 50 percent of the time.[24] And when they say they are 100 percent sure, they tend to be right about 70 to 85 percent of the time.[25]

Individuals whose intellectual and interpersonal abilities are *weakest* are most likely to overestimate their performance and ability.[26] So as managers and employees become more knowledgeable about an issue, they become less likely to display over-confidence.[27] Overconfidence is most likely to surface when organizational members are considering issues or problems that are outside their area of expertise.[28]

Anchoring Bias

The **anchoring bias** is a tendency to fixate on initial information and fail to ade-quately adjust for subsequent information.[29] It occurs because our mind appears to give a disproportionate amount of emphasis to the first information it receives.[30] Anchors are widely used by people in professions where persuasion skills are important—such as advertising, management, politics, real estate, and law. For instance, in a mock jury trial, the plaintiff's attorney asked one set of jurors to make an award in the range of $15 million to $50 million. The plaintiff's attorney asked another set of jurors for an award in the range of $50 million to $150 million. Consistent with the anchoring bias, the median awards were $15 million and $50 million, respectively.[31]

Consider the role of anchoring in negotiations. Any time a negotiation takes place, so does anchoring. As soon as someone states a number, your ability to ignore that number has been compromised. For instance, when a prospective employer asks how much you were making in your prior job, your answer typically anchors the employ-er's offer. You may want to keep this in mind when you negotiate your salary, but remember to set the anchor only as high as you realistically can. Finally, the more precise your anchor, the smaller the adjustment. Some research suggests people think of adjustment after an anchor is set as rounding off a number. If you suggest an initial target salary of $55 000, your boss will consider $50 000 to $60 000 a reasonable range for negotiation, but if you mention $55 650, your boss is more likely to con-sider $55 000 to $56 000 the range of likely values for negotiation.[32]

Confirmation Bias

The rational decision-making process assumes that we objectively gather information. But we do not. We *selectively* gather it. The **confirmation bias** represents a specific case of selective perception. We seek out information that reaffirms our past choices, and we discount information that contradicts them.[33] We also tend to accept at face value information that confirms our preconceived views, while we are critical and skeptical of information that challenges these views. Therefore, the information we gather is typically biased toward supporting views we already hold. This confirmation bias influences where we go to collect evidence because we tend to seek out sources most likely to tell us what we want to hear. It also leads us to give too much weight to supporting information and too little to contradictory information.[34]

Availability Bias

The **availability bias** is the tendency for people to base their judgments on informa-tion that is readily available.[35] Events that evoke emotions, that are particularly vivid, or that have occurred more recently tend to be more available in our memories. As a result, we tend to overestimate unlikely events such as an airplane crash, compared with more likely events such as car crashes. The availability bias can also explain why managers, when doing annual performance appraisals, tend to give more weight to recent behaviours of an employee than to those behaviours of six or nine months ago.

overconfidence bias Error in judgment that arises from being far too optimistic about one's own performance.

anchoring bias A tendency to fix-ate on initial information and fail to adequately adjust for subsequent information.

confirmation bias The tendency to seek out information that reaffirms past choices and to discount informa-tion that contradicts past judgments.

availability bias The tendency for people to base their judgments on information that is readily available to them rather than on complete data.

Escalation of Commitment

Some decision makers escalate commitment to a failing course of action.[36] **Escalation of commitment** refers to staying with a decision even when there is clear evidence that it's wrong. For example, a friend has been working for the same employer for four years. Although she admits that things are not going too well at work, she is determined to stay, rather than find another job. When asked to explain this seemingly nonrational choice of action, she responds: "I put a lot of time and effort into learning how to do this job."

Individuals escalate commitment to a failing course of action when they view themselves as responsible for the failure.[37] That is, they "throw good money after bad" to demonstrate that their initial decision was not wrong and to avoid having to admit they made a mistake. In fact, people who carefully gather and consider information consistent with the rational decision-making model are *more* likely to engage in escalation of commitment than those who spend less time thinking about their choices.[38] Perhaps they have invested so much time and energy into making their decisions that they have convinced themselves they are taking the right course of action and don't update their knowledge in the face of new information. Many organizations have suffered large losses because a manager was determined to prove his or her original decision was right by continuing to commit resources to a lost cause.

Randomness Error

Human beings have a lot of difficulty dealing with chance. Most of us like to believe we have some control over our world and our destiny. Our tendency to believe we can predict the outcome of random events is the **randomness error**.

Decision making becomes impaired when we try to create meaning out of random events, particularly when we turn imaginary patterns into superstitions.[39] These can be completely contrived ("I never make important decisions on Friday the 13th") or evolve from a certain pattern of behaviour that has been reinforced previously. For example, former NHL star goalie Patrick Roy—who is now the co-owner, general manager, and head coach of the Quebec Remparts of the Quebec Major Junior Hockey League—had a routine before every game he played. He skated "backwards towards the net before turning around at the last second, an act he believed made the goal shrink."[40] Superstitious behaviour can be debilitating when it affects daily judgments or biases major decisions.

Risk Aversion

Mathematically, we should find a 50–50 flip of the coin for $100 to be worth as much as a sure promise of $50. After all, the expected value of the gamble over a number of trials is $50. However, most people don't consider these options equally valuable. Rather, nearly everyone but committed gamblers would rather have the sure thing than a risky prospect.[41] For many people, a 50–50 flip of a coin even for $200 might not be worth as much as a sure promise of $50, even though the gamble is mathematically worth twice as much as the sure thing! This tendency to prefer a sure thing over a risky outcome is **risk aversion**.

Risk aversion has important implications. Ambitious people with power that can be taken away (most managers) appear to be especially risk averse, perhaps because they don't want to lose on a gamble everything they have worked so hard to achieve.[42] CEOs at risk of being terminated are also exceptionally risk averse, even when a riskier investment strategy is in their firms' best interests.[43]

Because people are less likely to escalate commitment where there is a great deal of uncertainty, the implications of risk aversion are not all bad.[44] When a risky investment is not paying off, most people would rather play it safe and cut their losses, but if they think the outcome is a sure thing, they will keep escalating.

escalation of commitment An increased commitment to a previous decision despite clear evidence suggesting that decision may have been incorrect.

randomness error The tendency of individuals to believe that they can predict the outcome of random events.

risk aversion The tendency to prefer a sure gain of a moderate amount over a riskier outcome, even if the riskier outcome might have a higher expected payoff.

Risk preference is sometimes reversed: People prefer to take their chances when trying to prevent a negative outcome.[45] They would rather take a 50–50 gamble on losing $100 than accept the certain loss of $50. Thus they will risk losing a lot of money at trial rather than settle out of court. Trying to cover up wrongdoing instead of admitting a mistake, despite the risk of truly catastrophic press coverage or even jail time, is another example. Stressful situations can make these risk preferences stronger. People will more likely engage in risk-seeking behaviour for negative outcomes, and risk-averse behaviour for positive outcomes, when under stress.[46]

Hindsight Bias

The **hindsight bias** is the tendency to believe falsely, after the outcome of an event is actually known, that we could have accurately predicted that outcome.[47] When we have accurate feedback on the outcome, we seem to be pretty good at concluding it was obvious. As Malcolm Gladwell, author of *Outliers*, *The Tipping Point*, and *What the Dog Saw: And Other Adventures*, writes, "What is clear in hindsight is rarely clear before the fact. It's an obvious point, but one that nonetheless bears repeating."[48]

The hindsight bias reduces our ability to learn from the past. It lets us think that we are better predictors than we really are and can make us falsely confident. If your actual predictive accuracy is only 40 percent, but you think it's 90 percent, you are likely to be less skeptical about your predictive skills.

OB in Action—Reducing Biases and Errors in Decision Making provides you with some ideas for improving your decision making. To learn more about your decision-making style, refer to the *Learning About Yourself Exercise* on pages 328–329.

OB in **ACTION**
Reducing Biases and Errors in Decision Making

→ **Focus on goals.** Clear goals make decision making easier and help you eliminate options that are inconsistent with your interests.

→ **Look for information that disconfirms** your **beliefs.** When we deliberately consider various ways we could be wrong, we challenge our tendencies to think we are smarter than we actually are.

→ **Don't create meaning** out of random events. Ask yourself if patterns can be meaningfully explained or whether they are merely coincidence. Don't attempt to create meaning out of coincidence.

→ **Increase** your **options.** The more alternatives you can generate, and the more diverse those alternatives, the greater your chance of finding an outstanding one.[49]

Group Decision Making

While a variety of decisions in both life and organizations are made at the individual level, the belief—as shown by the use of juries—that two heads are better than one has long been accepted as a basic component of North America's and many other countries' legal systems. Today, many decisions in organizations are made by groups, teams, or committees. In this section, we review group decision making and compare it with individual decision making.

3 What factors affect group decision making?

Groups vs. the Individual

Decision-making groups may be widely used in organizations, but are group decisions preferable to those made by an individual alone? The answer to this question depends on a number of factors we consider below.[50] See Exhibit 9-2 for a summary of our major points.

Strengths of Group Decision Making

Groups generate *more complete information and knowledge.* By combining the resources of several individuals, groups bring more input into the decision process. They offer *increased diversity of views.* This opens up the opportunity to consider more approaches and alternatives. Finally, groups lead to *increased acceptance of a solution.*[51] Many decisions fail after the final choice is made because people do not accept them. Group members who participated in making a decision are likely to support the decision enthusiastically and encourage others to accept it.

hindsight bias The tendency to believe falsely, after the outcome of an event is actually known, that one could have accurately predicted that outcome.

Exhibit 9-2: Group vs. Individual
Decision Making

EXHIBIT 9-2 Group vs. Individual Decision Making

Criteria of Effectiveness	Groups	Individuals
More complete information	✓	
Diversity of views	✓	
Decision quality	✓	
Accuracy	✓	
Creativity	✓	
Degree of acceptance	✓	
Speed		✓
Efficiency		✓

Weaknesses of Group Decision Making

Group decisions have their drawbacks. They are *time-consuming* because groups typically take more time to reach a solution. There are *conformity pressures*. The desire by group members to be accepted and considered an asset to the group can result in quashing any overt disagreement. Group discussion can be *dominated by one or a few members*. If they are low- and medium-ability members, the group's overall effectiveness will diminish. Finally, group decisions suffer from *ambiguous responsibility*. In an individual decision, it is clear who is accountable for the final outcome. In a group decision, the responsibility of any single member is watered down.

Effectiveness and Efficiency

Whether groups are more effective than individuals depends on how you define effectiveness. Group decisions are generally more *accurate* than the decisions of the average individual in a group, but they are less accurate than the judgments of the most accurate group member.[52] If decision effectiveness is defined in terms of *speed*, individuals are superior. If *creativity* is important, groups tend to be more effective than individuals. If effectiveness means the degree of *acceptance* the final solution achieves, the nod again goes to the group.[53]

But we cannot consider effectiveness without also assessing efficiency. Groups almost always stack up as a poor second to the individual decision maker. With few exceptions, group decision making consumes more work hours than if an individual were to tackle the same problem alone. The exceptions tend to be the instances in which, to achieve comparable quantities of diverse input, the single decision maker must spend a great deal of time reviewing files and talking to people.

Because groups can include members from diverse areas, the time spent searching for information can be reduced. However, as we noted, these advantages in efficiency tend to be the exception. Groups are generally less efficient than individuals. In deciding whether to use groups, then, consideration should be given to assessing whether increases in effectiveness are more than enough to offset the reductions in efficiency. This chapter's *Working with Others Exercise* on pages 330–332 gives you an opportunity to assess the effectiveness and efficiency of group decision making vs. individual decision making.

Groupthink and Groupshift

Two by-products of group decision making have the potential to affect the group's ability to appraise alternatives objectively and arrive at quality solutions: groupthink and groupshift.

Groupthink

Have you ever felt like speaking up in a meeting, classroom, or informal group, but decided against it? One reason might have been shyness. On the other hand, you might have been a victim of **groupthink**, a phenomenon in which group pressures for conformity prevent the group from critically appraising unusual, minority, or unpopular views. The individual's mental efficiency, reality testing, and moral judgment deteriorate as a result of group pressures.[54]

We have all seen the symptoms of the groupthink phenomenon:[55]

- *Illusion of invulnerability.* Group members become overconfident among themselves, allowing them to take extraordinary risks.

- *Assumption of morality.* Group members believe highly in the moral rightness of the group's objectives and do not feel the need to debate the ethics of their actions.

- *Rationalized resistance.* Group members rationalize any resistance to the assumptions they have made. No matter how strongly the evidence may contradict their basic assumptions, members behave so as to reinforce those assumptions continually.

- *Peer pressure.* Group members apply direct pressures on those who momentarily express doubts about any of the group's shared views or who question the validity of arguments supporting the alternative favoured by the majority.

- *Minimized doubts.* Group members who have doubts or hold differing points of view seek to avoid deviating from what appears to be group consensus by keeping silent about misgivings and even minimizing to themselves the importance of their doubts.

- *Illusion of unanimity.* If someone does not speak, it's assumed that he or she is in full agreement. In other words, abstention becomes viewed as a yes vote.

One place where groupthink has been shown to happen is among stock analysts, as *OB in the Street* shows.

in the STREET
Groupthink among Analysts

Why does stock performance have little to do with predictions? Waterloo-based Research In Motion (RIM) has been a great performer for shareholders over time.[56] With so many people carrying a BlackBerry, more and more people bought RIM's stock. When Barack Obama, who often carried two BlackBerrys on the presidential campaign trail in 2008, insisted that he would continue using one if elected (something none of his predecessors had done), sales and share prices went up even further.

Recent years have seen a turn in fortune for RIM, however. With strong competition from other producers of smartphones, RIM's sales started dropping, and so did its share price.

What did stock analysts do in the face of these drops? The majority continued to recommend buying RIM stock. In May 2011, 23 analysts were saying "buy" compared with 21 saying "hold" and 9 saying "sell." Some analysts suggested the share price could double in the next year, reaching $100 or more. At nearly the same time, RIM was getting ready to announce severe layoffs.

The analysts' opinions do not seem to reflect the reality of RIM's current struggles. So what are analysts thinking?

groupthink A phenomenon in which group pressures for conformity prevent the group from critically appraising unusual, minority, or unpopular views.

A McKinsey & Company study compared the results of S&P 500 companies from 1985 to 2010 to analysts' forecasts. The study found that "analysts overestimated earnings by nearly 100%," underestimating earnings only twice in 25 years.

Although analysts are supposed to do independent research, which should lead to independent assessments, this research does not happen. Christine Tan, a portfolio manager at Gluskin Sheff Associates in Toronto, suggests there are few incentives for analysts to go against the consensus of the market. If you do, and "you're wrong, you get fired," Tan says. In other words, analysts fear going against what others in the group might say (peer pressure), and they minimize their doubts, which are two of the symptoms of groupthink. ●

Do all groups suffer from groupthink? No. It seems to occur most often where there is a clear group identity, where members hold a positive image of their group, which they want to protect, and where the group perceives a collective threat to this positive image.[57] So groupthink is less a way to suppress dissenters than a means for a group to protect its positive image.

What can managers do to minimize groupthink?[58]

- *Monitor group size.* People grow more intimidated and hesitant as group size increases, and, although there is no magic number that will eliminate groupthink, individuals are likely to feel less personal responsibility when groups get larger than about 10.

- *Encourage group leaders to play an impartial role.* Leaders should actively seek input from all members and avoid expressing their own opinions, especially in the early stages of deliberation.

- *Appoint one group member to play the role of devil's advocate.* This member's role is to overtly challenge the majority position and offer divergent perspectives.

- *Stimulate active discussion of diverse alternatives to encourage dissenting views and more objective evaluations.* Group members might delay discussion of possible gains so they can first talk about the dangers or risks inherent in a decision. Requiring members to first focus on the negatives of an alternative makes the group less likely to stifle dissenting views and more likely to gain an objective evaluation.

While considerable anecdotal evidence indicates the negative implications of groupthink in organizational settings, not much actual empirical work has been conducted in organizations in this area.[59] In fact, researchers of groupthink have been criticized for suggesting that its effect is uniformly negative[60] and for overestimating the link between the decision-making process and its outcome.[61] A study of groupthink using 30 teams from five large corporations suggests that elements of groupthink may affect decision making differently. For instance, the illusion of invulnerability, belief in inherent group morality, and the illusion of unanimity were positively associated with team performance.[62] The most recent research suggests that we should be aware of groupthink conditions that lead to poor decisions, while realizing that not all groupthink symptoms harm decision making.

Groupshift

There are differences between group decisions and the individual decisions of group members.[63] Sometimes group decisions are more conservative. More often, they lean toward greater risk.[64] In either case, participants have engaged in **groupshift**, a phenomenon in which the initial positions of individual group members become exaggerated because of the interactions of the group.

What appears to happen in groups is that the discussion leads members toward a more extreme view of the position they already held. Conservative types become more

groupshift A phenomenon in which the initial positions of individual group members become exaggerated because of the interactions of the group.

cautious and more aggressive types assume more risk. The group discussion tends to exaggerate the initial position of the group.

The greater shift toward risk has generated several explanations.[65] It has been argued, for instance, that the discussion makes members more comfortable with one another, and, thus, more bold and daring. Another argument is that the group diffuses responsibility. Group decisions free any single member from accountability for the group's final choice, so greater risks can be taken. It's also likely that people take on extreme positions because they want to demonstrate how different they are from those outside the group.[66] People on the fringes of political or social movements take on more and more extreme positions just to prove they are really committed to the cause.

How should you use the findings on groupshift? Recognize that group decisions exaggerate the initial position of the individual members, that the shift has been shown more often to be toward greater risk, and that which way a group will shift is a function of the members' pre-discussion inclinations. *Case Incident—"If Two Heads Are Better Than One, Are Four Even Better?"* on page 333 considers the impact of groupshift on investment decisions.

Group Decision-Making Techniques

Groups can use a variety of techniques to stimulate decision making. We outline four of them below.

Interacting Groups

The most common form of group decision making takes place in **interacting groups**. Members meet face to face and rely on both verbal and nonverbal interaction to communicate with each other. All kinds of groups use this technique frequently, from groups organized to develop a class project, to a work team, to a senior management team. But as our discussion of groupthink demonstrates, interacting groups often censor themselves and pressure individual members toward conformity of opinion. *Brainstorming*, the *nominal group technique*, and *electronic meetings* have been proposed as ways to reduce many of the problems inherent in the traditional interacting group.

Brainstorming

Brainstorming uses an idea-generation process that specifically encourages any and all alternatives in a criticism-free environment.

In a typical brainstorming session, 6 to 12 people sit around a table. The group leader, or even another team member, states the problem in a clear manner so that all participants understand it. Members then "freewheel" as many alternatives as they can in a given period of time. No criticism is allowed, and all the alternatives are recorded for later discussion and analysis. One idea stimulates others and judgments of even the most bizarre suggestions are withheld until later to encourage group members to "think the unusual."

Brainstorming may indeed generate ideas—but not in a very efficient manner. Research consistently shows that individuals working alone generate more ideas than a group in a brainstorming session.[67] One reason for this is "production blocking." When people generate ideas in a group, many people are talking at once, which blocks the thought process and eventually impedes the sharing of ideas.[68] Another reason suggested by a 2011 study is fixation—group members start to fixate early on a limited number of solutions, rather than continuing to look for others.[69] One recent study suggests that goal-setting approaches might make brainstorming more effective.[70] Brainstorming, we should also note, is merely a process for generating ideas. The following two techniques go further by offering methods of actually arriving at a preferred solution.[71]

interacting groups Typical groups, in which members interact with each other face to face.

brainstorming An idea-generation process that specifically encourages any and all alternatives while withholding any criticism of those alternatives.

EXHIBIT 9-3 Nominal Group Technique

	Individual Activity	Group Activity	Individual Activity
Team members receive description of problem.	Individuals silently write down possible solutions.	Individuals take turns describing solutions to each other; group then discusses and evaluates ideas.	Individuals silently rank (or vote on) each solution presented.

Explore

Exhibit 9-3: Nominal Group Technique

Nominal Group Technique

The **nominal group technique** restricts discussion or interpersonal communication during the decision-making process; thus the term *nominal* (which means "in name only"). Group members are all physically present, as in a traditional committee meeting, but they operate independently. Specifically, a problem is presented and then the group takes the following steps:

- Members meet as a group, but before any discussion takes place each member independently writes down his or her ideas about the problem.

- After this silent period, each member presents one idea to the group. Group members take turns presenting a single idea until all ideas have been presented and recorded. No discussion takes place until all ideas have been recorded.

- The group discusses the ideas for clarity and evaluates them.

- Each group member silently and independently ranks the ideas. The idea with the highest overall ranking determines the final decision.

The steps of the nominal group technique are illustrated in Exhibit 9-3. The chief advantage of this technique is that it permits the group to meet formally but does not restrict independent thinking as the interacting group does.

A number of studies suggest that brainstorming by nominal groups is more effective than brainstorming by interacting groups. However, recent research suggests that nominal groups generate more ideas and more original ideas, but not necessarily more quality ideas.[72] Research generally shows that nominal groups outperform brainstorming groups.[73]

Electronic Meetings

The most recent approach to group decision making blends the nominal group technique with sophisticated computer technology.[74] It's called the computer-assisted group, or **electronic meeting**. Once the technology is in place, the concept is simple. As many as 50 people sit around a horseshoe-shaped table, which is empty except for a series of networked laptops. Issues are presented to the participants, and they type their responses into their computers. Individual comments (which are anonymous), as well as total votes, are displayed on a projection screen.

The major advantages of the electronic meeting are anonymity, honesty, and speed. This type of meeting also allows people to be brutally honest without penalty. It is fast because chit-chat is eliminated, discussions do not digress, and many participants can "talk" at once without stepping on one another's toes. However, evidence indicates that electronic meetings do not achieve most of their proposed benefits. They actually lead to *decreased* group effectiveness, require *more* time to complete tasks, and result in *reduced* member satisfaction compared with face-to-face groups.[75] Nevertheless, current enthusiasm for computer-mediated communications suggests that this technology is here to stay and is likely to increase in popularity in the future.

nominal group technique A group decision-making method in which individual members meet face to face to pool their judgments in a systematic but independent fashion.

electronic meeting A meeting in which members interact on computers, allowing for anonymity of comments and aggregation of votes.

EXHIBIT 9-4 Evaluating Group Effectiveness

Effectiveness Criteria	Type of Group			
	Interacting	Brainstorming	Nominal	Electronic
Number and quality of ideas	Low	Moderate	High	High
Social pressure	High	Low	Moderate	Low
Money costs	Low	Low	Low	High
Speed	Moderate	Moderate	Moderate	Moderate
Task orientation	Low	High	High	High
Potential for interpersonal conflict	High	Low	Moderate	Low
Commitment to solution	High	Not applicable	Moderate	Moderate
Development of group cohesiveness	High	High	Moderate	Low

Source: Based on J. K. Murnighan, "Group Decision Making: What Strategies Should You Use?" *Academy of Management Review*, February 1981, p. 61.

Each of these four group decision techniques has its own strengths and weaknesses. The choice depends on what criteria you want to emphasize and the cost-benefit trade-off. As Exhibit 9-4 indicates, an interacting group is good for achieving commitment to a solution, brainstorming develops group cohesiveness, the nominal group technique is an inexpensive means for generating a large number of ideas, and electronic meetings minimize social pressures and conflicts.

 Explore

Exhibit 9-4: Evaluating Group Effectiveness

Creativity in Organizational Decision Making

Although following the steps of the rational decision-making model will often improve decisions, a rational decision maker also needs **creativity**; that is, the ability to produce novel and useful ideas.[76] These are ideas that are different from what has been done before but that are appropriate to the problem or opportunity presented.

Why is creativity important to decision making? It allows the decision maker to more fully appraise and understand the problem, including seeing problems others cannot see. Such thinking is becoming more important.

4 How can we get more creative decisions?

PERSONAL INVENTORY ASSESSMENT

Learn About Yourself
Creative Style Indicator

Creative Potential

Most people have creative potential they can use when confronted with a decision-making problem. But to unleash that potential, they have to get out of the psychological ruts many of us fall into and learn how to think about a problem in divergent ways.

Exceptional creativity is scarce. We all know of creative geniuses in science (Albert Einstein), art (Pablo Picasso), and business (Steve Jobs). But what about the typical individual? Intelligent people and those who score high on openness to experience (see Chapter 2) are more likely to be creative.[77] Other traits of creative people include independence, self-confidence, risk-taking, a positive core self-evaluation, tolerance for ambiguity, a low need for structure, and perseverance.[78] A study of the lifetime creativity of 461 men and women found that fewer than 1 percent were exceptionally creative.[79] However, 10 percent were highly creative and about 60 percent were somewhat creative. These findings suggest that most of us have creative potential; we just need to learn to unleash it.

From Concepts to Skills on pages 334–335 provides suggestions on how you can become more effective at solving problems creatively.

PERSONAL INVENTORY ASSESSMENT

Learn About Yourself
How Creative Are You?

creativity The ability to produce novel and useful ideas.

Sometimes desperation can lead to creative decisions. General Motors Canada saw the challenge of producing the much-in-demand Chevrolet Equinox and GMC Terrain crossover utility vehicles as an opportunity to think creatively.[80] Rather than adding a new paint shop to GM's Ingersoll, Ontario-based Cami Automotive, which would have been expensive and time-consuming, management decided to ship the unpainted cars to an underutilized GM plant in Oshawa for painting and finishing. It was an unprecedented move, but one that allows the car to be produced much more quickly.

Three-Component Model of Creativity

What can individuals and organizations do to stimulate employee creativity? The best answer lies in the **three-component model of creativity**, which proposes that individual creativity essentially requires expertise, creative-thinking skills, and intrinsic task motivation[81] (see Exhibit 9-5). Studies confirm that the higher the level of each of these three components, the higher the creativity.

Expertise is the foundation for all creative work. Film writer, producer, and director Quentin Tarantino spent his youth working in a video rental store, where he built up an encyclopedic knowledge of movies. The potential for creativity is

Why are some people more creative than others?

EXHIBIT 9-5 The Three Components of Creativity

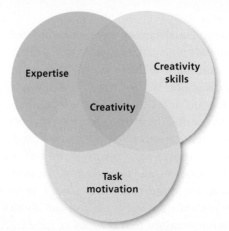

three-component model of creativity The proposition that individual creativity requires expertise, creative-thinking skills, and intrinsic task motivation.

Source: Copyright © 1997, by The Regents of the University of California. Reprinted from *The California Management Review* 40, no. 1. By permission of The Regents.

enhanced when individuals have abilities, knowledge, proficiencies, and similar expertise in their field of endeavour. You would not expect someone with a minimal knowledge of programming to be very creative as a software engineer.

The second component is *creative-thinking skills*. This encompasses personality characteristics associated with creativity, the ability to use analogies, and the talent to see the familiar in a different light.

A meta-analysis of 102 studies found that positive moods increase creativity, but it depended on what sort of positive mood was considered.[82] Moods such as happiness that encourage interaction with the world are more conducive to creativity than passive moods such as calm. This finding means that the common advice to relax and clear your mind to develop creative ideas may be misplaced. It would be better to get in an upbeat mood and then frame your work as an opportunity to have fun and experiment. Further, negative moods don't always affect creativity in the same way. Passive negative moods such as sadness don't seem to have much effect, but avoidance-oriented negative moods such as fear and anxiety decrease creativity. Feeling threatened reduces your desire to try new activities; risk aversion increases when you are scared. Active negative moods, such as anger, however, appear to enhance creativity, especially if you are taking your task seriously.

Being around others who are creative can actually make us more inspired, especially if we are creatively "stuck."[83] One study found that "weak ties" to creative people—knowing them but not well—facilitates creativity because the people are there as a resource if we need them, but they are not so close as to stunt our own independent thinking.[84]

Analogies allow decision makers to apply an idea from one context to another. One of the most famous examples was Alexander Graham Bell's observation that it might be possible to apply the way the ear operates to his "talking box." He noticed that the bones in the ear are operated by a delicate, thin membrane. He wondered why, then, a thicker and stronger piece of membrane should not be able to move a piece of steel. From that analogy, the telephone was conceived. Thinking in terms of analogies is a complex intellectual skill, which helps explain why cognitive ability is related to creativity. Demonstrating this effect, one study found that children who got high scores on cognitive ability tests at age 13 were significantly more likely to have made creative achievements in their professional lives 25 years later.[85]

Some people have developed their creative skills because they are able to see problems in a new way. They are able to make the strange familiar and the familiar strange.[86] For instance, most of us think of hens laying eggs. But how many of us have considered that a hen is only an egg's way of making another egg?

Creative people often love their work, to the point of seeming obsession. The final component in the three-component model of creativity is intrinsic *task motivation*. This is the desire to work on something because it's interesting, involving, exciting, satisfying, or personally challenging. It is what turns creativity *potential* into *actual* creative ideas.

Environmental stimulants that foster creativity include a culture that encourages the flow of ideas; fair and constructive judgment of ideas; rewards and recognition for creative work; sufficient financial, material, and information resources; freedom to decide what work is to be done and how to do it; a supervisor who communicates effectively, shows confidence in others, and supports the work group; and work group members who support and trust each other.[87]

Organizational Factors That Affect Creativity

In two decades of research analyzing the link between the work environment and creativity, six organizational factors have been found to *positively affect* your creativity at work:[88]

- *Challenge.* When people are matched up with the right assignments, their expertise and skills can be brought to the task of creative thinking. Individuals should be stretched, but not overwhelmed.

- *Freedom.* To be creative, once a person is given a project, he or she needs the freedom to determine the process. In other words, let the person decide how to tackle the problem. This heightens intrinsic motivation.

- *Resources.* Time and money are the two main resources that affect creativity. Thus, managers need to allot these resources carefully.

- *Work-group features.* In Chapter 5, our discussion of group composition and diversity concluded that diverse groups are likely to come up with more creative solutions. In addition to ensuring a diverse group of people, team members need to share excitement about the goal, must be willing to support each other through difficult periods, and must recognize one another's unique knowledge and perspectives.

- *Supervisory encouragement.* To sustain passion, most people need to feel that what they are doing matters to others. Managers can reward, collaborate, and communicate to nurture the creativity of individuals and teams.

- *Organizational support.* Creativity-supporting organizations reward creativity, and also make sure that there is information sharing and collaboration. They make sure that negative political problems do not get out of control.

Five organizational factors have been found to *block* your creativity at work:[89]

- *Expected evaluation.* Focusing on how your work is going to be evaluated.

- *Surveillance.* Being watched while you are working.

- *External motivators.* Focusing on external, tangible rewards.

- *Competition.* Facing win-lose situations with peers.

- *Constrained choice.* Being given limits on how you can do your work.

Canadian Tire built a better tent by giving people an environment that encouraged them to think creatively, as this *OB in the Workplace* shows.

in the WORKPLACE
Canadian Tire's "Innovation Room" Unleashes Creativity

Can playing with crayons help produce a better tent? Managers at Toronto-based Canadian Tire want better decisions than the kind that come from sitting around a boardroom table.[90] So they built an "innovation room" that is "a cross between a kindergarten classroom and a fantasy land."

To get new ideas for camping gear, they invited friends and family with an interest in camping to meet in the innovation room. The room included LEGO sets, crayons, a canoe, and a sundeck.

Managers were trying to create a new product—a tent with lighting—but were not sure how to develop a product that would sell. They left it to friends and family to get it right. By getting people together in the innovation room, where they could play and brainstorm, the idea emerged for a solar-lit tent. The tent is now a big seller.

"It's really about unlocking and unleashing creativity and getting people to just let loose and dream a little and have fun," says Glenn Butt, a senior vice-president at Canadian Tire. "It's a process that usually ends up with some very unique and different products and concepts." ●

What About Ethics in Decision Making?

 The owners of Invermere, BC-based Kicking Horse Coffee Company are committed to providing their customers with the best coffee possible.[91] "Quality is our number-one difference from others," says Elana Rosenfeld. "We take that seriously; we don't want to disappoint people if they are paying for this coffee." In 2007, the company faced a dilemma: how to respond to the increasing demand for more "green" coffee beans. The company had marketed itself as selling only organic beans, and those beans are harder to find, and more expensive. Nevertheless, Kicking Horse decided that despite supply challenges, they would no longer purchase any coffee beans that are not fair trade in origin. How can ethics influence business strategy?

5 What is ethics, and how can it be used for better decision making?

No contemporary examination of decision making would be complete without a discussion of ethics, because ethical considerations should be an important criterion in organizational decision making. **Ethics** is the study of moral values or principles that guide our behaviour and inform us whether actions are right or wrong. Ethical principles help us "do the right thing." In this section, we present four ways to frame decisions ethically and examine the factors that shape an individual's ethical decision-making behaviour. We also examine organizational responses to the demand for ethical behaviour, as well as consideration of ethical decisions when doing business in other cultures. To learn more about your ethical decision-making approach, see the *Ethical Dilemma Exercise* on page 332.

Four Ethical Decision Criteria

An individual can use four different criteria in making ethical choices.[92] The first is **utilitarianism**, in which decisions are made solely on the basis of their outcomes or consequences, ideally to provide the greatest good for the greatest number. This view dominates business decision making. It is consistent with goals such as efficiency, productivity, and high profits. By maximizing profits, for instance, a business executive can argue that he or she is securing the greatest good for the greatest number—as he or she hands out dismissal notices to 15 percent of the employees.

A second ethical criterion is to make decisions consistent with fundamental liberties and privileges as set forth in documents such as the Canadian Charter of Rights and Freedoms. An emphasis on *rights* in decision making means respecting and protecting the

Stewart Leibl, president of Perth's, a Winnipeg dry-cleaning chain, is a founding sponsor of the Koats for Kids program. The company's outlets are a drop-off point for no-longer-needed children's coats, which Perth's cleans free of charge before distributing them to children who have no winter coats. Leibl is going beyond utilitarian criteria when he says, "We all have a responsibility to contribute to the society that we live in." He is also looking at social justice.

ethics The study of moral values or principles that guide our behaviour and inform us whether actions are right or wrong.

utilitarianism A decision focused on outcomes or consequences that emphasizes the greatest good for the greatest number.

basic rights of individuals, such as the rights to privacy, free speech, and due process. This criterion protects **whistle-blowers** when they report unethical or illegal practices by their organizations to the media or to government agencies, using their right to free speech.

A third criterion is to impose and enforce rules fairly and impartially to ensure *justice* or an equitable distribution of benefits and costs. Union members typically favour this criterion. It justifies paying people the same wage for a given job, regardless of performance differences, and using seniority as the primary determination in making layoff decisions. A focus on justice protects the interests of the underrepresented and less powerful, but it can encourage a sense of entitlement that reduces risk-taking, innovation, and productivity.

A fourth ethical criterion is *care*. The ethics of care can be stated as follows: "The morally correct action is the one that expresses care in protecting the special relationships that individuals have with each other."[93] The care criterion suggests that individuals should be aware of the needs, desires, and well-being of those to whom they are closely connected. This perspective does remind us of the difficulty of being impartial in all decisions.

Decision makers, particularly in for-profit organizations, tend to feel safe and comfortable when they use utilitarianism, framing decisions as being in the best interests of "the organization" and stockholders. Critics of this perspective note that it can result in ignoring the rights of some individuals, particularly those with minority representation in the organization.[94] Using nonutilitarian criteria presents a solid challenge to today's managers because doing so involves far more ambiguities.

Factors That Influence Ethical Decision-Making Behaviour

What accounts for unethical behaviour in organizations? Is it immoral individuals or work environments that promote unethical activity? The answer is *both!* The evidence indicates that ethical or unethical actions are largely a function of both the individual's characteristics and the environment in which he or she works.[95] The model in Exhibit 9-6 illustrates factors affecting ethical decision making and emphasizes three factors: stage of moral development, locus of control, and the organizational environment.

Why do some people make more ethical decisions than others?

Stages of Moral Development

Stages of moral development assess a person's capacity to judge what is morally right.[96] Research suggests that there are three levels of moral development.[97] The higher one's moral development, the less dependent he or she is on outside influences and the more he or she will be predisposed to behave ethically. The first level is the preconventional level, the second is the conventional level, and the highest level is the principled level. These levels and their stages are described in Exhibit 9-7.

Explore

Exhibit 9-6: Factors Affecting Ethical Decision-Making Behaviour

whistle-blowers Individuals who report unethical practices by their employers to outsiders.

stages of moral development The developmental stages that explain a person's capacity to judge what is morally right.

EXHIBIT 9-6 Factors Affecting Ethical Decision-Making Behaviour

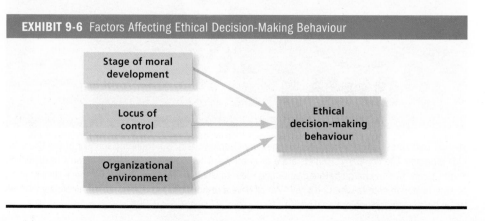

EXHIBIT 9-7 Stages of Moral Development

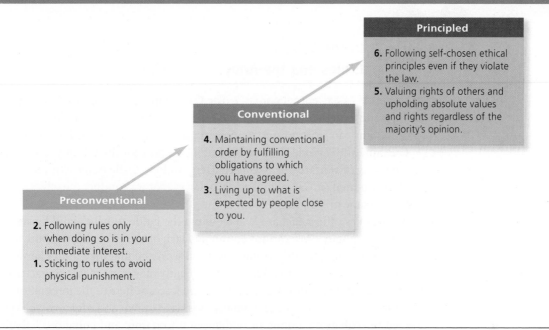

Principled

6. Following self-chosen ethical principles even if they violate the law.
5. Valuing rights of others and upholding absolute values and rights regardless of the majority's opinion.

Conventional

4. Maintaining conventional order by fulfilling obligations to which you have agreed.
3. Living up to what is expected by people close to you.

Preconventional

2. Following rules only when doing so is in your immediate interest.
1. Sticking to rules to avoid physical punishment.

Source: Based on L. Kohlberg, "Moral Stages and Moralization: The Cognitive-Developmental Approach," in *Moral Development and Behaviour: Theory, Research, and Social Issues,* ed. T. Lickona (New York: Holt, Rinehart and Winston, 1976), pp. 34–35.

Research indicates that people proceed through the stages one step at a time, though they do not necessarily reach the highest stage.[98] Most adults are at a mid-level of moral development—they are strongly influenced by peers and will follow an organization's rules and procedures. Those individuals who have progressed to the higher stages place increased value on the rights of others, regardless of the majority's opinion, and are likely to challenge organizational practices they personally believe are wrong. Those at the higher stages are most likely to make ethical decisions using the criteria of rights, justice, and care. A 2011 study by three psychologists from the University of Toronto found that people were likely to predict they would cheat more often than they engaged in actual cheating. The researchers suggested that the emotions experienced at the time that cheating is possible can weaken one's desire to cheat.[99]

Locus of Control

Research indicates that people with an external *locus of control* (that is, they believe their lives are controlled by outside forces, such as luck or chance) are less likely to take responsibility for the consequences of their behaviour and are more likely to rely on external influences to determine their behaviour. Those with an internal locus of control are more likely to rely on their own internal standards of right and wrong to guide their behaviour.

Organizational Environment

The *organizational environment* refers to an employee's perception of organizational expectations. Does the organizational culture encourage and support ethical behaviour by rewarding it or discourage unethical behaviour by punishing it? Characteristics of an organizational environment that are likely to foster high levels of ethical decision making include written codes of ethics; high levels of moral behaviour by senior management; realistic performance expectations; performance appraisals that evaluate means as well as ends; visible recognition and promotions for individuals who display high levels of moral behaviour; and visible punishment for those who act unethically. The Canadian Forces recently distributed a guide to its forces to underscore the need for ethical behaviour in warfare, as *OB in the Workplace* describes.

Explore

Exhibit 9-7: Stages of Moral Development

in the WORKPLACE
Ethics and the Army

Can a person be an "ethical warrior"? The Canadian Forces hopes so, and produced an ethics guide to help army personnel do the right thing.[100] The guide reminds soldiers that "we don't do" torture, and emphasizes moral courage alongside physical courage.

One aim of the guide is to ensure public support for the military when Canadians are engaging in warfare. Army chief Lt.Gen. Andrew Leslie notes that the military will not be supported "if Canadian society believes that we conduct ourselves in an unethical, inhumane or iniquitous manner."

Army ethics officer Richard Walker wrote the guide to help avoid lapses in behaviour in the military. "We cannot permit any lack of clarity . . . If somebody chooses to do the wrong thing for the wrong reasons, it won't be that they didn't know."

The guide is intended to address the ambiguity of warfare that is characteristic of the twenty-first century. While Canadian military forces adhere to the international rules of war, the enemies they faced in Somalia, Bosnia, Kosovo, and Afghanistan do not. This has led to "enhanced ambiguity, enhanced uncertainty and enhanced lethality," said Walker. The concern is that facing enemies who don't follow the international rules of war may encourage Canadian soldiers to engage in poor behaviour that will lead to psychological problems for them later. The guide reminds soldiers that those who "lose their humanity" in warfare will be emotionally scarred for life. "Respecting the dignity of all persons is essentially the moral precept that drives everything else," said Walker. ●

In summary, people who lack a strong moral sense are much less likely to make unethical decisions if they are constrained by an organizational environment that frowns on such behaviours. Conversely, righteous individuals can be corrupted by an organizational environment that permits or encourages unethical practices. In the next section, we consider how to formulate an ethical decision.

Making Ethical Decisions

While there are no clear-cut ways to differentiate ethical from unethical decision making, there are some questions you should consider.

Exhibit 9-8 illustrates a decision tree to guide ethical decision making. This tree is built on three of the ethical decision criteria—utilitarianism, rights, and justice—presented earlier. The first question you need to answer addresses self-interest vs. organizational goals.

The second question concerns the rights of other parties. If the decision violates the rights of someone else (his or her right to privacy, for instance), then the decision is unethical.

The final question that needs to be addressed relates to whether the decision conforms to standards of equity and justice. The department head who raises the performance evaluation of a favoured employee and lowers the evaluation of a disfavoured employee—and then uses these evaluations to justify giving the former a big raise and nothing to the latter—has treated the disfavoured employee unfairly.

Unfortunately, the answers to the questions in Exhibit 9-8 are often argued in ways to make unethical decisions seem ethical. Powerful people, for example, can become very adept at explaining self-serving behaviours in terms of the organization's best interests. Similarly, they can persuasively argue that unfair actions are really fair and just. Our point is that immoral people can justify almost any behaviour. Those who

EXHIBIT 9-8 Is a Decision Ethical?

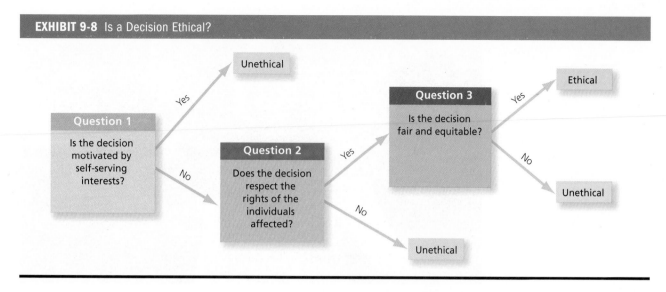

are powerful, articulate, and persuasive are the most likely to be able to get away with unethical actions successfully. When faced with an ethical dilemma, try to answer the questions in Exhibit 9-8 truthfully.

Corporate Social Responsibility

Elana Rosenfeld and Leo Johnson, founders of Kicking Horse Coffee Company, are committed to making the best coffee possible, but they also want to do so in ways that highlight corporate social responsibility.[101] They start with their employees, with whom they have built a relationship based on "trust, employee autonomy and a shared sense of mission." They restrict their purchases to fair trade growers, who provide healthy working environments for employees.

Rosenfeld and Johnson travel to visit their coffee bean suppliers in South America and other places, which enables them to report first-hand to their customers and employees "how fair trade coffee makes a real difference to the lives of those who were often exploited." Rosenfeld and Johnson also take the environment seriously. The cans their coffee is sold in are made of recycled steel, which can be recycled many times over. To what extent should companies be socially responsible?

Corporate social responsibility is an organization's responsibility to consider the impact of its decisions on society. Thus, organizations may try to better society through such things as charitable contributions or providing better wages to employees working in offshore factories. Organizations may engage in these practices because they feel pressured by society to do so, or they may seek ways to improve society because they feel it is the right thing to do.

Canadians want businesses to give back to society, according to a 2010 poll which found that Canadians' views of corporations are largely affected by whether businesses support charitable causes and protect the environment.[102] Oakville, Ontario-based Tim Hortons, which makes customers aware of its Children's Foundation, is well regarded by Canadians.[103]

Not everyone agrees that organizations should assume social responsibility. For example, economist Milton Friedman remarked in *Capitalism and Freedom* that "few trends could so thoroughly undermine the very foundations of our free society as the acceptance by corporate officials of a social responsibility other than to make as much money for their stockholders as possible."[104]

Joel Bakan, professor of law at the University of British Columbia, author of *The Corporation*,[105] and co-director of the documentary of the same name, is more critical of organizations than Friedman. Bakan suggests that today's corporations have many

※ Explore

Exhibit 9-8: Is a Decision Ethical?

6 What is corporate social responsibility?

corporate social responsibility
An organization's responsibility to consider the impact of its decisions on society.

Paul Nielsen (shown with his wife, Dayle) owns Calgary-based DumpRunner Waste Systems, a specialty garbage and debris removal company. He encourages an ethical approach to dealing with both clients and employees. He notes that in Calgary, business is built on handshakes and being true to your word, and people are expected to act ethically. Ethical behaviour may be easier for Nielsen than for some others. He says he is guided by his passion for being in business, rather than a "quest for money."

of the same characteristics as a psychopathic personality (self-interested, lacking empathy, manipulative, and reckless in their disregard of others). Bakan notes that even though companies have a tendency to act psychopathically, this is not why they are fixated on profits. Rather, their only legal responsibility is to maximize organizational profits for stockholders. He suggests changes in laws to encourage corporations to behave more socially responsibly.

Canadian senior executives have mixed feelings about the extent to which businesses should get involved in charitable giving, or forcing industry standards on foreign corporations. A 2011 poll found that 45 percent believe individual shareholders, not the company, should make personal decisions about giving to charity. Another 35 percent, however, felt corporations should donate to charities. One CEO explained, "Being a good corporate citizen means assisting those less fortunate—as long as it is done in the context of the entities' aims, objectives and employees' desires."[106] A 2011 poll conducted by COMPAS found that Canadian business leaders were not about imposing Canadian management values on Chinese employers, however. "We don't have the right to tell China how to run its economy," said one CEO. "We have the choice to buy, or not to buy."[107]

A recent survey found that Canadian and American MBA students are very interested in the subject of corporate social responsibility. Over 80 percent of respondents "believed business professionals should take into account social and environmental impacts when making decisions." Almost two-thirds of these respondents felt that corporate social responsibility should be part of core MBA classes and 60 percent said "they would seek socially responsible employment."[108]

LESSONS LEARNED

- Individuals often short-cut the decision making process and do not consider all options.
- Intuition leads to better results when supplemented with evidence and good judgment.
- Exceptional creativity is rare, but expertise, creative-thinking skills, and intrinsic task motivation encourage creativity.

SNAPSHOT SUMMARY

1 **How Should Decisions Be Made?**
The Rational Decision-Making Process

Summary and Implications

1 **Is there a right way to make decisions?** The rational decision-making model describes the six steps individuals take to make decisions: (1) Define the problem, (2) identify the criteria, (3) allocate weights to the criteria, (4) develop alternatives, (5) evaluate the alternatives, and (6) select the best alternative. This is an idealized model, and not every decision thoroughly follows these steps.

2 How do people actually make decisions? Most decisions in the real world do not follow the rational model. For instance, people are usually content to find an acceptable or reasonable solution to their problem rather than an optimizing one. Thus, decision makers may rely on bounded rationality, satisficing, and intuition in making decisions. They may also rely on judgment shortcuts, which can lead to overconfidence bias, anchoring bias, confirmation bias, availability bias, escalation of commitment, randomness error, risk aversion, and hindsight bias.

3 What factors affect group decision making? Groups generate more complete information and knowledge, they offer increased diversity of views, they generate higher-quality decisions, and they lead to increased acceptance of a solution. However, group decisions are time-consuming. They also lead to conformity pressures, and the group discussion can be dominated by one or a few members. Finally, group decisions suffer from ambiguous responsibility, and the responsibility of any single member is watered down. Groups can suffer from groupthink and/or groupshift. Under groupthink, the group emphasizes agreement above everything else, often shutting down individuals who express any disagreement with the group's actions. In groupshift, the group takes a more extreme position (either more conservative or more risky) than individuals would take on their own.

4 How can we get more creative decisions? While there is some evidence that individuals vary in their ability to be creative, research shows that individuals are more creative when they have expertise at the task at hand, creative-thinking skills, and are motivated by intrinsic interest. Five organizational factors have been found that can block creativity at work: (1) *expected evaluation*—focusing on how work is going to be evaluated; (2) *surveillance*—being watched while working; (3) *external motivators*—emphasizing external, tangible rewards; (4) *competition*—facing win-lose situations with peers; and (5) *constrained choice*—being given limits on how to do the work.

5 What is ethics, and how can it be used for better decision making? Ethics is the study of moral values or principles that guide our behaviour and inform us whether actions are right or wrong. Ethical principles help us "do the right thing." An individual can use four different criteria in making ethical choices. The first is the *utilitarian* criterion, in which decisions are made solely on the basis of their outcomes or consequences. The second is *rights*; this ethical criterion focuses on respecting and protecting the basic rights of individuals. The third is *justice*; this ethical criterion requires individuals to impose and enforce rules fairly and impartially so there is an equitable distribution of benefits and costs. The fourth is *care*; this ethical criterion suggests that we should be aware of the needs, desires, and well-being of those to whom we are closely connected. There are advantages and disadvantages to each of these criteria.

6 What is corporate social responsibility? Corporate social responsibility is defined as an organization's responsibility to consider the impact of its decisions on society. Thus, organizations may try to better society through such things as charitable contributions or providing better wages to employees working in offshore factories. Organizations may engage in these practices because they feel pressured by society to do so, or they may seek ways to improve society because they feel it is the right thing to do.

---

for Review

1. What is the rational decision-making model? Under what conditions is it applicable?

2. Describe organizational factors that might constrain decision makers.

3. What role does intuition play in effective decision making?

4. What is groupthink? What is its effect on decision-making quality?

5. What is groupshift? What is its effect on decision-making quality?

6. Identify five organizational factors that block creativity at work.

7. Describe the four criteria that individuals can use in making ethical decisions.

8. Are unethical decisions more a function of the individual decision maker or the decision maker's work environment? Explain.

9. What is corporate social responsibility, and why do companies engage in it?

for Critical Thinking

1. "For the most part, individual decision making in organizations is an irrational process." Do you agree or disagree? Discuss.

2. What factors do you think differentiate good decision makers from poor ones? Relate your answer to the six-step rational decision-making model.

3. Have you ever increased your commitment to a failed course of action? If so, analyze the follow-up decision to increase your commitment and explain why you behaved as you did.

4. If group decisions consistently achieve better-quality outcomes than those achieved by individuals, how did the phrase "a camel is a horse designed by a committee" become so popular and ingrained in our culture?

for You

- In some decision situations, you might consider following the rational decision-making model. Doing so will ensure that you examine a wider variety of options before committing to a particular decision.

- Analyze the decision situation and be aware of your biases. We all bring biases to the decisions we make.

- Combine rational analysis with intuition. As you gain experience, you should feel increasingly confident in using your intuition with your rational analysis.

- Use creativity-stimulation techniques. You can improve your overall decision-making effectiveness by searching for innovative solutions to problems. This can be as basic as telling yourself to think creatively and to look specifically for unique alternatives.

- When making decisions, you should consider their ethical implications. A quick way to do this is to ask yourself: Would I be embarrassed if this action were printed on the front page of the local newspaper?

OB at work

When in Doubt, Do!

Life is full of decisions and choices.[109] The real question is not "To be, or not to be" but rather "To do, or not to do?" For example, "Should I confront my professor about my mid-term grade?" "Should I buy a new car?" "Should I accept a new job?" "Should I choose this major?" Very often, we are unsure of our decision. In such cases, it is almost always better to choose action over inaction. In life, people more often regret inaction than action. Take the following simple example:

Say you carry an umbrella and it does not rain, or you don't carry an umbrella and it does rain. In which situation are you worse off? Would you rather experience the mild inconvenience of the extra weight of the umbrella or get drenched? Chances are you will regret inaction more than action. Research shows that after we make a decision, we indeed regret inaction more than action. Although we often regret actions in their immediate aftermath, over time these regrets decline markedly, whereas regrets over missed opportunities increase. Suppose you finally decide to take a trip to Europe. You have an amazing time, but a few weeks after you get back, your credit card bill arrives—and it isn't pretty. Unfortunately, you have to work overtime and miss a few dinners out with friends to pay off the bills. A few months down the road, however, you decide to reminisce by looking through your photos from the trip, and you cannot imagine not having gone. So, when in doubt, just do!

Act	State	
	Rain	**Shine**
Carry umbrella	Dry (except your feet!)	Inconvenience
Don't carry umbrella	Miserable drenching	Unqualified bliss

Wait! Not So Fast

It's just silly to think that, when in doubt, you should always act. People will undoubtedly make mistakes following such simple advice. For example, you are out of work, but you still decide to purchase your dream car—a BMW, fully loaded. Not the smartest idea. So why is the motto "just do it" dangerous? Because there are two types of regrets: hot regret, in which an individual kicks herself for having caused something bad, and wistful regret, in which she fantasizes about how else things might have turned out. The danger is that actions are more likely to lead to anguish or hot regret, and inaction is more likely to lead to wistful regret. So the bottom line is that we cannot apply simple rules such as "just do it" to important decisions.

LEARNING ABOUT **YOURSELF** EXERCISE

Decision-Making Style Questionnaire

Circle the response that comes closest to the way you usually feel or act. There are no right or wrong responses to any of these items.

1. I am more careful about

   a. people's feelings
   b. their rights

2. I usually get along better with

   a. imaginative people
   b. realistic people

3. It is a higher compliment to be called

   a. a person of real feeling
   b. a consistently reasonable person

4. In doing something with other people, it appeals more to me

   a. to do it in the accepted way
   b. to invent a way of my own

5. I get more annoyed at

   a. fancy theories
   b. people who do not like theories

6. It is higher praise to call someone

   a. a person of vision
   b. a person of common sense

7. I more often let

   a. my heart rule my head
   b. my head rule my heart

8. I think it is a worse fault

   a. to show too much warmth
   b. to be unsympathetic

9. If I were a teacher, I would rather teach

   a. courses involving theory
   b. factual courses

Which word in the following pairs appeals to you more? Circle *a* or *b*.

10. **a.** Compassion
    b. Foresight

11. **a.** Justice
    b. Mercy

12. **a.** Production
    b. Design

13. **a.** Gentle
    b. Firm

14. **a.** Uncritical
    b. Critical

15. **a.** Literal
    b. Figurative

16. **a.** Imaginative
    b. Matter-of-fact

Scoring Key:

Mark each of your responses on the following scales. Then use the point value column to arrive at your score. For example, if you answered *a* to the first question, you would check *1a* in the Feeling column. This response receives zero points when you add up the point value column. Instructions for classifying your scores are indicated following the scales.

LEARNING ABOUT **YOURSELF** EXERCISE (Continued)

Sensation	Point Value	Intuition	Point Value	Thinking	Point Value	Feeling	Point Value
2b _____	1	2a _____	2	1b _____	1	1a _____	0
4a _____	1	4b _____	1	3b _____	2	3a _____	1
5a _____	1	5b _____	1	7b _____	1	7a _____	1
6b _____	1	6a _____	0	8a _____	0	8b _____	1
9b _____	2	9a _____	2	10b _____	2	10a _____	1
12a _____	1	12b _____	0	11a _____	2	11b _____	1
15a _____	1	15b _____	1	13b _____	1	13a _____	1
16b _____	2	16a _____	0	14b _____	0	14a _____	1
Maximum Point Value	(10)		(7)		(9)		(7)

Circle *Intuition* if your Intuition score is equal to or greater than your Sensation score. Circle *Sensation* if your Sensation score is greater than your Intuition score. Circle *Feeling* if your Feeling score is greater than your Thinking score. Circle *Thinking* if your Thinking score is greater than your Feeling score.

A high score on *Intuition* indicates you see the world in holistic terms. You tend to be creative. A high score on *Sensation* indicates that you are realistic and see the world in terms of facts. A high score on *Feeling* means you make decisions based on gut feeling. A high score on *Thinking* indicates a highly logical and analytical approach to decision making.

Source: Based on a personality scale developed by D. Hellriegel, J. Slocum, and R. W. Woodman, *Organizational Behavior,* 3rd ed. (St. Paul, MN: West Publishing, 1983), pp. 127–141, and reproduced in J. M. Ivancevich and M. T. Matteson, *Organizational Behavior and Management,* 2nd ed. (Homewood, IL: BPI/Irwin, 1990), pp. 538–539.

PERSONAL INVENTORY ASSESSMENT

Creative Style Indicator: Creativity takes different forms. Use this scale to assess your own creative style when approaching problems at work.

How Creative Are You?: Some occupations require high levels of creativity, while others focus more on following rules. Use this scale to determine how creative you are. This information can help guide career decisions.

BREAKOUT **GROUP** EXERCISES

Form small groups to discuss the following topics, as assigned by your instructor:

1. Apply the rational decision-making model to deciding where your group might eat dinner this evening. How closely were you able to follow the rational model in making this decision?

2. The company that makes your favourite snack product has been accused of being weak in its social responsibility efforts. What impact will this have on your purchase of any more products from that company?

3. You have seen a classmate cheat on an exam or an assignment. Do you do something about this or ignore it?

WORKING WITH OTHERS EXERCISE

Wilderness Survival Exercise

You are a member of a hiking party. After reaching base camp on the first day, you decide to take a quick sunset hike by yourself. After a few exhilarating miles, you decide to return to camp. On your way back, you realize that you are lost. You have shouted for help to no avail. It is now dark and getting cold.

Your Task

Without communicating with anyone else in your group, read the following scenarios and choose the best answer. Keep track of your answers on a sheet of paper. You have 10 minutes to answer the 10 questions.

1. The first thing you decide to do is to build a fire. However, you have no matches, so you use the bow and drill method. What is the bow and drill method?

   a. A dry, soft stick is rubbed between one's hands against a board of supple green wood.

   b. A soft green stick is rubbed between one's hands against a hardwood board.

   c. A straight stick of wood is quickly rubbed back and forth against a dead tree.

   d. Two sticks (one being the bow, the other the drill) are struck to create a spark.

2. It occurs to you that you can also use the fire as a distress signal. When signalling with fire, how do you form the international distress signal?

   a. 2 fires

   b. 4 fires in a square

   c. 4 fires in a cross

   d. 3 fires in a line

3. You are very thirsty. You go to a nearby stream and collect some water in the small metal cup you have in your backpack. How long should you boil the water?

   a. 15 minutes

   b. A few seconds

   c. 1 hour

   d. It depends on the altitude.

4. You are very hungry, so you decide to eat what appear to be edible berries. When performing the universal edibility test, what should you do?

   a. Do not eat for 2 hours before the test.

   b. If the plant stings your lip, confirm the sting by holding it under your tongue for 15 minutes.

   c. If nothing bad has happened 2 hours after digestion, eat half a cup of the plant and wait again.

   d. Separate the plant into its basic components and eat each component, one at a time.

5. Next, you decide to build a shelter for the evening. In selecting a site, what do you *not* have to consider?

   a. It must contain material to make the type of shelter you need.

   b. It must be free of insects, reptiles, and poisonous plants.

   c. It must be large enough and level enough for you to lie down comfortably.

   d. It must be on a hill so you can signal rescuers and keep an eye on your surroundings.

6. In the shelter that you built, you notice a spider. You heard from a fellow hiker that black widow spiders populate the area. How do you identify a black widow spider?

   a. Its head and abdomen are black; its thorax is red.

   b. It is attracted to light.

WORKING WITH OTHERS EXERCISE (Continued)

c. It runs away from light.

d. It is a dark spider with a red or orange marking on the female's abdomen.

7. After getting some sleep, you notice that the night sky has cleared, so you decide to try to find your way back to base camp. You believe you should travel north and can use the North Star for navigation. How do you locate the North Star?

a. Hold your right hand up as far as you can and look between your index and middle fingers.

b. Find Sirius and look 60 degrees above it and to the right.

c. Look for the Big Dipper and follow the line created by its cup end.

d. Follow the line of Orion's belt.

8. You come across a fast-moving stream. What is the best way to cross it?

a. Find a spot downstream from a sandbar, where the water will be calmer.

b. Build a bridge.

c. Find a rocky area, as the water will be shallow and you will have hand- and footholds.

d. Find a level stretch where it breaks into a few channels.

9. After walking for about an hour, you feel several spiders in your clothes. You don't feel any pain, but you know some spider bites are painless. Which of these spider bites is painless?

a. Black widow

b. Brown recluse

c. Wolf spider

d. Harvestman (daddy longlegs)

10. You decide to eat some insects. Which insects should you avoid?

a. Adults that sting or bite

b. Caterpillars and insects that have a pungent odour

c. Hairy or brightly coloured ones

d. All of the above

Group Task

Break into groups of 5 or 6 people. Now imagine that your whole group is lost. Answer each question as a group, employing a consensus approach to reach each decision. Once the group comes to an agreement, write the decision down on the same sheet of paper that you used for your individual answers. You will have approximately 20 minutes for the group task.

Scoring Your Answers

Your instructor will provide you with the correct answers, which are based on expert judgments in these situations. Once you have received the answers, calculate (A) your individual score; (B) your group's score; (C) the average individual score in the group; and (D) the best individual score in the group. Write these down and consult with your group to ensure that these scores are accurate.

(A) Your individual score _____

(B) Your group's score _____

(C) Average individual score in group _____

(D) Best individual score in group _____

WORKING WITH OTHERS EXERCISE (Continued)

Discussion Questions

1. How did your group (B) perform relative to yourself (A)?

2. How did your group (B) perform relative to the average individual score in the group (C)?

3. How did your group (B) perform relative to the best individual score in the group (D)?

4. Compare your results with those of other groups. Did some groups do a better job of outperforming individuals than others?

5. What do these results tell you about the effectiveness of group decision making?

6. What can groups do to make group decision making more effective?

ETHICAL DILEMMA EXERCISE

Five Ethical Decisions: What Would You Do?

Assume that you are a middle manager in a company with about 1000 employees. How would you respond to each of the following situations?[110]

1. You are negotiating a contract with a potentially very large customer whose representative has hinted that you could almost certainly be assured of getting his business if you gave him and his wife an all-expenses-paid cruise to the Caribbean. You know the representative's employer would not approve of such a "payoff," but you have the discretion to authorize such an expenditure. What would you do?

2. You have an autographed CD by Drake and put it up for sale on eBay. So far, the highest bid is $74.50. A friend has offered you $100 for the CD, commenting that he could get $150 for it on eBay in a year. You know this is highly unlikely. Should you sell your friend the CD for what he offered ($100)? Do you have an obligation to tell your friend you have listed your CD on eBay?

3. Your company policy on reimbursement for meals while travelling on company business is that you will be repaid for your out-of-pocket costs, which are not to exceed $80 a day. You do not need receipts for these expenses—the company will take

your word. When travelling, you tend to eat at fast-food places and rarely spend more than $20 a day. Most of your colleagues submit reimbursement requests in the range of $55 to $60 a day regardless of what their actual expenses are. How much would you request for your meal reimbursements?

4. You are the manager at a gaming company, and you are responsible for hiring a group to outsource the production of a highly anticipated new game. Because your company is a giant in the industry, numerous companies are trying to get the bid. One of them offers you some kickbacks if you give that firm the bid, but ultimately, it is up to your bosses to decide on the company. You don't mention the incentive, but you push upper management to give the bid to the company that offered you the kickback. Is withholding the truth as bad as lying? Why or why not?

5. You have discovered that one of your closest friends at work has stolen a large sum of money from the company. Would you do nothing? Go directly to an executive to report the incident before talking about it with the offender? Confront the individual before taking action? Make contact with the individual with the goal of persuading that person to return the money?

CASE INCIDENT

"If Two Heads Are Better Than One, Are Four Even Better?"

Maggie Becker, age 24, is a marketing manager for Kavu, a small chain of coffee shops in eastern Ohio. Recently, Maggie's wealthy uncle passed away and left her, his only niece, $100 000. Maggie considers her current salary adequate to meet her current living expenses, so she would like to invest the money so that when she buys a house she will have a nice nest egg on which to draw.

One of Maggie's neighbours, Brian, is a financial advisor. Brian told Maggie that the array of investment options is virtually endless. She asked him to present her with two of the best options, and this is what he offered her:

1. A very low-risk AAA bond fund. With this option, based on the information Brian provided, Maggie estimates that after five years she stands virtually zero chance of losing money, with an expected gain of approximately $7000.

2. A moderate-risk mutual fund. Based on the information Brian provided her, Maggie estimates that with this option she stands a 50 percent chance of making $40 000 but also a 50 percent chance of losing $20 000.

Maggie prides herself on being rational and objective in her thinking. However, she is unsure of what to do in this case. Brian refuses to help her, telling her that she has already limited herself by asking for only two options. While driving to her parents' house for the weekend, Maggie finds herself vacillating between the two options. Her older brother is also visiting the folks this weekend, so Maggie decides to gather her family around the table after dinner, lay out the two options, and go with their decision. "You know the old saying—two heads are better than one," she says to herself, "so four heads should be even better."

Questions

1. Has Maggie made a good decision about the way she is going to make the decision?

2. Which investment would you choose? Why?

3. Which investment do you think most people would choose?

4. Based on what you have learned about groupshift, which investment do you think Maggie's family will choose?

FROM CONCEPTS TO SKILLS

Solving Problems Creatively

You can be more effective at solving problems creatively if you use the following 10 suggestions:[111]

1. *Think of yourself as creative.* Research shows that if you think you cannot be creative, you won't be. Believing in your ability to be creative is the first step to becoming more creative.

2. *Pay attention to your intuition.* Every individual has a subconscious mind that works well. Sometimes answers will come to you when you least expect them. Listen to that "inner voice." In fact, most creative people will keep notepads near their beds and write down ideas when the thoughts come to them.

3. *Move away from your comfort zone.* Every individual has a comfort zone in which certainty exists. But creativity and the known often do not mix. To be creative, you need to move away from the status quo and focus your mind on something new.

4. *Determine what you want to do.* This includes such things as taking time to understand a problem before beginning to try to resolve it, getting all the facts in mind, and trying to identify the most important facts.

5. *Think outside the box.* Use analogies whenever possible (for example, could you approach your problem like a fish out of water and look at what the fish does to cope? Or can you use the things you have to do to find your way when it's foggy to help you solve your problem?). Use different problem-solving strategies, such as verbal, visual, mathematical, or theatrical. Look at your problem from a different perspective or ask yourself what someone else, such as your grandmother, might do if faced with the same situation.

6. *Look for ways to do things better.* This may involve trying consciously to be original, not worrying about looking foolish, keeping an open mind, being alert to odd or puzzling facts, thinking of unconventional ways to use objects and the environment, discarding usual or habitual ways of doing things, and striving for objectivity by being as critical of your own ideas as you would be of someone else's.

7. *Find several right answers.* Being creative means continuing to look for other solutions even when you think you have solved the problem. A better, more creative solution just might be found.

8. *Believe in finding a workable solution.* Like believing in yourself, you also need to believe in your ideas. If you don't think you can find a solution, you probably won't.

9. *Brainstorm with others.* Creativity is not an isolated activity. Bouncing ideas off of others creates a synergistic effect.

10. *Turn creative ideas into action.* Coming up with creative ideas is only part of the process. Once the ideas are generated, they must be implemented. Keeping great ideas in your mind, or on papers that no one will read, does little to expand your creative abilities.

Practising Skills

Every time the phone rings, your stomach clenches and your palms start to sweat. And it's no wonder! As sales manager for Brinkers, a machine tool parts manufacturer, you are besieged by calls from customers who are upset about late deliveries. Your boss, Carter Hererra, acts as both production manager and scheduler. Every time your sales representatives negotiate a sale, it's up to Carter to determine whether production can actually meet the delivery date the customer specifies. Carter invariably says, "No problem." The good thing about this is that you make a lot of initial sales. The bad news is that production hardly ever meets the shipment dates that Carter authorizes. He does not seem to be all that concerned about the aftermath of late deliveries. He says, "Our customers know they're getting outstanding quality at a great price. Just let them try to match that anywhere. It can't be done. So even if they have to wait a couple of extra days or weeks, they're still getting the best deal they can." Somehow the customers do not see it that way, and they let you know about their unhappiness. Then it's up to you to try to smooth over the relationship. You know this problem has to be taken care of, but what possible solutions are there? After all, how are you going to keep from making your manager angry or making the customers angry? Use your knowledge of creative problem solving to come up with solutions.

Reinforcing Skills

1. Take 20 minutes to list as many medical or health-care-related jobs as you can that begin with the letter *r* (for instance, radiologist, registered nurse). If you run out of listings before time is up, it's okay to quit early. But try to be as creative as you can.

2. List on a piece of paper some common terms that apply to both *water* and *finance*. How many were you able to come up with?

MyManagementLab

Study, practise, and explore real business situations with these helpful resources:

- **Study Plan:** Check your understanding of chapter concepts with self-study quizzes.
- **Online Lesson Presentations:** Study key chapter topics and work through interactive assessments to test your knowledge and master management concepts.
- **Videos:** Learn more about the management practices and strategies of real companies.
- **Simulations:** Practise management decision-making in simulated business environments.

(P)(I)(A) PERSONAL INVENTORY ASSESSMENT

CHAPTER 10

Organizational Culture and Change

How does a pizza franchise business ensure quality control across the country? Developing a strong culture is part of the answer.

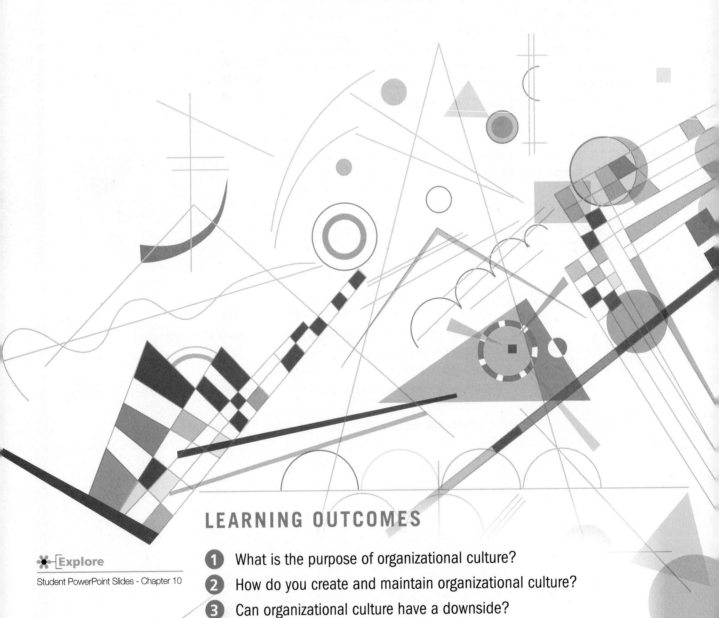

LEARNING OUTCOMES

1. What is the purpose of organizational culture?
2. How do you create and maintain organizational culture?
3. Can organizational culture have a downside?
4. How do organizations manage change?
5. Why do people and organizations resist change?

When you walk into one of Boston Pizza restaurant's locations across Canada, you will find many similarities, but a few differences too.[1] The Quebec restaurants carry poutine, while the Ontario restaurants have a meatball sub on the menu and use a different type of pepperoni on the pizzas than those made in BC and Quebec.

Despite these menu differences, the similarity that binds the Richmond, BC-based Boston Pizza restaurants throughout Canada and the United States is the strong organizational culture created by the company's co-owners, Jim Treliving and George Melville. The two men believe that a strong culture makes for a strong organization, and they emphasize the importance of finding the right people, having good systems in place, training employees, and communicating effectively.

The emphasis on a strong culture seems to be paying off for Boston Pizza. It has been named one of Canada's 10 Most Admired Corporate Cultures, and its three-year average revenue growth far exceeded industry standards and the TSX 60 Composite index.

In this chapter, we show that every organization has a culture. We examine how that culture reveals itself and the effect it has on the attitudes and behaviours of members of that organization. An understanding of what makes up an organization's culture and how culture is created, sustained, and learned enhances our ability to explain and predict the behaviour of people at work. We also look at different approaches organizations take to managing change.

THE BIG IDEA

A strong organizational culture can guide individual decisions and help everyone work together toward the same goals. Change is inevitable, and being able to adapt to change will help the process go more smoothly.

OB IS FOR EVERYONE

- What does organizational culture do?
- Is culture the same as rules?
- What kind of organizational culture would work best for you?
- Are there positive approaches to change?
- How do you respond to change?
- What makes organizations resist change?

LEARNING ABOUT YOURSELF

- Organizational Cultural Fit

What Is Organizational Culture?

① What is the purpose of organizational culture?

When Henry Mintzberg, professor at McGill University and one of the world's leading management experts, was asked to compare organizational structure and corporate culture, he said, "Culture is the soul of the organization—the beliefs and values, and how they are manifested. I think of the structure as the skeleton, and as the flesh and blood. And culture is the soul that holds the thing together and gives it life force."[2]

Mintzberg's culture metaphor provides a clear image of how to think about culture. Culture provides stability to an organization and gives employees a clear understanding of "the way things are done around here." Culture sets the tone for how organizations operate and how individuals within the organization interact. Think of the different impressions you have when a receptionist tells you that "Ms. Dettweiler" will be available in a moment, while at another organization you are told that "Emma" will be with you as soon as she gets off the phone. It's clear that in one organization the rules are more formal than in the other.

As we discuss organizational culture, you may want to remember that organizations differ considerably in the cultures they adopt. Consider the different cultures of Calgary-based WestJet Airlines and Montreal-based Air Canada. WestJet is viewed as having a "young, spunky, can-do environment, where customers will have more fun."[3] Air Canada, by contrast, is considered less helpful and friendly. One analyst even suggested that Air Canada staff "tend to make their customers feel stressed" by their confrontational behaviour.[4] Our discussion of culture should help you understand how these differences across organizations occur.

As you start to think about different organizations where you might work, you will want to research their cultures. For instance, some organizations' cultures are admired more than others: Toronto-based Shoppers Drug Mart, Calgary-based WestJet Airlines, Vancouver-based Ledcor Group, and Toronto-based Tangerine are 4 of the 10 companies named "Most Admired Corporate Cultures" of 2011. An organization that expects employees to work 15 hours a day may not be one in which you would like to work. You may want to complete the *Learning About Yourself Exercise* on page 361, which assesses whether you would be more comfortable in a formal, rule-oriented culture or a more informal, flexible culture.

PERSONAL INVENTORY ASSESSMENT

Learn About Yourself
Company Culture Assessment

PERSONAL INVENTORY ASSESSMENT

Learn About Yourself
Organizational Structure Assessment

Definition of Organizational Culture

Organizational culture refers to a system of shared meaning held by members that distinguishes the organization from other organizations.[5]

Seven primary characteristics capture the essence of an organization's culture:[6]

- *Innovation and risk-taking.* The degree to which employees are encouraged to be innovative and take risks.

- *Attention to detail.* The degree to which employees are expected to work with precision, analysis, and attention to detail.

PERSONAL INVENTORY ASSESSMENT

Learn About Yourself
Innovative Attitude Scale

- *Outcome orientation.* The degree to which management focuses on results, or outcomes, rather than on the techniques and processes used to achieve these outcomes.

- *People orientation.* The degree to which management decisions take into consideration the effect of outcomes on people within the organization.

- *Team orientation.* The degree to which work activities are organized around teams rather than individuals.

- *Aggressiveness.* The degree to which people are aggressive and competitive rather than easygoing and supportive.

organizational culture A system of shared meaning held by members that distinguishes the organization from other organizations.

EXHIBIT 10-1 Contrasting Organizational Cultures

Organization A	Organization B
• Managers must fully document all decisions.	• Management encourages and rewards risk-taking and change.
• Creative decisions, change, and risks are not encouraged.	• Employees are encouraged to "run with" ideas, and failures are treated as "learning experiences."
• Extensive rules and regulations exist for all employees.	• Employees have few rules and regulations to follow.
• Productivity is valued over employee morale.	• Productivity is balanced with treating its people right.
• Employees are encouraged to stay within their own department.	• Team members are encouraged to interact with people at all levels and functions.
• Individual effort is encouraged.	• Many rewards are team-based.

✳ Explore

Exhibit 10-1: Contrasting Organizational Cultures

- *Stability.* The degree to which organizational activities emphasize maintaining the status quo in contrast to growth.

Each of these characteristics exists on a continuum from low to high.

When individuals consider their organization in terms of these seven characteristics, they get a composite picture of the organization's culture. This picture becomes the basis for feelings of shared understanding that members have about the organization, how things are done in it, and the way members are supposed to behave. Exhibit 10-1 demonstrates how these characteristics can be mixed to create highly diverse organizations.

From Concepts to Skills on pages 366–367 offers ideas on how to read an organization's culture.

Levels of Culture

Because organizational culture has multiple levels,[7] the metaphor of an iceberg has often been used to describe it.[8] However, a simmering volcano may better represent the layers of culture: beliefs, values, and assumptions bubble below the surface, producing observable aspects of culture at the surface. Exhibit 10-2 reminds us that

EXHIBIT 10-2 Layers of Culture

✳ Explore

Exhibit 10-2: Layers of Culture

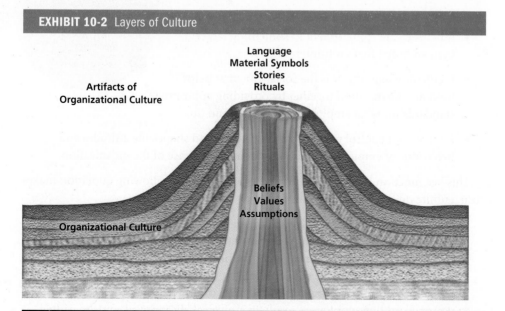

Language
Material Symbols
Stories
Rituals

Artifacts of
Organizational Culture

Beliefs
Values
Assumptions

Organizational Culture

Vancouver-based Playland amusement park hires hundreds of young people each summer to run the rides, sell tickets, and manage the games booths. Managers want to make sure that new employees will fit into the "fun culture" of the environment. Instead of one-on-one interviews, applicants are put into teams where they solve puzzles together while managers watch the group dynamics. Amy Nguyen (left) and Chloe Wong are two of the teens hired after they did well in the group interview.

culture is very visible at the level of **artifacts**. These are what you see, hear, and feel when you encounter an organization's culture. You may notice, for instance, that employees in two offices have very different dress policies, or one office displays great works of art while another posts company mottos on the wall.

Exhibit 10-2 also shows us that beliefs, values, and assumptions, unlike artifacts, are not always readily observable. Instead, we rely on the visible artifacts (material symbols, special language used, rituals carried out, and stories told to others) to help us uncover the organization's beliefs, values, and assumptions. **Beliefs** are the understandings of how objects and ideas relate to each other. **Values** are the stable, long-lasting beliefs about what is important. For instance, Winnipeg-based Palliser Furniture, a manufacturer of leather- and fabric-upholstered furniture, promotes the following corporate values: "demonstrate integrity in all relationships," "promote the dignity and value of each other," and "strive for excellence."[9] **Assumptions** are the taken-for-granted notions of how something should be. When basic assumptions are held by the entire group, members will have difficulty conceiving of another way of doing things. For instance, in Canada, some students hold a basic assumption that universities should not consider costs when setting tuition but that they should keep tuition low for greater access by students. Beliefs, values, and assumptions, if we can uncover them, help us understand why organizations do the things that we observe.

Functions of Culture

Culture performs a number of functions within an organization:

- It has a boundary-defining role because it creates distinction between one organization and others.

- It conveys a sense of identity to organization members.

- It helps create commitment to something larger than an individual's self-interest.

- It enhances stability; it is the social glue that helps hold the organization together by providing appropriate standards for what employees should say and do.

- It serves as a control mechanism that guides and shapes the attitudes and behaviour of employees, and helps them make sense of the organization.

What does organizational culture do?

This last function is of particular interest to us.[10] As the following quotation makes clear, culture defines the rules of the game:

Culture by definition is elusive, intangible, implicit, and taken for granted. But every organization develops a core set of assumptions, understandings, and implicit rules that govern day-to-day behaviour in the workplace. Until newcomers learn the rules, they are not accepted as full-fledged members of the organization. Transgressions of the rules on the part of high-level executives or front-line employees result in universal disapproval and powerful

artifacts Aspects of an organization's culture that an individual can see, hear, and feel.

beliefs The understandings of how objects and ideas relate to each other.

values The stable, long-lasting beliefs about what is important.

assumptions The taken-for-granted notions of how something should be.

penalties. Conformity to the rules becomes the primary basis for reward and upward mobility.[11]

Today's trend toward decentralized organizations makes culture more important than ever, but ironically it also makes establishing a strong culture more difficult. When formal authority and control systems are reduced, culture's *shared meaning* points everyone in the same direction. However, employees organized in teams may show greater allegiance to their team and its values than to the values of the organization as a whole. In virtual organizations, the lack of frequent face-to-face contact makes establishing a common set of norms very difficult. Strong leadership that communicates frequently about common goals and priorities is especially important in innovative organizations.[12]

Culture Creates Climate

If you have worked with someone whose positive attitude inspired you to do your best, or with a lacklustre team that drained your motivation, you have experienced the effects of climate. **Organizational climate** refers to the shared perceptions organizational members have about their organization and work environment.[13] This aspect of culture is like team spirit at the organizational level. When everyone has the same general feelings about what is important or how well things are working, the effect of these attitudes will be more than the sum of the individual parts. The same appears true for organizations. One meta-analysis found that across dozens of different samples, psychological climate was strongly related to individuals' level of job satisfaction, involvement, commitment, and motivation.[14] A positive overall workplace climate has been linked to higher customer satisfaction and financial performance as well.[15]

Dozens of dimensions of climate have been studied, including safety, justice, diversity, and customer service, to name a few.[16] A person who encounters a positive climate for performance will think about doing a good job more often and will believe others support his or her success. Someone who encounters a positive climate for diversity will feel more comfortable collaborating with co-workers regardless of their demographic background. Climate also influences the habits people adopt. If the climate for safety is positive, everyone wears safety gear and follows safety procedures even if individually they would not normally think very often about being safe. *OB in the Workplace* offers one example of an employee-first corporate culture.

in the WORKPLACE
Making Culture Work

What can a CEO do if employees don't buy into the company culture? Wadood Ibrahim, CEO of Winnipeg-based Protegra, believes in the importance of having a strong, employee-first corporate culture.[17] In fact, Protegra has been recognized for its corporate culture twice, placing first in the 2009 and 2011 "Best Small and Medium Employers in Canada" rankings conducted jointly by Queen's University Centre for Business Venturing and Aon Hewitt.

Protegra has an egalitarian culture at its core. Employees don't have corporate titles, and they are encouraged to participate in the employee share-ownership program.

After a period of growth in the early 2000s, the company's culture started to get muddied. The socialization process was not as strong as it should be, and communication

organizational climate The shared perceptions organizational members have about their organization and work environment.

about the company's values was lax. In order to make sure that everyone understood the company's culture, Ibrahim brought employees together to talk about what they saw as the company's core values. The common theme was respect, teamwork, and dependability. From his discussion with employees, Ibrahim codified the culture for his employees—"what Protegra was, what it aspired to be and how employees were expected to apply its values." This exercise led to 10 employees leaving, because they were not on board with the vision. Ibrahim saw this as a good thing: "We got alignment on values and vision," and the company has performed much better since.

In order to strengthen the company's culture further, in 2009 Ibrahim unveiled an internal website called "the Enduring Culture Machine." The site contains an in-depth explanation of Protegra's values and it's "meant to be a primer for new recruits, a communication tool for existing employees and a mechanism to protect and strengthen Protegra's culture over the long haul." Creativity and empowerment are still important, Ibrahim explains, "but [new staff] need to abide by basic company principles." ●

Do Organizations Have Uniform Cultures?

Organizational culture represents a common perception the organization's members hold. We should expect, therefore, that individuals with different backgrounds or at different levels in the organization will tend to describe its culture in similar terms.[18]

The fact that organizational culture has common properties does not mean that there cannot be subcultures within it. Most large organizations have a dominant culture and numerous sets of subcultures.[19]

A **dominant culture** expresses the core values that are shared by a majority of the organization's members. When we talk about an *organization's culture*, we are referring to

Organizational culture guides and shapes the attitudes of employees at New Zealand Air. One of the airline's guiding principles is to champion and promote New Zealand and its national heritage, both within the country and overseas. In this photo, a cabin crew member dressed in traditional Maori clothing and a pilot touch noses to represent the sharing of a single breath following a ceremony for the airline's purchase of a Boeing airplane in Everett, Washington. Such expressions of representing their country with pride create a strong bond among employees.

dominant culture A system of shared meaning that expresses the core values shared by a majority of the organization's members.

its dominant culture, which gives an organization its distinct personality.[20] **Subcultures** tend to develop in large organizations to reflect common problems, situations, or experiences faced by groups of members in the same department or location. The purchasing department can have a subculture that includes the **core values** of the dominant culture plus additional values unique to members of the purchasing department.

If organizations were composed only of numerous subcultures, organizational culture as an independent variable would be significantly less powerful. It is the "shared meaning" aspect of culture that makes it such a potent device for guiding and shaping behaviour. This is what allows us to say that Microsoft's culture values aggressiveness and risk-taking,[21] and then to use that information to better understand the behaviour of Microsoft executives and employees. But many organizations also have subcultures that can influence the behaviour of members.

Creating and Sustaining an Organization's Culture

One of the challenges Boston Pizza co-owners Jim Treliving and George Melville face in managing the 325 restaurants and more than 16 000 employees across Canada is making sure that everyone is on the same page.[22] The individual restaurants in the chain are not owned by the company. Instead, franchisees invest a considerable amount of money in order to gain the right to own a Boston Pizza restaurant. Thus, there could be a conflict between what the co-founders want done, and what a franchisee feels is best for his or her investment.

Treliving and Melville try to prevent this conflict by carefully vetting franchise candidates. Potential franchisees are informed of the initial $60 000 fee and start-up costs that could run between $1.5 and $2.4 million. Despite the size of their investment, franchisees must demonstrate a "willingness to adhere to the Boston Pizza system." Franchisees are given a lot of help in starting out, however.

When Hank Van Poelgeest opened up the first Boston Pizza restaurant in St. John's, Newfoundland, in January 2006, he naturally worried. A lot of preparation had gone into the opening, which involved months of planning, and a careful choice of location, and a team of nine people had been sent from head office to help hire and train staff. The new staff did a dress rehearsal of the grand opening four times to make sure nothing went wrong.

The preparation was so thorough that the opening exceeded all expectations. "We wanted to use the first couple of weeks as a slow beginning," says Van Poelgeest, "but we've never had a slow beginning." What role does culture play in creating high-performing employees?

An organization's culture does not pop out of thin air, and once established, it rarely fades away. Exhibit 10-3 summarizes how an organization's culture is established and sustained. We describe each part of this process on the next page.

2 How do you create and maintain organizational culture?

Is culture the same as rules?

How a Culture Begins

An organization's current customs, traditions, and general way of doing things owe a great deal to what it has done

EXHIBIT 10-3 How Organizational Cultures Form

Philosophy of organization's founders → Selection criteria → Top management / Socialization → Organization's culture

subcultures Mini-cultures within an organization, typically defined by department designations and geographical separation.

core values The primary, or dominant, values that are accepted throughout the organization.

before and how successful those previous endeavours have been. This leads us to the ultimate source of an organization's culture: its founders.[23]

Founders traditionally have a major impact on an organization's early culture. Free of previous customs or ideologies, they have a vision of what the organization should be. Because new organizations are typically small, it is possible for the founders to impose their vision on all organizational members. Jim Treliving, the founder of Boston Pizza, keeps his vision alive by stopping in at every Boston Pizza wherever he is travelling, shaking hands with the staff, and thanking them for their hard work. According to Treliving, "you take people in as franchisees and they become part of your family."[24]

Culture creation occurs in three ways.[25] First, founders hire and keep only employees who think and feel the way they do. Second, they indoctrinate and socialize these employees to their way of thinking and feeling. Finally, the founders' own behaviour encourages employees to identify with the founders and internalize those beliefs, values, and assumptions. When the organization succeeds, the founders' vision is seen as a primary determinant of that success. At that point, the founders' entire personality becomes embedded in the culture of the organization.

The culture at Toronto-based PCL, the largest general contracting organization in Canada, is still strongly influenced by the vision of Ernest Poole, who founded the company in 1906. "Poole's rules," which include "Employ highest grade people obtainable" and "Encourage integrity, loyalty and efficiencies," still influence the way the company hires and trains its employees long after the founder's death.[26] Other contemporary examples of founders who have had an immeasurable impact on their organizations' cultures are Ted Rogers of Toronto-based Rogers Communications, Frank Stronach of Aurora, Ontario-based Magna International, and Richard Branson of UK-based Virgin Group.

Keeping a Culture Alive

Once a culture is in place, practices within the organization maintain it by giving employees a set of similar experiences.[27] The selection process, performance evaluation criteria, training and career development activities, and promotion procedures ensure those hired fit in with the culture, reward those who support it, and penalize (even expel) those who challenge it. Three forces play a particularly important part in sustaining a culture: *selection* practices, the actions of *top management*, and *socialization* methods. Let's take a closer look at each.

Selection

The explicit goal of the selection process is to identify and hire individuals who have the knowledge, skills, and abilities to perform successfully.

The final decision, because it is significantly influenced by the decision maker's judgment of how well each candidate will fit into the organization, identifies people whose values are consistent with at least a good portion of the organization's values.[28]

Selection also provides information about the organization to applicants. Windsor, Ontario-based Windsor Family Credit Union makes job candidates go through a process that has as many as eight steps so that the organization and the employee can determine if they are a good fit for each other.[29] To signal to job candidates that dignity and respect are important parts of Kitchener, Ontario-based Mennonite Savings and Credit Union's culture, job candidates are provided with interview questions in advance. The credit union encourages two-way communication throughout the hiring process.[30] *OB in the Workplace* shows how one company's method of interviewing ensures that applicants are right for the job.

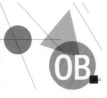

in the WORKPLACE
Playland's Interviews Are More Than Fun and Games

How does a company make sure an applicant is right for the job? At Playland, Vancouver's largest amusement park, applicants for a summer job don't do one-on-one interviews with managers or the human resource department.[31] Instead, they are asked to deconstruct a JENGA tower with a group of nine other applicants and answer a variety of "interesting questions." When an applicant removes a block from the tower, they answer a question printed on it.

Amy Nguyen, a 15-year-old high school student applying for her first job, had the following question: "There's a customer who had to line up a long time for food and he was very upset by the time he got to the front of the line. What would you do?"

"I said I would apologize, look cute and tell him, 'Let me see if my manager can do anything for you,'" says Nguyen. This answer got her a second interview, and she eventually got the job.

Jennifer Buensuceso, a PNE gaming manager at Playland, thinks the new way of hiring is much better than when she faced a one-on-one question and answer format when she was hired. She says the new method helps managers learn about the applicant's "team-building and individuality. You get to see them think out of the box."

This format is also good for nervous teens and those whose first language is not English. Getting them to play relaxes them and helps managers to see "who shows natural leadership skills, who's outgoing, who works well on a team and who's good at problem-solving."[32] ●

Careful hiring practices means that those who perceive a conflict between their values and those of the organization can remove themselves from the applicant pool. Selection, therefore, becomes a two-way street, allowing the employer or applicant to avoid a mismatch and sustaining an organization's culture by selecting out those individuals who might attack or undermine its core values.

Top Management
The actions of top management also have a major impact on the organization's culture.[33] Through words and actions, senior executives establish norms that filter through the organization about, for instance, whether risk-taking is desirable; how much freedom managers should give their employees; what is appropriate dress; what actions will pay off in terms of pay raises, promotions, and other rewards; and the like.

Socialization
No matter how effectively the organization recruits and selects new employees, they are not fully indoctrinated in the organization's culture and can disrupt beliefs and customs already in place. The process that helps new employees adapt to the prevailing culture is called **socialization**.[34] As a 2011 study suggests, socialization done well will develop a new employee's self-efficacy, hope, optimism, and resilience.[35]

New employees at the Japanese electronics company Sanyo are socialized through a particularly long training program. At their intensive five-month course, trainees eat and sleep together in company-subsidized dorms and are required to vacation together

What kind of organizational culture would work best for you?

socialization The process that adapts new employees to an organization's culture.

Monique Leroux, chair of the board, president, and CEO of Desjardins Group, recently led an organizational restructuring at Desjardins. To help accomplish this goal, she established 10 multidisciplinary teams with equal numbers of women and men on each, sending a clear message about gender equality to the cooperative. Leroux is a mentor to many women, and among her many activities geared to supporting women in a traditionally male-dominated financial industry, Leroux has also helped Desjardins launch scholarships and internships for young women interested in finance. Desjardins was named one of Canada's 10 Most Admired Corporate Cultures in 2011.

at company-owned resorts. They learn the Sanyo way of doing everything—from how to speak to managers to proper grooming and dress.[36] The company considers this program essential for transforming young employees, fresh out of school, into dedicated *kaisha senshi*, or corporate warriors.

An organization continues to socialize its employees throughout their career in the organization, which further contributes to sustaining the culture. (Sometimes, however, employees are not fully socialized. For instance, you will note in Exhibit 10-4 that the cartoon employees had learned they were supposed to wear checkerboard caps to work, but clearly did not know why.) As part of its continual socialization process, the CEO of Windsor, Ontario-based Windsor Family Credit Union takes employees to breakfast quarterly to find out about their questions, concerns, and their work.[37]

Explore

Exhibit 10-4

EXHIBIT 10-4

"I don't know how it started, either. All I know is that it's part of our corporate culture."

Source: © Mick Stevens/The New Yorker Collection/www.cartoonbank.com

This provides an opportunity to make sure employees understand the overall goals of the organization.

This chapter's *Ethical Dilemma Exercise* on page 364 explores whether you would be comfortable working in an organization whose culture accepts snooping on its employees.

The Liabilities of Organizational Culture

Culture enhances organizational commitment and increases the consistency of employee behaviour. These are clearly benefits to an organization. From an employee's standpoint, culture is valuable because it spells out how things are done and what is important. However, we should not ignore the potentially dysfunctional aspects of culture, especially of a strong culture, on an organization's effectiveness. As recent research suggests, cultures that strongly emphasize competition can lead to negative organizational consequences.[38]

We now consider culture's impact on change, diversity, and mergers and acquisitions.

3 Can organizational culture have a downside?

Barrier to Change

Culture is a liability when the shared values don't agree with those that will further the organization's effectiveness. For example, when an organization's environment is undergoing rapid change and its entrenched culture may no longer be appropriate. Consistency of behaviour, an asset in a stable environment, may then burden the organization and make it difficult to respond to changes. For many organizations with strong cultures, practices that led to previous successes can lead to failure when those practices no longer match up well with environmental needs.[39]

Barrier to Diversity

Hiring new employees who differ from the majority in race, gender, disability, or other characteristics creates a paradox:[40] Management demonstrates support for the differences that these employees bring to the workplace, but newcomers who wish to fit in must accept the organization's core cultural values. Because diverse behaviours and unique strengths are likely to diminish as people attempt to assimilate, strong cultures can become liabilities when they effectively eliminate these advantages.

By limiting the range of values and styles that are acceptable, strong cultures put considerable pressure on employees to conform. It is no coincidence that employees at Disney theme parks appear to be almost universally attractive, clean, and wholesome looking with bright smiles. That's the image the Walt Disney Company wants to project. It selects employees who will maintain that image. Once the theme-park employees are on the job, a strong culture—supported by formal rules and regulations—ensures that they will act in a relatively uniform and predictable way.

Organizations seek out and hire diverse individuals because of the new strengths they bring to the workplace. Yet these diverse behaviours and strengths are likely to diminish in strong cultures as people try to fit in. Strong cultures, therefore, can be liabilities when they effectively eliminate the unique strengths that people of different backgrounds bring to the organization. Moreover, strong cultures can also be liabilities when they support institutional bias or become insensitive to people who are different.

Barrier to Mergers and Acquisitions

Historically, when management looked at merger or acquisition decisions, the key factors were related to financial advantages or product synergy. In recent years, cultural compatibility has become the primary concern.[41] All things being equal, whether the acquisition actually works seems to have more to do with how well the two organizations' cultures match up.

Strategies for Merging Cultures

Organizations can use several strategies when considering how to merge the cultures of two organizations:[42]

- *Assimilation.* The entire new organization is determined to take on the culture of one of the merging organizations. This strategy works best when one of the organizations has a relatively weak culture. However, if a culture is simply imposed on an organization, it rarely works.

- *Separation.* The organizations remain separate and keep their individual cultures. This strategy works best when the organizations have little overlap in the industries in which they operate.

- *Integration.* A new culture is formed by merging parts of each of the organizations. This strategy works best when aspects of each organization's culture need to be improved.

Approaches to Managing Change

4 How do organizations manage change?

Our discussion of organizational culture as well as the issues that arise when organizations merge leads to a fundamental question for all organizations: How can change be managed? In what follows, we consider several approaches to managing change: Lewin's classic three-step model of the change process, Kotter's eight-step plan for implementing change, action research, and appreciative inquiry. We should also note that recent research emphasizes the need in change processes to manage the "hard stuff" as well as the "soft," or people, issues in order to be successful.[43]

Who is responsible for managing change in an organization? The answer is change agents.[44] **Change agents** can be managers or nonmanagers, employees of the organization, or outside consultants.

Lewin's Three-Step Model

Assuming that an organization has uncovered a need for change, how does it engage in the change process? Kurt Lewin argued that successful change in organizations should follow three steps, which are illustrated in Exhibit 10-5: **unfreezing** the status quo, **moving** to a new state, and **refreezing** the new change to make it permanent.[45] The value of this model can be seen in the following example, where the management of a large oil company decided to reorganize its marketing function in Western Canada.

The oil company had three regional offices in the West, located in Winnipeg, Calgary, and Vancouver. The decision was made to consolidate the marketing divisions of the three regional offices into a single regional office to be located in Calgary. The reorganization meant transferring more than 150 employees, eliminating some duplicate managerial positions, and instituting a new hierarchy of command.

The status quo can be considered to be an equilibrium state. To move from this equilibrium—to overcome the pressures of both individual resistance and group conformity—unfreezing is necessary. Exhibit 10-6 shows that unfreezing happens in

change agents People who act as catalysts and assume the responsibility for managing change.

unfreezing Change efforts to overcome the pressures of both individual resistance and group conformity.

moving Efforts to get employees involved in the change process.

refreezing Stabilizing a change intervention by balancing driving and restraining forces.

EXHIBIT 10-5 Lewin's Three-Step Change Model

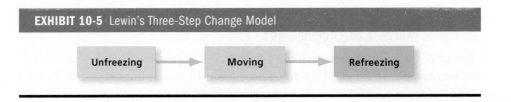

one of three ways. The **driving forces**, which direct behaviour away from the status quo, can be increased. The **restraining forces**, which hinder movement from the existing equilibrium, can be decreased. A third alternative is to *combine the first two approaches*. Companies that have been successful in the past are likely to encounter restraining forces because people question the need for change.[46] Similarly, research shows that companies with strong cultures excel at incremental change but are overcome by restraining forces against radical change.[47]

EXHIBIT 10-6 Unfreezing the Status Quo

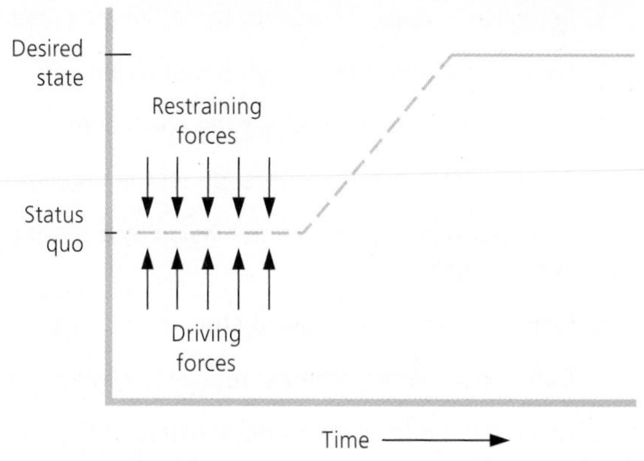

The oil company's management could expect employee resistance to the consolidation and outline its alternatives. Those in Winnipeg or Vancouver may not want to transfer to another city, pull youngsters out of school, make new friends, adapt to new co-workers, or undergo the reassignment of responsibilities. Positive incentives such as pay increases, liberal moving expenses, and low-cost mortgage funds for new homes in Calgary might encourage employees to accept the change. Management might also unfreeze acceptance of the status quo by removing restraining forces. It could counsel employees individually, hearing and clarifying each employee's specific concerns and apprehensions. Assuming that most of the fears are unjustified, the counsellor could assure the employees that there was nothing to fear and then demonstrate, through tangible evidence, that restraining forces are unwarranted. If resistance is extremely high, management may have to resort to both reducing resistance and increasing the attractiveness of the alternative if the unfreezing is to be successful.

Research on organizational change has shown that, to be effective, change has to happen quickly.[48] Organizations that build up to change do less well than those that get to and through the moving stage quickly.

Once the consolidation change has been implemented, to be successful the new situation must be refrozen so that it can be sustained over time. Without this last step, change likely will be short-lived and employees will try to revert to the previous equilibrium state. The objective of refreezing, then, is to stabilize the new situation by balancing the driving and restraining forces.

How could the oil company's management refreeze its consolidation change? By systematically replacing temporary forces with permanent ones. Management might impose a new bonus system tied to the specific changes desired. The formal rules and regulations governing the behaviour of those affected by the change could also be revised to reinforce the new situation. Over time, of course, the work group's own norms will evolve to sustain the new equilibrium. But until that point is reached, management will have to rely on more formal mechanisms.

The *Working with Others Exercise* on page 363 gives you the opportunity to identify driving and restraining forces for another company experiencing problems with change and to make some recommendations for change.

A key feature of Lewin's three-step model is its conception of change as an episodic activity, with a beginning, a middle, and an end. However, the structure of today's workplaces requires change to take place as an ongoing, if not chaotic, process. Certainly the adjustment that companies have made to the realities of e-commerce indicates a more chaotic change, rather than a controlled and planned change.

Kotter's Eight-Step Plan for Implementing Change

John Kotter, professor of leadership at Harvard Business School, built on Lewin's three-step model to create a more detailed approach for implementing change.[49]

Kotter began by listing common failures that occur when managers try to initiate change. These include the inability to create a sense of urgency about the need for

driving forces Forces that direct behaviour away from the status quo.

restraining forces Forces that hinder movement away from the status quo.

EXHIBIT 10-7 Kotter's Eight-Step Plan for Implementing Change
1. Establish a sense of urgency by creating a compelling reason for why change is needed.
2. Form a coalition with enough power to lead the change.
3. Create a new vision to direct the change and strategies for achieving the vision.
4. Communicate the vision throughout the organization.
5. Empower others to act on the vision by removing barriers to change and encouraging risk-taking and creative problem solving.
6. Plan for, create, and reward short-term "wins" that move the organization toward the new vision.
7. Consolidate improvements, reassess changes, and make necessary adjustments in the new programs.
8. Reinforce the changes by demonstrating the relationship between new behaviours and organizational success.

Source: Based on J. P. Kotter, *Leading Change* (Boston: Harvard Business School Press, 1996).

change; failure to create a coalition for managing the change process; the absence of a vision for change and to effectively communicate that vision; not removing obstacles that could impede the achievement of the vision; failure to provide short-term and achievable goals; the tendency to declare victory too soon; and not anchoring the changes in the organization's culture.

Kotter then established eight sequential steps to overcome these problems. These steps are listed in Exhibit 10-7.

Notice how Exhibit 10-7 builds on Lewin's model. Kotter's first four steps essentially represent the "unfreezing" stage. Steps 5 through 7 represent "moving." The final step works on "refreezing." Kotter's contribution lies in providing managers and change agents with a more detailed guide for implementing change successfully. This chapter's *Point/Counterpoint* on page 360 outlines the conditions under which cultural change is most likely to occur.

Action Research

Action research refers to a change process based on the systematic collection of data and then selection of a change action based on what the analyzed data indicate.[50] Its value is in providing a scientific method for managing planned change.

The process of action research, carried out by a change agent, consists of five steps:

1. *Diagnosis.* The change agent gathers information about problems, concerns, and needed changes from members of the organization by asking questions, reviewing records, and listening to the concerns of employees.

2. *Analysis.* The change agent organizes the information gathered into primary concerns, problem areas, and possible actions.

3. *Feedback.* The change agent shares with employees what has been found during diagnosis and analysis. The employees, with the help of the change agent, develop action plans for bringing about any needed change.

4. *Action.* The employees and the change agent carry out the specific actions they have identified to correct the problems.

5. *Evaluation.* The change agent evaluates the action plan's effectiveness, using the data gathered initially as a benchmark.

Action research provides at least two specific benefits for an organization. First, it is problem-focused. The change agent objectively looks for problems and the type of

action research A change process based on the systematic collection of data and then selection of a change action based on what the analyzed data indicate.

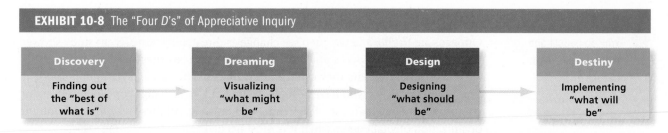

EXHIBIT 10-8 The "Four *D*'s" of Appreciative Inquiry

Discovery		Dreaming		Design		Destiny
Finding out the "best of what is"	→	Visualizing "what might be"	→	Designing "what should be"	→	Implementing "what will be"

Source: Based on D. L. Cooperrider and D. Whitney, *Collaborating for Change: Appreciative Inquiry* (San Francisco: Berrett-Koehler, 2000).

problem determines the type of change action. While this may seem intuitively obvious, a lot of change activities are not done this way. Rather, they are solution-centred. The change agent has a favourite solution—for example, implementing flextime, teams, or a process re-engineering program—and then seeks out problems that his or her solution fits. Second, because action research thoroughly involves employees in the process, it reduces resistance to change. Once employees have actively participated in the feedback stage, the change process typically takes on a momentum of its own under their sustained pressure to bring it about.

Appreciative Inquiry

Most organizational change approaches are problem-centred. They identify a problem or set of problems, then look for a solution. **Appreciative inquiry (AI)** accentuates the positive.[51] Rather than looking for problems to fix, this approach seeks to identify the unique qualities and special strengths of an organization, which can then be built on to improve performance. That is, it focuses on an organization's successes rather than on its problems.

> Are there positive approaches to change?

The appreciative inquiry process (see Exhibit 10-8) consists of four steps, or "Four *D*'s," often played out in a large-group meeting over a two- or three-day time period, and overseen by a trained change agent:

- *Discovery.* Identify what people think are the strengths of the organization. Employees recount times they felt the organization worked best or when they specifically felt most satisfied with their jobs.

- *Dreaming.* Employees use information from the discovery phase to speculate on possible futures for the organization, such as what the organization will be like in five years.

- *Design.* Based on the dream articulation, participants focus on finding a common vision of how the organization will look, and agree on its unique qualities.

- *Destiny.* In this final step, participants discuss how the organization is going to fulfill its dream, and they typically write action plans and develop implementation strategies.

AI has proven an effective change strategy in organizations such as Toronto-based Orchestras Canada, Ajax, Ontario-based Nokia Canada, Burnaby, BC-based TELUS, Calgary-based EnCana, and Toronto-based CBC.

The use of appreciative inquiry in organizations is relatively recent, and it has not yet been determined when it is most appropriately used for organizational change.[52] However, it does give us the opportunity of viewing change from a much more positive perspective.

appreciative inquiry (AI) An approach to change that seeks to identify the unique qualities and special strengths of an organization, which can then be built on to improve performance.

5 Why do people and organizations resist change?

Resistance to Change

Our egos are fragile, and we often see change as threatening. One recent study showed that even when employees are shown data that suggests they need to change, they latch onto whatever data they can find that suggests they are okay and don't need to change.[53] Employees who have negative feelings about a change cope by not thinking about it, increasing their use of sick time, and quitting. All these reactions can sap the organization of vital energy when it is most needed.[54]

Resistance to change can be positive if it leads to open discussion and debate.[55] These responses are usually preferable to apathy or silence and can indicate that members of the organization are engaged in the process, providing change agents an opportunity to explain the change effort. Change agents can also use resistance to modify the change to fit the preferences of other members of the organization. When they treat resistance only as a threat, rather than a point of view to be discussed, they may increase dysfunctional conflict.

Resistance to change does not necessarily surface in standardized ways. It can be overt, implicit, immediate, or deferred. It is easiest for management to deal with resistance when it is overt and immediate, such as complaints, a work slowdown, or a strike threat. The greater challenge is managing resistance that is implicit or deferred. These responses—loss of loyalty to the organization, loss of motivation to work, increased errors or mistakes, increased absenteeism—are more difficult to recognize. Deferred actions also cloud the link between the change and the reaction to it and may surface weeks, months, or even years later. Or a single change that in and of itself might have little impact becomes "the straw that breaks the camel's back" because resistance to earlier changes has been deferred and stockpiled.

Let's look at the sources of resistance. For analytical purposes, we have categorized them as individual and organizational sources. In the real world, the sources often overlap.

Individual Resistance

Individual sources of resistance to change reside in basic human characteristics such as perceptions, personalities, and needs. Exhibit 10-9 summarizes four reasons why individuals may resist change:[56]

How do you respond to change?

- *Self-interest.* People worry that they will lose something of value if change happens. Thus, they look after their own self-interests rather than those of the total organization.

- *Misunderstanding and lack of trust.* People resist change when they don't understand the nature of the change and fear that the cost of change will outweigh any potential gains for them. This often occurs when they don't trust those initiating the change.

- *Different assessments.* People resist change when they see it differently than their managers do and think the costs outweigh the benefits, even for the organization. Managers may assume that employees have the same information that they do, but this is not always the case.

- *Low tolerance for change.* People resist change because they worry that they don't have the skills and behaviour required of the new situation. They may feel that they are being asked to do too much, too quickly.

In addition to the above, individuals sometimes worry that being asked to change may indicate that what they have been doing in the past was somehow wrong. Managers

PERSONAL INVENTORY ASSESSMENT

Learn About Yourself
What's My Comfort with Change?

EXHIBIT 10-9 Sources of Individual Resistance to Change

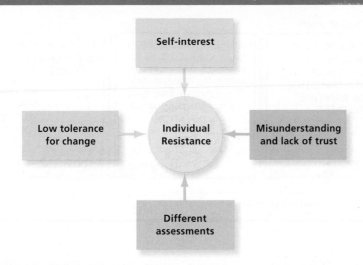

Source: Based on J. P. Kotter and L. A. Schlesinger, "Choosing Strategies for Change," *Harvard Business Review*, July–August 2008, pp. 107–109.

should not overlook the effects of peer pressure on an individual's response to change. As well, the manager's attitude (positive or negative) toward the change and his or her relationship with employees will affect an individual's response to change.

Cynicism

Employees often feel cynical about the change process, particularly if they have been through several rounds of change and nothing appears (to them) to have changed. One study identified sources of cynicism in the change process of a large unionized manufacturing plant.[57] The major elements contributing to the cynicism were as follows:

- Feeling uninformed about what was happening

- Lack of communication and respect from one's manager

- Lack of communication and respect from one's union representative

- Lack of opportunity for meaningful participation in decision making

The researchers also found that employees with negative personalities were more likely to be cynical about change. While organizations might not be able to change an individual's personality, they certainly have the ability to provide greater communication and respect, as well as opportunities to take part in decision making. The researchers found that cynicism about change led to such outcomes as lower commitment, less satisfaction, and reduced motivation to work hard. Exhibit 10-10 illustrates why some employees, particularly Dilbert, may have reason to feel cynical about organizational change. *Case Incident—Is a 5S Culture for You?* on page 365 looks at 5S, one approach companies are using to engage employees in cultural change.

Organizational Resistance

Organizations, by their very nature, are conservative.[58] They actively resist change. You don't have to look far to see evidence of this phenomenon. Government agencies want to continue doing what they have been doing for years,

What makes organizations resist change?

EXHIBIT 10-10

DILBERT BY SCOTT ADAMS

Source: Dilbert, reprinted by permission of Universal Uclick.

whether the need for their service changes or remains the same. Organized religions are deeply entrenched in their history. Attempts to change church doctrine require great persistence and patience. Educational institutions, which exist to open minds and challenge established ways of thinking, are themselves extremely resistant to change. Most school systems are using essentially the same teaching technologies today that they were 50 years ago. Similarly, most business firms appear highly resistant to change.

Six major sources of organizational resistance to change (shown in Exhibit 10-11) have been identified:[59]

- *Structural inertia.* Organizations have built-in mechanisms—such as their selection processes and formal regulations—to produce stability. When an organization is confronted with change, this structural inertia acts as a counterbalance to sustain stability.

- *Limited focus of change.* Organizations are made up of a number of interdependent subsystems. One cannot be changed without affecting the others. So limited changes in subsystems tend to be nullified by the larger system.

- *Group inertia.* Even if individuals want to change their behaviour, group norms may act as a constraint.

- *Threat to expertise.* Changes in organizational patterns may threaten the expertise of specialized groups.

EXHIBIT 10-11 Sources of Organizational Resistance to Change

Threat to established resource allocations

Structural inertia

Threat to established power relationships

Organizational Resistance

Limited focus of change

Threat to expertise

Group inertia

- *Threat to established power relationships.* Any redistribution of decision-making authority can threaten long-established power relationships within the organization.

- *Threat to established resource allocations.* Groups in the organization that control sizable resources often see change as a threat. They tend to be content with the way things are.

Overcoming Resistance to Change

It is important to note that not all change is good. Research has shown that sometimes an emphasis on making speedy decisions can lead to bad decisions. Sometimes the line between resisting needed change and falling into a "speed trap" is a fine one indeed.[60] What is more, sometimes in the "fog of change" those who are initiating change fail to realize the full magnitude of the effects they are causing or to estimate their true costs to the organization. Thus, although the perspective generally taken is that rapid, transformational change is good, this is not always the case. Change agents need to carefully think through the full implications.

Eight tactics can be used by change agents to deal with resistance to change.[61] Let's review them briefly.

PERSONAL INVENTORY ASSESSMENT

Learn About Yourself
Leading Positive Change

- *Education and communication.* Communicating the logic of a change can reduce resistance on two levels. First, it fights the effects of misinformation and poor communication: If employees receive the full facts and get any misunderstandings cleared up, resistance should subside. Second, communication can be helpful in "selling" the need for change. Research shows that change is more likely when the need for change is packaged properly.[62] A study of German companies revealed that changes are most effective when a company communicates its rationale, balancing various stakeholder (shareholders, employees, community, customers) interests, vs. a rationale based on shareholder interests only.[63]

- *Participation and involvement.* It's difficult for individuals to resist a change decision in which they have participated. Assuming that the participants have the expertise to make a meaningful contribution, their involvement can reduce resistance, obtain commitment, and increase the quality of the change decision. However, against these advantages are the negatives: potential for a poor solution and great consumption of time.

- *Building support and commitment.* When employees' fear and anxiety are high, employee counselling and therapy, new-skills training, or a short paid leave of absence may facilitate adjustment. When managers or employees have low emotional commitment to change, they favour the status quo and resist it.[64] So firing up employees can also help them emotionally commit to the change rather than embrace the status quo.

- *Developing positive relationships.* People are more willing to accept changes if they trust the managers implementing them.[65] One study surveyed 235 employees from a large housing corporation in the Netherlands that was experiencing a merger. Those who had a more positive relationship with their supervisors, and who felt that the work environment supported development, were much more positive about the change process.[66]

- *Implementing changes fairly.* One way organizations can minimize the negative impact of change is to make sure the change is implemented fairly. As we learned in Chapter 4, procedural fairness becomes especially important when employees perceive an outcome as negative, so it's crucial that employees see the reason for the change, and perceive implementation as consistent and fair.[67]

- *Manipulation and co-optation.* The term *manipulation* refers to covert influence attempts. Twisting and distorting facts to make them more attractive, withholding undesirable information, and creating false rumours to get employees to accept a change are all examples of manipulation. If management threatens to close a manufacturing plant whose employees are resisting an across-the-board pay cut, and if the threat is actually untrue, management is using manipulation. *Co-optation,* on the other hand, is a form of both manipulation and participation. It seeks to "buy off" the leaders of a resistance group by giving them a key role, seeking their advice not to find a better solution but to get their endorsement. Both manipulation and co-optation are relatively inexpensive ways to gain the support of adversaries, but they can backfire if the targets become aware they are being tricked or used. Once that is discovered, the change agent's credibility may drop to zero.

- *Selecting people who accept change.* Research suggests that the ability to easily accept and adapt to change is related to personality—some people simply have more positive attitudes about change than others.[68] Such individuals are open to experience, take a positive attitude toward change, are willing to take risks, and are flexible in their behaviour. One study of managers in the United States, Europe, and Asia found that those with a positive self-concept and high risk tolerance coped better with organizational change. A study of 258 police officers found that those higher in growth-needs strength, internal locus of control, and internal work motivation had more positive attitudes about organizational change efforts.[69] Another study found that selecting people based on a resistance-to-change scale worked well in eliminating those who tended to react emotionally to change or to be rigid.[70] Individuals higher in general mental ability are also better able to learn and adapt to changes in the workplace.[71] In sum, an impressive body of evidence shows organizations can facilitate change by selecting people predisposed to accept it.

- *Explicit and implicit coercion.* Coercion is the application of direct threats or force upon the resisters. If management really is determined to close a manufacturing plant whose employees don't accept a pay cut, the company is using coercion. Other examples are threats of transfer, loss of promotions, negative performance evaluations, and a poor letter of recommendation. The advantages and drawbacks of coercion are approximately the same as those for manipulation and co-optation.

As you read *OB in the Workplace,* consider which of the above steps the president of the National Research Council (NRC) used to introduce changes to his staff.

OB in the WORKPLACE
The NRC Changes Its Research Focus to "Market Drivers"

How can leading scientists be convinced to move from basic to applied research? John McDougall, president of the Ottawa-based National Research Council (NRC), Canada's largest science institute, warned his staff in March 2011 that radical change was coming to the organization.[72] In trying to motivate acceptance of the change, he wrote in a memo dated March 2 that "history is an anchor that ties us to the past rather than a sail that catches the wind to power us forward."

He also announced changes in budgeting practices for the NRC, which has an annual budget of $749 million and 4280 employees. Existing research budgets would be reduced by 20 percent and directed to projects of senior management's choice. Eventually, senior management would control 80 percent of research funds.

Many of the scientists that work at the NRC did not react positively to the change. McDougall favours applied research—what he referred to as "market drivers" that can immediately benefit industry and government—but many scientists also see value in basic research.

McDougall's memo noted that senior managers are generally "rallying behind the new agenda. Those who are still hesitant will need our help to develop their courage and conviction." It also promised to "reward good performance (and) find ways to deal with weak performance."

Essentially, McDougall was giving his staff no choice but to get on board—he would control the budget and the reward system, and they would either have to comply or find work elsewhere.

McDougall's memo ended by telling employees that they needed to get "the right attitude and the right behaviour . . . In the months ahead—stay proud, get excited, continue to work and remember 'WE ARE ALL NRC.'" ●

The Politics of Change

No discussion of resistance to change would be complete without a brief mention of the politics of change. Because change invariably threatens the status quo, it inherently implies political activity.[73]

Politics suggests that the demand for change is more likely to come from outside change agents, employees who are new to the organization (who have less invested in the status quo) or managers who are slightly removed from the main power structure. Managers who have spent their entire careers with a single organization and eventually achieve a senior position in the hierarchy are often major impediments to change. It is a very real threat to their status and position. Yet they may be expected to implement changes to demonstrate that they are not merely caretakers.

By acting as change agents, senior managers can convey to stockholders, suppliers, employees, and customers that they are addressing problems and adapting to a dynamic environment. Of course, as you might guess, when forced to introduce change, these long-time power holders tend to introduce incremental change. Radical change is too threatening. This explains why boards of directors that recognize the need for rapid and radical change often turn to outside candidates for new leadership.[74]

You may remember that we discussed politics in Chapter 7 and gave some suggestions on how to more effectively encourage people to go along with your ideas. That chapter also indicated how individuals acquire power, which provides further insight into the ability of some individuals to resist change. *OB in Action—How to Speed Up the Pace of Change* provides some tips for increasing the pace of change.

in ACTION
How to Speed Up the Pace of Change

→ Compel executives to **confront reality** and **agree on ground rules** for working together.

→ Run **a no-slack launch**, and ensure **early, visible victories**.

→ **Limit change initiatives** to three or four.

→ **Move ahead quickly** and confront those not on board.

→ Get **all employees engaged**.

→ **Anticipate** and **defuse** postlaunch blues, midcourse overconfidence, and the feeling of perpetual motion.[75]

✓•⌐**Practise**

((•⌐**Listen**

Audio Chapter Summary

Summary and Implications

1 **What is the purpose of organizational culture?**   Organizational culture is a system of shared meaning held by members that distinguishes the organization from other organizations. Culture provides stability to an organization and gives employees a clear understanding of "the way things are done around here."

2 **How do you create and maintain organizational culture?**   The original culture of an organization is derived from the founder's philosophy. That philosophy then influences what types of employees are hired. The culture of the organization is then reinforced by top management, who signal what is acceptable behaviour and what is not. Employees are socialized into the culture, and will be more easily socialized to the extent that the employee's values match those of the organization.

3 **Can organizational culture have a downside?**   Many of culture's functions are valuable for both the organization and the employee. Culture enhances organizational commitment and increases the consistency of employee behaviour. Culture also reduces ambiguity for employees by telling them what is important and how things are done. However, a strong culture can have a negative effect, such as Enron's pressure-cooker culture, which led to the company's ultimate collapse. Culture can act as a barrier to change, it can make it difficult to create an inclusive environment, and it can hinder the success of mergers and acquisitions.

4 **How do organizations manage change?**   Kurt Lewin argued that successful change in organizations should follow three steps: *unfreezing* the status quo, *moving* to a new state, and *refreezing* the new change to make it permanent. John Kotter built on Lewin's three-step model to create a more detailed eight-step plan for implementing change. Another approach to managing change is action research. *Action research* refers to a change process based on the systematic collection of data and the selection of a change action based on what the analyzed data indicate. Some organizations use appreciative inquiry to manage change. *Appreciative inquiry* seeks to identify the unique qualities and special strengths of an organization, which can then be built on to improve performance.

5 **Why do people and organizations resist change?**   Individuals resist change because of basic human characteristics such as perceptions, personalities, and needs. Organizations resist change because they are conservative, and because change is difficult. The status quo is often preferred by those who feel they have the most to lose if change goes ahead.

MyManagementLab   Study, practise, and explore real business situations with these helpful resources:

- **Study Plan:** Check your understanding of chapter concepts with self-study quizzes.
- **Online Lesson Presentations:** Study key chapter topics and work through interactive assessments to test your knowledge and master management concepts.
- **Videos:** Learn more about the management practices and strategies of real companies.
- **Simulations:** Practise management decision-making in simulated business environments.

P **I** **A** PERSONAL INVENTORY ASSESSMENT

OB at Work

for Review

1. How can an outsider assess an organization's culture?

2. Why do subcultures develop in an organization?'

3. Can an employee survive in an organization if he or she rejects its core values? Explain.

4. What benefits can socialization provide for the organization? For the new employee?

5. How can culture be a liability to an organization?

6. How does Lewin's three-step model of change deal with resistance to change?

7. How does Kotter's eight-step plan for implementing change deal with resistance to change?

8. What are the factors that lead individuals to resist change?

9. What are the factors that lead organizations to resist change?

for Critical Thinking

1. Is socialization brainwashing? Explain.

2. Can you identify a set of characteristics that describes your college's or university's culture? Compare them with several of your peers' lists. How closely do they agree?

3. "Resistance to change is an irrational response." Do you agree or disagree? Explain.

for You

- Carefully consider the culture of any organization at which you are thinking of being employed. You will feel more comfortable in cultures that share your values and expectations.

- When you work in groups on student projects, the groups create mini-cultures of their own. Be aware of the values and norms that are being supported early on in the group's life, as these will greatly influence the group's culture.

- Be aware that change is a fact of life. If you need to change something in yourself, be aware of the importance of creating new systems to replace the old. Saying you want to be healthier, without specifying that you intend to go to the gym three times a week, or eat five servings of fruits and vegetables a day, means that change likely will not occur. It's important to specify goals and behaviours as part of that change.

OB at work

POINT

COUNTERPOINT

Organizational Culture Does Not Change

An organization's culture is made up of relatively stable characteristics. It develops over many years and is rooted in deeply held values to which employees are strongly committed. In addition, there are a number of forces continually operating to maintain a given culture. These would include written statements about the organization's mission and philosophy, the design of physical spaces and buildings, the dominant leadership style, hiring criteria, past promotion practices, entrenched rituals, popular stories about key people and events, the organization's historical performance evaluation criteria, and the organization's formal structure.

Selection and promotion policies are particularly important devices that work against cultural change. Employees chose the organization because they perceived their values as a "good fit" with those of the organization. They become comfortable with that fit and will strongly resist efforts to disturb the equilibrium.

Those in control in organizations will also select senior managers who will continue the current culture. Even attempts to change a culture by going outside the organization to hire a new chief executive are unlikely to be effective. The evidence indicates that the culture is more likely to change the executive than the other way around. Why? It's too entrenched, and change becomes a potential threat to member self-interest.

We are not saying that culture can never be changed. In the unusual case when an organization confronts a survival-threatening crisis—a crisis universally acknowledged as a true life- or-death situation—members of the organization will be responsive to efforts at cultural change. However, anything less than a crisis is unlikely to be effective in bringing about cultural change.

How to Change an Organization's Culture

Changing an organization's culture is extremely difficult, but it *can* be done. The evidence suggests that cultural change is most likely to occur when most or all of the following conditions exist:

- *A dramatic crisis.* This is the shock that undermines the status quo and calls into question the relevance of the current culture. Examples of these crises might be a surprising financial setback, the loss of a major customer, or a dramatic technological breakthrough by a competitor.
- *Turnover in leadership.* New top leadership, which can provide an alternative set of key values, may be perceived as more capable of responding to the crisis. This would definitely be the organization's chief executive, but also might need to include all senior management positions.
- *Young and small organization.* The younger the organization is, the less entrenched its culture will be. It is also easier for management to communicate its new values when the organization is small.
- *Weak culture.* The more widely held a culture is and the higher the agreement among members on its values, the more difficult it will be to change. Conversely, weak cultures are more open to change than strong ones.

Efforts directed at changing organizational culture don't usually yield immediate or dramatic results. For, in the final analysis, cultural change is a lengthy process—measured in years, not months. But we can ask the question "Can culture be changed?" and the answer is "Yes!"

LEARNING ABOUT **YOURSELF** EXERCISE

What Kind of Organizational Culture Fits You Best?

For each of the following statements, circle the level of agreement or disagreement that you personally feel:

SA = Strongly agree

A = Agree

U = Uncertain

D = Disagree

SD = Strongly disagree

1. I like being part of a team and having my performance assessed in terms of my contribution to the team.	SA	A	U	D	SD
2. No person's needs should be compromised in order for a department to achieve its goals.	SA	A	U	D	SD
3. I like the thrill and excitement of taking risks.	SA	A	U	D	SD
4. If a person's job performance is inadequate, it's irrelevant how much effort he or she made.	SA	A	U	D	SD
5. I like things to be stable and predictable.	SA	A	U	D	SD
6. I prefer managers who provide detailed and rational explanations for their decisions.	SA	A	U	D	SD
7. I like to work where there isn't a great deal of pressure and where people are essentially easygoing.	SA	A	U	D	SD

Scoring Key:

For items 1, 2, 3, 4, and 7, score as follows: Strongly agree = +2, Agree = +1, Uncertain = 0, Disagree = −1, Strongly disagree = −2.

For items 5 and 6, reverse the score (Strongly agree = −2, and so on). Add up your total. Your score will fall somewhere between +14 and −14.

What does your score mean? The lower your score, the more comfortable you will be in a formal, mechanistic, rule-oriented, and structured culture. This is often associated with large corporations and government agencies. Positive scores indicate a preference for informal, humanistic, flexible, and innovative cultures, which are more likely to be found in research units, advertising firms, high-tech companies, and small businesses.

PERSONAL INVENTORY ASSESSMENT

Company Culture Assessment: Employees usually work best when there is alignment between the company culture and their own cultural preferences. Use this scale to assess which culture is the best fit for you.

Organizational Structure Assessment: Personality as well as other factors can influence which organizational structure you prefer. Use this scale to determine what type of cultural structure would be the best fit for you.

Innovation Attitude Scale: What is your attitude toward innovation? Use this scale to help determine if you would work well in occupations and industries that require high levels of innovation.

What's My Comfort with Change?: Some people deal well with change while others do not. Use this scale to determine your own comfort with change. This information can help in career selection, since some occupations and industries experience more change than others.

Leading Positive Change: Change leaders require a complex mix of skills and abilities. Use this scale to assess your ability to lead positive change within an organization.

BREAKOUT **GROUP** EXERCISES

Form small groups to discuss the following topics, as assigned by your instructor:

1. Identify artifacts of culture in your current or previous workplace. From these artifacts, would you conclude that the organization has a strong or weak culture?

2. Have you or someone you know worked somewhere where the culture was strong? What was your reaction to that strong culture? Did you like that environment, or would you prefer to work where there is a weaker culture? Why?

3. Reflect on either the culture of one of your classes or the culture of the organization where you work, and identify characteristics of that culture that could be changed. How might these changes be made?

WORKING WITH OTHERS EXERCISE

The Beacon Aircraft Company

Objectives

1. To illustrate how forces for change and stability must be managed in organizational change programs.

2. To illustrate the effects of alternative change techniques on the relative strength of forces for change and forces for stability.[76]

The Situation

The marketing division of the Beacon Aircraft Company has undergone two reorganizations in the past two years. Initially, its structure changed from a functional one, in which employees were organized within departments, to a matrix form, in which employees from several different functions reported both to their own manager and to a project manager. But the matrix structure did not satisfy some functional managers. They complained that the structure confused the authority and responsibility relationships.

In reaction to these complaints, the marketing manager revised Beacon's structure back to the functional form. This new structure had a marketing group and several project groups. The project groups were managed by project managers with a few general staff members, but no functional specialists, such as people from marketing, were assigned to these groups.

After the change, some problems began to surface. Project managers complained that they could not obtain adequate assistance from functional staff members. It not only took more time to obtain necessary assistance, but it also created problems in establishing stable relationships with functional staff members. Since these problems affected their services to customers, project managers demanded a change in the organizational structure—probably again toward a matrix structure. Faced with these complaints and demands from project managers, the vice-president is pondering another reorganization. He has requested an outside consultant to help him in the reorganization plan.

The Procedure

1. Divide yourselves into groups of 5 to 7 and take the role of consultants.

2. Each group identifies the driving and restraining forces found in the firm. List these forces.

The Driving Forces	The Restraining Forces
_____	_____
_____	_____
_____	_____
_____	_____

3. Each group develops a set of strategies for increasing the driving forces and another set for reducing the restraining forces.

4. Each group prepares a list of changes it wants to introduce.

5. The class reassembles and hears each group's recommendations.

OB at work

Is There Room for Snooping in an Organization's Culture?

Although some of the spying Hewlett-Packard performed on some members of its board of directors in 2006 appeared to violate California law, much of it was legal. Moreover, many companies spy on their employees—sometimes with and sometimes without their knowledge or consent. Organizations differ in their culture of surveillance. Some differences are due to the type of business. A US Department of Defense contractor has more reason—perhaps even an obligation—to spy on its employees than does an orange juice producer.

However, surveillance in most industries is on the upswing. There are several reasons for this, including the huge growth of two sectors with theft and security problems (services and information technology, respectively) and the increased availability of surveillance technology.

Consider the following surveillance actions and, for each action, decide whether it would never be ethical (mark *N*), would sometimes be ethical (mark *S*), or would always be ethical (mark *A*). For those you mark *S*, indicate what factors your judgment would depend on.

1. Sifting through an employee's trash for evidence of wrongdoing

2. Periodically reading email messages for disclosure of confidential information or inappropriate use

3. Conducting video surveillance of workspace

4. Monitoring websites visited by employees and determining the appropriateness and work-relatedness of those visited

5. Recording phone conversations

6. Posing as a job candidate, an investor, a customer, or a colleague (when the real purpose is to solicit information)

Would you be less likely to work for an employer that engaged in some of these methods? Why or why not? Do you think use of surveillance says something about an organization's culture?

Is a 5S Culture for You?

Jay Scovie looked at his workspace.[77] He took pride in how nice and tidy he had made it look. As it turns out, his pride was misplaced. Sweeping visible clutter from your workspace by packing it into boxes hidden in a closet was not acceptable to his employer, Japanese manufacturer Kyocera. Scovie's habit drew the attention of Dan Brown, Kyocera's newly appointed inspector. "It became a topic of repeated conversation," Scovie said.

Why the obsession with order? Kyocera has joined a growing list of organizations that base their culture on 5S, a concept borrowed from lean manufacturing and based on five phases or principles:

1. **Sorting** (*Seiri*). Going through all tools, materials, and supplies so as to keep only what is essential.

2. **Straightening** (*Seiton*). Arranging tools, supplies, equipment, and parts in a manner that promotes maximum efficiency. For everything there should be a place, and everything should be in its place.

3. **Shining** (*Seiso*). Systematic cleaning to make the workplace and workspace as clean and neat as possible. At the end of the shift or workday, everything is left as it was when the workday started.

4. **Standardizing** (*Seiketsu*). Knowing exactly what your responsibilities are to keep the first three S's.

5. **Sustaining** (*Shitsuke*). Maintaining and reviewing standards, rigorous review, and inspection to ensure order does not slowly slip back into disorder or chaos.

Other companies are following Kyocera in making 5S an important part of their culture, including London, Ontario-based 3M Canada, Markham, Ontario-based Steelcase, and St. Thomas, Ontario-based Waltec. Lawn mower manufacturer Toro organizes printer output according to 5S principles, and Virginia Mason Hospital in Seattle uses 5S to coordinate office space and arrange the placement of medical equipment, such as stethoscopes. Paul Levy, president and CEO of Beth Israel Deaconess Medical Center in Boston, has used 5S to reduce errors and time lost searching for equipment.

At Kyocera, Brown exercises some discretion—he asked one employee to remove a hook on her door while allowing another to keep a whale figurine on her desk. "You have to figure out how to balance being too picky with upholding the purpose of the program," he said. While Brown was happy with Scovie's desk (if not the closet), he wanted to look inside. Scovie tried to redirect the conversation but relented when Brown pressed. Inside one of Scovie's desk drawers was a box full of CDs, small electronic devices, and items Kyocera no longer makes. "Obviously, we're at the sorting stage here," Scovie told Brown.

Questions

1. What would you see as the value in Kyocera using 5S?

2. What are some advantages and disadvantages of trying to impose a similar culture in Canadian companies?

3. What might your response be to having to engage in the 5S principles in your workplace?

FROM CONCEPTS TO SKILLS

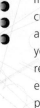

How to "Read" an Organization's Culture

The ability to read and assess an organization's culture can be a valuable skill.[78]

If you are looking for a job, you will want to choose an employer whose culture is compatible with your values and in which you will feel comfortable. If you can accurately assess a prospective employer's culture before you make your decision, you may be able to save yourself a lot of grief and reduce the likelihood of making a poor choice. Similarly, you will undoubtedly have business transactions with numerous organizations during your professional career. You will be trying to sell a product or service, negotiate a contract, arrange a joint venture, or you may merely be seeking out which individual in an organization controls certain decisions. The ability to assess another organization's culture can be a definite plus in successfully completing these pursuits.

For the sake of simplicity, we will approach the problem of reading an organization's culture from that of a job applicant. We will assume that you are interviewing for a job. Here is a list of things you can do and questions to ask to help learn about a potential employer's culture:

- Observe the physical surroundings. Pay attention to signs, pictures, style of dress, length of hair, degree of openness between offices, and office furnishings and arrangements.

- With whom are you meeting? Just the person who would be your immediate manager? Or potential colleagues, managers from other departments, or senior executives? Afterwards, based on what they revealed, to what degree do people other than the immediate manager have input into hiring decisions?

- How would you characterize the style of the people you met? Formal? Casual? Serious? Jovial?

- Does the organization have formal rules and regulations printed in a human resource policy manual? If so, how detailed are these policies?

- Ask questions of the people you meet. The most valid and reliable information tends to come from asking the same questions of many people (to see how closely their responses align) and by talking with boundary spanners. *Boundary spanners* are employees whose work links them to the external environment. This includes jobs such as human resource interviewer, salesperson, purchasing agent, labour negotiator, public relations specialist, and company lawyer.

Questions that will give you insights into organizational processes and practices might include the following:

- What is the background of the founders?

- What is the background of current senior managers? What are their functional specializations? Were they promoted from within or hired from outside?

- How does the organization integrate new employees? Is there an orientation program? Training? If so, could you describe these features?

- How does your manager define his or her job success? (Amount of profit? Serving customers? Meeting deadlines? Acquiring budget increases?)

- How would you define fairness in terms of reward allocations?

- Can you identify some people here who are on the "fast track"? What do you think has put them on the fast track?

- Can you identify someone who seems to be considered a deviant in the organization? How has the organization responded to this person?

- Can you describe a decision that someone made here that was well received?

- Can you describe a decision that did not work out well? What were the consequences for the decision maker?

- Could you describe a crisis or critical event that has occurred recently in the organization? How did top management respond? What was learned from this experience?

Practising Skills

You are the nursing supervisor at a community hospital employing both emergency-room and floor nurses. Each of these teams of nurses tends to work almost exclusively with others doing the same job. In your professional reading, you have come across the concept of cross-training nursing teams and giving them more varied responsibilities, which in turn has been shown to both improve patient care and lower costs. You call the two team leaders, Sue and Scott, into your office to explain that you want the nursing teams to move to this approach. To your surprise, they are both opposed to the idea. Sue says she and the other emergency-room nurses feel they are needed in the ER, where they fill the most vital role in the hospital. They work special hours when needed, do whatever tasks are required, and often work in difficult and stressful circumstances. They think the floor nurses have relatively easy jobs for the pay they receive. Scott, the leader of the floor nurse team, tells you that his group believes the ER nurses lack the special training and extra experience that the floor nurses bring to the hospital. The floor nurses claim they have the heaviest responsibilities and do the most exacting work. Because they have ongoing contact with patients and families, they believe they should not be called away from vital floor duties to help the ER nurses complete their tasks. Now that you are faced with this resistance, how can you most effectively introduce the cross-training model?

Reinforcing Skills

1. Choose two courses that you are taking this term, ideally in different faculties, and describe the culture of the classroom in each. What are the similarities and differences? What values about learning might you infer from your observations of culture?

2. Compare the atmosphere or feeling you get from various organizations. Because of the number and wide variety that you will find, it will probably be easiest for you to do this exercise using restaurants, retail stores, or banks. Based on the atmosphere that you observe, what type of organizational culture do you think these organizations might have? If you can, interview three employees at each organization for their descriptions of their organization's culture.

3. Think about changes (major and minor) that you have dealt with over the past year. Perhaps these changes involved other people and perhaps they were personal. Did you resist the change? Did others resist the change? How did you overcome your resistance or the resistance of others to the change?

4. Interview a manager at three different organizations about a change he or she has introduced. What was the manager's experience in bringing in the change? How did the manager manage resistance to the change?

ENDNOTES

Chapter 1

1 Vignette based on C. Atchison, "The Gen Y Whisperer," *PROFIT*, June 1, 2011, http://www.profitguide.com/manage-grow/human-resources/the-gen-y-whisperer-30187; thanks to Grail Noble for her input.

2 See, for instance, C. Heath and S. B. Sitkin, "Big-B versus Big-O: What Is *Organizational* About Organizational Behavior?" *Journal of Organizational Behavior* 22 (2001), pp. 43–58. For a review of what one eminent researcher believes *should* be included in organizational behaviour, based on survey data, see J. B. Miner, "The Rated Importance, Scientific Validity, and Practical Usefulness of Organizational Behavior Theories: A Quantitative Review," *Academy of Management Learning & Education* 2, no. 3 (September 2003), pp. 250–268.

3 C. R. Farquhar and J. A. Longair, *Creating High-Performance Organizations with People*, Report R164–96 (Ottawa: The Conference Board of Canada, 1996).

4 W. Immen, "People Skills Win Out, Survey Finds," *Globe and Mail*, October 23, 2009, p. B15.

5 See, for instance, J. Lane And T. Hirsch, "Mind the Gap: No 'People Skills, No Job,'" *Globe and Mail*, September 6, 2012.

6 These companies were named in the 100 Top Employers for 2012. See http://www.canadastop100.com/national/

7 I. S. Fulmer, B. Gerhart, and K. S. Scott, "Are the 100 Best Better? An Empirical Investigation of the Relationship Between Being a 'Great Place to Work' and Firm Performance," *Personnel Psychology*, Winter 2003, pp. 965–993.

8 S. E. Humphrey, J. D. Nahrgang, and F. P. Morgeson, "Integrating Motivational, Social, and Contextual Work Design Features: A Meta-analytic Summary and Theoretical Extension of the Work Design Literature," *Journal of Applied Psychology* 92, no. 5 (2007), pp. 1332–1356.

9 *The 2002 National Study of the Changing Workforce* (New York: Families and Work Institute, 2002).

10 Statistics Canada, *Canadian Business Patterns Database*, December 2011.

11 http://www.ic.gc.ca/eic/site/061.nsf/eng/02719.html

12 Statistics Canada, *Canadian Business Patterns Database*, December 2011; and http://www.ic.gc.ca/eic/site/061.nsf/eng/02719.html.

13 Vignette based on C. Atchison, "The Gen Y Whisperer," *PROFIT*, June 1, 2011, http://www.profitguide.com/manage-grow/human-resources/the-gen-y-whisperer-30187

14 See, for example, M. J. Driver, "Cognitive Psychology: An Interactionist View"; R. H. Hall, "Organizational Behavior: A Sociological Perspective"; and C. Hardy, "The Contribution of Political Science to Organizational Behavior," all in J. W. Lorsch, ed., *Handbook of Organizational Behavior* (Englewood Cliffs, NJ: Prentice Hall, 1987), pp. 62–108.

15 Based on W. Chuang and B. Lee, "An Empirical Evaluation of the Overconfidence Hypothesis," *Journal of Banking and Finance*, September 2006, pp. 2489–2515; and A. R. Drake, J. Wong, and S. B. Salter, "Empowerment, Motivation, and Performance: Examining the Impact of Feedback and Incentives on Nonman-agement Employees," *Behavioral Research in Accounting* 19 (2007), pp. 71–89.

16 D. M. Rousseau and S. McCarthy, "Educating Managers from an Evidence-Based Perspective," *Academy of Management Learning & Education* 6, no. 1 (2007), pp. 84–101.

17 K. Holland, "Inside the Minds of Your Employees," *New Yorker*, January 28, 2007.

18 "Fifty Organizations Named to Aon Hewitt's Annual Best Employers in Canada List," October 20, 2011, https://ceplb03.hewitt.com/bestemployers/canada/pdfs/AonHewittBest-Employers2012.pdf

19 S. Brearton and J. Daly, "The 50 Best Companies to Work for in Canada," *Report on Business*, March 21, 2009, http://www.theglobeandmail.com/report-on-business/rob-magazine/the-fifty-best-companies-to-work-for-in-canada/article503896/

20 R. T. Mowday, L. W. Porter, and R. M. Steers, *Employee Organization Linkages: The Psychology of Commitment, Absenteeism, and Turnover* (New York: Academic Press, 1982).

21 Vignette based on C. Atchison, "The Gen Y Whisperer," *PROFIT*, June 1, 2011, http://www.profitguide.com/manage-grow/human-resources/the-gen-y-whisperer-30187

22 J. Morrissy, "Canadian Workers among Most Dissatisfied in World," *Vancouver Sun*, June 25, 2011; and B. Lindenberg, "Employee Engagement: Do Benefits Make a Difference?" *Benefits Canada*, July 28, 2011, http://www.benefitscanada.com/benefits/other/employee-engagement-do-employee-benefits-make-a-difference-18960

23 "2011 Best Workplaces in Canada," Great Places to Work, http://www.greatplacetowork.ca/news/index.php?date=1494; and http://www.microsoft.com/canada/potential/investing_in_canadian_communities.aspx

24 T. A. Judge, C. J. Thoresen, J. E. Bono, and G. R. Patton, "The Job Satisfaction–Job Performance Relationship: A Qualitative and Quantitative Review," *Psychological Bulletin* 127 (2001), pp. 376–407; and M. Riketta, "The Causal Relation between Job Attitudes and Performance: A Meta-analysis of Panel Studies," *Journal of Applied Psychology* 93, no. 2 (2008), pp. 472–481.

25 S. C. Payne and S. S. Webber, "Effects of Service Provider Attitudes and Employment Status on Citizenship Behaviors and Customers' Attitudes and Loyalty Behavior," *Journal of Applied Psychology* 91, no. 2 (2006), pp. 365–378; and H. Liao and D. E. Rupp, "The Impact of Justice Climate and Justice Orientation on Work Outcomes: A Cross-Level Multifoci Framework," *Journal of Applied Psychology* 90, no. 2 (2005), pp. 242–256.

26 S. Findlay, "Employee Loyalty Takes a Nasty Fall," *Macleans.ca*, July 30, 2009.

27 B. Dumaine, "The New Non-Manager Managers," *Fortune*, February 22, 1993, pp. 80–84.

28 "Wanted: Teammates, Crew Members, and Cast Members: But No Employees," *Wall Street Journal*, April 30, 1996, p. A1.

29 S. Ross, "U.S. Managers Fail to Fit the Bill in New Workplace: Study," *Reuters News Agency*, November 19, 1999.

30 C. Atchison, "Secrets of Canada's Best Bosses," *PROFIT*, February 16, 2011, http://www.profitguide.com/manage-grow/leadership/secrets-of-canada%E2%80%99s-best-bosses-30084

31 D. M. Mayer, M. Kuenzi, R. Greenbaum, M. Bardes, and R. Salvador, "How Low Does Ethical Leadership Flow? Test of a Trickle-Down Model," *Organizational Behavior and Human Decision Processes* 108, no. 1 (2009), pp. 1–13; and A. Ardichvili, J. A. Mitchell, and D. Jondle, "Characteristics of Ethical Business Cultures," *Journal of Business Ethics* 85, no. 4 (2009), pp. 445–451.

32 The Conference Board of Canada, *Employability Skills 2000+*, http://www.conferenceboard.ca/topics/education/learning-tools/employability-skills.aspx

33 T. Belford, "Strategy for the New Economy," *Financial Post* (*National Post*), March 14, 2005, p. FP9.

34 From G. Johnson, "Bombardier: Giving Women Wings," *Globe and Mail*, February 20, 2011, http://theglobeandmail.com/report-on-business/careers/top-employers/bombardier-giving-women-wings/article567311/?service=mobile

35 Based on http://www.sgicanada.ca/sk/about/articles/2012/calendarcontest.html; http://www.eluta.ca/diversity-at-sgi; http://www.sgi.sk.ca/careers/whatweoffer.html; and K.-A. Riess, "SGI among Top 100 Diversity Employers," *StarPhoenix*, April 5, 2008, p. F12.

36 June 2011 figures, as reported at http://www.statcan.gc.ca/subjects-sujets/labour-travail/lfs-epa/t110708a2-eng.htm

37 See, for instance, M. Workman and W. Bommer, "Redesigning Computer Call Center Work: A Longitudinal Field Experiment," *Journal of Organizational Behavior*, May 2004, pp. 317–337.

38 Statistics Canada, "Study: Temporary Employment in the Downturn (1997–2009)," *The Daily*, November 26, 2010, http://www.statcan.gc.ca/daily-quotidien/101126/dq101126b-eng.htm

39 http://www.statcan.gc.ca/subjects-sujets/labour-travail/lfs-epa/t110708a1-eng.htm

40 Seasonally adjusted numbers. See Statistics Canada, "Study: Temporary Employment in the Downturn (1997–2009)," *The Daily*, November 26, 2010, http://www.statcan.gc.ca/daily-quotidien/101126/dq101126b-eng.htm

41 Statistics Canada, "Study: Temporary Employment in the Downturn (1997–2009)," *The Daily*, November 26, 2010, http://www.statcan.gc.ca/daily-quotidien/101126/dq101126b-eng.htm

42 P. Drucker, *Management: Tasks, Responsibilities, Practices* (New York: Harper & Row, 1974).

43 H. Evanschitzky, C. Groening, V. Mittal, and M. Wunderlich, "How Employer and Employee Satisfaction Affect Customer Satisfaction: An Application to Franchise Services," *Journal of Service Research* 14, no. 2 (2010), p. 136.

44 A. J. Rucci, S. P. Kirn, and R. T. Quinn, "The Employee–Customer–Profit Chain at Sears," *Harvard Business Review*, January–February 1998, pp. 83–97.

45 D. W. Organ, *Organizational Citizenship Behavior: The Good Soldier Syndrome* (Lexington, MA: Lexington Books, 1988), p. 4.

46 M. G. Ehrhart and S. E. Naumann, "Organizational Citizenship Behavior in Work Groups: A Group Norms Approach," *Journal of Applied Psychology* 89, no. 6 (December 1, 2004), pp. 960–974.

47 "Corporate Culture," *Canadian HR Reporter* 17, no. 21 (December 6, 2004), pp. 7–11.

48 See, for example, P. M. Podsakoff and S. B. MacKenzie, "Organizational Citizenship Behavior and Sales Unit Effectiveness," *Journal of Marketing Research*, August 1994, pp. 351–363; P. M. Podsakoff, M. Ahearne, and S. B. MacKenzie, "Organizational Citizenship Behavior and the Quantity and Quality of Work Group Performance," *Journal of Applied Psychology*, April 1997, pp. 262–270; L. A. Bettencourt, K. Gwinner, and M. L. Meuter, "A Comparison of Attitude, Personality, and Knowledge Predictors of Service-Oriented Organizational Citizenship Behaviors," *Journal of Applied Psychology* 86 (2001), pp. 29–41; and E. W. Morrison, "Organizational Citizenship Behavior as a Critical Link Between HRM Practices and Service Quality," *Human Resource Management* 35 (1996), pp. 493–512.

49 See, for instance, V. S. Major, K. J. Klein, and M. G. Ehrhart, "Work Time, Work Interference with Family, and Psychological Distress," *Journal of Applied Psychology*, June 2002, pp. 427–436; D. Brady, "Rethinking the Rat Race," *BusinessWeek*, August 26, 2002, pp. 142–143; J. M. Brett and L. K. Stroh, "Working 61 Plus Hours a Week: Why Do Managers Do It?" *Journal of Applied Psychology*, February 2003, pp. 67–78.

50 See, for instance, *The 2002 National Study of the Changing Workforce* (New York: Families and Work Institute, 2002).

51 Cited in S. Armour, "Workers Put Family First Despite Slow Economy, Jobless Fears," *USA Today*, June 2, 2002, p. B3.

52 M. Peters, "Generation Y: Challenging Employers to Provide Balance," *Family Connections* 12, no. 2 (Summer 2008), http://www.bccf.ca/all/resources/generation-y-challenging-employers-provide-balance

53 F. Luthans and C. M. Youssef, "Emerging Positive Organizational Behavior," *Journal of Management*, June 2007, pp. 321–349; and J. E. Dutton and S. Sonenshein, "Positive Organizational Scholarship," in *Encyclopedia of Positive Psychology*, ed. C. Cooper and J. Barling (Thousand Oaks, CA: Sage, 2007).

54 L. M. Roberts, G. Spreitzer, J. Dutton, R. Quinn, E. Heaphy, and B. Barker, "How to Play to Your Strengths," *Harvard Business Review*, January 2005, pp. 1–6; and L. M. Roberts, J. E. Dutton, G. M. Spreitzer, E. D. Heaphy, and R. E. Quinn, "Composing the Reflected Best-Self Portrait: Becoming Extraordinary in Work Organizations," *Academy of Management Review* 30, no. 4 (2005), pp. 712–736.

55 D. Flavelle, "Rona Sees Growth Here: Home Reno Sales Flat during Make-or-Break Season but Canadian Retailer Keeps Faith in Diversification," *Toronto Star*, April 20, 2011, p. B1.

56 Based on "Lying at Work Could Get You Fired," *UPI*, March 5, 2006; "Brain Scans Detect More Activity in Those Who Lie," *Reuters*, November 29, 2004; and P. Ekman and E. L. Rosenberg, *What the Face Reveals: Basic and Applied Studies of Spontaneous Expression Using the Facial Action Coding System (CAPS)*, 2nd ed. (New York: Oxford University Press, 2004).

57 Based on K. H. Hammonds, "Handle with Care," *Fast Company*, August 2002, pp. 103–107.

58 R. E. Quinn, *Beyond Rational Management: Mastering the Paradoxes and Competing Demands of High Performance* (San Francisco: Jossey-Bass, 1991); R. E. Quinn, S. R. Faerman, M. P. Thompson, and M. R. McGrath, *Becoming a Master Manager: A Competency Framework* (New York: John Wiley & Sons, 1990); and K. Cameron and R. E. Quinn, *Diagnosing and Changing Organizational Culture: Based on the Competing Values Framework* (Reading, MA: Addison Wesley Longman, 1999).

59 R. E. Quinn, S. R. Faerman, M. P. Thompson, and M. R. McGrath, *Becoming a Master Manager: A Competency Framework* (New York: John Wiley & Sons, 1990).

60 D. Maley, "Canada's Top Women CEOs," *Maclean's*, October 20, 1997, pp. 52+.

61 Written by Nancy Langton and Joy Begley © 1999. (The events described are based on an actual situation, although the participants, as well as the centre, have been disguised.)

Chapter 2

1 Vignette based on http://www.retailcouncil.org/news/media/press/2007/pr20070516.asp; "Wal-Mart Canada Named One of Canada's Best Employers," http://www.newswire.ca/en/releases/archive/January2007/02/c2780.html; "Walmart Canada to Open First Supercentre in Manitoba," *Canada NewsWire*,

May 12, 2011; and C. Persaud, "Walmart Canada to Face Steep Competition Once Target Arrives," *MarketNews,* July 8, 2011, http://www.marketnews.ca/LatestNewsHeadlines/Walmart-CanadatoFaceSteepCompetitionOnceTargetArrives.html; and http://www.workplaceinstitute.org/press-releases/2011-best-employers-awards-winners/

2 B. Nyhan and J. Reifler, "When Corrections Fail: The Persistence of Political Misperceptions" *Political Behavior* 32, no. 2 (2010), pp. 303–330.

3 D. Wood, P. Harms, and S. Vazire, "Perceiver Effects as Projective Tests: What Your Perceptions of Others Say About You," *Journal of Personality and Social Psychology* 99, no. 1 (2010), pp. 174–190.

4 H. H. Kelley, "Attribution in Social Interaction," in *Attribution: Perceiving the Causes of Behavior,* ed. E. Jones, D. Kanouse, H. Kelley, N. Nisbett, S. Valins, and B. Weiner (Morristown, NJ: General Learning Press, 1972).

5 See L. Ross, "The Intuitive Psychologist and His Shortcomings," in *Advances in Experimental Social Psychology,* vol. 10, ed. L. Berkowitz (Orlando, FL: Academic Press, 1977), pp. 174–220; and A. G. Miller and T. Lawson, "The Effect of an Informational Option on the Fundamental Attribution Error," *Personality and Social Psychology Bulletin,* June 1989, pp. 194–204.

6 M. J. Young, M. W. Morris, V. M. Scherwin. "Managerial Mystique: Magical Thinking in Judgments of Managers' Vision, Charisma, and Magnetism," *Journal of Management,* May 2011, published online before print, http://jom.sagepub.com/content/early/2011/04/29/0149206311406284

7 Columbia Business School, "Dynamics Behind Magical Thinking and Charismatic Leadership Revealed," *ScienceDaily,* July 15, 2011.

8 N. Epley and D. Dunning, "Feeling 'Holier Than Thou': Are Self-Serving Assessments Produced by Errors in Self- or Social Predictions?" *Journal of Personality and Social Psychology* 79, no. 6 (2000), pp. 861–875.

9 Based on N. Hall, "Lawyer Awarded $100,000 By B.C. Human Rights Tribunal for Discrimination," *Vancouver Sun,* July 18, 2011; and *Gichuru v. The Law Society of British Columbia* (No. 9), 2011 BCHRT 185, http://bit.ly/ndnd4O

10 M. C. Frame, K. J. Roberto, A. E. Schwab, and C. T. Harris, "What Is Important on the Job? Differences across Gender, Perspective, and Job Level," *Journal of Applied Social Psychology* 40, no. 1 (January 2010), pp. 36–56.

11 S. E. Asch, "Forming Impressions of Personality," *Journal of Abnormal and Social Psychology,* July 1946, pp. 258–290.

12 A. Parducci, "Category Judgment: A Range-Frequency Model," *Psychological Review* 72, no. 6 (November 1965), pp. 407–418; D. M. O'Reilly, R. A. Leitch, and D. H. Wedell, "The Effects of Immediate Context on Auditors' Judgments of Loan Quality," *Auditing* 23, no. 1 (2004), pp. 89–105; and J. DeCoster and H. M. Claypool, "A Meta-analysis of Priming Effects on Impression Formation Supporting a General Model of Information Biases," *Personality & Social Psychology Review* 8, no. 1 (2004), pp. 2–27.

13 http://www.timescolonist.com/entertainment/UVic+grad+student+launches+First+Nations+music+website/5594608/story.html#ixzz1bugKFx8q

14 See, for example, G. N. Powell, "The Good Manager: Business Students' Stereotypes of Japanese Managers Versus Stereotypes of American Managers," *Group & Organizational Management,* March 1992, pp. 44–56; C. Ostroff and L. E. Atwater, "Does Whom You Work with Matter? Effects of Referent Group Gender and Age Composition on Managers' Compensation," *Journal of Applied Psychology,* August 2003, pp. 725–740; M. E. Heilman, A. S. Wallen, D. Fuchs, and M. M. Tamkins, "Penalties for Success: Reactions to Women Who Succeed at Male Gender-Typed Tasks," *Journal of Applied Psychology,* June 2004, pp. 416–427; and R. A. Posthuma and M. A. Campion, "Age Stereotypes

in the Workplace: Common Stereotypes, Moderators, and Future Research Directions," *Journal of Management* 35, no. 1 (2009), pp. 158–188.

15 J. L. Eberhardt, P. G. Davies, V. J. Purdic-Vaughns, and S. L. Johnson, "Looking Deathworthy: Perceived Stereotypicality of Black Defendants Predicts Capital-Sentencing Outcomes," *Psychological Science* 17, no. 5 (2006), pp. 383–386.

16 J. C. Ziegert and P. J. Hanges, "Employment Discrimination: The Role of Implicit Attitudes, Motivation, and a Climate for Racial Bias," *Journal of Applied Psychology* 90, no. 3 (May 2005), pp. 553–562; and D. Pager and L. Quillian, "Walking the Talk? What Employers Say Versus What They Do," *American Sociological Review* 70, no. 3 (June 2005), pp. 355–380.

17 J. D. Remedios, A. L. Chasteen, and J. D. Paek, "Not All Prejudices Are Experienced Equally: Comparing Experiences Of Racism And Sexism In Female Minorities," *Group Processes & Intergroup Relations,* June 11, 2011, published online before print, http://gpi.sagepub.com/content/early/2011/06/17/1368430211411594

18 K. A. Martin, A. R. Sinden, J. C. Fleming, "Inactivity May Be Hazardous to Your Image: The Effects of Exercise Participation on Impression Formation," *Journal of Sport & Exercise Psychology* 22, no. 4 (December 2000), pp. 283–291.

19 F. Yuan and R. W. Woodman, "Innovative Behavior in the Workplace: The Role of Performance and Image Outcome Expectations." *Academy of Management Journal* 53, no. 2 (2010), pp. 323–342.

20 J. K. Harter, F. L. Schmidt, J. W. Asplund, E. A. Killham, and S. Agrawal, "Causal Impact of Employee Work Perceptions on the Bottom Line of Organizations," *Perspectives on Psychological Science* 5, no. 4 (2010), pp. 378–389.

21 Y. H. Kim, C. Y. Chiu, and Z. Zou, "Know Thyself: Misperceptions of Actual Performance Undermine Achievement Motivation, Future Performance, and Subjective Well-Being," *Journal of Personality and Social Psychology* 99, no. 3 (2010), pp. 395–409.

22 H. G. Heneman III and T. A. Judge, *Staffing Organizations* (Middleton, WI: Mendota House, 2006).

23 J. Willis and A. Todorov, "First Impressions: Making Up Your Mind After a 100ms Exposure to a Face," *Psychological Science,* July 2006, pp. 592–598.

24 See, for example, E. C. Webster, *Decision Making in the Employment Interview* (Montreal: McGill University, Industrial Relations Center, 1964).

25 See, for example, K. F. E. Wong and J. Y. Y. Kwong, "Effects of Rater Goals on Rating Patterns: Evidence from an Experimental Field Study," *Journal of Applied Psychology* 92, no. 2 (2007), pp. 577–585; and S. E. DeVoe and S. S. Iyengar, "Managers' Theories of Subordinates: A Cross-Cultural Examination of Manager Perceptions of Motivation and Appraisal of Performance," *Organizational Behavior and Human Decision Processes,* January 2004, pp. 47–61.

26 D. B. McNatt and T. A. Judge, "Boundary Conditions of the Galatea Effect: A Field Experiment and Constructive Replication," *Academy of Management Journal,* August 2004, pp. 550–565; O. B. Davidson and D. Eden, "Remedial Self-Fulfilling Prophecy: Two Field Experiments to Prevent Golem Effects Among Disadvantaged Women," *Journal of Applied Psychology,* June 2000, pp. 386–398; D. Eden, "Self-Fulfilling Prophecies in Organizations," in *Organizational Behavior: The State of the Science,* 2nd ed., ed. J. Greenberg (Mahwah, NJ: Lawrence Erlbaum, 2003), pp. 91–122; and G. Natanovich and D. Eden, "Pygmalion Effects Among Outreach Supervisors and Tutors: Extending Sex Generalizability," *Journal of Applied Psychology* 93, no. 6 (2008), pp. 1382–1389.

27 See, for example, K. F. E. Wong and J. Y. Y. Kwong, "Effects of Rater Goals on Rating Patterns: Evidence from an Experimental

Field Study," *Journal of Applied Psychology* 92, no. 2 (2007), pp. 577–585; and S. E. DeVoe and S. S. Iyengar, "Managers' Theories of Subordinates: A Cross-Cultural Examination of Manager Perceptions of Motivation and Appraisal of Performance," *Organizational Behavior and Human Decision Processes*, January 2004, pp. 47–61.

28 Vignette based on "Personality Counts: Walmart's Frugal, but Target Charms," *CNN Money*, August 19, 2011, http://management. fortune.cnn.com/2011/08/19/personality-counts-walmart-is-frugal-but-target-charms/; and "Target Plans up to 135 Canadian Stores by 2013," *Toronto Star*, September 23, 2011, http://www. thestar.com/business/article/1058457—target-finalizes-its-canadian-stores-inks-deal-with-sobeys

29 G. W. Allport, *Personality: A Psychological Interpretation* (New York: Holt, Rinehart and Winston, 1937), p. 48.

30 K. I. van der Zee, J. N. Zaal, and J. Piekstra, "Validation of the Multicultural Personality Questionnaire in the Context of Personnel Selection," *European Journal of Personality* 17 (2003), pp. S77–S100.

31 S. A. Birkeland, T. M. Manson, J. L. Kisamore, M. T. Brannick, and M. A. Smith, "A Meta-analytic Investigation of Job Applicant Faking on Personality Measures," *International Journal of Selection and Assessment* 14, no. 14 (2006), pp. 317–335.

32 T. A. Judge, C. A. Higgins, C. J. Thoresen, and M. R. Barrick, "The Big Five Personality Traits, General Mental Ability, and Career Success across the Life Span," *Personnel Psychology* 52, no. 3 (1999), pp. 621–652.

33 See D. T. Lykken, T. J. Bouchard Jr., M. McGue, and A. Tellegen, "Heritability of Interests: A Twin Study," *Journal of Applied Psychology*, August 1993, pp. 649–661; R. D. Arvey and T. J. Bouchard Jr., "Genetics, Twins, and Organizational Behavior," in *Research in Organizational Behavior*, vol. 16, ed. B. M. Staw and L. L. Cummings (Greenwich, CT: JAI Press, 1994), pp. 65–66; D. Lykken and A. Tellegen, "Happiness Is a Stochastic Phenomenon," *Psychological Science*, May 1996, pp. 186–189; and W. Wright, *Born That Way: Genes, Behavior, Personality* (New York: Knopf, 1998).

34 S. Srivastava, O. P. John, and S. D. Gosling, "Development of Personality in Early and Middle Adulthood: Set Like Plaster or Persistent Change?" *Journal of Personality and Social Psychology*, May 2003, pp. 1041–1053; and B. W. Roberts, K. E. Walton, and W. Viechtbauer, "Patterns of Mean-Level Change in Personality Traits across the Life Course: A Meta-analysis of Longitudinal Studies," *Psychological Bulletin* 132, no. 1 (2006), pp. 1–25.

35 S. E. Hampson and L. R. Goldberg, "A First Large Cohort Study of Personality Trait Stability Over the 40 Years between Elementary School and Midlife," *Journal of Personality and Social Psychology* 91, no. 4 (2006), pp. 763–779.

36 See A. H. Buss, "Personality as Traits," *American Psychologist*, November 1989, pp. 1378–1388; and D. G. Winter, O. P. John, A. J. Stewart, E. C. Klohnen, and L. E. Duncan, "Traits and Motives: Toward an Integration of Two Traditions in Personality Research," *Psychological Review*, April 1998, pp. 230–250.

37 See, for instance, G. W. Allport and H. S. Odbert, "Trait Names, A Psycholexical Study," *Psychological Monographs* 47, no. 211 (1936); and R. B. Cattell, "Personality Pinned Down," *Psychology Today*, July 1973, pp. 40–46.

38 R. B. Kennedy and D. A. Kennedy, "Using the Myers-Briggs Type Indicator in Career Counseling," *Journal of Employment Counseling*, March 2004, pp. 38–44.

39 G. N. Landrum, *Profiles of Genius* (New York: Prometheus, 1993).

40 See, for instance, D. J. Pittenger, "Cautionary Comments Regarding the Myers-Briggs Type Indicator," *Consulting Psychology Journal: Practice and Research*, Summer 2005, pp. 210–221; L. Bess and R. J. Harvey, "Bimodal Score Distributions and the Myers-Briggs Type Indicator: Fact or Artifact?" *Journal of Personality*

Assessment, February 2002, pp. 176–186; R. M. Capraro and M. M. Capraro, "Myers-Briggs Type Indicator Score Reliability across Studies: A Meta-analytic Reliability Generalization Study," *Educational and Psychological Measurement*, August 2002, pp. 590–602; and R. C. Arnau, B. A. Green, D. H. Rosen, D. H. Gleaves, and J. G. Melancon, "Are Jungian Preferences Really Categorical? An Empirical Investigation Using Taxometric Analysis," *Personality and Individual Differences*, January 2003, pp. 233–251.

41 See, for example, J. M. Digman, "Personality Structure: Emergence of the Five-Factor Model," in M. R. Rosenzweig and L. W. Porter, eds., *Annual Review of Psychology*, vol. 41 (Palo Alto, CA: Annual Reviews, 1990), pp. 417–440; D. B. Smith, P. J. Hanges, and M. W. Dickson, "Personnel Selection and the Five-Factor Model: Reexamining the Effects of Applicant's Frame of Reference," *Journal of Applied Psychology*, April 2001, pp. 304–315; and M. R. Barrick and M. K. Mount, "Yes, Personality Matters: Moving On to More Important Matters," *Human Performance* 18, no. 4 (2005), pp. 359–372.

42 J. B. Hirsh, J. B. Peterson, "Predicting creativity and academic success with a 'Fake-Proof' measure of the Big Five," *Journal of Research in Personality*, 42 (2008), pp. 1323–1333.

43 "New Fake-Proof Personality Test Created," *ScienceDaily*, October 8, 2008, http://www.sciencedaily.com/releases/2008/10/081007102849.htm

44 See, for instance, M. R. Barrick and M. K. Mount, "The Big Five Personality Dimensions and Job Performance: A Meta-analysis," *Personnel Psychology*, Spring 1991, pp. 1–26; G. M. Hurtz and J. J. Donovan, "Personality and Job Performance: The Big Five Revisited," *Journal of Applied Psychology*, December 2000, pp. 869–879; J. Hogan and B. Holland, "Using Theory to Evaluate Personality and Job-Performance Relations: A Socioanalytic Perspective," *Journal of Applied Psychology*, February 2003, pp. 100–112; and M. R. Barrick and M. K. Mount, "Select on Conscientiousness and Emotional Stability," in *Handbook of Principles of Organizational Behavior*, ed. E. A. Locke (Malden, MA: Blackwell, 2004), pp. 15–28.

45 M. K. Mount, M. R. Barrick, and J. P. Strauss, "Validity of Observer Ratings of the Big Five Personality Factors," *Journal of Applied Psychology*, April 1994, p. 272. Additionally confirmed by G. M. Hurtz and J. J. Donovan, "Personality and Job Performance: The Big Five Revisited," *Journal of Applied Psychology* 85 (2000), pp. 869–879; and M. R. Barrick, M. K. Mount, and T. A. Judge, "The FFM Personality Dimensions and Job Performance: Meta-analysis of Meta-analyses," *International Journal of Selection and Assessment* 9 (2001), pp. 9–30.

46 A. E. Poropat, "A Meta-analysis of the Five-Factor Model of Personality and Academic Performance," *Psychological Bulletin* 135, no. 2 (2009), pp. 322–338.

47 F. L. Schmidt and J. E. Hunter, "The Validity and Utility of Selection Methods in Personnel Psychology: Practical and Theoretical Implications of 85 Years of Research Findings," *Psychological Bulletin*, September 1998, p. 272.

48 T. A. Judge and J. E. Bono, "A Rose by Any Other Name. Are Self-Esteem, Generalized Self-Efficacy, Neuroticism, and Locus of Control Indicators of a Common Construct?" in *Personality Psychology in the Workplace*, ed. B. W. Roberts and R. Hogan (Washington, DC: American Psychological Association), pp. 93–118.

49 A. Erez and T. A. Judge, "Relationship of Core Self-Evaluations to Goal Setting, Motivation, and Performance," *Journal of Applied Psychology* 86, no. 6 (2001), pp. 1270–1279.

50 A. N. Salvaggio, B. Schneider, L. H. Nishi, D. M. Mayer, A. Ramesh, and J. S. Lyon, "Manager Personality, Manager Service Quality Orientation, and Service Climate: Test of a Model," *Journal of Applied Psychology* 92, no. 6 (2007), pp. 1741–1750; B. A. Scott and T. A. Judge, "The Popularity Contest at Work: Who Wins, Why, and What Do They Receive?" *Journal of Applied Psychology* 94, no. 1 (2009), pp. 20–33; and T. A. Judge and

C. Hurst, "How the Rich (and Happy) Get Richer (and Happier): Relationship of Core Self-Evaluations to Trajectories in Attaining Work Success," *Journal of Applied Psychology* 93, no. 4 (2008), pp. 849–863.

51 U. Malmendier and G. Tate, "CEO Overconfidence and Corporate Investment," *Journal of Finance* 60, no. 6 (December 2005), pp. 2661–2700.

52 J. J. Dahling, B. G. Whitaker, and P. E. Levy, "The Development and Validation of a New Machiavellianism Scale," *Journal of Management* 35, no. 2 (2009), pp. 219–257.

53 R. Christie and F. L. Geis, *Studies in Machiavellianism* (New York: Academic Press, 1970), p. 312; and N. V. Ramanaiah, A. Byravan, and F. R. J. Detwiler, "Revised Neo Personality Inventory Profiles of Machiavellian and Non-Machiavellian People," *Psychological Reports*, October 1994, pp. 937–938.

54 J. J. Dahling, B. G. Whitaker, and P. E. Levy, "The Development and Validation of a New Machiavellianism Scale," *Journal of Management* 35, no. 2 (2009), pp. 219–257.

55 R. Christie and F. L. Geis, *Studies in Machiavellianism* (New York: Academic Press, 1970).

56 C. Sedikides, E. A. Rudich, A. P. Gregg, M. Kumashiro, and C. Rusbult, "Are Normal Narcissists Psychologically Healthy? Self-Esteem Matters," *Journal of Personality and Social Psychology* 87, no. 3 (2004), pp. 400–416, reviews some of the literature on narcissism.

57 M. Elias, "Study: Today's Youth Think Quite Highly of Themselves," *USA Today*, November 19, 2008, p. 7D; and K. H. Trzesniewski, M. B. Donnellan, and R. W. Robins, "Do Today's Young People Really Think They Are So Extraordinary?" *Psychological Science* 19, no. 2 (2008), pp. 181–188.

58 A. B. Brunell, S. Staats, J. Barden, and J. M. Hupp, "Narcissism and Academic Dishonesty: The Exhibitionism Dimension and the Lack of Guilt," *Personality and Individual Differences* 50, no. 3 (2011), pp. 323–328.

59 M. Maccoby, "Narcissistic Leaders: The Incredible Pros, the Inevitable Cons," *Harvard Business Review*, January–February 2000, pp. 69–77, http://www.maccoby.com/Articles/NarLeaders.shtml

60 W. K. Campbell and C. A. Foster, "Narcissism and Commitment in Romantic Relationships: An Investment Model Analysis," *Personality and Social Psychology Bulletin* 28, no. 4 (2002), pp. 484–495.

61 T. A. Judge, J. A. LePine, and B. L. Rich, "The Narcissistic Personality: Relationship with Inflated Self-Ratings of Leadership and with Task and Contextual Performance," *Journal of Applied Psychology* 91, no. 4 (2006), pp. 762–776.

62 J. Goncalo, F. J. Flynn, and S. H. Kim, "Are Two Narcissists Better Than One? The Link between Narcissism, Perceived Creativity, and Creative Performance," *Personality and Social Psychology Bulletin* 36, no.11 (2010), pp. 1484–1495.

63 See M. Snyder, *Public Appearances/Private Realities: The Psychology of Self-Monitoring* (New York: W. H. Freeman, 1987); and S. W. Gangestad and M. Snyder, "Self-Monitoring: Appraisal and Reappraisal," *Psychological Bulletin*, July 2000, pp. 530–555.

64 See M. Snyder, *Public Appearances/Private Realities: The Psychology of Self-Monitoring* (New York: W. H. Freeman, 1987).

65 H. Oh and M. Kilduff, "The Ripple Effect of Personality on Social Structure: Self-Monitoring Origins of Network Brokerage," *Journal of Applied Psychology* 93, no. 5 (2008), pp. 1155–1164; and A. Mehra, M. Kilduff, and D. J. Brass, "The Social Networks of High and Low Self-Monitors: Implications for Workplace Performance," *Administrative Science Quarterly*, March 2001, pp. 121–146.

66 D. V. Day, D. J. Schleicher, A. L. Unckless, and N. J. Hiller, "Self-Monitoring Personality at Work: A Meta-analytic Investigation

of Construct Validity," *Journal of Applied Psychology*, April 2002, pp. 390–401.

67 R. N. Taylor and M. D. Dunnette, "Influence of Dogmatism, Risk-Taking Propensity, and Intelligence on Decision-Making Strategies for a Sample of Industrial Managers," *Journal of Applied Psychology*, August 1974, pp. 420–423.

68 I. L. Janis and L. Mann, *Decision Making: A Psychological Analysis of Conflict, Choice, and Commitment* (New York: Free Press, 1977); W. H. Stewart Jr. and L. Roth, "Risk Propensity Differences between Entrepreneurs and Managers: A Meta-analytic Review," *Journal of Applied Psychology*, February 2001, pp. 145–153; J. B. Miner and N. S. Raju, "Risk Propensity Differences between Managers and Entrepreneurs and between Low- and High-Growth Entrepreneurs: A Reply in a More Conservative Vein," *Journal of Applied Psychology* 89, no. 1 (2004), pp. 3–13; and W. H. Stewart Jr. and P. L. Roth, "Data Quality Affects Meta-analytic Conclusions: A Response to Miner and Raju (2004) Concerning Entrepreneurial Risk Propensity," *Journal of Applied Psychology* 89, no. 1 (2004), pp. 14–21.

69 J. K. Maner, J. A. Richey, K. Cromer, M. Mallott, C. W. Lejuez, T. E. Joiner, and N. B. Schmidt, "Dispositional Anxiety and Risk-Avoidant Decision Making," *Personality and Individual Differences* 42, no. 4 (2007), pp. 665–675.

70 M. Friedman and R. H. Rosenman, *Type A Behavior and Your Heart* (New York: Alfred A. Knopf, 1974), p. 84.

71 M. Friedman and R. H. Rosenman, *Type A Behavior and Your Heart* (New York: Alfred A. Knopf, 1974), pp. 84–85.

72 K. W. Cook, C. A. Vance, and E. Spector, "The Relation of Candidate Personality with Selection-Interview Outcomes," *Journal of Applied Social Psychology* 30 (2000), pp. 867–885.

73 M. Friedman and R. H. Rosenman, *Type A Behavior and Your Heart* (New York: Alfred A. Knopf, 1974), p. 86.

74 J. M. Crant, "Proactive Behavior in Organizations," *Journal of Management* 26, no. 3 (2000), p. 436.

75 S. E. Seibert, M. L. Kraimer, and J. M. Crant, "What Do Proactive People Do? A Longitudinal Model Linking Proactive Personality and Career Success," *Personnel Psychology*, Winter 2001, p. 850; and J. A. Thompson, "Proactive Personality and Job Performance: A Social Capital Perspective," *Journal of Applied Psychology* 90, no. 5 (2005), pp. 1011–1017.

76 T. S. Bateman and J. M. Crant, "The Proactive Component of Organizational Behavior: A Measure and Correlates," *Journal of Organizational Behavior*, March 1993, pp. 103–118; A. L. Frohman, "Igniting Organizational Change from Below: The Power of Personal Initiative," *Organizational Dynamics*, Winter 1997, pp. 39–53; and J. M. Crant and T. S. Bateman, "Charismatic Leadership Viewed from Above: The Impact of Proactive Personality," *Journal of Organizational Behavior*, February 2000, pp. 63–75.

77 J. M. Crant, "Proactive Behavior in Organizations," *Journal of Management* 26, no. 3 (2000), p. 436.

78 See, for instance, R. C. Becherer and J. G. Maurer, "The Proactive Personality Disposition and Entrepreneurial Behavior among Small Company Presidents," *Journal of Small Business Management*, January 1999, pp. 28–36.

79 S. E. Seibert, J. M. Crant, and M. L. Kraimer, "Proactive Personality and Career Success," *Journal of Applied Psychology*, June 1999, pp. 416–427; and S. E. Seibert, M. L. Kraimer, and J. M. Crant, "What Do Proactive People Do? A Longitudinal Model Linking Proactive Personality and Career Success," *Personnel Psychology*, Winter 2001, p. 850; F. J. Flynn and D. R. Ames, "What's Good for the Goose May Not Be as Good for the Gander: The Benefits of Self-Monitoring for Men and Women in Task Groups and Dyadic Conflicts," *Journal of Applied Psychology* 91, no. 2 (2006), pp. 272–281; and J. D. Kammeyer-Mueller and C. R. Wanberg, "Unwrapping the Organizational Entry Process: Disentangling

Multiple Antecedents and Their Pathways to Adjustment," *Journal of Applied Psychology* 88, no. 5 (2003), pp. 779–794.

80 See, for instance, R. R. McCrae and P. T. Costa, Jr., "Personality Trait Structure as a Human Universal," *American Psychologist,* May 1997, pp. 509–516; S. Yamagata, A. Suzuki, J. Ando, Y. Ono, K. Yutaka, N. Kijima, K. Yoshimura, F. Ostendorf, A. Angleitner, R. Riemann, F. M. Spinath, W. J. Livesley, and K. L. Jang, "Is the Genetic Structure of Human Personality Universal? A Cross-Cultural Twin Study from North America, Europe, and Asia," *Journal of Personality and Social Psychology* 90, no. 6 (2006), pp. 987–998; H. C. Triandis and E. M. Suh, "Cultural Influences on Personality," in *Annual Review of Psychology,* vol. 53, ed. S. T. Fiske, D. L. Schacter, and C. Zahn-Waxler (Palo Alto, CA: Annual Reviews, 2002), pp. 133–160; R. R. McCrae and J. Allik, *The Five-Factor Model of Personality across Cultures* (New York: Kluwer Academic/ Plenum, 2002); and R. R. McCrae, P. T. Costa Jr., T. A. Martin, V. E. Oryol, A. A. Rukavishnikov, I. G. Senin, M. Hřebíčková, and T. Urbanek, "Consensual Validation of Personality Traits across Cultures," *Journal of Research in Personality* 38, no. 2 (2004), pp. 179–201.

81 A. T. Church and M. S. Katigbak, "Trait Psychology in the Philippines," *American Behavioral Scientist,* September 2000, pp. 73–94.

82 J. F. Salgado, "The Five Factor Model of Personality and Job Performance in the European Community," *Journal of Applied Psychology,* February 1997, pp. 30–43.

83 See, for example, D. B. Turban, C. K. Stevens, and F. K. Lee, "Effects of Conscientiousness and Extraversion on New Labor Market Entrants' Job Search: The Mediating Role of Metacognitive Activities and Positive Emotions," *Personnel Psychology* 62 no. 3 (2009), p. 553.

84 S. von Stumm, B. Hell, T. Chamorro-Premuzic, "The Hungry Mind: Intellectual Curiosity Is the Third Pillar of Academic Performance," *Perspectives on Psychological Science* 2 no. 6 (2011), p. 574.

85 J. Pickard, "Misuse of Tests Leads to Unfair Recruitment," *People Management* 2, no. 25 (1996), p. 7.

86 J. Pickard, "Misuse of Tests Leads to Unfair Recruitment," *People Management* 2, no. 25 (1996), p. 7.

87 Vignette based on "Trail Workers Test Walmart's Resistance to Unions," August 15, 2010, *Nelson Life,* http://nelsonlife.com/550/trail-workers-test-walmarts-resistance-to-unions/; and http://www.ratemyemployer.ca/employer/employer.aspx?empID=7575&l=en

88 See, for instance, C. D. Fisher and N. M. Ashkanasy, "The Emerging Role of Emotions in Work Life: An Introduction," *Journal of Organizational Behavior,* Special Issue 2000, pp. 123–129; N. M. Ashkanasy, C. E. J. Hartel, and W. J. Zerbe, eds., *Emotions in the Workplace: Research, Theory, and Practice* (Westport, CT: Quorum Books, 2000); N. M. Ashkanasy and C. S. Daus, "Emotion in the Workplace: The New Challenge for Managers," *Academy of Management Executive,* February 2002, pp. 76–86; and N. M. Ashkanasy, C. E. J. Hartel, and C. S. Daus, "Diversity and Emotion: The New Frontiers in Organizational Behavior Research," *Journal of Management* 28, no. 3 (2002), pp. 307–338.

89 See, for example, L. L. Putnam and D. K. Mumby, "Organizations, Emotion and the Myth of Rationality," in *Emotion in Organizations,* ed. S. Fineman (Thousand Oaks, CA: Sage, 1993), pp. 36–57; and J. Martin, K. Knopoff, and C. Beckman, "An Alternative to Bureaucratic Impersonality and Emotional Labor: Bounded Emotionality at the Body Shop," *Administrative Science Quarterly,* June 1998, pp. 429–469.

90 B. E. Ashforth and R. H. Humphrey, "Emotion in the Workplace: A Reappraisal," *Human Relations,* February 1995, pp. 97–125.

91 S. G. Barsade and D. E. Gibson, "Why Does Affect Matter in Organizations?" *Academy of Management Perspectives,* February 2007, pp. 36–59.

92 See N. H. Frijda, "Moods, Emotion Episodes and Emotions," in *Handbook of Emotions,* ed. M. Lewis and J. M. Haviland (New York: Guilford Press, 1993), pp. 381–403.

93 H. M. Weiss and R. Cropanzano, "Affective Events Theory," in *Research in Organizational Behavior,* vol. 18, ed. B. M. Staw and L. L. Cummings (Greenwich, CT: JAI Press, 1996), pp. 17–19.

94 See P. Ekman and R. J. Davidson, eds., *The Nature of Emotions: Fundamental Questions* (Oxford, UK: Oxford University Press, 1994).

95 N. H. Frijda, "Moods, Emotion Episodes and Emotions," in *Handbook of Emotions,* ed. M. Lewis and J. M. Haviland (New York: Guilford Press, 1993), pp. 381–403.

96 See P. Ekman and R. J. Davidson, eds., *The Nature of Emotions: Fundamental Questions* (Oxford, UK: Oxford University Press, 1994).

97 K. Sanford and A. J. Grace, "Emotion and Underlying Concerns during Couples' Conflict: An Investigation of within-Person Change," *Personal Relationships* 18, no. 1 (2011), pp. 96–109.

98 Baylor University, "Exploring How Partners Perceive Each Other's Emotion during a Relationship Fight," *ScienceDaily,* December 16, 2010, http://www.sciencedaily.com/releases/2010/12/101216161514.htm

99 See J. A. Morris and D. C. Feldman, "Managing Emotions in the Workplace," *Journal of Managerial Issues* 9, no. 3 (1997), pp. 257–274; S. Mann, *Hiding What We Feel, Faking What We Don't: Understanding the Role of Your Emotions at Work* (New York: HarperCollins, 1999); and S. M. Kruml and D. Geddes, "Catching Fire without Burning Out: Is There an Ideal Way to Perform Emotion Labor?" in *Emotions in the Workplace,* ed. N. M. Ashkansay, C. E. J. Hartel, and W. J. Zerbe (New York: Quorum Books, 2000), pp. 177–188.

100 P. Ekman, W. V. Friesen, and M. O'Sullivan, "Smiles When Lying," in *What the Face Reveals: Basic and Applied Studies of Spontaneous Expression Using the Facial Action Coding System (FACS),* ed. P. Ekman and E. L. Rosenberg (London: Oxford University Press, 1997), pp. 201–216.

101 A. Grandey, "Emotion Regulation in the Workplace: A New Way to Conceptualize Emotional Labor," *Journal of Occupational Health Psychology* 5, no. 1 (2000), pp. 95–110; and R. Cropanzano, D. E. Rupp, and Z. S. Byrne, "The Relationship of Emotional Exhaustion to Work Attitudes, Job Performance, and Organizational Citizenship Behavior," *Journal of Applied Psychology,* February 2003, pp. 160–169.

102 A. R. Hochschild, "Emotion Work, Feeling Rules, and Social Structure," *American Journal of Sociology,* November 1979, pp. 551–575; W. C. Tsai, "Determinants and Consequences of Employee Displayed Positive Emotions," *Journal of Management* 27, no. 4 (2001), pp. 497–512; M. W. Kramer and J. A. Hess, "Communication Rules for the Display of Emotions in Organizational Settings," *Management Communication Quarterly,* August 2002, pp. 66–80; and J. M. Diefendorff and E. M. Richard, "Antecedents and Consequences of Emotional Display Rule Perceptions," *Journal of Applied Psychology,* April 2003, pp. 284–294.

103 B. M. DePaulo, "Nonverbal Behavior and Self-Presentation," *Psychological Bulletin,* March 1992, pp. 203–243.

104 C. S. Hunt, "Although I Might Be Laughing Loud and Hearty, Deep Inside I'm Blue: Individual Perceptions Regarding Feeling and Displaying Emotions at Work" (paper presented at the Academy of Management Conference, Cincinnati, OH, August 1996), p. 3.

105 R. C. Solomon, "Back to Basics: On the Very Idea of 'Basic Emotions,'" *Journal for the Theory of Social Behaviour* 32, no. 2 (2002), pp. 115–144.

106 C. M. Brotheridge and R. T. Lee, "Development and Validation of the Emotional Labour Scale," *Journal of Occupational & Organizational Psychology* 76, no. 3 (September 2003), pp. 365–379.

107 A. A. Grandey, "When 'the Show Must Go On': Surface Acting and Deep Acting as Determinants of Emotional Exhaustion and Peer-Rated Service Delivery," *Academy of Management Journal,* February 2003, pp. 86–96; and A. A. Grandey, D. N. Dickter, and H. Sin, "The Customer Is Not Always Right: Customer Aggression and Emotion Regulation of Service Employees," *Journal of Organizational Behavior* 25, no. 3 (May 2004), pp. 397–418.

108 J. P. Trougakos, D. J. Beal, S. G. Green, and H. M. Weiss, "Making the Break Count: An Episodic Examination of Recovery Activities, Emotional Experiences, and Positive Affective Displays," *Academy of Management Journal* 51, no. 1 (2008), pp. 131–146.

109 S. Brassen, M. Gamer, and C. "Büchel, Anterior Cingulate Activation Is Related to a Positivity Bias and Emotional Stability in Successful Aging," *Biological Psychiatry* 70, no. 2 (2011), pp. 131–137.

110 A. R. Damasio, *Descartes' Error: Emotion, Reason, and the Human Brain* (New York: Quill, 1994).

111 N. M. Ashkanasy, and C. S. Daus, "Emotion in the Workplace: The New Challenge for Managers," *Academy of Management Executive* 16, no. 1 (2002), pp. 76–86.

112 T. Sy, S. Cote, and R. Saavedra, "The Contagious Leader: Impact of the Leader's Mood on the Mood of Group Members, Group Affective Tone, and Group Processes," *Journal of Applied Psychology* 90, no. 2 (March 2005), pp. 295–305.

113 Based on D. R. Caruso, J. D. Mayer, and P. Salovey, "Emotional Intelligence and Emotional Leadership," in *Multiple Intelligences and Leadership,* ed. R. E. Riggio, S. E. Murphy, and F. J. Pirozzolo (Mahwah, NJ: Lawrence Erlbaum, 2002), p. 70.

114 This section is based on Daniel Goleman, *Emotional Intelligence* (New York: Bantam, 1995); P. Salovey and D. Grewal, "The Science of Emotional Intelligence," *Current Directions in Psychological Science* 14, no. 6 (2005), pp. 281–285; M. Davies, L. Stankov, and R. D. Roberts, "Emotional Intelligence: In Search of an Elusive Construct," *Journal of Personality and Social Psychology,* October 1998, pp. 989–1015; D. Geddes and R. R. Callister, "Crossing the Line(s): A Dual Threshold Model of Anger in Organizations," *Academy of Management Review* 32, no. 3 (2007), pp. 721–746; and J. Ciarrochi, J. P. Forgas, and J. D. Mayer, eds., *Emotional Intelligence in Everyday Life* (Philadelphia: Psychology Press, 2001).

115 M. Seo and L. F. Barrett, "Being Emotional During Decision Making—Good or Bad? An Empirical Investigation," *Academy of Management Journal* 50, no. 4 (2007), pp. 923–940.

116 E. H. O'Boyle, R. H. Humphrey, J. M. Pollack, T. H. Hawver, and P. A. Story, "The Relation between Emotional Intelligence And Job Performance: A Meta-analysis," *Journal of Organizational Behavior* 32, no. 5 (July 2011), pp. 788–818.

117 F. I. Greenstein, *The Presidential Difference: Leadership Style from FDR to Clinton* (Princeton, NJ: Princeton University Press, 2001).

118 M. Maccoby, "To Win the Respect of Followers, Leaders Need Personality Intelligence," *Ivey Business Journal* 72, no. 3 (May–June 2008); J. Reid, "The Resilient Leader: Why EQ Matters," *Business Journal* 72, no. 3 (May–June 2008); and P. Wieand, J. Birchfield, and M. C. Johnson III, "The New Leadership Challenge: Removing the Emotional Barriers to Sustainable Performance in a Flat World," *Ivey Business Journal* 72, no. 4 (July–August 2008).

119 J. Rowlands, "Soft Skills Give Hard Edge," *Globe and Mail,* June 9, 2004, p. C8.

120 P. Wieand, J. Birchfield, and M. C. Johnson III, "The New Leadership Challenge: Removing the Emotional Barriers to Sustainable Performance in a Flat World," *Ivey Business Journal* 72, no. 4 (July–August 2008).

121 C. Cherniss, "The Business Case for Emotional Intelligence," *Consortium for Research on Emotional Intelligence in Organizations,* 1999, http://www.eiconsortium.org/reports/business_case_for_ei.html

122 E. H. O'Boyle, R. H. Humphrey, J. M. Pollack, T. H. Hawver, and P. A. Story, "The Relation between Emotional Intelligence and Job Performance: A Meta-analysis," *Journal of Organizational Behavior* 32, no. 5 (July 2011), pp. 788–818.

123 K. S. Law, C. Wong, and L. J. Song, "The Construct and Criterion Validity of Emotional Intelligence and Its Potential Utility for Management Studies," *Journal of Applied Psychology* 89, no. 3 (2004), pp. 483–496.

124 H. A. Elfenbein and N. Ambady, "Predicting Workplace Outcomes from the Ability to Eavesdrop on Feelings," *Journal of Applied Psychology* 87, no. 5 (October 2002), pp. 963–971.

125 S. Côté, P. N. Lopes, P. Salovey, and C. T. H. Miners, "Emotional Intelligence and Leadership Emergence in Small Groups," *The Leadership Quarterly* 21, no. 3, (June 2010), pp. 496–508.

126 R. Bar-On, D. Tranel, N. L. Denburg, and A. Bechara, "Exploring the Neurological Substrate of Emotional and Social Intelligence," *Brain* 126, no. 8 (August 2003), pp. 1790–1800.

127 P. A. Vernon, K. V. Petrides, D. Bratko, J. A. Schermer, "A Behavioral Genetic Study of Trait Emotional Intelligence," *Emotion* 8, no. 5 (2008), pp. 635–642.

128 E. A. Locke, "Why Emotional Intelligence Is an Invalid Concept," *Journal of Organizational Behavior* 26, no. 4 (June 2005), pp. 425–431.

129 J. M. Conte, "A Review and Critique of Emotional Intelligence Measures," *Journal of Organizational Behavior* 26, no. 4 (June 2005), pp. 433–440; and M. Davies, L. Stankov, and R. D. Roberts, "Emotional Intelligence: In Search of an Elusive Construct," *Journal of Personality and Social Psychology* 75, no. 4 (1998), pp. 989–1015.

130 T. Decker, "Is Emotional Intelligence a Viable Concept?" *Academy of Management Review* 28, no. 2 (April 2003), pp. 433–440; and M. Davies, L. Stankov, and R. D. Roberts, "Emotional Intelligence: In Search of an Elusive Construct," *Journal of Personality and Social Psychology* 75, no. 4 (1998), pp. 989–1015.

131 F. J. Landy, "Some Historical and Scientific Issues Related to Research on Emotional Intelligence," *Journal of Organizational Behavior* 26, no. 4 (June 2005), pp. 411–424.

132 S. L. Robinson and R. J. Bennett, "A Typology of Deviant Workplace Behaviors: A Multidimensional Scaling Study," *Academy of Management Journal,* April 1995, p. 556.

133 S. L. Robinson and R. J. Bennett, "A Typology of Deviant Workplace Behaviors: A Multidimensional Scaling Study," *Academy of Management Journal,* April 1995, pp. 555–572.

134 Based on A. G. Bedeian, "Workplace Envy," *Organizational Dynamics,* Spring 1995, p. 50.

135 A. G. Bedeian, "Workplace Envy," *Organizational Dynamics,* Spring 1995, p. 54.

136 S. C. Douglas, C. Kiewitz, M. Martinko, P. Harvey, Y. Kim, and J. U. Chun, "Cognitions, Emotions, and Evaluations: An Elaboration Likelihood Model for Workplace Aggression," *Academy of Management Review* 33, no. 2 (2008), pp. 425–451.

137 K. Lee and N. J. Allen, "Organizational Citizenship Behavior and Workplace Deviance: The Role of Affect and Cognition," *Journal of Applied Psychology* 87, no. 1 (2002), pp. 131–142; and T. A. Judge, B. A. Scott, and R. Ilies, "Hostility, Job Attitudes, and Workplace Deviance: Test of a Multilevel Model," *Journal of Applied Psychology* 91, no. 1 (2006), pp. 126–138.

138 H. M. Weiss and R. Cropanzano, "Affective Events Theory," in *Research in Organizational Behavior,* vol. 18, ed. B. M. Staw and L. L. Cummings (Greenwich, CT: JAI Press, 1996), p. 55.

139 H. Liao and A. Chuang, "A Multilevel Investigation of Factors Influencing Employee Service Performance and Customer Outcomes," *Academy of Management Journal* 47, no. 1 (2004), pp. 41–58.

140 D. J. Beal, J. P. Trougakos, H. M. Weiss, and S. G. Green, "Episodic Processes in Emotional Labor: Perceptions of Affective Delivery and Regulation Strategies," *Journal of Applied Psychology* 91, no. 5 (2006), pp. 1057–1065.

141 Cited in S. W. Floyd, J. Roos, and F. Kellermanns, *Innovating Strategy Process* (Blackwell Publishing, 2005), p. 66.

142 D. Zapf and M. Holz, "On the Positive and Negative Effects of Emotion Work in Organizations," *European Journal of Work and Organizational Psychology* 15, no. 1 (2006), pp. 1–28.

143 D. Zapf, "Emotion Work and Psychological Well-Being: A Review of the Literature and Some Conceptual Considerations," *Human Resource Management Review* 12, no. 2 (2002), pp. 237–268.

144 J. E. Bono and M. A. Vey, "Toward Understanding Emotional Management at Work: A Quantitative Review of Emotional Labor Research," in *Emotions in Organizational Behavior*, ed. C. E. Härtel and W. J. Zerbe (Mahwah, NJ: Lawrence Erlbaum, 2005), pp. 213–233.

145 This dilemma is based on R. R. Hastings, "Survey: The Demographics of Tattoos and Piercings," *HR Week*, February 2007, http://www.shrm.org; H. Wessel, "Taboo of Tattoos in the Workplace," *Orlando (Florida) Sentinel*, May 28, 2007, http://www.tmcnet.com/usubmit/2007/05/28/2666555.htm; S. O'Donnell, "Popularity of Piercing Pokes Holes in Traditional Workplace Standards," *Edmonton Journal*, March 12, 2006, p. A1; and K. Dedyna, "Picture-Perfect Workers? TATTOOS: Inky Designs Gain Acceptance with Bosses, Clients," *Province* (Vancouver), August 28, 2005, p. A50.

146 J. Perrone and M. H. Vickers, "Emotions as Strategic Game in a Hostile Workplace: An Exemplar Case," *Employee Responsibilities and Rights Journal* 16, no. 3 (2004), pp. 167–178.

147 Based on V. P. Richmond, J. C. McCroskey, and S. K. Payne, *Nonverbal Behavior in Interpersonal Relations*, 2nd ed. (Englewood Cliffs, NJ: Prentice Hall, 1991), pp. 117–138; and L. A. King, "Ambivalence Over Emotional Expression and Reading Emotions in Situations and Faces," *Journal of Personality and Social Psychology*, March 1998, pp. 753–762.

Chapter 3

1 Vignette based on http://www.casinoregina.com/corporate/aboutus

2 M. Rokeach, *The Nature of Human Values* (New York: Free Press, 1973), p. 5.

3 See, for instance, B. Meglino and E. Ravlin, "Individual Values in Organizations," *Journal of Management* 24, no. 3 (1998), pp. 351–389.

4 M. Rokeach and S. J. Ball-Rokeach, "Stability and Change in American Value Priorities, 1968–1981," *American Psychologist*, May 1989, pp. 775–784.

5 M. Rokeach, *The Nature of Human Values* (New York: Free Press, 1973), p. 6.

6 M. Rokeach, *The Nature of Human Values* (New York: Free Press, 1973), p. 56.

7 M. Rokeach, *The Nature of Human Values* (New York: Free Press, 1973), p. 56.

8 J. M. Munson and B. Z. Posner, "The Factorial Validity of a Modified Rokeach Value Survey for Four Diverse Samples," *Educational and Psychological Measurement*, Winter 1980, pp. 1073–1079; and W. C. Frederick and J. Weber, "The Values of Corporate Managers and Their Critics: An Empirical Description and Normative Implications," in *Business Ethics: Research Issues and Empirical Studies*, ed. W. C. Frederick and L. E. Preston (Greenwich, CT: JAI Press, 1990), pp. 123–144.

9 W. C. Frederick and J. Weber, "The Values of Corporate Managers and Their Critics: An Empirical Description and Normative Implications," in *Business Ethics: Research Issues and Empirical Studies*, ed. W. C. Frederick and L. E. Preston (Greenwich, CT: JAI Press, 1990), pp. 123–144.

10 W. C. Frederick and J. Weber, "The Values of Corporate Managers and Their Critics: An Empirical Description and Normative Implications," in *Business Ethics: Research Issues and Empirical Studies*, ed. W. C. Frederick and L. E. Preston (Greenwich, CT: JAI Press, 1990), p. 132.

11 K. Hodgson, *A Rock and a Hard Place: How to Make Ethical Business Decisions When the Choices Are Tough* (New York: AMACOM, 1992), pp. 66–67.

12 Based on A. Judd, "Vancouver Man Fired over Riot Facebook Comments," *Global News*, June 17, 2011, http://www.globaltvbc.com/Vancouver+fired+over+riot+Facebook+comments/4965316/story.html; and V. Lu, "Vancouver Rioters Got Rowdy, Then Got Fired," *thestar.com*, June 23, 2011.

13 K. Hodgson, "Adapting Ethical Decisions to a Global Marketplace," *Management Review* 81, no. 5 (May 1992), pp. 53–57. Reprinted by permission.

14 Vignette based on http://www.casinoregina.com/corporate/aboutus

15 G. Hofstede, *Culture's Consequences: International Differences in Work-Related Values* (Beverly Hills, CA: Sage, 1980); G. Hofstede, *Cultures and Organizations: Software of the Mind* (London: McGraw-Hill, 1991); G. Hofstede, "Cultural Constraints in Management Theories," *Academy of Management Executive* 7, no. 1 (1993), pp. 81–94; G. Hofstede and M. F. Peterson, "National Values and Organizational Practices," in *Handbook of Organizational Culture and Climate*, ed. N. M. Ashkanasy, C. M. Wilderom, and M. F. Peterson (Thousand Oaks, CA: Sage, 2000), pp. 401–416; and G. Hofstede, *Culture's Consequences: Comparing Values, Behaviors, Institutions, and Organizations Across Nations*, 2nd ed. (Thousand Oaks, CA: Sage, 2001). For criticism of this research, see B. McSweeney, "Hofstede's Model of National Cultural Differences and Their Consequences: A Triumph of Faith—A Failure of Analysis," *Human Relations* 55, no. 1 (2002), pp. 89–118.

16 G. Hofstede, Dimensionalizing Cultures: The Hofstede Model in Context. Online Readings in Psychology and Culture, Unit 2, 2011. Retrieved from http://scholarworks.gvsu.edu/orpc/vol2/iss1/8.

17 G. Hofstede, Dimensionalizing Cultures: The Hofstede Model in Context. Online Readings in Psychology and Culture, Unit 2, 2011. Retrieved from http://scholarworks.gvsu.edu/orpc/vol2/iss1/8.

18 G. Hofstede and M. H. Bond, "The Confucius Connection: From Cultural Roots to Economic Growth," *Organizational Dynamics*, Spring 1988, pp. 12–13.

19 G. Hofstede, G. J. Hofstede, M. Minkov, *Cultures and Organizations, Software of the Mind*, 3rd rev. ed. (New York: McGrawHill, 2010), p. 35.

20 M. H. Bond, "Reclaiming the Individual from Hofstede's Ecological Analysis—A 20-Year Odyssey: Comment on Oyserman et al. (2002)," *Psychological Bulletin* 128, no. 1 (2002), pp. 73–77; G. Hofstede, "The Pitfalls of Cross-National Survey Research: A Reply to the Article by Spector et al. on the Psychometric Properties of the Hofstede Values Survey Module 1994," *Applied Psychology: An International Review* 51, no. 1 (2002), pp. 170–178; and T. Fang, "A Critique of Hofstede's Fifth National Culture Dimension," *International Journal of Cross-Cultural Management* 3, no. 3 (2003), pp. 347–368.

21 See A. Harzing and G. Hofstede, "Planned Change in Organizations: The Influence of National Culture," in *Research in the Sociology of Organizations, Cross Cultural Analysis of Organizations*, vol. 14, ed. P. A. Bamberger, M. Erez, and S. B. Bacharach (Greenwich, CT: JAI Press, 1996), pp. 297–340. The five usual criticisms and Hofstede's responses (in parentheses) are (1) Surveys are not a suitable way to measure cultural differences (answer: they should not be the only way); (2) Nations are not the proper units for studying cultures (answer: they are usually the only kind of units available for comparison); (3) A study of the subsidiaries of one company cannot provide information about entire national cultures (answer: what was measured were differences among national cultures, and any set of functionally equivalent samples can supply information about such differences); (4) The IBM data are old and therefore obsolete (answer: the dimensions found are assumed to have century-old roots; they have been validated against all kinds of external measurements; and recent replications show no loss of validity); and (5) Four or five dimensions are not enough (answer: additional dimensions should be statistically independent of the dimensions defined earlier; they should be valid on the basis of correlations with external measures; candidates are welcome to apply). See A. Harzing and G. Hofstede, "Planned Change in Organizations: The Influence of National Culture," in *Research in the Sociology of Organizations, Cross Cultural Analysis of Organizations*, vol. 14, ed. P. A. Bamberger, M. Erez, and S. B. Bacharach (Greenwich, CT: JAI Press, 1996), pp. 297–340.

22 M. Javidan and R. J. House, "Cultural Acumen for the Global Manager: Lessons from Project GLOBE," *Organizational Dynamics* 29, no. 4 (2001), pp. 289–305; and R. J. House, P. J. Hanges, M. Javidan, and P. W. Dorfman, eds., *Leadership, Culture, and Organizations: The GLOBE Study of 62 Societies* (Thousand Oaks, CA: Sage, 2004).

23 P. C. Early, "Leading Cultural Research in the Future: A Matter of Paradigms and Taste," *Journal of International Business Studies*, September 2006, pp. 922–931; G. Hofstede, "What Did GLOBE Really Measure? Researchers' Minds versus Respondents' Minds," *Journal of International Business Studies*, September 2006, pp. 882–896; and M. Javidan, R. J. House, P. W. Dorfman, P. J. Hanges, and M. S. de Luque, "Conceptualizing and Measuring Cultures and Their Consequences: A Comparative Review of GLOBE's and Hofstede's Approaches," *Journal of International Business Studies*, September 2006, pp. 897–914.

24 B. Meglino, E. C. Ravlin, and C. L. Adkins, "A Work Values Approach to Corporate Culture: A Field Test of the Value Congruence Process and Its Relationship to Individual Outcomes," *Journal of Applied Psychology* 74 (1989), pp. 424–432.

25 B. Z. Posner, J. M. Kouzes, and W. H. Schmidt, "Shared Values Make a Difference: An Empirical Test of Corporate Culture," *Human Resource Management* 24 (1985), pp. 293–310; and A. L. Balazas, "Value Congruency: The Case of the 'Socially Responsible' Firm," *Journal of Business Research* 20 (1990), pp. 171–181.

26 C. A. O'Reilly, J. Chatman, and D. Caldwell, "People and Organizational Culture: A Q-Sort Approach to Assessing Person-Organizational Fit," *Academy of Management Journal* 34 (1991), pp. 487–516.

27 C. Enz and C. K. Schwenk, "Performance and Sharing of Organizational Values" (paper presented at the annual meeting of the Academy of Management, Washington, DC, 1989).

28 Based on D. Sankey, "Non-Profits Look to Diversify Staff; Youth, Visible Minorities Not Usually Part of Sector's Workforce," *Vancouver Sun*, July 9, 2011, p. D12.

29 See, for example, *The Multigenerational Workforce* (Alexandria, VA: Society for Human Resource Management, 2009); and M. Adams, *Sex in the Snow* (Toronto: Penguin, 1997).

30 K. W. Smola and C. D. Sutton, "Generational Differences: Revisiting Generational Work Values for the New Millennium," *Journal of Organizational Behavior* 23 (2002), pp. 363–382; and K. Mellahi and C. Guermat, "Does Age Matter? An Empirical Examination of the Effect of Age on Managerial Values and Practices in India," *Journal of World Business* 39, no. 2 (2004), pp. 199–215.

31 J. Timm, "Leadership Q&A: Robert Dutton," *Canadian Business*, June 22, 2011, http://www.canadianbusiness.com/article/30752—leadership-q-a-robert-dutton

32 N. A. Hira, "You Raised Them, Now Manage Them," *Fortune*, May 28, 2007, pp. 38–46; R. R. Hastings, "Surveys Shed Light on Generation Y Career Goals," *SHRM Online*, March 2007, http://www.shrm.org; and S. Jayson, "The 'Millennials' Come of Age," *USA Today*, June 29, 2006, pp. 1D, 2D.

33 B. Tulgan, *Not Everyone Gets a Trophy: How to Manage Generation Y* (San Francisco, CA: Jossey-Bass, 2009).

34 Statistics Canada, "Census of Population," *The Daily*, February 11, 2003.

35 S. A. Hewlett, L. Sherbin, and K. Sumberg "How Gen Y & Boomers Will Reshape Your Agenda," *Harvard Business Review*, July/August 2009, pp. 71–76.

36 Statistics Canada, "2006 Census: Immigration, Citizenship, Language, Mobility and Migration," *The Daily*, December 4, 2007; and "2006 Census: Ethnic Origin, Visible Minorities, Place of Work and Mode of Transportation," *The Daily*, April 2, 2008.

37 Statistics Canada, "Immigration in Canada: A Portrait of the Foreign-born Population, 2006 Census: Immigrants in Metropolitan Areas," http://www12.statcan.ca/english/census06/analysis/ immcit/city_life.cfm

38 K. Young, "Language: Allophones on the Rise," *National Post*, December 4, 2007.

39 K. Young, "Language: Allophones on the Rise," *National Post*, December 4, 2007.

40 Statistics Canada, "Ethnic Diversity Survey, 2002," *The Daily*, September 29, 2003.

41 http://www.marketingcharts.com/television/american-vs-canadian-youth-lifestyles-values-differ-10588/

42 M. Adams, *Fire and Ice: The United States, Canada and the Myth of Converging Values* (Toronto: Penguin Canada, 2003).

43 M. Adams, *Fire and Ice: The United States, Canada and the Myth of Converging Values* (Toronto: Penguin Canada, 2003).

44 "The Choice in Quebec," *Maclean's*, October 30, 1995, pp. 18–33.

45 R. N. Kanungo and J. K. Bhatnagar, "Achievement Orientation and Occupational Values: A Comparative Study of Young French and English Canadians," *Canadian Journal of Behavioural Science* 12 (1978), pp. 384–392; M. W. McCarrey, S. Edwards, and R. Jones, "Personal Values of Canadian Anglophone and Francophone Employees and Ethnolinguistic Group Membership, Sex and Position Level," *Journal of Psychology* 104 (1978), pp. 175–184; M. W. McCarrey, S. Edwards, and R. Jones, "The Influence of Ethnolinguistic Group Membership, Sex, and Position Level on Motivational Orientation of Canadian Anglophone and Francophone Employees," *Canadian Journal of Behavioural Science* 9 (1977), pp. 274–282; M. W. McCarrey, Y. Gasse, and L. F. Moore, "Work Value Goals and Instrumentalities: A Comparison of Canadian West-Coast Anglophone and Quebec City Francophone Managers," *International Review of Applied Psychology* 33 (1984), pp. 291–303; and S. C. Jain and D. A. Ralston, "The North American Free Trade Agreement: An Overview," in *NAFTA: A Three-Way Partnership for Free Trade and Growth*, ed. S. C. Jain and D. A. Ralston (Storrs, CT: University of Connecticut, 1996), pp. 3–7.

46 M. Major, M. McCarrey, P. Mercier, and Y. Gasse, "Meanings of Work and Personal Values of Canadian Anglophone and Francophone Middle Managers," *Canadian Journal of Administrative Sciences*, September 1994, pp. 251–263.

47 R. N. Kanungo and J. K. Bhatnagar, "Achievement Orientation and Occupational Values: A Comparative Study of Young French and English Canadians," *Canadian Journal of Behavioural Science* 12 (1978), pp. 384–392.

48 V. Mann-Feder and V. Savicki, "Burnout in Anglophone and Francophone Child and Youth Workers in Canada: A Cross-Cultural Comparison," *Child & Youth Care Forum* 32, no. 6 (2003), p. 345.

49 R. N. Kanungo and J. K. Bhatnagar, "Achievement Orientation and Occupational Values: A Comparative Study of Young French and English Canadians," *Canadian Journal of Behavioural Science* 12 (1978), pp. 384–392.

50 V. Mann-Feder and V. Savicki, "Burnout in Anglophone and Francophone Child and Youth Workers in Canada: A Cross-Cultural Comparison," *Child & Youth Care Forum* 32, no. 6 (2003), pp. 337–354.

51 N. J. Adler and J. L. Graham, "Cross-Cultural Interaction: The International Comparison Fallacy?" *Journal of International Business Studies* 20 (1989), pp. 515–537.

52 N. J. Adler, J. L. Graham, and T. S. Gehrke, "Business Negotiations in Canada, Mexico, and the United States," *Journal of Business Research* 15 (1987), pp. 411–429.

53 H. C. Jain, J. Normand, and R. N. Kanungo, "Job Motivation of Canadian Anglophone and Francophone Hospital Employees," *Canadian Journal of Behavioural Science*, April 1979, pp. 160–163; and R. N. Kanungo, G. J. Gorn, and H. J. Dauderis, "Motivational Orientation of Canadian Anglophone and Francophone Managers," *Canadian Journal of Behavioural Science*, April 1976, pp. 107–121.

54 M. Major, M. McCarrey, P. Mercier, and Y. Gasse, "Meanings of Work and Personal Values of Canadian Anglophone and Francophone Middle Managers," *Canadian Journal of Administrative Sciences*, September 1994, pp. 251–263.

55 K. L. Gibson, S. J. Mckelvie, and A. F. De Man, "Personality and Culture: A Comparison of Francophones and Anglophones in Québec," *Journal of Social Psychology* 148, no. 2 (2008), pp. 133–165.

56 G. Bouchard, F. Rocher, and G. Rocher, *Les Francophones Québécois* (Montreal: Bowne de Montréal, 1991).

57 K. L. Gibson, S. J. Mckelvie, and A. F. De Man, "Personality and Culture: A Comparison of Francophones and Anglophones in Québec," *Journal of Social Psychology* 148, no. 2 (2008), pp. 133–165.

58 C. P. Egri, D. A. Ralston, C. S. Murray, and J. D. Nicholson, "Managers in the NAFTA Countries: A Cross-Cultural Comparison of Attitudes toward Upward Influence Strategies," *Journal of International Management* 6, no. 2 (2000), pp. 149–171.

59 C. P. Egri, D. A. Ralston, C. S. Murray, and J. D. Nicholson, "Managers in the NAFTA Countries: A Cross-Cultural Comparison of Attitudes toward Upward Influence Strategies," *Journal of International Management* 6, no. 2 (2000), p. 164.

60 G. Hamilton, "B.C. First Nation Logging Firm Wins National Award," *Vancouver Sun*, July 14, 2011, p. C2.

61 G. Hamilton, "B.C. First Nation Logging Firm Wins National Award," *Vancouver Sun*, July 14, 2011, p. C2.

62 L. Redpath and M. O. Nielsen, "A Comparison of Native Culture, Non-Native Culture and New Management Ideology," *Canadian Journal of Administrative Sciences* 14, no. 3 (1997), p. 327.

63 G. C. Anders and K. K. Anders, "Incompatible Goals in Unconventional Organizations: The Politics of Alaska Native Corporations," *Organization Studies* 7 (1986), pp. 213–233; G. Dacks, "Worker-Controlled Native Enterprises: A Vehicle for Community Development in Northern Canada?" *Canadian Journal of Native Studies* 3 (1983), pp. 289–310; L. P. Dana, "Self-Employment in the Canadian Sub-Arctic: An Exploratory Study," *Canadian Journal of Administrative Sciences* 13 (1996), pp. 65–77.

64 L. Redpath and M. O. Nielsen, "A Comparison of Native Culture, Non-Native Culture and New Management Ideology," *Canadian Journal of Administrative Sciences* 14, no. 3 (1997), p. 327.

65 R. B. Anderson, "The Business Economy of the First Nations in Saskatchewan: A Contingency Perspective," *Canadian Journal of Native Studies* 2 (1995), pp. 309–345.

66 E. Struzik, "'Win-Win Scenario' Possible for Resource Industry, Aboriginals," *Edmonton Journal*, April 6, 2003, p. A12.

67 http://www.highlevelwoodlands.com

68 D. C. Natcher and C. G. Hickey, "Putting the Community Back into Community-Based Resource Management: A Criteria and Indicators Approach to Sustainability," *Human Organization* 61, no. 4 (2002), pp. 350–363.

69 http://www.cuslm.ca/foresterie/sfmn/nouvelles/LUM-Webb.pdf

70 Discussion based on L. Redpath and M. O. Nielsen, "A Comparison of Native Culture, Non-Native Culture and New Management Ideology," *Canadian Journal of Administrative Sciences* 14, no. 3 (1997), pp. 327–339.

71 Discussion based on L. Redpath and M. O. Nielsen, "A Comparison of Native Culture, Non-Native Culture and New Management Ideology," *Canadian Journal of Administrative Sciences* 14, no. 3 (1997), pp. 327–339.

72 D. Grigg and J. Newman, "Five Ways to Foster Bonds, Win Trust in Business," *Ottawa Citizen*, April 23, 2003, p. F12.

73 T. Chui, K. Tran, and J. Flanders, "Chinese Canadians: Enriching the Cultural Mosaic," *Canadian Social Trends* 76 (Spring 2005).

74 Statistics Canada, "Canada's Visible Minority Population in 2017," *The Daily*, March 22, 2005.

75 I. Y. M. Yeung and R. L. Tung, "Achieving Business Success in Confucian Societies: The Importance of Guanxi (Connections)," *Organizational Dynamics: Special Report*, 1998, pp. 72–83.

76 I. Y. M. Yeung and R. L. Tung, "Achieving Business Success in Confucian Societies: The Importance of Guanxi (Connections)," *Organizational Dynamics: Special Report*, 1998, p. 73.

77 Vignette based on K. Blevins, "Casino Workers in Regina Going Back to Work on Tuesday," *Leader-Post*, July 25, 2010, http://communities.canada.com/reginaleaderpost/print.aspx?postid=337941

78 D. A. Harrison, D. A. Newman, and P. L. Roth, "How Important Are Job Attitudes? Meta-analytic Comparisons of Integrative Behavioral Outcomes and Time Sequences," *Academy of Management Journal* 49, no. 2 (2006), pp. 305–325.

79 M. Riketta, "The Causal Relation between Job Attitudes and Performance: A Meta-analysis of Panel Studies," *Journal of Applied Psychology* 93, no. 2 (2008), pp. 472–481.

80 D. P. Moynihan and S. K. Pandey, "Finding Workable Levers over Work Motivation: Comparing Job Satisfaction, Job Involvement, and Organizational Commitment," *Administration & Society* 39, no. 7 (2007), pp. 803–832.

81 For problems with the concept of job satisfaction, see R. Hodson, "Workplace Behaviors," *Work and Occupations*, August 1991, pp. 271–290; and H. M. Weiss and R. Cropanzano, "Affective Events Theory: A Theoretical Discussion of the Structure, Causes and Consequences of Affective Experiences at Work," in *Research in Organizational Behavior*, vol. 18, ed. B. M. Staw and L. L. Cummings (Greenwich, CT: JAI Press, 1996), pp. 1–3.

82 J. Morrissy, "Canadian Workers among Most Dissatisfied in World," *Vancouver Sun*, June 25, 2011.

83 J. Barling, E. K. Kelloway, and R. D. Iverson, "High-Quality Work, Job Satisfaction, and Occupational Injuries," *Journal of Applied Psychology* 88, no. 2 (2003), pp. 276–283; and F. W. Bond and D. Bunce, "The Role of Acceptance and Job Control in Mental Health, Job Satisfaction, and Work Performance," *Journal of Applied Psychology* 88, no. 6 (2003), pp. 1057–1067.

84 S. E. Humphrey, J. D. Nahrgang, and F. P. Morgeson, "Integrating Motivational, Social, and Contextual Work Design Features: A Meta-analytic Summary and Theoretical Extension of the

Work Design Literature," *Journal of Applied Psychology* 92, no. 5 (2007), pp. 1332–1356; and D. S. Chiaburu and D. A. Harrison, "Do Peers Make the Place? Conceptual Synthesis and Meta-analysis of Coworker Effect on Perceptions, Attitudes, OCBs, and Performance," *Journal of Applied Psychology* 93, no. 5 (2008), pp. 1082–1103.

85 E. Diener, E. Sandvik, L. Seidlitz, and M. Diener, "The Relationship between Income and Subjective Well-Being: Relative or Absolute?" *Social Indicators Research* 28 (1993), pp. 195–223.

86 E. Diener, E. Sandvik, L. Seidlitz, and M. Diener, "The Relationship Between Income and Subjective Well-Being: Relative or Absolute?" *Social Indicators Research* 28 (1993), pp. 195–223.

87 E. Diener and M. E. P. Seligman, "Beyond Money: Toward an Economy of Well-Being," *Psychological Science in the Public Interest* 5, no. 1 (2004), pp. 1–31; and A. Grant, "Money = Happiness? That's Rich: Here's the Science behind the Axiom," *(South Mississippi) Sun Herald*, January 8, 2005.

88 E. Diener, E. Sandvik, L. Seidlitz, and M. Diener, "The Relationship between Income and Subjective Well-Being: Relative or Absolute?" *Social Indicators Research* 28 (1993), pp. 195–223.

89 T. A. Judge and C. Hurst, "The Benefits and Possible Costs of Positive Core Self-Evaluations: A Review and Agenda for Future Research," in *Positive Organizational Behavior*, ed. D. Nelson and C. L. Cooper (London, UK: Sage Publications, 2007), pp. 159–174.

90 M. T. Iaffaldano and M. Muchinsky, "Job Satisfaction and Job Performance: A Meta-analysis," *Psychological Bulletin*, March 1985, pp. 251–273.

91 T. A. Judge, C. J. Thoresen, J. E. Bono, and G. K. Patton, "The Job Satisfaction–Job Performance Relationship: A Qualitative and Quantitative Review," *Psychological Bulletin*, May 2001, pp. 376–407; and T. Judge, S. Parker, A. E. Colbert, D. Heller, and R. Ilies, "Job Satisfaction: A Cross-Cultural Review," in *Handbook of Industrial, Work, & Organizational Psychology*, vol. 2, ed. N. Anderson, D. S. Ones, H. K. Sinangil, and C. Viswesvaran (Thousand Oaks, CA: Sage, 2001), p. 41.

92 M. Riketta, "The Causal Relation between Job Attitudes and Performance: A Meta-Analysis of Panel Studies," *Journal of Applied Psychology* 93, no. 2 (2008), pp. 472–481.

93 C. N. Greene, "The Satisfaction–Performance Controversy," *Business Horizons*, February 1972, pp. 31–41; E. E. Lawler III, *Motivation in Organizations* (Monterey, CA: Brooks/Cole, 1973); and M. M. Petty, G. W. McGee, and J. W. Cavender, "A Meta-analysis of the Relationship between Individual Job Satisfaction and Individual Performance," *Academy of Management Review*, October 1984, pp. 712–721.

94 C. Ostroff, "The Relationship between Satisfaction, Attitudes, and Performance: An Organizational Level Analysis," *Journal of Applied Psychology*, December 1992, pp. 963–974; A. M. Ryan, M. J. Schmit, and R. Johnson, "Attitudes and Effectiveness: Examining Relations at an Organizational Level," *Personnel Psychology*, Winter 1996, pp. 853–882; and J. K. Harter, F. L. Schmidt, and T. L. Hayes, "Business-Unit Level Relationship Between Employee Satisfaction, Employee Engagement, and Business Outcomes: A Meta-analysis," *Journal of Applied Psychology*, April 2002, pp. 268–279.

95 D. W. Organ, *Organizational Citizenship Behavior: The Good Soldier Syndrome* (Lexington, MA: Lexington Books, 1988), p. 4.

96 D. W. Organ, *Organizational Citizenship Behavior: The Good Soldier Syndrome* (Lexington, MA: Lexington Books, 1988); and C. A. Smith, D. W. Organ, and J. P. Near, "Organizational Citizenship Behavior: Its Nature and Antecedents," *Journal of Applied Psychology*, 1983, pp. 653–663.

97 J. Farh, C. Zhong, and D. W. Organ, "Organizational Citizenship Behavior in the People's Republic of China," *Organization Science* 15, no. 2 (2004), pp. 241–253.

98 J. M. George and A. P. Brief, "Feeling Good–Doing Good: A Conceptual Analysis of the Mood at Work—Organizational Spontaneity Relationship," *Psychological Bulletin* 112 (2002), pp. 310–329; and S. Wagner and M. Rush, "Altruistic Organizational Citizenship Behavior: Context, Disposition and Age," *Journal of Social Psychology* 140 (2002), pp. 379–391.

99 S. D. Salamon and Y. Deutsch, "OCB as a Handicap: An Evolutionary Psychological Perspective," *Journal of Organizational Behavior* 27, no. 2 (2006), pp. 185–199.

100 P. E. Spector, *Job Satisfaction: Application, Assessment, Causes, and Consequences* (Thousand Oaks, CA: Sage, 1997), pp. 57–58.

101 P. M. Podsakoff, S. B. MacKenzie, J. B. Paine, and D. G. Bachrach, "Organizational Citizenship Behaviors: A Critical Review of the Theoretical and Empirical Literature and Suggestions for Future Research," *Journal of Management* 26, no. 3 (2000), pp. 513–563.

102 B. J. Hoffman, C. A. Blair, J. P. Maeriac, and D. J. Woehr, "Expanding the Criterion Domain? A Quantitative Review of the OCB Literature," *Journal of Applied Psychology* 92, no. 2 (2007), pp. 555–566; and J. A. LePine, A. Erez, and D. E. Johnson, "The Nature and Dimensionality of Organizational Citizenship Behavior: A Critical Review and Meta-analysis," *Journal of Applied Psychology*, February 2002, pp. 52–65.

103 S. L. Blader and T. R. Tyler, "Testing and Extending the Group Engagement Model: Linkages between Social Identity, Procedural Justice, Economic Outcomes, and Extrarole Behavior," *Journal of Applied Psychology* 94, no. 2 (2009), pp. 445–464; J. Fahr, P. M. Podsakoff, and D. W. Organ, "Accounting for Organizational Citizenship Behavior: Leader Fairness and Task Scope versus Satisfaction," *Journal of Management*, December 1990, pp. 705–722; and M. A. Konovsky and D. W. Organ, "Dispositional and Contextual Determinants of Organizational Citizenship Behavior," *Journal of Organizational Behavior*, May 1996, pp. 253–266.

104 D. S. Chiaburu and D. A. Harrison, "Do Peers Make the Place? Conceptual Synthesis and Meta-analysis of Coworker Effect on Perceptions, Attitudes, OCBs, and Performance," *Journal of Applied Psychology* 93, no. 5 (2008), pp. 1082–1103; and J. R. Spence, D. L. Ferris, D. J. Brown, and D. Heller, "Understanding Daily Citizenship Behaviors: A Social Comparison Perspective," *Journal of Organizational Behavior* 32, no. 4 (2011), pp. 547–571.

105 See, for instance, E. Naumann and D. W. Jackson Jr., "One More Time: How Do You Satisfy Customers?" *Business Horizons*, May–June 1999, pp. 71–76; D. J. Koys, "The Effects of Employee Satisfaction, Organizational Citizenship Behavior, and Turnover on Organizational Effectiveness: A Unit-Level, Longitudinal Study," *Personnel Psychology*, Spring 2001, pp. 101–114; J. Griffith, "Do Satisfied Employees Satisfy Customers? Support-Services Staff Morale and Satisfaction among Public School Administrators, Students, and Parents," *Journal of Applied Social Psychology*, August 2001, pp. 1627–1658; and C. Vandenberghe, K. Bentein, R. Michon, J. Chebat, M. Tremblay, and J. Fils, "An Examination of the Role of Perceived Support and Employee Commitment in Employee-Customer Encounters," *Journal of Applied Psychology* 92, no. 4 (2007), pp. 1177–1187.

106 M. J. Bitner, B. H. Booms, and L. A. Mohr, "Critical Service Encounters: The Employee's Viewpoint," *Journal of Marketing*, October 1994, pp. 95–106.

107 P. E. Spector, S. Fox, L. M. Penney, K. Bruursema, A. Goh, and S. Kessler, "The Dimensionality of Counterproductivity: Are All Counterproductive Behaviors Created Equal?" *Journal of Vocational Behavior* 68, no. 3 (2006), pp. 446–460; and D. S. Chiaburu and D. A. Harrison, "Do Peers Make the Place? Conceptual Synthesis and Meta-analysis of Coworker Effect on Perceptions, Attitudes, OCBs, and Performance," *Journal of Applied Psychology* 93, no. 5 (2008), pp. 1082–1103.

108 S. M. Puffer, "Prosocial Behavior, Noncompliant Behavior, and Work Performance among Commission Salespeople," *Journal of Applied Psychology*, November 1987, pp. 615–621; J. Hogan and R. Hogan, "How to Measure Employee Reliability," *Journal of Applied Psychology*, May 1989, pp. 273–279; and C. D. Fisher and E. A. Locke, "The New Look in Job Satisfaction Research and Theory," in *Job Satisfaction*, ed. C. J. Cranny, P. C. Smith, and E. F. Stone (New York: Lexington Books, 1992), pp. 165–194.

109 R. B. Freeman, "Job Satisfaction as an Economic Variable," *American Economic Review*, January 1978, pp. 135–141.

110 G. J. Blau and K. R. Boal, "Conceptualizing How Job Involvement and Organizational Commitment Affect Turnover and Absenteeism," *Academy of Management Review*, April 1987, p. 290.

111 N. J. Allen and J. P. Meyer, "The Measurement and Antecedents of Affective, Continuance, and Normative Commitment to the Organization," *Journal of Occupational Psychology* 63 (1990), pp. 1–18; and J. P Meyer, N. J. Allen, and C. A. Smith, "Commitment to Organizations and Occupations: Extension and Test of a Three-Component Conceptualization," *Journal of Applied Psychology* 78 (1993), pp. 538–551.

112 M. Riketta, "Attitudinal Organizational Commitment and Job Performance: A Meta-analysis," *Journal of Organizational Behavior*, March 2002, pp. 257–266.

113 T. A. Wright and D. G. Bonett, "The Moderating Effects of Employee Tenure on the Relation between Organizational Commitment and Job Performance: A Meta-analysis," *Journal of Applied Psychology*, December 2002, pp. 1183–1190.

114 See, for instance, W. Hom, R. Katerberg, and C. L. Hulin, "Comparative Examination of Three Approaches to the Prediction of Turnover," *Journal of Applied Psychology*, June 1979, pp. 280–290; H. Angle and J. Perry, "Organizational Commitment: Individual and Organizational Influence," *Work and Occupations*, May 1983, pp. 123–146; J. L. Pierce and R. B. Dunham, "Organizational Commitment: Pre-Employment Propensity and Initial Work Experiences," *Journal of Management*, Spring 1987, pp. 163–178; and T. Simons and Q. Roberson, "Why Managers Should Care About Fairness: The Effects of Aggregate Justice Perceptions on Organizational Outcomes," *Journal of Applied Psychology* 88, no. 3 (2003), pp. 432–443.

115 Y. Gong, K. S. Law, S. Chang, and K. R. Xin, "Human Resources Management and Firm Performance: The Differential Role of Managerial Affective and Continuance Commitment," *Journal of Applied Psychology* 94, no. 1 (2009), pp. 263–275.

116 A. A. Luchak and I. R. Gellatly, "A Comparison of Linear and Nonlinear Relations between Organizational Commitment and Work Outcomes," *Journal of Applied Psychology* 92, no. 3 (2007), pp. 786–793.

117 J. R. Katzenback and J. A. Santamaria, "Firing up the Front Line," *Harvard Business Review*, May–June 1999, p. 109.

118 See, for example, J. M. Diefendorff, D. J. Brown, and A. M. Kamin, "Examining the Roles of Job Involvement and Work Centrality in Predicting Organizational Citizenship Behaviors and Job Performance," *Journal of Organizational Behavior*, February 2002, pp. 93–108.

119 Based on G. J. Blau and K. R. Boal, "Conceptualizing How Job Involvement and Organizational Commitment Affect Turnover and Absenteeism," *Academy of Management Review*, April 1987, p. 290.

120 G. Chen and R. J. Klimoski, "The Impact of Expectations on Newcomer Performance in Teams as Mediated by Work Characteristics, Social Exchanges, and Empowerment," *Academy of Management Journal* 46, no. 5 (2003), pp. 591–607; A. Ergeneli, G. Saglam, and S. Metin, "Psychological Empowerment and Its Relationship to Trust in Immediate Managers," *Journal of Business Research*, January 2007, pp. 41–49; and S. E. Seibert, S. R. Silver, and W. A. Randolph, "Taking Empowerment to the Next Level: A Multiple-Level Model of Empowerment, Performance, and Satisfaction," *Academy of Management Journal* 47, no. 3 (2004), pp. 332–349.

121 J. M. Diefendorff, D. J. Brown, A. M. Kamin, and R. G. Lord, "Examining the Roles of Job Involvement and Work Centrality in Predicting Organizational Citizenship Behaviors and Job Performance," *Journal of Organizational Behavior*, February 2002, pp. 93–108.

122 M. R. Barrick, M. K. Mount, and J. P. Strauss, "Antecedents of Involuntary Turnover Due to a Reduction in Force," *Personnel Psychology* 47, no. 3 (1994), pp. 515–535.

123 D. R. May, R. L. Gilson, and L. M. Harter, "The Psychological Conditions of Meaningfulness, Safety and Availability and the Engagement of the Human Spirit at Work," *Journal of Occupational and Organizational Psychology* 77, no. 1 (2004), pp. 11–37.

124 "Building a Better Workforce," *PROFIT*, February 16, 2011, http://www.profitguide.com/article/10084—building-a-better-workforce—page0

125 J. K. Harter, F. L. Schmidt, and T. L. Hayes, "Business-Unit-Level Relationship between Employee Satisfaction, Employee Engagement, and Business Outcomes: A Meta-analysis," *Journal of Applied Psychology* 87, no. 2 (2002), pp. 268–279.

126 W. H. Macey and B. Schneider, "The Meaning of Employee Engagement," *Industrial and Organizational Psychology* 1 (2008), pp. 3–30.

127 A. Saks, "The Meaning and Bleeding of Employee Engagement: How Muddy Is the Water?" *Industrial and Organizational Psychology* 1 (2008), pp. 40–43.

128 A. B. Bakker, "An Evidence-Based Model of Work Engagement," *Current Directions in Psychological Science* 20, no. 4 (August 2011), pp. 265–269.

129 E. A. Locke, "The Nature and Causes of Job Satisfaction," in *Handbook of Industrial and Organizational Psychology*, ed. M. D. Dunnette (Chicago: Rand McNally, 1976), pp. 1319–1328.

130 See, for instance, T. A. Judge and S. Watanabe, "Another Look at the Job Satisfaction–Life Satisfaction Relationship," *Journal of Applied Psychology*, December 1993, pp. 939–948; R. D. Arvey, B. P. McCall, T. J. Bouchard Jr., and P. Taubman, "Genetic Influences on Job Satisfaction and Work Values," *Personality and Individual Differences*, July 1994, pp. 21–33; and D. Lykken and A. Tellegen, "Happiness Is a Stochastic Phenomenon," *Psychological Science*, May 1996, pp. 186–189.

131 This exercise is based on M. Allen, "Here Comes the Bribe," *Entrepreneur*, October 2000, p. 48.

132 J. Zaslow, "From Attitude to Gratitude: This Is No Time for Complaints," *Wall Street Journal*, March 4, 2009, p. D1; A. M. Wood, S. Joseph, and J. Maltby, "Gratitude Uniquely Predicts Satisfaction with Life: Incremental Validity above the Domains and Facets of the Five Factor Model," *Personality and Individual Differences* 45, no. 1 (2008), pp. 49–54; and R. A. Emmons, "Gratitude, Subjective Well-Being, and the Brain," in *The Science of Subjective Well-Being*, ed. M. Eid and R. J. Larsen (New York: Guilford Press, 2008), pp. 469–489.

OB on the Edge: Stress at Work

1 Based on J. Newman and D. Grigg, "Road to Health Pays Off for B.C. Trucking Firm," *Edmonton Journal*, July 2, 2011, p. C5.

2 Paragraph based on D. Hansen, "Worker Who Felt 'Thrown Away' Wins," *Vancouver Sun*, August 16, 2006.

3 Statistics Canada, "Perceived Life Stress, Quite a Lot, by Sex, by Province and Territory, 2010," http://www40.statcan.ca/l01/cst01/health107b-eng.htm

4 K. MacQueen, "Workplace Stress Costs Us Dearly, and Yet Nobody Knows What It Is or How to Deal with It," *Maclean's*, October 15, 2007.

5 K. MacQueen, "Workplace Stress Costs Us Dearly, and Yet Nobody Knows What It Is or How to Deal with It," *Maclean's*, October 15, 2007.

6 L. Duxbury and C. Higgins, "2001 National Work-Life Conflict Study," as reported in J. Campbell, "'Organizational Anorexia' Puts Stress on Employees," *Ottawa Citizen*, July 4, 2002.

7 K. Harding, "Balance Tops List of Job Desires," *Globe and Mail*, May 7, 2003, pp. C1, C6.

8 V. Galt, "Productivity Buckling under the Strain of Stress, CEOs Say," *Globe and Mail*, June 9, 2005, p. B1.

9 "Canadian Workers among Most Stressed," *Worklife Report* 14, no. 2 (2002), pp. 8–9.

10 N. Ayed, "Absenteeism Up Since 1993," *Canadian Press Newswire*, March 25, 1998.

11 N. Ayed, "Absenteeism Up Since 1993," *Canadian Press Newswire*, March 25, 1998.

12 Adapted from R. S. Schuler, "Definition and Conceptualization of Stress in Organizations," *Organizational Behavior and Human Performance*, April 1980, p. 189. For an updated review of definitions, see C. L. Cooper, P. J. Dewe, and M. P. O'Driscoll, *Organizational Stress: A Review and Critique of Theory, Research, and Applications* (Thousand Oaks, CA: Sage, 2002).

13 See, for instance, M. A. Cavanaugh, W. R. Boswell, M. V. Roehling, and J. W. Boudreau, "An Empirical Examination of Self-Reported Work Stress among U.S. Managers," *Journal of Applied Psychology*, February 2000, pp. 65–74.

14 Based on *Health* magazine as it appeared in Centers for Disease Control and Prevention, US Department of Health and Human Services, "*Helicobacter pylori* and Peptic Ulcer Disease—Myths," http://www.cdc.gov/ulcer/myth.htm

15 N. P. Podsakoff, J. A. LePine, and M. A. LePine, "Differential Challenge-Hindrance Stressor Relationships with Job Attitudes, Turnover Intentions, Turnover, and Withdrawal Behavior: A Meta-analysis," *Journal of Applied Psychology* 92, no. 2 (2007), pp. 438–454; and J. A. LePine, M. A. LePine, and C. L. Jackson, "Challenge and Hindrance Stress: Relationships with Exhaustion, Motivation to Learn, and Learning Performance," *Journal of Applied Psychology*, October 2004, pp. 883–891.

16 S. Gilboa, A. Shirom, Y. Fried, and C. Cooper, "A Meta-analysis of Work Demand Stressors and Job Performance: Examining Main and Moderating Effects," *Personnel Psychology* 61, no. 2 (2008), pp. 227–271.

17 J. C. Wallace, B. D. Edwards, T. Arnold, M. L. Frazier, and D. M. Finch, "Work Stressors, Role-Based Performance, and the Moderating Influence of Organizational Support," *Journal of Applied Psychology* 94, no. 1 (2009), pp. 254–262.

18 L. W. Hunter and S. M. B. Thatcher, "Feeling the Heat: Effects of Stress, Commitment, and Job Experience on Job Performance," *Academy of Management Journal* 50, no. 4 (2007), pp. 953–968.

19 J. de Jonge and C. Dormann, "Stressors, Resources, and Strain at Work: A Longitudinal Test of the Triple-Match Principle," *Journal of Applied Psychology* 91, no. 5 (2006), pp. 1359–1374; K. Daniels, N. Beesley, A. Cheyne, and V. Wimalasiri, "Coping Processes Linking the Demands-Control-Support Model, Affect and Risky Decisions at Work," *Human Relations* 61, no. 6 (2008), pp. 845–874; and M. van den Tooren and J. de Jonge, "Managing Job Stress in Nursing: What Kind of Resources Do We Need?" *Journal of Advanced Nursing* 63, no. 1 (2008), pp. 75–84.

20 This section is adapted from C. L. Cooper and R. Payne, *Stress at Work* (London: Wiley, 1978); S. Parasuraman and J. A. Alutto, "Sources and Outcomes of Stress in Organizational Settings: Toward the Development of a Structural Model," *Academy of Management Journal* 27, no. 2 (June 1984), pp. 330–350; and P. M. Hart and C. L. Cooper, "Occupational Stress: Toward a More Integrated Framework," in *Handbook of Industrial, Work and Organizational Psychology*, vol. 2, ed. N. Anderson, D. S. Ones, H. K. Sinangil, and C. Viswesvaran (London: Sage, 2001), pp. 93–114.

21 E. A. Rafferty and M. A. Griffin, "Perceptions of Organizational Change: A Stress and Coping Perspective," *Journal of Applied Psychology* 71, no. 5 (2007), pp. 1154–1162.

22 See, for example, M. L. Fox, D. J. Dwyer, and D. C. Ganster, "Effects of Stressful Job Demands and Control of Physiological and Attitudinal Outcomes in a Hospital Setting," *Academy of Management Journal*, April 1993, pp. 289–318.

23 G. W. Evans and D. Johnson, "Stress and Open-Office Noise," *Journal of Applied Psychology*, October 2000, pp. 779–783.

24 T. M. Glomb, J. D. Kammeyer-Mueller, and M. Rotundo, "Emotional Labor Demands and Compensating Wage Differentials," *Journal of Applied Psychology*, August 2004, pp. 700–714; and A. A. Grandey, "When 'The Show Must Go On': Surface Acting and Deep Acting as Determinants of Emotional Exhaustion and Peer-Rated Service Delivery," *Academy of Management Journal*, February 2003, pp. 86–96.

25 S. Lim, L. M. Cortina, and V. J. Magley, "Personal and Workgroup Incivility: Impact on Work and Health Outcomes," *Journal of Applied Psychology* 93, no. 1 (2008), pp. 95–107; N. T. Buchanan and L. F. Fitzgerald, "Effects of Racial and Sexual Harassment on Work and the Psychological Well-Being of African American Women," *Journal of Occupational Health Psychology* 13, no. 2 (2008), pp. 137–151; C. R. Willness, P. Steel, and K. Lee, "A Meta-analysis of the Antecedents and Consequences of Workplace Sexual Harassment," *Personnel Psychology* 60, no. 1 (2007), pp. 127–162; and B. Moreno-Jiménez, A. Rodríguez-Muñoz, J. C. Pastor, A. I. Sanz-Vergel, and E. Garrosa, "The Moderating Effects of Psychological Detachment and Thoughts of Revenge in Workplace Bullying," *Personality and Individual Differences* 46, no. 3 (2009), pp. 359–364.

26 V. S. Major, K. J. Klein, and M. G. Ehrhart, "Work Time, Work Interference with Family, and Psychological Distress," *Journal of Applied Psychology*, June 2002, pp. 427–436; see also P. E. Spector, C. L. Cooper, S. Poelmans, T. D. Allen, M. O'Driscoll, J. I. Sanchez, O. L. Siu, P. Dewe, P. Hart, L. Lu, L. F. R. De Moreas, G. M. Ostrognay, K. Sparks, P. Wong, and S. Yu, "A Cross-National Comparative Study of Work-Family Stressors, Working Hours, and Well-Being: China and Latin America versus the Anglo World," *Personnel Psychology*, Spring 2004, pp. 119–142.

27 D. L. Nelson and C. Sutton, "Chronic Work Stress and Coping: A Longitudinal Study and Suggested New Directions," *Academy of Management Journal*, December 1990, pp. 859–869.

28 H. Selye, *The Stress of Life* (New York: McGraw-Hill, 1976).

29 FactBox based on A. Picard, "The Working Wounded," *Globe and Mail*, June 22, 2008; and Statistics Canada, "Study: Work Absences in 2010," *The Daily*, May 25, 2011, http://www.statcan.gc.ca/daily-quotidien/110525/dq110525e-eng.htm; Statistics Canada, "Perceived Life Stress, 2009," http://www.statcan.gc.ca/pub/82-229-x/2009001/status/pls-eng.htm; and Canadian Newswire, "Vacation Deprivation Continues but Canadians Still Value Vacations in Today's Economy, Expedia.ca Survey Finds," May 13, 2009, http://www.newswire.ca/en/releases/archive/May2009/13/c2818.html

30 R. S. Schuler, "Definition and Conceptualization of Stress in Organizations," *Organizational Behavior and Human Performance*, April 1980, p. 191; and R. L. Kahn and P. Byosiere, "Stress in Organizations," *Organizational Behavior and Human Performance*, April 1980, pp. 604–610.

31 See T. A. Beehr and J. E. Newman, "Job Stress, Employee Health, and Organizational Effectiveness: A Facet Analysis, Model, and Literature Review," *Personnel Psychology*, Winter 1978, pp. 665–699; and B. D. Steffy and J. W. Jones, "Workplace Stress and Indicators of Coronary-Disease Risk," *Academy of Management Journal*, September 1988, pp. 686–698.

32 J. Schaubroeck, J. R. Jones, and J. L. Xie, "Individual Differences in Utilizing Control to Cope with Job Demands: Effects on Susceptibility to Infectious Disease," *Journal of Applied Psychology*, April 2001, pp. 265–278.

33 KPMG Canada, compensation letter, July 1998.

34 B. D. Steffy and J. W. Jones, "Workplace Stress and Indicators of Coronary-Disease Risk," *Academy of Management Journal* 31 (1988), p. 687.

35 C. L. Cooper and J. Marshall, "Occupational Sources of Stress: A Review of the Literature Relating to Coronary Heart Disease and Mental Ill Health," *Journal of Occupational Psychology* 49, no. 1 (1976), pp. 11–28.

36 J. R. Hackman and G. R. Oldham, "Development of the Job Diagnostic Survey," *Journal of Applied Psychology*, April 1975, pp. 159–170.

37 J. L. Xie and G. Johns, "Job Scope and Stress: Can Job Scope Be Too High?" *Academy of Management Journal*, October 1995, pp. 1288–1309.

38 S. J. Motowidlo, J. S. Packard, and M. R. Manning, "Occupational Stress: Its Causes and Consequences for Job Performance," *Journal of Applied Psychology*, November 1987, pp. 619–620.

39 See, for instance, R. C. Cummings, "Job Stress and the Buffering Effect of Supervisory Support," *Group & Organization Studies*, March 1990, pp. 92–104; M. R. Manning, C. N. Jackson, and M. R. Fusilier, "Occupational Stress, Social Support, and the Cost of Health Care," *Academy of Management Journal*, June 1996, pp. 738–750; and P. D. Bliese and T. W. Britt, "Social Support, Group Consensus and Stressor-Strain Relationships: Social Context Matters," *Journal of Organizational Behavior*, June 2001, pp. 425–436.

40 R. Williams, *The Trusting Heart: Great News About Type A Behavior* (New York: Times Books, 1989).

41 D. C. Ganster, W. E. Sime, and B. T. Mayes, "Type A Behavior in the Work Setting: A Review and Some New Data," in *In Search of Coronary-Prone Behavior: Beyond Type A*, ed. A. W. Siegman and T. M. Dembroski (Hillsdale, NJ: Erlbaum, 1989), pp. 117–118; and B. K. Houston, "Cardiovascular and Neuroendocrine Reactivity, Global Type A, and Components of Type A," in *Type A Behavior Pattern: Research, Theory, and Intervention*, ed. B. K. Houston and C. R. Snyder (New York: Wiley, 1988), pp. 212–253.

42 T. H. Macan, "Time Management: Test of a Process Model," *Journal of Applied Psychology*, June 1994, pp. 381–391.

43 See, for example, G. Lawrence-Ell, *The Invisible Clock: A Practical Revolution in Finding Time for Everyone and Everything* (Seaside Park, NJ: Kingsland Hall, 2002).

44 S. A. Devi, "Aging Brain: Prevention of Oxidative Stress by Vitamin E and Exercise," *Scientific World Journal* 9 (2009), pp. 366–372. See also J. Kiely and G. Hodgson, "Stress in the Prison Service: The Benefits of Exercise Programs," *Human Relations*, June 1990, pp. 551–572.

45 E. J. Forbes and R. J. Pekala, "Psychophysiological Effects of Several Stress Management Techniques," *Psychological Reports*, February 1993, pp. 19–27; and G. Smith, "Meditation, the New Balm for Corporate Stress," *BusinessWeek*, May 10, 1993, pp. 86–87.

46 J. Lee, "How to Fight That Debilitating Stress in Your Workplace," *Vancouver Sun*, April 5, 1999, p. C3. Reprinted with permission.

47 "Wellness Program at Work Helps Employees Improve Themselves Mentally and Physically," *Gazette* (Montreal), July 12, 2008, http://www.canada.com/montrealgazette/news/working/story.html?id=ca89add0-8f3d-4fa6-bfc5-4b05ed9e8cf5

48 H. Staseson, "Can Perk Help Massage Bottom Line? On-Site Therapeutic Sessions Are Used by an Increasingly Diverse Group of Employers Hoping to Improve Staff Performance," *Globe and Mail*, July 3, 2002, p. C1.

49 Health Canada, "Wellness Programs Offer Healthy Return, Study Finds," *Report Bulletin*, #224, October 2001, p. 1.

50 H. Staseson, "Can Perk Help Massage Bottom Line? On-Site Therapeutic Sessions Are Used by an Increasingly Diverse Group of Employers Hoping to Improve Staff Performance," *Globe and Mail*, July 3, 2002, p. C1.

51 "Cdn Employers Not Measuring Wellness Outcomes: Survey," *Benefits Canada*, May 4, 2011, http://www.benefitscanada.com/news/cnd-employers-not-measuring-wellness-outcomes-survey-16510

52 Based on S. Martin, "Money Is the Stressor for Americans," *Monitor on Psychology*, December 2008, pp. 28–29; *Helicobacter pylori and Peptic Ulcer Disease*, Centers for Disease Control and Prevention, U.S. Department of Health and Human Services, http://www.cdc.gov/ulcer; and M. Maynard, "Maybe the Toughest Job Aloft," *New York Times*, August 15, 2006, pp. C1, C6.

53 P. M. Wright, "Operationalization of Goal Difficulty as a Moderator of the Goal Difficulty-Performance Relationship," *Journal of Applied Psychology*, June 1990, pp. 227–234; E. A. Locke and G. P. Latham, "Building a Practically Useful Theory of Goal Setting and Task Motivation: A 35-Year Odyssey," *American Psychologist* 57, no. 9 (2002), pp. 705–717; and K. L. Langeland, C. M. Johnson, and T. C. Mawhinney, "Improving Staff Performance in a Community Mental Health Setting: Job Analysis, Training, Goal Setting, Feedback, and Years of Data," *Journal of Organizational Behavior Management*, 1998, pp. 21–43.

54 E. R. Greenglass and L. Fiksenbaum, "Proactive Coping, Positive Affect, and Well-Being: Testing for Mediation Using Path Analysis," *European Psychologist* 14, no. 1 (2009), pp. 29–39; and P. Miquelon and R. J. Vallerand, "Goal Motives, Well-Being, and Physical Health: Happiness and Self-Realization as Psychological Resources under Challenge," *Motivation and Emotion* 30, no. 4 (2006), pp. 259–272.

55 S. E. Jackson, "Participation in Decision Making as a Strategy for Reducing Job-Related Strain," *Journal of Applied Psychology*, February 1983, pp. 3–19.

56 S. Greengard, "It's About Time," *IndustryWeek*, February 7, 2000, pp. 47–50; and S. Nayyar, "Gimme a Break," *American Demographics*, June 2002, p. 6.

57 See, for instance, B. Leonard, "Health Care Costs Increase Interest in Wellness Programs," *HR Magazine*, September 2001, pp. 35–36; and "Healthy, Happy and Productive," *Training*, February 2003, p. 16.

58 K. M. Richardson and H. R. Rothstein, "Effects of Occupational Stress Management Intervention Programs: A Meta-analysis," *Journal of Occupational Health Psychology* 13, no. 1 (2008), pp. 69–93.

Chapter 4

1 Vignette based on N. Watts, "Chan Finishes Off Podium in Fifth, Lysacek Takes Gold," *Toronto Observer*, February 19, 2010, http://www.torontoobserver.ca/2010/02/19/chan-finishes-off-podium-in-fifth-lysacek-takes-gold/; and L. Ewing, "Figure Skating's Code of Points Practically Takes a Statistician to Decipher," *Canadian Press*, February 8, 2010.

2 See, for instance, T. R. Mitchell, "Matching Motivational Strategies with Organizational Contexts," in *Research in Organizational Behavior*, vol. 19, ed. L. L. Cummings and B. M. Staw (Greenwich, CT: JAI Press, 1997), pp. 60–62.

3 D. McGregor, *The Human Side of Enterprise* (New York: McGraw-Hill, 1960). For an updated analysis of Theory X and Theory Y constructs, see R. J. Summers and S. F. Cronshaw, "A Study of McGregor's Theory X, Theory Y and the Influence of Theory X, Theory Y Assumptions on Causal Attributions for Instances of Worker Poor Performance," in *Organizational Behavior*, ed. S. L. McShane, ASAC 1988 Conference Proceedings, 9, part 5, Halifax, 1988, pp. 115–123.

4   K. W. Thomas, *Intrinsic Motivation at Work* (San Francisco: Berrett-Koehler, 2000); and K. W. Thomas, "Intrinsic Motivation and How It Works," *Training,* October 2000, pp. 130–135.

5   A. Kohn, *Punished by Rewards* (Boston: Houghton Mifflin, 1993).

6   C. P. Alderfer, "An Empirical Test of a New Theory of Human Needs," *Organizational Behavior and Human Performance,* May 1969, pp. 142–175.

7   D. C. McClelland, *The Achieving Society* (New York: Van Nostrand Reinhold, 1961); J. W. Atkinson and J. O. Raynor, *Motivation and Achievement* (Washington, DC: Winston, 1974); D. C. McClelland, *Power: The Inner Experience* (New York: Irvington, 1975); M. J. Stahl, *Managerial and Technical Motivation: Assessing Needs for Achievement, Power, and Affiliation* (New York: Praeger, 1986); and D. G. Winter, "The Motivational Dimensions of Leadership: Power, Achievement, and Affiliation," in *Multiple Intelligences and Leadership,* ed. R. E. Riggio, S. E. Murphy, and F. J. Pirozzolo (Mahwah, NJ: Lawrence Erlbaum, 2002), pp. 119–138.

8   A. H. Maslow, *Motivation and Personality* (New York: Harper and Row, 1954).

9   C. Conley, *Peak: How Great Companies Get Their Mojo From Maslow* (San Francisco: Jossey-Bass, 2007).

10 K. Korman, J. H. Greenhaus, and I. J. Badin, "Personnel Attitudes and Motivation," in *Annual Review of Psychology,* ed. M. R. Rosenzweig and L. W. Porter (Palo Alto, CA: Annual Reviews, 1977), p. 178; and M. A. Wahba and L. G. Bridwell, "Maslow Reconsidered: A Review of Research on the Need Hierarchy Theory," *Organizational Behavior and Human Performance,* April 1976, pp. 212–240.

11 L. Tay and E. Diener, "Needs and Subjective Well-Being around the World," *Journal of Personality and Social Psychology,* June 20, 2011, published online before print, http://psycnet.apa.org/?&fa=main.doiLanding&doi=10.1037/a0023779

12 C. P. Alderfer, "An Empirical Test of a New Theory of Human Needs," *Organizational Behavior and Human Performance,* May 1969, pp. 142–175.

13 C. P. Schneider and C. P. Alderfer, "Three Studies of Measures of Need Satisfaction in Organizations," *Administrative Science Quarterly,* December 1973, pp. 489–505; and I. Borg and M. Braun, "Work Values in East and West Germany: Different Weights, but Identical Structures," *Journal of Organizational Behavior* 17, Special Issue (1996), pp. 541–555.

14 F. Herzberg, B. Mausner, and B. Snyderman, *The Motivation to Work* (New York: Wiley, 1959).

15 R. J. House and L. A. Wigdor, "Herzberg's Dual-Factor Theory of Job Satisfaction and Motivations: A Review of the Evidence and Criticism," *Personnel Psychology,* Winter 1967, pp. 369–389; D. P. Schwab and L. L. Cummings, "Theories of Performance and Satisfaction: A Review," *Industrial Relations,* October 1970, pp. 403–430; R. J. Caston and R. Braito, "A Specification Issue in Job Satisfaction Research," *Sociological Perspectives,* April 1985, pp. 175–197; and J. Phillipchuk and J. Whittaker, "An Inquiry into the Continuing Relevance of Herzberg's Motivation Theory," *Engineering Management Journal* 8, no. 1 (1996), pp. 15–20.

16 R. J. House and L. A. Wigdor, "Herzberg's Dual-Factor Theory of Job Satisfaction and Motivations: A Review of the Evidence and Criticism," *Personnel Psychology,* Winter 1967, pp. 369–389; D. P. Schwab and L. L. Cummings, "Theories of Performance and Satisfaction: A Review," *Industrial Relations,* October 1970, pp. 403–430; and R. J. Caston and R. Braito, "A Specification Issue in Job Satisfaction Research," *Sociological Perspectives,* April 1985, pp. 175–197.

17 D. C. McClelland, *The Achieving Society* (New York: Van Nostrand Reinhold, 1961); J. W. Atkinson and J. O. Raynor, *Motivation and Achievement* (Washington, DC: Winston, 1974); D. C. McClelland, *Power: The Inner Experience* (New York: Irvington, 1975); and M. J. Stahl, *Managerial and Technical Motivation:*

Assessing Needs for Achievement, Power, and Affiliation (New York: Praeger, 1986).

18 D. C. McClelland, *The Achieving Society* (New York: Van Nostrand Reinhold, 1961).

19 D. C. McClelland and D. G. Winter, *Motivating Economic Achievement* (New York: The Free Press, 1969); and J. B. Miner, N. R. Smith, and J. S. Bracker, "Role of Entrepreneurial Task Motivation in the Growth of Technologically Innovative Firms: Interpretations from Follow-up Data," *Journal of Applied Psychology,* October 1994, pp. 627–630.

20 D. C. McClelland, *Power: The Inner Experience* (New York: Irvington, 1975); D. C. McClelland and D. H. Burnham, "Power Is the Great Motivator," *Harvard Business Review,* March–April 1976, pp. 100–110; and R. E. Boyatzis, "The Need for Close Relationships and the Manager's Job," in *Organizational Psychology: Readings on Human Behavior in Organizations,* 4th ed., ed. D. A. Kolb, I. M. Rubin, and J. M. McIntyre (Upper Saddle River, NJ: Prentice Hall, 1984), pp. 81–86.

21 D. G. Winter, "The Motivational Dimensions of Leadership: Power, Achievement, and Affiliation," in *Multiple Intelligences and Leadership,* ed. R. E. Riggio, S. E. Murphy, and F. J. Pirozzolo (Mahwah, NJ: Lawrence Erlbaum, 2002), pp. 119–138.

22 J. B. Miner, *Studies in Management Education* (New York: Springer, 1965).

23 Vignette based on P. J. Kwong, "With Lessons Learned, Chan Ready to Defend His Title," *cbcsports.ca,* July 11, 2011, http://www.cbc.ca/sports/blogs/pjkwong/2011/07/with-lessons-learned-chan-ready-to-defend-his-title.html; and "Chan Wins World Figure Skating Title," *Toronto Sun,* http://www.toronto-sun.com/2011/04/28/chan-wins-world-figure-skating-title

24 V. H. Vroom, *Work and Motivation* (New York: John Wiley, 1964).

25 R. Sinclair, "A&A: LPGA Golfer Alena Sharp," *CBC.ca,* February 18, 2011, http://www.cbc.ca/sports/moresports/story/2011/02/13/sp-lpga-sharp.html

26 See, for example, H. G. Heneman III, and D. P. Schwab, "Evaluation of Research on Expectancy Theory Prediction of Employee Performance," *Psychological Bulletin,* July 1972, pp. 1–9; T. R. Mitchell, "Expectancy Models of Job Satisfaction, Occupational Preference and Effort: A Theoretical, Methodological and Empirical Appraisal," *Psychological Bulletin,* November 1974, pp. 1053–1077; and L. Reinharth and M. A. Wahba, "Expectancy Theory as a Predictor of Work Motivation, Effort Expenditure, and Job Performance," *Academy of Management Journal,* September 1975, pp. 502–537.

27 See, for example, L. W. Porter and E. E. Lawler III, *Managerial Attitudes and Performance* (Homewood, IL: Richard D. Irwin, 1968); D. F. Parker and L. Dyer, "Expectancy Theory as a Within-Person Behavioral Choice Model: An Empirical Test of Some Conceptual and Methodological Refinements," *Organizational Behavior and Human Performance,* October 1976, pp. 97–117; H. J. Arnold, "A Test of the Multiplicative Hypothesis of Expectancy-Valence Theories of Work Motivation," *Academy of Management Journal,* April 1981, pp. 128–141; J. P. Wanous, T. L. Keon, and J. C. Latack, "Expectancy Theory and Occupational/Organizational Choices: A Review and Test," *Organizational Behaviour and Human Performance,* August 1983, pp. 66–86; and W. Van Eerde and H. Thierry, "Vroom's Expectancy Models and Work-Related Criteria: A Meta-analysis," *Journal of Applied Psychology* 81 (October 1996), pp. 575–586.

28 P. C. Earley, *Face, Harmony, and Social Structure: An Analysis of Organizational Behavior across Cultures* (New York: Oxford University Press, 1997); R. M. Steers and C. Sanchez-Runde, "Culture, Motivation, and Work Behavior," in *Handbook of Cross-Cultural Management,* ed. M. Gannon and K. Newman (London: Blackwell, 2001), pp. 190–215; and H. C. Triandis, "Motivation and Achievement in Collectivist and Individualistic

Cultures," in *Advances in Motivation and Achievement*, vol. 9, ed. M. Maehr and P. Pintrich (Greenwich, CT: JAI Press, 1995), pp. 1–30.

29 E. A. Locke, "Toward a Theory of Task Motivation and Incentives," *Organizational Behavior and Human Performance*, May 1968, pp. 157–189; and G. H. Seijts, G. P. Latham, K. Tasa, and B. Latham, "Goal Setting and Goal Orientation: An Integration of Two Different yet Related Literatures," *Academy of Management Journal* 47, no. 2 (2004), pp. 227–239.

30 P. C. Earley, P. Wojnaroski, and W. Prest, "Task Planning and Energy Expended: Exploration of How Goals Influence Performance," *Journal of Applied Psychology*, February 1987, pp. 107–114.

31 See, for instance, Morisano, D., J. B. Hirsh, J. B. Peterson, R. O. Pihl, and B. M. Shore, "Setting, Elaborating, and Reflecting on Personal Goals Improves Academic Performance," *Journal of Applied Psychology* 95, no. 2 (2010), pp. 255–264.

32 "KEY Group Survey Finds Nearly Half of All Employees Have No Set Performance Goals," *IPMA-HR Bulletin*, March 10, 2006, p. 1; S. Hamm, "SAP Dangles a Big, Fat Carrot," *BusinessWeek*, May 22, 2006, pp. 67–68; and "P&G CEO Wields High Expectations but No Whip," *USA Today*, February 19, 2007, p. 3B.

33 See, for instance, S. J. Carroll and H. L. Tosi, *Management by Objectives: Applications and Research* (New York: Macmillan, 1973); and R. Rodgers and J. E. Hunter, "Impact of Management by Objectives on Organizational Productivity," *Journal of Applied Psychology*, April 1991, pp. 322–336.

34 Based on L. Bourgon, "The End of Clock-Punching?" *Canadian Business*, September 27, 2010; "Building a Better Workforce," *PROFIT*, February 16, 2011, http://www.profitguide.com/article/10084—building-a-better-workforce—page0; and C. Ressler and J. Thompson, *Why Work Sucks and How to Fix It* (New York: Penguin, 2008).

35 M. Craemer, "Motivating Employees in the 21st Century," *Seattle Post-Intelligencer*, April 5, 2010, http://blog.seattlepi.com/workplacewrangler/2010/04/05/motivating-employees-in-the-21st-century/

36 E. A. Locke and G. P. Latham, *A Theory of Goal Setting and Task Performance* (Englewood Cliffs, NJ: Prentice Hall, 1980).

37 G. P. Latham and E. A. Locke, "Enhancing the Benefits and Overcoming the Pitfalls of Goal Setting," *Organizational Dynamics* 35, no. 6, pp. 332–340; L. D. Ordóñez, M. E. Schweitzer, A. D. Galinsky, and M. Bazerman, "Goals Gone Wild: The Systematic Side Effects of Overprescribing Goal Setting," *Academy of Management Perspectives* 23, no. 1 (2009), pp. 6–16; and E. A. Locke and G. P. Latham, "Has Goal Setting Gone Wild, or Have Its Attackers Abandoned Good Scholarship?" *Academy of Management Perspectives* 23, no. 1 (2009), pp. 17–23.

38 A. Bandura, *Self-Efficacy: The Exercise of Control* (New York: Freeman, 1997). See also M. Salanova, S. Llorens, and W. Schaufeli, "'Yes, I Can, I Feel Good, and I Just Do It!' On Gain Cycles and Spirals of Efficacy Beliefs, Affect, and Engagement," *Applied Psychology: An International Review* 60, no. 2 (2011), pp. 255–285.

39 A. D. Stajkovic and F. Luthans, "Self-Efficacy and Work-Related Performance: A Meta-analysis," *Psychological Bulletin*, September 1998, pp. 240–261; and A. Bandura, "Cultivate Self-Efficacy for Personal and Organizational Effectiveness," in *Handbook of Principles of Organizational Behavior*, ed. E. Locke (Malden, MA: Blackwell, 2004), pp. 120–136.

40 A. Bandura and D. Cervone, "Differential Engagement in Self-Reactive Influences in Cognitively-Based Motivation," *Organizational Behavior and Human Decision Processes*, August 1986, pp. 92–113.

41 Vignette based on C. Cole, "Figure Skating's Code of Points System Has Opened Up the Podium," *Vancouver Sun*, February 6, 2010, http://www.vancouversun.com/news/regional/Figure+skating+Code+Points+system+opened+podium/2532110/story.html

42 J. S. Adams, "Inequity in Social Exchanges," in *Advances in Experimental Social Psychology*, ed. L. Berkowitz (New York: Academic Press, 1965), pp. 267–300.

43 See, for example, E. Walster, G. W. Walster, and W. G. Scott, *Equity: Theory and Research* (Boston: Allyn and Bacon, 1978); and J. Greenberg, "Cognitive Reevaluation of Outcomes in Response to Underpayment Inequity," *Academy of Management Journal*, March 1989, pp. 174–184.

44 P. S. Goodman and A. Friedman, "An Examination of Adams' Theory of Inequity," *Administrative Science Quarterly*, September 1971, pp. 271–288; R. P. Vecchio, "An Individual-Differences Interpretation of the Conflicting Predictions Generated by Equity Theory and Expectancy Theory," *Journal of Applied Psychology*, August 1981, pp. 470–481; R. T. Mowday, "Equity Theory Predictions of Behavior in Organizations," in *Motivation and Work Behavior*, 6th ed., ed. R. Steers, L. W. Porter, and G. Bigley (New York: McGraw-Hill, 1996), pp. 111–131; R. W. Griffeth and S. Gaertner, "A Role for Equity Theory in the Turnover Process: An Empirical Test," *Journal of Applied Social Psychology*, May 2001, pp. 1017–1037; and L. K. Scheer, N. Kumar, and J.-B. E. M. Steenkamp, "Reactions to Perceived Inequity in U.S. and Dutch Interorganizational Relationships," *Academy of Management* 46, no. 3 (2003), pp. 303–316.

45 See, for example, K. S. Sauley and A. G. Bedeian, "Equity Sensitivity: Construction of a Measure and Examination of Its Psycho-metric Properties," *Journal of Management* 26, no. 5 (2000), pp. 885–910; and M. N. Bing and S. M. Burroughs, "The Predictive and Interactive Effects of Equity Sensitivity in Teamwork-Oriented Organizations," *Journal of Organizational Behavior*, May 2001, pp. 271–290.

46 J. Greenberg and S. Ornstein, "High Status Job Title as Compensation for Underpayment: A Test of Equity Theory," *Journal of Applied Psychology*, May 1983, pp. 285–297; and J. Greenberg, "Equity and Workplace Status: A Field Experiment," *Journal of Applied Psychology*, November 1988, pp. 606–613.

47 See, for instance, J. Greenberg, *The Quest for Justice on the Job* (Thousand Oaks, CA: Sage, 1996); R. Cropanzano and J. Greenberg, "Progress in Organizational Justice: Tunneling through the Maze," in *International Review of Industrial and Organizational Psychology*, vol. 12, ed. C. L. Cooper and I. T. Robertson (New York: Wiley, 1997); J. A. Colquitt, D. E. Conlon, M. J. Wesson, C. O. L. H. Porter, and K. Y. Ng, "Justice at the Millennium: A Meta-analytic Review of the 25 Years of Organizational Justice Research," *Journal of Applied Psychology*, June 2001, pp. 425–445; T. Simons and Q. Roberson, "Why Managers Should Care About Fairness: The Effects of Aggregate Justice Perceptions on Organizational Outcomes," *Journal of Applied Psychology*, June 2003, pp. 432–443; and G. P. Latham and C. C. Pinder, "Work Motivation Theory and Research at the Dawn of the Twenty-First Century," *Annual Review of Psychology* 56 (2005), pp. 485–516.

48 O. Janssen, C. K. Lam, and X. Huang, "Emotional Exhaustion and Job Performance: The Moderating Roles of Distributive Justice and Positive Affect," *Journal of Organizational Behavior* 31, no. 6 (2010), pp. 787–809.

49 K. Leung, K. Tong, and S. S. Ho, "Effects of Interactional Justice on Egocentric Bias in Resource Allocation Decisions," *Journal of Applied Psychology* 89, no. 3 (2004), pp. 405–415.

50 "Americans Feel They Pay Fair Share of Taxes, Says Poll," *NaturalNews.com*, May 2, 2005, http://www.naturalnews.com/007297.html

51 R. E. Johnson, C.-H. Chang, and C. Rosen, "'Who I Am Depends on How Fairly I'm Treated': Effects of Justice on Self-Identity and Regulatory Focus," *Journal of Applied Social Psychology* 40, no. 12 (2010), pp. 3020–3058.

52 G. S. Leventhal, "What Should Be Done with Equity Theory? New Approaches to the Study of Fairness in Social Relationships," in *Social Exchange: Advances in Theory and Research*, ed.

K. Gergen, M. Greenberg, and R. Willis (New York: Plenum, 1980), pp. 27–55.

53 D. P. Skarlicki and R. Folger, "Retaliation in the Workplace: The Roles of Distributive, Procedural, and Interactional Justice," *Journal of Applied Psychology* 82, no. 3 (1997), pp. 434–443.

54 R. Cropanzano, C. A. Prehar, and P. Y. Chen, "Using Social Exchange Theory to Distinguish Procedural from Interactional Justice," *Group & Organization Management* 27, no. 3 (2002), pp. 324–351; and S. G. Roch and L. R. Shanock, "Organizational Justice in an Exchange Framework: Clarifying Organizational Justice Dimensions," *Journal of Management*, April 2006, pp. 299–322.

55 J. A. Colquitt, D. E. Conlon, M. J. Wesson, C. O. L. H. Porter, and K. Y. Ng, "Justice at the Millennium: A Meta-Analytic Review of the 25 Years of Organizational Justice Research," *Journal of Applied Psychology*, June 2001, pp. 425–445.

56 D. P. Skarlicki and R. Folger, "Retaliation in the Workplace: The Roles of Distributive, Procedural and Interactional Justice," *Journal of Applied Psychology* 82, no. 3 (1997), pp. 434–443.

57 E. Deci and R. Ryan, eds., *Handbook of Self-Determination Research* (Rochester, NY: University of Rochester Press, 2002); R. Ryan and E. Deci, "Self-Determination Theory and the Facilitation of Intrinsic Motivation, Social Development, and Well-Being," *American Psychologist* 55, no. 1 (2000), pp. 68–78; and M. Gagné and E. L. Deci, "Self-Determination Theory and Work Motivation," *Journal of Organizational Behavior* 26, no. 4 (2005), pp. 331–362.

58 E. L. Deci, R. Koestner, and R. M. Ryan, "A Meta-analytic Review of Experiments Examining the Effects of Extrinsic Rewards on Intrinsic Motivation," *Psychological Bulletin* 125, no. 6 (1999), pp. 627–668; N. Houlfort, R. Koestner, M. Joussemet, A. Nantel-Vivier, and N. Lekes, "The Impact of Performance-Contingent Rewards on Perceived Autonomy and Competence," *Motivation & Emotion* 26, no. 4 (2002), pp. 279–295; G. J. Greguras and J. M. Diefendorff, "Different Fits Satisfy Different Needs: Linking Person-Environment Fit to Employee Commitment and Performance Using Self-Determination Theory," *Journal of Applied Psychology* 94, no. 2 (2009), pp. 465–477; and M. P. Moreno-Jiménez and M. C. H. Villodres, "Prediction of Burnout in Volunteers," *Journal of Applied Social Psychology* 40, no. 7 (2010), pp. 1798–1818.

59 R. Eisenberger and L. Rhoades, "Incremental Effects of Reward on Creativity," *Journal of Personality and Social Psychology* 81, no. 4 (2001), 728–741; and R. Eisenberger, W. D. Pierce, and J. Cameron, "Effects of Reward on Intrinsic Motivation—Negative, Neutral, and Positive: Comment on Deci, Koestner, and Ryan (1999)," *Psychological Bulletin* 125, no. 6 (1999), pp. 677–691.

60 M. Burgess, M. E. Enzle, and R. Schmaltz, "Defeating the Potentially Deleterious Effects of Externally Imposed Deadlines: Practitioners' Rules-of-Thumb," *Personality and Social Psychology Bulletin* 30, no. 7 (2004), pp. 868–877.

61 K. W. Thomas, E. Jansen, and W. G. Tymon Jr., "Navigating in the Realm of Theory: An Empowering View of Construct Development," in *Research in Organizational Change and Development*, vol. 10, ed. W. A. Pasmore and R. W. Woodman (Greenwich, CT: JAI Press, 1997), pp. 1–30.

62 T. R. Mitchell and A. E. Mickel, "The Meaning of Money: An Individual-Difference Perspective," *Academy of Management*, July 1999, pp. 568–578.

63 T. A. Judge, R. F. Piccolo, J. C. Podsakoff, and B. L. Rich, "The Relationship between Pay Satisfaction and Job Satisfaction," *Journal of Vocational Behavior* 77 (2010), 157–167.

64 R. Fischer and D. Boer, "What Is More Important for National Well-Being: Money or Autonomy? A Meta-analysis of Well-Being, Burnout, and Anxiety across 63 Societies," *Journal of Personality and Social Psychology*, July 2011, pp. 164–184.

65 S. A. Hewlett, L. Sherbin, and K. Sumberg "How Gen Y & Boomers Will Reshape Your Agenda," *Harvard Business Review*, July/August 2009, pp. 71–76.

66 This paragraph is based on T. R. Mitchell and A. E. Mickel, "The Meaning of Money: An Individual-Difference Perspective," *Academy of Management*, July 1999, pp. 568–578. The reader may want to refer to the myriad of references cited in the article.

67 S. A. Hewlett, L. Sherbin, and K. Sumberg "How Gen Y & Boomers Will Reshape Your Agenda," *Harvard Business Review*, July/August 2009, pp. 71–76.

68 Cited in S. Caudron, "The Top 20 Ways to Motivate Employees," *IndustryWeek*, April 3, 1995, pp. 15–16. See also B. Nelson, "Try Praise," *Inc.*, September 1996, p. 115.

69 Our definition of a formal recognition system is based on S. E. Markham, K. D. Scott, and G. H. McKee, "Recognizing Good Attendance: A Longitudinal, Quasi-Experimental Field Study," *Personnel Psychology*, Autumn 2002, p. 641.

70 S. J. Peterson and F. Luthans, "The Impact of Financial and Nonfinancial Incentives on Business Unit Outcomes over Time," *Journal of Applied Psychology* 91, no. 1 (2006), pp. 156–165.

71 "Building a Better Workforce," *PROFIT*, February 16, 2011, http://www.profitguide.com/article/10084—building-a-better-workforce—page0; and http://www.rlsolutions.com/Careers/Benefits.aspx

72 B. Scudamore, "Pump up Employee Passion," *PROFIT*, October 13, 2010, http://www.profitguide.com/article/6574—pump-up-employee-passion

73 Hewitt Associates, "Employers Willing to Pay for High Performance," news release, September 8, 2004, http://was4.hewitt.com/hewitt/resource/newsroom/pressrel/2004/09-08-04eng.htm

74 See also D. A. Johnson and A. M. Dickinson, "Employee-of-the-Month Programs: Do They Really Work?" *Journal of Organizational Behavior Management* 30, no. 4 (2010), pp. 308–324.

75 "Praise Beats Raise as Best Motivator, Survey Shows," *Vancouver Sun*, September 10, 1994.

76 S. L. Rynes, B. Gerhart, and L. Parks, "Personnel Psychology: Performance Evaluation and Pay for Performance," *Annual Review of Psychology* 56, no. 1 (2005), p. 572.

77 Based on J. R. Schuster and P. K. Zingheim, "The New Variable Pay: Key Design Issues," *Compensation & Benefits Review*, March–April 1993, p. 28; K. S. Abosch, "Variable Pay: Do We Have the Basics in Place?" *Compensation & Benefits Review*, July–August 1998, pp. 12–22; and K. M. Kuhn and M. D. Yockey, "Variable Pay as a Risky Choice: Determinants of the Relative Attractiveness of Incentive Plans," *Organizational Behavior and Human Decision Processes*, March 2003, pp. 323–341.

78 "Canada's General Motors Workers to Get Up to 16 Per Cent of Salary in Bonuses," *Canadian Press*, February 14, 2011.

79 "Canada's General Motors Workers to Get Up to 16 Per Cent of Salary in Bonuses," *Canadian Press*, February 14, 2011.

80 "2010 Global Salary Increase & Variable Pay Budget Trends," http://compforce.typepad.com/compensation_force/2010/02/2010-global-salary-increase-variable-pay-budget-trends.html

81 E. Willes "Give Buono Credit for Lions Revival," *Gazette* (Montreal), September 25, 2011.

82 E. Arita, "Teething Troubles Aside, Merit-Based Pay Catching On," *Japan Times*, April 23, 2004, http://search.japantimes.co.jp/cgi-bin/nb20040423a3.html

83 G. D. Jenkins Jr., N. Gupta, A. Mitra, and J. D. Shaw, "Are Financial Incentives Related to Performance? A Meta-analytic Review of Empirical Research," *Journal of Applied Psychology*, October 1998, pp. 777–787; and S. L. Rynes, B. Gerhart, and L. Parks, "Personnel

Psychology: Performance Evaluation and Pay for Performance," *Annual Review of Psychology* 56, no. 1 (2005), pp. 571–600.

84 "Many Companies Fail to Achieve Success with Pay-for-Performance Programs," *Hewitt & Associates News and Information*, June 9, 2004; and J. Pfeffer, *What Were They Thinking? Unconventional Wisdom About Management* (Boston: Harvard Business School Press, 2007).

85 E. J. Castilla and S. Benard, "The Paradox of Meritocracy in Organizations," *Administrative Science Quarterly* 55, no. 4 (2010), pp. 543–576.

86 "Bonus Pay in Canada," *Manpower Argus*, September 1996, p. 5; E. White, "Employers Increasingly Favor Bonuses to Raises," *Wall Street Journal*, August 28, 2006, p. B3; and J. S. Lublin, "Boards Tie CEO Pay More Tightly to Performance," *Wall Street Journal*, February 21, 2006, pp. A1, A14.

87 N. Byrnes, "Pain, But No Layoffs at Nucor," *BusinessWeek*, March 26, 2009, http://www.businessweek.com

88 See, for instance, S. C. Hanlon, D. G. Meyer, and R. R. Taylor, "Consequences of Gainsharing," *Group & Organization Management*, March 1994, pp. 87–111; J. G. Belcher Jr., "Gainsharing and Variable Pay: The State of the Art," *Compensation & Benefits Review*, May–June 1994, pp. 50–60; and T. M. Welbourne and L. R. Gomez Mejia, "Gainsharing: A Critical Review and a Future Research Agenda," *Journal of Management* 21, no. 3 (1995), pp. 559–609.

89 Employment Policy Foundation, *U.S. Wage and Productivity Growth Attainable through Gainsharing*, May 10, 2000.

90 T. M. Welbourne and C. J. Ferrante, "To Monitor or Not to Monitor: A Study of Individual Outcomes from Monitoring One's Peers under Gainsharing and Merit Pay," *Group & Organization Management* 33, no. 2 (2008), pp. 139–162.

91 T. M. Welbourne and L. R. Gomez-Mejia, "Gainsharing: A Critical Review and a Future Research Agenda," *Journal of Management* 21, no. 3 (1995), pp. 559–609.

92 B. Jang, "WestJet Charts Bold New Path," *Globe and Mail*, March 27, 2010.

93 M. Gooderham, "A Piece of the Pie as Motivational Tool," *Globe and Mail*, November 20, 2007, p. B8.

94 R. J. Long, "Patterns of Workplace Innovations in Canada," *Relations Industrielles* 44, no. 4 (1989), pp. 805–826; R. J. Long, "Motives for Profit Sharing: A Study of Canadian Chief Executive Officers," *Relations Industrielles* 52, no. 4 (1997), pp. 712–723; T. H. Wagar and R. J. Long, "Profit Sharing in Canada: Incidences and Predictors," *Proceedings of the Administrative Sciences Association of Canada* (Human Resources Division), 1995, pp. 97–105.

95 N. Chi and T. Han, "Exploring the Linkages Between Formal Ownership and Psychological Ownership for the Organization: The Mediating Role of Organizational Justice," *Journal of Occupational and Organizational Psychology* 81, no. 4 (2008), pp. 691–711.

96 See K. M. Young, ed., *The Expanding Role of ESOPs in Public Companies* (New York: Quorum, 1990); J. L. Pierce and C. A. Furo, "Employee Ownership: Implications for Management," *Organizational Dynamics*, Winter 1990, pp. 32–43; J. Blasi and D. L. Druse, *The New Owners: The Mass Emergence of Employee Ownership in Public Companies and What It Means to American Business* (Champaign, IL: Harper Business, 1991); F. T. Adams and G. B. Hansen, *Putting Democracy to Work: A Practical Guide for Starting and Managing Worker-Owned Businesses* (San Francisco: Berrett-Koehler, 1993); and A. A. Buchko, "The Effects of Employee Ownership on Employee Attitudes: An Integrated Causal Model and Path Analysis," *Journal of Management Studies*, July 1993, pp. 633–656.

97 K. Vermond, "Worker as Shareholder: Is It Worth It?" *Globe and Mail*, March 29, 2008, p. B21.

98 A. A. Buchko, "The Effects of Employee Ownership on Employee Attitudes: An Integrated Causal Model and Path Analysis," *Journal of Management Studies*, July 1993, pp. 633–656.

99 C. M. Rosen and M. Quarrey, "How Well Is Employee Ownership Working?" *Harvard Business Review*, September–October 1987, pp. 126–132.

100 W. N. Davidson and D. L. Worrell, "ESOP's Fables: The Influence of Employee Stock Ownership Plans on Corporate Stock Prices and Subsequent Operating Performance," *Human Resource Planning*, 1994, pp. 69–85.

101 J. L. Pierce and C. A. Furo, "Employee Ownership: Implications for Management," *Organizational Dynamics*, Winter 1990, pp. 32–43; and S. Kaufman, "ESOPs' Appeal on the Increase," *Nation's Business*, June 1997, p. 43.

102 See data in D. Stamps, "A Piece of the Action," *Training*, March 1996, p. 66.

103 X. Zhang, K. M. Bartol, K. G. Smith, M. D. Pfarrer, and D. M. Khanin, "CEOs on the Edge: Earnings Manipulation and Stock-Based Incentive Misalignment," *Academy of Management Journal* 51, no. 2 (2008), pp. 241–258.

104 C. G. Hanson and W. D. Bell, *Profit Sharing and Profitability: How Profit Sharing Promotes Business Success* (London: Kogan Page, 1987); M. Magnan and S. St-Onge, "Profit Sharing and Firm Performance: A Comparative and Longitudinal Analysis" (paper presented at the 58th annual meeting of the Academy of Management, San Diego, CA, August 1998); and D. D'Art and T. Turner, "Profit Sharing, Firm Performance, and Union Influence in Selected European Countries," *Personnel Review* 33, no. 3 (2004), pp. 335–350.

105 T. M. Welbourne and L. R. Gomez-Mejia, "Gainsharing: A Critical Review and a Future Research Agenda," *Journal of Management* 21, no. 3 (1995), pp. 559–609.

106 E. P. Lazear, "Performance Pay and Productivity," *American Economic Review* 90, no. 5 (December 2000), pp. 1346–1361. See also S. Oah, and J.-H. Lee. "Effects of Hourly, Low-Incentive, and High-Incentive Pay on Simulated Work Productivity: Initial Findings with a New Laboratory Method," *Journal of Organizational Behavior Management* 31, no. 1 (2011), pp. 21–42.

107 C. B. Cadsby, F. Song, and F. Tapon, "Sorting and Incentive Effects of Pay for Performance: An Experimental Investigation," *Academy of Management Journal* 50, no. 2 (2007), pp. 387–405.

108 J. Pfeffer and N. Langton, "The Effects of Wage Dispersion on Satisfaction, Productivity, and Working Collaboratively: Evidence from College and University Faculty," *Administrative Science Quarterly* 38, no. 3 (1983), pp. 382–407.

109 "Risk and Reward: More Canadian Companies Are Experimenting with Variable Pay," *Maclean's*, January 8, 1996, pp. 26–27.

110 "Risk and Reward: More Canadian Companies Are Experimenting with Variable Pay," *Maclean's*, January 8, 1996, pp. 26–27.

111 P. K. Zingheim and J. R. Schuster, "Introduction: How Are the New Pay Tools Being Deployed?" *Compensation & Benefits Review*, July–August 1995, pp. 10–11.

112 *OB in the Street* based on "In Pursuit of Level Playing Fields," *Globe and Mail*, March 9, 2002, p. S1.

113 T. Denison, "Formula for Success," August 13, 2004, http://www.collegecolours.com/columns/004.html and J. McElroy, "Full-Ride Athletic Scholarships Still on Hold," *Macleans.ca*, June 4, 2010, http://oncampus.macleans.ca/education/2010/06/04/full-ride-athletic-scholarships-still-on-hold/

114 J. R. Hackman and G. R. Oldham, "Motivation Through the Design of Work: Test of a Theory," *Organizational Behavior and Human Performance*, August 1976, pp. 250–279.

115 J. R. Hackman and G. R. Oldham, *Work Redesign* (Reading, MA: Addison Wesley, 1980).

116 J. R. Hackman, "Work Design," in *Improving Life at Work*, ed. J. R. Hackman and J. L. Suttle (Santa Monica, CA: Goodyear, 1977), pp. 132–133.

117 J. R. Hackman, "Work Design," in *Improving Life at Work*, ed. J. R. Hackman and J. L. Suttle (Santa Monica, CA: Goodyear, 1977), p. 129.

118 J. S. Lublin, "It's Shape-up Time for Performance Reviews," *Wall Street Journal*, October 3, 1994, p. B1.

119 Much of this section is based on H. H. Meyer, "A Solution to the Performance Appraisal Feedback Enigma," *Academy of Management Executive*, February 1991, pp. 68–76.

120 T. D. Schelhardt, "It's Time to Evaluate Your Work, and All Involved Are Groaning," *Wall Street Journal*, November 19, 1996, p. A1.

121 R. J. Burke, "Why Performance Appraisal Systems Fail," *Personnel Administration*, June 1972, pp. 32–40.

122 B. D. Cawley, L. M. Keeping, and P. E. Levy, "Participation in the Performance Appraisal Process and Employee Reactions: A Meta-analytic Review of Field Investigations," *Journal of Applied Psychology*, August 1998, pp. 615–633; and P. E. Levy, and J. R. Williams, "The Social Context of Performance Appraisal: A Review and Framework for the Future," *Journal of Management* 30, no. 6 (2004), pp. 881–905.

123 List directly quoted from R. Kreitner and A. Kinicki, *Organizational Behavior*, 6th ed. (New York: McGraw-Hill/Irwin, 2004), p. 335.

124 S. Kerr, "On the Folly of Rewarding A, While Hoping for B," *Academy of Management Executive* 9, no. 1 (1995), pp. 7–14.

125 D. Turner, "Atlanta Schools Created Culture of Cheating, Fear, Intimidation," *Huffington Post*, July 16, 2011, http://www.huffingtonpost.com/2011/07/16/atlanta-schools-created-c_n_900635.html

126 "More on the Folly," *Academy of Management Executive* 9, no. 1 (1995), pp. 15–16.

127 M. Parker, "Strategies for Creating a Culture of Innovation," *Canadian Business Online*, August 29, 2007.

128 A. Kohn, *Punished by Rewards* (Boston: Houghton Mifflin, 1993), p. 181.

129 A. Kohn, *Punished by Rewards* (Boston: Houghton Mifflin, 1993), p. 181.

130 A. Kohn, *Punished by Rewards* (Boston: Houghton Mifflin, 1993), p. 186. See also P. R. Scholtes, "An Elaboration of Deming's Teachings on Performance Appraisal," in *Performance Appraisal: Perspectives on a Quality Management Approach*, ed. G. N. McLean, S. R. Damme, and R. A. Swanson (Alexandria, VA: American Society for Training and Development, 1990); and H. H. Meyer, E. Kay, and J. R. P. French Jr., "Split Roles in Performance Appraisal," *Harvard Business Review*, 1965, excerpts reprinted in "HBR Retrospect," *Harvard Business Review*, January–February 1989, p. 26; W.-U. Meyer, M. Bachmann, U. Biermann, M. Hempelmann, F.-O. Ploeger, and H. Spiller, "The Informational Value of Evaluative Behavior: Influences of Praise and Blame on Perceptions of Ability," *Journal of Educational Psychology* 71 (1979), pp. 259–268; and A. Halachmi and M. Holzer, "Merit Pay, Performance Targeting, and Productivity," *Review of Public Personnel Administration* 7 (1987), pp. 80–91.

131 A. S. Blinder, "Introduction," in *Paying for Productivity: A Look at the Evidence*, ed. A. S. Blinder (Washington, DC: Brookings Institution, 1990).

132 A. Kohn, *Punished by Rewards* (Boston: Houghton Mifflin, 1993), p. 187.

133 D. Tjosvold, *Working Together to Get Things Done: Managing for Organizational Productivity* (Lexington, MA: Lexington Books, 1986); P. R. Scholtes, *The Team Handbook: How to Use Teams to Improve Quality* (Madison, WI: Joiner Associates, 1988); and A.

Kohn, *No Contest: The Case Against Competition*, rev. ed. (Boston: Houghton Mifflin, 1992).

134 E. L. Deci, "Applications of Research on the Effects of Rewards," in *The Hidden Costs of Rewards: New Perspectives on the Psychology of Human Motivation*, ed. M. R. Lepper and D. Green (Hillsdale, NJ: Erlbaum, 1978).

135 S. E. Perry, *San Francisco Scavengers: Dirty Work and the Pride of Ownership* (Berkeley: University of California Press, 1978).

136 A. Kohn, *Punished by Rewards* (Boston: Houghton Mifflin, 1993), p. 192.

137 T. H. Naylor, "Redefining Corporate Motivation, Swedish Style," *Christian Century*, May 30–June 6, 1990, pp. 566–570; R. A. Karasek, T. Thorell, J. E. Schwartz, P. L. Schnall, C. F. Pieper, and J. L. Michela, "Job Characteristics in Relation to the Prevalence of Myocardial Infarction in the US Health Examination Survey (HES) and the Health and Nutrition Examination Survey (HANES)," *American Journal of Public Health* 78 (1988), pp. 910–916; and D. P. Levin, "Toyota Plant in Kentucky Is Font of Ideas for the U.S.," *New York Times*, May 5, 1992, pp. A1, D8.

138 M. Bosquet, "The Prison Factory," reprinted from *Le Nouvel Observateur* in *Working Papers for a New Society*, Spring 1973, pp. 20–27; J. Holusha, "Grace Pastiak's 'Web of Inclusion,'" *New York Times*, May 5, 1991, pp. F1, F6; J. Simmons and W. Mares, *Working Together: Employee Participation in Action* (New York: New York University Press, 1985); D. I. Levine and L. D'Andrea Tyson, "Participation, Productivity, and the Firm's Environment," in *Paying for Productivity: A Look at the Evidence*, ed. A. S. Blinder (Washington, DC: Brookings Institution, 1990); and W. F. Whyte, "Worker Participation: International and Historical Perspectives," *Journal of Applied Behavioral Science* 19 (1983), pp. 395–407.

139 J. A. Ross, "Japan: Does Money Motivate?" *Harvard Business Review*, September–October 1997. See also R. B. Money and J. L. Graham, "Salesperson Performance, Pay, and Job Satisfaction: Tests of a Model Using Data Collected in the U.S. and Japan" (working paper, University of South Carolina, 1997).

140 N. J. Adler, *International Dimensions of Organizational Behavior*, 3rd ed. (Cincinnati, OH: South Western, 1997), p. 158.

141 A. Kohn, *Punished by Rewards* (Boston: Houghton Mifflin, 1993).

142 W. G. Ouchi, *Theory Z* (New York: Avon Books, 1982); "Bosses' Pay," *Economist*, February 1, 1992, pp. 19–22; and W. Edwards Deming, *Out of the Crisis* (Cambridge: MIT Center for Advanced Engineering Study, 1986).

143 J. Pfeffer, *The Human Equation: Building Profits by Putting People First* (Boston: Harvard Business School Press, 1998).

144 G. Hofstede, "Motivation, Leadership, and Organization: Do American Theories Apply Abroad?" *Organizational Dynamics*, Summer 1980, p. 55.

145 J. K. Giacobbe-Miller, D. J. Miller, and V. I. Victorov, "A Comparison of Russian and U.S. Pay Allocation Decisions, Distributive Justice Judgments, and Productivity under Different Payment Conditions," *Personnel Psychology*, Spring 1998, pp. 137–163.

146 S. L. Mueller and L. D. Clarke, "Political-Economic Context and Sensitivity to Equity: Differences between the United States and the Transition Economies of Central and Eastern Europe," *Academy of Management Journal*, June 1998, pp. 319–329.

147 Based on K. Izuma, D. N. Saito, and N. Sadato, "Processing of Social and Monetary Rewards in the Human Striatum," *Neuron* 58, no. 2 (2008), pp. 284–294; "The Most Praised Generation Goes to Work," *Gainesville (Florida) Sun*, April 29, 2007, pp. 5G, 6G; J. Zaslow, "In Praise of Less Praise," *Wall Street Journal*, May 3, 2007, p. D1; S. Loewy and J. Bailey, "The Effects of Graphic Feedback, Goal-Setting, and Manager Praise on Customer Service Behaviors," *Journal of Organizational Behavior Management* 27, no. 3 (2007), pp. 15–26; and J. S. Seiter and E. Dutson, "The Effect of Compliments on Tipping Behavior in Hairstyling Salons," *Journal of Applied Social Psychology* 37, no. 9 (2007), pp. 1999–2007.

148 Exercise developed by Steve Robbins, with special thanks to Professor Penny Wright (San Diego State University) for her suggestions during the development of this exercise. Exercise modified by Nancy Langton.

149 E. Church, "Market Recovery Delivers Executive Payout Bonanza," *Globe and Mail*, May 4, 2005, pp. B1, B9; "Gimme Gimme: Greed, the Most Insidious of Sins, Has Once Again Embraced a Decade," *Financial Post*, September 28/30, 1996, pp. 24–25; and I. McGugan, "A Crapshoot Called Compensation," *Canadian Business*, July 1995, pp. 67–70.

150 J. McFarland, "Who Earned What Last Year, and Why?" *Globe and Mail*, May 29, 2011, http://www.theglobeandmail.com/report-on-business/careers/management/executive-compensation/who-earned-what-last-year-and-why/article2038061/

151 Based on average weekly earnings for 2010, found at http://www40.statcan.ca/l01/cst01/labr79-eng.htm

152 Based on C. Benedict, "The Bullying Boss," *New York Times*, June 22, 2004, p. F1.

153 Based on S. P. Robbins and D. A. DeCenzo, *Fundamentals of Management*, 4th ed. (Upper Saddle River, NJ: Prentice Hall, 2004), p. 85.

Chapter 5

1 Vignette based on http://www.cirquedusoleil.com; "Cirque du Soleil on Teamwork and Creativity," *Business Banter*, June 28, 2011, http://businessbanter.wordpress.com/2011/06/28/cirque-du-soleil-on-teamwork-and-creativity/; G. Collins, "Run Away to the Circus? No Need. It's Staying Here," *New York Times*, April 29, 2009, p. C1; and A. Tesolin, "Igniting the Creative Spark at Cirque du Soleil—Arupa Tesolin Interviews Lyn Heward Creative Leader at Cirque," *SelfGrowth.com*, http://www.selfgrowth.com/articles/Igniting_the_Creative_Spark_at_Cirque_du_Soleil.html

2 J. R. Katzenbach and D. K. Smith, *The Wisdom of Teams: Creating the High-Performance Organization* (New York: Harper Business, 1999), p. 45.

3 J. R. Katzenbach and D. K. Smith, *The Wisdom of Teams: Creating the High-Performance Organization* (New York: Harper Business, 1999), p. 214.

4 See, for example, D. Tjosvold, *Team Organization: An Enduring Competitive Advantage* (Chichester, UK: Wiley, 1991); S. A. Mohrman, S. G. Cohen, and A. M. Mohrman Jr., *Designing Team-Based Organizations* (San Francisco: Jossey-Bass, 1995); P. MacMillan, *The Performance Factor: Unlocking the Secrets of Teamwork* (Nashville, TN: Broadman and Holman, 2001); and E. Salas, C. A. Bowers, and E. Edens, eds., *Improving Teamwork in Organizations: Applications of Resource Management Training* (Mahwah, NJ: Lawrence Erlbaum, 2002).

5 B. W. Tuckman, "Developmental Sequences in Small Groups," *Psychological Bulletin*, June 1965, pp. 384–399; B. W. Tuckman and M. C. Jensen, "Stages of Small-Group Development Revisited," *Group and Organizational Studies*, December 1977, pp. 419–427; and M. F. Maples, "Group Development: Extending Tuckman's Theory," *Journal for Specialists in Group Work*, Fall 1988, pp. 17–23.

6 R. C. Ginnett, "The Airline Cockpit Crew," in *Groups That Work (and Those That Don't)*, ed. J. R. Hackman (San Francisco: Jossey-Bass, 1990).

7 C. J. G. Gersick, "Time and Transition in Work Teams: Toward a New Model of Group Development," *Academy of Management Journal*, March 1988, pp. 9–41; C. J. G. Gersick, "Marking Time: Predictable Transitions in Task Groups," *Academy of Management Journal*, June 1989, pp. 274–309; E. Romanelli and M. L. Tushman, "Organizational Transformation as Punctuated Equilibrium: An Empirical Test," *Academy of Management Journal*,

October 1994, pp. 1141–1166; B. M. Lichtenstein, "Evolution or Transformation: A Critique and Alternative to Punctuated Equilibrium," in *Academy of Management Best Paper Proceedings*, ed. D. P. Moore (National Academy of Management Conference, Vancouver, 1995), pp. 291–295; and A. Seers and S. Woodruff, "Temporal Pacing in Task Forces: Group Development or Deadline Pressure?" *Journal of Management* 23, no. 2 (1997), pp. 169–187.

8 C. J. G. Gersick, "Time and Transition in Work Teams: Toward a New Model of Group Development," *Academy of Management Journal*, March 1988, pp. 9–41; M. J. Waller, J. M. Conte, C. B. Gibson, and M. A. Carpenter, "The Effect of Individual Perceptions of Deadlines on Team Performance," *Academy of Management Review*, October 2001, pp. 586–600; G. A. Okhuysen and M. J. Waller, "Focusing on Midpoint Transitions: An Analysis of Boundary Conditions," *Academy of Management Journal* 45 (2002), pp. 1056–1065; and M. J. Waller, M. E. Zellmer-Bruhn, and R. C. Giambatista, "Watching the Clock: Group Pacing Behavior Under Dynamic Deadlines," *Academy of Management Journal* 45 (2002), pp. 1046–1055.

9 A. Chang, P. Bordia, and J. Duck, "Punctuated Equilibrium and Linear Progression: Toward a New Understanding of Group Development," *Academy of Management Journal* 46, no. 1 (2003), pp. 106–117.

10 K. L. Bettenhausen, "Five Years of Groups Research: What We Have Learned and What Needs to Be Addressed," *Journal of Management* 17 (1991), pp. 345–381; and R. A. Guzzo and G. P. Shea, "Group Performance and Intergroup Relations in Organizations," in *Handbook of Industrial and Organizational Psychology*, 2nd ed., vol. 3, ed. M. D. Dunnette and L. M. Hough (Palo Alto, CA: Consulting Psychologists Press, 1992), pp. 269–313.

11 A. Chang, P. Bordia, and J. Duck, "Punctuated Equilibrium and Linear Progression: Toward a New Understanding of Group Development," *Academy of Management Journal* 46, no. 1 (2003), pp. 106–117; and S. G. S. Lim and J. K. Murnighan, "Phases, Deadlines, and the Bargaining Process," *Organizational Behavior and Human Decision Processes* 58 (1994), pp. 153–171.

12 Vignette based on A. Tesolin, "Igniting the Creative Spark at Cirque du Soleil—Arupa Tesolin Interviews Lyn Heward Creative Leader at Cirque," *SelfGrowth.com*, http://www.selfgrowth.com/articles/Igniting_the_Creative_Spark_at_Cirque_du_Soleil.html; and M. Baghai and J. Quigley, "Cirque du Soleil: A Very Different Vision of Teamwork," *Fast Company*, February 4, 2011.

13 See, for instance, D. L. Gladstein, "Groups in Context: A Model of Task Group Effectiveness," *Administrative Science Quarterly*, December 1984, pp. 499–517; J. R. Hackman, "The Design of Work Teams," in *Handbook of Organizational Behavior*, ed. J. W. Lorsch (Englewood Cliffs, NJ: Prentice Hall, 1987), pp. 315–342; M. A. Campion, G. J. Medsker, and C. A. Higgs, "Relations between Work Group Characteristics and Effectiveness: Implications for Designing Effective Work Groups," *Personnel Psychology*, 1993; and R. A. Guzzo and M. W. Dickson, "Teams in Organizations: Recent Research on Performance and Effectiveness," in *Annual Review of Psychology*, vol. 47, ed. J. T. Spence, J. M. Darley, and D. J. Foss, 1996, pp. 307–338.

14 D. E. Hyatt and T. M. Ruddy, "An Examination of the Relationship between Work Group Characteristics and Performance: Once More into the Breach," *Personnel Psychology*, Autumn 1997, p. 555.

15 This model is based on D. R. Ilgen, J. R. Hollenbeck, M. Johnson, and D. Jundt, "Teams in Organizations: From Input-Process-Output Models to IMOI Models," *Annual Review of Psychology* 56, no. 1 (2005), pp. 517–543; M. A. Campion, E. M. Papper, and G. J. Medsker, "Relations between Work Team Characteristics and Effectiveness: A Replication and Extension," *Personnel Psychology*, Summer 1996, pp. 429–452; D. E. Hyatt and T. M. Ruddy, "An Examination of the Relationship

between Work Group Characteristics and Performance: Once More into the Breach," *Personnel Psychology*, Autumn 1997, pp. 553–585; S. G. Cohen and D. E. Bailey, "What Makes Teams Work: Group Effectiveness Research from the Shop Floor to the Executive Suite," *Journal of Management* 23, no. 3 (1997), pp. 239–290; G. A. Neuman and J. Wright, "Team Effectiveness: Beyond Skills and Cognitive Ability," *Journal of Applied Psychology*, June 1999, pp. 376–389; and L. Thompson, *Making the Team* (Upper Saddle River, NJ: Prentice Hall, 2000), pp. 18–33.

16 *OB in the Street* based on J. McIntosh, "On The Road to the 2010 Olympics," thestar.com, February 10, 2008; M. Petrie, "Canada's Skeleton Crew Made Peace to Improve," *CanWest News Service*, February 21, 2005; and B. Graveland, "Pain Credits Team for Win," *Edmonton Journal*, February 22, 2005, p. D3.

17 M. Petrie, "Canada's Skeleton Crew Made Peace to Improve," *CanWest News Service*, February 21, 2005.

18 B. Graveland, "Pain Credits Team for Win," *Edmonton Journal*, February 22, 2005, p. D3.

19 See M. Mattson, T. V. Mumford, and G. S. Sintay, "Taking Teams to Task: A Normative Model for Designing or Recalibrating Work Teams" (paper presented at the National Academy of Management Conference, Chicago, August 1999); and G. L. Stewart and M. R. Barrick, "Team Structure and Performance: Assessing the Mediating Role of Intrateam Process and the Moderating Role of Task Type," *Academy of Management Journal*, April 2000, pp. 135–148.

20 Based on W. G. Dyer, R. H. Daines, and W. C. Giauque, *The Challenge of Management* (New York: Harcourt Brace Jovanovich, 1990), p. 343.

21 E. M. Stark, "Interdependence and Preference for Group Work: Main and Congruence Effects on the Satisfaction and Performance of Group Members," *Journal of Management* 26, no. 2 (2000), pp. 259–279; and J. W. Bishop, K. D. Scott, and S. M. Burroughs, "Support, Commitment, and Employee Outcomes in a Team Environment," *Journal of Management* 26, no. 6 (2000), pp. 1113–1132.

22 J. R. Hackman, *Leading Teams* (Boston: Harvard Business School Press, 2002).

23 P. Balkundi and D. A. Harrison, "Ties, Leaders, and Time in Teams: Strong Inference About Network Structure's Effects on Team Viability and Performance," *Academy of Management Journal* 49, no. 1 (2006), pp. 49–68; G. Chen, B. L. Kirkman, R. Kanfer, D. Allen, and B. Rosen, "A Multilevel Study of Leadership, Empowerment, and Performance in Teams," *Journal of Applied Psychology* 92, no. 2 (2007), pp. 331–346; L. A. DeChurch and M. A. Marks, "Leadership in Multiteam Systems," *Journal of Applied Psychology* 91, no. 2 (2006), pp. 311–329; A. Srivastava, K. M. Bartol, and E. A. Locke, "Empowering Leadership in Management Teams: Effects on Knowledge Sharing, Efficacy, and Performance," *Academy of Management Journal* 49, no. 6 (2006), pp. 1239–1251; J. E. Mathieu, K. K. Gilson, and T. M. Ruddy, "Empowerment and Team Effectiveness: An Empirical Test of an Integrated Model," *Journal of Applied Psychology* 91, no. 1 (2006), pp. 97–108; and K. J. Klein, A. P. Knight, J. C. Ziegert, B. C. Lim, and J. L. Saltz, "When Team Members' Values Differ: The Moderating Role of Team Leadership," *Organizational Behavior & Human Decision Processes* 114, no. 1 (2011), pp. 25–36.

24 W. Immen, "The More Women in Groups, the Better," *Globe and Mail*, April 27, 2005, p. C3; and J. L. Berdahl and C. Anderson, "Men, Women, and Leadership Centralization in Groups over Time," *Group Dynamics: Theory, Research, and Practice* 9, no. 1 (2005), pp. 45–57.

25 J. L. Berdahl and C. Anderson, "Men, Women, and Leadership Centralization in Groups over Time," *Group Dynamics: Theory, Research, and Practice* 9, no. 1 (2005), pp. 45–57.

26 R. Wageman, J. R. Hackman, and E. V. Lehman, "Development of the Team Diagnostic Survey" (working paper, Tuck School, Dartmouth College, Hanover, NH, 2004).

27 J. R. Hackman and R. Wageman, "A Theory of Team Coaching," *Academy of Management Review* 30, no. 2 (April 2005), pp. 269–287.

28 R. I. Beekun, "Assessing the Effectiveness of Sociotechnical Interventions: Antidote or Fad?" *Human Relations*, October 1989, pp. 877–897.

29 S. G. Cohen, G. E. Ledford, and G. M. Spreitzer, "A Predictive Model of Self-Managing Work Team Effectiveness," *Human Relations*, May 1996, pp. 643–676.

30 D. R. Ilgen, J. R. Hollenbeck, M. Johnson, and D. Jundt, "Teams in Organizations: From Input-Process-Output Models to IMOI Models," *Annual Review of Psychology* 56, no. 1 (2005), pp. 517–543.

31 K. T. Dirks, "Trust in Leadership and Team Performance: Evidence from NCAA Basketball," *Journal of Applied Psychology*, December 2000, pp. 1004–1012; and M. Williams, "In Whom We Trust: Group Membership as an Affective Context for Trust Development," *Academy of Management Review*, July 2001, pp. 377–396.

32 "Relationship Building Breeds Success," *National Post*, August 11, 2008, p. FP7.

33 P. L. Schindler and C. C. Thomas, "The Structure of Interpersonal Trust in the Workplace," *Psychological Reports*, October 1993, pp. 563–573.

34 See S. T. Johnson, "Work Teams: What's Ahead in Work Design and Rewards Management," *Compensation & Benefits Review*, March–April 1993, pp. 35–41; and A. M. Saunier and E. J. Hawk, "Realizing the Potential of Teams Through Team-Based Rewards," *Compensation & Benefits Review*, July–August 1994, pp. 24–33.

35 M. J. Pearsall, M. S. Christian, A. P. J. Ellis, "Motivating Interdependent Teams: Individual Rewards, Shared Rewards, or Something in between?" *Journal of Applied Psychology* 95, no. 1 (2010), pp. 183–191.

36 K. Merriman, "Low-Trust Teams Prefer Individualized Pay," *Harvard Business Review*, 86, no. 11 (November 2008), p. 32.

37 J. Pfeffer and N. Langton, "The Effect of Wage Dispersion on Satisfaction, Productivity, and Working Collaboratively: Evidence from College and University Faculty," *Administrative Science Quarterly* 38 (1993), pp. 382–407.

38 M. Bloom, "The Performance Effects of Pay Dispersion on Individuals and Organizations," *Academy of Management Journal* 42 (1999), pp. 25–40.

39 For a more detailed breakdown on team skills, see M. J. Stevens and M. A. Campion, "The Knowledge, Skill, and Ability Requirements for Teamwork: Implications for Human Resource Management," *Journal of Management*, Summer 1994, pp. 503–530.

40 S. T. Bell, "Deep-Level Composition Variables as Predictors of Team Performance: A Meta-analysis," *Journal of Applied Psychology* 92, no. 3 (2007), pp. 595–615; and M. R. Barrick, G. L. Stewart, J. M. Neubert, and M. K. Mount, "Relating Member Ability and Personality to Work-Team Processes and Team Effectiveness," *Journal of Applied Psychology* 83, no. 3 (1998), pp. 377–391.

41 K. Tasa, G. J. Sears, and A. C. H. Schat, "Personality and Teamwork Behavior in Context: The Cross-Level Moderating Role of Collective Efficacy," *Journal of Organizational Behavior* 32, no. 1 (2011), pp. 65–85.

42 A. Ellis, J. R. Hollenbeck, and D. R. Ilgen, "Team Learning: Collectively Connecting the Dots," *Journal of Applied Psychology* 88, no. 5 (2003), pp. 821–835; C. O. L. H. Porter, J. R. Hollenbeck, and D. R. Ilgen, "Backing Up Behaviors in Teams: The Role of Personality and Legitimacy of Need," *Journal of Applied Psychology* 88, no. 3 (June 2003), pp. 391–403; A. Colquitt, J. R. Hollenbeck, and D. R. Ilgen, "Computer-Assisted Communication and Team Decision-Making Performance: The Moderating Effect of Openness to Experience," *Journal of Applied Psychology* 87, no. 2 (April 2002), pp. 402–410; J. A. LePine, J. R. Hollenbeck, D. R. Ilgen, and J. Hedlund, "The Effects of Individual Differences on the Performance of Hierarchical Decision Making Teams: Much More Than G," *Journal of Applied Psychology* 82, no. 5 (1997), pp. 803–811; C. Jackson and J. LePine, "Peer Responses to a Team's Weakest Link," *Journal of Applied Psychology* 88, no. 3 (2003), pp. 459–475; and J. LePine, "Team Adaptation and Postchange Performance," *Journal of Applied Psychology* 88, no. 1 (2003), pp. 27–39.

43 S. E. Humphrey, F. P. Morgeson, and M. J. Mannor, "Developing a Theory of the Strategic Core of Teams: A Role Composition Model of Team Performance," *Journal of Applied Psychology* 94, no. 1 (2009), pp. 48–61.

44 E. Sundstrom, K. P. Meuse, and D. Futrell, "Work Teams: Applications and Effectiveness," *American Psychologist*, February 1990, pp. 120–133.

45 See M. F. Peterson, P. B. Smith, A. Akande, S. Ayestaran, S. Bochner, V. Callan, N. Guk Cho, J. Correia Jesuino, M. D'Amorim, P.H. François, K. Hofmann, P. L. Koopman, K. Leung, T. K. Lim, S. Mortazavi, J. Munene, M. Radford, A. Ropo, G. Savage, B. Setiadi, T. N. Sinha, R. Sorenson, and C. Viedge, "Role Conflict, Ambiguity, and Overload: A 21-Nation Study," *Academy of Management Journal*, April 1995, pp. 429–452.

46 See, for instance, M. Sashkin and K. J. Kiser, *Putting Total Quality Management to Work* (San Francisco: Berrett-Koehler, 1993); and J. R. Hackman and R. Wageman, "Total Quality Management: Empirical, Conceptual and Practical Issues," *Administrative Science Quarterly*, June 1995, pp. 309–342.

47 A. Joshi and H. Roh, "The Role of Context in Work Team Diversity Research: A Meta-analytic Review," *Academy of Management Journal* 52, no. 3 (2009), pp. 599--627; and S. K. Horwitz and I. B. Horwitz, "The Effects of Team Diversity on Team Outcomes: A Meta-analytic Review of Team Demography," *Journal of Management* 33, no. 6 (2007), pp. 987–1015.

48 G. S. Van Der Vegt, J. S. Bunderson, and A. Oosterhof, "Expertness Diversity and Interpersonal Helping in Teams: Why Those Who Need the Most Help End Up Getting the Least," *Academy of Management Journal* 49, no. 5 (2006), pp. 877–893.

49 See D. R. Comer, "A Model of Social Loafing in Real Work Groups," *Human Relations*, June 1995, pp. 647–667.

50 W. Moede, "Die Richtlinien der Leistungs-Psychologie," *Industrielle Psychotechnik* 4 (1927), pp. 193–207. See also D. A. Kravitz and B. Martin, "Ringelmann Rediscovered: The Original Article," *Journal of Personality and Social Psychology*, May 1986, pp. 936–941.

51 See, for example, J. A. Shepperd, "Productivity Loss in Performance Groups: A Motivation Analysis," *Psychological Bulletin*, January 1993, pp. 67–81; and S. J. Karau and K. D. Williams, "Social Loafing: A Meta-Analytic Review and Theoretical Integration," *Journal of Personality and Social Psychology*, October 1993, pp. 681–706.

52 D. E. Hyatt and T. M. Ruddy, "An Examination of the Relationship between Work Group Characteristics and Performance: Once More into the Breach," *Personnel Psychology*, Autumn 1997, p. 555; and J. D. Shaw, M. K. Duffy, and E. M. Stark, "Interdependence and Preference for Group Work: Main and Congruence Effects on the Satisfaction and Performance of Group Members," *Journal of Management* 26, no. 2 (2000), pp. 259–279.

53 R. Wageman, "Critical Success Factors for Creating Superb Self-Managing Teams," *Organizational Dynamics*, Summer 1997, p. 55.

54 M. A. Campion, E. M. Papper, and G. J. Medsker, "Relations between Work Team Characteristics and Effectiveness: A Replication and Extension," *Personnel Psychology*, Summer 1996, p. 430.

55 M. A. Campion, E. M. Papper, and G. J. Medsker, "Relations between Work Team Characteristics and Effectiveness: A Replication and Extension," *Personnel Psychology*, Summer 1996, p. 430.

56 J. A. LePine, R. F. Piccolo, C. L. Jackson, J. E. Mathieu, and J. R. Saul, "A Meta-analysis of Teamwork Processes: Tests of a Multidimensional Model and Relationships with Team Effectiveness Criteria," *Personnel Psychology* 61 (2008), pp. 273–307; and J. E. Mathieu and T. L. Rapp, "Laying the Foundation for Successful Team Performance Trajectories: The Roles of Team Charters and Performance Strategies," *Journal of Applied Psychology* 94, no. 1 (2009), pp. 90–103.

57 I. D. Steiner, *Group Processes and Productivity* (New York: Academic Press, 1972).

58 J. A. LePine, R. F. Piccolo, C. L. Jackson, J. E. Mathieu, and J. R. Saul, "A Meta-analysis of Teamwork Processes: Tests of a Multidimensional Model and Relationships with Team Effectiveness Criteria," *Personnel Psychology* 61 (2008), pp. 273–307; and J. E. Mathieu and T. L. Rapp, "Laying the Foundation for Successful Team Performance Trajectories: The Roles of Team Charters and Performance Strategies," *Journal of Applied Psychology* 94, no. 1 (2009), pp. 90–103.

59 J. E. Mathieu and W. Schulze, "The Influence of Team Knowledge and Formal Plans on Episodic Team Process–Performance Relationships," *Academy of Management Journal* 49, no. 3 (2006), pp. 605–619.

60 A. Gurtner, F. Tschan, N. K. Semmer, and C. Nagele, "Getting Groups to Develop Good Strategies: Effects of Reflexivity Interventions on Team Process, Team Performance, and Shared Mental Models," *Organizational Behavior and Human Decision Processes* 102 (2007), pp. 127–142; M. C. Schippers, D. N. Den Hartog, and P. L. Koopman, "Reflexivity in Teams: A Measure and Correlates," *Applied Psychology: An International Review* 56, no. 2 (2007), pp. 189–211; and C. S. Burke, K. C. Stagl, E. Salas, L. Pierce, and D. Kendall, "Understanding Team Adaptation: A Conceptual Analysis and Model," *Journal of Applied Psychology* 91, no. 6 (2006), pp. 1189–1207.

61 E. Weldon and L. R. Weingart, "Group Goals and Group Performance," *British Journal of Social Psychology*, Spring 1993, pp. 307–334.

62 R. A. Guzzo, P. R. Yost, R. J. Campbell, and G. P. Shea, "Potency in Groups: Articulating a Construct," *British Journal of Social Psychology*, March 1993, pp. 87–106; S. J. Zaccaro, V. Blair, C. Peterson, and M. Zazanis, "Collective Efficacy," in *Self-Efficacy, Adaptation and Adjustment: Theory, Research and Application*, ed. J. E. Maddux (New York: Plenum, 1995), pp. 308–330; and D. L. Feltz and C. D. Lirgg, "Perceived Team and Player Efficacy in Hockey," *Journal of Applied Psychology*, August 1998, pp. 557–564.

63 For some of the controversy surrounding the definition of cohesion, see J. Keyton and J. Springston, "Redefining Cohesiveness in Groups," *Small Group Research*, May 1990, pp. 234–254.

64 C. R. Evans and K. L. Dion, "Group Cohesion and Performance: A Meta-analysis," *Small Group Research*, May 1991, pp. 175–186; B. Mullen and C. Cooper, "The Relation between Group Cohesiveness and Performance: An Integration," *Psychological Bulletin*, March 1994, pp. 210–227; S. M. Gully, D. J. Devine, and D. J. Whitney, "A Meta-analysis of Cohesion and Performance: Effects of Level of Analysis and Task Interdependence," *Small Group Research*, 1995, pp. 497–520; and P. M. Podsakoff, S. B. MacKenzie, and M. Ahearne, "Moderating Effects of Goal Acceptance on the Relationship between Group Cohesiveness and Productivity," *Journal of Applied Psychology*, December 1997, pp. 974–983.

65 A. Chang and P. Bordia, "A Multidimensional Approach to the Group Cohesion–Group Performance Relationship," *Small Group Research*, August 2001, pp. 379–405.

66 Submitted by Don Miskiman, Chair, Department of Management, and U-C Professor of Management, Malaspina University-College, Nanaimo, BC. With permission.

67 Paragraph based on R. Kreitner and A. Kinicki, *Organizational Behavior*, 6th ed. (New York: Irwin, 2004), pp. 459–461.

68 R. Kreitner and A. Kinicki, *Organizational Behavior*, 6th ed. (New York: Irwin, 2004), p. 460. Reprinted by permission of McGraw Hill Education.

69 A. P. J. Ellis, "System Breakdown: The Role of Mental Models and Transactive Memory on the Relationships between Acute Stress and Team Performance," *Academy of Management Journal* 49, no. 3 (2006), pp. 576–589.

70 S. W. J. Kozlowski and D. R. Ilgen, "Enhancing the Effectiveness of Work Groups and Teams," *Psychological Science in the Public Interest*, December 2006, pp. 77–124; and B. D. Edwards, E. A. Day, W. Arthur, Jr., and S. T. Bell, "Relationships among Team Ability Composition, Team Mental Models, and Team Performance," *Journal of Applied Psychology* 91, no. 3 (2006), pp. 727–736.

71 K. M. Eisenhardt, J. L. Kahwajy, and L. J. Bourgeois III, "How Management Teams Can Have a Good Fight," *Harvard Business Review*, July–August 1997, p. 78.

72 K. J. Behfar, R. S. Peterson, E. A. Mannix, and W. M. K. Trochim, "The Critical Role of Conflict Resolution in Teams: A Close Look at the Links between Conflict Type, Conflict Management Strategies, and Team Outcomes," *Journal of Applied Psychology* 93, no. 1 (2008), pp. 170–188.

73 K. M. Eisenhardt, J. L. Kahwajy, and L. J. Bourgeois III, "How Management Teams Can Have a Good Fight," *Harvard Business Review*, July–August 1997, p. 78.

74 K. A. Jehn, S. Rispens, and S M. B. Thatcher, "The Effects of Conflict Asymmetry on Work Group and Individual Outcomes," *Academy of Management Journal* 53, no, 3 (2010), pp. 596–616.

75 Based on K. M. Eisenhardt, J. L. Kahwajy, and L. J. Bourgeois III, "How Management Teams Can Have a Good Fight," *Harvard Business Review*, July–August 1997, p. 78.

76 K. Hess, *Creating the High-Performance Team* (New York: Wiley, 1987).

77 See, for example, C. M. Fiol and E. J. O'Connor, "Identification in Face-to-Face, Hybrid, and Pure Virtual Teams: Untangling the Contradictions," *Organization Science* 16, no. 1 (January–February 2005), pp. 19–32; L. L. Martins, L. L. Gilson, and M. T. Maynard, "Virtual Teams: What Do We Know and Where Do We Go from Here?" *Journal of Management* 30, no. 6 (December 2004), pp. 805–835; D. Duarte and N. T. Snyder, *Mastering Virtual Teams: Strategies, Tools, and Techniques* (San Francisco: Jossey-Bass, 1999); M. L. Maznevski and K. M. Chudoba, "Bridging Space Over Time: Global Virtual Team Dynamics and Effectiveness," *Organization Science*, September–October 2000, pp. 473–492; and J. Katzenbach and D. Smith, "Virtual Teaming," *Forbes*, May 21, 2001, pp. 48–51.

78 B. B. Baltes, M. W. Dickson, M. P. Sherman, C. C. Bauer, and J. S. LaGanke, "Computer-Mediated Communication and Group Decision Making: A Meta-analysis," *Organizational Behaviour and Human Decision Processes* 87, no. 1 (2002), pp. 156–179.

79 J. M. Wilson, S. G. Straus, and B. McEvily, "All in Due Time: The Development of Trust in Computer-Mediated and Face-to-Face Teams," *Organizational Behavior and Human Decision Processes* 99, no. 1 (2006), pp. 16–33; and S. L. Jarvenpaa, K. Knoll, and D. E. Leidner, "Is Anybody Out There? Antecedents of Trust in Global Virtual Teams," *Journal of Management Information Systems*, Spring 1998, pp. 29–64.

80 This section based on A. Majchrzak, A. Malhotra, J. Stamps, and J. Lipnack, "Can Absence Make a Team Grow Stronger?" *Harvard Business Review* 82, no. 5 (May 2004), pp. 131–136.

81 A. Malhotra, A. Majchrzak, and B. Rosen, "Leading Virtual Teams," *Academy of Management Perspectives*, February 2007, pp. 60–70; and J. M. Wilson, S. S. Straus, and B. McEvily, "All in Due Time: The Development of Trust in Computer- Mediated and Face-to-Face Teams," *Organizational Behavior and Human Decision Processes* 19 (2006), pp. 16–33.

82 C. E. Naquin and R. O. Tynan, "The Team Halo Effect: Why Teams Are Not Blamed for Their Failures," *Journal of Applied Psychology*, April 2003, pp. 332–340.

83 C. Joinson, "Managing Virtual Teams," *HR Magazine*, June 2002, p. 71. Reprinted with the permission of *HR Magazine*, published by the Society for Human Resource Management, Alexandria, VA.

84 D. Brown, "Innovative HR Ineffective in Manufacturing Firms," *Canadian HR Reporter*, April 7, 2003, pp. 1–2.

85 R. Forrester and A. B. Drexler, "A Model for Team-Based Organization Performance," *Academy of Management Executive*, August 1999, p. 47. See also S. A. Mohrman, with S. G. Cohen and A. M. Mohrman Jr., *Designing Team-Based Organizations* (San Francisco: Jossey-Bass, 1995); and J. H. Shonk, *Team-Based Organizations* (Homewood, IL: Business One Irwin, 1992).

86 Based on J. Berger and D. Pope, "When Losing Leads to Winning," working paper, Wharton School of Business, University of Pennsylvania (2009); J. Senécal, T. M. Loughead, and G. A. Bloom, "A Season-Long Team-Building Intervention: Examining the Effect of Team Goal Setting on Cohesion," *Journal of Sport & Exercise Psychology* 30, no. 2 (2008), pp. 186–199; N. Katz, "Sports Teams as a Model for Workplace Teams: Lessons and Liabilities," *Academy of Management Executive*, August 2001, pp. 56–67; and "Talent Inc.," *New Yorker*, July 22, 2002, http://www.newyorker.com/archive/2002/07/22/020722on_onlineonly01

87 Association for Psychological Science, "Cross-Cultural Perspective Can Help Teamwork in the Workplace," *ScienceDaily*, August 10, 2010, http://www.sciencedaily.com/releases/2010/08/100810122041.htm

88 Based on A. Webb, "The Trials and Tribulations of Teamwork," *Automotive News*, March 2, 2009, http://www.autonews.com; J. K. Liker and M. Hoseus, "Toyota's Powerful HR," *Human Resource Executive*, November 1, 2008, http://www.hreonline.com; J. K. Liker and M. Hoseus, *Toyota Culture: The Heart and Soul of the Toyota Way* (New York: McGraw-Hill, 2008); and D. Kiley, "The Toyota Way to No. 1," *BusinessWeek*, April 26, 2007, http://www.businessweek.com

89 Based on S. P. Robbins and P. L. Hunsaker, *Training in Interpersonal Skills*, 2nd ed. (Upper Saddle River, NJ: Prentice Hall, 1996), pp. 168–184.

Chapter 6

1 Vignette based on M. Ormsby, "Brawl Brewing in Girls' Hockey," *Toronto Star*, November 11, 2009.

2 "Employers Cite Communication Skills, Honesty/Integrity as Key for Job Candidates," *IPMA-HR Bulletin*, March 23, 2007, p. 1.

3 J. Langan-Fox, "Communication in Organizations: Speed, Diversity, Networks, and Influence on Organizational Effectiveness, Human Health, and Relationships," in *Handbook of Industrial, Work and Organizational Psychology*, vol. 2, ed. N. Anderson, D. S. Ones, H. K. Sinangil, and C. Viswesvaran (Thousand Oaks, CA: Sage, 2001), p. 190.

4 J. C. McCroskey, J. A. Daly, and G. Sorenson, "Personality Correlates of Communication Apprehension," *Human Communication Research*, Spring 1976, pp. 376–380.

5 See R. L. Daft and R. H. Lengel, "Information Richness: A New Approach to Managerial Behavior and Organization Design," in *Research in Organizational Behavior*, vol. 6, ed. B. M. Staw and L. L. Cummings (Greenwich, CT: JAI Press, 1984), pp. 191–233;

R. E. Rice and D. E. Shook, "Relationships of Job Categories and Organizational Levels to Use of Communication Channels, Including Electronic Mail: A Meta-Analysis and Extension," *Journal of Management Studies*, March 1990, pp. 195–229; R. E. Rice, "Task Analyzability, Use of New Media, and Effectiveness," *Organization Science*, November 1992, pp. 475–500; S. G. Straus and J. E. McGrath, "Does the Medium Matter? The Interaction of Task Type and Technology on Group Performance and Member Reaction," *Journal of Applied Psychology*, February 1994, pp. 87–97; J. Webster and L. K. Trevino, "Rational and Social Theories as Complementary Explanations of Communication Media Choices: Two Policy-Capturing Studies," *Academy of Management Journal*, December 1995, pp. 1544–1572; and L. K. Trevino, J. Webster, and E. W. Stein, "Making Connections: Complementary Influences on Communication Media Choices, Attitudes, and Use," *Organization Science*, March–April 2000, pp. 163–182.

6 "Building a Better Workforce," *PROFIT*, February 16, 2011, http://www.profitguide.com/article/10084—building-a-better-workforce—page0

7 I. Austen, "Telling Tales Out of School, on YouTube," *New York Times*, November 27, 2006; and D. Rogers, "Quebec Students Suspended for Posting Teacher's Outburst Online," *Ottawa Citizen*, November 25, 2006.

8 R. L. Daft, R. H. Lengel, and L. K. Trevino, "Message Equivocality, Media Selection, and Manager Performance: Implications for Information Systems," *MIS Quarterly*, September 1987, pp. 355–368.

9 P. Brent, "How to Arm, Not Alarm, Your Staff in Crisis," *Canadian Business*, March 14, 2011, p. 68.

10 "Virtual Pink Slips Start Coming Online," *Vancouver Sun*, July 3, 1999, p. D15.

11 T. M. Burton and R. E. Silverman, "Lots of Empty Spaces in Cerner Parking Lot Get CEO Riled Up," *Wall Street Journal*, March 30, 2001, p. B3; and E. Wong, "A Stinging Office Memo Boomerangs," *New York Times*, April 5, 2001, p. C1.

12 Vignette based on M. Ormsby, "Brawl Brewing in Girls' Hockey," *Toronto Star*, November 11, 2009.

13 K. Savitsky, B. Keysar, N. Epley, T. Carter, and A. Swanson, "The Closeness-Communication Bias: Increased Egocentrism among Friends versus Strangers," *Journal of Experimental Social Psychology* 47, no. 1 (2011), pp. 269–273.

14 M. Richtel, "Lost in Email, Tech Firms Face Self-Made Beast," *New York Times*, June 14, 2008.

15 J. Sandberg, "The Jargon Jumble," *Wall Street Journal*, October 24, 2006, p. B1.

16 E. W. Morrison and F. J. Milliken, "Organizational Silence: A Barrier to Change and Development in a Pluralistic World," *Academy of Management Review* 25, no. 4 (2000), pp. 706–725; and B. E. Ashforth and V. Anand, "The Normalization of Corruption in Organizations," *Research in Organizational Behavior* 25 (2003), pp. 1–52.

17 F. J. Milliken, E. W. Morrison, and P. F. Hewlin, "An Exploratory Study of Employee Silence: Issues That Employees Don't Communicate Upward and Why," *Journal of Management Studies* 40, no. 6 (2003), pp. 1453–1476.

18 This paragraph is based on J. O'Toole and W. Bennis, "What's Needed Next: A Culture of Candor," *Harvard Business Review*, June 2009, pp. 54–61.

19 M. Gladwell, *Outliers* (New York: Little, Borwn, and Company, 2008), p. 184.

20 S. Tangirala and R. Ramunujam, "Employee Silence on Critical Work Issues: The Cross-Level Effects of Procedural Justice Climate," *Personnel Psychology* 61, no. 1 (2008), pp. 37–68; and F. Bowen and K. Blackmon, "Spirals of Silence: The Dynamic Effects of Diversity on Organizational Voice," *Journal of Management Studies* 40, no. 6 (2003), pp. 1393–1417.

21 C. G. Pinder and K. P. Harlos, "Silent Organizational Behavior" (paper presented at the Western Academy of Management Conference, March 2000).

22 L. S. Rashotte, "What Does That Smile Mean? The Meaning of Nonverbal Behaviors in Social Interaction," *Social Psychology Quarterly*, March 2002, pp. 92–102.

23 R. L. Birdwhistell, *Introduction to Kinesics* (Louisville, KY: University of Louisville Press, 1952).

24 J. Fast, *Body Language* (Philadelphia, PA: M. Evan, 1970), p. 7.

25 A. Mehrabian, *Nonverbal Communication* (Chicago: Aldine-Atherton, 1972).

26 N. M. Henley, "Body Politics Revisited: What Do We Know Today?" in *Gender, Power, and Communication in Human Relationships*, ed. P. J. Kalbfleisch and M. J. Cody (Hillsdale, NJ: Erlbaum, 1995), pp. 27–61.

27 E. T. Hall, *The Hidden Dimension*, 2nd ed. (Garden City, NY: Anchor Books/Doubleday, 1966).

28 H. Weeks, "Taking the Stress Out of Stressful Conversations," *Harvard Business Review*, July–August 2001, pp. 112–119.

29 B. Gates, "How I Work," *Fortune*, April 17, 2006, http://www.money.cnn.com

30 "Email Brings Costs and Fatigue," *Western News* (UWO), July 9, 2004, http://communications.uwo.ca/com/western_news/stories/email_brings_costs_and_fatigue_20040709432320/

31 K. Macklem, "You've Got Too Much Mail," *Maclean's*, January 30, 2006, pp. 20–21.

32 S. Radicati, ed., *Email Statistics Report, 2011–2015* (Palo Alto, CA: The Radicati Group, 2011), http://www.radicati.com/wp/wp-content/uploads/2011/05/Email-Statistics-Report-2011-2015-Executive-Summary.pdf

33 K. Macklem, "You've Got Too Much Mail," *Maclean's*, January 30, 2006, pp. 20–21.

34 D. Brady, "*!#?@ the Email. Can We Talk?" *BusinessWeek*, December 4, 2006, p. 109.

35 E. Binney, "Is Email the New Pink Slip?" *HR Magazine*, November 2006, pp. 32–33; and R. L. Rundle, "Critical Case: How an Email Rant Jolted a Big HMO," *Wall Street Journal*, April 24, 2007, pp. A1, A16.

36 M. Healy, "Communication Fatigue Disrupts Marketing Messages," *globeandmail.com*, July 20, 2012.

37 R. Stross, "The Daily Struggle to Avoid Burial by Email," *New York Times*, April 21, 2008, p. BU5; and H. Rhodes, "You've Got Mail . . . Again," *Gainesville Sun*, September 29, 2008, pp. 1D, 6D.

38 C. Byron, "Carrying Too Heavy a Load? The Communication and Miscommunication of Emotion by Email," *Academy of Management Review* 33, no. 2 (2008), pp. 309–327.

39 D. Goleman, "Flame First, Think Later: New Clues to Email Misbehavior," *New York Times*, February 20, 2007, p. D5; and E. Krell, "The Unintended Word," *HR Magazine*, August 2006, pp. 50–54.

40 R. Zeidner, "Keeping Email in Check," *HR Magazine*, June 2007, pp. 70–74; "Email May Be Hazardous to Your Career," *Fortune*, May 14, 2007, p. 24; "More Firms Fire Employees for Email Violations," *Gainesville Sun* (Florida), June 6, 2006, p. B1.

41 Based on S. Proudfoot, "1 in 3 Workers Admit to Improper Email; Stories of Career-Killing Gaffes Leave Many Unfazed, Study Finds," *Edmonton Journal*, June 25, 2008, p. A1; E. Church, "Employers Read Email as Fair Game," *Globe and Mail*, April 14, 1998, p. B16; and J. Kay, "Someone Will Watch Over Me: Think Your Office Emails Are Private? Think Again," *National Post Business*, January 2001, pp. 59–64.

42 J. Kay, "Someone Will Watch Over Me: Think Your Office Emails Are Private? Think Again," *National Post Business*, January 2001, pp. 59–64.

43 E. Church, "Employers Read Email as Fair Game," *Globe and Mail*, April 14, 1998, p. B16.

44 A. Harmon, "Appeal of Instant Messaging Extends into the Workplace," *New York Times*, March 11, 2003, p. A1.

45 http://www.cwta.ca/CWTASite/english/industryfacts.html

46 J. Bow, "Business Jumps on Text-Messaging Wave," *Business Edge*, April 5, 2007, p. 12.

47 A. Williams, "Mind Your BlackBerry or Mind Your Manners," *New York Times*, June 21, 2009, http://www.nytimes.com

48 "Survey Finds Mixed Reviews on Checking Email During Meetings," *IPMA-HR Bulletin*, April 27, 2007, p. 1.

49 K. Gurchiek, "Shoddy Writing Can Trip Up Employees, Organizations," *SHRM Online*, April 27, 2006, pp. 1–2.

50 D. Lidsky, "It's Not Just Who You Know," *Fast Company*, May 2007, p. 56.

51 Based on D. Bell, "Probe Will Examine Cop's Online Comments," *Nanaimo Daily News*, March 31, 2010, p. A4; and D. Bell, "Mountie's Posts on Facebook Raise Hackles," *Times-Colonist*, March 27, 2010, p. A1.

52 http://blog.nielsen.com/nielsenwire/online_mobile/buzz-in-the-blogosphere-millions-more-bloggers-and-blog-readers/

53 Based on "At Many Companies, Hunt for Leakers Expands Arsenal of Monitoring Tactics," *Wall Street Journal*, September 11, 2006, pp. B1, B3; and B. J. Alge, G. A. Ballinger, S. Tangirala, and J. L. Oakley, "Information Privacy in Organizations: Empowering Creative and Extra-Role Performance," *Journal of Applied Psychology* 91, no. 1 (2006), pp. 221–232.

54 J. Castaldo, "Are You Sure You Really Want To Tweet That, Boss?" *Canadian Business*, November 22, 2010.

55 http://ec2-107-21-125-140.compute-1.amazonaws.com/wp-content/themes/ceo/assets/F500-Social-CEO-Index.pdf

56 See D. Tannen, *You Just Don't Understand: Women and Men in Conversation* (New York: Ballantine Books, 1991); and D. Tannen, *Talking from 9 to 5* (New York: William Morrow, 1995).

57 D. Goldsmith and P. Fulfs, "You Just Don't Have the Evidence: An Analysis of Claims and Evidence in Deborah Tannen's *You Just Don't Understand*," in *Communications Yearbook*, vol. 22, ed. M. Roloff (Thousand Oaks, CA: Sage, 1999).

58 N. Langton, "Differences in Communication Styles: Asking for a Raise," in *Organizational Behavior: Experiences and Cases*, 4th ed., ed. D. Marcic (St. Paul, MN: West Publishing, 1995).

59 See M. Munter, "Cross-Cultural Communication for Managers," *Business Horizons*, May–June 1993, pp. 75–76.

60 N. Adler, *International Dimensions of Organizational Behavior*, 4th ed. (Cincinnati, OH: South Western, 2002), p. 94.

61 See, for instance, C. F. Fink, "Some Conceptual Difficulties in Theory of Social Conflict," *Journal of Conflict Resolution*, December 1968, pp. 412–460. For an updated review of the conflict literature, see J. A. Wall Jr. and R. R. Callister, "Conflict and Its Management," *Journal of Management* 21, no. 3 (1995), pp. 515–558.

62 L. L. Putnam and M. S. Poole, "Conflict and Negotiation," in *Handbook of Organizational Communication: An Inter-disciplinary Perspective*, ed. F. M. Jablin, L. L. Putnam, K. H. Roberts, and L. W. Porter (Newbury Park, CA: Sage, 1987), pp. 549–599.

63 K. W. Thomas, "Conflict and Negotiation Processes in Organizations," in *Handbook of Industrial and Organizational Psychology*, vol. 3, 2nd ed., ed. M. D. Dunnette and L. M. Hough (Palo Alto, CA: Consulting Psychologists Press, 1992), pp. 651–717.

64 For a comprehensive review of this approach, also called the interactionist approach, see C. De Dreu and E. Van de Vliert (eds.), *Using Conflict in Organizations* (London: Sage, 1997).

65 K. Jehn, "A Multimethod Examination of the Benefits and Detriments of Intragroup Conflict," *Administrative Science Quarterly*, June 1995, pp. 256–282; K. A. Jehn, "A Qualitative Analysis of Conflict Types and Dimensions in Organizational Groups," *Administrative Science Quarterly*, September 1997, pp. 530–557; K. A. Jehn and E. A. Mannix, "The Dynamic Nature of Conflict: A Longitudinal Study of Intragroup Conflict and Group Performance," *Academy of Management Journal*, April 2001, pp. 238–251; C. K. W. De Dreu and A. E. M. Van Vianen, "Managing Relationship Conflict and the Effectiveness of Organizational Teams," *Journal of Organizational Behavior*, May 2001, pp. 309–328; and K. A. Jehn and C. Bendersky, "Intragroup Conflict in Organizations: A Contingency Perspective on the Conflict-Outcome Relationship," in *Research in Organizational Behavior*, vol. 25, ed. R. M. Kramer and B. M. Staw (Oxford, UK: Elsevier, 2003), pp. 199–210.

66 A. C. Amason, "Distinguishing the Effects of Functional and Dysfunctional Conflict on Strategic Decision Making: Resolving a Paradox for Top Management Teams," *Academy of Management Journal* 39, no. 1 (1996), pp. 123–148.

67 "Survey Shows Managers Have Their Hands Full Resolving Staff Personality Conflicts," *IPMA-HR Bulletin*, November 3, 2006.

68 D. Tjosvold, "Cooperative and Competitive Goal Approach to Conflict: Accomplishments and Challenges," *Applied Psychology: An International Review* 47, no. 3 (1998), pp. 285–342.

69 K. W. Thomas, "Conflict and Negotiation Processes in Organizations," in *Handbook of Industrial and Organizational Psychology*, vol. 3, 2nd ed., ed. M. D. Dunnette and L. M. Hough (Palo Alto, CA: Consulting Psychologists Press, 1992), pp. 651–717.

70 C. K. W. De Dreu, A. Evers, B. Beersma, E. S. Kluwer, and A. Nauta, "A Theory-Based Measure of Conflict Management Strategies in the Workplace," *Journal of Organizational Behavior* 22, no. 6 (September 2001), pp. 645–668. See also D. G. Pruitt and J. Rubin, *Social Conflict: Escalation, Stalemate and Settlement* (New York: Random House, 1986).

71 C. K. W. De Dreu, A. Evers, B. Beersma, E. S. Kluwer, and A. Nauta, "A Theory-Based Measure of Conflict Management Strategies in the Workplace," *Journal of Organizational Behavior* 22, no. 6 (September 2001), pp. 645–668.

72 R. A. Baron, "Personality and Organizational Conflict: Effects of the Type A Behavior Pattern and Self-Monitoring," *Organizational Behavior and Human Decision Processes*, October 1989, pp. 281–296; A. Drory and I. Ritov, "Effects of Work Experience and Opponent's Power on Conflict Management Styles," *International Journal of Conflict Management* 8 (1997), pp. 148–161; R. J. Sternberg and L. J. Soriano, "Styles of Conflict Resolution," *Journal of Personality and Social Psychology*, July 1984, pp. 115–126; and R. J. Volkema and T. J. Bergmann, "Conflict Styles as Indicators of Behavioral Patterns in Interpersonal Conflicts," *Journal of Social Psychology*, February 1995, pp. 5–15.

73 These ideas are based on S. P. Robbins, *Managing Organizational Conflict: A Nontraditional Approach* (Upper Saddle River, NJ: Prentice Hall, 1974), pp. 59–89.

74 Based on K. W. Thomas, "Toward Multidemensional Values in Teaching: The Example of Conflict Behaviours," *Academy of Management Review*, July 1977, p. 487; and C. K. W. De Dreu, A. Evers, B. Beersma, E. S. Kluwer, and A. Nauta, "A Theory-Based Measure of Conflict Management Strategies in the Workplace," *Journal of Organizational Behaviour* 22, no. 6 (September 2001). pp. 645–688.

75 "Managers Spend More Than 6 Hours Per Week Handling Staff Conflicts: Survey," *hrreporter.com*, March 23, 2011.

76 R. D. Ramsey, "Interpersonal Conflicts," *SuperVision* 66, no. 4 (April 2005), pp. 14–17.

77 M. A. Von Glinow, D. L. Shapiro, and J. M. Brett, "Can We Talk, and Should We? Managing Emotional Conflict in Multicultural Teams," *Academy of Management Review* 29, no. 4 (October 2004), pp. 578–592.

78 R. Kreitner and A. Kinicki, *Organizational Behavior*, 6th ed. (New York: McGraw Hill, 2004), p. 492, Table 14-1. Reprinted by permission of McGraw Hill Education.

79 J. A. Wall Jr., *Negotiation: Theory and Practice* (Glenview, IL: Scott, Foresman, 1985).

80 http://www.gov.sk.ca/news?newsId=db80bb4e-28ae-49d0-819f-bb9e328081bd

81 http://www.gov.sk.ca/news?newsId=9c8ad8fa-d115-479a-8937-2ecfeaad195e

82 This model is based on R. J. Lewicki, "Bargaining and Negotiation," *Exchange: The Organizational Behavior Teaching Journal* 6, no. 2 (1981), pp. 39–40; and B. S. Moskal, "The Art of the Deal," *IndustryWeek*, January 18, 1993, p. 23.

83 J. C. Magee, A. D. Galinsky, and D. H. Gruenfeld, "Power, Propensity to Negotiate, and Moving First in Competitive Interactions," *Personality and Social Psychology Bulletin*, February 2007, pp. 200–212.

84 Based on G. Ku, A. D. Galinsky, and J. K. Murnighan, "Starting Low but Ending High: A Reversal of the Anchoring Effect in Auctions," *Journal of Personality and Social Psychology* 90 (June 2006), pp. 975–986; K. Sherstyuk, "A Comparison of First Price Multi-Object Auctions," *Experimental Economics* 12, no. 1 (2009), pp. 42–64; and R. M. Isaac, T. C. Salmon, and A. Zillante, "A Theory of Jump Bidding in Ascending Auctions," *Journal of Economic Behavior & Organization* 62, no. 1 (2007), pp. 144–164.

85 D. A. Moore, "Myopic Prediction, Self-Destructive Secrecy, and the Unexpected Benefits of Revealing Final Deadlines in Negotiation," *Organizational Behavior and Human Decision Processes*, July 2004, pp. 125–139.

86 J. R. Curhan, H. A. Elfenbein, and H. Xu, "What Do People Value When They Negotiate? Mapping the Domain of Subjective Value in Negotiation," *Journal of Personality and Social Psychology* 91, no. 3 (2007), pp. 493–512.

87 S. S. Wiltermuth and M. A. Neale, "Too Much Information: The Perils of Nondiagnostic Information in Negotiations," *Journal of Applied Psychology* 96, no. 1 (2011), pp. 192–201.

88 R. Fisher and W. Ury, *Getting to Yes: Negotiating Agreement Without Giving In*, 2nd ed. (New York: Penguin Books, 1991).

89 P. H. Kim and A. R. Fragale, "Choosing the Path to Bargaining Power: An Empirical Comparison of BATNAs and Contributions in Negotiation," *Journal of Applied Psychology* 90, no. 2 (March 2005), pp. 373–381.

90 M. H. Bazerman and M. A. Neale, *Negotiating Rationally* (New York: Free Press, 1992), pp. 67–68.

91 R. P. Larrick and G. Wu, "Claiming a Large Slice of a Small Pie: Asymmetric Disconfirmation in Negotiation," *Journal of Personality and Social Psychology* 93, no. 2 (2007), pp. 212–233.

92 R. Fisher and W. Ury, *Getting to Yes: Negotiating Agreement without Giving In*, 2nd ed. (New York: Penguin Books, 1991).

93 M. Marks and C. Harold, "Who Asks and Who Receives in Salary Negotiation," *Journal of Organizational Behavior* 32, no. 3 (2011), pp. 371–394.

94 R. Fisher and W. Ury, *Getting to Yes: Negotiating Agreement without Giving In*, 2nd ed. (New York: Penguin Books, 1991).

95 S. A. Hellweg and S. L. Phillips, "Communication and Productivity in Organizations: A State-of-the-Art Review," in *Proceedings of the 40th Annual Academy of Management Conference*, Detroit, 1980, pp. 188–192.

96 The points presented here were influenced by E. Van de Vliert, "Escalative Intervention in Small-Group Conflicts," *Journal of Applied Behavioral Science*, Winter 1985, pp. 19–36.

97 Q. Reade, "Workplace Conflict Is Time-consuming Problem for Business," *PersonnelToday.com*, September 30, 2004, http://www.personneltoday.co.uk

98 Based on R. Cohen, "Bad Bidness," *New York Times Magazine*, September 2, 2006, p. 22; M. E. Schweitzer, "Deception in Negotiations," in *Wharton on Making Decisions*, ed. S. J. Hoch and H. C. Kunreuther (New York: Wiley, 2001), pp. 187–200; and M. Diener, "Fair Enough," *Entrepreneur*, January 2002, pp. 100–102.

99 Based on M. E. Schweitzer, "Deception in Negotiations," in *Wharton on Making Decisions*, ed. S. J. Hoch and H. C. Kunreuther (New York: Wiley, 2001), pp. 187–200; and M. Diener, "Fair Enough," *Entrepreneur*, January 2002, pp. 100–102.

100 "Dianna Abdala," *Wikipedia* (en.wikipedia.org/wiki/Dianna_Abdala); and J. Sandberg, "Infamous Email Writers Aren't Always Killing Their Careers After All," *Wall Street Journal*, February 21, 2006, p. B1.

101 These suggestions are based on J. A. Wall Jr. and M. W. Blum, "Negotiations," *Journal of Management*, June 1991, pp. 278–282; and J. S. Pouliot, "Eight Steps to Success in Negotiating," *Nation's Business*, April 1999, pp. 40–42.

Chapter 7

1 Vignette based on "Tim Hortons' Extra-Large Trouble Trouble," *Macleans.ca*, September 7, 2010, http://www2.macleans.ca/2010/09/07/extra-large-trouble-trouble; and M. Friscolanti, "Tim Hortons: Rolling in Dough," *Macleans.ca*, September 6, 2011, http://www2.macleans.ca/2011/09/06/rolling-in-dough

2 Based on B. M. Bass, *Bass & Stogdill's Handbook of Leadership*, 3rd ed. (New York: Free Press, 1990).

3 D. H. Gruenfeld, M. E. Inesi, J. C. Magee, and A. D. Galinsky, "Power and the Objectification of Social Targets," *Journal of Personality and Social Psychology* 95, no. 1 (2008), pp. 111–127; A. D. Galinsky, J. C. Magee, D. H. Gruenfeld, J. A. Whitson, and K. A. Liljenquist, "Power Reduces the Press of the Situation: Implications for Creativity, Conformity, and Dissonance," *Journal of Personality and Social Psychology* 95, no. 6 (2008), pp. 1450–1466; and J. C. Magee and C. A. Langner, "How Personalized and Socialized Power Motivation Facilitate Antisocial and Prosocial Decision-Making," *Journal of Research in Personality* 42, no. 6 (2008), pp. 1547–1559.

4 R. M. Kanter, "Power Failure in Management Circuits," *Harvard Business Review*, July–August 1979, p. 65.

5 Power Outage: A Loss of Social Power Distorts How Money Is Represented," *ScienceDaily*, July 26, 2010, http://www.sciencedaily.com/releases/2010/06/100607151320.htm; and D. Dubois, D. D. Rucker, and A. D. Galinsky, "The Accentuation Bias: Money Literally Looms Larger (and Sometimes Smaller) to the Powerless," *Social Psychological and Personality Science* 1, no. 3 (2010), pp. 199–205.

6 G. A. Van Kleef, A. C. Homan, C. Finkenauer, S. Gundemir, E. Stamkou, "Breaking the Rules to Rise to Power: How Norm Violators Gain Power in the Eyes of Others," *Social Psychological and Personality Science*, January 26, 2011, published online before print http://spp.sagepub.com/content/early/2011/01/20/1948550611398416

7 J. Lammers, D. A. Stapel, and A. Galinsky, "Power Increases Hypocrisy: Moralizing in Reasoning, Immunity and Behavior," *Psychological Science* 21, no. 5 (2010), pp. 737–744.

8 S. Prashad, "Fill Your Power Gap," *Globe and Mail*, July 23, 2003, p. C3.

9 T. B. Lawrence, M. K. Mauws, B. Dyck, and R. F. Kleysen, "The Politics of Organizational Learning: Integrating Power into the 4I Framework," *Academy of Management Review* 30, no. 1 (January 2005), pp. 180–191.

10 J. R. P. French Jr. and B. Raven, "The Bases of Social Power," in *Studies in Social Power*, ed. D. Cartwright (Ann Arbor, MI: University of Michigan, Institute for Social Research, 1959),

pp. 150–167. For an update on French and Raven's work, see D. E. Frost and A. J. Stahelski, "The Systematic Measurement of French and Raven's Bases of Social Power in Workgroups," *Journal of Applied Social Psychology*, April 1988, pp. 375–389; T. R. Hinkin and C. A. Schriesheim, "Development and Application of New Scales to Measure the French and Raven (1959) Bases of Social Power," *Journal of Applied Psychology*, August 1989, pp. 561–567; and G. E. Littlepage, J. L. Van Hein, K. M. Cohen, and L. L. Janiec, "Evaluation and Comparison of Three Instruments Designed to Measure Organizational Power and Influence Tactics," *Journal of Applied Social Psychology*, January 16–31, 1993, pp. 107–125.

11 B. H. Raven, "Social Influence and Power," in *Current Studies in Social Psychology*, ed. I. D. Steiner and M. Fishbein (New York: Holt, Rinehart and Winston, 1965), pp. 371–382.

12 E. A. Ward, "Social Power Bases of Managers: Emergence of a New Factor," *Journal of Social Psychology*, February 2001, pp. 144–147.

13 S. R. Giessner and T. W. Schubert, "High in the Hierarchy: How Vertical Location and Judgments of Leaders' Power Are Interrelated," *Organizational Behavior and Human Decision Processes* 104, no. 1 (2007), pp. 30–44.

14 D. Hickson, C. Hinings, C. Lee, R. Schneck, and J. Pennings, "A Strategic Contingencies Theory of Intra-Organizational Power," *Administrative Science Quarterly* 16 (1971), pp. 216–229; and J. W. Dean Jr. and J. R. Evans, *Total Quality: Management, Organization, and Strategy* (Minneapolis-St. Paul, MN: West, 1994).

15 G. Yukl, H. Kim, and C. M. Falbe, "Antecedents of Influence Outcomes," *Journal of Applied Psychology* 81, no. 3 (June 1, 1996), pp. 309–317.

16 P. P. Carson, K. D. Carson, and C. W. Roe, "Social Power Bases: A Meta-analytic Examination of Interrelationships and Outcomes," *Journal of Applied Social Psychology* 23, no. 14 (1993), pp. 1150–1169.

17 Cited in J. R. Carlson, D. S. Carlson, and L. L. Wadsworth, "The Relationship between Individual Power Moves and Group Agreement Type: An Examination and Model," *S.A.M. Advanced Management Journal* 65, no. 4 (2000), pp. 44–51.

18 C. M. Falbe and G. Yukl, "Consequences for Managers of Using Single Tactics and Combinations of Tactics," *Academy of Management Journal* 35 (1992), pp. 638–652.

19 Vignette based on "Tim Hortons' Extra-Large Trouble Trouble," *Macleans.ca*, September 7, 2010, http://www2.macleans.ca/2010/09/07/extra-large-trouble-trouble

20 R. E. Emerson, "Power-Dependence Relations," *American Sociological Review* 27 (1962), pp. 31–41.

21 Thanks are due to an anonymous reviewer for supplying this insight.

22 H. Mintzberg, *Power in and around Organizations* (Englewood Cliffs, NJ: Prentice Hall, 1983), p. 24.

23 Vignette based on M. Friscolanti, "Tim Hortons: Rolling in Dough," *Macleans.ca*, September 6, 2011, http://www2.macleans.ca/2011/09/06/rolling-in-dough

24 See, for example, D. Kipnis, S. M. Schmidt, C. Swaffin-Smith, and I. Wilkinson, "Patterns of Managerial Influence: Shotgun Managers, Tacticians, and Bystanders," *Organizational Dynamics*, Winter 1984, pp. 58–67; T. Case, L. Dosier, G. Murkison, and B. Keys, "How Managers Influence Superiors: A Study of Upward Influence Tactics," *Leadership and Organization Development Journal* 9, no. 4 (1988), pp. 25–31; D. Kipnis and S. M. Schmidt, "Upward-Influence Styles: Relationship with Performance Evaluations, Salary, and Stress," *Administrative Science Quarterly*, December 1988, pp. 528–542; G. Yukl and C. M. Falbe, "Influence Tactics and Objectives in Upward, Downward, and Lateral Influence Attempts," *Journal of Applied Psychology*, April 1990,

pp. 132–140; G. Yukl, H. Kim, and C. M. Falbe, "Antecedents of Influence Outcomes," *Journal of Applied Psychology*, June 1996, pp. 309–317; K. E. Lauterbach and B. J. Weiner, "Dynamics of Upward Influence: How Male and Female Managers Get Their Way," *Leadership Quarterly*, Spring 1996, pp. 87–107; K. R. Xin and A. S. Tsui, "Different Strokes for Different Folks? Influence Tactics by Asian-American and Caucasian-American Managers," *Leadership Quarterly*, Spring 1996, pp. 109–132; S. J. Wayne, R. C. Liden, I. K. Graf, and G. R. Ferris, "The Role of Upward Influence Tactics in Human Resource Decisions," *Personnel Psychology*, Winter 1997, pp. 979–1006; and C. A. Higgins and T. A. Judge, "The Effect of Applicant Influence Tactics on Recruiter Perceptions of Fit and Hiring Recommendations: A Field Study," *Journal of Applied Psychology* 89, no. 4 (August 2004), pp. 622–632.

25 This section adapted from G. Yukl, C. M. Falbe, and J. Y. Youn, "Patterns of Influence Behavior for Managers," *Group & Organization Studies* 18, no. 1 (March 1993), p. 7.

26 G. Yukl, *Leadership in Organizations*, 5th ed. (Upper Saddle River, NJ: Prentice Hall, 2002), pp. 141–174; G. R. Ferris, W. A. Hochwarter, C. Douglas, F. R. Blass, R. W. Kolodinksy, and D. C. Treadway, "Social Influence Processes in Organizations and Human Resource Systems," in *Research in Personnel and Human Resources Management*, vol. 21, ed. G. R. Ferris and J. J. Martocchio (Oxford, UK: JAI Press/Elsevier, 2003), pp. 65–127; and C. A. Higgins, T. A. Judge, and G. R. Ferris, "Influence Tactics and Work Outcomes: A Meta-analysis," *Journal of Organizational Behavior*, March 2003, pp. 89–106.

27 C. M. Falbe and G. Yukl, "Consequences for Managers of Using Single Influence Tactics and Combinations of Tactics," *Academy of Management Journal*, July 1992, pp. 638–653.

28 R. E. Petty and P. Briñol, "Persuasion: From Single to Multiple to MetaCognitive Processes," *Perspectives on Psychological Science* 3, no. 2 (2008), pp. 137–147.

29 I. Stern and J. D. Westphal, "Stealthy Footsteps to the Boardroom: Executives' Backgrounds, Sophisticated Interpersonal Influence Behavior, and Board Appointments," *Administrative Science Quarterly* 55, no. 2 (2010), pp. 278–319; and G. Yukl, *Leadership in Organizations*, 5th ed. (Upper Saddle River, NJ: Prentice Hall, 2002), pp. 141–174.

30 N. K. Grant, L. R. Fabrigar, and Heidi Lim, "Exploring the Efficacy of Compliments as a Tactic for Securing Compliance," *Basic & Applied Social Psychology* 32, no. 3 (2010), pp. 226–233.

31 C. M. Falbe and G. Yukl, "Consequences for Managers of Using Single Influence Tactics and Combinations of Tactics," *Academy of Management Journal*, July 1992, pp. 638–653.

32 A. W. Kruglanski, A. Pierro, and E. T. Higgins, "Regulatory Mode and Preferred Leadership Styles: How Fit Increases Job Satisfaction," *Basic and Applied Social Psychology* 29, no. 2 (2007), pp. 137–149; and A. Pierro, L. Cicero, and B. H. Raven, "Motivated Compliance with Bases of Social Power," *Journal of Applied Social Psychology* 38, no. 7 (2008), pp. 1921–1944.

33 "Building a Better Workforce," *PROFIT*, February 16, 2011, http://www.profitguide.com/article/10084—building-a-better-workforce—page0

34 This is the definition given by R. Forrester, "Empowerment: Rejuvenating a Potent Idea," *Academy of Management Executive*, August 2000, pp. 67–80.

35 R. E. Quinn and G. M. Spreitzer, "The Road to Empowerment: Seven Questions Every Leader Should Consider," *Organizational Dynamics*, Autumn 1997, p. 38.

36 C. Argyris, "Empowerment: The Emperor's New Clothes," *Harvard Business Review*, May–June 1998.

37 Concordia University, "Freedom's Just Another Word for Employee Satisfaction," *ScienceDaily*, January 24, 2011, http://www.sciencedaily.com/releases/2011/01/110124102944.htm

38 J. Schaubroeck, J. R. Jones, and J. L. Xie, "Individual Differences in Utilizing Control to Cope with Job Demands: Effects on Susceptibility to Infectious Disease," *Journal of Applied Psychology*, April 2001, pp. 265–278.

39 "Delta Promotes Empowerment," *Globe and Mail*, May 31, 1999, Advertising Supplement, p. C5.

40 T. Lee and C. M. Brotheridge, "When the Prey Becomes the Predator: Bullying as Predictor of Reciprocal Bullying, Coping, and Well-Being" (working paper, University of Regina, 2005).

41 N. J. Fast and S. Chen, "When the Boss Feels Inadequate: Power, Incompetence, and Aggression." *Psychological Science* 20, no. 11 (2009), pp. 1406–1413.

42 University of California-Berkeley, "Bosses Who Feel Inadequate Are More Likely to Bully," *ScienceDaily*, October 15, 2009, http://www.sciencedaily.com/releases/2009/10/091014102209.htm

43 M. S. Hershcovis and J. Barling, "Comparing the Outcomes of Sexual Harassment and Workplace Aggression: A Meta-analysis" (paper presented at the Seventh International Conference on Work, Stress and Health, Washington, DC, March 8, 2008).

44 Quebec Labour Standards, s. 81.18, *Psychological Harassment at Work*.

45 http://www.benefitscanada.com/benefits/other/b-c-s-anti-bullying-law-in-effect-30348

46 S. Stecklow, "Sexual-Harassment Cases Plague U.N.," *Wall Street Journal*, May 21, 2009, p. A1.

47 *Janzen v. Platy Enterprises Ltd.* [1989] 10 C.H.R.R. D/6205 SCC.

48 The following section is based on J. N. Cleveland and M. E. Kerst, "Sexual Harassment and Perceptions of Power: An Under-Articulated Relationship," *Journal of Vocational Behavior*, February 1993, pp. 49–67.

49 C. Bass, "University Bans Faculty-Student Sex," *Yale Alumni Magazine*, March/April 2010, http://yalealumnimagazine.com/issues/2010_03/lv_sex015.html

50 http://www2.carleton.ca/equity/human-rights/policy/1307-2/#SEXUAL%20HARASSMENT

51 C. Hill and E. Silva, *Drawing The Line: Sexual Harassment On Campus* (Washington, DC: American Association of University Women, 2005).

52 H. Burnett-Nichols, "Don't Touch, Do Tell," *University Affairs*, March 8, 2010, http://www.universityaffairs.ca/dont-touch-do-tell.aspx

53 C. R. Willness, P. Steel, and K. Lee, "A Meta-analysis of the Antecedents and Consequences of Workplace Sexual Harassment," *Personnel Psychology* 60 (2007), pp. 127–162.

54 See, for instance, "Car Dealership Settles Same Sex Harassment Lawsuit," *Associated Press*, June 28, 1999.

55 Vignette based on "Tim Hortons' Extra-Large Trouble Trouble," *Macleans.ca*, September 7, 2010, http://www2.macleans.ca/2010/09/07/extra-large-trouble-trouble

56 S. A. Culbert and J. J. McDonough, *The Invisible War: Pursuing Self-Interest at Work* (New York: John Wiley, 1980), p. 6.

57 H. Mintzberg, *Power in and around Organizations* (Englewood Cliffs, NJ: Prentice Hall, 1983), p. 26.

58 T. Cole, "Who Loves Ya?" *Report on Business Magazine*, April 1999, p. 54.

59 D. Farrell and J. C. Petersen, "Patterns of Political Behavior in Organizations," *Academy of Management Review*, July 1982, p. 405. For a thoughtful analysis of the academic controversies underlying any definition of organizational politics, see A. Drory and T. Romm, "The Definition of Organizational Politics: A Review," *Human Relations*, November 1990, pp. 1133–1154; and R. S. Cropanzano, K. M. Kacmar, and D. P. Bozeman, "Organizational Politics, Justice, and Support: Their Differences and Similarities," in *Organizational Politics, Justice and Support: Managing Social Climate at Work*, ed. R. S. Cropanzano and K. M. Kacmar (Westport, CT: Quorum Books, 1995), pp. 1–18.

60 P. Dawson and D. Buchanan, "The Way It Really Happened: Competing Narratives in the Political Process of Technological Change," *Human Relations* 58, no. 7 (2005), pp. 845–865; A. Spicer, "The Political Process of Inscribing a New Technology," *Human Relations* 58, no. 7 (2005), pp. 867–890; and J. Swan and H. Scarbrough, "The Politics of Networked Innovation," *Human Relations* 58, no. 7 (2005), pp. 913–943.

61 J. Pfeffer, *Power in Organizations* (Marshfield, MA: Pittman, 1981).

62 G. R. Ferris, G. S. Russ, and P. M. Fandt, "Politics in Organizations," in *Impression Management in Organizations*, ed. R. A. Giacalone and P. Rosenfeld (Newbury Park, CA: Sage, 1989), pp. 143–170; and K. M. Kacmar, D. P. Bozeman, D. S. Carlson, and W. P. Anthony, "An Examination of the Perceptions of Organizational Politics Model: Replication and Extension," *Human Relations*, March 1999, pp. 383–416.

63 K. M. Kacmar and R. A. Baron, "Organizational Politics: The State of the Field, Links to Related Processes, and an Agenda for Future Research," in *Research in Personnel and Human Resources Management*, vol. 17, ed. G. R. Ferris (Greenwich, CT: JAI Press, 1999); and M. Valle and L. A. Witt, "The Moderating Effect of Teamwork Perceptions on the Organizational Politics–Job Satisfaction Relationship," *Journal of Social Psychology*, June 2001, pp. 379–388.

64 G. R. Ferris, D. D. Frink, M. C. Galang, J. Zhou, K. M. Kacmar, and J. L. Howard, "Perceptions of Organizational Politics: Prediction, Stress-Related Implications, and Outcomes," *Human Relations*, February 1996, pp. 233–266; K. M. Kacmar, D. P. Bozeman, D. S. Carlson, and W. P. Anthony, "An Examination of the Perceptions of Organizational Politics Model; Replication and Extension," *Human Relations*, March 1999, p. 388; and J. M. L. Poon, "Situational Antecedents and Outcomes of Organizational Politics Perceptions," *Journal of Managerial Psychology* 18, no. 2 (2003), pp. 138–155.

65 C. Kiewitz, W. A. Hochwarter, G. R. Ferris, and S. L. Castro, "The Role of Psychological Climate in Neutralizing the Effects of Organizational Politics on Work Outcomes," *Journal of Applied Social Psychology*, June 2002, pp. 1189–1207; and J. M. L. Poon, "Situational Antecedents and Outcomes of Organizational Politics Perceptions," *Journal of Managerial Psychology* 18, no. 2 (2003), pp. 138–155.

66 K. M. Kacmar and R. A. Baron, "Organizational Politics: The State of the Field, Links to Related Processes, and an Agenda for Future Research," in *Research in Personnel and Human Resources Management*, vol. 17, ed. G. R. Ferris (Greenwich, CT: JAI Press, 1999); and M. Valle and L. A. Witt, "The Moderating Effect of Teamwork Perceptions on the Organizational Politics–Job Satisfaction Relationship," *Journal of Social Psychology*, June 2001, pp. 379–388.

67 R. W. Allen, D. L. Madison, L. W. Porter, P. A. Renwick, and B. T. Mayes, "Organizational Politics: Tactics and Characteristics of Its Actors," *California Management Review*, Fall 1979, pp. 77–83.

68 See, for instance, W. L. Gardner and M. J. Martinko, "Impression Management in Organizations," *Journal of Management*, June 1988, pp. 321–338; M. C. Bolino and W. H. Turnley, "More Than One Way to Make an Impression: Exploring Profiles of Impression Management," *Journal of Management* 29, no. 2 (2003), pp. 141–160; S. Zivnuska, K. M. Kacmar, L. A. Witt, D. S. Carlson, and V. K. Bratton, "Interactive Effects of Impression Management and Organizational Politics on Job Performance," *Journal of Organizational Behavior*, August 2004, pp. 627–640; and M. C. Bolino, K. M. Kacmar, W. H. Turnley, and J. B. Gilstrap, "A Multi-Level Review of Impression Management Motives and Behaviors," *Journal of Management* 34, no. 6 (2008), pp. 1080–1109.

69 M. R. Leary and R. M. Kowalski, "Impression Management: A Literature Review and Two-Component Model," *Psychological Bulletin,* January 1990, p. 40.

70 W. L. Gardner and M. J. Martinko, "Impression Management in Organizations," *Journal of Management,* June 1988, p. 333.

71 R. A. Baron, "Impression Management by Applicants during Employment Interviews: The 'Too Much of a Good Thing' Effect," in *The Employment Interview: Theory, Research, and Practice,* ed. R. W. Eder and G. R. Ferris (Newbury Park, CA: Sage, 1989), pp. 204–215.

72 A. P. J. Ellis, B. J. West, A. M. Ryan, and R. P. DeShon, "The Use of Impression Management Tactics in Structural Interviews: A Function of Question Type?" *Journal of Applied Psychology,* December 2002, pp. 1200–1208.

73 C. K. Stevens and A. L. Kristof, "Making the Right Impression: A Field Study of Applicant Impression Management during Job Interviews," *Journal of Applied Psychology* 80 (1995), pp. 587–606; and L. A. McFarland, A. M. Ryan, and S. D. Kriska, "Impression Management Use and Effectiveness Across Assessment Methods," *Journal of Management* 29, no. 5 (2003), pp. 641–661; C. A. Higgins and T. A. Judge, "The Effect of Applicant Influence Tactics on Recruiter Perceptions of Fit and Hiring Recommendations: A Field Study," *Journal of Applied Psychology* 89, no. 4 (2004), pp. 622–632; and W. C. Tsai, C. C. Chen, and S. F. Chiu, "Exploring Boundaries of the Effects of Applicant Impression Management Tactics in Job Interviews," *Journal of Management,* February 2005, pp. 108–125.

74 D. C. Gilmore and G. R. Ferris, "The Effects of Applicant Impression Management Tactics on Interviewer Judgments," *Journal of Management,* December 1989, pp. 557–564.

75 C. K. Stevens and A. L. Kristof, "Making the Right Impression: A Field Study of Applicant Impression Management during Job Interviews," *Journal of Applied Psychology* 80 (1995), pp. 587–606.

76 C. A. Higgins, T. A. Judge, and G. R. Ferris, "Influence Tactics and Work Outcomes: A Meta-analysis," *Journal of Organizational Behavior,* March 2003, pp. 89–106.

77 C. A. Higgins, T. A. Judge, and G. R. Ferris, "Influence Tactics and Work Outcomes: A Meta-analysis," *Journal of Organizational Behavior,* March 2003, pp. 89–106.

78 K. J. Harris, K. M. Kacmar, S. Zivnuska, and J. D. Shaw, "The Impact of Political Skill on Impression Management Effectiveness," *Journal of Applied Psychology* 92, no. 1 (2007), pp. 278–285; and D. C. Treadway, G. R. Ferris, A. B. Duke, G. L. Adams, and J. B. Thatcher, "The Moderating Role of Subordinate Political Skill on Supervisors' Impressions of Subordinate Ingratiation and Ratings of Subordinate Interpersonal Facilitation," *Journal of Applied Psychology* 92, no. 3 (2007), pp. 848–855.

79 J. M. Maslyn and D. B. Fedor, "Perceptions of Politics: Does Measuring Different Foci Matter?" *Journal of Applied Psychology* 84 (1998), pp. 645–653; and L. G. Nye and L. A. Witt, "Dimensionality and Construct Validity of the Perceptions of Organizational Politics Scale," *Educational and Psychological Measurement* 53 (1993), pp. 821–829.

80 G. R. Ferris, D. D. Frink, D. I. Bhawuk, J. Zhou, and D. C. Gilmore, "Reactions of Diverse Groups to Politics in the Workplace," *Journal of Management* 22 (1996), pp. 23–44; K. M. Kacmar, D. P. Bozeman, D. S. Carlson, and W. P. Anthony, "An Examination of the Perceptions of Organizational Politics Model: Replication and Extension," *Human Relations* 52 (1999), pp. 383–416.

81 T. P. Anderson, "Creating Measures of Dysfunctional Office and Organizational Politics: The DOOP and Short-Form DOOP Scales," *Psychology: A Journal of Human Behavior* 31 (1994), pp. 24–34.

82 G. R. Ferris, D. D. Frink, D. I. Bhawuk, J. Zhou, and D. C. Gilmore, "Reactions of Diverse Groups to Politics in the Workplace," *Journal of Management* 22 (1996), pp. 23–44; and K. M. Kacmar,

D. P. Bozeman, D. S. Carlson, and W. P. Anthony, "An Examination of the Perceptions of Organizational Politics Model: Replication and Extension," *Human Relations* 52 (1999), pp. 383–416.

83 K. M. Kacmar, D. P. Bozeman, D. S. Carlson, and W. P. Anthony, "An Examination of the Perceptions of Organizational Politics Model: Replication and Extension," *Human Relations* 52 (1999), pp. 383–416; J. M. Maslyn and D. B. Fedor, "Perceptions of Politics: Does Measuring Different Foci Matter?" *Journal of Applied Psychology* 84 (1998), pp. 645–653.

84 M. Warshaw, "The Good Guy's (and Gal's) Guide to Office Politics," *Fast Company,* April 1998, p. 156.

85 G. Yukl, C. M. Falbe, and J. Y. Youn, "Patterns of Influence Behavior for Managers," *Group & Organization Studies* 18, no. 1 (March 1993), p. 7.

86 A. Salz, "Graduation Banquet Speech Raising Questions," *Edmonton Sun,* June 12, 2011, http://www.edmontonsun.com/2011/06/12/graduation-banquet-speech-raising-questions

87 This exercise was inspired by one found in J. R. Gordon, *Organizational Behavior,* 2nd ed. (Englewood Cliffs, NJ: Prentice Hall, 1992), pp. 499–502.

88 Based on D. Kadlec, "Did Sandy Play Dirty?" *Time,* November 25, 2002.

89 Based on S. Armour, "'Business Casual' Causes Confusion," *USA Today,* July 10, 2007, pp. 1B, 2B; T. McMahon, "Toeing the Line on Flip-Flops; Questions & Answers," *National Post,* June 14, 2011, p. A.9; and M. Harris, "Dress-Code Debate Divides Many Workplaces," *Nanaimo Daily News,* February 16, 2011, p. A.9.

90 *From Concepts to Skills* based on S. P. Robbins and P. L. Hunsaker, *Training in Interpersonal Skills: Tips for Managing People at Work,* 2nd ed. (Upper Saddle River, NJ: Prentice Hall, 1996), pp. 131–134.

OB on the Edge: The Toxic Workplace

1 C. Cole, "Lions Punt Printers after On-Air Tirade; QB Confronted Teammate at End of Sunday's OT Loss at Winnipeg," *Calgary Herald,* October 14, 2010, p. 6.

2 C. Cole, "B.C. Lions Release Casey Printers for His Onfield Tirade at Teammate," *Vancouver Sun,* October 13, 2010, http://www.vancouversun.com/sports/Casey+Printers+released+Lions+after+team+epic+collapse/3664346/story.html

3 L. M. Anderson and C. M. Pearson, "Tit for Tat? The Spiraling Effect of Incivility in the Workplace," *Academy of Management Review* 24, no. 3 (1999), pp. 452–471.

4 L. M. Anderson and C. M. Pearson, "Tit for Tat? The Spiraling Effect of Incivility in the Workplace," *Academy of Management Review* 24, no. 3 (1999), pp. 452–471. For further discussion of this, see R. A. Baron and J. H. Neuman, "Workplace Violence and Workplace Aggression: Evidence on Their Relative Frequency and Potential Causes," *Aggressive Behavior* 22 (1996), pp. 161–173; C. C. Chen and W. Eastman, "Towards a Civic Culture for Multicultural Organizations," *Journal of Applied Behavioral Science* 33 (1997), pp. 454–470; J. H. Neuman and R. A. Baron, "Aggression in the Workplace," in *Antisocial Behavior in Organizations,* ed. R. A. Giacalone and J. Greenberg (Thousand Oaks, CA: Sage, 1997), pp. 37–67.

5 L. M. Anderson and C. M. Pearson, "Tit for Tat? The Spiraling Effect of Incivility in the Workplace," *Academy of Management Review* 24, no. 3 (1999), pp. 452–471.

6 L. M. Anderson and C. M. Pearson, "Tit for Tat? The Spiraling Effect of Incivility in the Workplace," *Academy of Management Review* 24, no. 3 (1999), pp. 452–471.

7 R. Corelli, "Dishing Out Rudeness: Complaints Abound as Customers Are Ignored, Berated," *Maclean's,* January 11, 1999, p. 44.

8 R. Corelli, "Dishing Out Rudeness: Complaints Abound as Customers Are Ignored, Berated," *Maclean's*, January 11, 1999, p. 44.

9 "Definition of Workplace Bullying," *Workforce Bullying Institute*, http://www.workplacebullying.org/individuals/problem/definition/

10 http://www.workplacebullying.org/research/WBI-Zogby-2007Survey.html

11 C. Porath and C. Pearson, "How Toxic Colleagues Corrode Performance," *Harvard Business Review*, April 2009, p. 24.

12 A. M. Hansen and R. Persson, "Frequency of Bullying at Work, Physiological Response, and Mental Health," *Journal of Psychosomatic Research* 70, no. 1 (January 2011), pp. 19–27.

13 B. L. Lovell and R. T. Lee, "Impact of Workplace Bullying on Emotional and Physical Well-Being: A Longitudinal Collective Case Study," *Journal of Aggression, Maltreatment & Trauma* 20, no. 3 (April 2011), pp. 344–357.

14 R. Corelli, "Dishing Out Rudeness: Complaints Abound as Customers Are Ignored, Berated," *Maclean's*, January 11, 1999, p. 44.

15 R. Corelli, "Dishing Out Rudeness: Complaints Abound as Customers Are Ignored, Berated," *Maclean's*, January 11, 1999, p. 44.

16 R. A. Baron and J. H. Neuman, "Workplace Violence and Workplace Aggression: Evidence on Their Relative Frequency and Potential Causes," *Aggressive Behavior* 22 (1996), pp. 161–173; C. MacKinnon, *Only Words* (New York: Basic Books, 1994); J. Marks, "The American Uncivil Wars," *U.S. News & World Report*, April 22, 1996, pp. 66–72; and L. P. Spratlen, "Workplace Mistreatment: Its Relationship to Interpersonal Violence," *Journal of Psychosocial Nursing* 32, no. 12 (1994), pp. 5–6.

17 Information in this paragraph based on A. Hanon and C. Castagna, "Gunman Sought Revenge," *Edmonton Sun*, March 12, 2010; and L. Drake, S. McKeen, R. Warnica, and R. Cormier, "Angry Worker Blamed in Fatal Shooting," *Calgary Herald*, March 13, 2010.

18 W. M. Glenn, "An Employee's Survival Guide: An ILO Survey of Workplaces in 32 Countries Ranked Argentina the Most Violent, Followed by Romania, France and Then, Surprisingly, Canada," *Occupational Health & Safety*, April–May 2002, p. 28 passim.

19 D. Flavelle, "Managers Cited for Increase in 'Work Rage,'" *Vancouver Sun*, April 11, 2000, pp. D1, D11; and "Profile of Workplace Victimization Incidents," *Statistics Canada*, 2007, http://www.statcan.ca/english/research/85F0033MIE/2007013/findings/profile.htm

20 http://www.csmonitor.com/USA/Society/2010/0107/ABB-shooting-Economy-may-play-role-in-workplace-violence

21 E. Wulfhorst, "Desk Rage Spoils Workplace for Many Americans," *Reuters*, July 10, 2008, http://www.reuters.com/article/newsOne/idUSN0947145320080710

22 S. James, "Long Hours Linked to Rising Toll from Stress," *Financial Post (National Post)*, August 6, 2003, p. FP12.

23 "Profile of Workplace Victimization Incidents," *Statistics Canada*, 2007, http://www.statcan.ca/english/research/85F0033MIE/2007013/findings/profile.htm

24 W. M. Glenn, "An Employee's Survival Guide: An ILO Survey of Workplaces in 32 Countries Ranked Argentina the Most Violent, Followed by Romania, France and Then, Surprisingly, Canada," *Occupational Health & Safety*, April–May 2002, p. 28 passim.

25 W. M. Glenn, "An Employee's Survival Guide: An ILO Survey of Workplaces in 32 Countries Ranked Argentina the Most Violent, Followed by Romania, France and Then, Surprisingly, Canada," *Occupational Health & Safety*, April–May 2002, p. 28 passim.

26 http://www.nstu.ca/images/pklot/NSTU%20Teacher%20Stress%20Survey%20Report_final.pdf

27 A. M. Webber, "Danger: Toxic Company," *Fast Company*, November 1998, pp. 152–157.

28 D. Flavelle, "Managers Cited for Increase in 'Work Rage,'" *Vancouver Sun*, April 11, 2000, pp. D1, D11; and G. Smith, *Work Rage* (Toronto: HarperCollins Canada, 2000).

29 "Work Rage," *BCBusiness Magazine*, January 2001, p. 23.

30 D. Flavelle, "Managers Cited for Increase in 'Work Rage,'" *Vancouver Sun*, April 11, 2000, pp. D1, D11.

31 A. Skogstad, T. Torsheim, S. Einarsen, and L.J. Hauge, "Testing the Work Environment Hypothesis of Bullying on a Group Level of Analysis: Psychosocial Factors as Precursors of Observed Workplace Bullying," *Applied Psychology: An International Review* 60, no. 3 (July 2011), pp. 475–495.

32 D. Geddes, and L. T. Stickney, "The Trouble with Sanctions: Organizational Responses to Deviant Anger Displays at Work," *Human Relations* 64, no. 2 (February 2011), pp. 201–230.

33 H. Levinson, *Emotional Health in the World of Work* (Boston: South End Press, 1964); and E. Schein, *Organizational Psychology* (Englewood Cliffs, NJ: Prentice Hall, 1980).

34 Barry Ray, "Who's Afraid of the Big Bad Boss? Plenty of Us, New FSU Study Shows," *FSU News*, December 4, 2006, http://www.fsu.edu/news/2006/12/04/bad.boss/

35 D. Abma, "Bad Managers a Problem in Canadian Workplaces: Survey," *Financial Post*, January 19, 2011.

36 E. W. Morrison and S. L. Robinson, "When Employees Feel Betrayed: A Model of How Psychological Contract Violation Develops," *Academy of Management Journal* 22 (1997), pp. 226–256; S. L. Robinson, "Trust and Breach of the Psychological Contract," *Administrative Science Quarterly* 41 (1996), pp. 574–599; and S. L. Robinson, M. S. Kraatz, and D. M. Rousseau, "Changing Obligations and the Psychological Contract: A Longitudinal Study," *Academy of Management Journal* 37 (1994), pp. 137–152. A recent study suggests that perceptions of the psychological contract vary by culture: D. C. Thomas, S. R. Fitzsimmons, E. C. Ravlin, K. Au, B. Z. Ekelund, and C. Barzantny, "Psychological Contracts across Cultures," *Organization Studies* 31, no. 11 (2010), pp. 1437–1458.

37 T. R. Tyler and P. Dogoey, "Trust in Organizational Authorities: The Influence of Motive Attributions on Willingness to Accept Decisions," in *Trust in Organizations*, ed. R. M. Kramer and T. R. Tyler (Thousand Oaks, CA: Sage, 1996), pp. 246–260.

38 S. Montes and D. Zweig, "Do Promises Matter? An Exploration of the Role of Promises in Psychological Contract Breach," *Journal of Applied Psychology* 94, no. 5 (2009), pp. 1243–1260.

39 A. M. Webber, "Danger: Toxic Company," *Fast Company*, November 1998, pp. 152–157.

40 Based on A. McKee, "Neutralize Your Toxic Boss," *Harvard Business School Conversation Starter*, January 20, 2009, http://blogs.harvardbusiness.org; and "Toxic Bosses: How to Live with the S.O.B," *BusinessWeek*, August 14, 2008, http://www.businessweek.com

41 A. M. Webber, "Danger: Toxic Company," *Fast Company*, November 1998, pp. 152–157.

42 P. Frost, *Toxic Emotions at Work* (Cambridge, MA: Harvard Business School Press, 2003).

43 R. Bacal, "Toxic Organizations—Welcome to the Fire of an Unhealthy Workplace," *Work 911.com*, 2000, http://www.work911.com/articles/toxicorgs.htm

44 "Men More Likely to Be Rude in Workplace, Survey Shows," *Vancouver Sun*, August 16, 1999, p. B10.

45 D. E. Gibson and S. G. Barsade, "The Experience of Anger at Work: Lessons from the Chronically Angry" (paper presented at the annual meetings of the Academy of Management, Chicago, August 11, 1999).

46 D. E. Gibson and S. G. Barsade, "The Experience of Anger at Work: Lessons from the Chronically Angry" (paper presented at the annual meetings of the Academy of Management, Chicago, August 11, 1999).

47 R. Corelli, "Dishing Out Rudeness: Complaints Abound as Customers Are Ignored, Berated," *Maclean's*, January 11, 1999, p. 44.

48 P. Frost and S. Robinson, "The Toxic Handler: Organizational Hero—and Casualty," *Harvard Business Review*, July–August 1999, p. 101 (Reprint 99406).

49 P. Frost and S. Robinson, "The Toxic Handler: Organizational Hero—and Casualty," *Harvard Business Review*, July–August 1999, p. 101 (Reprint 99406).

50 P. Frost and S. Robinson, "The Toxic Handler: Organizational Hero—and Casualty," *Harvard Business Review*, July–August 1999, p. 101 (Reprint 99406).

Chapter 8

1 Vignette based on National Defence, "Canadian Forces Snowbirds to Gain Leadership Depth," (news release), January 9, 2010, http://www.snowbirds.dnd.ca/v2/nr-sp/nr-sp-eng.asp?cat=2&id=321; J. Graham, "She's the Boss: Snowbirds First Female Pilot to Lead Aerobatic Squad," *Canadian Press*, May 2, 2010, http://www.cbc.ca/canada/saskatchewan/story/2010/05/02/sask-snowbirds.html#ixzz0mv2nPxRr; and C. Coward, "Five Questions with a Snowbird," *Hamilton Spectator*, November 5, 2011, http://www.thespec.com/localprofile/article/620542—five-questions-with-a-snowbird

2 J. P. Kotter, "What Leaders Really Do," *Harvard Business Review*, May–June 1990, pp. 103–111.

3 R. N. Kanungo, "Leadership in Organizations: Looking Ahead to the 21st Century," *Canadian Psychology* 39, no. 1–2 (1998), p. 77. For more evidence of this consensus, see N. Adler, *International Dimensions of Organizational Behavior*, 3rd ed. (Cincinnati, OH: South-Western College Publishing, 1997); R. J. House, "Leadership in the Twenty-First Century," in *The Changing Nature of Work*, ed. A. Howard (San Francisco: Jossey-Bass, 1995), pp. 411–450; R. N. Kanungo and M. Mendonca, *Ethical Dimensions of Leadership* (Thousand Oaks, CA: Sage Publications, 1996); and A. Zaleznik, "The Leadership Gap," *Academy of Management Executive* 4, no. 1 (1990), pp. 7–22.

4 Vignette based on J. Graham, "She's the Boss: Snowbirds First Female Pilot to Lead Aerobatic Squad," *Canadian Press*, May 2, 2010, http://www.cbc.ca/canada/saskatchewan/story/2010/05/02/sask-snowbirds.html#ixzz0mv2nPxRr

5 Based on D. Fost, "Survey Finds Many Workers Mistrust Bosses," *San Francisco Chronicle*, January 3, 2007, http://www.sfgate.com; and T. Weiss, "The Narcissistic CEO," *Forbes*, August 29, 2006, http://www.forbes.com

6 C. C. Eckel, E. Fatas, and R. Wilson, "Cooperation and Status in Organizations," *Journal of Public Economic Theory* 12, no. 4 (2010), pp. 737–762.

7 J. G. Geier, "A Trait Approach to the Study of Leadership in Small Groups," *Journal of Communication*, December 1967, pp. 316–323.

8 S. A. Kirkpatrick and E. A. Locke, "Leadership: Do Traits Matter?" *Academy of Management Executive*, May 1991, pp. 48–60; and S. J. Zaccaro, R. J. Foti, and D. A. Kenny, "Self-Monitoring and Trait-Based Variance in Leadership: An Investigation of Leader Flexibility across Multiple Group Situations," *Journal of Applied Psychology*, April 1991, pp. 308–315.

9 See T. A. Judge, J. E. Bono, R. Ilies, and M. Werner, "Personality and Leadership: A Review" (paper presented at the 15th Annual Conference of the Society for Industrial and Organizational Psychology, New Orleans, 2000); and T. A. Judge, J. E. Bono, R. Ilies, and M. W. Gerhardt, "Personality and Leadership: A Qualitative and Quantitative Review," *Journal of Applied Psychology*, August 2002, pp. 765–780.

10 T. A. Judge, J. E. Bono, R. Ilies, and M. Werner, "Personality and Leadership: A Review" (paper presented at the 15th Annual Conference of the Society for Industrial and Organizational Psychology, New Orleans, 2000).

11 D. R. Ames and F. J. Flynn, "What Breaks a Leader: The Curvilinear Relation between Assertiveness and Leadership," *Journal of Personality and Social Psychology* 92, no. 2 (2007), pp. 307–324.

12 K. Ng, S. Ang, and K. Chan, "Personality and Leader Effectiveness: A Moderated Mediation Model of Leadership Self-Efficacy, Job Demands, and Job Autonomy," *Journal of Applied Psychology* 93, no. 4 (2008), pp. 733–743.

13 This section is based on D. Goleman, "What Makes a Leader?" *Harvard Business Review*, November–December 1998, pp. 93–102; J. M. George, "Emotions and Leadership: The Role of Emotional Intelligence," *Human Relations*, August 2000, pp. 1027–1055; C. S. Wong and K. S. Law, "The Effects of Leader and Follower Emotional Intelligence on Performance and Attitude: An Exploratory Study," *Leadership Quarterly*, June 2002, pp. 243–274; and D. R. Caruso and C. J. Wolfe, "Emotional Intelligence and Leadership Development," in *Leader Development for Transforming Organizations: Growing Leaders for Tomorrow*, ed. D. David and S. J. Zaccaro (Mahwah, NJ: Lawrence Erlbaum, 2004), pp. 237–263.

14 J. Champy, "The Hidden Qualities of Great Leaders," *Fast Company*, November 2003, p. 135.

15 J. Antonakis, "Why 'Emotional Intelligence' Does Not Predict Leadership Effectiveness: A Comment on Prati, Douglas, Ferris, Ammeter, and Buckley (2003)," *International Journal of Organizational Analysis* 11 (2003), pp. 355–361. See also M. Zeidner, G. Matthews, and R. D. Roberts, "Emotional Intelligence in the Workplace: A Critical Review," *Applied Psychology: An International Review* 53 (2004), pp. 371–399; and F. Walter, M. S. Cole, and R. H. Humphrey, "Emotional Intelligence: Sine Qua Non of Leadership or Folderol?" *Academy of Management Perspectives* 25, no. 1 (2011), pp. 45–59.

16 T. A. Judge, J. E. Bono, R. Ilies, and M. Werner, "Personality and Leadership: A Review" (paper presented at the 15th Annual Conference of the Society for Industrial and Organizational Psychology, New Orleans, 2000); R. G. Lord, C. L. DeVader, and G. M. Alliger, "A Meta-analysis of the Relation between Personality Traits and Leadership Perceptions: An Application of Validity Generalization Procedures," *Journal of Applied Psychology*, August 1986, pp. 402–410; and J. A. Smith and R. J. Foti, "A Pattern Approach to the Study of Leader Emergence," *Leadership Quarterly*, Summer 1998, pp. 147–160.

17 R. M. Stogdill and A. E. Coons (eds.), *Leader Behavior: Its Description and Measurement*, Research Monograph no. 88 (Columbus: Ohio State University, Bureau of Business Research, 1951). This research is updated in C. A. Schriesheim, C. C. Cogliser, and L. L. Neider, "Is It 'Trustworthy'? A Multiple-Levels-of-Analysis Reexamination of an Ohio State Leadership Study, with Implications for Future Research," *Leadership Quarterly*, Summer 1995, pp. 111–145; and T. A. Judge, R. F. Piccolo, and R. Ilies, "The Forgotten Ones? The Validity of Consideration and Initiating Structure in Leadership Research," *Journal of Applied Psychology*, February 2004, pp. 36–51.

18 R. M. Stogdill and A. E. Coons, eds., *Leader Behavior: Its Description and Measurement*, Research Monograph no. 88 (Columbus: Ohio State University, Bureau of Business Research, 1951). This research is updated in S. Kerr, C. A. Schriesheim, C. J. Murphy, and R. M. Stogdill, "Toward a Contingency Theory of Leadership Based upon the Consideration and Initiating Structure Literature," *Organizational Behavior and Human Performance*, August 1974, pp. 62–82; and C. A. Schriesheim, C. C. Cogliser, and L. L. Neider, "Is It 'Trustworthy'? A Multiple-Levels-of-Analysis Reexamination of an Ohio State Leadership Study, with Implications for Future Research," *Leadership Quarterly*, Summer 1995, pp. 111–145.

19 D. Akst, "The Rewards of Recognizing a Job Well Done," *Wall Street Journal*, January 31, 2007, p. D9.

20 R. Kahn and D. Katz, "Leadership Practices in Relation to Productivity and Morale," in *Group Dynamics: Research and Theory*, 2nd ed., ed. D. Cartwright and A. Zander (Elmsford, NY: Row, Paterson, 1960).

21 T. A. Judge, R. F. Piccolo, and R. Ilies, "The Forgotten Ones? The Validity of Consideration and Initiating Structure in Leadership Research," *Journal of Applied Psychology*, February 2004, pp. 36–51.

22 G. Yukl and D. D. Van Fleet, "Theory and Research on Leadership in Organizations," in *Handbook of Industrial and Organizational Psychology*, vol. 2, ed. M. D. Dunnette and L. M. Hough (Palo Alto, CA: Consulting Psychologists Press, 1992), pp. 147–197.

23 For a critical review, see A. K. Korman, "'Consideration,' 'Initiating Structure' and Organizational Criteria—A Review," *Personnel Psychology* 19 (1966), pp. 349–361. For a more supportive review, see S. Kerr and C. Schriesheim, "Consideration, Initiating Structure, and Organizational Criteria—An Update of Korman's 1966 Review," *Personnel Psychology* 27 (1974), pp. 555–568.

24 Based on G. Johns and A. M. Saks, *Organizational Behaviour*, 5th ed. (Toronto: Pearson Education Canada, 2001), p. 276.

25 A. J. Mayo and N. Nohria, "Zeitgeist Leadership," *Harvard Business Review* 83, no. 10 (2005), pp. 45–60.

26 See, for instance, P. M. Podsakoff, S. B. MacKenzie, M. Ahearne, and W. H. Bommer, "Searching for a Needle in a Haystack: Trying to Identify the Illusive Moderators of Leadership Behavior," *Journal of Management* 1, no. 3 (1995), pp. 422–470.

27 H. Wang, K. S. Law, R. D. Hackett, D. Wang, and Z. X. Chen, "Leader-Member Exchange as a Mediator of the Relationship between Transformational Leadership and Followers' Performance and Organizational Citizenship Behavior," *Academy of Management Journal* 48, no. 3 (June 2005), pp. 420–432.

28 F. E. Fiedler, *A Theory of Leadership Effectiveness* (New York: McGraw-Hill, 1967).

29 Cited in R. J. House and R. N. Aditya, "The Social Scientific Study of Leadership: Quo Vadis?" *Journal of Management* 23, no. 3 (1997), p. 422.

30 G. Johns and A. M. Saks, *Organizational Behaviour*, 5th ed. (Toronto: Pearson Education Canada, 2001), pp. 278–279.

31 For controversy surrounding the Fiedler LPC scale, see A. Bryman, "Leadership in Organizations," in *Handbook of Organization Studies*, ed. S. R. Clegg, C. Hardy, and W. R. Nord (London: Sage, 1996), pp. 279–280; A. Bryman, *Leadership and Organizations* (London: Routledge and Kegan Paul, 1986); and T. Peters and N. Austin, *A Passion for Excellence* (New York: Random House, 1985). For supportive evidence on the Fiedler model, see L. H. Peters, D. D. Hartke, and J. T. Pohlmann, "Fiedler's Contingency Theory of Leadership: An Application of the Meta-analysis Procedures of Schmidt and Hunter," *Psychological Bulletin*, March 1985, pp. 274–285; C. A. Schriesheim, B. J. Tepper, and L. A. Tetrault, "Least Preferred Co-Worker Score, Situational Control, and Leadership Effectiveness: A Meta-analysis of Contingency Model Performance Predictions," *Journal of Applied Psychology*, August 1994, pp. 561–573; and R. Ayman, M. M. Chemers, and F. Fiedler, "The Contingency Model of Leadership Effectiveness: Its Levels of Analysis," *Leadership Quarterly*, Summer 1995, pp. 147–167. For evidence that LPC scores are not stable, see, for instance, R. W. Rice, "Psychometric Properties of the Esteem for the Least Preferred Coworker (LPC) Scale," *Academy of Management Review*, January 1978, pp. 106–118; C. A. Schriesheim, B. D. Bannister, and W. H. Money, "Psychometric Properties of the LPC Scale: An Extension of Rice's Review," *Academy of Management Review*, April 1979, pp. 287–290; and J. K. Kennedy, J. M. Houston, M. A. Korgaard, and D. D. Gallo, "Construct Space of the Least Preferred Co-worker (LPC) Scale," *Educational & Psychological Measurement*, Fall 1987, pp. 807–814. For difficulty in applying Fiedler's model, see E. H. Schein, *Organizational Psychology*, 3rd ed. (Englewood Cliffs, NJ: Prentice

Hall, 1980), pp. 116–117; and B. Kabanoff, "A Critique of Leader Match and Its Implications for Leadership Research," *Personnel Psychology*, Winter 1981, pp. 749–764. For evidence that Hersey and Blanchard's model has received little attention from researchers, see R. K. Hambleton and R. Gumpert, "The Validity of Hersey and Blanchard's Theory of Leader Effectiveness," *Group & Organization Studies*, June 1982, pp. 225–242; C. L. Graeff, "The Situational Leadership Theory: A Critical View," *Academy of Management Review*, April 1983, pp. 285–291; R. P. Vecchio, "Situational Leadership Theory: An Examination of a Prescriptive Theory," *Journal of Applied Psychology*, August 1987, pp. 444–451; J. R. Goodson, G. W. McGee, and J. F. Cashman, "Situational Leadership Theory: A Test of Leadership Prescriptions," *Group & Organization Studies*, December 1989, pp. 446–461; W. Blank, J. R. Weitzel, and S. G. Green, "A Test of the Situational Leadership Theory," *Personnel Psychology*, Autumn 1990, pp. 579–597; and W. R. Norris and R. P. Vecchio, "Situational Leadership Theory: A Replication," *Group & Organization Management*, September 1992, pp. 331–342. For evidence of partial support for the theory, see R. P. Vecchio, "Situational Leadership Theory: An Examination of a Prescriptive Theory," *Journal of Applied Psychology*, August 1987, pp. 444–451; and W. R. Norris and R. P. Vecchio, "Situational Leadership Theory: A Replication," *Group & Organization Management*, September 1992, pp. 331–342; and for evidence of no support for Hersey and Blanchard, see W. Blank, J. R. Weitzel, and S. G. Green, "A Test of the Situational Leadership Theory," *Personnel Psychology*, Autumn 1990, pp. 579–597.

32 P. Hersey and K. H. Blanchard, "So You Want to Know Your Leadership Style?" *Training and Development Journal*, February 1974, pp. 1–15; and P. Hersey, K. H. Blanchard, and D. E. Johnson, *Management of Organizational Behavior: Leading Human Resources*, 8th ed. (Upper Saddle River, NJ: Prentice Hall, 2001), cited in C. F. Fernandez and R. P. Vecchio, "Situational Leadership Theory Revisited: A Test of an ACROSS-Jobs Perspective," *Leadership Quarterly* 8, no. 1 (1997), p. 67. See also http://www.situational.com/leadership.htm

33 See, for instance, C. F. Fernandez and R. P. Vecchio, "Situational Leadership Theory Revisited: A Test of an across-Jobs Perspective," *Leadership Quarterly* 8, no. 1 (1997), pp. 67–84; C. L. Graeff, "Evolution of Situational Leadership Theory: A Critical Review," *Leadership Quarterly* 8, no. 2 (1997), pp. 153–170; and R. P. Vecchio and K. J. Boatwright, "Preferences for Idealized Styles of Supervision," *Leadership Quarterly*, August 2002, pp. 327–342.

34 M. G. Evans, "The Effects of Supervisory Behavior on the Path-Goal Relationship," *Organizational Behavior and Human Performance* 5 (1970), pp. 277–298; M. G. Evans, "Leadership and Motivation: A Core Concept," *Academy of Management Journal* 13 (1970), pp. 91–102; R. J. House, "A Path-Goal Theory of Leader Effectiveness," *Administrative Science Quarterly*, September 1971, pp. 321–338; R. J. House and T. R. Mitchell, "Path-Goal Theory of Leadership," *Journal of Contemporary Business*, Autumn 1974, p. 86; M. G. Evans, "Leadership," in *Organizational Behavior*, ed. S. Kerr (Columbus, OH: Grid Publishing, 1979); R. J. House, "Retrospective Comment," in *The Great Writings in Management and Organizational Behavior*, 2nd ed., ed. L. E. Boone and D. D. Bowen (New York: Random House, 1987), pp. 354–364; and M. G. Evans, "Fuhrungstheorien, Wegziel-theorie," in *Handworterbuch Der Fuhrung*, 2nd ed., ed. A. Kieser, G. Reber, and R. Wunderer, trans. G. Reber (Stuttgart, Germany: Schaffer Poeschal Verlag, 1995), pp. 1075–1091.

35 G. R. Jones, J. M. George, C. W. L. Hill, and N. Langton, *Contemporary Management* (Toronto: McGraw-Hill Ryerson, 2002), p. 392.

36 See J. C. Wofford and L. Z. Liska, "Path-Goal Theories of Leadership: A Meta-analysis," *Journal of Management*, Winter 1993, pp. 857–876; M. G. Evans, "R.J. House's 'A Path-Goal Theory of Leader Effectiveness,'" *Leadership Quarterly*, Fall 1996, pp. 305–309;

C. A. Schriesheim and L. L. Neider, "Path-Goal Leadership Theory: The Long and Winding Road," *Leadership Quarterly*, Fall 1996, pp. 317–321; A. Somech, "The Effects of Leadership Style and Team Process on Performance and Innovation in Functionally Heterogeneous Teams," *Journal of Management* 32, no. 1 (2006), pp. 132–157; and S. Yun, S. Faraj, and H. P. Sims, "Contingent Leadership and Effectiveness of Trauma Resuscitation Teams," *Journal of Applied Psychology* 90, no. 6 (2005), pp. 1288–1296.

37 T. Sy, "What Do You Think of Followers? Examining the Content, Structure, and Consequences of Implicit Followership Theories," *Organizational Behavior and Human Decision Processes* 113, no. 2 (2010), pp. 73–84.

38 S. Kerr and J. M. Jermier, "Substitutes for Leadership: Their Meaning and Measurement," *Organizational Behavior and Human Performance*, December 1978, pp. 375–403; J. P. Howell and P. W. Dorfman, "Substitutes for Leadership: Test of a Construct," *Academy of Management Journal*, December 1981, pp. 714–728; J. P. Howell, P. W. Dorfman, and S. Kerr, "Leadership and Substitutes for Leadership," *Journal of Applied Behavioral Science* 22, no. 1 (1986), pp. 29–46; J. P. Howell, D. E. Bowen, P. W. Dorfman, S. Kerr, and P. M. Podsakoff, "Substitutes for Leadership: Effective Alternatives to Ineffective Leadership," *Organizational Dynamics*, Summer 1990, pp. 21–38; P. M. Podsakoff, B. P. Niehoff, S. B. MacKenzie, and M. L. Williams, "Do Substitutes for Leadership Really Substitute for Leadership? An Empirical Examination of Kerr and Jermier's Situational Leadership Model," *Organizational Behavior and Human Decision Processes*, February 1993, pp. 1–44; P. M. Podsakoff and S. B. MacKenzie, "An Examination of Substitutes for Leadership within a Levels-of-Analysis Framework," *Leadership Quarterly*, Fall 1995, pp. 289–328; P. M. Podsakoff, S. B. MacKenzie, and W. H. Bommer, "Transformational Leader Behaviors and Substitutes for Leadership as Determinants of Employee Satisfaction, Commitment, Trust, and Organizational Citizenship Behaviors," *Journal of Management* 22, no. 2 (1996), pp. 259–298; P. M. Podsakoff, S. B. MacKenzie, and W. H. Bommer, "Meta-analysis of the Relationships between Kerr and Jermier's Substitutes for Leadership and Employee Attitudes, Role Perceptions, and Performance," *Journal of Applied Psychology*, August 1996, pp. 380–399; and J. M. Jermier and S. Kerr, "'Substitutes for Leadership: Their Meaning and Measurement'—Contextual Recollections and Current Observations," *Leadership Quarterly* 8, no. 2 (1997), pp. 95–101.

39 S. D. Dionne, F. J. Yammarino, L. E. Atwater, and L. R. James, "Neutralizing Substitutes for Leadership Theory: Leadership Effects and Common-Source Bias," *Journal of Applied Psychology* 87 (2002), pp. 454–464; and J. R. Villa, J. P. Howell, P. W. Dorfman, and D. L. Daniel, "Problems with Detecting Moderators in Leadership Research Using Moderated Multiple Regression," *Leadership Quarterly* 14 (2002), pp. 3–23.

40 Vignette based on J. Graham, "She's the Boss: Snowbirds First Female Pilot to Lead Aerobatic Squad," *Canadian Press*, May 2, 2010, http://www.cbc.ca/canada/saskatchewan/story/2010/05/02/sask-snowbirds.html#ixzz0mv2nPxRr; and C. Coward, "Five Questions with a Snowbird," *Hamilton Spectator*, November 5, 2011, http://www.thespec.com/localprofile/article/620542—five-questions-with-a-snowbird

41 M. Weber, *The Theory of Social and Economic Organization*, trans. A. M. Henderson and T. Parsons (New York: The Free Press, 1947).

42 J. A. Conger and R. N. Kanungo, "Behavioral Dimensions of Charismatic Leadership," in *Charismatic Leadership*, ed. J. A. Conger and R. N. Kanungo (San Francisco: Jossey-Bass, 1988), p. 79.

43 J. A. Conger and R. N. Kanungo, *Charismatic Leadership in Organizations* (Thousand Oaks, CA: Sage, 1998); and R. Awamleh and W. L. Gardner, "Perceptions of Leader Charisma and

Effectiveness: The Effects of Vision Content, Delivery, and Organizational Performance," *Leadership Quarterly*, Fall 1999, pp. 345–373.

44 B. Shamir, R. J. House, and M. B. Arthur, "The Motivational Effects of Charismatic Leadership: A Self-Concept Theory," *Organization Science*, November 1993, pp. 577–594.

45 R. Kark, B. Shamir, and G. Chen, "The Two Faces of Transformational Leadership: Empowerment and Dependency," *Journal of Applied Psychology* 88, no. 2 (2003), pp. 246–255.

46 D. N. Den Hartog, A. H. B. De Hoogh, and A. E. Keegan, "The Interactive Effects of Belongingness and Charisma on Helping and Compliance," *Journal of Applied Psychology* 92, no. 4 (2007), pp. 1131–1139.

47 A. Erez, V. F. Misangyi, D. E. Johnson, M. A. LePine, and K. C. Halverson, "Stirring the Hearts of Followers: Charismatic Leadership as the Transferal of Affect," *Journal of Applied Psychology* 93, no. 3 (2008), pp. 602–615. For reviews on the role of vision in leadership, see S. J. Zaccaro, "Visionary and Inspirational Models of Executive Leadership: Empirical Review and Evaluation," in *The Nature of Executive Leadership: A Conceptual and Empirical Analysis of Success*, ed. S. J. Zaccaro (Washington, DC: American Psychological Association, 2001), pp. 259–278; and M. Hauser and R. J. House, "Lead through Vision and Values," in *Handbook of Principles of Organizational Behavior*, ed. E. A. Locke (Malden, MA: Blackwell, 2004), pp. 257–273.

48 D. A. Waldman, B. M. Bass, and F. J. Yammarino, "Adding to Contingent-Reward Behavior: The Augmenting Effect of Charismatic Leadership," *Group & Organization Studies*, December 1990, pp. 381–394; and S. A. Kirkpatrick and E. A. Locke, "Direct and Indirect Effects of Three Core Charismatic Leadership Components on Performance and Attitudes," *Journal of Applied Psychology*, February 1996, pp. 36–51.

49 A. H. B. de Hoogh, D. N. den Hartog, P. L. Koopman, H. Thierry, P. T. van den Berg, and J. G. van der Weide, "Charismatic Leadership, Environmental Dynamism, and Performance," *European Journal of Work & Organizational Psychology*, December 2004, pp. 447–471; S. Harvey, M. Martin, and D. Stout, "Instructor's Transformational Leadership: University Student Attitudes and Ratings," *Psychological Reports*, April 2003, pp. 395–402; and D. A. Waldman, M. Javidan, and P. Varella, "Charismatic Leadership at the Strategic Level: A New Application of Upper Echelons Theory," *Leadership Quarterly*, June 2004, pp. 355–380.

50 R. J. House, "A 1976 Theory of Charismatic Leadership," in *Leadership: The Cutting Edge*, ed. J. G. Hunt and L. L. Larson (Carbondale, IL: Southern Illinois University Press, 1977), pp. 189–207; and Robert J. House and Ram N. Aditya, "The Social Scientific Study of Leadership," *Journal of Management* 23, no. 3 (1997), p. 441.

51 J. C. Pastor, M. Mayo, and B. Shamir, "Adding Fuel to Fire: The Impact of Followers' Arousal on Ratings of Charisma," *Journal of Applied Psychology* 92, no. 6 (2007), pp. 1584–1596.

52 F. Cohen, S. Solomon, M. Maxfield, T. Pyszczynski, and J. Greenberg, "Fatal Attraction: The Effects of Mortality Salience on Evaluations of Charismatic, Task-Oriented, and Relationship-Oriented Leaders," *Psychological Science*, December 2004, pp. 846–851; and M. G. Ehrhart and K. J. Klein, "Predicting Followers' Preferences for Charismatic Leadership: The Influence of Follower Values and Personality," *Leadership Quarterly*, Summer 2001, pp. 153–179.

53 K. Levine, R. Muenchen, and A. Brooks, "Measuring Transformational and Charismatic Leadership: Why Isn't Charisma Measured?" *Communication Monographs* 77, no. 4 (2010), pp. 576–591.

54 J. A. Conger, *The Charismatic Leader: Behind the Mystique of Exceptional Leadership* (San Francisco: Jossey-Bass, 1989); R. Hogan, R. Raskin, and D. Fazzini, "The Dark Side of Charisma," in *Measures of Leadership*, ed. K. E. Clark and M. B. Clark (West Orange, NJ: Leadership Library of America, 1990); D. Sankowsky, "The Charismatic Leader as Narcissist: Understanding the Abuse of Power," *Organizational Dynamics*, Spring 1995, pp. 57–71; and J. O'Connor, M. D. Mumford, T. C. Clifton, T. L. Gessner, and M. S. Connelly, "Charismatic Leaders and Destructiveness: An Historiometric Study," *Leadership Quarterly*, Winter 1995, pp. 529–555.

55 K. Yakabuski, "Henri-Paul Rousseau Was the King of Quebec's Pension Fund and His Returns the Envy of Many," *Globe and Mail*, January 31, 2009, p. B1.

56 G. Pitts, "Scandals Part of Natural Cycles of Excess," *Globe and Mail*, June 28, 2002, pp. B1, B5.

57 J. Collins, "Level 5 Leadership: The Triumph of Humility and Fierce Resolve," *Harvard Business Review*, January 2001, pp. 67–76; J. Collins, "Good to Great," *Fast Company*, October 2001, pp. 90–104; J. Collins, "The Misguided Mix-up," *Executive Excellence*, December 2002, pp. 3–4; and H. L. Tosi, V. F. Misangyi, A. Fanelli, D. A. Waldman, and F. J. Yammarino, "CEO Charisma, Compensation, and Firm Performance," *The Leadership Quarterly* 15 (2004), pp. 405–420.

58 See, for instance, B. M. Bass, B. J. Avolio, D. I. Jung, and Y. Berson, "Predicting Unit Performance by Assessing Transformational and Transactional Leadership," *Journal of Applied Psychology*, April 2003, pp. 207–218; and T. A. Judge and R. F. Piccolo, "Transformational and Transactional Leadership: A Meta-analytic Test of Their Relative Validity," *Journal of Applied Psychology*, October 2004, pp. 755–768.

59 N. W. Chi, Y. Y. Chung, and W. C. Tsai, "How Do Happy Leaders Enhance Team Success? The Mediating Roles of Transformational Leadership, Group Affective Tone, and Team Processes," *Journal of Applied Social Psychology* 41, no. 6 (2011), pp. 1421–1454.

60 B. M. Bass, "Leadership: Good, Better, Best," *Organizational Dynamics*, Winter 1985, pp. 26–40; and J. Seltzer and B. M. Bass, "Transformational Leadership: Beyond Initiation and Consideration," *Journal of Management*, December 1990, pp. 693–703.

61 T. R. Hinkin and C. A. Schriesheim, "An Examination of 'Nonleadership': From Laissez-Faire Leadership to Leader Reward Omission and Punishment Omission," *Journal of Applied Psychology* 93, no. 6 (2008), pp. 1234–1248.

62 S. J. Shin and J. Zhou, "Transformational Leadership, Conservation, and Creativity: Evidence from Korea," *Academy of Management Journal*, December 2003, pp. 703–714; V. J. García-Morales, F. J. Lloréns-Montes, and A. J. Verdú-Jover, "The Effects of Transformational Leadership on Organizational Performance Through Knowledge and Innovation," *British Journal of Management* 19, no. 4 (2008), pp. 299–313; and S. A. Eisenbeiss, D. van Knippenberg, and S. Boerner, "Transformational Leadership and Team Innovation: Integrating Team Climate Principles," *Journal of Applied Psychology* 93, no. 6 (2008), pp. 1438–1446.

63 Y. Ling, Z. Simsek, M. H. Lubatkin, and J. F. Veiga, "Transformational Leadership's Role in Promoting Corporate Entrepreneurship: Examining the CEO-TMT Interface," *Academy of Management Journal* 51, no. 3 (2008), pp. 557–576.

64 A. E. Colbert, A. E. Kristof-Brown, B. H. Bradley, and M. R. Barrick, "CEO Transformational Leadership: The Role of Goal Importance Congruence in Top Management Teams," *Academy of Management Journal* 51, no. 1 (2008), pp. 81–96.

65 D. Zohar and O. Tenne-Gazit, "Transformational Leadership and Group Interaction as Climate Antecedents: A Social Network Analysis," *Journal of Applied Psychology* 93, no. 4 (2008), pp. 744–757.

66 F. O. Walumbwa, B. J. Avolio, and W. Zhu, "How Transformational Leadership Weaves Its Influence on Individual Job Performance: The Role of Identification and Efficacy Beliefs," *Personnel Psychology* 61, no. 4 (2008), pp. 793–825.

67 J. E. Bono and T. A. Judge, "Self-Concordance at Work: Toward Understanding the Motivational Effects of Transformational Leaders," *Academy of Management Journal*, October 2003, pp. 554–571; Y. Berson and B. J. Avolio, "Transformational Leadership and the Dissemination of Organizational Goals: A Case Study of a Telecommunication Firm," *Leadership Quarterly*, October 2004, pp. 625–646; and J. Schaubroeck, S. S. K. Lam, and S. E. Cha, "Embracing Transformational Leadership: Team Values and the Impact of Leader Behavior on Team Performance," *Journal of Applied Psychology* 92, no. 4 (2007), pp. 1020–1030.

68 J. R. Baum, E. A. Locke, and S. A. Kirkpatrick, "A Longitudinal Study of the Relation of Vision and Vision Communication to Venture Growth in Entrepreneurial Firms," *Journal of Applied Psychology*, February 2000, pp. 43–54.

69 B. J. Avolio, W. Zhu, W. Koh, and P. Bhatia, "Transformational Leadership and Organizational Commitment: Mediating Role of Psychological Empowerment and Moderating Role of Structural Distance," *Journal of Organizational Behavior*, December 2004, pp. 951–968; and T. Dvir, N. Kass, and B. Shamir, "The Emotional Bond: Vision and Organizational Commitment Among High-Tech Employees," *Journal of Organizational Change Management* 17, no. 2 (2004), pp. 126–143.

70 R. T. Keller, "Transformational Leadership, Initiating Structure, and Substitutes for Leadership: A Longitudinal Study of Research and Development Project Team Performance," *Journal of Applied Psychology* 91, no. 1 (2006), pp. 202–210.

71 T. A. Judge and R. F. Piccolo, "Transformational and Transactional Leadership: A Meta-analytic Test of Their Relative Validity," *Journal of Applied Psychology*, October 2004, pp. 755–768.

72 Y. Ling, Z. Simsek, M. H. Lubatkin, and J. F. Veiga, "The Impact of Transformational CEOs on the Performance of Small- to Medium-Sized Firms: Does Organizational Context Matter?" *Journal of Applied Psychology* 93, no. 4 (2008), pp. 923–934.

73 J. Schaubroeck, S. S. K. Lam, and S. E. Cha, "Embracing Transformational Leadership: Team Values and the Impact of Leader Behavior on Team Performance," *Journal of Applied Psychology* 92, no. 4 (2007), pp. 1020–1030.

74 H. Hetland, G. M. Sandal, and T. B. Johnsen, "Burnout in the Information Technology Sector: Does Leadership Matter?" *European Journal of Work and Organizational Psychology* 16, no. 1 (2007), pp. 58–75; and K. B. Lowe, K. G. Kroeck, and N. Sivasubramaniam, "Effectiveness Correlates of Transformational and Transactional Leadership: A Meta-analytic Review of the MLQ Literature," *Leadership Quarterly*, Fall 1996, pp. 385–425.

75 See, for instance, J. Barling, T. Weber, and E. K. Kelloway, "Effects of Transformational Leadership Training on Attitudinal and Financial Outcomes: A Field Experiment," *Journal of Applied Psychology*, December 1996, pp. 827–832; T. Dvir, D. Eden, and B. J. Avolio, "Impact of Transformational Leadership on Follower Development and Performance: A Field Experiment," *Academy of Management Journal*, August 2002, pp. 735–744; and R. A. Hassan, B. A. Fuwad, and A. I. Rauf, "Pre-Training Motivation and the Effectiveness of Transformational Leadership Training: An Experiment," *Academy of Strategic Management Journal* 9, no. 2 (2010), pp. 1–8.

76 R. N. Kanungo, "Leadership in Organizations: Looking Ahead to the 21st Century," *Canadian Psychology* 39, no. 1–2 (1998), p. 78.

77 B. J. Avolio and B. M. Bass, "Transformational Leadership, Charisma and Beyond," working paper, School of Management, State University of New York, Binghamton, 1985, p. 14.

78 Vignette based on A. McCuaig, "Pilot Flies into Literary World," *Medicine Hat News*, http://www.medicinehatnews.com/local-entertainment/pilot-flies-into-literary-world-11252011.html

79 D. Ancona, E. Backman, and H. Bresman, "X-Teams: New Ways of Leading in a New World," *Ivey Business Journal* 72, no. 3 (May–June 2008), http://www.iveybusinessjournal.com/-article.asp?intArticle_ID=755

80 See, for example, L. J. Zachary, *The Mentor's Guide: Facilitating Effective Learning Relationships* (San Francisco: Jossey-Bass, 2000); M. Murray, *Beyond the Myths and Magic of Mentoring: How to Facilitate an Effective Mentoring Process*, rev. ed. (New York: Wiley, 2001); and F. Warner, "Inside Intel's Mentoring Movement," *Fast Company*, April 2002, pp. 116–120.

81 B. R. Ragins and J. L. Cotton, "Easier Said than Done: Gender Differences in Perceived Barriers to Gaining a Mentor," *Academy of Management Journal* 34, no. 4 (1993), pp. 939–951; C. R. Wanberg, E. T. Welsh, and S. A. Hezlett, "Mentoring Research: A Review and Dynamic Process Model," in G. R. Ferris and J. J. Martocchio (eds.), *Research in Personnel and Human Resources Management*, vol. 22 (Greenwich, CT: Elsevier Science, 2003), pp. 39–124; and T. D. Allen, "Protégé Selection by Mentors: Contributing Individual and Organizational Factors," *Journal of Vocational Behavior* 65, no. 3 (2004), pp. 469–483.

82 T. D. Allen, M. L. Poteet, J. E. A. Russell, and G. H. Dobbins, "A Field Study of Factors Related to Supervisors' Willingness to Mentor Others," *Journal of Vocational Behavior* 50, no. 1 (1997), pp. 1–22; S. Aryee, Y. W. Chay, and J. Chew, "The Motivation to Mentor Among Managerial Employees in the Maintenance Career Stage: An Interactionist Perspective," *Group and Organization Management* 21, no. 3 (1996), pp. 261–277; L. T. Eby, A. L. Lockwood, and M. Butts, "Perceived Support for Mentoring: A Multiple Perspectives Approach," *Journal of Vocational Behavior* 68, no. 2 (2006), pp. 267–291; and T. D. Allen, E. Lentz, and R. Day, "Career Success Outcomes Associated with Mentoring Others: A Comparison of Mentors and Nonmentors," *Journal of Career Development* 32, no. 3 (2006), pp. 272–285.

83 See, for example, D. A. Thomas, "The Impact of Race on Managers' Experiences of Developmental Relationships: An Intra-Organizational Study," *Journal of Organizational Behavior*, November 1990, pp. 479–492; K. E. Kram and D. T. Hall, "Mentoring in a Context of Diversity and Turbulence," in *Managing Diversity*, ed. E. E. Kossek and S. A. Lobel (Cambridge, MA: Blackwell, 1996), pp. 108–136; M. N. Ruderman and M. W. Hughes-James, "Leadership Development across Race and Gender," in *The Center for Creative Leadership Handbook of Leadership Development*, ed. C. D. McCauley, R. S. Moxley, and E. Van Velsor (San Francisco: Jossey-Bass, 1998), pp. 291–335; and B. R. Ragins and J. L. Cotton, "Mentor Functions and Outcomes: A Comparison of Men and Women in Formal and Informal Mentoring Relationships," *Journal of Applied Psychology*, August 1999, pp. 529–550.

84 J. A. Wilson and N. S. Elman, "Organizational Benefits of Mentoring," *Academy of Management Executive*, November 1990, p. 90.

85 D. Zielinski, "Mentoring Up," *Training* 37, no. 10 (October 2000), pp. 136–141.

86 J. M. Hunt and J. R. Weintraub, "Learning Developmental Coaching," *Journal of Management Education* 28, no. 1 (February 2004), pp. 39–61.

87 J. Mills, "Subordinate Perceptions of Managerial Coaching Practices," *Proceedings*, Academy of Management, Chicago, 1986, pp. 113–116.

88 C. C. Manz and H. P. Sims Jr., *The New SuperLeadership: Leading Others to Lead Themselves* (San Francisco: Berrett-Koehler Publishers, 2001).

89 A. Bandura, "Self-Reinforcement: Theoretical and Methodological Considerations," *Behaviorism* 4 (1976), pp. 135–155; P. W. Corrigan, C. J. Wallace, and M. L. Schade, "Learning Medication Self-Management Skills in Schizophrenia; Relationships With Cognitive Deficits and Psychiatric Symptom," *Behavior Therapy*, Winter 1994, pp. 5–15; A. S. Bellack, "A Comparison of Self-Reinforcement and Self-Monitoring in a Weight Reduction Program," *Behavior Therapy* 7 (1976), pp. 68–75; T. A. Eckman, W. C. Wirshing, and S. R. Marder, "Technique for Training Schizophrenic Patients in Illness Self-Management: A Controlled Trial," *American Journal of Psychiatry* 149 (1992), pp. 1549–1555; J. J. Felixbrod and K. D. O'Leary, "Effect of Reinforcement on Children's Academic Behavior as a Function of Self-Determined and Externally Imposed Contingencies," *Journal of Applied Behavior Analysis* 6 (1973), pp. 141–150; A. J. Litrownik, L. R. Franzini, and D. Skenderian, "The Effects of Locus of Reinforcement Control on a Concept Identification Task," *Psychological Reports* 39 (1976), pp. 159–165; P. D. McGorry, "Psychoeducation in First-Episode Psychosis: A Therapeutic Process," *Psychiatry*, November 1995, pp. 313–328; G. S. Parcel, P. R. Swank, and M. J. Mariotto, "Self-Management of Cystic Fibrosis: A Structural Model for Educational and Behavioral Variables," *Social Science and Medicine* 38 (1994), pp. 1307–1315; G. E. Speidel, "Motivating Effect of Contingent Self-Reward," *Journal of Experimental Psychology* 102 (1974), pp. 528–530.

90 D. B. Jeffrey, "A Comparison of the Effects of External Control and Self-Control on the Modification and Maintenance of Weight," *Journal of Abnormal Psychology* 83 (1974), pp. 404–410.

91 C. C. Manz and H. P. Sims Jr., *The New SuperLeadership: Leading Others to Lead Themselves* (San Francisco: Berrett-Koehler, 2001).

92 J. Kelly and S. Nadler, "Leading From Below," *Wall Street Journal*, March 3, 2007, pp. R4, R10.

93 See, for instance, J. H. Zenger, E. Musselwhite, K. Hurson, and C. Perrin, *Leading Teams: Mastering the New Role* (Homewood, IL: Business One Irwin, 1994); and M. Frohman, "Nothing Kills Teams Like Ill-Prepared Leaders," *IndustryWeek*, October 2, 1995, pp. 72–76.

94 M. Frohman, "Nothing Kills Teams Like Ill-Prepared Leaders," *IndustryWeek*, October 2, 1995, p. 93.

95 M. Frohman, "Nothing Kills Teams Like Ill-Prepared Leaders," *IndustryWeek*, October 2, 1995, p. 100.

96 J. R. Katzenbach and D. K. Smith, *The Wisdom of Teams: Creating the High-Performance Organization* (Boston, MA: Harvard Business School, 1993).

97 N. Steckler and N. Fondas, "Building Team Leader Effectiveness: A Diagnostic Tool," *Organizational Dynamics*, Winter 1995, p. 20.

98 R. S. Wellins, W. C. Byham, and G. R. Dixon, *Inside Teams* (San Francisco: Jossey-Bass, 1994), p. 318.

99 N. Steckler and N. Fondas, "Building Team Leader Effectiveness: A Diagnostic Tool," *Organizational Dynamics*, Winter 1995, p. 21.

100 L. A. Hambley, T. A. O'Neill, and T. J. B. Kline, "Virtual Team Leadership: The Effects of Leadership Style and Communication Medium on Team Interaction Styles and Outcomes," *Organizational Behavior and Human Decision Processes* 103 (2007), pp. 1–20; and B. J. Avolio and S. S. Kahai, "Adding the 'E' to E-Leadership: How It May Impact Your Leadership," *Organizational Dynamics* 31, no. 4 (2003), 325–338.

101 J. Howell and K. Hall-Merenda, "Leading From a Distance," in *Leadership: Achieving Exceptional Performance*, A Special Supplement Prepared by the Richard Ivey School of Business, *Globe and Mail*, May 15, 1998, pp. C1, C2.

102 S. J. Zaccaro and P. Bader, "E-Leadership and the Challenges of Leading E-Teams: Minimizing the Bad and Maximizing the Good," *Organizational Dynamics* 31, no. 4 (2003), pp. 381–385.

103 C. E. Naquin and G. D. Paulson, "Online Bargaining and Interpersonal Trust," *Journal of Applied Psychology*, February 2003, pp. 113–120.

104 B. Shamir, "Leadership in Boundaryless Organizations: Disposable or Indispensable?" *European Journal of Work and Organizational Psychology* 8, no. 1 (1999), pp. 49–71.

105 R. M. Kanter, *The Change Masters: Innovation and Entrepreneurship in the American Corporation* (New York: Simon and Schuster, 1983).

106 R. A. Heifetz, *Leadership Without Easy Answers* (Cambridge, MA: Harvard University Press, 1996), p. 205.

107 R. A. Heifetz, *Leadership Without Easy Answers* (Cambridge, MA: Harvard University Press, 1996), p. 205.

108 R. A. Heifetz, *Leadership Without Easy Answers* (Cambridge, MA: Harvard University Press, 1996), p. 188.

109 Vignette based on C. Coward, "Five Questions with a Snowbird," *Hamilton Spectator*, November 5, 2011, http://www.thespec.com/localprofile/article/620542—five-questions-with-a-snowbird; and J. Graham, "She's the Boss: Snowbirds First Female Pilot to Lead Aerobatic Squad," *Canadian Press*, May 2, 2010, http://www.cbc.ca/canada/saskatchewan/story/2010/05/02/sask-snowbirds.html#ixzz0mv2nPxRr

110 F. O. Walumbwa, F. Luthans, J. B. Avey, and A. Oke, "Authentically Leading Groups: The Mediating Role of Collective Psychological Capital And Trust," *Journal of Organizational Behavior* 32, no. 1 (2011), pp. 4–24.

111 R. Ilies, F. P. Morgeson, and J. D. Nahrgang, "Authentic Leadership and Eudaemonic Wellbeing: Understanding Leader-Follower Outcomes," *Leadership Quarterly* 16 (2005), pp. 373–394.

112 This section is based on E. P. Hollander, "Ethical Challenges in the Leader–Follower Relationship," *Business Ethics Quarterly*, January 1995, pp. 55–65; J. C. Rost, "Leadership: A Discussion About Ethics," *Business Ethics Quarterly*, January 1995, pp. 129–142; L. K. Treviño, M. Brown, and L. P. Hartman, "A Qualitative Investigation of Perceived Executive Ethical Leadership: Perceptions From Inside and Outside the Executive Suite," *Human Relations*, January 2003, pp. 5–37; and R. M. Fulmer, "The Challenge of Ethical Leadership," *Organizational Dynamics* 33, no. 3 (2004), pp. 307–317.

113 J. L. Lunsford, "Piloting Boeing's New Course," *Wall Street Journal*, June 13, 2006, pp. B1, B3.

114 J. M. Burns, *Leadership* (New York: Harper & Row, 1978).

115 J. M. Howell and B. J. Avolio, "The Ethics of Charismatic Leadership: Submission or Liberation?" *Academy of Management Executive*, May 1992, pp. 43–55.

116 D. van Knippenberg, D. De Cremer, and B. van Knippenberg, "Leadership and Fairness: The State of the Art," *European Journal of Work and Organizational Psychology* 16, no. 2 (2007), pp. 113–140.

117 M. E. Brown and L. K. Treviño, "Socialized Charismatic Leadership, Values Congruence, and Deviance in Work Groups," *Journal of Applied Psychology* 91, no. 4 (2006), pp. 954–962.

118 M. E. Brown and L. K. Treviño, "Leader-Follower Values Congruence: Are Socialized Charismatic Leaders Better Able to Achieve It?" *Journal of Applied Psychology* 94, no. 2 (2009), pp. 478–490.

119 J. G. Clawson, *Level Three Leadership* (Upper Saddle River, NJ: Prentice Hall, 1999), pp. 46–49.

120 All labour force data based on "Women in Management in Canada (2011)," *Catalyst*, August 2011, http://www.catalyst.org/publication/247/women-in-management-in-canada

121 The material in this section is based on J. Cliff, N. Langton, and H. Aldrich, "Walking The Talk? Gendered Rhetoric vs. Action in Small Firms," *Organizational Studies* 26, no. 1 (2005), pp. 63–91; S. Helgesen, *The Female Advantage: Women's Ways of Leadership* (New York: Doubleday, 1990); A. H. Eagly and B. T. Johnson, "Gender and Leadership Style: A Meta-analysis," *Psychological Bulletin*, September 1990, pp. 233–256; A. H. Eagly and S. J. Karau, "Gender and the Emergence of Leaders: A Meta-analysis," *Journal of Personality and Social Psychology*, May 1991, pp. 685–710; J. B. Rosener, "Ways Women Lead," *Harvard Business Review*, November–December 1990, pp. 119–125; A. H. Eagly, M. G. Makhijani, and B. G. Klonsky, "Gender and the Evaluation of Leaders: A Meta-analysis," *Psychological Bulletin*, January 1992, pp. 3–22; A. H. Eagly, S. J. Karau, and B. T. Johnson, "Gender and Leadership Style Among School Principals: A Meta-analysis," *Educational Administration Quarterly*, February 1992, pp. 76–102; L. R. Offermann and C. Beil, "Achievement Styles of Women Leaders and Their Peers," *Psychology of Women Quarterly*, March 1992, pp. 37–56; R. L. Kent and S. E. Moss, "Effects of Size and Gender Role on Leader Emergence," *Academy of Management Journal*, October 1994, pp. 1335–1346; C. Lee, "The Feminization of Management," *Training*, November 1994, pp. 25–31; H. Collingwood, "Women as Managers: Not Just Different: Better," *Working Woman*, November 1995, p. 14; J. B. Rosener, *America's Competitive Secret: Women Managers* (New York: Oxford University Press, 1995).

122 A. H. Eagly, "Female Leadership Advantage and Disadvantage: Resolving the Contradictions," *Psychology of Women Quarterly*, March 2007, pp. 1–12; and A. H. Eagly, M. C. Johannesen-Schmidt, and M. L. van Engen, "Transformational, Transactional, and Laissez-Faire Leadership Styles: A Meta-analysis Comparing Women and Men," *Psychological Bulletin*, July 2003, pp. 569–591.

123 O. A. O'Neill and C. A. O'Reilly III, "Reducing the Backlash Effect: Self-Monitoring and Women's Promotions," *Journal of Occupational and Organizational Psychology* 84, no. 4 (2011), pp. 825–832.

124 http://www.sciencedaily.com/releases/2011/01/110119114954.htm

125 B. Orser, *Creating High Performance Organizations: Leveraging Women's Leadership* (Ottawa: The Conference Board of Canada, 2000).

126 J. M. Norvilitis and H. M. Reid, "Evidence for an Association between Gender-Role Identity and a Measure of Executive Function," *Psychological Reports*, February 2002, pp. 35–45; W. H. Decker and D. M. Rotondo, "Relationships Among Gender, Type of Humor, and Perceived Leader Effectiveness," *Journal of Managerial Issues*, Winter 2001, pp. 450–465; H. Aguinis and S. K. R. Adams, "Social-Role Versus Structural Models of Gender and Influence Use in Organizations: A Strong Inference Approach," *Group & Organization Management*, December 1998, pp. 414–446; and A. H. Eagly, S. J. Karau, and M. G. Makhijani, "Gender and the Effectiveness of Leaders: A Meta-analysis," *Psychological Bulletin* 117 (1995), pp. 125–145.

127 A. H. Eagly, M. C. Johannesen-Schmidt, and M. L. van Engen, "Transformational, Transactional, and Laissez-Faire Leadership Styles: A Meta-analysis Comparing Women and Men," *Psychological Bulletin* 129, no. 4 (July 2003), pp. 569–591; K. M. Bartol, D. C. Martin, and J. A. Kromkowski, "Leadership and the Glass Ceiling: Gender and Ethnic Influences on Leader Behaviors at Middle and Executive Managerial Levels," *Journal of Leadership & Organizational Studies*, Winter 2003, pp. 8–19; and R. Sharpe, "As Leaders, Women Rule," *BusinessWeek*, November 20, 2000, pp. 74–84.

128 J. Zenger and J. Folkman, "Are Women Better Leaders than Men?" *HBR Blog Network*, March 15, 2012, http://blogs.hbr.org/cs/2012/03/a_study_in_leadership_women_do.html

129 Based on R. D. Arvey, Z. Zhang, and B. J. Avolio, "Developmental and Genetic Determinants of Leadership Role Occupancy Among Women," *Journal of Applied Psychology*, May 2007, pp. 693–706.

130 M. Pandya, "Warren Buffett on Investing and Leadership: I'm Wired for This Game," *Wharton Leadership Digest* 3, no. 7 (April 1999), http://leadership.wharton.upenn.edu/digest/04-99.shtml

131 This exercise is based on J. M. Howell and P. J. Frost, "A Laboratory Study of Charismatic Leadership," *Organizational Behavior and Human Decision Processes*, April 1989, pp. 243–269.

132 Based on T. W. Martin, "Whole Foods to Sell 31 Stores in FTC Deal," *Wall Street Journal*, March 7, 2009, p. B5; M. Fraser and

S. Dutta, "Yes, CEOs Should Facebook and Twitter," *Forbes*, March 11, 2009, http://www.forbes.com; D. Kesmodel and J. R. Wilke, "Whole Foods Is Hot, Wild Oats a Dud—So Said 'Rahodeb,'" *Wall Street Journal*, July 12, 2007, pp. A1, A10; G. Farrell and P. Davidson, "Whole Foods' CEO Was Busy Guy Online," *USA Today*, July 13, 2007, p. 4B; and http://money.cnn.com/magazines/fortune/best-companies/2012/full_list/

133 Based on D. Koeppel, "A Tough Transition: Friend to Supervisor," *New York Times*, March 16, 2003, p. BU-12.

134 Based on J. M. Howell and P. J. Frost, "A Laboratory Study of Charismatic Leadership," *Organizational Behavior and Human Decision Processes*, April 1989, pp. 243–269.

Chapter 9

1 Vignette based on J. Warrillow, "Reframe a Supply Problem to Build Anticipation," *Globe and Mail*, October 5, 2011, http://www.theglobeandmail.com/report-on-business/small-business/sb-growth/day-today/reframe-a-supply-problem-to-build-anticipation/article2190385/; and J. Warrillow, *Built to Sell: Creating a Business That Can Thrive without You* (New York: Portfolio, 2011).

2 W. Pounds, "The Process of Problem Finding," *Industrial Management Review*, Fall 1969, pp. 1–19.

3 See H. A. Simon, "Rationality in Psychology and Economics," *Journal of Business*, October 1986, pp. 209–224; and A. Langley, "In Search of Rationality: The Purposes Behind the Use of Formal Analysis in Organizations," *Administrative Science Quarterly*, December 1989, pp. 598–631.

4 For a review of the rational decision-making model, see E. F. Harrison, *The Managerial Decision Making Process*, 5th ed. (Boston: Houghton Mifflin, 1999), pp. 75–102.

5 https://www.cibc.com/ca/inside-cibc/community-matters/funding-guidelines.html

6 J. G. March, *A Primer on Decision Making* (New York: Free Press, 1994), pp. 2–7.

7 Vignette based on J. Warrillow, "Reframe a Supply Problem to Build Anticipation," *Globe and Mail*, October 5, 2011, http://www. theglobeandmail.com/report-on-business/small-business/sb-growth/day-today/reframe-a-supply-problem-to-build-anticipation/article2190385/

8 D. L. Rados, "Selection and Evaluation of Alternatives in Repetitive Decision Making," *Administrative Science Quarterly*, June 1972, pp. 196–206.

9 M. Bazerman, *Judgment in Managerial Decision Making*, 3rd ed. (New York: Wiley, 1994), p. 5.

10 J. E. Russo, K. A. Carlson, and M. G. Meloy, "Choosing an Inferior Alternative," *Psychological Science* 17, no. 10 (2006), pp. 899–904.

11 See, for instance, L. R. Beach, *The Psychology of Decision Making* (Thousand Oaks, CA: Sage, 1997).

12 See H. A. Simon, *Administrative Behavior*, 4th ed. (New York: Free Press, 1997); and M. Augier, "Simon Says: Bounded Rationality Matters," *Journal of Management Inquiry*, September 2001, pp. 268–275. Individuals may also be constrained by time, which makes them focus their deliberations on fewer aspects of alternatives. For further discussion of this point, see J. W. Payne, J. R. Bettman, and E. J. Johnson, "Behavioral Decision Research: A Constructive Processing Perspective," *Annual Review of Psychology* 43, no. 1 (1992), pp. 87–131.

13 G. Gigerenzer, "Why Heuristics Work," *Perspectives on Psychological Science* 3, no. 1 (2008), pp. 20–29; and A. K. Shah and D. M. Oppenheimer, "Heuristics Made Easy: An Effort-Reduction Framework," *Psychological Bulletin* 134, no. 2 (2008), pp. 207–222.

14 See T. Gilovich, D. Griffin, and D. Kahneman, *Heuristics and Biases: The Psychology of Intuitive Judgment* (New York: Cambridge University Press, 2002).

15 E. Dane and M. G. Pratt, "Exploring Intuition and Its Role in Managerial Decision Making," *Academy of Management Review* 32, no. 1 (2007), pp. 33–54.

16 P. D. Brown, "Some Hunches About Intuition," *New York Times*, November 17, 2007, p. B5.

17 P. D. Brown, "Some Hunches About Intuition," *New York Times*, November 17, 2007, p. B5.

18 See, for instance, L. A. Burke and M. K. Miller, "Taking the Mystery Out of Intuitive Decision Making," *Academy of Management Executive*, November 1999, pp. 91–99; N. Khatri and H. A. Ng, "The Role of Intuition in Strategic Decision Making," *Human Relations*, January 2000, pp. 57–86; J. A. Andersen, "Intuition in Managers: Are Intuitive Managers More Effective?" *Journal of Managerial Psychology* 15, no. 1–2 (2000), pp. 46–63; D. Myers, *Intuition: Its Powers and Perils* (New Haven, CT: Yale University Press, 2002); and L. Simpson, "Basic Instincts," *Training*, January 2003, pp. 56–59.

19 See, for instance, L. A. Burke and M. K. Miller, "Taking the Mystery Out of Intuitive Decision Making," *Academy of Management Executive*, November 1999, pp. 91–99.

20 B. D. Dunn and H. C. Galton, "Listening to Your Heart: How Interoception Shapes Emotion Experience and Intuitive Decision Making," *Psychological Science* 21 no. 12 (December 2010), pp. 1835–1844.

21 S. P. Robbins, *Decide & Conquer: Making Winning Decisions and Taking Control of Your Life* (Upper Saddle River, NJ: Financial Times/Prentice Hall, 2004), p. 13.

22 Based on P. Cohen, "Stand Still: Use Penalty-Kick Wisdom to Make Your Decisions," *National Post*, March 8, 2008, p. FW9.

23 S. Plous, *The Psychology of Judgment and Decision Making* (New York: McGraw-Hill, 1993), p. 217.

24 S. Lichtenstein and B. Fischhoff, "Do Those Who Know More Also Know More About How Much They Know?" *Organizational Behavior and Human Performance*, December 1977, pp. 159–183.

25 B. Fischhoff, P. Slovic, and S. Lichtenstein, "Knowing with Certainty: The Appropriateness of Extreme Confidence," *Journal of Experimental Psychology: Human Perception and Performance*, November 1977, pp. 552–564.

26 J. Kruger and D. Dunning, "Unskilled and Unaware of It: How Difficulties in Recognizing One's Own Incompetence Lead to Inflated Self-Assessments," *Journal of Personality and Social Psychology*, November 1999, pp. 1121–1134.

27 B. Fischhoff, P. Slovic, and S. Lichtenstein, "Knowing with Certainty: The Appropriateness of Extreme Confidence," *Journal of Experimental Psychology* 3 (1977), pp. 552–564.

28 J. Kruger and D. Dunning, "Unskilled and Unaware of It: How Difficulties in Recognizing One's Own Incompetence Lead to Inflated Self-Assessments," *Journal of Personality and Social Psychology*, November 1999, pp. 1121–1134.

29 See, for instance, A. Tversky and D. Kahneman, "Judgment Under Uncertainty: Heuristics and Biases," *Science*, September 1974, pp. 1124–1131.

30 J. S. Hammond, R. L. Keeney, and H. Raiffa, *Smart Choices* (Boston: HBS Press, 1999), p. 191.

31 R. Hastie, D. A. Schkade, and J. W. Payne, "Juror Judgments in Civil Cases: Effects of Plaintiff's Requests and Plaintiff's Identity on Punitive Damage Awards," *Law and Human Behavior*, August 1999, pp. 445–470.

32 C. Janiszewski and D. Uy, "Precision of the Anchor Influences the Amount of Adjustment," *Psychological Science* 19, no. 2 (2008), pp. 121–127.

33 See R. S. Nickerson, "Confirmation Bias: A Ubiquitous Phenomenon in Many Guises," *Review of General Psychology*, June 1998, pp. 175–220; and E. Jonas, S. Schultz-Hardt, D. Frey, and N. Thelen, "Confirmation Bias in Sequential Information Search after Preliminary Decisions," *Journal of Personality and Social Psychology*, April 2001, pp. 557–571.

34 B. Nyhan and J. Reifler, "When Corrections Fail: The Persistence of Political Misperceptions," *Political Behavior* 32, no. 2 (2010), pp. 303–330.

35 See A. Tversky and D. Kahneman, "Availability: A Heuristic for Judging Frequency and Probability," in *Judgment under Uncertainty: Heuristics and Biases*, ed. D. Kahneman, P. Slovic, and A. Tversky (Cambridge, UK: Cambridge University Press, 1982), pp. 163–178; and B. J. Bushman and G. L. Wells, "Narrative Impressions of Literature: The Availability Bias and the Corrective Properties of Meta-analytic Approaches," *Personality and Social Psychology Bulletin*, September 2001, pp. 1123–1130.

36 See B. M. Staw, "The Escalation of Commitment to a Course of Action," *Academy of Management Review*, October 1981, pp. 577–587; and H. Moon, "Looking Forward and Looking Back: Integrating Completion and Sunk-Cost Effects Within an Escalation-of-Commitment Progress Decision," *Journal of Applied Psychology*, February 2001, pp. 104–113.

37 B. M. Staw, "Knee-Deep in the Big Muddy: A Study of Escalating Commitment to a Chosen Course of Action," *Organizational Behavior and Human Performance* 16 (1976), pp. 27–44; and B. M. Staw, "The Escalation of Commitment: An Update and Appraisal," in *Organizational Decision Making*, ed. Z. Shapira (New York; Cambridge University Press, 1997), pp. 121–215.

38 K. F. E. Wong, J. Y. Y. Kwong, and C. K. Ng, "When Thinking Rationally Increases Biases: The Role of Rational Thinking Style in Escalation of Commitment," *Applied Psychology: An International Review* 57, no. 2 (2008), pp. 246–271.

39 See, for instance, A. James and A. Wells, "Death Beliefs, Superstitious Beliefs and Health Anxiety," *British Journal of Clinical Psychology*, March 2002, pp. 43–53.

40 http://lilomag.com/2011/06/04/10-most-superstitious-famous-athletes/

41 See, for example, D. J. Keys and B. Schwartz, "Leaky Rationality: How Research on Behavioral Decision Making Challenges Normative Standards of Rationality," *Psychological Science* 2, no. 2 (2007), pp. 162–180; and U. Simonsohn, "Direct Risk Aversion: Evidence from Risky Prospects Valued Below Their Worst Outcome," *Psychological Science* 20, no. 6 (2009), pp. 686–692.

42 J. K. Maner, M. T. Gailliot, D. A. Butz, and B. M. Peruche, "Power, Risk, and the Status Quo: Does Power Promote Riskier or More Conservative Decision Making," *Personality and Social Psychology Bulletin* 33, no. 4 (2007), pp. 451–462.

43 A. Chakraborty, S. Sheikh, and N. Subramanian, "Termination Risk and Managerial Risk Taking," *Journal of Corporate Finance* 13 (2007), pp. 170–188.

44 X. He and V. Mittal, "The Effect of Decision Risk and Project Stage on Escalation of Commitment," *Organizational Behavior and Human Decision Processes* 103, no. 2 (2007), pp. 225–237.

45 D. Kahneman and A. Tversky, "Prospect Theory: An Analysis of Decisions under Risk," *Econometrica* 47, no. 2 (1979), pp. 263–291; and P. Bryant and R. Dunford, "The Influence of Regulatory Focus on Risky Decision-Making," *Applied Psychology: An International Review* 57, no. 2 (2008), pp. 335–359.

46 A. J. Porcelli and M. R. Delgado, "Acute Stress Modulates Risk Taking in Financial Decision Making," *Psychological Science* 20, no. 3 (2009), pp. 278–283.

47 R. L. Guilbault, F. B. Bryant, J. H. Brockway, and E. J. Posavac, "A Meta-analysis of Research on Hindsight Bias," *Basic and Applied Social Psychology*, September 2004, pp. 103–117; and L. Werth, F. Strack, and J. Foerster, "Certainty and Uncertainty: The Two Faces of the Hindsight Bias," *Organizational Behavior and Human Decision Processes*, March 2002, pp. 323–341.

48 M. Gladwell, "Connecting the Dots," *New Yorker*, March 10, 2003.

49 S. P. Robbins, *Decide & Conquer: Making Winning Decisions and Taking Control of Your Life* (Upper Saddle River, NJ: Financial Times/Prentice Hall, 2004), pp. 164–168.

50 See N. R. F. Maier, "Assets and Liabilities in Group Problem Solving: The Need for an Integrative Function," *Psychological Review*, April 1967, pp. 239–249; G. W. Hill, "Group versus Individual Performance: Are N+1 Heads Better Than One?" *Psychological Bulletin*, May 1982, pp. 517–539; M. D. Johnson and J. R. Hollenbeck, "Collective Wisdom as an Oxymoron: Team-Based Structures as Impediments to Learning," in *Research Companion to the Dysfunctional Workplace: Management, Challenges and Symptoms*, ed. J. Langan-Fox, C. L. Cooper, and R. J. Klimoski (Northampton, MA: Edward Elgar Publishing, 2007), pp. 319–331; and R. F. Martell and M. R. Borg, "A Comparison of the Behavioral Rating Accuracy of Groups and Individuals," *Journal of Applied Psychology*, February 1993, pp. 43–50.

51 See, for example, W. C. Swap and Associates, *Group Decision Making* (Newbury Park, CA: Sage, 1984).

52 D. Gigone and R. Hastie "Proper Analysis of the Accuracy of Group Judgments," *Psychological Bulletin* 121, no. 1 (January 1997), pp. 149–167; and B. L. Bonner, S. D. Sillito, and M. R. Baumann, "Collective Estimation: Accuracy, Expertise, and Extroversion as Sources of Intra-Group Influence," *Organizational Behavior and Human Decision Processes* 103 (2007), pp. 121–133.

53 See, for example, W. C. Swap and Associates, *Group Decision Making* (Newbury Park, CA: Sage, 1984).

54 I. L. Janis, *Groupthink* (Boston: Houghton Mifflin, 1982); W. Park, "A Review of Research on Groupthink," *Journal of Behavioral Decision Making*, July 1990, pp. 229–245; C. P. Neck and G. Moorhead, "Groupthink Remodeled: The Importance of Leadership, Time Pressure, and Methodical Decision Making Procedures," *Human Relations*, May 1995, pp. 537–558; and J. N. Choi and M. U. Kim, "The Organizational Application of Groupthink and Its Limits in Organizations," *Journal of Applied Psychology*, April 1999, pp. 297–306.

55 Based on I. L. Janis, *Groupthink: Psychological Studies of Policy Decisions and Fiascoes*, 2nd ed. (Boston: Houghton Mifflin, 1982), p. 244.

56 Based on J. Castaldo, "Analysis Paralysis," *Canadian Business*, May 6, 2011.

57 M. E. Turner and A. R. Pratkanis, "Mitigating Groupthink by Stimulating Constructive Conflict," in *Using Conflict in Organizations*, ed. C. De Dreu and E. Van de Vliert (London: Sage, 1997), pp. 53–71.

58 See N. R. F. Maier, *Principles of Human Relations* (New York: John Wiley, 1952); I. L. Janis, *Groupthink: Psychological Studies of Policy Decisions and Fiascoes*, 2nd ed. (Boston: Houghton Mifflin, 1982); and C. R. Leana, "A Partial Test of Janis' Groupthink Model: Effects of Group Cohesiveness and Leader Behavior on Defective Decision Making," *Journal of Management*, Spring 1985, pp. 5–17.

59 J. N. Choi and M. U. Kim, "The Organizational Application of Groupthink and Its Limitations in Organizations," *Journal of Applied Psychology* 84 (1999), pp. 297–306.

60 J. Longley and D. G. Pruitt, "Groupthink: A Critique of Janis' Theory," in *Review of Personality and Social Psychology*, ed. L. Wheeler (Newbury Park, CA: Sage, 1980), pp. 507–513; and J. A. Sniezek, "Groups under Uncertainty: An Examination of Confidence in Group Decision Making," *Organizational Behavior and Human Decision Processes* 52 (1992), pp. 124–155.

61 C. McCauley, "The Nature of Social Influence in Groupthink: Compliance and Internalization," *Journal of Personality and*

Social Psychology 57 (1989), pp. 250–260; P. E. Tetlock, R. S. Peterson, C. McGuire, S. Chang, and P. Feld, "Assessing Political Group Dynamics: A Test of the Groupthink Model," *Journal of Personality and Social Psychology* 63 (1992), pp. 781–796; S. Graham, "A Review of Attribution Theory in Achievement Contexts," *Educational Psychology Review* 3 (1991), pp. 5–39; and G. Moorhead and J. R. Montanari, "An Empirical Investigation of the Groupthink Phenomenon," *Human Relations* 39 (1986), pp. 399–410.

62 J. N. Choi and M. U. Kim, "The Organizational Application of Groupthink and Its Limitations in Organizations," *Journal of Applied Psychology* 84 (1999), pp. 297–306.

63 See D. J. Isenberg, "Group Polarization: A Critical Review and Meta-analysis," *Journal of Personality and Social Psychology*, December 1986, pp. 1141–1151; J. L. Hale and F. J. Boster, "Comparing Effect Coded Models of Choice Shifts," *Communication Research Reports*, April 1988, pp. 180–186; and P. W. Paese, M. Bieser, and M. E. Tubbs, "Framing Effects and Choice Shifts in Group Decision Making," *Organizational Behavior & Human Decision Processes*, October 1993, pp. 149–165.

64 See, for example, N. Kogan and M. A. Wallach, "Risk Taking as a Function of the Situation, the Person, and the Group," in *New Directions in Psychology*, vol. 3 (New York: Holt, Rinehart and Winston, 1967); and M. A. Wallach, N. Kogan, and D. J. Bem, "Group Influence on Individual Risk Taking," *Journal of Abnormal and Social Psychology* 65 (1962), pp. 75–86.

65 R. D. Clark III, "Group-Induced Shift toward Risk: A Critical Appraisal," *Psychological Bulletin*, October 1971, pp. 251–270.

66 Z. Krizan and R. S. Baron, "Group Polarization and Choice-Dilemmas: How Important Is Self-Categorization?" *European Journal of Social Psychology* 37, no. 1 (2007), pp. 191–201.

67 N. W. Kohn and S. M. Smith, "Collaborative Fixation: Effects of Others' Ideas on Brainstorming," *Applied Cognitive Psychology* 25, no. 3 (2011), pp. 359–371.

68 N. L. Kerr and R. S. Tindale, "Group Performance and Decision-Making," *Annual Review of Psychology* 55 (2004), pp. 623–655.

69 N. W. Kohn and S. M. Smith, "Collaborative Fixation: Effects of Others' Ideas on Brainstorming," *Applied Cognitive Psychology* 25, no. 3 (2011), pp. 359–371; and S. M. Smith, "The Constraining Effects of Initial Ideas," In *Group Creativity*, ed. P. B. Paulus and B. A. Nijstad (New York: Oxford University Press, 2003), pp. 15–31.

70 R. C. Litchfield, "Brainstorming Reconsidered: A Goal-Based View," *Academy of Management Review* 33, no. 3 (2008), pp. 649–668.

71 See A. L. Delbecq, A. H. Van deVen, and D. H. Gustafson, *Group Techniques for Program Planning: A Guide to Nominal and Delphi Processes* (Glenview, IL: Scott, Foresman, 1975); and W. M. Fox, "Anonymity and Other Keys to Successful Problem-Solving Meetings," *National Productivity Review*, Spring 1989, pp. 145–156.

72 E. F. Rietzschel, B. A. Nijstad, and W. Stroebe, "Productivity Is Not Enough: A Comparison of Interactive and Nominal Brainstorming Groups on Idea Generation and Selection," *Journal of Experimental Social Psychology* 42, no. 2 (2006), pp. 244–251.

73 C. Faure, "Beyond Brainstorming: Effects of Different Group Procedures on Selection of Ideas and Satisfaction With the Process," *Journal of Creative Behavior* 38 (2004), pp. 13–34.

74 See, for instance, A. R. Dennis and J. S. Valacich, "Computer Brainstorms: More Heads Are Better Than One," *Journal of Applied Psychology*, August 1993, pp. 531–537; R. B. Gallupe and W. H. Cooper, "Brainstorming Electronically," *Sloan Management Review*, Fall 1993, pp. 27–36; and A. B. Hollingshead and J. E. McGrath, "Computer-Assisted Groups: A Critical Review of the Empirical Research," in *Team Effectiveness and Decision Making in Organizations*, ed. R. A. Guzzo and E. Salas (San Francisco: Jossey-Bass, 1995), pp. 46–78.

75 B. B. Baltes, M. W. Dickson, M. P. Sherman, C. C. Bauer, and J. LaGanke, "Computer-Mediated Communication and Group Decision Making: A Meta-analysis," *Organizational Behavior and Human Decision Processes*, January 2002, pp. 156–179.

76 T. M. Amabile, "A Model of Creativity and Innovation in Organizations," in *Research in Organizational Behavior*, vol. 10, ed. B. M. Staw and L. L. Cummings (Greenwich, CT: JAI Press, 1988), p. 126; and J. E. Perry-Smith and C. E. Shalley, "The Social Side of Creativity: A Static and Dynamic Social Network Perspective," *Academy of Management Review*, January 2003, pp. 89–106.

77 G. J. Feist and F. X. Barron, "Predicting Creativity from Early to Late Adulthood: Intellect, Potential, and Personality," *Journal of Research in Personality*, April 2003, pp. 62–88.

78 R. W. Woodman, J. E. Sawyer, and R. W. Griffin, "Toward a Theory of Organizational Creativity," *Academy of Management Review*, April 1993, p. 298; J. M. George and J. Zhou, "When Openness to Experience and Conscientiousness Are Related to Creative Behavior: An Interactional Approach," *Journal of Applied Psychology*, June 2001, pp. 513–524; and E. F. Rietzschel, C. K. W. de Dreu, and B. A. Nijstad, "Personal Need for Structure and Creative Performance: The Moderating Influence of Fear of Invalidity," *Personality and Social Psychology Bulletin*, June 2007, pp. 855–866.

79 Cited in C. G. Morris, *Psychology: An Introduction*, 9th ed. (Upper Saddle River, NJ: Prentice Hall, 1996), p. 344.

80 G. Keenan, "GM Shows a Nimble Touch in Oshawa," *Globe and Mail*, March 27, 2010. Caption from GM: "Auto workers at the General Motors Canada assembly line in Oshawa, Ont."

81 This section is based on T. M. Amabile, "Motivating Creativity in Organizations: On Doing What You Love and Loving What You Do," *California Management Review* 40, no. 1 (Fall 1997), pp. 39–58.

82 M. Baas, C. K. W. De Dreu, and B. A. Nijstad, "A Meta-analysis of 25 Years of Mood-Creativity Research: Hedonic Tone, Activation, or Regulatory Focus?" *Psychological Bulletin* 134, no. 6 (2008), pp. 779–806.

83 J. Zhou, "When the Presence of Creative Coworkers Is Related to Creativity: Role of Supervisor Close Monitoring, Developmental Feedback, and Creative Personality," *Journal of Applied Psychology* 88, no. 3 (June 2003), pp. 413–422.

84 J. E. Perry-Smith, "Social Yet Creative: The Role of Social Relationships in Facilitating Individual Creativity," *Academy of Management Journal* 49, no. 1 (2006), pp. 85–101.

85 G. Park, D. Lubinski, and C. P. Benbow, "Contrasting Intellectual Patterns Predict Creativity in the Arts and Sciences," *Psychological Science* 18, no. 11 (2007), pp. 948–952.

86 W. J. J. Gordon, *Synectics* (New York: Harper & Row, 1961).

87 See C. E. Shalley, J. Zhou, and G. R. Oldham, "The Effects of Personal and Contextual Characteristics on Creativity: Where Should We Go from Here?" *Journal of Management*, November 2004, pp. 933–958; G. Hirst, D. Van Knippenberg, and J. Zhou, "A Cross-Level Perspective on Employee Creativity: Goal Orientation, Team Learning Behavior, and Individual Creativity," *Academy of Management Journal* 52, no. 2 (2009), pp. 280–293; and C. E. Shalley, L. L. Gilson, and T. C. Blum, "Interactive Effects of Growth Need Strength, Work Context, and Job Complexity on Self-Reported Creative Performance," *Academy of Management Journal* 52, no. 3 (2009), pp. 489–505.

88 M. Amabile, "How to Kill Creativity," *Harvard Business Review*, September–October 1998, pp. 76–87; H. S. Choi and L. Thompson, "Old Wine in a New Bottle: Impact of Membership Change on Group Creativity," *Organizational Behavior and Human Decision Processes* 98, no. 2 (2005), pp. 121–132; R. Florida and J. Goodnight, "Managing for Creativity," *Harvard Business Review*, July 2005, pp. 124+; L. L. Gilson, J. E. Mathieu, C. E. Shalley, and T. R. Ruddy, "Creativity and Standardization: Complementary

or Conflicting Drivers of Team Effectiveness?" *Academy of Management Journal* 48, no. 3 (2005), pp. 521–531; and K. G. Smith, C. J. Collins, and K. D. Clark, "Existing Knowledge, Knowledge Creation Capability, and the Rate of New Product Introduction in High-Technology Firms," *Academy of Management Journal* 48, no. 2 (2005), pp. 346–357.

89 Cited in T. Stevens, "Creativity Killers," *IndustryWeek*, January 23, 1995, p. 63.

90 M. Strauss, "Retailers Tap into War-Room Creativity of Employees," *Globe and Mail*, March 12, 2007, p. B1.

91 Vignette based on A. Trang, "'Kick Ass' Coffee," *Advantage*, November–December 2011, pp. 75–76; and http://www. kickinghorsecoffee.com/en/story

92 G. F. Cavanagh, D. J. Moberg, and M. Valasquez, "The Ethics of Organizational Politics," *Academy of Management Journal*, June 1981, pp. 363–374.

93 P. L. Schumann, "A Moral Principles Framework for Human Resource Management Ethics," *Human Resource Management Review* 11 (Spring–Summer 2001), pp. 93–111.

94 See, for example, T. Machan, ed., *Commerce and Morality* (Totowa, NJ: Rowman and Littlefield, 1988).

95 L. K. Trevino, "Ethical Decision Making in Organizations: A Person-Situation Interactionist Model," *Academy of Management Review*, July 1986, pp. 601–617; and L. K. Trevino and S. A. Youngblood, "Bad Apples in Bad Barrels: A Causal Analysis of Ethical Decision Making Behavior," *Journal of Applied Psychology*, August 1990, pp. 378–385.

96 See L. Kohlberg, *Essays in Moral Development: The Philosophy of Moral Development*, vol. 1 (New York: Harper & Row, 1981); L. Kohlberg, *Essays in Moral Development: The Psychology of Moral Development*, vol. 2 (New York: Harper & Row, 1984); and R. S. Snell, "Complementing Kohlberg: Mapping the Ethical Reasoning Used by Managers for Their Own Dilemma Cases," *Human Relations*, January 1996, pp. 23–50.

97 L. Kohlberg, *Essays in Moral Development: The Philosophy of Moral Development*, vol. 1 (New York: Harper & Row, 1981); L. Kohlberg, *Essays in Moral Development: The Philosophy of Moral Development*, vol. 2 (New York: Harper & Row, 1984); and R. S. Snell, "Complementing Kohlberg: Mapping the Ethical Reasoning Used by Managers for Their Own Dilemma Cases," *Human Relations*, January 1996, pp. 23–49.

98 J. Weber, "Managers' Moral Reasoning: Assessing Their Responses to Three Moral Dilemmas," *Human Relations*, July 1990, pp. 687–702; and S. B. Knouse and R. A. Giacalone, "Ethical Decision-Making in Business: Behavioral Issues and Concerns," *Journal of Business Ethics*, May 1992, pp. 369–377.

99 R. Teper, M. Inzlicht, and E. Page-Gould, "Are We More Moral Than We Think? Exploring the Role of Affect in Moral Behavior and Moral and Moral Forecasting," *Psychological Science*, April 2011.

100 J. O'Neill, "Canadian Forces Distributing Ethics Guide," *Vancouver Sun*, March 3, 2010.

101 Vignette based on J. Warrillow, "Reframe a Supply Problem to Build Anticipation," *Globe and Mail*, October 5, 2011, http:// www. theglobeandmail.com/report-on-business/small-business/sb-growth/day-today/reframe-a-supply-problem-to-build-anticipation/article2190385/

102 J. Castaldo, "Those Emotional Canadians!" *Canadian Business*, May 10, 2010, pp. 32–33.

103 M. McClearn, "Brands We Trust: On a First-Name Basis," *Canadian Business*, April 7, 2011.

104 M. Friedman, *Capitalism and Freedom* (Chicago: University of Chicago Press, 1962).

105 J. Bakan, *The Corporation* (Toronto: Big Picture Media Corporation, 2003).

106 J. Nelson, "The CEO Poll: Should Companies Give to Charity?" *Canadian Business*, April 7, 2011.

107 J. Castaldo, "The CEO Poll: The Trouble with Outsourcing," *Canadian Business*, April 7, 2011.

108 http://www.greenbiz.com/news/2006/10/25/survey-shows-mba-students-believe-business-should-be-agent-social-change

109 Based on T. Gilovich, V. H. Medvec, and D. Kahneman, "Varieties of Regret: A Debate and Partial Resolution," *Psychological Review* 105 (1998), pp. 602–605. See also M. Tsiros and V. Mittal, "Regret: A Model of Its Antecedents and Consequences in Consumer Decision Making," *Journal of Consumer Research*, March 2000, pp. 401–417.

110 Several of these scenarios are based on D. R. Altany, "Torn between Halo and Horns," *IndustryWeek*, March 15, 1993, pp. 15–20.

111 Based on J. Calano and J. Salzman, "Ten Ways to Fire Up Your Creativity," *Working Woman*, July 1989, p. 94; J. V. Anderson, "Mind Mapping: A Tool for Creative Thinking," *Business Horizons*, January–February 1993, pp. 42–46; M. Loeb, "Ten Commandments for Managing Creative People," *Fortune*, January 16, 1995, pp. 135–136; and M. Henricks, "Good Thinking," *Entrepreneur*, May 1996, pp. 70–73.

Chapter 10

1 Vignette based on M. Parker, "Identifying Enablers and Blockers of Cultural Transformation," *Canadian Business*, May 17, 2007; E. Lazarus, "Building the Perfect Franchise," *PROFIT*, February 2006, p. 48ff; M. Parker, "Why Can't Employers See the Paradox?" *Financial Post*, March 19, 2008, p. WK7; Boston Pizza Press Kit, http://www.bostonpizza.com; "Boston Pizza Reports Higher Second-Quarter Net Income, Same Store Sales," *Canadian Press*, August 10, 2011; and http://www.bostonpizza.com/assets/mediacentre/documents/pdf/Boston_Pizza_Quick_Facts.pdf

2 "Organization Man: Henry Mintzberg Has Some Common Sense Observations About the Ways We Run Companies," *Financial Post*, November 22/24, 1997, pp. 14–16.

3 K. McArthur, "Air Canada Tells Employees to Crack a Smile More Often," *Globe and Mail*, March 14, 2002, pp. B1, B2.

4 K. McArthur, "Air Canada Tells Employees to Crack a Smile More Often," *Globe and Mail*, March 14, 2002, pp. B1, B2.

5 See, for example, H. S. Becker, "Culture: A Sociological View," *Yale Review*, Summer 1982, pp. 513–527; and E. H. Schein, *Organizational Culture and Leadership* (San Francisco: Jossey-Bass, 1985), p. 168.

6 This seven-item description is based on C. A. O'Reilly III, J. Chatman, and D. F. Caldwell, "People and Organizational Culture: A Profile Comparison Approach to Assessing Person-Organization Fit," *Academy of Management Journal*, September 1991, pp. 487–516; and J. A. Chatman and K. A. Jehn, "Assessing the Relationship between Industry Characteristics and Organizational Culture: How Different Can You Be?" *Academy of Management Journal*, June 1994, pp. 522–553. For a description of other popular measures, see A. Xenikou and A. Furnham, "A Correlational and Factor Analytic Study of Four Questionnaire Measures of Organizational Culture," *Human Relations*, March 1996, pp. 349–371. For a review of cultural dimensions, see N. M. Ashkanasy, C. P. M. Wilderom, and M. F. Peterson, eds., *Handbook of Organizational Culture and Climate* (Thousand Oaks, CA: Sage, 2000), pp. 131–145.

7 E. Schein, "Coming to a New Awareness of Organizational Culture," *Sloan Management Review*, Winter 1984, pp. 3–16; E. Schein, *Organizational Culture and Leadership*, 2nd ed. (San Francisco, CA: Jossey-Bass, 1992); and E. Schein, "What Is Culture?" in *Reframing Organizational Culture*, ed. P. J. Frost, L. F. Moore, M. R. Louis, C. C. Lundberg, and J. Martin (Newbury Park, CA: Sage, 1991), pp. 243–253.

8 T. G. Stroup Jr., "Leadership and Organizational Culture: Actions Speak Louder Than Words," *Military Review* 76, no. 1 (January–February 1996), pp. 44–49; B. Moingeon and B. Ramanantsoa, "Understanding Corporate Identity: The French School of Thought," *European Journal of Marketing* 31, no. 5/6 (1997), pp. 383–395; A. P. D. Van Luxemburg, J. M. Ulijn, and N. Amare, "The Contribution of Electronic Communication Media to the Design Process: Communicative and Cultural Implications," *IEEE Transactions on Professional Communication* 45, no. 4 (December 2002), pp. 250–264; L. D. McLean, "Organizational Culture's Influence on Creativity and Innovation: A Review of the Literature and Implications for Human Resource Development," *Advances in Developing Human Resources* 7, no. 2 (May 2005), pp. 226–246; and V. J. Friedman and A. B. Antal, "Negotiating Reality: A Theory of Action Approach to Intercultural Competence," *Management Learning* 36, no. 1 (2005), pp. 69–86.

9 See http://www.palliser.com/CompanyInfo.php

10 See C. A. O'Reilly and J. A. Chatman, "Culture as Social Control: Corporations, Cultures, and Commitment," in *Research in Organizational Behavior*, vol. 18, ed. B. M. Staw and L. L. Cummings (Greenwich, CT: JAI Press, 1996), pp. 157–200.

11 T. E. Deal and A. A. Kennedy, "Culture: A New Look Through Old Lenses," *Journal of Applied Behavioral Science*, November 1983, p. 501.

12 Y. Ling, Z. Simsek, M. H. Lubatkin, and J. F. Veiga, "Transformational Leadership's Role in Promoting Corporate Entrepreneurship: Examining the CEO-TMT Interface," *Academy of Management Journal* 51, no. 3 (2008), pp. 557–576; and A. Malhotra, A. Majchrzak, and B. Rosen, "Leading Virtual Teams," *Academy of Management Perspectives* 21, no. 1 (2007), pp. 60–70.

13 D. Denison, "What Is the Difference between Organizational Culture and Organizational Climate? A Native's Point of View on a Decade of Paradigm Wars," *Academy of Management Review* 21 (1996) pp. 519–654; and L. R. James, C. C. Choi, C. E. Ko, P. K. McNeil, M. K. Minton, M. A. Wright, and K. Kim, "Organizational and Psychological Climate: A Review of Theory and Research," *European Journal of Work and Organizational Psychology* 17, no. 1 (2008), pp. 5–32.

14 J. Z. Carr, A. M. Schmidt, J. K. Ford, and R. P. DeShon, "Climate Perceptions Matter: A Meta-analytic Path Analysis Relating Molar Climate, Cognitive and Affective States, and Individual Level Work Outcomes," *Journal of Applied Psychology* 88, no. 4 (2003), pp. 605–619.

15 M. Schulte, C. Ostroff, S. Shmulyian, and A. Kinicki, "Organizational Climate Configurations: Relationships to Collective Attitudes, Customer Satisfaction, and Financial Performance," *Journal of Applied Psychology* 94, no. 3 (2009), pp. 618–634.

16 See, for example, Z. S. Byrne, J. Stoner, K. R. Thompson, and W. Hochwarter, "The Interactive Effects of Conscientiousness, Work Effort, and Psychological Climate on Job Performance," *Journal of Vocational Behavior* 66, no. 2 (2005), pp. 326–338; D. S. Pugh, J. Dietz, A. P. Brief, and J. W. Wiley, "Looking Inside and Out: The Impact of Employee and Community Demographic Composition on Organizational Diversity Climate," *Journal of Applied Psychology* 93, no. 6 (2008), pp. 1422–1428; and J. C. Wallace, E. Popp, and S. Mondore, "Safety Climate as a Mediator between Foundation Climates and Occupational Accidents: A Group-Level Investigation," *Journal of Applied Psychology* 91, no. 3 (2006), pp. 681–688.

17 C. Atchison, "Secrets of Canada's Best Bosses," *PROFIT*, February 16, 2011, http://www.profitguide.com/manage-grow/leadership/secrets-of-canada%e2%80%99s-best-bosses-30084

18 The view that there will be consistency among perceptions of organizational culture has been called the "integration" perspective. For a review of this perspective and conflicting approaches, see D. Meyerson and J. Martin, "Cultural Change: An Integration of Three Different Views," *Journal of Management Studies*, November 1987, pp. 623–647; and P. J. Frost, L. F. Moore, M. R. Louis, C. C. Lundberg, and J. Martin, eds., *Reframing Organizational Culture* (Newbury Park, CA: Sage Publications, 1991).

19 See J. M. Jermier, J. W. Slocum Jr., L. W. Fry, and J. Gaines, "Organizational Subcultures in a Soft Bureaucracy: Resistance Behind the Myth and Facade of an Official Culture," *Organization Science*, May 1991, pp. 170–194; S. A. Sackmann, "Culture and Subcultures: An Analysis of Organizational Knowledge," *Administrative Science Quarterly*, March 1992, pp. 140–161; R. F. Zammuto, "Mapping Organizational Cultures and Subcultures: Looking Inside and across Hospitals" (paper presented at the 1995 National Academy of Management Conference, Vancouver, August 1995); and G. Hofstede, "Identifying Organizational Subcultures: An Empirical Approach," *Journal of Management Studies*, January 1998, pp. 1–12.

20 T. A. Timmerman, "Do Organizations Have Personalities?" (paper presented at the 1996 National Academy of Management Conference, Cincinnati, OH, August 1996).

21 S. Hamm, "No Letup—and No Apologies," *BusinessWeek*, October 26, 1998, pp. 58–64.

22 Vignette based on "Rising on Three Pillars Strategy; 10 Most Admired Corporate Cultures," *Financial Post*, November 26, 2008, p. WK4; and http://www.bostonpizza.com/en/about/PressKit.aspx

23 E. H. Schein, "The Role of the Founder in Creating Organizational Culture," *Organizational Dynamics*, Summer 1983, pp. 13–28.

24 http://www.bostonpizza.com/.../Website_PressKit_PDFs_JAN2010_JimTreliving_...

25 E. H. Schein, "Leadership and Organizational Culture," in *The Leader of the Future*, ed. F. Hesselbein, M. Goldsmith, and R. Beckhard (San Francisco: Jossey-Bass, 1996), pp. 61–62.

26 "PCL's Biggest Investment: Its People," *National Post*, September 2, 2008, p. FP10.

27 See, for example, J. R. Harrison and G. R. Carroll, "Keeping the Faith: A Model of Cultural Transmission in Formal Organizations," *Administrative Science Quarterly*, December 1991, pp. 552–582.

28 See B. Schneider, "The People Make the Place," *Personnel Psychology*, Autumn 1987, pp. 437–453; J. A. Chatman, "Matching People and Organizations: Selection and Socialization in Public Accounting Firms," *Administrative Science Quarterly*, September 1991, pp. 459–484; D. E. Bowen, G. E. Ledford Jr., and B. R. Nathan, "Hiring for the Organization, Not the Job," *Academy of Management Executive*, November 1991, pp. 35–51; B. Schneider, H. W. Goldstein, and D. B. Smith, "The ASA Framework: An Update," *Personnel Psychology*, Winter 1995, pp. 747–773; and A. L. Kristof, "Person-Organization Fit: An Integrative Review of Its Conceptualizations, Measurement, and Implications," *Personnel Psychology*, Spring 1996, pp. 1–49.

29 "Building a Better Workforce," *PROFIT*, February 16, 2011, http://www.profitguide.com/article/10084—building-a-better-workforce—page0

30 "Building a Better Workforce," *PROFIT*, February 16, 2011, http://www.profitguide.com/article/10084—building-a-better-workforce—page0

31 S. Fralic, "Even Playland's Interviews Are Fun for Job-Seekers," *Vancouver Sun*, Monday, July 14, 2008, http://www.canada.com/vancouversun/news/story.html?id=7ba15dd4-cbe8-4a09-a08c-cce86c73a694

32 S. Fralic, "Even Playland's Interviews Are Fun for Job-Seekers," *Vancouver Sun*, Monday, July 14, 2008, http://www.canada.com/vancouversun/news/story.html?id=7ba15dd4-cbe8-4a09-a08c-cce86c73a694

33 D. C. Hambrick and P. A. Mason, "Upper Echelons: The Organi-zation as a Reflection of Its Top Managers," *Academy of Manage-ment Review*, April 1984, pp. 193–206; B. P. Niehoff, C. A. Enz, and R. A. Grover, "The Impact of Top-Management Actions on Employee Attitudes and Perceptions," *Group and Organization Studies*, September 1990, pp. 337–352; and H. M. Trice and J. M. Beyer, "Cultural Leadership in Organizations," *Organiza-tion Science*, May 1991, pp. 149–169.

34 See, for instance, J. P. Wanous, *Organizational Entry*, 2nd ed. (New York: Addison Wesley, 1992); G. T. Chao, A. M. O'Leary-Kelly, S. Wolf, H. J. Klein, and P. D. Gardner, "Organizational Socialization: Its Content and Consequences," *Journal of Applied Psychology*, October 1994, pp. 730–743; B. E. Ashforth, A. M. Saks, and R. T. Lee, "Socialization and Newcomer Adjustment: The Role of Organizational Context," *Human Relations*, July 1998, pp. 897–926; D. A. Major, "Effective Newcomer Social-ization into High-Performance Organizational Cultures," in *Handbook of Organizational Culture & Climate*, ed. N. M. Ash-kanasy, C. P. M. Wilderom, and M. F. Peterson (Thousand Oaks, CA: Sage, 2000), pp. 355–368; and D. M. Cable and C. K. Parsons, "Socialization Tactics and Person-Organization Fit," *Personnel Psychology*, Spring 2001, pp. 1–23.

35 A. M. Saks and J. A. Gruman, "Organizational Socialization and Positive Organizational Behaviour: Implications for Theory, Research, and Practice," *Canadian Journal of Administrative Sci-ences* 28, no. 1 (2011), pp. 4–16.

36 J. Impoco, "Basic Training, Sanyo Style," *U.S. News & World Report*, July 13, 1992, pp. 46–48.

37 "Building a Better Workforce," *PROFIT*, February 16, 2011, http://www.profitguide.com/article/10084—building-a-better-workforce—page0.

38 G. Probst and S. Raisch, "Organizational Crisis: The Logic of Fail-ure," *Academy of Management Executive* 19, no. 1 (February 2005), pp. 90–105; D. L. Ferrin and K. T. Dirks, "The Use of Rewards to Increase and Decrease Trust: Mediating Processes and Differential Effects," *Organizational Science* 14, no. 1 (2003), pp. 18–31; J. R. Dunn and M. E. Schweitzer, "Too Good to Be Trusted? Relative Performance, Envy, and Trust," *Academy of Management Best Con-ference Paper Proceedings*, 2004, CM, pp. B1–B6.

39 See, for instance, D. Miller, "What Happens After Success: The Perils of Excellence," *Journal of Management Studies*, May 1994, pp. 11–38.

40 See T. Cox Jr., *Cultural Diversity in Organizations: Theory, Research & Practice* (San Francisco: Berrett-Koehler, 1993), pp. 162–170; L. Grensing-Pophal, "Hiring to Fit Your Corporate Culture," *HR Magazine*, August 1999, pp. 50–54; and D. L. Stone, E. F. Stone-Romero, and K. M. Lukaszewski, "The Impact of Cultural Values on the Acceptance and Effectiveness of Human Resource Man-agement Policies and Practices," *Human Resource Management Review* 17, no. 2 (2007), pp. 152–165.

41 A. F. Buono and J. L. Bowditch, *The Human Side of Mergers and Acquisitions: Managing Collisions Between People, Cultures, and Organizations* (San Francisco: Jossey-Bass, 1989); S. Cartwright and C. L. Cooper, "The Role of Culture Compatibility in Suc-cessful Organizational Marriages," *Academy of Management Exec-utive*, May 1993, pp. 57–70; R. J. Grossman, "Irreconcilable Differences," *HR Magazine*, April 1999, pp. 42–48; J. Veiga, M. Lubatkin, R. Calori, and P. Very, "Measuring Organizational Culture Clashes: A Two-Nation Post-Hoc Analysis of a Cultural Compatibility Index," *Human Relations*, April 2000, pp. 539–557; and E. Krell, "Merging Corporate Cultures," *Training*, May 2001, pp. 68–78.

42 K. W. Smith, "A Brand-New Culture for the Merged Firm," *Merg-ers and Acquisitions* 35, no. 6 (June 2000), pp. 45–50.

43 H. L. Sirkin, P. Keenan, and A. Jackson, "The Hard Side of Change Management," *Harvard Business Review*, October 1, 2005, pp. 108–118.

44 See, for instance, K. H. Hammonds, "Practical Radicals," *Fast Company*, September 2000, pp. 162–174; and P. C. Judge, "Change Agents," *Fast Company*, November 2000, pp. 216–226.

45 K. Lewin, *Field Theory in Social Science* (New York: Harper and Row, 1951).

46 P. G. Audia, E. A. Locke, and K. G. Smith, "The Paradox of Suc-cess: An Archival and a Laboratory Study of Strategic Persistence Following Radical Environmental Change," *Academy of Manage-ment Journal*, October 2000, pp. 837–853.

47 J. B. Sorensen, "The Strength of Corporate Culture and the Reli-ability of Firm Performance," *Administrative Science Quarterly*, March 2002, pp. 70–91.

48 J. Amis, T. Slack, and C. R. Hinings, "The Pace, Sequence, and Linearity of Radical Change," *Academy of Management Journal*, February 2004, pp. 15–39; and E. Autio, H. J. Sapienza, and J. G. Almeida, "Effects of Age at Entry, Knowledge Intensity, and Imitability on International Growth," *Academy of Management Journal*, October 2000, pp. 909–924.

49 J. P. Kotter, "Leading Changes: Why Transformation Efforts Fail," *Harvard Business Review*, March–April 1995, pp. 59–67; and J. P. Kotter, *Leading Change* (Boston: Harvard Business School Press, 1996).

50 See, for example, A. B. Shani and W. A. Pasmore, "Organization Inquiry: Towards a New Model of the Action Research Process," in *Contemporary Organization Development: Current Thinking and Applications*, eds. D. D. Warrick (Glenview, IL: Scott, Foresman, 1985), pp. 438–448; and C. Eden and C. Huxham, "Action Research for the Study of Organizations," in *Handbook of Orga-nization Studies*, eds. S. R. Clegg, C. Hardy, and W. R. Nord (Lon-don: Sage, 1996).

51 See, for example, G. R. Bushe, "Advances in Appreciative Inquiry as an Organization Development Intervention," *Organizational Development Journal*, Summer 1999, pp. 61–68; D. L. Cooper-rider and D. Whitney, *Collaborating for Change: Appreciative Inquiry* (San Francisco: Berrett-Koehler, 2000); R. Fry, F. Barrett, J. Seiling, and D. Whitney, eds., *Appreciative Inquiry & Organiza-tional Transformation: Reports from the Field* (Westport, CT: Quo-rum, 2002); J. K. Barge and C. Oliver, "Working with Appreciation in Managerial Practice," *Academy of Management Review*, January 2003, pp. 124–142; and D. van der Haar and D. M. Hosking, "Evaluating Appreciative Inquiry: A Relational Constructionist Perspective," *Human Relations*, August 2004, pp. 1017–1036.

52 G. R. Bushe, "Advances in Appreciative Inquiry as an Organiza-tion Development Intervention," *Organization Development Jour-nal* 17, no. 2 (Summer 1999), pp. 61–68.

53 P. G. Audia and S. Brion, "Reluctant to Change: Self-Enhancing Responses to Diverging Performance Measures," *Organizational Behavior and Human Decision Processes* 102 (2007), pp. 255–269.

54 M. Fugate, A. J. Kinicki, and G. E. Prussia, "Employee Coping with Organizational Change: An Examination of Alternative Theoretical Perspectives and Models," *Personnel Psychology* 61, no. 1 (2008), pp. 1–36.

55 J. D. Ford, L. W. Ford, and A. D'Amelio, "Resistance to Change: The Rest of the Story," *Academy of Management Review* 33, no. 2 (2008), pp. 362–377.

56 J. P. Kotter and L. A. Schlesinger, "Choosing Strategies for Change," *Harvard Business Review*, July–August 2008, pp. 130–139.

57 A. E. Reichers, J. P. Wanous, and J. T. Austin, "Understanding and Managing Cynicism About Organizational Change," *Acad-emy of Management Executive* 11 (1997), pp. 48–59.

58 R. H. Hall, *Organizations: Structures, Processes, and Outcomes*, 4th ed. (Englewood Cliffs, NJ: Prentice Hall, 1987), p. 29.

59 D. Katz and R. L. Kahn, *The Social Psychology of Organizations*, 2nd ed. (New York: John Wiley & Sons, 1978), pp. 714–715.

60 M. T. Hannan, L. Pólos, and G. R. Carroll, "The Fog of Change: Opacity and Asperity in Organizations," *Administrative Science Quarterly*, September 2003. pp. 399–432.

61 J. P. Kotter and L. A. Schlesinger, "Choosing Strategies for Change," *Harvard Business Review*, March–April 1979, pp. 106–114.

62 J. E. Dutton, S. J. Ashford, R. M. O'Neill, and K. A. Lawrence, "Moves That Matter: Issue Selling and Organizational Change," *Academy of Management Journal*, August 2001, pp. 716–736.

63 P. C. Fiss and E. J. Zajac, "The Symbolic Management of Strategic Change: Sensegiving via Framing and Decoupling," *Academy of Management Journal* 49, no. 6 (2006), pp. 1173–1193.

64 Q. N. Huy, "Emotional Balancing of Organizational Continuity and Radical Change: The Contribution of Middle Managers," *Administrative Science Quarterly*, March 2002, pp. 31–69; D. M. Herold, D. B. Fedor, and S. D. Caldwell, "Beyond Change Management: A Multilevel Investigation of Contextual and Personal Influences on Employees' Commitment to Change," *Journal of Applied Psychology* 92, no. 4 (2007), pp. 942–951; and G. B. Cunningham, "The Relationships among Commitment to Change, Coping with Change, and Turnover Intentions," *European Journal of Work and Organizational Psychology* 15, no. 1 (2006), pp. 29–45.

65 J. P. Kotter, "Leading Change: Why Transformational Efforts Fail," *Harvard Business Review*, January 2007, pp. 96–103.

66 K. van Dam, S. Oreg, and B. Schyns, "Daily Work Contexts and Resistance to Organisational Change: The Role of Leader-Member Exchange, Development Climate, and Change Process Characteristics," *Applied Psychology: An International Review* 57, no. 2 (2008), pp. 313–334.

67 D. B. Fedor, S. Caldwell, and D. M. Herold, "The Effects of Organizational Changes on Employee Commitment: A Multilevel Investigation," *Personnel Psychology* 59 (2006), pp. 1–29.

68 S. Oreg, "Personality, Context, and Resistance to Organizational Change," *European Journal of Work and Organizational Psychology* 15, no. 1 (2006), pp. 73–101.

69 S. M. Elias, "Employee Commitment in Times of Change: Assessing the Importance of Attitudes toward Organizational Change," *Journal of Management* 35, no. 1 (2009), pp. 37–55.

70 J. A. LePine, J. A. Colquitt, and A. Erez, "Adaptability to Changing Task Contexts: Effects of General Cognitive Ability, Conscientiousness, and Openness to Experience," *Personnel Psychology*, Fall 2000, pp. 563–593; T. A. Judge, C. J. Thoresen, V. Pucik, and T. M. Welbourne, "Managerial Coping with Organizational Change: A Dispositional Perspective," *Journal of Applied Psychology*, February 1999, pp. 107–122; and S. Oreg, "Resistance to Change: Developing an Individual Differences Measure," *Journal of Applied Psychology*, August 2003, pp. 680–693.

71 J. W. B. Lang and P. D. Bliese, "General Mental Ability and Two Types of Adaptation to Unforeseen Change: Applying Discontinuous Growth Models to the Task-Change Paradigm," *Journal of Applied Psychology* 94, no. 2 (2009), pp. 411–428.

72 Based on T. Spears, "New NRC Boss Shifts Focus to Economic Development, Less Pure Research," *Postmedia News*, March 19, 2011.

73 See J. Pfeffer, *Managing with Power: Politics and Influence in Organizations* (Boston: Harvard Business School Press, 1992), pp. 7, 318–320; and D. Knights and D. McCabe, "When 'Life Is but a Dream': Obliterating Politics Through Business Process Reengineering?" *Human Relations*, June 1998, pp. 761–798.

74 See, for instance, W. Ocasio, "Political Dynamics and the Circulation of Power: CEO Succession in U.S. Industrial Corporations, 1960–1990," *Administrative Science Quarterly*, June 1994, pp. 285–312.

75 R. H. Miles, "Accelerating Corporate Transformations (Don't Lose Your Nerve!)," *Harvard Business Review*, January/February 2010, pp. 68–75.

76 Adapted from K. H. Chung and L. C. Megginson, *Organizational Behavior*, Copyright © 1981 by K. H. Chung and L. C. Megginson. Reprinted by permission of HarperCollins Publishers, Inc.

77 J. Jargon, "Neatness Counts at Kyocera and Others in the 5S Club," *Wall Street Journal*, October 27, 2008, pp. A1, A15; R. Gapp, R. Fisher, and K. Kobayashi, "Implementing 5S within a Japanese Context: An Integrated Management System," *Management Decision* 46, no. 4 (2008), pp. 565–579; and R. Hough, "5S Implementation Methodology," *Management Services* 52, no. 2 (2008), pp. 44–45.

78 Ideas in *From Concepts to Skills* were influenced by A. L. Wilkins, "The Culture Audit: A Tool for Understanding Organizations," *Organizational Dynamics*, Autumn 1983, pp. 24–38; H. M. Trice and J. M. Beyer, *The Cultures of Work Organizations* (Englewood Cliffs, NJ: Prentice Hall, 1993), pp. 358–362; H. Lancaster, "To Avoid a Job Failure, Learn the Culture of a Company First," *Wall Street Journal*, July 14, 1998, p. B1; and M. Belliveau, "4 Ways to Read a Company," *Fast Company*, October 1998, p. 158.

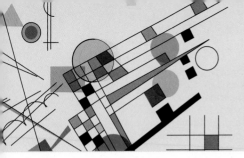

GLOSSARY/SUBJECT INDEX

The page on which the key term is defined is printed in boldface.

A

Aboriginal values, 86–87

absenteeism, 4, 93

abuse of power, 239–241

acceptance, 310

Access to Information Act, 203

accommodation, 86

accountability, 160, 178

accuracy, 310

accurate information, 129

achievement-oriented leader, 273

acquisitions, 347–348

action plans, 125

action research. A change process based on the systematic collection of data and then selection of a change action based on what the analyzed data indicate. **350**–351

adjourning. The final stage in group development for temporary groups, where attention is directed toward wrapping up activities rather than task performance. 162–**163**, 165

affect. A broad range of feelings that people experience. **53,** 54

affective commitment. The strength of an individual's emotional attachment to, identification with, and involvement in the organization; an individual's emotional attachment to and identification with an organization, and a belief in its values. **10, 93**

affective conflict. Conflict that is emotional and aimed at a person rather than an issue. **208**

aggressiveness, 338

agreeableness. A personality factor that describes the degree to which someone is good-natured, cooperative, warm, and trusting. **45,** 268

Alderfer's ERG theory, 116, 120

analysts, 311

anchoring bias. A tendency to fixate on initial information and fail to adequately adjust for subsequent information. **307**

anglophone values, 84–86

antagonistic relationships, 92

anthropology, 6

anti-bullying labour legislation, 240

appraisals, 42

appreciative inquiry (AI). An approach to change that seeks to identify the unique qualities and special strengths of an organization, which can then be built on to improve performance. 351

artifacts. Aspects of an organization's culture that an individual can see, hear, and feel. **340**

Asia, 77

Asian values, 87–88

assimilation, 348

assumption of morality, 311

assumptions. The taken-for-granted notions of how something should be. **340**

athletes, and scholarships, 138–139

attention, 124

attention to detail, 338

attitudes. Positive or negative feelings about objects, people, or events. **88**
  changing attitudes, 102–103
  employee engagement, 95
  job involvement, 95
  job satisfaction, 88–93
  organizational commitment, 93–95

attribution theory. The theory that when we observe what seems to be atypical behaviour by an individual, we attempt to determine whether it is internally or externally caused. **35**–37
  distortion of attributions, 36–37
  fundamental attribution error, 36–37

Australia, 18, 77

Austria, 146

authentic leaders. Leaders who know who they are, know what they believe in and value, and act on these values and beliefs openly and candidly. Their followers would consider them to be ethical people. **287**

authentic motivation, 145

authoritative command, 211

autonomy. The degree to which the job provides substantial freedom, independence, and discretion to the individual in scheduling the work and determining the procedures to be used in carrying it out. **140**

availability bias. The tendency for people to base their judgments on information that is readily available to them rather than on complete data. **307**

avoiding, 210, 211

B

Baby Boomer, 16, 80, 81, 82, 132, 133

backstabbing, 59

bad bosses, 267

bargaining. *See* negotiation

bargaining strategies, 213–215

bargaining zone. The zone between each party's resistance point, assuming that there is overlap in this range. **216**

barriers to effective communication, 196–200
  barriers between women and men, 206
  cultural barriers to communication, 206–208
  defensiveness, 196

differences in perceptions, 207
  emotions, 196
  filtering, 196
  information overload, 197
  language, 197
  nonverbal communication, 198–199
  selective perception, 196
  semantics, 206
  silence, 198
  stress, 199–200
  tone differences, 207
  word connotations, 206–207

bases of power, 230–233, 242

BATNA. The *best* alternative *to a negotiated* agreement; the outcome an individual faces if negotiations fail. **216**

behaviour
  consensus, 36
  consistency, 36
  destructive illegal behaviours, 85
  destructive legal behaviours, 85
  deviant behaviours, 58–59
  distinctiveness, 36
  externally caused behaviour, 35
  internally caused behaviour, 35
  political behaviour, 59, 242
  self-reinforced behaviour, 283
  three rules about behaviour, 36

behavioural accounting, 7

behavioural economics, 7

behavioural finance, 7

behavioural theories of leadership. Theories that propose that specific behaviours differentiate leaders from nonleaders. **269**–270

beliefs. The understandings of how objects and ideas relate to each other. **340**

bias
  anchoring bias, 307
  availability bias, 307
  confirmation bias, 307
  hindsight bias, 309
  overconfidence bias, 306–307

bidding behaviour, 214

Big Five Personality Model, 44, 45–46, 47, 52, 170, 268

Bill C-28, 200

blog (web log). A website where entries are written, and generally displayed in reverse chronological order, about news, events, and personal diary entries. **205**

body language, 199

bonus. An individual-based incentive plan that rewards employees for recent performance rather than historical performance. **135**–136

Boomers. *See* Baby Boomer

bounded rationality. Limitations on a person's ability to interpret, process, and act on information. **304**–305

F

face-to-face conversation, 193
facial expressions, 54, 199
fair process and treatment, 127, 128–130
fairness, 288
"fake proof" personality test, 46
family, 107
federal government, 124
feedback. The degree to which individuals obtain direct and clear information about the effectiveness of their performance. **140**
  in communication, 192
  and compensation, 144–145
  effective feedback, 142
  as extrinsic reward, 131
  and motivation, 147
  performance feedback, 142
  performance-rewards relationship, 125
  praise, 150
feeling types, 44
felt emotions. An individual's actual emotions. **55**
femininity. A national culture attribute that sees little differentiation between male and female roles; women are treated as the equals of men in all respects. **77,** 79
Fiedler contingency model. A leadership theory that proposes that effective group performance depends on the proper match between the leader's style and the degree to which the situation gives the leader control. **271**–272
field studies, 8
"50 Best Employers in Canada" (Hewitt), 10
fights in relationships, 54–55
filtering. A sender's manipulation of information so that it will be seen more favourably by the receiver. **196**
finance, and OB, 7
financial scandals, 278
Finland, 77
Fire and Ice (Adams), 84
five-stage model, 161–163
fixed pie. The belief that there is only a set amount of goods or services to be divided up between the parties. **213**
forcing, 210, 211
formal channels. Communication channels established by an organization to transmit messages related to the professional activities of members. **192**
former Communist countries, 147
forming. The first stage in group development, characterized by much uncertainty. **161,** 165
four D's of appreciative inquiry, 351
francophone values, 84–86
free riders, 175
freedom, 318
French, 84–86
front-line information, 286
functional conflict. Conflict that supports the goals of the group and improves its performance. **208**

fundamental attribution error. The tendency to underestimate the influence of external factors and overestimate the influence of internal factors when making judgments about the behaviour of others. **36**–37
future orientation, 79

G

gainsharing. A group-based incentive plan in which improvements in group productivity determine the total amount of money to be shared. **136**
gender
  and communication, 206
  and leadership, 288–289
gender differentiation, 79
general dependency postulate, 234–235
general moral principles, 75, 76
Generation Nexters, 81
Generation X, 16, 80, 81, 82
Generation Y, 16, 80, 81–82, 132, 133
  see also Millennials
generational differences, 80–82
generational mix, 16
Germany, 18, 52, 146
"get out of my way or get trampled" approach, 85
gift, 101
Global Leadership and Organizational Behavior Effectiveness (GLOBE) research program, 79
globalization, 21
GLOBE framework for assessing cultures, 79
goal. What an individual is trying to accomplish. **123,** 126, 147, 176
goal setting, 131, 156–157
goal-setting theory. A theory that says that specific and difficult goals, with feedback, lead to higher performance. **123**–125, 126, 127
good, 76
good citizenship behaviours, 19
Great Britain. *See* United Kingdom
greatest good for the greatest number, 76
ground rules for negotiation, 216–217
group. Two or more people with a common relationship. 4, **160**
  challenges at the group level, 15–17
  cohesiveness, 137, 177, 178
  five-stage model, 161–163
  generational mix, 16
  group processes, levels of, 175
  and incentive pay, 137–138
  leaders, 312
  punctuated-equilibrium model, 163–165
  size, 312
  stages of group development, 161–165
  vs. team, 160–161
  workforce diversity, 16–17
  working with others, 15–16
group-based incentives, 136
group decision making, 309–315
  brainstorming, 313
  effectiveness, 310
  efficiency, 310
  electronic meeting, 314

evaluation of group effectiveness, 315
  groups *vs.* the individual, 309–310
  groupshift, 312–313
  groupthink, 310–312
  interacting groups, 313
  nominal group technique, 314
  strengths of, 309–310
  techniques, 313–315
  weaknesses of, 310
group diversity. The presence of a heterogeneous mix of individuals within a group. **172**–173
group inertia, 354
groups
  and creativity, 318
groupshift. A phenomenon in which the initial positions of individual group members become exaggerated because of the interactions of the group. **312**–313
groupthink. A phenomenon in which group pressures for conformity prevent the group from critically appraising unusual, minority, or unpopular views. 310–312, **311**
growth needs, 116
guanxi, 87
gut feelings, 9

H

halo effect. Drawing a general impression of an individual on the basis of a single characteristic. **38**–39
harassment, 198, 239–241
hard disciplines, and soft OB concepts, 7
Hawthorne studies, 90
heredity, 43–44
Hersey and Blanchard's Situational Leadership® (SL), 272
Herzberg's motivation-hygiene theory, 116–118, 120
heuristics. Judgment shortcuts in decision making. **40**
hierarchy of needs theory. A hierarchy of five needs—physiological, safety, social, esteem, and self-actualization—in which, as each need is substantially satisfied, the next need becomes dominant. **115**–116, 120, 146
high job characteristics, 140
high Machs, 48–49
high performing, 165
higher-order needs. Needs that are satisfied internally, such as social, esteem, and self-actualization needs. **115**
hijab, 40
hindrance stressors, 106
hindsight bias. The tendency to believe falsely, after the outcome of an event is actually known, that one could have accurately predicted that outcome. **309**
Hodgson's general moral principles, 75, 76
Hofstede's framework for assessing cultures, 76–79
Hong Kong, 87
human variable, 211
humane orientation, 79

top management, 345
and uniform cultures, 342–343
values, 340
organizational environment, 321–322
organizational justice. An overall perception of what is fair in the workplace, composed of distributive, procedural, and interactional justice. **128**
organizational personalities, 42
organizational resistance to change, 353–355
organizational support, 318
organizers, 45
outcome orientation, 338
Outliers (Gladwell), 198
overarching goals, 211
overconfidence bias. Error in judgment that arises from being far too optimistic about one's own performance. 306–**307**

P

Pakistan, 52
paraverbal cues, 179
part-timers, 18
participative leader, 273
path-goal theory. A leadership theory that says it is the leader's job to assist followers in attaining their goals and to provide the necessary direction and/or support to ensure that their individual goals are compatible with the overall goals of the group or organization. **272**–274
pay for performance. *See* variable-pay programs
paying back, 247
peer pressure, 311
people orientation, 338
perceiver, 34
perceiving types, 44
perception. The process by which individuals select, organize, and interpret their sensory impressions in order to give meaning to their environment. **34**
and conflicts in relationships, 54–55
differences in, and communication, 207
employment interviews, 41
factors influencing perception, 34–35
of fairness, 130
importance of perception, 41–42
of justice, 129
perceptual errors, 35–41
performance evaluations, 42
performance expectations, 41
selective perception, 37–38, 196
and stress, 108
perceptual errors, 35–41
attribution theory, 35–37
contrast effects, 39
halo effect, 38–39
projection, 39–40
selective perception, 37–38, 196
stereotyping, 40
performance evaluations, 42
teams, 169–170
performance expectations, 41
performance feedback, 142
performance orientation, 79
performance-rewards relationship, 122

performing. The fourth stage in group development, when the group is fully functional. **162,** 165
persistence, 114, 124
personal appeals, 236
personal best, 20
personal relationships, 107
personality. The stable patterns of behaviour and consistent internal states that determine how an individual reacts to and interacts with others. **42**
Big Five Personality Model, 44, 45–46, 47, 52, 170, 268
changes in, 43–44
core self-evaluations, 48
cultural bias, and personality tests, 52–53
determinants of, 43–44
"fake proof" personality test, 46
and heredity, 43–44
and job satisfaction, 89–90
Machiavellianism, 48–49
measuring personality, 42–43
Myers-Briggs Type Indicator (MBTI), 44–45
narcissism, 49
and national culture, 52–53
organizational personalities, 42
personality attributes influencing OB, 46–52
personality traits, 44–46
proactive personality, 52
risk-taking, 50
self-monitoring, 49–50
and stress, 107, 108–109
and teams, 170–172
Type A personality, 50–51, 108–109, 132
Type B personality, 51–52, 108
personality conflicts, 212
personality traits. Enduring characteristics that describe an individual's behaviour. **44**–46
Philippines, 77
physical activity, 109
physical distance, 199
physical sciences, 9
piece-rate pay plan. An individual based incentive plan in which employees are paid a fixed sum for each unit of production completed. **134**
Point/Counterpoint, 9–10
conflict, 221
decision making, 327
display rules, 61
impression management, 250
job satisfaction, 98
leadership, 293
organizational culture, and change, 360
praise, 150
quick fix to OB issues, 24
sports teams, as models, 184
political behaviour. Those activities that influence, or attempt to influence, the distribution of advantages and disadvantages within the organization. 59, **242**
politicking, 244, 256–257
politics, 241–247
of change, 357
impression management, 245–246
making office politics work, 246–247
politicking, 244, 256–257
reality of politics, 242–244

types of political activity, 245
in your workplace, 243
ponzi scheme, 278
position power, 271
positions, 212
positive moods, 317
positive organizational behaviour, 20
positive organizational scholarship. An area of OB research that concerns how organizations develop human strengths, foster vitality and resilience, and unlock potential. **20**
positive relationships, 355
positive social relationships, 5
positive work environment, 20–21
power. A capacity that A has to influence the behaviour of B, so that B acts in accordance with A's wishes. **230**
abuse of power, 239–241
bases of power, 230–233, 242
coercive power, 231, 233
dependency, 230, 234–235
evaluation of bases of power, 233
expert power, 231, 232–233
information power, 231, 233
legitimate power, 231–232, 233
need for power (nPow), 118
politics, 241–247
position power, 271
potential for power, 230
referent power, 231, 233
reward power, 231, 233
power distance. A national culture attribute that describes the extent to which a society accepts that power in institutions and organizations is distributed unequally. **76,** 77, 79
power relationships, 355
praise, 150
prejudice. An unfounded dislike of a person or group based on their belonging to a particular stereotyped group. **40–41**
pressure, 236
Privacy Act, 203
privacy issues, 202
proactive personality. A person who identifies opportunities, shows initiative, takes action, and perseveres until meaningful change occurs. **52**
problem. A discrepancy between some current state of affairs and some desired state. **302**
problem clarity, 303
problem solving, 160, 170, 210, 211, 217–218, 334–335
procedural justice. The perceived fairness of the process used to determine the distribution of rewards. **129**
process, 129
process control, 129
process theories of motivation, 115, 120–126
expectancy theory, 121–122, 127, 133, 142–143
goal-setting theory, 123–125, 126, 127
self-efficacy theory, 125–126
social cognitive theory, 126
social learning theory, 126
process variables and team effectiveness, 175–178

production-oriented leader. A leader who emphasizes the technical or task aspects of the job. **269**

productivity. A performance measure including effectiveness and efficiency. 4, **19**
exit and neglect behaviours, 93
groups and productivity, 137–138
and job satisfaction, 90–91
task-oriented, 271
variable-pay programs, 134–138

profit-sharing plan. An organization-wide plan in which the employer shares profits with employees based on a predetermined formula. **136**

projection. Attributing one's own characteristics to other people. **39**–40

promise keeping, 288

promises, 76

protégés, 282

proxemics. The study of physical space in interpersonal relationships. **199**

psychological contract, 260–261

psychological empowerment. Employees' belief in the degree to which they affect their work environment, their competence, the meaningfulness of their job, and their perceived autonomy in their work. **95**

psychological harassment, 240

psychology, 6

punctuated-equilibrium model, 163–165

Punished by Rewards (Kohn), 114, 144

Pygmalion effect, 41

Q

quality, 19

quick fix to OB issues, 24

R

randomness error. The tendency of individuals to believe that they can predict the outcome of random events. **308**

rational. Refers to choices that are consistent and value-maximizing within specified constraints. **302**

rational decision-making model. A six-step decision-making model that describes how individuals should behave in order to maximize some outcome. **302**–303

rational persuasion, 236

rational thinking, and emotions, 56

rationality, myth of, 53

rationalized resistance, 311

readiness, 272

reading an organization's culture, 366–367

reading emotions, 70–71

receiver, 192

referent power. Influence based on possession by an individual of desirable resources or personal traits. 231, **233**

reflected best-self, 20

reflexivity. A characteristic of effective teams, allowing them to reflect on and adjust their master plan when necessary. **176**

refreezing. Stabilizing a change intervention by balancing driving and restraining forces. **348,** 350

relatedness needs, 116

relationship-oriented, 271

relaxation techniques, 109

research methods, 8

resistance, 233

resistance point, 216

resistance to change, 352–357
cynicism, 353
individual resistance, 352–353
organizational resistance, 353–355
overcoming resistance to change, 355–356
politics of change, 357

resource allocations, 355

resources, 106, 211, 318

resources, adequacy of, 168

respect, 76

respect for the individual, 288

restraining forces. Forces that hinder movement away from the status quo. **349**

restraint. A national culture attribute that emphasizes the importance of controlling the gratification of needs. **77**

Results-Only Work Environment (ROWE), 123–124

reward power. Power that achieves compliance based on the ability to distribute rewards that others view as valuable. **231**

rewards
cognitive evaluation theory, 127, 130
elimination of rewards, 144–145
equity theory, 127–128, 146
extrinsic rewards, 130–131
fair process and treatment, 127, 128–130
intrinsic rewards, 130–131, 132
management reward follies, 144
responses to reward system, 126–131
rewards, and desired performance, 147
self-determination theory, 130, 131
signals sent by rewards, 142–144
teams, 169–170

rewards-personal goals relationship, 122

right to self-determination, 76

rights, 319–320

risk aversion. The tendency to prefer a sure gain of a moderate amount over a riskier outcome, even if the riskier outcome might have a higher expected payoff. **308**–309

risk-taking. A person's willingness to take chances or risks. **50,** 338

Rokeach value survey, 74–75

role. A set of expected behaviours of a person in a given position in a social unit. **172,** 173

role conflict. A situation in which an individual finds that complying with one role requirement may make it more difficult to comply with another. **172**

role demands, 107

role expectations. How others believe a person should act in a given situation. **172**

role stress, 110

routine messages, 194

rudeness, 258

Russia, 146, 147, 206

S

sabbaticals, 110

satisfaction, 117

satisfice. To provide a solution that is both satisfactory and sufficient. **304**–305

satisfiers, 117

scarcity, and dependency, 235

scholarships, 138–139

selection, 344–345, 356

selective perception. People's selective interpretation of what they *see* based on their interests, background, experience, and attitudes. **37**–38, 196

self-actualization. The drive to become what a person is capable of becoming. **115**

self-determination, 76, 239

self-determination theory. A theory of motivation that is concerned with the beneficial effects of intrinsic motivation and the harmful effects of extrinsic motivation. **130,** 131

self-efficacy. An individual's belief that he or she is capable of performing a task. **125**

self-efficacy theory, 125–126

self-esteem, 132

self-fulfilling prophecy. A concept that proposes a person will behave in ways consistent with how he or she is perceived by others. **41**

self-interest, 352

self-leadership, 283–284

self-management, 283–284

self-monitoring. A personality trait that measures an individual's ability to adjust behaviour to external, situational factors. **49**–50

self-promotion, 246

self-reinforced behaviour, 283

self-report measures, 42–43

self-serving bias. The tendency for individuals to attribute their own successes to internal factors while putting the blame for failures on external factors. **37**

semantics, 206

sender, 192

sensing types, 44

sensitive messages, 195

separation, 348

service jobs, 18

sexual harassment. Unwelcome behaviour of a sexual nature in the workplace that negatively affects the work environment or leads to adverse job-related consequences for the employee. **240**–241

shirkers, 187

short-term hires, 18

short-term orientation. A national culture attribute that emphasizes the past and present, respect for tradition, and fulfillment of social obligations. **77,** 79

silence, 198

situation, 34, 35

situational, or contingency, theories. Theories that propose that leadership effectiveness is dependent on the situation. **270**–274

NAME AND ORGANIZATION INDEX

Toronto Leaside Girls Hockey Association
(TLGHA), 191, 196
Town of Ajax, 136
Toyota, 188
Toyota Motor Company, 207
Toyota USA, 188
Trans-Fair Canada, 301
Transport Canada, 124
Treliving, Jim, 337, 343, 344
Trudeau, Pierre, 275, 293
Tsi Del Del, 86
Tulgan, Bruce, 82
Tung, Rosalie, 87
Twenge, Jean, 150
Twitter, 205

U

United Food and Commercial Workers
(UFCW), 68
United Nations, 240
United Way, 271
Université du Québec à Montréal, 239
University of Alberta, 86
University of British Columbia, 241, 323
University of Illinois, 139
University of Kentucky, 155
University of Manitoba, 240, 259
University of Massachusetts, 247
University of New Brunswick, 241
University of North Carolina, 155, 258
University of Northern British Columbia, 105
University of Ottawa, 85, 139
University of Toronto, 41, 46, 123, 272
University of Western Ontario, 93
UPS, 13, 27
Upverter, 204
Ury, W., 217
US Armed Forces, 45
US Department of Defense, 364

V

Valeant Pharmaceuticals Intl. Inc., 154f
Van Maanen, John, 173n

Vancouver Canucks, 5, 75, 134, 217
Vanderbroek, Sophie, 235
Vermeulen, Rob, 205
Virgin Group, 18, 51, 267, 278, 344
Virginia Mason Hospital, 365
Vista Projects, 95
Vroom, Victor, 121

W

Wagner, Shannon, 105
Walker, Richard, 322
Wall & Associates, 21
Wall Street Journal, 101
Wallach, M.A., 65n
Walmart, 42, 143, 240
Walmart Canada, 33–34, 53
Walt Disney Company. see Disney
Waltec, 365
Walton, Roland, 229
Wang, Chloe, 340
Warren, Robert, 259
Waterstone Human Capital, 33, 237
Weber, J., 75n
Weber, M., 37n
Weber, Max, 276
Weightman, Mike, 171
Weill, Stanford, 254
Weir, Johnny, 244
Welch, Jack, 20, 150, 293
Wendy's, 241
Werner, Jessa, 205
Western Electric, 90
WestJet Airlines, 82, 136, 237, 338
Wharton School (University of Pennsylvania),
150, 272
Whetten, D.A., 186n
White Spot, 68
Whitney, D., 351n
Whole Foods, 296
Wild Oats, 296
Wilfrid Laurier Golden Hawks, 139
Wilson, Fred, 201
Wilson, O'Neill, 258

Windsor Family Credit Union, 344, 346
Winnipeg Blue Bombers, 258
Wolfe, R.N., 63n
Woodman, R.W., 329n
Woodworth, Michael, 204
Workplace Bullying and Trauma Institute, 155
World Bank, 240
WorldCom, 75
WorldofGood.com, 90
Wright, Barb, 213

X

Xerox Corporation, 235
Xie, Jia Lin, 238
XING, 204

Y

Yahoo!, 195, 202
Yale University, 241
Yale University School of Management, 163
Yamana Gold Inc., 154f
Yanashita, Koichi, 134
Yellow House Events, 3, 5–6, 11
Yeung, Irene, 87
York University, 91
Young, Bill, 289
YouTube, 76, 193, 194
Yukl, G., 231n

Z

Zaslow, Jeffrey, 101
Zellers, 42
Zetsche, Dieter, 188
Zhou, J., 243n
Zingheim, Patricia, 138
ZoomInfo, 204
Zuckerberg, Mark, 277
Zweig, David, 261

LIST OF CANADIAN COMPANIES

PHOTO CREDITS